PELICAN BOOKS

The Worm in the Bud

The son of an engineer, Ronald Pearsall was born in 1927 in Birmingham, and his interest in the nineteenth century stems from his memories of what was the most Victorian of cities. He has been a professional musician, a journalist, and has lectured for the army and for the British Council. In 1967 he left London to have more time for serious work, and now lives in an old Sussex rectory. He is at present working on an extended study of the Victorian occult.

Besides contributing to many British periodicals, including the *Quarterly Review*, *Army Quarterly* and *History Today*, Ronald Pearsall has been published in the United States, Canada, Australia and Holland. *The Worm in the Bud* is at present being translated into German and Italian. The author of a wide variety of articles and reviews, he has also edited and introduced reprints of various Victorian 'underground' classics.

Ronald Pearsall

The Worm in the Bud

The World of
Victorian Sexuality

Penguin Books

Penguin Books Ltd, Harmondsworth, Middlesex, England
Penguin Books Australia Ltd, Ringwood, Victoria, Australia

—

First published by Weidenfeld & Nicolson 1969
Published in Pelican Books 1971
Copyright © Ronald Pearsall, 1969

—

Made and printed in Great Britain
by Hazell Watson & Viney Ltd,
Aylesbury, Bucks
Set in Linotype Granjon

Contents

Part Two
The Victorian Buried Life

Duke: And what's her history?
Viola: A blank, my lord. She never told her love,
But let concealment, like a worm i' the bud,
Feed on her damask cheek...

Twelfth Night by William Shakespeare
Act II, Scene 4

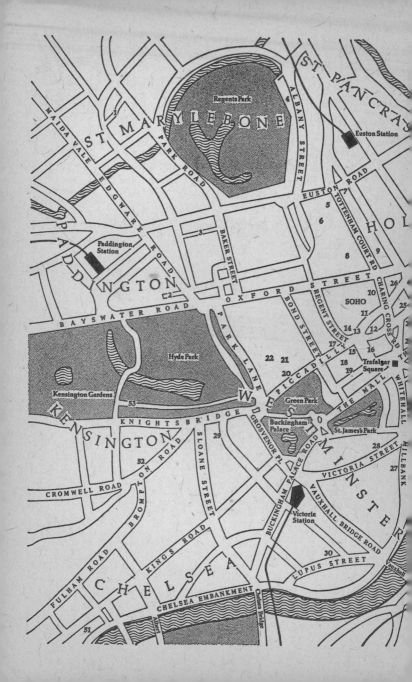

Key to the
Sin Map of London

1 Circus Road. It was in this road that there existed the flagellation establishment frequented by Swinburne. In this road Bradlaugh lived when he was being prosecuted for distributing birth control literature, hiding suspect books beneath floorboards.

2 Connaught Terrace, Edgware Road. A leading demi-mondaine of the 1850s lived here, Amy Johnson, alias Hope, alias Scott.

3 York Street. A brothel for the 'sole accommodation of a noble duke, and he far advanced in years'.

4 Albany Street. Because of its proximity to Albany Barracks, a centre of Victorian homosexuality.

5 Fitzroy Street contained a homosexual introducing house, much used during the Oscar Wilde period.

6 Cleveland Street. A homosexual introducing house used by Lord Arthur Somerset and others.

7 New Road, now the Euston Road, contained *tableaux vivants*, Victorian strip tease.

8 Charlotte Street, where lived the prostitute Mrs Billings over an auctioneers.

9 Bedford Square. The nineties publisher Leonard Smithers had a house in this square, the haunt of the Yellow Book set (Wilde, Beardsley, Dowson, etc. – though Wilde never actually contributed to the Yellow Book).

10 Soho Square. Smithers opened his first 'Arcadian' bookshop here.

11 Church Street, Soho, contained Madame Audray's introducing house.

12 Empire Theatre of Varieties, which had a notorious prom-

enade given over to high-priced prostitutes.

13 The Casino, Great Windmill Street, a popular rendezvous for prostitutes.

14 Willis's, Brewer Street, 'indelicacy in the dancing'.

15 Piccadilly Circus. From here to Waterloo Steps the best of the under-fifteens. On the site of the Criterion Theatre, the pornographic writer Sellon, author of *The Ups and Downs of Life* (perhaps the rarest piece of Victorian pornography), blew out his brains.

16 The Haymarket, the centre of high-class perambulating prostitution.

17 Burlington Arcade, where the prostitutes flocked in the winter. They had arrangements with the shopkeepers so that assignments could be delicately negotiated.

18 Jermyn Street, where Mrs Clarke, a celebrated courtesan of the fifties, lived. Her house was recognized by the shoes in the window below.

19 Bury Street, where Madame de Landeau kept an introducing house.

20 Piccadilly, where the pornographic publisher Hotten set up shop at number 151b.

21 Charles Street, the Victoria Saloon.

22 Chesterfield Street, where the demi-mondaine 'Skittles' Walters lived.
'Skittles' was the most famous courtesan of the time, befriended by Gladstone, kept by Lord Hartington, for a time leader of the Liberal party.

23 The Lowther Rooms, Adelaide Street, famous for 'the three Miss Butterworths' and their 'pas de Venus' and the theatre whores who gathered here.

24 The Feathers night-house, Hart Street.

25 The Ship, James Street, haunt of 'market porters, doxies, high and low pads'.

26 The Seven Dials, a low area and rookery, famous for its obscene sheet music.

27 Westminster Abbey. In the thirties a notorious homosexual case occurred when William Bankes, M.P., was accused of 'standing behind the screen of a place for making water against Westminster Abbey walls, in company with a soldier named Flower, and of having been surprised with his breeches and braces unbuttoned at ten at night, his companion's dress being in similar disorder'.

28 Site of the Almonary, pulled down because it was a centre of vice.

29 Wilton Crescent. Here lived Laura Bell, a well-known prostitute.

30 Lupus Street, where there was an introducing house for the special benefit of Members of Parliament.

31 Holywell Street, the centre of the dirty-book and obscene print trades.

32 Drury Lane and Wych Street, where the cheaper street woman operated.

33 The Shades, Adam Street, Adelphi, a celebrated subterranean establishment.

34 The Coal Hole, Strand, where

'a smart smutty song could occasionally be heard'.

35   The Union, Bow Street, 'flashy in the extreme'. A visitor was 'often indulged with a lewd song or half-naked dance'.

36   The Albert Saloon, Brydges Street, the home ground of three well-known prostitutes, Louisa Seymour, Kate Lacey, and Jane Smith.

37   The White Swan, Wych Street, 'scarcely better than a brothel'.

38   The Haunch of Venison, Bell Yard, Fleet Street, 'the resort of all abandoned women who reside in those places'.

39   The Castle Tavern, Holborn, 'crack crib in the sport world'.

40   The Three Tuns, Fetter Lane, 'the songs sung are of the beastly description'.

41   The Twelve Bells, Bride Lane, 'exhibition of low characters'.

42   The Clerkenwell House of Correction. Here the pornographic publisher Dugdale died in the sixties.

43   Brunswick Square, an area popular among homosexuals. It was here that the transvestites Boulton and Park were discovered by the police 'larking about'.

44   The Cross Keys, Gracechurch Street. 'Private rooms can be had here either by day or night; the charge for a sleeping room for self and lady is 4s, but for a short visit the mere calling for wine is deemed sufficient.'

45   The Nag's Head, Tower Hill, 'a low Cock-and-hen club'.

46   Old Garrick Tavern, Leman Street, 'a famous depot for black-eyed Jewesses'.

47   Dock Street, where Katherine Keeley kept a child brothel.

48   Betty Street, where Mrs Maxwell kept a child brothel.

49   Vauxhall Gardens, the fun place for mid Victorians. It closed in 1859.

50   The Surrey Theatre. Being south of the river and therefore unfashionable, it was much frequented by the respectable in search of excitement.

51   Cremorne Gardens, not so popular as Vauxhall, flourished 1845 to 1877. It became so notorious that its licence was withdrawn.

52   Brompton Square. At 36 lived a demi-mondaine 'at the top of the tree' (said Gladstone). Gladstone persuaded her to renounce her wicked ways.

53   Rotten Row, where the cream of the courtesans rode in their carriages, displaying their charms. In the fifties or sixties, one of the sights of London.

Introduction

I F the Victorians had one golden rule, it was that it was better to be preoccupied by than occupied with sex, and many of their seeming inconsistencies and hypocrisies stem from an inability to reevaluate this maxim. The victims were predominantly the middle classes, who modelled their behaviour and thought processes on those of the upper classes, or what they thought was the behaviour and thought processes of the upper classes. The middle classes were mistaken; the upper classes did not give a damn about conventional morality, and pursued their libidinous pleasures with a gusto only tempered by occasional panic. When one speaks of the Victorians as if they were a peculiar species of animal, one is predominantly thinking of the Victorian middle class, painstakingly evolving an image for itself, mistaking the genteel for the pure, and distressed by the all too evident intrusion of the animal in man.

Sexual intercourse was a deed of darkness; sexual desire was something the well-bred man and woman should not have; anomalies and perversions were hurriedly thrust from the mind into a nether region where they festered and broke into strange cankers. Gentility was not programmed into the physical relationships between the sexes, and the refusal to recognize this had an effect that is still apparent today, for just as the middle class tried to emulate the upper classes, so did the emancipated and respectable working class reject the promiscuity and easygoing ways of their ancestors in the effort to achieve a simulacrum of middle classdom; the repressions of the nineteenth-century middle class have been passed on to the aspiring working classes in a sociological musical chairs.

Those in the middle classes were anxious to be reassured that there was a sexual norm, and they were communicated to by those members of the same class whose duty it was to reassure, the doctors and the clergy. It was also their duty to frighten those who happened to stray from this supposed sexual norm. The doctors were more successful, with their threats of cancer and an early death for those who enjoyed sex enough to indulge excessively; in the growing climate of agnosticism, many men were willing to take a chance on the clergyman's prognostications.

The impudence and arrogance of the medical profession in laying down the law on something that they knew nothing at all about can, in retrospect, only be marvelled at. The power that they exercised over a credulous middle class can hardly be over-estimated. Preferring self-assured dogma to pragmatic investigation, the doctors established for their patients a code of sexual behaviour that was utterly arbitrary. The result was clear – repression when their strictures were obeyed, guilt and alarm when they were not. The wives suffered more than the men, and hysteria, neurasthenia, and complex anxiety states stalked through the middle-class *purlieus*. Forbidden by these unwritten laws of middle-class existence not only to indulge in sex but to enjoy what there was of it, many women found that they became child-rearing vegetables while their husbands shelved their guilt and made use of the vast army of prostitutes, which may have numbered 120,000 in London alone.

The huge number of prostitutes catered to all kinds and conditions of men, and their presence on the streets was a constant promise to middle-class men and a perpetual threat to middle-class women. The unspoken agreement not to notice this gay flaunting species – what a French writer called the fouled hindquarters of English life – served to exacerbate domestic lack of communication on sexual matters. The higher-priced prostitutes, with their fashionable French tricks, and the alluring décor of their establishments, were attractive to happily married husbands who were simply bored with the lack of excitement of their domestic sexual life. It was understood that a marriage contract deliberately wrote out fun; a wife was there to raise a family, a prostitute for enjoyment. A respectable married professional man could expect more response from a prostitute who knew the basic sexual demands of her customers far better than the so-called experts, and who was willing to provide services that today are considered normal shading into off-beat but that were then the ultimate in the untalked about, the staple diet of Victorian pornography. With this division of interests, the second establishment of the rich man can be seen as a supplement and not a duplication.

The conventionally respectable middle-class man, by pretending that he was more moral than he really was, even to himself, compromised his integrity, and the guilt and unease that simmered to the surface was reflected in the way he conducted himself in society, in the day to day business of living. It was not only an age of optimism and an age of transition, but an age of anxiety. With their attempt to attribute a reason for everything, the Victorians pinned this anxiety on to the decline of religion, but more frequently it was simply a failure to live up to their printed circuits. By striving too hard for an almost unattainable level of sexual respectability, by refusing to admit that they were constantly falling down on this target, the middle-class Victorians found that the whole subject of sex became forbidden, confused, and diffused into the most unlikely areas. The more repressed could see sex in everything, the shape of a grand piano became indecent and its legs were draped to avoid giving offence to tender minded young ladies. The English language became a mine-field; not only, predictably, did breasts become bosom, but legs became limbs or, to point the argument even more powerfully, 'unmentionables'. The most innocuous of relationships between men and women were conducted at fever-pitch, and the whole paraphernalia of etiquette was brought into play to regulate what in the eighteenth century and in the Regency had been a quiet normal boy-meets-girl situation.

The middle classes became increasingly the dominant force in Victorian *mores*, and the lesser members of the aristocracy found themselves forced to toe the middle-class line. When upper-class sexual misdoings were reported in a by-and-large hostile press it could mean their complete social undoing, and their attitude towards this great uncomprehended middle stratum of society became more and more tetchy and querulous as their own governing power became reduced by the various reform bills giving suffrage to the lowlier members of this abhorrent species. The upper classes were always happier with the poor, whose rabbity sex lives were more easily understood, and whose morals ('do what you want when you feel like it') were not so far removed from their own.

When sex ceased to be talked about openly it went underground. No society has been so eager to welcome pornography and indecent engravings as the Victorian. When pornography became a commercial proposition early in the reign, its potentialities were immediately seen by the traders in pornography, and obscene photographs were produced by the hundred thousand. When sex reared its ugly head – the Freudian simile is particularly Victorian – in such a manner as not to be ignored, the repressed and inhibited classes overreacted, and this can be seen time and time again by the chorus of prurient horror that was evoked every time a sexual scandal broke surface in the pages of the popular press. The journalists played up to this; *Reynold's Newspaper* built up a circulation of more than 250,000 by pandering to this taste for salacious details, details notably lacking in what the present age takes for a mirror of the times, the quasi-realistic novels of Dickens and Trollope.

The tacit agreement to pretend that sex was not as it really was permeated the period, especially the years from 1850 onward. Not only was there no reconciliation between personal sexual behaviour and the respectable sexual norm, but there was no attempt to make such a reconciliation. We call this failing hypocrisy, but hypocrisy surely presupposes a conscious and deliberate course of action. The Victorian middle classes acted on a level that was hardly more than instinctive; when sex sema-phored its presence, reason retired in confusion.

In such a time, those who were not afflicted by the climate of repression stand out with uncommon clarity. Swinburne, work-ing out his flagellation mania in an establishment in St John's Wood; Rossetti, commuting between the virginal Elizabeth Siddal and his fat whores; Boulton and Park, gaily flaunting their transvestism in the theatres of the Strand – not only do these stand larger than life, they make their so-so-respectable contemporaries look like their photographs in old family albums – sepia-coloured and wooden. That this is so is due to the triumph of nineteenth-century image-making. The Vic-torians conducted their public relations not for themselves, but for us; they wanted to appear to posterity as good, noble, pure in word, heart, and deed; and that they have succeeded so well is due not only to the energy with which they tackled this pro-ject, but to our own laziness in preferring the easy stereotype to the reality.

People do not alter much in a hundred years; the difference lies in the accommodation to the age in which they live, in their susceptibility to outside forces. Because opportunities for divorce were minimal in the nineteenth century (7,321 divorces between 1858 and 1887), it does not mean that the British were fifty times more faithful than the Americans (328,716 divorces between 1867 and 1886); because the Oscar Wilde case was treated by the press as if it were a unique visitation it does not mean that the ratio of homosexuality to heterosexuality was less than it is today (reckoned by Kinsey at about six per cent); be-cause Queen Victoria is supposed to have not known what Les-bianism was, it does not mean that her subjects were no wiser.

The men and women in this book are not an alien species, but ourselves, planted in an age when it was difficult to be honest with oneself, where guilt and alarm filtered out of the personal into the public sphere, when private sexual proclivities were thought to be unique to oneself, and uniquely damning. Harassed beyond measure, the procreative instinct manifested itself in ways that to the thoughtless are funny, to the perceptive, pathetic. The northern confectioner who sold obscene-shaped sweets was sent to prison, a middle-aged officer with a fine war service was sent to prison, dismissed from the army, and hounded out of the country because he kissed a pretty girl in a railway compartment, while respectable women subjected themselves to a system of tight lacing that could slice into their livers as this was the only way they could daintily display the heaving bosoms that were forced upwards by their corsets.

The propagandists of birth control received short shrift at the hands of the three main forces of chastisement – the magistrates, the police and the press; that birth control methods became increasingly widely known and used indicates that there was a ground swell of common sense amidst all the doublethink, obscurantism and devious conniving of the establishment. It is interesting to note that the class that was most indignant at the mere mention of birth control, a subject considered so filthy it could only be referred to by the euphemism Malthusianism, was the most eager to make use of the surreptitious information being put into circulation by under-the-counter booksellers. It is revealing that the class that was pathologically most anxious to read the pornography that was being drafted into the British Museum Reading Room was that which considered that it, individually or collectively, had a divine duty to keep anything like it out of the hands of the working classes. In a word, it was not fair; the middle class used their privilege to imposed views and conditions that they considered right, if not holy, keeping in their hands the means of contracting out if private needs ran counter to public proclamation. That they did this unconsciously does not mean that it was any the less true.

The second half of the nineteenth century was particularly replete with a specific type of man – he with the righteous countenance and the sticky palms. The prurient thrived in the climate of repression; some sought to hide the mainsprings of these elusive desires under a genteel enamelling, venturing into the East End of London ostensibly to do social work, trying to convert prostitutes into respectable working girls, indulging in an orgy of over-compensation if their professions allowed them to pontificate on any aspect of sex. That they succeeded in impressing their auditors with their boundless disinterestedness and detachment must ever be marvellous, though the Victorians were endlessly credulous, especially when told anything by their 'betters'. Unacquainted with Freud, whose name was not known *at all* until the nineties, the prurient did not realize how they revealed themselves in their deeds or their comments, how their own special interests were shown up when they rapturously exchanged anecdotes of rape and mutilation during the 1857 Indian Mutiny, when they thronged the streets to buy the *Pall Mall Gazette* when its editor was sensationally publicizing the white slave traffic (a heading such as 'Girls Strapped Down' had the readers slavering), when they stood in groups knitted in mutual congratulations to hiss Oscar Wilde on his way to Reading Gaol.

Yet despite all this, despite the curtains of respectability that were intermittently dropped and hoisted, people could get all that they wanted in the way of sex provided that they did not make a song and a dance about it. It was easier for those who had thrown off the shackles of class, but it was not difficult for the passing respectable. The banker who kept a mistress in St John's Wood, the floggee with a few pounds to spare to be 'chastised', the transvestite with theatrical tastes and a trunk of women's clothes, the man with a penchant for young virgins, the homosexual with a liking for stable boys, provided that they did not deliberately set themselves up for martyrdom by tilting at the cumbrous mechanisms of the establishment or clash with the law on one of its periodic bouts of dirt hunting – these enthusiasts were as free to pursue their cravings as they would have been in any other age. Indeed, present-day writers assert that it was a good deal less hazardous being a homosexual in the eighteen-nineties than it is today.

Heterosexual adventurers found it easy to stray in all the price ranges. Prostitutes advertised themselves through cards in windows ('Beds to Let'), through sandwich-board men parading up and down the Haymarket and Bond Street, and in the men about town's pocketbooks, and they were on view in marvellously variegated drinking houses and gin palaces, in the music halls – which often had a promenade especially for the gay ladies – in the numerous dancing saloons, in the pleasure gardens of Highbury Barn, Vauxhall and Cremorne, and in the night houses. In the public houses a man and his pick-up could get a room by merely calling for wine, and in the streets the prostitutes perambulated like so many flagships on review at Spithead, armed with a variety of time-honoured phrases of welcome ('Are you good-natured, dear?'). There were even strip joints under the coy name of *tableaux vivants*.

When one considers all this, the contrast between the furtive gloom of the agonized and repressed, and the gay life so evidently there for all to see, it is small wonder that one makes rash generalizations about the Victorians and sex at one's peril.

Part One
The Imperious Desire

He meets, by heavenly chance express,
  The destined maid; some hidden hand
Unveils to him that loveliness
  Which others cannot understand.
His merits in her presence grow,
  To match the promise in her eyes,
And round her happy footsteps blow
  The authentic airs of Paradise.
For joy of her he cannot sleep;
  Her beauty haunts him all the night;
It melts his heart, it makes him weep
  For wonder, worship, and delight.
O, paradox of love, he longs,
  Most humble when he most aspires,
To suffer scorn and cruel wrongs
  From her he honours and desires.
Her graces make him rich, and ask
  No guerdon; this imperial style
Affronts him; he disdains to bask,
  The pensioner of her priceless smile.
He prays for some hard thing to do,
  Some work of fame and labour immense,

To stretch the languid bulk and thew
  Of love's fresh-born magnipotence.
No smallest boon were bought too dear,
  Though barter'd for his love-sick life;
Yet trusts he, with undaunted cheer,
  To vanquish heaven, and call her Wife.
He notes how queens of sweetness still
  Neglect their crowns, and stoop to mate;
How, self-consign'd with lavish will,
  They ask but love proportionate;
How swift pursuit by small degrees,
  Love's tactic, works like miracle;
How valour, clothed in courtesies,
  Brings down the haughtiest citadel;
And therefore, though he merits not
  To kiss the braid upon her skirt,
His hope, discouraged ne'er a jot,
  Out-soars all possible desert.

The Angel in the House
Canto III – 'The Lover'
by Coventry Patmore

I

The Aristocracy

Albert and Victoria

In 1837 a girl of eighteen became Queen of England. Her uncle, the King of the Belgians, thought that he would be able to manipulate her and the fortunes of England, and so did her mother, the Duchess of Kent. They were both wrong. Queen Victoria speedily proved that she was not to be trifled with; the languid court etiquette of earlier days, with the gentlemen mumbling drunkenly over the port, was no more; after the ladies left at dinner, the gentlemen were allowed a mere five minutes to collect themselves. She arranged her marriage with the same precision.

Germany was the stud of nineteenth-century monarchy, and Victoria selected her husband from one of the smaller and poorer states, Coburg. Of the sons of the Duke and Duchess of Coburg, it was fortunate that it was upon Albert that Victoria's affections rested, for Albert's brother Ernest was a notorious profligate in the Coburg tradition, and although in early life the two brothers had been inseparable, as time went by Ernest had to be forcibly kept away from England. His presence, Albert told him, was 'not desired'. Ernest was urged to marry. 'I cannot imagine that the *chronique scandaleuse*, be it ever so rich, prevent you from living virtuously, with a virtuous wife,' [1] Albert wrote to him.

Victoria had first met the brothers in May 1836. Albert she considered extremely handsome, while Ernest was good-natured, honest, and had an intelligent countenance. Within a fortnight there was no question where her affections lay. She wrote to the King of the Belgians, 'Allow me, then, my dearest Uncle, to tell you how delighted I am with him, and how much I like him in every way. He possesses every quality that could be desired to render me completely happy. He is so sensible, so kind, and so good, and so amiable too. He has, besides, the most pleasing and delightful exterior and appearance you can possibly see.'² They all went to see, appropriately enough, the opera *I Puritani*.

Three years later, the brothers reappeared for a second inspection. Ernest was dismissed cursorily, but there is a note of ecstasy in Victoria's account to her uncle of Albert; his '*beauty* is *most striking*, and he is so amiable and unaffected – in short, very *fascinating*', so much so that she decided not to wait too long before marrying him. 'My mind is quite made up – and I told Albert this morning of it. ... He seems *perfection*, and I think I have the prospect of very great happiness before me.'³

Albert was timid and retiring, and although it was his duty to be the consort of this enthusiastic young woman, his coolness towards the prospect was known to Victoria. 'I shall do everything in my power to render the sacrifice he has made as small as I can,' she wrote. Albert told Victoria's mother of his 'dread of being unequal' to the position. On his way to England for the wedding he passed through Brussels, where he saw the King of the Belgians. Albert, reported the King to Victoria, was 'rather exasperated about various things, and pretty full of grievances'.⁴ Yet no doubt Albert knew that he could have done worse. Though not strictly speaking pretty, Victoria had a vivacity that made her appear so. Objectively, the periodical the *Town* described her: 'Her Majesty is short, and not well proportioned; her bust is somewhat fine; her mouth is imbecile in expression; her teeth are irregular but sound; her feet are not small, and her hands are not white.' Albert 'is of the height of five feet ten inches; his figure is not well-proportioned; in walking he has a stoop'. They did not appear to be a well-matched couple. In addition, their temperaments were poles apart; Albert was prim and prudish, while Victoria had inherited the sensuality of her Hanoverian forefathers, and eagerly welcomed not only the pomp and circumstance of a royal wedding, but its consummation. Eventually she was to assimilate much of Albert's prudery, but in these early years no one could have been, to use the word in its best understood sense, less Victorian.

The marriage was a great occasion for everyone – for British industry (the Queen was dressed entirely in articles of British manufacture, her vast white dress of Spitalfields silk, her veil of Honiton lace, her Coventry ribbons, her gloves London-made from English kid); for Lord Melbourne to show off his ability with the Sword of State (at the Coronation he was said to have looked like a butcher); for eccentric Uncle Augustus to sob throughout the ceremony; while for the oafish Duke of Cambridge it was an opportunity to give a running commentary.

Early in the morning Victoria had written a note to be taken by hand to Albert. 'Dearest – How are you today, and have you slept well? I have rested very well, and feel very comfortable today. What weather! I believe, however, the rain will cease. Send one word when you, my most dearly beloved bridegroom, will be ready.'[5]

For several days Victoria had been subject to nerves and tantrums. Her pet physician, Sir James Clark, perhaps the most incompetent royal doctor of all time, had pronounced measles, but, as usual, he was wrong. Albert had had his own maladies, stemming from the stormy channel crossing. The crowds waiting to see him land at Dover were no consolation, though he managed to bow to them, 'no common effort'.

At Buckingham Palace the red carpets were put out, and Prince Albert emerged in the role of a British field marshal, with the ribbon of the Order of the Garter across his breast. There were trumpets, lowering of colours, and presentations of arms. The marriage was solemnized at the Chapel Royal, St James', with peers and peeresses in various hues, gold on the altars, and masses of orange blossom. The Duchess of Kent made a grand entry in velvet and ermine. The train of the

Queen's dress was carried by twelve ladies, and they appealed particularly to the anonymous writer of *The Times*, ('ladies more beautiful never graced palace, hall, or country green').

Thus the official picture. But for weeks the jokes had been circulating, from the amiable pun – 'Saxe-Humbug' and 'Go-to-her' (Gotha) – to the most scurrilous of *double-entendre* – a form of humour that remains the basis of the sex joke. 'You peril my reputation,' wrote Robert Monteith[6] to the minor literary man Richard Monckton Milnes, 'I receive notelets from you containing the last indecencies on the subject of Royal venery; I burn with chaste and loyal indignation, shout with laughter, and end with showing the documents right and left . . .'[7]

Prince Albert – shy, diffident, stooping – was perfectly set up for the wits. Being German he could be quoted in comic broken English, and being a foreigner he could be sneered at with the inner knowledge that there would be few to take his part. Great play could also be made with the location of Windsor, and the various towns that lay between it and London, and especially helpful was the fact that a nearby town was conveniently named Maidenhead. This furnished ample material.

One of the anecdotes was given a title 'An Obstacle Removed'.[8]

'Incapable as Lord Melbourne and his colleagues have been in managing the affairs of this country, still it must be confessed that they merit some little applause from the public in consequence of throwing open Maidenhead-gate, which hitherto has been a passage for the private convenience of Her Majesty; and although it is a perfect Whig measure, not being open to all parties, still some benefit is conferred upon the country. As Prince Albert possessed the privilege of riding through it at his pleasure, and it will possibly be the thoroughfare through which the future kings of England will pass, it is no longer called Maidenhead-gate, but Albert-lodge.'

Other jokes were in the format of question and answer:

'So Albert goes with the Queen to Windsor after the ceremony.'
'He'll go further before morning.'
'How so?'

'Why, he'll go in at Bushy, pass Virginia Water, on through Maiden-head, and leave Staines behind.'

In some of the humour, personalities intruded. There were a large number of disgruntled uncle-type figures still around, in particular the Duke of Cumberland, the obnoxious one-eyed tyrant next in line to the throne. However, Prince George of Cambridge was credited with a mock Valentine addressed ostensibly to the Queen:

> May the 'tiffle' speedily take him,
> May he nab him by surprise,
> Cramps and spavins soon o'ertake him,
> Trout-fed beggar – damn his eyes!
> Cruel, cruel, oh! my jewel!
> Thus to sear a heart for love,
> For a crowdie water-gruel,
> Spooney German, *sucking* dove.[9]

As is the case in most sex jokes, repetition of the standard symbolism becomes a bore, and it is in the parodying of popular songs of the period that there does emerge a raffish agreeable humour:

Air – 'The Mountain Sprite'

> In yon great castle there dwelt alone,
> A maid, whose life all had calmly flown,
> Till Melbourne sought her, by day and night,
> To wed with a magless German wight.
>
> So he from Gotha came wandering o'er,
> At the *golden* sands of this island shore;
> A rich bride sparkled before his sight –
> 'I'm in a good thing,' quoth the German wight.
>
> Old Baroness Lehzen, one sunny day,
> As snug in her bed on her back she lay,
> Persuaded the maid, with all her might,
> To marry the magless German wight.
>
> And now, from the turret of yon great tower,
> Down to the grove and the myrtle bower,
> All over these grounds you may feast your sight,
> With the wide domain of the German wight.

> One night, spurred on by a dazzling look,
> The German boldly his pencil took,
> And, guided only by a dim rushlight,
> He succeeded in making a German wight.
>
> 'Of all the wights by land or sea'
> Exclaimed he, 'then there is none like thee,
> You shall reign over millions in sovereign might,
> A monarch I've made' quoth the German wight.[10]

With the men about town, the deadpan approach to the royal wedding was favoured. A mock news item printed on 8 February – three days before the wedding – said that 'Her Majesty has given the most peremptory orders that the following papers shall be in her bed chamber on the night of her marriage: Four *Posts*, with double sheets, one *Standard*, two *Globes*, one *Examiner*, and no *Observer*. The four *Posts*, with sheets, John Bull finds. Prince Albert, however, has undertaken to supply her Majesty every evening with the *Standard* and *Globes*.'

The news that Prince Albert would be married in the uniform of a British field marshal was also incorporated into the saga. At Melton, the Marquis of Waterford and his mistress, the prostitute Louisa Turner, discussed it, and Louisa is supposed to have riposted, 'Whatever the officers might think of the matter, she trusted that the privates under his command would, in the hour of need, stand stiff before him.'

The fact of Albert being a German is used in the anecdote:

'How did you get on all night?' asked the Baroness Lehzen. 'Sometimes von side, sometimes oder,' responded Albert.

The unfortunate contretemps over Albert's allowance was also not forgotten. What are the board wages of Prince Albert? A quarter of a crown a day and the whole of a sovereign at night. Who gave Prince Albert his first sovereign? The Archbishop of Canterbury. The Prince bored a hole in it, and spit in it for luck. Nor was the fact that the Queen proposed to the Prince overlooked. Why is Her Majesty the most celebrated composer of the day? Because her overture to Prince Albert is known all over the world.

Occasionally anecdotes are related with a volume of circumstantial detail that make them possible genuine items of repartee. During the forties there was considerable controversy about the Corn Laws, a state subsidy that kept foreign grain out of the country and British farmers happy with inflated prices for their wheat. 'What is the use of all this botheration about the Corn Laws?' Dillon Browne M.P. is supposed to have asked at Ben Morgan's in Maiden Lane, 'has not the little Queen – the saints preserve her – settled the question by opening her port for the reception of foreign seed?' On the other hand, an anecdote spoken between Palmerston and Melbourne is *most* improbable:

'Melbourne, my old cock, I'll give you a riddle.'
'Say on.'
'When Prince Albert marries the Queen, and is fixed in his high blown fortune, why will he resemble a hospital?'
'Can't say,' said Melbourne, after a vain attempt to appear thoughtful.
'Why, because he'll be supported by voluntary contributions.'

Two decades later this would have been followed by 'collapse of stout party,' but Victorian humour had not yet reached the level sanctified in *Punch* of the sixties. This joke was published in the weekly the *Town*, a malignant periodical that stumbled on for four years, and was printed on 4 January, five weeks before the royal marriage. The wedding served as material for many months, and in April and May the humorous writers were still ringing the changes on these early Freudian symbols.

'You have not seen all the *beauties of England* yet,' observed Lord Paget to the Prince, after he had *dismounted* from a *riding* excursion with the Queen; 'there are some counties remarkable for their scenery. I dare say your highness will *like hunts*!'
'Vare much! Vare much!' replied Albert, 'I have been in several, and do like them all vare much!'
Vic blushed up to her top-knot, till Albert took off her attention by performing a *pirouette* on one of her corns.
It is whispered in the highest circles that the *row* will shortly become a more favourite diversion in all *quarters*, as the Queen intends patronizing nautical *recreations*. Albert is engaged to accompany her,

during the approaching *season*, in several delightful excursions *below the Brest*.

The schoolboyish infantility of this humour presents a not often observed facet of early Victorian England, and would not have received such widespread acceptance but for the pathological hatred felt by many for Prince Albert. Immediately prior to her wedding, Victoria was also going through a period of disdain; it was widely believed that she was being manipulated by her ex-governess Baroness Lehzen and by the mysterious Baron Stockmar, who acted as the eyes and ears of the King of the Belgians. It was also well known that she did not see eye to eye with the great hero of the century, the Duke of Wellington, a man now in his dotage who could always reckon on the biggest of all cheers. It was also known that Victoria had considered not inviting Wellington to the wedding because of her aversion to all Tories.

The Duke was not accustomed to being reluctantly invited to weddings, nor did he relish being called, as the Queen had done, a rebel. Shortly after the wedding he had a severe stroke, the worst he had ever had. 'The character of the Duke is much changed by these attacks. He is irritable, violent, and has no control whatever of his temper. It is lamentable.' [11] So wrote that assiduous observer of the social scene, Lady Holland.

Early in the morning of 11 February the Queen and the Prince were observed walking in the grounds of Windsor Castle. 'Strange that a bridal night should be so short,' commented Greville, who had the opportunity to observe all that happened about the Queen, and who brought to all the gossip he recorded a certain malicious melancholy.

The sharp-eyed news hawks of the period also acquired this information about the royal early rising, but they, worn out, no doubt, by the task of thinking up constant streams of double meanings, could do very little with it:

> If *we* were satisfied with lying
> From twelve to eight, I cannot see
> Why meddling fools should now be trying
> To bring discredit upon *me*.

Whatever the outsiders thought of the Queen's wedding night, and however many thousands of words of obscene fantasy had been written about it, the Queen was quite evidently more than satisfied. She may have disposed of her uncle, the King of the Belgians, as a political force to be reckoned with in England, but her affection for him bubbled over in a letter she wrote to him after the early morning walk at Windsor.

I write to you from here, the happiest, happiest Being that ever existed. Really, I do not think it *possible* for any one in the world to be *happier*, or as happy as I am. He is an Angel, and his kindness and affection for me is really touching. To look in those dear eyes, and that dear sunny face, is enough to make me adore him. What I can do to make him happy will be my greatest delight. Independent of my great personal happiness, the reception we both met with yesterday was the most gratifying and enthusiastic I ever experienced. . .[12]

This happiness communicated itself to all those who could look at the alliance objectively. Wrote Dickens to the poet and professional eccentric Walter Savage Landor:

Society is unhinged here by her majesty's marriage, and I am sorry to add that I have fallen hopelessly in love with the Queen, and wander up and down with vague and dismal thoughts of running away to some uninhabited island with a maid of honour, to be entrapped by conspiracy for that purpose. Can you suggest any particular young person, serving in such a capacity, who would suit me?[13]

All the world, it is optimistically postulated, loves a lover.

Among the debauched and world-weary aristocracy, however, there was a note of envy. The Duchess of Bedford had the idea that the Queen was 'excessively in love' with Albert, 'but he not a bit with her'. Greville confided that Albert gave the impression 'of not being happy'. The detached and objective Peel was heard to mention that the Queen 'had quite the manner of a woman in love with a man'. On the third night, Greville pretended to be shocked when the Queen got together a party for dancing, a diversion of which she was very fond. 'Her best friends,' he wrote, 'are shocked and hurt at her not conforming more than she is doing to English customs and at not continuing for a short space in that retirement, which modesty and native delicacy generally prescribe . . .'[14]

The Queen was not conforming to the image that had been wished on her by the popular press.[15] She had outbid the journalists who had dwelt with relish on the details of her wedding night thinking that this would shock and hurt her, journalists who had forgotten that she was a Hanoverian, and had clearly inherited their zest, gusto, and their sensuality. The idea, so strenuously advocated, that the Queen was a mock-modest prude does not bear the slightest examination; she was a Prince Albert-orientated creature, and did not care who knew it.

Life at Court

One of the crosses the Queen had to bear was sexual immorality at court. The interminable formalities of Windsor encouraged a certain laxness when visitors escaped from the Presence, though most of them managed to avoid the *faux pas* committed by Palmerston who had affectionate relations with one of Her Majesty's Ladies of the Bedchamber, and who, one night, in pursuit of her, went into the wrong bedroom, the distressed occupant of which raised the alarm.[16]

The gaming tables were whisked away, though whist and billiards remained reputable diversions. Prince Albert had an organ installed ('the first of instruments; the only instrument for expressing one's feelings').[17] Music was the art favoured at court. 'Just conceive anything so awful as a round table,' wrote Mary Bulteel, a Maid of Honor '– with Royalties sitting around it – a whist table – Prince Consort and Uncle Charles at billiards – *a dead silence* – me quite alone at the end of the room, with a very resonant pianoforte, and nothing but my voice heard through the room.'[18] Spiritualism was later a passing interest of the court, especially that variety of it concerned with table turning.

The Queen speedily became pregnant, was surprised by her

bouncing good health, but suffered severely during her twelve-hour labour. She was also peeved because it was not the expected son, and until the Princess Royal was christened she was referred to as 'the Child'. To the Queen, child-bearing was the 'shadow-side' of marriage, the *Schattenseite*, an attitude that was taken up enthusiastically towards the end of the century by the suffragettes ('I know it must be very horrid to go, as it were, a beast to the shambles,' wrote Josephine Butler to a woman about to be confined, in 1893).

Soon after the birth of Princess Victoria Adelaide Mary Louise ('Vicky'), the Queen became pregnant again. The mothers of Britain, inundated with their own children, were pleased; the Queen was one of them, helpless before the vast forces of nature. They also, said Lord Grey elegantly, came to 'estimate and admire the beauty of domestic life beyond reproach, or the possibility of reproach, of which the Queen and he [the Prince] set so noble an example'.[19] How different from the raffish life of the aristocracy, or 'the almost entire extinction of sexual decency which is one of the darkest stains upon the character of the manufacturing population'.[20]

However, the elderly reprobates of the Regency era were dying off. Lord Hertford took a party of whores to an inn in Richmond, dined them and wined them, returned home, was violently sick, and was dead within three days. Lord Melbourne, for whom Victoria's affection had dwindled, had a stroke, but put it down to lumbago and 'suppressed gout'. One of the uncles, the Duke of Sussex, the one who had sobbed throughout the Queen's wedding ceremony, expressed a firm wish to be buried in the new public cemetery at Kensal Green, London. Prince Albert's father in the monarch-producing state of Coburg died, largely unlamented. Lord Brougham 'conducted himself strangely indeed at the Drawing Room, got *into conversation* with the Queen and Albert, offering to carry letters to Paris for her, and then turning most familiarly to her, "and *parcels* also" '.[21]

The atrophy of court life was made worse by the lack of humour of the Prince, though he had a partiality for practical jokes, a propensity he passed on to the Prince of Wales. If some-

one caught a foot in a mat or nearly fell into the fire or out of a
window, 'the mirth of the whole Royal Family, led by the
Prince, knew no bounds'.[22] Lord Granville, a refugee from the
Regency way of life, said that he would never tell his best stories
to the royal couple since pretending to pinch one's finger in
the door would answer better. For those whose sense of humour
was more advanced, there might well be the glacial, 'We are not
amused.'

Child followed child in rapid succession. After the Princess
Royal and the Prince of Wales there was Alice (25 April 1843)
and Alfred (6 August 1844), then Helena, Louise, Arthur,
Leopold, and Beatrice. The fervent ardor of the Prince Consort
was undimmed. 'I hope tomorrow at half-past six to fall into
your arms,' he wrote in 1851, though whatever these intima-
tions of pneumatic bliss really indicate, sex *qua* sex did not have
the Queen's whole-hearted approval. 'That despising of our
poor degraded sex (for what else is it, as we poor creatures are
born for Man's pleasure and amusement) ... is a little in all
clever men's natures; dear Papa even is not quite exempt though
he would not admit it.'[23] So she wrote with what was then
devastating frankness to her eldest daughter in 1859. Nevertheless, although she was so often in what she described as 'that
unhappy condition', the Queen would have nothing to do with
birth control. It was, she considered, a 'horrid thing'.

One of the Prince of Wales's favourite farces was *My Awful
Dad*. Whether this means anything other than that this was the
cultural level of the Prince of Wales is a moot point, though it
does appear that there were times when Prince Albert was, indeed, the most awful of dads, directing the Prince of Wales
along the lines totally alien to the temperament of this, his first-
born son. The Prince of Wales was cut off almost entirely from
his contemporaries as a boy; it was a rare occasion when he
managed to evade the parental scrutiny, such as a walking tour
in the Lake District in 1857, but even then his companions
were hand-picked, and any divergencies from the straight and
narrow would be sure to be reported back to Prince Albert.

Naturally enough, Queen Victoria wanted the Prince of
Wales ('Bertie') to be a carbon copy of her husband, and the

fact that he was not prejudiced her against him in a most un-motherly way. She wrote to the Queen of Prussia:

I find no especial pleasure or compensation in the company of the elder children, only very occasionally do I find the rather intimate intercourse with them either easy or agreeable. ... I only feel properly *à mon aise* and quite happy when Albert is with me. ... I cannot get used to the fact that Vicky [the eldest daughter, the Princess Royal] is almost grown up. . .[24]

She had not found a formula for dealing with adolescents, while Albert pursued his aim of making the Prince of Wales into the minor German professor with artistic tastes. The walking tour of the Lake District having turned out well, the young prince was despatched to Konigswinter, near Bonn, with the customary entourage. Here the Prince of Wales displayed amorous tendencies that were later to get out of hand, and kissed a pretty girl, a harmless incident that was, characteristic-ally, reported back to England, and which was referred to by Gladstone, then Chancellor of the Exchequer, as 'this squalid debauch'. Gladstone had a peculiar way of looking at the sins of the world, and his propensities towards helping fallen women were already causing raised eyebrows amongst his colleagues; one need not take too much notice of his strictures, though the fact that a mere kiss was described as a squalid debauch leads one to suspect that there *may* have been more in it than a mere kiss.

The deprecation of Queen Victoria could have done little to bolster up the self confidence of the Prince of Wales. His per-sonal income had recently been lifted from £100 to £500 a year. He spent more money on clothes, which, again, was a black mark in the eyes of the prematurely aged Prince Albert, still only in his late thirties, act as an elder statesman as he might. Despite the fact that the Prince of Wales shone in fashionable society, the Queen complained that he was 'a very dull com-panion', and that, in his dislike of clever books, he was a caricature of herself. Her husband was more ruthless: 'Bertie's propensity is indescribable laziness,' he wrote aggressively, 'I never in my life met such a thorough and cunning lazybones.'[25]

The disappointment that the royal pair felt over their off-spring was brought to the boil when the Prince of Wales was despatched to Curragh Camp, in Ireland, for a ten-week course of infantry training. No doubt the intention was good, and there would be few hardships for Bertie in the role of a staff colonel attached to the First Battalion, Grenadier Guards, and should he play his part adequately it would be a fine advertisement for the volunteer movement, brought into being by fear of war. However, the Prince of Wales proved as difficult to drill as to educate, and his presumption in asking to command a company was put down with contempt by the CO, a Colonel Percy, who told the Prince that he was imperfect in his drill, and that his word of command was indistinct.

Whatever the hardships of the army, they were compensated for by a new freedom. There were no sycophants to write back all the news. A young actress was smuggled into the Prince of Wales's quarters by amiable brother officers, and this became the first of the Prince's fully-fledged affairs. The girl's name was Nellie Clifden, and she boasted of her conquest; the person to whose ears the news came was, predictably, Stockmar, and this was information too good to keep to oneself, though in any event the affair was known on the continent, and was shortly to be confirmed by a clubland gossip, Lord Torrington.

It was unfortunate at the time that Prince Albert was going through a particularly bleak spell. Overwork had led to deep depression and melancholy; he had once said to Victoria that he did not cling to life (as she did) and that, if he had a severe illness, he would go under. 'I should not struggle for life. I have no tenacity of life.' [26] At breakfast he wore a wig to keep out the cold. There was also the Trent affair, an occasion when the British were interfering inadvisedly with the progress of the American Civil War. It is said by the keenest supporters of Prince Albert that it was his dispatch that saved Britain and America from war, but be that as it may, it was one more burden to be carried, and carried alone, as the Queen was prostrate with grief over the death of her mother, and was indulging in extensive self-recrimination.

The news of the Prince of Wales's escapade could hardly

have come at a more inauspicious time, and he wrote to his
son 'with a heavy heart upon a subject which has caused me the
greatest pain I have yet felt in this life'. The Prince of Wales
replied that he had yielded to temptation, that the affair was at
an end, and that he was contrite, but that he would not name
the officers who had led him into disgrace, a gesture that Albert
warmly commended. Albert forgave his son this 'evil deed'
that gave him 'terrible pain' and said that in future the Prince
of Wales must fight 'a valiant fight'. It was also essential that
there should be an early marriage with someone from the royal
vortex of Europe.

Prince Albert was already in poor physical condition; for a
long time he had been suffering from stomach trouble. He developed headache and pains in the back and legs, but the royal
doctors again blundered – 'there was no cause for alarm' said
Dr Jenner. On 14 December 1861, Albert died of typhoid fever.
In her distress, the Queen blamed the Prince of Wales ('I never
can or shall look at him without a shudder. ... Beloved Papa
told him that I could not be told all the disgusting details.'[27]
So she wrote to her daughter.)

What had happened to the robust sensuality of the Hanovers,
what had happened to the unconcern with which the Queen
had discussed such matters with Lord Melbourne in the old
days? 'The Q's conduct in this matter is hardly sane but as we
know it has never been otherwise,' wrote Lord Clarendon to the
Duchess of Manchester, and as for the Prince of Wales, 'the
poor boy asks nothing better than to devote himself to comforting his Mother'.[29] It was also unfortunate that the Prince of
Wales had arrived at the deathbed in a rather gay mood, not
realizing the seriousness of the case, as his informant, Princess
Alice, had taken the word of the doctors regarding the condition of her father.

If one era had ended when Prince Albert had died, another
began on 10 March 1863. This was the day Bertie, Prince of
Wales, married Princess Alexandra of Denmark, one of the
poorer relations of Europe. 'Her parents were not so rich as
most London shopkeepers; had from seven hundred to a

thousand a year,' wrote Jane Welsh Carlyle brightly, adding more sombrely that 'I also feel a sympathy with her in the prospect of the bother she will have by-and-by.'[29]

And bother there assuredly was. The Prince of Wales made profligacy in high circles respectable, he brought the gaming tables back into his own sector of the court, and he made horse racing the sport of kings; he borrowed money from international financiers (Hirsch and Cassel) and a series of 'innocent flirtations' brought him as a witness in a divorce case and threatened him with high scandal in others. When this is considered, there is no need to wonder why he became one of the most popular men in the country. All the world loves a lover, but even more so when he captures the heart of beauties like Lillie Langtry, and when he can actually make money with race horses (his stallions earned £269,495 in stud fees, and his horses won £146,345), and all this on a mere £100,000 [30] a year !

Gone were the days when visitors to Windsor who wanted to smoke had to lie in the fireplace so that the smoke would go up the chimney. Gone were the days when the slightest word out of place would be dealt with with punctilious severity. The second half of the nineteenth century had two courts : Windsor–Buckingham Palace–Osborne–Balmoral and Marlborough House–Sandringham. There was no question which was the most brilliant. At Windsor, the main event was the Presence, at which 'the Queen proceeded slowly round the assembly, moving as it were on castors',[31] and, secondly, the meals, prepared by cooks of vast experience, eaten silently and quickly (the Queen ate quickly and it was the custom to whip the plates away as soon as she had finished).

By the sixties, photography was a massive and flourishing industry, and the royal family was not exempt from the probing lens. The photographs taken at the time are uncommonly revealing (early nude photographs, for example, invariably show pubic hair). A photograph of Queen Victoria, with the Prince and Princess of Wales, on the day of the marriage, depict a raffish young man with a receding chin (a Hanoverian legacy) and fuzz on the cheek, an elongated cupid's-bow mouth, and the heavy-lidded eyes one tends to associate with the Prince in later days when he was Edward VII. Alexandra was unquestionably a beautiful girl, who steadily got more beautiful, reaching her peak probably in the late eighties. A fascinating Marlborough House group photograph of 1889 makes it clear that she was ravishingly pretty. Unfortunately she became increasingly deaf, though a limp she had was no disadvantage, as it was imitated by great ladies and became known in this adopted form as the 'Alexandra limp'. She emerges from the royal tangles of the nineteenth century with her glamour and her virtue intact, and her one liaison, with Colonel the Honorable Oliver Montagu, was conducted on a lofty platonic plane, though when he died in 1893 she was desolate.

The photographs of the Queen dating from the 1860s present something of a dilemma. In most of them she is depicted gazing with a mournful sanctimonious air at a bust of Prince Albert, and in her voluminous widow's garb (including hood) she appears to us as a parody of that omniscient nineteenth-century comic figure, the poor forlorn widow-woman, a sort of Queen Gummidge. There is none of the charm of her early years, and none of the majesty she was later to command effortlessly. When she went into her ostentatious display of grief in 1861, it is not to be wondered at that the main sentiment felt by her statesmen (and her relatives) was one of irritation. Death, after all, was always present, and Prince Albert had exceeded the average expectation of life for that century which was forty.

Victoria wanted the best of both worlds (the best of *three* worlds if one includes the hereafter [32] – she took a very dim view of the Creator's impudence in taking away her beloved Albert). She wished to go into seclusion yet continue to rule the country; she wished the Prince of Wales to be a responsible member of the royal clan yet refused to give him a job to do.

The honeymoon was at Osborne, depicted by the Crown Prince of Prussia as one great gloomy vault filled with the relics of the Prince Consort, but the return to London was described by Disraeli as a royal public honeymoon spread over months. The Prince of Wales's life might be said to be a series of honeymoons, though his wife was usually kept in the picture, whether or not she was expected to receive the new favourites. 'At no time for the last sixty or seventy years was frivolity, the love of pleasure, self-indulgence, luxury, and idleness (producing ignorance) carried to such an excess as now in the Higher Classes, and it resembles the time before the first French Revolution.' [33] So wrote the Queen to the Prince of Wales. She was happier about the Lower Orders, whom she identified with the kowtowing local worthies and the gruff, rough-grained servants at Balmoral.

The Prince of Wales was more in touch with reality. He drew the Queen's attention to mob behaviour, to the 'roughs' who were beginning to leave the squalid fastnesses in the East End and were venturing 'up West', to riot in Hyde Park and attend inflammatory meetings in Trafalgar Square. He conceded that a great proportion of the Aristocracy, 'or Upper Ten Thousand', were self-indulgent, idle, absorbed in amusement, but protested that this was worse in other countries. He agreed that the Aristocracy ought to lead a useful life – but ought to have their pleasures. In a similar way he later pontificated on gambling; it was evil – except if one could afford it.

The fashionable world became oriented to the activities of the Prince of Wales. Yachting at Cowes became fashionable; sermons at those churches favoured by the Prince's presence were to last no longer than ten minutes. There were chores, of course, the laying of foundation stones and the inspection of institutions, chores which had to be carried out while the Queen was 'on a dreary sad pinnacle of solitary grandeur' organizing the deification of Prince Albert, represented today by Martin's biography, which took fourteen years to write, and the Albert Memorial.

During the 1860s the Queen became reconciled to the nature of the Prince of Wales. Perhaps, after all, he was not responsible for the death of her husband by the Curragh Camp escapade. He had, unquestionably, 'a loving affectionate heart ... was simple and unassuming ... full of good and amiable qualities ... was nice and unpretending'. This feeling was not counteracted by news that the Prince was dipping into capital to pay gaming losses.

Alexandra, like all the royal ladies, began to build up a large family, and the stresses made her ill. The Prince's escapades began, and gossip circulated about attentions to ladies in St Petersburg, Moscow and Paris. No one appeared surprised, or much concerned; these places were a long way away, and the personages concerned were not likely to complain. More damaging things were happening nearer home.

In February 1870 Sir Charles Mordaunt, one of the fast set so much distrusted by Queen Victoria, filed a petition for divorce from his twenty-one-year-old wife. Shortly after the birth of her first child, Lady Mordaunt had told her husband, 'Charlie, you are not the father of that child. Lord Cole is the father of it, and I am the cause of its blindness.' She had sat silent for a quarter of an hour, and had then burst into tears, declaring, 'Charlie, I have been very wicked; I have done very wrong.'

That any member of the fast set should have been surprised at such a circumstance must give us pause. Mordaunt asked who the villains were, with whom had she done very wrong. Lady Mordaunt replied, 'With Lord Cole, the Prince of Wales, and others, often, and in open day.'

In due course, the Prince was served with a subpoena to appear at court, though it was not he who was cited with Lord Cole, but Sir Frederick Johnstone. Lady Mordaunt's father claimed that she was insane (as, indeed, she was) and this invalidated the accusation. Nevertheless, the Prince of Wales had written twelve letters to Lady Mordaunt, though these were dismissed an innocuous by the Lord Chancellor, Lord Hatherley, to whom the Prince went, after confiding in his wife. Hatherley professed that no 'useful object' would be served in the 'extra ordinary step' of sending a subpoena to the Prince, though he realized the implications. It was, he said, 'as bad as a revolution as affecting [the Prince of] Wales'. Gossip was all very well, but the presence of the heir apparent in the witness box in an age when divorce cases received the maximum publicity could hardly foster the cause of the monarchy. Divorce was humorous, though not quite so funny as breach of promise, the cases of which had the courts in stitches.

The Queen, when the Prince told her about the subpoena,

was surprisingly understanding. She declared that she had every confidence in his innocence, but that in future he would do better to be more circumspect. 'Believe me,' she wrote to the Princess Royal, 'children are a terrible anxiety, and the sorrow they cause is far greater than the pleasure they give.' Although the case would not be rigged, there was evidence that the judge would protect the Prince 'from any improper questions', though the Prince himself was alarmed at the prospect of being cross-examined. Nothing like this could have happened to Prince Albert. 'The fact of the Prince of Wales's intimate acquaintance with a young married woman being publicly proclaimed,' wrote the Queen to the Lord Chancellor, 'will show an amount of imprudence which cannot but damage him in the eyes of the middle and lower classes, which is most deeply to be lamented in these days when the higher classes, in their frivolous, selfish and pleasure-seeking lives, do more to increase the spirit of democracy than anything else.'[34] One need not be surprised that democracy was a naughty word to the great Queen.

The Prince was cross-examined for seven minutes, and acquitted himself well, 'painful and lowering' as it was to his mother. He denied that he had committed adultery, and he was not cross-examined by the formidable Sergeant Ballantine. Thus the Mordaunt case was less dangerous to the stability of the monarchy than it might have been, though the Prince of Wales had the rare and unpleasant experience of being booed in the street. As for Mordaunt, the case went badly, his petition being rejected on account of his wife's insanity. Five years later, Mordaunt tried again. He limited his attention to Lord Cole, and this economy succeeded. He was granted his petition.

The Marlborough House Set

Oscar Wilde once said that his three favourite women were Queen Victoria, Lillie Langtry and Sarah Bernhardt. It is odd that one of these was the Prince of Wales's mother, and that two were his mistresses. It must be that they had something in common, or that the Prince, when pursuing his doxies, was really in search of a mother-figure. A quality they assuredly did share was presence; to James Agate, one-time arbiter of the theatre's fate, Bernhardt was 'the divine Sarah', even after she had lost a leg, and even after she had made an ill-fated excursion into silent films (she did not die until 1923).

An actress was defined in a serial feature in a dim satirical weekly of 1868, the *Tomahawk*, as 'a creature'. Sarah Bernhardt was more than this; to Lady Frederick Cavendish she was a 'a woman of notorious, shameless character. ... Not content with being run after on the stage, this woman is asked to respectable people's houses to act, and even to luncheon and dinner; and all the world goes. It is an outrageous scandal !' [35]

Among the aristocracy, the adulterous liaison was accepted throughout the nineteenth century, forming an admirable illustration of Saint-Simon's definition of free love as 'men and women giving themselves to several without ceasing to be united as a couple'. However, Sarah Bernhardt was something of an outsider, someone difficult to accept, basically 'a creature'. On 1 July 1881 Ferdinand de Rothschild, at the Prince of Wales' request, gave a midnight supper party at his house in Piccadilly to allow the Duc d'Aumâle to meet Sarah Bernhardt. The fashionable ladies present refused to speak to the actress, and the whole affair was a dismal frost, made worse by the fact that the Duc D'Aumâle was deaf. The Prince of Wales's patronage never ceased, and Sarah Bernhardt had her place at the coronation, when Bertie, or 'Tum-Tum' as he was known to his closest friends, was miraculously transformed into King Edward VII (this place was in a special box inside Westminster Abbey, and the occupants included Mrs Hartman, Lady Kilmorey, Mrs Arthur Paget, and the reigning royal lady, Mrs George Keppel. This was known as 'the King's Loose Box', not only among the racing fraternity.)

It is difficult for sophisticates of the twentieth century to get excited about these Junoesque creatures of the Victorian age. They appear as so many cows come to pasture, an impression conveyed by the statuesque poses inflicted on them by photographers. The soulful look, in which the pupil of the eye is tucked away beneath the eyelid, seems to us affected; in this, the grand age of the uplifting corset, the breasts have a melon-like size, look, and, perhaps, texture.

Lillie Langtry was, according to the drama critic of *Punch*, Clement Scott, 'of too solid a physique for any light skittish movement' – on the stage, that is – but she rapidly established herself as the reigning beauty of the hour. She became the darling of the painters and the photographers, serving as model for Millais when he was painting the 'Jersey Lily' (thus the nickname), and for G. F. Watts, the bearded patriarch of the art world, and ex-husband of another theatrical lady, Ellen Terry. She was photographed holding, affectionately and senti-mentally, a dead bird, and the music halls thought this amusing, and a song came out:

> I have been photographed like this,
> I have been photographed like that,
> But I have never been photoed
> As a raving maniac.

Like 'Bertie', Lillie Langtry came from a dubious family tree – morally speaking. Her father, the Dean of Jersey, 'was a damned nuisance ... couldn't be trusted with any woman anywhere'.[36] The Prince of Wales met her on 24 May 1877 at the house of Arctic explorer Sir Allen Young; Mrs Langtry's husband con-veniently disappeared into the background (it was a handy piece of court etiquette that when anyone was engaged with the Prince of Wales, all outsiders, even husbands, were to depart from the room).

The life of Lillie Langtry was garish in the extreme. Among her lovers were Crown Prince Rudolf of Austria, a Texan cattle-puncher named Moreton Frewen, King Leopold, George Alexander Baird ('the Squire') who died worth £831,719 and who blacked her eyes (this cost him £50,000), and James Tod-hunter Sloan from Indiana. There was also Ernest Terah Hooley, who bought as a frivolity the royal yacht *Britannia* for £10,000, and the megalomaniac Whitaker Wright, who spent £250,000 in buying Lea Park, Witley, and a further £400,000 on improvements, one of which was a room beneath the lake to watch the fishes. The sporting magazine *Pink 'Un* was at this time serving out the double meanings: 'We heard Mrs Langtry has lost her parrot; for this we are sorry. That the lady possessed such a bird we were unaware, but we knew she had a cockatoo!'

Mrs Langtry was one of those sufficiently intimate with the Prince to play practical jokes on him, such as pretending her soup was cold so that he could taste it and burn his mouth, and slipping ice cream down his neck. It was speculated that Gladstone was also interested in her; Gladstone was certainly unworldly enough to give her the code sign that meant any letters to him were unopened by secretaries, and unworldly enough to give her advice. Although, according to Dr Andrew Clark (Gladstone's physician), Gladstone had 'a flawlessly proportioned figure like some ancient Greek statue', this side of Gladstone did not interest Mrs Langtry. When the rumours were circulating about Gladstone and her, she proclaimed indignantly that it 'was completely absurd and untrue. At that time I had the whole of London society at my call. Why should I have given my favours to a man of that age?' [37] though she said, saucily, at a different time, 'What does it matter what people say as long as they don't actually know?'

There was no question where the Prince of Wales stood. When she decided that she wanted to go on the stage, the Prince brought his weight to bear, and she almost immediately played the lead in several plays, under the auspices of the Bancrofts, who had cornered the Victorian market in problem plays (especially those by their friend, the prolific Tom Robertson).

Donating Lillie Langtry to the stage was only one of 'the many gracious acts by which his Royal Highness has honoured, and endeared himself to, the theatrical profession'.[38] It is not every woman in her late twenties who can decide to go on the stage on hardly more than an impulse and within a few months be able to play the heroine (in *Ours*, by the ubiquitous Tom Robertson). It is hardly to be wondered at that for more than half a century contemporary theatre was dead.

The ability to run with the hares and hunt with the hounds

was probably no more prevalent in the nineteenth century than it is today, though the toadying attitude towards the Prince of Wales does sometimes stick in the throat. The ambiguous attitude towards sin led to some odd attitudes on the part of the press, even that section of the press that called itself satirical.

There were few journalists who did not take the Prince's protestations of innocence in the Mordaunt case with a pinch of salt. There were fewer still who did not go into fits of righteous indignation against those taking such a view:

But when we know the stories to be lies, to be based upon prurient fancies, and to be uttered by poisonous tongues, then, indeed, is our conduct contemptible – then, indeed, is our manhood our curse, our chivalry a sound – meaning nothing! ... The Prince of Wales may not be a milk-sop or a Saint, but he is the Heir Apparent to our Throne, the son of our Queen, and the husband of Alexandra. As such his honour should be as precious to us as our own.[39]

How such an idyllic state differed from Paris! There

Adultery is King on the Boulevards. Ah! that sounds too horrible. But it is true. ... The ducks and drakes our neighbours make with the conjugal code set the circles widening until they fall with a ripple on our shores and vibrate into the heart of London life.[40] [However] in France there is something refined about sin. A halo of sentimentality shines round the head of the breaker of the seventh commandment, and the faithless wife has always an air about her of dying pathetically to slow, soft, and solemn music.[41]

There may have been something refined about Paris sin, but the great advantage of Paris sin to the Marlborough House set was that it was discreet. As Francis Place, the adventurous writer on birth control, put it, in France, 'although a woman may indulge in gallantry, she never injures her husband by introducing into his family a spurious issue'. Well, hardly ever, though with Englishmen there was always a danger. The Frenchmen knew about sex, and were adept at *coitus interruptus*, known as *la chamade*, the retreat, *la prudence*, or *la discrétion*. 'Women of honour,' recorded Place prosaically, 'will rarely trust themselves to the discretion of an Englishman.'

What *exactly* went on in Paris between the Prince of Wales and the *demi-mondaines* will possibly be ever hidden from us, for no figure of the century has been handled in such a cavalier manner by the image makers. The effort by many to present the Prince in a favourable light has led to the most preposterous doublethink. In 1878 Lord Redesdale was standing talking to a friend in the Marlborough Club (a club formed by the Prince of Wales after taking umbrage against one of the older clubs). The friend observed the Prince of Wales nearby, the centre of 'a happy, joyous band'. 'See!' said the friend. 'Is there any one of those men who would not lay down his life for him?' If that were the case, how much more would his friends protect the image of the heir apparent? The *Dictionary of National Biography* asserted that 'at times he enjoyed practical joking at the expense of his friends'. Not a bit of it, asserted Lord Redesdale, 'never either as Prince or King did I, during nearly half a century, see him take active part in any such games himself. He was always mindful of his dignity. . . .'[42] As Prince of Wales, states the *Encyclopaedia Britannica*, 'he was exemplary . . . in his scrupulous detachment from party politics'. The divinity that hedges kings was indeed working overtime on behalf of the princely image.

At a ball given by the Prince in 1870, his friend Christopher Sykes became hopelessly drunk and had to be put to bed. To make it more amusing when he came to, the Prince arranged for a dead sea gull to be laid beside him. This was such a jolly jape that the following night a live trussed rabbit was substituted.[43] In Paris, the Prince and his set arranged for a group of 'policemen' to descend on Madame de Courval, a friend who happened to be running gaming tables. However, the Prince kept his fun within limits, unlike his friend Robert Bristowe, who, to get rid of two servants who would not accept their discharge — knowing, it is said, the master's good nature — bought a jaguar and installed it in his house in Clarges Street, Mayfair. He let it loose in the hall, and rang for the servants, after rushing into the dining room and locking himself in. Naturally enough the servants refused to come, not relishing a tiff with the jaguar. Eventually, Bristowe bored a hole in the dining-room door and spent a gay hour shooting at the jaguar with a revolver, eventually killing it. This was extreme, even for Victorian practical joking, never noted for its subtlety.

As for what the *Encyclopaedia Britannica* maintained to be the Prince of Wales's 'scrupulous detachment' from party politics (in an article written by the editor of the eleventh edition of 1910–11, Hugh Chisholm), there is ample evidence that he was a keen dabbler, though never so forceful as his mother. Gladstone observed with his customary acerbity the Prince's 'total want of political judgement, either inherited or acquired', and it was hardly the action of a scrupulously detached prince to write to the Queen (23 December 1877) urging her to wage war on Russia, otherwise 'we shall never be able to hold our head up again in the eyes of the world'. Fortunately the days of Palmerston were gone forever; otherwise the Prince, with such an irresistible argument, could easily have involved Britain in a war no more satisfactory than the disastrous Crimean War.

The Top Ten Thousand

One of the reasons why sexual morality was so lax among the Marlborough House set was that there were so few diversions apart from baccarat – 'baccy' in the circle – charades, masked balls, and whist. There were far more who wished to play other kinds of games. With this in mind, the rooms were allocated at the great country houses so that there would be as little inconvenience in sleeping around as was consistent with discretion.

A Dr Lewis wrote that 'there are many whose pride forbids all external indulgences, but who permit lascivious fancies to run riot through their imagination' (*In a Nutshell*, 1883). This class hardly existed in the Top Ten Thousand. Lady Arundel, who lived with the painter Basil Hodges, proclaimed brightly to Mrs Panton, 'I don't think there are half a dozen certificates to be had among the lot, and no one that I can see is a penny the worse.' Many of these liaisons were maintained over the years, almost like marriages; others were taken up and dropped to suit the protagonists. Basil Hodges was one of the more unfortunate, as Lady Arundel left him suddenly; he did not despair, but always kept a lamp burning in her bedroom and dainty garments at the ready in case she returned to him suddenly one night in the tradition of Victorian melodrama.

The liaisons were accepted – Lord Torrington and Lady Molesworth, Lord Abingdon and Lady Jersey, Lord Hartington and the Duchess of Manchester, Lord Walpole and Lady Lincoln. 'That libertinism of the most demoralizing character,' [44] wrote Francis Newman (brother of the famous churchman John Henry Newman), 'flourishes in London, in Paris, and in New York, cannot be a secret.'

When such aristocratic liaisons were not accepted, then inconvenience could arise. This was especially true when husbands would not accept the fact that their wives were unfaithful to them, though it was considered ill-bred to proclaim it to the world, and even more so when it was found that the Prince of Wales had been writing to these wives. This had happened in the Mordaunt case, and it was to happen again in the potentially more electric Blandford incident.

On 11 October 1875, the Prince of Wales set out to show the flag in India, taking with him a miscellaneous group of eighteen people, including, to Queen Victoria's disgust, Charles Beresford, the ringleader of the practical joking set, the lunatic fringe of the Marlborough House clique. Also in the party was Lord Aylesford, known as 'Sporting Joe' to his friends. Four months after leaving England, Lord Aylesford received a letter from his wife telling him that she intended to elope with Lord Blandford, brother of Randolph Churchill, later the seventh Duke of Marlborough. Lady Aylesford's brother had also been a member of the Prince of Wales's troupe; he had received information four days earlier than his brother-in-law, and had begun his journey home.

The Prince of Wales was incensed by the behaviour of Blandford; he was 'the greatest blackguard alive'. Aylesford was not displeased by this show of royal partiality and made it known. Into this delicate situation, Lord Randolph Churchill – 'Goose-

Lord Randolph. Lord Randolph had just acquired the post of secretary of state for India in Lord Salisbury's administration, and even royalty admired political success, especially unexpected success.

One of the brightest stars in the Marlborough House firmament was Lord Hartington, known to the set and to most politicians as 'Harty Tarty'. He was eccentric, he was intelligent, and he came from the Cavendish family, which meant that he would be, when his turn came to be Duke of Devonshire, enormously rich. The Prince of Wales used wealth as one of his favourite guide-lines. A convenient way of measuring wealth among the noble families was the size of the annual income from rent. In the case of the Duke of Devonshire, it was £181,000 per annum from 200,000 acres, an income that was completed by dividends on stocks and shares, royalties, and any money deriving from the Duchess of Devonshire. Hartington's father was the seventh Duke of Devonshire.

Hartington was thus born into social grandeur and was made soon aware that he was not as other men. The efforts to fight against the heritage was too much, as it was easier to accept the gifts of the gods, whether it was money, or whether it was women. For the type of women euphemistically known as *demimondaines*, the high-priced whores with their bijou residences in St John's Wood and their landaus and phaetons emblazoned with the coats of arms of their protectors, those of the Hartington ilk were willing victims (though Hartington's own particular woman, 'Skittles' Walters, lived in Chesterfield Street).

What is perhaps surprising is that Hartington had a distinguished career. When Disraeli went to the country in 1880, certain that he would be returned, it would be Hartington who would be leading the Liberal opposition. Owing to Gladstone's return from his grumpy retirement, Disraeli was soundly trounced; on the brink of premiership, the basic second-rateness of Hartington showed through, and, but for that, Britain might well have had a prime minister who had kept the best-known whore – 'Skittles' Walters – in the kingdom. For many years, Hartington had as his mistress the Duchess of Manchester, a liaison eventually confirmed by his marriage to her.

Besides major figures such as Hartington and Beresford, the Marlborough House set had its transient figures. Some of these people were phony, and some were cheats (occasionally they shot or poisoned themselves when they were found out). There were crazed eccentrics such as Christopher Sykes, and there were doddering rakes from the days when Queen Victoria was courting her Albert. In addition, there was the licentious European nobility – the King of Holland who followed his mistress to Paris to see if she was deceiving him (she was), the complete roster of French rulers, and dozens of miscellaneous princes going to and from the spas of central Europe (the most notorious of which was Baden), interspersing these health-giving visits with tripe to what many people considered the sewer of Europe – Paris.

To those who were not his intimates, Hartington in his prime cannot have been a prepossessing individual. He has been described by his contemporaries as a 'heavy swell', and he had the 'haw hawy' type of voice ridiculed by *Punch*. He dressed badly, in ill-fitting tails, which did not close behind him as he walked, and his lemon-coloured trousers were notorious. It was averred that his incredible rudeness and gaucherie were a cover for shyness, and it was reported that he said that the happiest day of his life was when his pig took a first prize at an agricultural show. His honesty was also interpreted as rudeness. During the American Civil War, as many British aristocrats did, he supported the south, and on finding himself in New York at the beginning of the war, and at a masked ball given in his honour, he allowed a secession badge to be pinned to his clothing, though it was pulled off by one of his friends before injury was done to him.

In his Paris days he was visiting a well-known banker whose wife had run off with the groom. In the baron's collection of *objets d'art* was a half-length nude sculpture of a bacchante (with 'passion-maddened' eyes). 'Isn't it beautiful?' the banker asked. 'It is, indeed,' agreed Hartington, 'the first Madame — , I suppose?' [46] In the Houses of Parliament, Hartington's voice carried little weight. He had no oratory, no sophistication, no effortless charm. His commonsensical words fell like lead. On

one occasion, he was so bored with his own utterances, that he
yawned in the middle of one of his statements, explaining it by
admitting that this lapse was because what he was saying 'was
so damned dull'.

When he became Duke of Devonshire, the Duchess of Manchester (née Countess Louise von Alten) was 'made an honest
woman of'. She is one of the charmers of the period, individu-
alistic, free of pedantry, and so unshocked by her own flaunting
of her relationship with Hartington that everyone else accepted
it. Only occasionally was attention drawn to the fact, such as
when the boor and card-cheat Sir William Gordon-Cumming
asked her loudly in a gossip-conscious company, 'When is Harty
Tarty going to make an honest woman of you?' The Queen also
feared the influence of the carefree Duchess when, after Disraeli
had failed to conquer the country in 1880, it was necessary to
summon Hartington to form a government (he was not 'a hard
worker' she protested). As it happened, her reluctance to put her
faith in someone who was a member of the frivolous Marlborough House set did not matter, as Hartington, well aware of
his deficiencies, refused to form a government (after all, what
had Gladstone been stomping up and down the country for if it
was not to be prime minister?).

The Duchess of Manchester, who was described as surpass-
ingly beautiful, had what E. F. Benson called 'the unswerving
relentlessness of a steam-roller about her'.[47] When an impudent
friend asked her about the rumour that Devonshire House was
to be sold, she replied: 'Yes, perfectly true. We are proposing
to live at Clapham Junction instead. So convenient a train
service.'

The Marlborough House set continued for almost forty years.
There were vicissitudes, and friends who overstepped the mark
between familiarity and offensiveness were summarily dealt with.
At Sandringham, Sir Frederick Johnstone (one of the co-
respondents in the Mordaunt divorce case) had become very
drunk; the Prince of Wales pointed this out, 'Freddy, Freddy,
you're very drunk.' Johnstone pointed to the Prince's belly, and
imitating the princely rolling 'r's, proclaimed, 'Tum-Tum,
you're ve*rr*y fat!' Johnstone was out of the house before break-

fast the following morning. Thus the minor tragedies of the rich.

Much of the spite directed against the *dolce vita* of the aristocracy was motivated by envy. The Prince of Wales's circle was relatively open, as money, in sufficient quantities, could buy a way in, but other sets were exclusive. The Marlborough House set was the coarse buffoon of the coteries. There were others where the exclusiveness has resisted the historian, because of the use of a private language in letters and of pet names. Eliza and Joseph were the Queen and Prince Albert, but who were the Midge, the Flea, the Duffer, the Lively Mouse, the Cold Cow? We are a long way from the schoolboyish pseudonyms of the Prince of Wales's circle – the Tum-Tum, Sporting Joe, and so on. Or are we?

2

The Lesser Infortune

The Leisure Classes

THE leisure class is a parasite, and its exponents in the nineteenth century were as distasteful a bunch as one could wish for, professional idlers who desperately tried to stave off the collapse of the three-tier social system. That they did so, and are still doing so, says much for the innate conservatism of Britain. There were two basic leisure classes – those who were forced into the state through unemployment (the poor), and those who were born into it (the rich), many of whom found the forced inactivity irksome and who redeemed themselves by doing something tolerably useful, though they had to tread the class line and not try too hard. The aim of the rich leisure class was to demonstrate that they were too well-bred to work, and they did this in three ways: (a) conspicuous consumption; (b) conspicuous leisure; and (c) vicarious consumption. They ate more, were overdressed, lived in houses too large for them, flaunted their leisure habits, had too many servants, and prattled about God's good taste in making them Superior People. Unfortunately for them they could not keep their satisfaction to themselves, and overflowed into print where their narrow minds and vapid sentiments are ossified for the benefit of anyone who cares to spend a small sum on aristocratic memoirs in second-hand bookshops. The more astute were aware that things were changing – 'We are whirled about, and hooted around, and rung up as if we were parcels, booking clerks, or office boys' [1] – and threw spanners into the government machine when it appeared that civilization was moving too fast.

Nature abhoring a vacuum and the devil finding work for idle hands to do, the leisure class was open to all kinds of temptation, and this produced the classic nineteenth-century situation – the desire to submit to temptation countered by the desire to conform. The loss of virtue of a young maiden of the leisure class was social death, adultery by a matron of this class could result in every attribute of this class being stripped away, and although the high-flying aristocracy of the Marlborough House set were able to cut corners, far more members of the leisure class were forced into an endless round of petty unsatisfying 'pleasures', interspersed with interludes sniping at the lower orders and at the rising middle classes who were themselves becoming members of the leisure class. This was especially true of the distaff side. The men had found a way to cut through the boredom inflicted by their station in life. 'Our amusements were very simple ones,' wrote the Countess of Cardigan defensively. 'After lunch we walked over Cannock Chase, and those ladies who did not care for walking rode sturdy little ponies. We returned to tea, and after dinner there was music, cards or dancing. We thoroughly enjoyed ourselves and nobody was bored, although we did not smoke cigarettes, lose money at Bridge, or scour the country in motor-cars to kill time.' [2] It was characteristic of the Countess of Cardigan that she did not pen her memoirs herself, but had them – vicarious activity again – ghosted. Those women who found walks, flower arranging and cards too too unrewarding even for their exalted position threw themselves into mock serious pursuits. Lady Dorothy Nevill had many 'things with which to pass my time, including a model farm with a Dutch dairy, situated amidst the lovely surroundings. In a little wooded hollow, not far from the house, stood a fair-sized cottage, and here I established a model laundry, where a certain number of poor girls were trained for domestic service, not always, I am bound to say, with very satisfactory results.' [3]

Occasionally the whiff of adultery came too close to the ladies of the leisure class for comfort, and contemporaries of Lady Colin Campbell must have drawn in their breath when they heard her novel defence when accused of adultery with Lord Blandford and others (including a Captain Shaw of the fire brigade, an incident that encouraged W. S. Gilbert to incorporate him in one of his operettas).[4] Lady Colin's defence was that she was too *busy* to participate in any adultery, and for the benefit of a court that must have been mentally curled up in hysterics she accounted for her day. She had to run a house in Cadogan Square; act as hostess for her M.P. husband; write letters, articles for the *Queen* and other journals, and novels; perform as a singer at charity concerts, for which she was in constant demand; teach working girls at night school; and ladle out soup for the denizens of Stepney. It was clearly a defence that would have been impossible for many of her class to put forward, but it helped that Lord Blandford, with whom she was supposed to have spent a weekend at a hotel in Purfleet as Mr and Mrs Perry, had conceded that the woman with whom he had consorted was a woman of the streets and not Lady Colin.

What was a man of the leisure class to do with his life? Politics, perhaps. The House of Commons was a rich man's preserve. When the twenty-three-year-old William Harcourt wanted to enter politics, his by no means poor father wrote to him, warning him against it 'unless you were to tell me candidly that you have been *accepted* by a girl with £20,000'.[5] Some place in the royal household, perhaps, such as Lord Ribblesdale obtained: 'I found my Lord-in-Waitingship most agreeable – the pay was good, the service light, my Royal Mistress most kind, the yoke unexacting. ... A "wait" lasted a fortnight. One year, thanks to the hazards of the roster, I only did two or three days' waiting, another only four or five.'[6] Perhaps the Foreign Office, a haven for aristocratic reactionaries, which did little work. Cobden slated it in 1860 – 'the delay which has taken place is attributable to our Foreign Office, to their habitual procrastination, the desire to meddle, and I fear also to the willingness on the part of some of the officials in that department to find fault with *my* performance. My position is that of a poacher, and their feeling towards me is akin to that of gamekeepers towards a trespasser in quest of game.'[7] Naturally – Cobden was basically not one of them. Lord Redesdale was one of the inmates of the Foreign Office, and his memoirs reveal an almost surrealist nonchalance with regard to its functioning.

For those with a penchant for the quiet life there was the established church, but far more popular for the younger sons, especially those with a propensity towards kicking up merry hell, was the army. Until the Cardwell reforms in the last quarter of the century, it was usual to buy one's commission at great cost. Being an officer was a way of being decorative without being vulgar; the aristocratic country gentlemen could not display conspicuous waste with any degree of certainty (they had to sublimate it by dressing up their servants in imposing livery), but this inhibition did not apply to the officer. Unless he was dispatched off to the deplorable and new-fangled camp at Aldershot, the life of the British officer was the epitome of the leisurely way of life. If he attempted to take some interest in his profession he was heavily disillusioned – in 1884 a young officer in Malta was fined by his mess for gossiping about the Peninsular War; his true vocation was fun, particularly women and cards.

Occasionally the demarcation line between gentleman-idler and officer-idler was blurred. At the start of the Crimean War, the 'TGs' – the 'Travelling Gentlemen' – went out with their officer friends. 'We wish to pitch our tent in your camp – the 18th,' requested 'Two Brothers', joint authors of *Our Tent in the Crimea* (1856). 'Very well,' said the commanding officer, 'I'll see to getting you some ground.' Along with the troops went the camp followers, wives and sweethearts for the officers, sluts for the common soldiers. Lord Raglan had picked his site for disembarkation partly because it was a suitable place for the grand yachts of his officers. The only passing gentleman Lord Raglan was not pleased to have around the place was William Howard Russell, the first war correspondent ('By God, Sir, I'd as soon see the devil!' declared General Pennefather). The wives, sweethearts and camp followers in the Crimea were supplemented by Florence Nightingale's nurses who, although dressed in an ill-fitting outfit of grey tweed dress, grey worsted jacket, plain white cap and short woollen cloak, were fair game. When one soldier pounced on one of the nurses, his mate pointed out 'Let her alone, don't you see she's one of Miss Nightingale's women?' The old officer type was confused by the inroad of nurses, especially the nuns. They would not react to military orders. During one spectacular muddle, a militia major was heard to shout, 'Halt! Those damned white sisters have gone again.'

Even in the diabolical conditions of the Crimea, the leisure class had it their own way. 'Very tolerable structures have been raised for the occupation of individuals,' wrote Dr Marlow of the Twenty-Eighth Regiment, 'while men labouring under disease are left on the damp ground in a leaky tent.' When the weather was extra cold, many officers threw up their commissions and went home, one of them being indignantly surprised when he was cut in his club – this was Lord George Paget, who redeemed himself by going back. Not that it was cowardice that drove the officers back – Lord George Paget was one of those who went onward with the six hundred during the Charge of the Light Brigade – but merely that the rude Russian winter was not playing fair with them, would not bend the rules to suit the English leisure class. This impulsive contracting out of an alien environment is not peculiar to the nineteenth century.

Many officers had a good war in the Crimea, and would have sympathized with the Prince of Wales ('I like the Russians. Their women are charming and most accomplished').[8] Nevertheless, Scutari and Balaclava did not quite compensate for the loss of the amenities of, say, St James's or the Tower of London, that bastion of high life on the very tip of the East End (only a quarter of a mile to the Ratcliffe Highway). The Tower of London was a good place from which to venture into the low life, the night houses such as the 'Raleigh', entered through a tunnel, or Sally Sutherland's night house, eventually taken over by the 'Raleigh' as its card room. Cards were played for enormous stakes, the games being watched by 'fielders', who did not play, but betted on the players. When the cards were turning against them, the rich young subalterns thought about going elsewhere.

'What are you going to do, George?' inquired a youngster; 'why not have a look in at Kate Hamilton's? This is all damned rot, and I've put my name down for 2 A.M.'[9]

Putting one's name down was a formality indicating to the sentry when the officer would return to the Tower. The subalterns who had bought their way into their regiment – it was possible to go from bottom to top of a regiment through the clink of gold coins – were willing victims for the sharps, who sometimes did pimping on the side. In the world of the night house, being an officer did not necessarily mean being a gentleman as well. One man 'was partial to shuffling the cards with their faces towards him, and placing a king at the bottom of the pack. This he explained was mere force of habit, and when remonstrated with – as he often had been – added that he was superstitious, and that one of his superstitions took this form.'

There was little to stop officers taking women back to the Tower, but accommodation houses were plentiful and more discreet. Before the Embankment was built, the river was edged with lodging houses, many with long balconies tippling over the Thames, from which the night birds could view Bankside, the notorious stews of Shakespeare's London. For a higher quality stray, the officers could get a cab to Burlington Arcade, then in its full glory. One of the strollers here in the sixties was Nelly Clifton, sometimes spelled Clifden or Cliffden, the nymph of the *pavé* the Prince of Wales had had when he was doing what passed as military service in the Curragh, Ireland. The officers in their fancy hats, the shako, and their ostentatious uniforms, were often set upon by thugs and footpads. Even the comparatively respectable places, such as Evans's, were beset by pickpockets, and frequently officers armed themselves to the teeth. One of the worst areas for the officer to traverse in his search for fun was 'the Dials' (Seven Dials, now the region just south of New Oxford Street). This was a refuge for Irish villains, and odds were offered against anyone's coming out of it intact. One Irishman named Corrigan tried it; his faith in his ancestry let him down – blood was not thicker than water. He emerged breathless and running at one o'clock in the morning, with a remnant of a shirt on his back. As soon as he had recovered, he described the slaughter he had inflicted on his attackers. These existed solely in his own mind, and decidedly not the minds of his listeners. Seven Dials was not only a haven for desperadoes; it was also the centre of the scurrilous broadsheet world. This fact worked to Corrigan's discomfiture – a verse issued hot from the presses, 'Oh, pray for the souls that Corrigan killed.'

Madness stalked the leisure class, whether it manifested itself in the feverish activity of Lord Hastings, or in the dottiness of Sir Charles Ross, who visited London every season for a fortnight, subsisting on mutton chops and steak, and who once frightened an old lady by emerging naked from beneath a furze bush with his ribs painted black. Lord Hastings was a Regency buck thirty years out of his time; after his breakfast of mackerel fried in gin and caviar on toast, he would look around for someone to share his frantic urge for excitement:

By Gad, old man, I'm damned glad to see you! To begin with, you must dine with me at eight – here. I've asked Prince Hohenlohe and Baron Spaum, and young Beust and Count Adelberg, and if you'll swear on a sack of bibles not to repeat it, I expect two live Ambassadors – it's always as well to have a sacred person or two handy in case of a row with the police. First we go to Endell Street – to Faultless's pit. I've got a match for a monkey with Hamilton to beat his champion bird, The Sweep, and after that I've arranged with a detective to take us the rounds in the Ratcliffe Highway. No dressing, old man; the kit you came over in is the ticket, and a sovereign or two in silver distributed amongst your pockets; you're bound to have a fist in every wrinkle of your person – why, if you're dancing with a beauty she'll be going over you all the time. I often used to laugh and shout out, 'Go it, I'm not a bit ticklish!' – still, what the hell does it matter? [10]

'Society is not a sphere where Christian charity is much practised,' wrote Lady Greville starchily, 'and, to those who stand by, it must afford food for a good deal of reflection.' [11] The women of society were condemned to rot in idleness, occasionally rising from their sloth to defend their husbands ('men who shoot, or hunt, or play cricket all the year round work as hard for their pleasure as the lower orders do for their daily bread'). What could the young lady of the leisure class do? She could hunt, ride, or skate – on ice, of course; roller skating was 'common'. In the season she could go to a ball every night. In the autumn it was OK to go to a watering place and swim and, toward the end of the century, play tennis. There was Scotland for the grouse and partidge shooting, occupations hallowed by the past example of the Queen, while winter brought, according to Lady Greville, 'a long drag through the coverts or over the turnips'. Exclusive country clubs, such as Hurlingham, catered for the more energetic. The daily procession of the high-priced prostitutes in Hyde Park had demoted this pursuit for respectable folk – the favoured time was now the evening. What did the leisure class do about Sunday? Lady Greville was crisp and honest about this: 'Sunday has long been rather a stumbling-block in England to those who love to amuse themselves; it does not appeal much to Society at large, for a day of enforced rest to people who never have any work in particular to do loses all *raison d'être*.' Sunday in town was tackled by the introduction of the Sunday luncheon; this was soon taken over by the middle class. The Sunday luncheon could be spread over three hours, and merged gracefully into the fashionable Sunday home, the salons of Lady Molesworth and Lady Waldegrave. The pontiffs were snooty about the tendency of the lower orders to catch on to the pursuits they themselves had started – the Sunday on the river. The rabble 'tear up sheaves of water-lilies by the root, and cut big branches of the May trees that droop over, touching the water with their snowy, heavy-scented blossom, and fill the boat with river stuff and wild flowers that, held in hot hands, die before they arrive at their destination; and return to their little back shops and dingy workrooms with their nostrils full of the smell of the real country'.[12]

The leisure class was also the manipulating class, and one of the things it tried to manipulate was communication with posterity. The intoxication it achieved when contemplating its own virtues was insufficiently heady to influence our own age. What Charles Reade aptly described as prurient prudency leaves us cool and contemptuous; likewise the feverish snobbishness, brought to a nasty yellow head by a pushing middle class – who whatever its faults was not afraid of hard work – and an increasingly unruly lower class. 'We have seen that the race for amusement and the forces of toil and play increase in speed and complexity daily,' wrote Lady Greville, obscurely but pertinently. No book of aristocratic memoirs is complete without the sad reflection that the old rapport between the upper and the lower classes is gone forever, and the corollary that the upper classes would see that the lower classes would be punished for it. 'Personally, I do not fear Labour,' wrote Lady Norah Bentinck, 'and I have the greatest faith in the British working man.'[13] It was not a sentiment that was widely shared by her contemporaries.

The vocal section of the leisure class was repeatedly let down by its more irresponsible members, and the presence of a prying and scandal-hungry press made it difficult to preserve the chaste image. Occasionally it was necessary to make an example of one of them. When Lady Twiss was revealed as someone possibly once a prostitute and certainly once 'common' her doom was sealed. The posture of the Queen fortified the purity band. Despite the fame of her husband, Lady Millais was never received at court on account of the annulment of her marriage with Ruskin. No doubt the more stupid members of the leisure class thought that everything in the garden was lovely, that titled lord and titled lady were always beyond reproach, but most were aware that they were involved in a huge public relations scheme. As Lady Norah Bentinck put it in ineffably characteristic metaphor : 'Wonderful, mysterious, grand, clever old England, who keeps the Ritz Hotel front-door closed on Sundays and the side-door open !'

The girls of the rich middle classes were not to be envied either. Could their parents, wrote Alys Pearsall-Smith,

for one single moment get a glimpse into the hearts of their quiet, uncomplaining daughters, they would be astonished and perhaps horrified. 'What can our daughters want more than they have now?' they would ask. 'They have a good home and every comfort, and the society of their parents' friends; perhaps a carriage to drive in and horses to ride. What more can they possibly desire?' To such parents I would reply: Your daughter wants herself.[14]

These daughters who wanted themselves were beset by problems, not the least of which was the establishment of some kind of *modus operandi* regarding men. Man in the abstract they knew; man in the particular the middle-class daughter was stranger to, unless she had the advantage of loquacious servants, as had the offspring of the aristocrat. The middle class tended to keep their own servants under a strict scrutiny, with buttoned-up lips. Man in the abstract they knew from the products of romantic and hack writers, the fashion-plate soldiery of Ouida who conversed in high campese, the priggish titled heroes of Charlotte Yonge – the hero of her best-selling *The Heir of Redclyffe* of 1853 was 'right-minded ... very well informed ... noble', and the stereotypes of the anonymous writers who turned out serials for the respectable middle-class periodicals. The main appeal of such mass-produced heroes can be judged by a typical specimen. In *Walter's Word* of 1875, the writer sums up essential man:

A lean, dark face, with well-formed and what are called speaking features; the mouth hard when in rest, but capable of much expression, and improved rather than otherwise by its delicate black moustache; the eyes large and lustrous ... the nose aquiline, the forehead high; altogether a very handsome face, nor marred – to the female eye at least – by a certain haughtiness of aspect...[15]

To render him thoroughly irresistible to women readers, he had also been wounded in the Crimean War – not too badly, of course, just enough to have an arm in a picturesque sling.

Tom of *Tom's Wife*, serialized in 1881, is out of the same barrel, but rusticated a little:

He was a proficient in all the sports and pastimes of a rural life, and had a fair knowledge of farming and agriculture. His frank, good-humoured nature had won for him the good-will of all who knew him; while many a bright eye flashed and fair face flushed their testimony to the young Squire's good looks as he rode through the village on his stout roan mare. His bright blue eyes, golden-brown curls, and fair complexion – though tanned to a darker hue by the sun – all bespoke his Saxon origin.[16]

Such creations are not so different from the heroes of contemporary women's magazine fiction, and obviously editors knew that this was the kind of basic man for the class of readers who

subscribed to the journal from which both extracts come. The
sexual pneuma of these creatures is nil. Of all the writers who
could have explored the sexual nexus between man and woman,
none was better equipped than Dickens, but like his contemporaries he fought shy of the explicit, bringing, for instance,
Major Bagstock in *Dombey and Son* to the boil, and then using
analogies to indicate the major's roaring sexuality. Those
novelists who prided themselves on penetrating the veil of prudery were no more successful. Of the man who was supposed to
be the last word in daring, Grant Allen, the most shocking thing
he did was to entitle one of his books, *The Woman Who Did*
('The Woman Who Did' became a fetish like 'The Girl of the
Period'. The magazine revealingly named the *Adult* advertised
for women who did).

In 1895, when *The Woman Who Did* was published, it was
possible for girls to ask themselves, 'Did what?' She would
'array herself in the white garb of affiance for her bridal evening', and 'her cheek was aglow with virginal shrinking'. But
what then? For those who had not undergone ordeal by girls'
school, and consequent 'contamination', when the Adonis in his
velvet collar, and his black striped trousers, his white waistcoat,
and his sister-embroidered braces, disrobed himself of these
there might be some shocks. Five years after her unconsummated marriage, Euphemia Ruskin revealed to her father: 'I
had never been told the duties of married persons to each other
and knew little or nothing about their relations in the closest
union on earth.' [17] Mrs Ruskin may have been playing it up a
little, but there were certainly many new wives to whom a
rampant penis was visually a traumatic experience, an experience that had nothing to do with the polite mottoes that authorities on marriage had been babbling since the rise of the genteel
marriage. A wife should be 'a companion who will raise the
tone of his mind from . . . low anxieties and vulgar cares', wrote
Mrs Sarah Ellis (*The Wives of England; Their Relative Duties,
Domestic Influence, and Social Obligations*, 1843). What, many
a bride must have asked herself, had this to do with her present
predicament? Those who followed diligently the path of
righteousness as laid down by the Reverend Spurgeon, the Vic-

torian's Billy Graham, might well recall one of his pronouncements and submit with grace to this curious behaviour of a man
who had until then been the soul of delicacy: 'He has many
objects in life which she does not quite understand,' wrote
Spurgeon apropos of husbands, 'but she believes in them all, and
everything which she can do to promote them, she delights to
perform.'

Pleasure of woman in sex was part of the prohibitory mechanism of the age. 'If the married female conceives every second
year, during the nine months that follow conception she experiences no great sexual excitement. The consequence is that sexual
desire in the male is somewhat diminished, and the act of coition
takes place but rarely,' wrote Dr William Acton in *Functions
and Disorders of the Reproductive Organs*. This, it is implied, is
how it should be, in 1857. In the early forties writers on sexual
matters were more flowery but not so definite:

The facilities which nature has given to woman in her department
of procreation are very varied, and she may be said even to have submitted herself to their control. She can admit the intercourse of the
opposite sex with consequence, she can behold the most libidinous
acts without being moved, and even set bounds to passion in the very
act of intercourse itself; but, to enjoy a female who participates in,
and is desirous of promoting the pleasure she would derive is comparatively as different as the connexion [*sic*] with an animated and
lifeless object.[18]

'The best mothers, wives, and managers of households,' countered Acton, 'know little or nothing of sexual indulgences. Love
of home, children, and domestic duties, are the only passions
they feel. ... She submits to her husband, but only to please him;
and, but for the desire of maternity, would far rather be relieved
from his attentions.' Acton's message triumphed. He was addressing the medical man, not the lay reader, and the doctors
transmitted the message on. For the rutting slum dwellers
Acton might well not have existed, and had he been alone in
pushing through his own personal mission, his influence would
have been negligible. However, he appeared on the scene at the
right time, and made manifest views that many held and

wanted others to hold. Interference was a prime ingredient in *laissez-faire* so far as others were concerned.

In theory, women were inhibited from admiring man in all his gross physical completeness. The primary male sexual characteristics were barred from discussion and conversation, the fig-leaf brigade cast stony eyes on statues and pictures that dared to make very much of penis and testicles, and the notion that women could obtain pleasure from sexual intercourse was one that led naturally to cancer of the womb through over-indulgence or insanity ('nymphomania, a form of insanity which those accustomed to visit lunatic asylums must be fully conversant with' – Acton). It was an inhibition that only operated through the middle echeleons of society; as the middle echelons had acquired the greatest share of power, their views had the greatest coverage, though the aristocracy still lived it up regardless of nonconformist distaste, and the only poor who were influenced were those aspiring to the middle class. The sexual appeal of man to woman therefore went underground, and it might be supposed that hard-core pornography echoes with the shrill ecstasy of lady pornographers released from silence.

Not a bit of it. The proscriptions on depicting basic man appeal from the woman's point of view have affected the dirty book trade. There are only a couple of books in the canon known to be written by women, and these are feeling-orientated rather than thing-orientated. Could it be that Acton's words had bitten deep, that he and his disciples, the medical profession, had convinced women that pleasure in sex was (a) disgusting; (b) more important – dangerous? Could it be that twentieth-century revelations by Kinsey on the sexual nature of woman are not applicable to nineteenth-century woman?

Certainly nineteenth-century writers postulated woman's reaction to copulation, but they are men projecting themselves in the role of women.

I quickly felt his finger again introducing the head of that terrible engine I had felt before, and which now felt like a pillar of ivory entering me. ... I was on the altar, and, butcher-like, he was determined to complete the sacrifice; indeed, my cries seemed only to excite him to the finishing of my ruin, and sucking my lips and breasts with fury, he unrelentingly rooted up all obstacles my virginity offered.

Never, oh never shall I forget the delicious transports that followed the stiff insertion; and then, ah me! by what thrilling degrees did he, by his luxurious movements, fiery kisses, and strange touches of his hand to the most crimson parts of my body, reduce me to a voluptuous state of insensibility.

These two extracts from *The Lustful Turk* of 1828 sum up the predicament. This is how the writer imagines how he would have felt had he been the woman, if he had been beset by the sadism and masochism that made him want to write in the role of woman, anyway.

Masher and Swell

Where, one might ask, are the dandies of yesteryear? The Regency bucks lasted well into Victoria's reign, but there came a time when their trembling hands folded the cravats no more. They were replaced by the swell and the masher. Swells and mashers belonged to a decidedly lower hierarchy than the dandies, and they did not eschew vulgarity; painfully aware that their social pretensions were hollow, they reacted aggressively. Unlike the dandies, whose mode of attire was an expression of their essence, the swells and mashers were orientated to an outside object – to women. Their primary characteristics were that they were jaunty and not very bright, and although basically they belonged to lowly social groups, their equivalent could be found among the upper classes, as J. K. Stephen, a young university poet who later went insane through being hit on the head by a windmill, observed:

> As I was waiting for the tardy tram,
> I met what purported to be a man.
> What seemed to pass for its material frame,
> The semblance of a suit of clothes had on,
> Fit emblem of the grand sartorial art
> And worthy of a more sublime abode,

Its coat and waistcoat were of weird design
Adapted to the fashion's latest whim.
I think it wore an Athenaeum tie.
White flannels draped its too ethereal limbs
And in its vacant eye there glared a glass.[19]

T. W. Barrett, a music hall draw, sang of John the Masher
(*circa* 1880):

I am the sort of fellow you will meet with every day,
I captivate each pretty girl that comes across my way,
I always wear the very best of thirty shilling suits,
You'll find I always wear a pair of gaiters o'er my boots;
My necktie is my latest choice in colour and in taste,
My diamonds are the brightest and best of Paris paste,
I know the drapers' shops where all the cheap kid gloves are sold,
And my rings they are plated, well, with eighteen carat gold.

I'm known by all the Totties in the Town,
They know my name, but they prefer to call me Captain Brown,
My chain's the latest pattern, there's none that can surpass,
It's warranted to be all solid eighteen carat brass;
My watch, real German silver, it never leaves my fob,
It came direct from Birmingham, and cost me fifteen bob,
And as I walk along the streets the girls I cannot pass,
They're sure to have a look at me and my sixpenny eye glass.

The rise of the swell came in with the greater leisure time of the
working people. The half holiday on Saturday meant that there
were increased opportunities for the *hoi polloi* to enjoy the facilities that had once been the prerogative of their superiors, and,
dressed up, they were more inclined to leave their native haunts
for 'up West':

I'm a Street up the Strandity, cane in my handity,
Doing the grandity Sweller,
Very much Baronly, See Nelly Farrenly,
Short dresses and boots rather tall,
Awfully rollicking, fearfully frollicking,
Number one Masher of all.

But now I'm a cute wide awakeity, others' views takeity,
Up to each racketty sweller,
Queer in my speechity, very knee breechity,
Stammer and stutter and dwall,
Flowers of rarcity round Leicester Squareity,
A pushity shoveity loveity doveity
Hottest young Masher of all.

But now I'm a don't care a figity, awfully bigity,
Wonderful collarly feller,
Five o'clock teaity, weak at the kneeity, a
Kensington Gardeny sweller;
Bertie and Gusity, from university, do, dear boy, give us a call,
A slasherty, dasherty, casherty masherty
Mashiest Masher of all.[20]

This was one of Charles Godfrey's songs, from about 1882.
It offered a wry self-deprecation and a vaunting egotism. We, he
proclaimed, are as good as they. The disparity between the life
one led on weekends and the workaday life was emphasized by
T. W. Barrett again from the eighties:

I'm a dooced big toff of a fellow,
My make up I reckon's immense,
I live in a manner peculiar,
I'm somewhat devoid tho' of sense;
By profession I am a tripe dresser,
Sometimes I'm a trusser of fowls,
But at night I'm all there as a Masher,
When I mouch out the same as the owls.

In another context, this would be self-knocking copy, but in the
music halls, the sounding board of the working class, this irony
was well understood. Outsiders were unpleasantly aware of the
growing self-assertion of those whom they had confidently written off as subject peoples living somewhere to the east of the City.
Just as society was breaking up, so did the division between
those who were gents and those who were not become increasingly hazy. 'Society as it used to be – a somewhat exclusive
body of people, all of them distinguished either for their rank,

their intellect, or their wit – is no more,' [21] wrote a high priest-
ess of the old order, Lady Dorothy Nevill. Similarly, it was difficult to discern between the socially acceptable and the socially
unacceptable through dress. Costermongers were no longer content to be sartorially minded merely with a gay and gaudy scarf;
small tailors in Whitechapel were turning out excellent copies of
West End modes at a fraction of the price for the East End
swells. Admittedly the effect might be spoiled by a little too
much flash, but the nobs were not notably possessed of good
taste. In the eighties and the nineties the iron grip of the middle
classes was being relaxed – not through choice, but through
necessity. Bicycling parties were held in Battersea Park, and an
intruder from one of the lesser classes could mingle with the toffs
with a confidence that had not been possible when the unit of
transport was the horse and the locale was Rotten Row.

The lower orders could be picked out by the observant by the
assured way with which they dealt with their women. Although
the winds of change were making hay of the traditional barriers
between the sexes, the middle classes had not come to terms with
boy meets girl, the casual sexual encounter. Even at Christmas,
when seasonly good will might well have made the elders a little
more lax in their moral attitudes, the young man had constantly
to watch himself during, for example, blind man's buff. 'Watch
this man carefully,' requested the newspaper *Day and Night*
ominously, 'and you will see that every time he comes in contact with the lovely young girls who are joining in the game, his
hands by some strange accident fall upon their swelling busts, or
resting on the bare shoulders, seem to wander as it were involun-
tarily on to forbidden ground.' [22] The working classes had few
of these inhibitions; they flirted outrageously, pleased and excited by the new extravagance of their dress, delighted by the
wonders of London that had once been outside the pale.

> I'd take her to see the Aquarium,
> I'd take her to see the 'Zoo',
> I'd take her to see the Waxwork Show
> The Crystal Palace, too.
> Oh! yes if she'd only be true to me,
> 'T would fill me with delight,

And I'd bring her to see the Music Halls
Every Saturday night.[23]

The well-bred gentility of middle-class girls was totally lacking
among the lower-class donahs:

> My gal's a out-and-outer,
> That is she's not a muff,
> There's no two ways about her,
> She's a proper bit of stuff.
> When on Sunday dress'd all in her best,
> She's flash but she's discreet,
> She's as straight as any sausage,
> And a dozen times more sweet.
>
> Oh, you ought to see my Sarah,
> She's a spiffin bit of stuff,
> You'll never find a fairer,
> She's nature in the rough,
> She's never out of collar,
> So excuse me if I holler –
> Whoe, – ain't I nuts on
> Blooming little Sarah.

They had qualities of no mean order:

> She can sing, she can play the piano,
> She can jump, she can dance, she can run,
> In fact she's a modern Taglioni,
> And Sims Reeves rolled into one.
> And who would not love such a beauty,
> Like an angel dropped from above,
> May I be stung to death with flies
> If ever I cease to love,
> May I have to live on pigeon's milk
> If ever I cease to love.[24]

Similarly the chaste courtship of legend was not for them:

> My arms I'd round her taper waist
> Her lovely form I pressed,
> Her beauteous face reclining
> Upon my manly chest,

> I kissed her twice upon her lips
> I wish I'd done it thrice,
> I whispered oh, it's naughty,
> She said, it is so nice.

The women were not backward in making their own inclinations known:

> Come to me closer, love,
> Come closer, dear,
> Place your arm 'round me,
> I will make you feel queer.
> Fondle and kiss me
> When no one is near,
> For you know I'm a
> Modest young maiden.

It was sometimes necessary to use ungentlemanly methods to obtain one's ends:

> I met a little charmer,
>   So did I,
> And said I wouldn't harm her,
>   So did I,
> I took her into Short's,
> And stood her wine by quarts,
>   So did I,

It was considered allowable for swells and mashers to be unscrupulous in their dealings with women, and innocents and widows were fair game. Similarly, men who were tricked into marriage had only themselves to blame, and there are innumerable merry anecdotes and songs of the man who married a sweet young thing, only to find that he had got a parched virgin of forty, who unscrewed wooden legs and arms and took off a wig to reveal a billiard-ball-smooth head.

> I'm rather fond of widows who
> Have got a little tin,
> I go in for the 'Spooney' and
> I'm pretty sure to win.
> I vow eternal love, until
> They name the happy day.

By then I've borrowed a score or more
So takes myself away.[25]

Beyond the cockiness and the self-assurance lay the awareness that swelldom was a transitional state, that soon domesticity would rear its wearisome head, that the ravishing beauties in their chignons and fancy boots would fade before they were thirty into bedraggled drabs, that it would be farewell the Aquarium and Hampstead Heath. It was back to the buildings or to the cosy insanitary fug of tunnel-back slum with a mother-in-law yelling the odds.

Love in the East End

The working-classes of the nineteenth-century urban scene consisted of two main currents (a) those who wanted to better themselves; and (b) those who were content to stay as they were. Current (a) can further be subdivided into (1) those who wanted to ascend into the middle class; and (2) those who were quite happy with their own. These currents were not readily discerned by the 'superior' classes, and if they were, the efforts to get above themselves by the poor were treated cynically or as a comical built-in foible. Max Beerbohm is not an outstandingly abhorrent creature, but on the subject he can be disgustingly snide. Writing to William Rothenstein he said:

Such lots of pretty, common girls walking up and down – all brown with the sun and dressed like sailors – casting vulgar glances from heavenly eyes and bubbling out Cockney jargon from perfect lips. You would revel in them but I confess they do not attract me: apart from the fact that I have an ideal, I don't think the lower orders ought to be attractive – it brings Beauty into disrepute.[26]

He was writing in the nineties, when the fight to keep the lower orders buttoned down was well nigh lost. There is also a tongue-in-cheek uneasiness that would have been unlikely two decades earlier, when the poor knew their place – or at least, were thought to. From *Queen*, 18 September 1875:

It may sound illiberal to say so, but it is a truth all the same – unrefined manners for the most part belong to unrefined natures, and the ignorance which misplaces h's and marries plural nouns to singular verbs goes deeper into the whole being than mere grammar. A vulgar woman who says 'you was' and 'they is' lacks more than technical education. She lacks all that refinement which is produced by the study of literature and history, all that perception of moral beauty which grows with the contemplation of artistic loveliness, all the social sweetness and grace of temper which are the result of good breeding begun from early years.

Such writers would have liked to have kept the poor and the uneducated in reserves. To a certain extent, they succeeded in doing so. The East End was sacred to the underprivileged, even when they were not necessarily the poor. Traders and small businessmen when they had made their pile still preferred to remain in the area, where they understood its culture and were not forced to conform to new aesthetic standards. The East End had a language of its own, originally invented as a secret form of communication between villains but later taken up by costermongers and the passably respectable. An extended use of the idiom was made by Pierce Egan [27] in his *Life in London* of 1821 :

Lascars, blacks, jack tars, coal-heavers, dustmen, women of colour, old and young, and a sprinkling of the remnants of once fine girls, &c, were all *jigging* together, provided the *teazer of the catgut* was not *bilked* of his *duce*. *Heavey wet* was the cooling beverage, but frequently overtaken by *flashes of lightning*. The *covey* was no *scholard*, as he asserted, and, therefore, he held the pot with one hand and took the *blunt* with the other, to prevent the trouble of *chalking*, or making mistakes.

On the sudden appearance of our '*swell TRIO*', and the CORIN-THIAN'S friend, among these unsophisticated sons and daughters of Nature, their *ogles* were on the roll, under an apprehension that the *beaks* were out on the *nose*; but it was soon made 'all right', by one of the *mollishers* whispering, loud enough to be heard by most of the party, 'that she understood as how the *gemmen* had only dropped in for to have a *bit of a spree*, and there was no doubt that they *voud* stand a *drap* of *summut* to make them all *cumfurable*, and likewise prove good customers to the *crib*'. On the *office* being given, the *stund-still* was instantly removed; and the *kidwys* and *kiddiesses* were footing the *double-shuffle* against each other with as much *gig* as the 'We we-e-e-ps' exert themselves on the first of May . . .

This esoteric jargon contains a number of ingredients. The uneducated often have a lazy way of speaking; it was, and is, too much trouble to annunciate long words correctly ('gemmen = 'gentlemen', 'cumfurable' = 'comfortable') just as it was, and is, to bother to sound aspirates. A characteristic feature of East End speech was to turn every 'w' into 'v' (voud' = 'would'). Nevertheless, the jargon provided a basis for the 'flash' language of the forties and fifties, when every would-be blade thought it exceedingly smart to get the vocabulary off pat. One senses that Pierce Egan in the extract above was swanking rather. Henry Mayhew's reportage has more the ring of truth; he was in at the childhood of rhyming slang, and one of his contacts explained it to him about 1850:

The cadgers' talk is quite different now to what it was in the days of Billy [William IV, who reigned from 1830 until Victoria's accession]. You see the flats got awake to it, so in course we had to alter the patter. The new style of cadgers' cant is nothing like the thieves' cant, and is done all on the rhyming principle. This way's the caper. Suppose I want to ask a pal to come and have a glass of rum and smoke a pipe of tobacco, and have a game at cards with some blokes at home with me, I should say, if there were any flats present, 'Splodger, will you have a *Jack-surpass* of *finger-and-thumb*, and blow your yard of *tripe* of nosey me *knacker*, and have a touch of the *broads* with me and the other heaps of *coke* at my *drum*.'

Just because the East Enders were poor, there are no grounds for the theory that they were stupid as well. Endless ingenuity was used in verbal trickery, and working men had vocabularies that a brainwashed television-gawping college lad of today would envy. They delighted to turn the changes on respectable words ('physiognomy' became 'phiz'), and this semantic adventurousness was taken over by exponents of the flash language, where genteelisms acquire a new persona from their juxtaposition with coarse Anglo-Saxon. In *Yokels' Preceptor*, a handbook for men about town, the prostitutes are listed – Elephant Bet,

Finnikin Fan, Yarmouth Bloater, Flabby Poll, Fair Eliza, and the Black Mott. Elephant Bet was 'the walking dunnyken, the elephant squash arse', Finnikin Fan 'this shickster from her affectation gained this cognomen'. She is quoted as saying to one customer, 'It's no go, I can't take you, you'd give me the uglies.' The vernacular of the forties and fifties illustrates a rip-roaring sense of language. It is a great pity it fizzles out.

Life in the East End was harsh, violent and crude. Love and marriage had frequently to be crammed in, and they were treated with a wry cynicism by the protagonists and the observers. The *liebeslied* of the poor was the music hall song, and the thousands of ditties that have survived give one invaluable clues to the way the poor felt about sex, courtship and marriage, but they remain only clues. It was an oral culture, not a written one. Many of the songs were written by professionals who had only a fuzzy idea of the way their audience lived, and others dealt with an idyllic Arcadia that performer and audience treated as real though both knew that it did not exist. There was a convention that the poor knew all about the countryside, the convenient fiction of:

> I met her by the lake, I met her by the spring,
> I met her in the brake, and heard the thrushes sing,
> I met her by the river, and wandered round the crook,
> Left her at the cottage door a kiss upon her cheek.

Songs that have reached us in a printed format do not often stress sex except by implication. The songs themselves are found in three varieties – ordinary sheet music, frequently with lithographed covers by specialists in the genre such as Concanen, fairly expensive; collections of music hall songs, words only, in small type on poor paper, with a garish and incompetent black-and-white cover design; broadsheets selling at a half-penny, often dealing with some scandal, sexual or macabre, printed on antique wooden presses on diversely coloured paper. There were about ten publishers who dealt in these 'ha'penny sheets', the leading one of which was Disley of Seven Dials. They ran closer to the wind than the other publications. One hawker said, 'Songs if they're over religious don't sell at all; though a tidy moral does werry well. But a good, awful murder's the thing. I've knowed a man sell a ream a day of them – that's twenty dozen you know.' These broadsheets were turned off the press in great quantities – 30,000 or 40,000 at a time. The author got a shilling a song, or a glass of rum, a slice of cake, and sixty copies, which were run off for him as he was drinking his rum and nibbling his vittals.

Sexual oddities sold even better than murders. At the Royal Mortar Tavern in London Road, the publican Frederick Brown had a barman, ex-navy. It was discovered that she was a woman. The broad sheets on this sold in their thousands.[28] During the Mordaunt divorce case, in which the Prince of Wales was involved, culminating in his appearance in the witness box, *The Infidelities of a Prince* was sold in Fleet Street. One book 'will contain a portrait and biographical memoir of the young and extremely pretty Lady Mordaunt, with many pleasing reminiscences'. Such books were sold in Holywell Street under plain cover; one prurient purchaser found that he had bought Dr Watt's hymns in sealed cover. The purveyors of broad sheets made use of the defence of Lady Mordaunt that she was mad:

> Now this gay Lady —
> Cannot be right, or hardly,
> She said she loved other men,
> Much better than her Charley.
> Some say it was her dodge,
> And nothing but hanky panky,
> While others say all fudge,
> She is trying to act cranky.
>
> This lady's appetite,
> It really is enormous,
> But whether wrong or right,
> The papers will inform us,
> She is fond of veal and ham,
> To feed she is a glutton,
> She got tired of Charley's lamb,
> And longed for royal mutton.

This was published by Disley, who did not disdain lesser tidbits:

> At Epping Sessions, there this case occurred,
> And she said, now only think,
> That the doctor, Mr Saunders,
> With her played at tiddly-wink.

The sex life of the working class could be horrendous. Rape was considered hardly an enormity, and sexual assault on young, middle-aged, and old was commonplace. Hell, said Shelley, was a smoky and populous place much like London. One cannot be surprised that immorality was rife; one is only amazed that there were little oases of decency that managed to withstand the sand sweeping in from all quarters. An excessive interest in murder on the part of the uneducated was pandered to by 'penny-a-liners' and hack playwrights. Sweeney Todd, the Demon Barber of Fleet Street, who cut his victims' throats as they were being shaved and had the bodies made into sausages, made his debut in 1842 at the Britannia Theatre, Hoxton. By 1843, a character in Dickens's *Martin Chuzzlewit* was hoping that no one would think that he had been made into meat pies. Dickens ever had his finger on the public pulse.

'Orrible murder was intriguing because it was, generally speaking, outside the scope of the poor. Various folk heroes arose such as Dick Turpin. *Gentleman Jack* was a marathon yarn that ran for four years in the fifties, and some of these 'novels' were published by the kingpin of pornography, William Dugdale. Sexual misbehaviour among the nobs was also highly readable, though among themselves it was too commonplace to be worth mentioning. When sex was dealt with in the penny novel it was with the heavy hand of melodrama.

'I do not understand your meaning, Father Wilkinson,' Mrs Cherwynd resumed, 'in speaking about temptation being too great.'

And the fair woman rose, and looked around the small room. There was a frightful amount of carnal longing in that woman's eye.

Her nostrils dilated, and her lip quivered, and she attempted to breathe!

If the following comparison may not be considered too strong, would it not suggest to one the picture of a beast of prey, gloating upon his victim?

For the fair woman knew she was irresistible.

She soon felt that, by the wild stare of her confessor.
A smile of triumph appeared again upon her lip.
'If one sin by thought, or by deed,' she asked, 'which is worse?'

This extract is from *The Outsiders of Society* of the early sixties.

The fascination of the extreme situation operates throughout all levels of society, but the lower classes did not get so steamed up about sex as the middle, or especially as the upper. Part of this was due to a lack of imagination, to a prosaic concern with essentials, the head-line mentality. Part was due to a comparative absence of repression and inhibition, the hallmarks of any sophisticated society.

Not that there is not tenderness in the love songs of the working classes, though it may be disguised in whimsy:

> Love is certain to be known
> Where a woman's to be found:
> When one has the first attack
> It's like raspberry jam running down one's back.

There are other staple ingredients. The music hall songs are full of young men who have been trapped into marriage by widows of forty or by women who are not quite what they appeared:

> She's cheeks like lilies, eyes like sloes,
> And fingers long and taper,
> Her hair is red, to match her nose,
> And mostly worn in paper.

There is the predicament of the man who married a woman with one leg:

> Her leg comes down with a dot and carry one,
> As she stumps along so gaily;
> There's many a worse girl
> (Though she's queer about the pins)
> Than my lovely Sarah Bailey.

[spoken] 'Shake a leg!' I thought I should have expired when mother mentioned it. Father said, 'Put your best leg foremost; get married, and put your legs under your own mahogany.' Legs! Three between the two of us – a matrimonial tripod. I brought her home, and you should have seen the look of astonishment when. . . (Chorus ad lib.)

A theme often reiterated was the young man in the clutches of a woman who wants the best years of his life and does not greatly care how she gets them:

> I'd sooner be by a Serpent stung, or hugg'd by a grizzly Bear
> Or crush'd by one of Pickford's Vans, or blown into the Air,
> I'd rather be by Marwood Hung – or slowly fade away,
> Than have the least connection with deceitful Emma Hay.[29]

Bamboozled into marriage, the men have to face new facts of life:

> I rise each morn at six o'clock, because it's her desire,
> And minus trousers, socks or shoes, I light the kitchen fire,
> I wait upon her hand and foot, but if I out should be,
> And get home rather late at night, she kindly waits on me.

[spoken] – with a big stick, of course it's very kind of her to sit up for me, it's very kind of her to open the door for me, but when she carries her kindness to the extent of prostrating me on the one and eleven-penny door mat, then I fail to dream of the day when ... [Chorus]

[spoken] She has a playful habit of getting me into a snug corner, and practising the art of self defence on my poor frontispiece [*sic*] until she's tired and I daren't show my perogative [*sic*] for ... [Chorus]

[spoken] Yes, and she put my pipe out the day after we were married – I can't get a smoke unless I either poke my head up the chimney or go down to the summer house and do a whiff behind the scarlet runners.

Innocent into virago was always very popular:

> When I first courted Nancy she was, oh, so very shy,
> And when I kissed her first she broke my nose and black'd my eye;
> She was barmaid at a tripe shop, where I often used to call,
> But now she's a professional at some big Concert Hall

[spoken] Yes, she's a professional at — It's right, she sweeps the floor and dusts the tables.

Another favourite theme is the young man who is smitten with a girl who does not care for him:

Nancy fancied a soldier, Nancy fancied a snob,
Nancy fancied a nobleman who wasn't worth a bob.
Nancy fancied a sailor who's sailing on the sea,
She fancied a slop with a carroty mop, but never once fancied me.

> I feel like beef without mustard,
> Or a woman that's had a divorce,
> I feel like a crab on a fishmonger's slab
> Or a cove who his senses has lost.
> I feel like tea without sugar,
> Or very bad fourpenny ale.
> For the loss of Jemima, my foolish Jemima,
> Who after the Prince did sail.

When they were not bemoaning the loss of their fair ones or re-counting the hazards of married life, the music hall stars adopted the roles of swells. Many of them, because of their popularity, became the authentic article. Leybourne was driven from theatre to theatre to sing his best-selling song 'Champagne Charlie is my name', much to the disgust of the resident celebrities. The all-conquering male captivated the Cockney audience:

> I was the boy for bewitching 'em
> Whether good humour'd or coy;
> All cried when I was beseeching 'em,
> 'Do what you will with me, joy.'

The great stars mocked their audience. In his persona of a swell, Vance had some spoken business: 'Yaas, the drinking habits of the populace are simply disgusting. What the deuce do they want with beer in the middle of the day? They're not up all night at halls and parties, and they don't get jolly in the small hours.'

Music hall comediennes established the convention that it was a girl's duty to say no even when she meant yes, to put up a front of modesty in such a saucy manner as to make nonsense of the premise. Lottie Collins was one of the great names of the nineties, graduating to stardom from being an expert with a jump-rope. Her performance of 'Ta-ra-ra *Boom*-de-ay' was a quasisexual experience, starting quietly with the pert verse and working up to a crescendo with the chorus, just as Mac-Dermott did, with his elbows working into his sides and his feet tapping out the rhythm. In her large Gainsborough hat, short skirt of red silk, and the blossoming of white petticoats, Lottie Collins began:

> A smart and stylish girl you see,
> The belle of high society;
> Fond of fun as fond could be
> When it's on the strict Q T
> Not too young, and not too old,
> Not too timid, not to bold,
> But just the very thing, I'm told,
> That in your arms, you'd like to hold!
>   Ta-ra-ra *Boom-de-ay*! . . .

With the opening of the chorus, Miss Collins put her hands on her hips in wanton barmaid style, and broke into a dance, the nearest British approach to the cancan. Lottie Collins was one of the highest paid of the music hall ladies; in 1892, she was paid £150 a week for a fifteen-minute nightly turn. She became a cult figure, as did Vesta Tilley who did male impersonations, as 'the Piccadilly Johnny with the little glass eye [i.e., a monocle] and a demure little girl turn in white frock ('Our Lodger's such a Nice Young Man'). Marie Lloyd took her stage name from *Lloyd's Newspaper*. Born in 1870, she started her career at the Eagle near Islington, becoming increasingly proficient in the art of the suggestive wink and nod, falling foul of the licensing authorities whom she further acerbated by a private rendition of her own version of 'Come into the Garden, Maud'. The music hall was the voice of a largely inarticulate class, but it was the voice of the 'improved' working class. For the drunken lay-abouts who propped up the bars of Bethnal Green, for the totally submerged Irish immigrants who set up their own fes-tering nexus in Rosemary Lane (it led off the Minories by the Tower of London), for the wife-beaters and sewer workers, the innuendo of Leybourne and the sauciness of Marie Lloyd were as remote as they were to the middle classes who only went to the theatre when they were assured of the niceness of the play.

The sex life projected by the music hall ethos is wanton but uncomplicated, unperverted but not altogether respectable. The donah [30] could be a wife or a mistress, and no one was worried which. The audience had a cynical awareness of what went on outside their *purlieus*. They could be stirred up by a patriotic number, and from the evidence of song sheets they could even be moved by the deaths of Disraeli and Gladstone. They were also familiar with fashionable West End scandals and trends:

> I'm a very Sunflowery, Aprily showery,
> Eastcheapy, Towery man.
>
> I'm a very aesthetic young man,
> A non energetic young man;
>
> Slippity, sloppity over the shoppity,
> Flippity flop young man.
>
> I'm a bitter and mildly
> Naturely childy,
> Oscary Wyldy man.
>
> I'm a Fuller's earth colour young man,
> A greeny and 'Yuller' young man
> Pretty externally 'Patience' and 'Colonely'
> Utterly utter young man.[31]

Many of the songs contain advice to the audience on romantic matters:

> When courting don't write spooney letters,
> To your fair one, for love, or for sport,
> For should you but break any promise,
> They are sure to be read out in court.
> When you wed, do not wed the fam'ly as well,
> For that will not a Paradise make,
> Above all close the door to your mother-in-law,
> Or – that's where you'll make the mistake.

Music hall monologues occasionally go into more intimate detail. Dealing with a kiss:

Don't jump like a trout for a fly, and smack a woman on the neck, on the ear, on the corner of her forehead, or on the end of her nose, or knock off her lace fall. The gentleman should be a little taller. He should have a clean face, a kind eye, and a mouth full of expression.

Don't kiss everybody. Don't sit down to it; Stand up. . . . Her left
hand is in your right; let there be an impression on that, not like the
grip of a vice, but a gentle clasp, full of electricity, thought, and
respect . . . (Be brave but don't be in a hurry). Her lips are almost
open. Lean slightly forward with your head, not the body. Take
good aim, the lips meet; the eyes close; the heart opens; the soul rides
the storms, troubles and sorrows of life (don't be in a hurry); heaven
opens before you; the world shoots under your feet, as a meteor
flashes across the evening sky (don't be afraid); the nerves dance
before the just-erected altar of love as zephyrs dance with the dew-
dimmed flowers; the heart forgets its bitterness, and the heart [*sic*]
of kissing is learned.

Sentimentality and briskness mixed well in the music hall. It
was entertainment of the people, by the people, and for the
people. It had an indigenous naïvety and a directness that was
not equalled in the upper strata of life, and the crispness of its
sentiments and the often acrid realism throw many of the art
products of the time into the shade. The lugubrious tempori-
zing of the late Victorian sociologists – the Webbs and the
Booths, and the middle-class identification game of George Gissing, must be seen against the backdrop of the 'alls. Lottie Collins, Marie Lloyd, Ethel Victor, Vesta Tilley and a galaxy of
vivacious ladies opened up a quarter of a century of fun until the
pattern was dashed by the First World War. It may be that the
blueprint of a culture more inherently stable than those that
actually succeeded was drafted by these endearing and very
talented performers.

3

A Dream of Fair Women

Sex Appeal

W H E N the great writers of the century came to examine professionally the grass roots of the irresistible sexual attractions of woman – they fell by the wayside, and contented themselves merely with an account of minor secondary sexual characteristics. In fact, as Havelock Ellis wisely states in *Man and Woman*, 1894, 'The sexes are not greatly attracted by any purely aesthetic qualities; it is the womanly qualities of the woman which are attractive to the man, the manly qualities of the man which are attractive to the woman.'

At its most extreme, the concentration of the minor secondary characteristics could result in a mere catalogue that had no relevance to the woman being described, and only served to fill in space. Thus an extract from the popular novelist Ouida lyricized: 'The marigolds and the sunflowers had given her the ripe rich gold to tint her hair; the lupins had lent their azure for her eyes; the moss-rose buds had made her pretty mouth; the arum lilies had uncurled their softness for her skin; and the lime blossoms had given her their frank, fresh, innocent fragrance.' Occasionally the emphasis on one select portion of the anatomy gives to the writing a sickly fetishist air – the *vers de société* poet H. Cholmondeley-Pennell writing on a finger (1884):

> O Finger with the circlet slight,
> That keeps it warm and cosy,
> Wee winsome third left-handed doight
> So white and warm and rosy, –
> More taper digits there may be,
> More lips may kiss and cling on,
> This tiny finger's best to me –
> The one I put the ring on.[1]

In some of these minor poets, one is inclined to believe that there is a degree of substitution. The effort to project what Havelock Ellis calls womanly qualities is hampered by the vetoe on certain words and certain parts of the body. The tone of the above verse is very similar to the tone of many pornographic poems calculated to excite such as this extract from a poem 'On Enjoyment'.[2]

> With what rapture do I view
> The soft bosom's glassy hue!
> Now my wanton fingers rove
> O'er the beauteous mounds of love!
> Now my eager lips I close.
> On each blooming blushing rose!
> Now my eager hand I slip
> O'er the glossy marble hip;
> And on each round, swelling thigh
> Cast my charm'd delighted eye;

or this:

> Can I forget the beauteous Emma's charms,
> The soft elysium of her circling arms;
> The wanton jerk of those elastic hips,
> Which made the ermin'd sages lick their lips.

and favourite analogies such as:

> How the snowy hillocks rise!
> Parted by the luscious vale.

and

> Know you the valley, sequester'd, inviting,
> That shelters the fountain, of purest delight.

It cannot be stressed too often that Victorian writers even of the hackish variety dropped into verse with often astonishing ease, and were adept at using the poetic language in which 'a spade' is 'a digging implement', and 'a fish' was 'of the finny breed'. They used analogies and metaphors with an adroitness that would need to be explained to a reader who only saw verse on birthday or Christmas cards or heard it in television jingles; but when the message was in danger of being taken at its face value these writers used italics to point the double meaning. At the same time – the early forties – as the magazine the *Exquisite* was publishing the above specimens, the *Town* was catering for a slightly more worldly market. It did not publish long semi-pornographical stories in serial form as did the *Exquisite*, but crisp, mock news items, and accounts of the suddenly popular sport, prize fighting. The editor, 'Baron' Renton Nicholson, was especially partial to the double meaning:

'I have been to Covent Garden to see a new *piece* . . . I call it "My Market Woman"; it has *carrotty* hair, a *turn-up* nose, lips *redish*, a dress like scarlet runners, *pea* green. It lodges on the first floor, and therefore I call it my middle dish of vegetables.'

'Indeed you are an ingenious fellow, for, to speak in the words of Shakspere, you have given to *hairy something* a local habitation and a name.'

The aim of such work was totally different from that of the pornographic magazine. The *Town* amused and did not excite; when it indulged in descriptions of the sex act, it could be witty and cool. During the winter of 1840 – not long after the royal marriage – Queen Victoria and her Albert were very keen on ice skating. In the issue of the *Town* of 26 December, leaving the Christmas spirit in abeyance, was a paragraph entitled 'Her Majesty upon the Ice'; which ran:

During every day favourable for the purpose, Prince Albert pushed Her Majesty, in the arm chair. It was, we are assured, a most interesting sight, the prince leaning fondly over her, and directing each motion with the most exquisite skill, grace and gentleness, while Her Majesty's beautifully expressive countenance clearly indicated the high degree of delight she derived from the exhilarating [*sic*] exercise and his unremitting exertion.

Cowardly it might have been – the Queen and her husband having no opportunity to answer back – but the sophistication and worldliness of such material are an agreeable antidote to the sadism and perversities of the underground pornographic magazines that flowered briefly during the middle-class-dominated decades, the sixties and the seventies. The *Town* might have encouraged smut, but its heart and its genitals were in the right place.

Although saucy and suggestive, the *Exquisite* occasionally went out of its way to obey the proprieties, rather unnecessarily, as it had a limited circulation. For example, there is no reason, except a misplaced squeamishness, why breasts and thighs are not written in full in the following:

> While her b—s and t—s
> Sink and rise
> Like stormy waves on a milky main.

Unlike the *Town*, the *Exquisite* did set out to raise sexual appetites:

> On a gilded couch the lady lies,
> And bends on her lover her beaming eyes –
> With snowy brow and snowy breast,
> Silken hair and silken vest
> And mantle rich and rare;
> While her faithful robes contrive to show
> More of her leg than is quite 'comme il faut'.
>
> Polished hips and bosom swelling
> And her shame and terror telling,
> The mount of Venus,
> Kissing between as
> Fine pair of legs as Thetis could boast;
> And the curls of dark hair
> That lay clustering there,
> And shaded the lips that mortals love most.

The centres of interest of the pornographic writers were, as might be expected, the genitalia, pubic hair, the breasts, the buttocks, and the legs, more or less in that order. Not a word about eyebrows, or even eyes, and even the rounded shoulder was not deemed worth a mention except in passing from one salacious area to another. That this was a romantic decade is evidenced by 'A Paphian Lyric':

> Oh! soft are the hills, and made for reclining,
>> Whose velvet-like slopes grot and fountain conceal
> Reposed on that throne, let man scorn all repining,
> And prove that to *live* is supremely to *feel*.

or 'The Curl':

> Sweet graceful curl, with golden hue,
> That decks a gem so rare;
> Soft silken tress, each fond caress,
> But makes thee look more fair.
> Dame Nature, in a jealous mood,
> To watch o'er joys, that thrill the soul,
> And guard the lips of Love.

Between 1840 and 1860 exists a curious hiatus, unbroken except for the occasional handbook for men about town. This lack was possibly an accident of history; possibly more pornographic material was destroyed, or perhaps during these twenty years the suppression of naughty books was beginning to be felt. Unquestionably the police were more proficient.

Certainly the mood of later pornographic literature was drastically changed. Whatever their errors of taste, and irrespective of some indiscriminate mud-throwing, journalists of the forties were writers; in other words, they manipulated the subject. In the second generation of Victorian pornographers, it was the other way about – the subject manipulated the writer (which might well be the definition of a hack). Readers were not interested in stylistic tricks, the ability of the writer to come to grips with the work, nor were they concerned with grammar or spelling. They wanted the raw meat laced plentifully with spice. The comparisons one must make are not with respectable fiction writers, but the hack writers of serials for the prim and proper *Chambers's Journal* and *Once a Week*.

A characteristic of pornography of the sixties was that the language was unexceptional, the vocabulary almost identical with that of the hack romantic writer as in this extract from *The Three Chums – A Tale of London Every Day Life*:

Harry secured the sofa, where he sat with Mrs Lovejoy on his lap, and one of his hands inside the bosom of her dressing gown, whilst her hands, at least one of them, was God knows where, and very evidently gave him considerable pleasure, to judge by the sparkle of his eyes, and the way he caressed her, as well as the frequent kisses they exchanged.

or this from *The Disembodied Spirit*:

I could inhale the sweets of her delicious breath, and here I could also catch glimpses of part of her lovely breasts, as they rose and fell in the calm undulations of innocent sleep, rendered more and more excited by the partial view thus obtained, I longed for a more complete sight of these rounded globes.

Her rounded, softly moulded chin, gradually merging into the white column of her neck, the last gradually swelling until it ended in two round swelling breasts parted between, and crowned each with a delicious pink bud.

Her legs had opened wide, and as I gazed my eyes dwelt on each softly rounded limb from taper ankle to glowing thigh; her hand, meantime prompted perhaps by some incident of her dream, wandered down till it rested between her quivering thighs, and unconsciously played with the short curling hair that covered that lovely spot, excited or tittled with this unusual occupation, a pair of scarlet pouting lips, whilst the soft mound above thrilled as if longing for some unknown pleasure.

The characteristics that constituted sex appeal, one can see, were no different in 1860 from 1960. The modifications that were made in the appearance of woman dressed – the tiny waist, the dress reaching almost to the ground, and the uplift of breasts – had not made any impact on basic womanly qualities. It has been noted that pornography produced at the present time has all the qualities present in pornography produced a century ago, and this has been explained in terms of authors emulating earlier erotica, of carrying on a tradition because it was simply easier. It is possibly truer that the writers of erotica have seized on basic elements, that they lacked the technical equipment to utilize extras such as fashion or accessories. The writers of the serial stories in the respectable magazines were forced by their medium to use such props, though their aim was still to create a certain excitement in their male readers, if only to insure that such readers bothered to carry on with the next episode. The tone of William Cyples's *A Change of Luck* bears an astonishing resemblance to the above extracts: 'Eyes flashed most brightly, arms were gracefully weaved in glimpses of white motion, the proud form was bent in the lowest of elegant courtesies; there were soft witcheries of touching finger-tips upon the gloved palm; a fragrant incense of warm, scented breath enwrapped him, as the only half-concealed bosom rose and fell.'

The aesthetic qualities as a spontaneous combustible between man and woman apparently having been oversold, the popular periodicals had to get over to their readers sex appeal of woman to man, and man to woman, with a narrow spectrum of experience available. This was a problem also to women who wanted desperately to get married, and who made use of the *Matrimonial News*, a journal started in the early 1870s. Anonymity was guaranteed by the use of a number, but advertisers were requested to send to the editor their *carte* as an indication of good faith. Typical of the advertisements was:

6872 – A respectable servant-girl, aged 27, nice appearance, very respectable family, and who has saved up about £100, would like to correspond with a steady respectable man about 35, with a view to marriage. Address and carte with Editor.

Respectability as a surrogate for womanly qualities may have won for number 6872 a husband – no one can say, though 'nice appearance' would hardly charm the birds off the trees. Number 6543 had surely the better idea of enticing a mate, prefacing her advertisement with a quote:

> Oh, woman, in our hours of ease,
> Uncertain, coy, and hard to please;
> When pain or sickness rend the brow,
> A ministering angel thou.

A Young widow, highly connected, dark hair and eyes, considered pretty, good figure, clever, and amusing, possessing a small income, desires to marry. She does not deny that she might at times realise the two first lines of the couplet [*sic*] quoted above, but she can assure any gentleman willing to make the experiment that she is as certain to be true to the conclusion.

Some of the women described themselves as of 'a jolly disposition', and in one issue of *Matrimonial News*, of 350 advertisements, only one lady admitted that she was 'not pretty', though, she added, 'considered very ladylike, and with fascinating manners'. There were men too, who wished to get married, and they were faced with the problem of reconciling dignity and the insertion of an advertisement. 6883 was:

A Merchant in Lanarkshire (bachelor), aged 38, fair complexion, 6 feet, plain and simple in tastes and habits, of a religious cast of mind, though by no means ascetic, income from £500 to £600, wishes to correspond with an English county lady over 23, one with similar means preferred; must be warm hearted and a loving disposition, have head as well as hands in domestic affairs, and above all 'piety' is indispensably requisite. Editor has carte and address.

A Martian, acquainted with the undeniable fact that marriage is a civilized way of regulating the sexual behaviour of man and woman, would, provided it had them, rub its eyes if confronted with such advertisements. In the world of the printed word, a world that has only the most tentative relations with the world of real life, marriage and sex were, in the nineteenth century, successfully divorced, just as another indissoluble duo — sexual intercourse and the end result, children — were not referred to in erotic writings.

The writers of nineteenth-century erotica being principally male (though pseudonyms are occasionally female even when the writers are men), and the readers of erotica likewise, the descriptive passages are mainly concerned with the sex appeal of women. Occasionally there is mention of a 'pego' of astounding dimensions, especially in third-generation Victorian pornography when the note of sadism has become, to continue the metaphor in a way the Victorians themselves would have liked, a giant organ swell (a penis of massive size would create more havoc among the virgins that skip through sadistic pornography; in several instances, Negroes were introduced to provide just this ingredient).

A large section of the descriptions are masturbatory fantasies, a voyeur's eye view. This is frequently indicated by the title of the story or the verse. Thus 'Kissi-Kissi: or What I saw in a Garret' of 1860:

> There was the pure and snowy skin,
> Revealing currents warm within,
> The graceful peak where beauty sits,
> The swelling globes, the panting teats,
> The fair abdomen, and the loins,
> Where each fair thigh its fellow joins.
> He saw all these but fixed his eyes
> Most on the spot where 'twixt the thighs,
> The rosy entrance to her heart
> Lay like a rosebud rent apart;
> For it, unlike to older girls,
> Was yet unhid by clustering curls –
> Save such a down as one might find
> Upon a peach's luscious rind.

The nineteenth-century obsession with young girls' sexual potential is evident in the above, as it is from a further extract from *The Three Chums*, a serial in *The Boudoir* that stretches over all three volumes: 'They had slits in their dresses, so that both of his hands found employment exploring and groping on the one side of the soft incipient moss of the elder one's grot, as well as the hairless slit of her little sister.'

Sometimes writers and editors were aware that occasional readers had more mature tastes. Again the unknown author of *The Three Chums* (possibly it was the publisher Dugdale himself) wrote: 'Although so bulky, Mrs Lovejoy was what some would term a truly splendid woman, not more than forty, very pleasing face and rich brown hair; whilst her open night dress displayed all the splendours of her mature bosom's magnificent orbs, as white as snow and ornamented by the most seductive strawberry nipples.'

Third-generation pornography, the eighties onward, permitted itself liberties. Though some descriptions of sexual charm could well have taken their place in the pornographic magazines of the sixties, the writers tended more to use ancillaries. The following is quite unexceptional and would have been unremarkable in one of the more hot-blooded romantic tales for the wider public: 'Annie, a finely developed blonde, with deep blue eyes, pouting red lips, and a full heaving bosom, which to me looked like a perfect volcano of smothered desires.'

It is also clear that the climate of repression had given to hitherto ordinary attributes of woman an added piquancy. From *Sub-Umbra, or Sport Amongst the She-Noodles*: 'What can be more pleasing than to talk of fun with pretty girls, the beauties of their legs and bosoms, and all about them? How I should love to see your lovely calf at this moment, especially after the glimpses I have already had of a divine ankle.'

However, these are brief interludes, though the triumvirate of vagina, clitoris, and pubic area are supplemented: 'I could see the lips of her plump pouting cunny, deliciously feathered, with soft light down, her lovely legs, drawers, stockings, pretty boots, making a *tout ensemble*, which as I write and describe them cause Mr Priapus to swell in my breeches.'

Observation was also replaced by participation as one of the mechanisms of excitation; Lesbiansim was engaging the attention of the enthusiasts for this type of literature. In *Lady Pokingham: Or They All Do It* (1880) the writer is purporting to be a woman, added gilt to the gingerbread: 'What a delightfully pouting little slit you have, Beatrice,' she explained, patting my Mons Veneris, 'we shall make a beautiful contrast, mine is a light blonde, and yours will be brunette. See my little curly parsley bed is already half-an-inch long.'

A lengthy extract from *Voluptuous Confessions of a French Lady of Fashion* might well be the definitive summary of the basic womanly qualities as the nineteenth-century erotic writer saw them:

Then she took a delicate cambric chemise, trimmed with lace, and advancing towards the full-length mirror of the wardrobe, looked in the glass for a minute or two, and by a graceful movement of her shoulders let slip the chemise she had on, which arrested in its downward course for a second by the swelling of her hips, soon fell twisted at her feet. The fall of her back and her backside were both admirable. At the bottom of her white and polished belly, her luxurious ebony fleece, the length and thickness of which constituted a true rarity, could be plainly seen. The contrast of this enormous black spot upon a body so white gave to Bertha a peculiar appearance of strange voluptuousness.

My mouth, rather large and very sensual, was furnished with fine teeth; a black mole, on the right side of my upper lip, gave piqauncy to my physiognomy. I had an admirable bust, the breasts apart, firm and well placed; my figure was neat and supple with voluminous buttocks that were perfectly handsome, and the mount of Venus, very much pronounced, protected a nook that, it appears, was a rare and pure pattern, both in form and exceptional voluptuous quality. Without possessing the rare bush of my aunt, I was well provided in that way, and by a singular peculiarity the pretty fur continued much lower down, by a silky growth of short moss, that shadowed with its dark line the furrow separating the neighbouring twin globes.

That this was 1860 and not 1960 might possibly be deduced from the appearance of a word that was once highly regarded by midcultists – physiognomy – and by mention of a material that has gone the way of red flannel – cambric. That this was 1860 is confirmed by a passage of dialogue that occurs between these two extracts:

'My adored one, how lovely you are! What admirable hips! What an adorable – ARSE!'
'Oh! Alfred! What is that naughty word?'
'Don't be frightened, darling; lovers can say anything. Those words, out of place in colder moments, add fresh relish to the sweet mystery of love. You will soon say them too, and understand their charm.'

For some reason, the writer or printer had added a question mark after 'love'. Perhaps this was a word that came alien to him, a word that had somehow infiltrated in from the world of Tennyson or Ouida. It was not a disastrous admission, however, and did not wreck the flimsy premise that laid down that sex could be isolated from every other aspect of human life, especially as the circulation of the magazine in which this suspect word appeared was only three hundred.

Just as Queen Victoria found out and promulgated that child-bearing was the shadow-side of marriage, so pornography was the shadow-side of the man–woman relationship. It is curious that the full expression of man's attitude towards woman can only be found in ill-printed and semiliterate magazines and books. 'Women and love always constitute the subject of conversation wherever there is a meeting of intellectual people socially brought together by eating and drinking,' wrote Edmond de Goncourt in his journal. 'Our talk at dinner was at first smutty, and Turgenev listened to us with the open-mouthed wonder of a barbarian who only makes love very naturally.' A now forgotten writer, W. L. George (1882–1926) wrote in 1918 that if a novelist were to develop his characters evenly, a three hundred-page novel might extend to five hundred – two hundred pages for sex preoccupations. Our literary characters are lop-sided because their ordinary traits are fully portrayed while their sex life is cloaked, minimized or left out. ... The novelist may discuss anything but the main preoccupation of life ...' (*A Novelist on Novels*). Time has rendered this minor figure's strictures obsolete, but when he wrote unquestionably he had fact on his side. This emasculation exasperated Frank Harris so much that he was induced to write his autobiography, *My Life and Loves* (1925). Much of his loving was done in the Victorian period, but he, too, was shackled by the remnants of Victorian respectability that clung around him:

... and the worst of it all is that the highest function of man has been degraded by foul words so that it is almost impossible to write the body's hymn of joy as it should be written. The poets have been almost as guilty in this respect as the priests: Aristophanes and Rabelais are ribald, dirty, Boccaccio cynical, while Ovid leers cold-bloodedly and Zola, like Chaucer, finds it difficult to suit language to his desires.

When it comes to the point, however, Frank Harris becomes a good deal more pornographic than any of them, and his reluctance to use what he calls the 'foul words' he partially overcomes ('her pussy', 'her sex', 'her cunny').

From the scandal papers, such as *Rosenberg's Little Journal* of 1886, there were uneasy indications that they too would like to use the freedom enjoyed by the small circulation pornographic magazines. But the editors were always aware that the long arm of the law was ready for them. Editors of such papers tend to be cynical. 'From the costermonger who seeks his 'Judy' in the slums of Whitechapel to the prince whose jackal is always on the look-out for a pretty actress or a frail aristocrat, men are all pretty much alike.' Such editors incline to the misogynistical when they deal with the charms of woman:

Woman is very lovely. See her pink and white complexion, her frizzy gold hair, her lovely black lashes to her sparkling eyes, her swelling bosom, her elegant shape, her shining teeth, and she is a picture quite too sweet to behold. Add to all these charms a loving and clinging manner, and you are a gone coon. You lead this lovely creature to the hymeneal altar on the first proximo; on the second proximo you discover that her head is as smooth as a bladder of lard, that her teeth take out, that her swelling bust is made of india-rubber, that she wears a bustle as big as a piano, that her complexion washes off, that she makes up her eye lashes. You have married a heap of dry, yellow, wrinkled skin and bone – a hairless, toothless, complexionless, bustless, formless thing – that howls at you for hinting that she married you under false pretences.[3]

Here is the real world, away from the restricted area where men would pay a guinea for thirty pages of quintessential sex. Journalists were also critical of the latitude permitted to Victorian high art. 'Goodall's canvas, representing King David being supported by a semi nude tart, commands general admiration', stated *Tittle Tattle* on 19 May 1888, 'and ought to be exhibited at the Westminster Aquarium. If this tart were reproduced on the front page of this journal, Warren would have a fit, and order out the police, while good old Bridge would tumble into the coal scuttle with fright.' Bridge was known as 'the Bow Street Solon'.[4] There were consolations. If readers could not afford to purchase dirty books, there were cheaper ways of titillation. In *Day and Night*, modestly naughty, but hardly worth while being locked away in the British Museum newspaper library's private case (a room built like a small nuclear shelter), there was an advertisement (9 September 1871) '100 Beautiful Female Photographs for 18 stamps, just imported (sealed). G. Wright, 3 St Marks-road, Kensington-park, London. Coloured Cartes 1/– Transparent Cards 3/6 each Don Juan 1/6 Secrets for Ladies 1/–.'

Public affirmation of the sexual charms of working-class girls was even more closely restricted. One of the chief outlets was the music hall song. Charles Leybourne (sometimes Leyburne) was a prolific producer of lyrics, and he echoes the sentiments of the romantic serials with extra sentimental mock-humorous quirks:

> She's got a little ankle, she's got a little foot,
> And pretty little fingers running taper,
> Her waist is round and small, her mouth is best of all,
> With ruby lips not twice as thick as paper.

This was a falling off from earlier working class songs, of the quasi-folk variety:

> As I walked out one morning I met a buxom lass,
> Belonging to a dairy man, she had a field of grass,
> It grew between two mountains at the foot of a rising hill,
> She bir'd [*sic*] me to cut it down while the birds did sweetly sing.
>
> She said, my lusty young man, will you now begin,
> My grass is in good order, I long to have it down,
> It is such pleasant weather I long to clear the ground,
> So get your scythe in order to mow my meadow down.

This kind of song – this particular one being issued by William Pratt, 82 Digbeth, Birmingham, 'the Cheapest Song Warehouse in England' – is a parallel to the publications for men about town. Songs for the mass audience were vilely printed in broadsheet form; the most famous of the printers and publishers was Jemmy Catnach, who bought an old wooden press in 1813 and never looked back.

An odd feature of the music hall song was the anti sex-

appeal element, and some of the lyrics seem to be potent anti-
aphrodisiacs:

> Her beauty and praise I mean to disclose,
> She's dirty and lazy with a short snuffy nose,
> She's a disgrace to the women wherever she goes
> And her clothes all in tatters are hanging,
> With a beard on her lip like a wandering Jew,
> Not a tooth in her head that is sound only two,
> And a shift on her back neither black white or blue
> That never was wet with a washing.
>
> We met beside the mountain stream,
> Damp tulips deck'd her chalk white brow
> Her voice was like the night owl's scream,
> Her eyes – alas! I see them now!
> Her hair look'd purple in the sun,
> Her teeth – they were a guinea a set,
> Her age! she was forty-one;
> She weighed but sixteen stone – and – yet
>   I could not say I loved her,
>   Nor bid her join my lot,
>   I could not say I loved her,
>   I tried – but no! could not.
>
> We met once more 'neath gas-light glare,
> Amid the fierce and wild quadrille.
> She was – they said – a millionaire,
> I spoke – her answer haunts me still.
> She lisp'd, 'I'm thine. Wealth, beauty, all,
> My income's twenty-five pounds ten,
> We'll live near gaswork at Vauxhall,
> Say, dost thou love me now?' – and then –
>   I could not say I loved her,
>   Nor bid her join my lot,
>   I could not say I loved her,
>   I tried – but no! could not.

The poor were pragmatic and acrid. Life was real and life
was earnest, and they had no time for the airy-fairy fantasies of
their betters. If they were ugly they could not substitute their
own wispy inadequate tresses the 'Fairy Fringe', price one

guinea, or the 'New Hunting Chignon', three guineas, or dye them with 'Aureoline' (peroxide) at ten shillings and sixpence a bottle. If their complexions were pallid or spotty, toilet masks and 'Ivorine cream' were not within their budget, and if their breasts were sagging, corsets were often outside their sphere. Nor did they buy 'patent palpitators' and 'bust improvers' to augment their home-grown products. They expected little, and they got little. The visions conjured up for the rich by the small band of dedicated men were not for them. From *La Rose d'Amour*, a serial in the magazine *The Pearl* (1879): [5]

She had a temptingly small foot, giving tokens of the excellent smallness of the delicious slit, which nature had placed between a pair of ripe fleshy thighs, backed by a pair of fair buttocks, beautifully rising up, swelling out into bold relief from the adjacent parts. A belly, white and soft as a bed of snow, a waist slender as a nymph, a neck like a swan, a small mouth, inlaid with two rows of ivory, lips rosy and pouting, cheeks soft as the velvet down of an overripe peach, languishing dark eyes, sparkling and beaming with a lascivious fire, shaded by long silken lashes, while her auburn hair fell in a profusion of ringlets over her neck and shoulders, half concealing a pair of large globes, rivalling alabaster in whiteness, tipped with nipples hard and red as rose-buds, in fact she was 'perfection personified'.

These undoubted charms would not have appealed to the philosopher Herbert Spencer. Looking back on his life, he recalls his friendship with the Potters of Upper Hamilton Terrace. 'Well, what do you think of Miss Potter?' he was asked. 'Any other young fellow would have launched out into unmeasured praise. But my reply was: – 'I do not quite like the shape of her head ... it seems probable that this abnormal tendency to criticize has been a chief factor in the continuance of my celibate life ...' [6]

The Submissive Woman

A factor that worked against the New Woman and the emancipationist was the submissive instinct in woman. Lilia, in Tennyson's 'The Princess' (1847), was an early exponent of women's rights:

> 'Ah, were I something great! I wish I were
> Some mighty poetess, I would shame you then,
> That love to keep us children! O I wish
> That I were some great princess, I would build
> Far off from men a college like a man's,
> And I would teach them all that men are taught;
> We are twice as quick!' And here she shook aside
> The hand that play'd the patron with her curls.

A stanza later, Lilia realizes the pretentiousness of this posture:

> Petulant she spoke, and at herself she laugh'd;
> A rosebud set with little wilful thorns,
> And sweet as English air could make her, she:

Had she been a character of half a century later, there would have been no need for such a rebuttal, and by that time, any way, there was many 'a college like a man's'. Tennyson was not only the greatest of English poets; he could also sum up a type in a crisp sentence. The rosebuds set with little wilful thorns struggled against their dichotomy for the rest of the century, and many of them are still struggling. Their reason told them that they were the equals of men, their instincts forced them into an attitude of sexual submission, both physically and mentally. This attitude was rationalized with brutal relish by the seventh Duke of Northumberland ('man in the beginning was ordained to rule over the woman'), with more civility by Havelock Ellis: 'Women, it is true, remain nearer than men to the infantile state: but, on the other hand, men approach more nearly than women to the ape-like and senile state.' Woman as a child was even more exasperatingly offensive to the emancipationists than woman as man's plaything. Ellis reasoning is interesting; whether it is valid or not, one may judge for oneself: 'Nature has made women more like children in order that they may better understand and care for children, and in the gift of children Nature has given to women a massive and sustained physiological joy to which there is nothing in men's lives to correspond. Nature has done her best to make women healthy and glad, and has on the whole been content to let men run somewhat wild.' [7]

Ellis offers the proposition that the societies that are most favourable to woman are primitive, and that militant and highly cultured periods are hostile. The masculine cultures of Greece and Rome degraded woman and suppressed natural emotion, and Ellis quotes with approval the historical notion that these civilizations faltered and collapsed because of the inferior role they inflicted on woman. The nineteenth century was complex and confused, and in its subterranean levels it produced sub-cultures of unprecedented primitiveness and brutality, that were not, however, particularly favourable to women or, indeed, anyone. Its technology was sophisticated, and the century was militant and highly cultured. The situation of woman in this incoherent society was equally uncertain. Those who were desperately anxious to eradicate the image of submissive woman, the 'love, honour and obey' syndrome of the marriage service, had a fifth column in their own ranks, in the person-ages of women who were quite happy with the existing order of things. 'Every step made towards identity of habits,' wrote Mrs Lynn Linton (the *Nineteenth Century*, 1891), 'is a step down-wards in refinement and delicacy – wherein lies the essential core of civilization.' Mrs Linton sneered at the brave new women who smoked in public, and drew a parallel with them and 'ancient dames with "whiskin" beards about their "mou's", withered and unsightly worn out, and no longer women in desirableness or beauty,' who smoked black cutty-pipes in the north of England.

Mrs Linton drew a picture of the young woman who had thrown off the habit of submission. It is not so depressing as, perhaps, she imagined it would be: 'A superbly dressed young woman, bust, arms, and shoulders bare, and gleaming white and warm beneath the subdued light of a luxurious dinner-table – a beautiful young creature, painted, dyed, and powdered according to the mode – her lips red with wine and moist with liqueur ...'

A reply to the Mrs Lintons of the nineties was made, rationally and with dignity, by Kathleen Cuffe, who asked for the free use of a latchkey, permission to go to music halls alone without being treated like a whore, and allowed to go for walks 'without having first provided herself with an unhappy maid or attendant of some description, presumably to prevent her from losing her way or getting run over'. Miss Cuffe pointed out, logically, that if a young married woman can go out alone (she 'does not wear her wedding-ring in her nose or other prominent spot to assure the passer-by of her social status'), why not the single girl? Why should a single girl not be able to have a friendship with a man? 'It does indeed seem a mistaken system that prevents a man and a girl knowing anything in reality of each other's characters until they are engaged.' [8] Unknown to Kathleen Cuffe, these fences were in the process of being torn down.

The submissive instincts were rationalized by many as the necessity of sacrificing oneself for the children. Mona Caird took up this point with vigour: 'The affairs of the present are carried on by the adult population, not by the children; and if the generations of adults are going to renounce, age after age, their own chances of development – resigning, as so many mothers do, opportunities of intellectual progress and spiritual enlightenment for the sake of their children – how in the name of common sense will they benefit humanity.' [9]

The children would merely have to go through the same rigmarole themselves.

Is the submission of the female an instinct at all? That most rational of psychologists, William McDougall, felt unquestionably: 'There is undoubtedly some considerable difference between the male and the female of most species, as regards not only the receptive but also the executive side of the instinct [i.e., the mating instinct]. The male is more aggressive and active and usually takes the initiative' (*An Outline of Psychology*, 1923). Unlike Freud and the psychoanalysts, for whom mammals lesser than man might well have not existed, McDougall studied closely the behaviour of animals in the hope and the conviction that such attention would throw light on to human

behaviour. This trend has over the last few decades been more
and more pronounced.

In the nineteenth century, the instinct to submit took innumerable turns. It could be treated on a lofty philosophical
plane, as by Coventry Patmore: '*Between unequals sweet is
equal love*'; and the fact is that there is no love, and therefore
no sweetness, which is not thus conditioned; and the greater
the inequality the greater the sweetness.' From the far-famed
poet of married love, this is significant, and if it is at all ambiguous – as Patmore's statements tend to be – this ambiguity is
destroyed shortly afterwards in the same work (*Religio Poetae*
1893 – he too had been struck by the Latin blight): 'She only
really loves and desires to become what he loves and desires her
to be.' The superiority of man and the innate inferiority of
woman had been stressed by Patmore's mentor, Swedenborg:
'The man is born intellectual, and the female is born volitional.'

The attitude of 'cultured' man was expressed admirably by
Ruskin in *Sesame and Lilies* 1868:

The relations of the womanly to the manly nature, their different
capacities of intellect or virtue, seem never to have been yet estimated
with entire consent. We hear of the 'mission' and of the 'rights' of
Woman, as if these could ever be separate from the mission and the
rights of Man – as if she and her lord were creatures of independent
kind, and of irreconcilable claim. This, at least, is wrong. And not
less wrong – is the idea that woman is only the shadow and attendant image of her lord, owing him a thoughtless and servile obedience,
and supported altogether in her weakness by the pre-eminence of his
fortitude.

This, I say, is the most foolish of all errors respecting her who was
made to be the helpmate of man. As if he could be helped effectively
by a shadow, or worthily by a slave!

Ruskin is nowhere more self-revealing than in this sage-like
pronouncement, with its loaded language and devastating hypocrisy. By putting 'mission' and 'rights' in quotes, Ruskin is
coyly sneering, 'she and her lord' points out their basic relationship, and although Ruskin was ostensibly on the side of
equality, few emancipationists would have concurred with his

righteous view that woman 'was made to be the helpmate of man' or that she should be 'supported altogether in her weakness by the pre-eminence of his fortitude'. In view of his own disastrous encounters with woman in all her aspects, it might be surprising that Ruskin can lay down the line so firmly. 'The man's work for his own home is, as has been said, to secure its maintenance, progress, and defense; the woman's to secure its order, comfort, and loveliness.' Ruskin and, to do him justice, millions of his contemporaries, were thrusting submission on to woman: (a) because it was good for them; (b) because it was good for the men; (c) because it preserved the social *status quo*; (d) because it stopped women from getting above themselves; (e) because it kept the home running smoothly; and (f) because it perpetuated a sentimental notion of the man–woman relationship.

Men read and listened to Ruskin because this was what they wanted to have confirmed, and women read and listened because he was emphasizing the role in life that had been hammered into them since they were toddlers. They did not spot the clues, that Ruskin was defining an ideal environment and relationship, that by writing about it he would hope it would come true, did not discern the curious terminology of another of his paeans – also in *Sesame and Lilies* – upon the domestic life: 'This is the true nature of home – it is the place of Peace; the shelter, not only from all injury, but from all terror, doubt, and division. In so far as it is not this, it is not home; so far as the anxieties of the outer life penetrate into it, and the inconsistently minded, unknown, unloved, or hostile society of the outer world is allowed by either husband or wife to cross the threshold, it ceases to be home . . ." The home, in fact, as womb.

The nineteenth-century reader was being conned by someone who had no experience of the subject on which he was pontificating, though even the most receptive reader might well have had second thoughts about a manic little extract from one of Ruskin's dottier books, *Arrows of the Chace* (the pseudo-antique spelling is always suspect in the nineteenth century): 'Woman's work is as refreshing as the dew's and as defined as the moon's, but it is not the rain's, nor the sun's.'

The *Saturday Review* said much the same thing as Ruskin in less flowery, cruder, and more acceptable language: 'It is no small thing that half the human race should habitually take a purer and more sentimental view of life than those who have to do the dirty work' (6 May 1871).

The handbooks on etiquette emphasized the necessity of the wife's sinking her dignity when the occasion arose – it was better to be sycophantic than left alone. In her book *The Women of England*, Sarah Ellis tells her reader how to behave if her husband likes to go out in the evening without her.

The rational woman, whose conversation on this occasion is to serve her purpose more effectually than tears, knows better than to speak of what her husband would probably consider a most unreasonable subject of complaint. She tries to recollect some incident, some trait of character, or some anecdote of what has lately occurred within her knowledge, and relates it in her most lively and piquant manner. If conscious of beauty, she tries a little raillery, and plays gently upon some of her husband's not unpleasing peculiarities, looking all the while as disengaged and unsuspecting as she can. If his attention become fixed, she gives her conversation a more serious turn, and plunges at once into some theme of deep and absorbing interest. If her companion grows restless, she changes the subject, and again recollects something laughable to relate to him. Yet all the while her own poor heart is aching with the feverish anxiety that vacillates between the extremes of hope and fear.

That the message was understood and accepted is clear from the fact that *The Women of England* went through sixteen editions between 1838 and 1841, and from her accounts of her early life with Albert, it might appear that Queen Victoria had read and profited from it. *Punch* was amused by such books, and parodied them: 'Never contradict him, dear, but fall in with all his little wishes and whims, however unreasonable. In short, devote yourself to him entirely. Your turn will come.' And with many wives, it did; a pretence at submission worked wonders.

The Victorian male not only wanted a submissive wife, but expected it. In *Letters to a Young Man About Town* (1853)

Thackeray wrote: 'An exquisite slave is what we want for the most part; a humble, flattering, smiling, tea-making, pianoforte-playing being, who laughs at our jokes however old they may be, coaxes us and wheedles us in our humours, and' – the sting in the tail – 'fondly lies to us through life.' Thackeray assured his readers that there were more clever women in the world than one might imagine. They trod a tight rope preserving an image, though on occasions when dealing with a more than usually obtuse and self-satisfied husband the temptations to drop the pretence must have been irresistible. Many of the admirers of Elizabeth Barrett Browning's novel in verse *Aurora Leigh* (1856) nodded when they came across:

> And I breathe large at home. I drop my cloak,
> Unclasp my girdle, loose the band that ties
> My hair . . . now could I but unloose my soul!
> We are sepulchred alive in this close world,
> And want more room.

The efforts to perpetuate a *modus vivendi* that clipped in with society's expectations frequently produced conflicts that drove despairing wives to invalid beds. 'Tragic health was, in a manner, the only solution for her of the practical problem of life,' [10] said Henry James of his sister, Alice (a brave woman who faced with great heroism the fact that she was dying of cancer of the breast). Tragic health was for many the only solution for practical problems of marriage. Intelligent and sensitive women found that they were yoked to boobies who had complacently accepted all the fodder of masculine superiority. They either had to pretend to a submission that was foreign to them, or rock the marital boat, though behind the lace curtains rational couples made their own adjustments. Many men realized upon marriage that, despite all precepts, they were the submissive parties, and when there were two anxious to act out such a role there was confusion, and the expectations of society were welcome in that they forced on such a couple the necessity to work out a compromise.

Many working-class girls went into marriage chronically inferior. In 1847 the first evening school for women was opened in Birmingham, and volunteer teachers were shocked at the domestic deficiencies of their pupils. They had been coached in needlework and the making of small largely useless articles of clothing almost since they had been weaned, and the teachers were shattered at the ignorance of the women with whom they were confronted. Of thirty-six pupils, only three had any ability at all with needle and thread, and those three were dressmakers; similarly the women could not cook ('the broth she attempts to make is bits of hard meat and vegetables floating in warm water, probably smoked'),[11] could not make bread, could not read or write, and were the prey of unscrupulous shopkeepers. Beatrice Potter, later to be married to the Fabian Sidney Webb, was aghast when she saw the conditions under which working-class women lived, their status hardly being more than that of animals, humiliated and worked upon by any representative of authority who happened to be handy, whether it was doctor, magistrate, or workhouse master. 'She is dreadfully bothered with the *weltschmerz*, the uselessness of life etc. etc,' wrote the *Pall Mall Gazette* of Miss Potter. It was small wonder that for such working-class women the life of prostitution was often a release and, for the more thoughtful, a means of revenge on men who held all the cards in the relationships of the sexes.

The lives of working-class women demonstrate an extra dimension in submissiveness. Theirs was a world where the strong equably beat the weak, where the wife was a skivvy who did the chores and an object to be used for sex, where even the courtship ritual had a perfunctory prosaic animal quality. Thus the song:

> At last she consented, away we both went,
> Five shillings in lobsters and oysters I spent,
> Six drops of brandy for her I did pay,
> Down by the dark arches under the railway.

The instinct of woman to submit was brought to a pitch of self-degradation, and the bullying of petty officialdom added to their uncomprehending woe. Poor women were things to be sued, to be shunted around, appertainments of a profession.

The case of Ann Ferry, wife of a dock labourer, is interesting if only because of its typicality.

Mrs Ferry, who lived in one of the key submerged areas, Bethnal Green, was heavily pregnant. Because she had no money, she had to beg for admission to a maternity hospital, or, as it was known then, a lying-in hospital. She obtained an order for admission to the hospital in the City Road, but fell down ill in the street, and a cab was called. The cabman, not used to carrying passengers of his own class, was not disposed to be charitable, and demanded five shillings for his services. (In view of her social status, Mrs Ferry should have travelled in one of the straw-lined swaying omnibuses where the fare would have been a penny or twopence.) As she had no money, a collection was made on the spot, and the cabman raised seven shillings. The woman fell down again, and the child was born. Her sister went to a Mr Massingham, the parish doctor, not a physician, after first having to apply to the parish relieving officer. It was now six-thirty o'clock in the evening, and the doctor said that he would call in the morning, despite the sister's distress at the state of Mrs Ferry, and left her a bottle of medicine. At 10.30 a.m. there was still no sign of the parish doctor, and the sister called again on him, to find him reading the newspaper. He told her that he could not visit her until the following day, but he still did not come, and Mrs Ferry's daughter, age fifteen, called on him and told him, 'Mother is dying.' 'Fiddle de dee!' the doctor is reported to have retorted. 'Nonsense. If your mother was put to bed yesterday, it can't be said that she will die today.' The girl cried. 'It's no use your crying. It's no use you kicking up that noise here; it won't bring her back again.' At noon, Mrs Ferry died. The only strange thing about this sordid case of 1871 is that it came before the courts at all. The jury said that the doctor was inhuman, but that was the extent of his punishment, though no doubt Hippocrates was revolving in his grave.

The atrocious conditions under which the poor lived played their part in producing a level of brutality that is still evident in those parts of industrial Britain that are still basically slums, such as the Aston district of Birmingham and the Gorbals district of Glasgow. Today there are only occasional vestiges of the overcrowding noted in Wyld Court, Drury Lane, at the opening of Victoria's reign:

Witness found two beds in the room, the first containing the defendant and his three daughters aged seventeen, sixteen, fifteen, and a boy aged six. The second bed contained a man and his wife, who were paying eightpence per week for the lodging.

The first bed contained the defendant, his wife, a boy of sixteen, and a girl of fourteen, with another boy of ten, and an infant. In the second bed there were a woman, a girl, and a child; in the third bed a man, his wife, a girl of sixteen, and two boys (twelve and seven); with a fourth bed, a woman and two boys; and in the fifth a man. There were no partitions of any kind to separate the sexes. The total number of persons in the room was twenty, but seven only were allowed.[12]

Under these conditions, wrote Edwin Chadwick in his *Report on the Sanitary Condition of the Labouring Population* of the same epoch (1842), 'adult life, exposed to such miasmata, gives way'. Only when one considers these factors, the overcrowding, the filth, the brutality, the poor's rejection by the bulk of their betters, does one realize the full implications of the subjugation of working-class woman. Many made desperate efforts to struggle from their impasse. In 1889, when the worst conditions in London had probably been ameliorated, Elizabeth Smith, aged thirty-six of Holloway, London, tried to drown herself in the New River. Constable 537N stopped her. 'Oh, do let me drown myself. My husband has been knocking me about.' The husband complained that he did not know why his wife should want to commit suicide. 'Yes, you do,' replied his wife. 'You told me to do it. A month ago you broke one of my fingers, and five years ago you broke one of my ribs.' Again, she was not exceptional. There were thousands of Mrs Smiths who were perambulating punching-bags, whose role was a perpetual subjection, who knew this, and only wanted to get through life with as few bruises as possible. Even in these nasty squalid depths, nineteenth-century society was oriented to make dominance.

There are two types of submissiveness, physical and spiritual. It was not to be expected that the established Church would upset the apple cart. 'A woman's position is one of subjection,' wrote the Reverend F. W. Robertson in 1849, 'mythically described as a curse in the Book of Genesis. Well, but I ween that all curses are blessings in disguise. Labour among thorns and thistles – man's best health.' [13] Robertson, whose earnestness and mournful mien did much to nullify the bracing air of Brighton where he officiated, and who is a key figure in mid Victorian theology for no very clear reason, believed that this subjection was a good thing, that woman's menial drudgery did 'a great deal to strengthen with the sense of duty done, self-control and power'. The Church used the submissive instincts of woman with a skill that frequently approached the Machiavellian, and this was especially evident in the High Church convents set up by Pusey. The Protestant nun is something of an anomaly, and the ritualistic sisterhoods framed on the models of the Roman Catholic Church tended to attract the betwixt and between, women who did not want to become brides of Christ sufficiently to go the whole hog and join the Roman Catholic Church, women who wished to submit to the discipline of a closed society but did not want to outrage convention by turning against their family faith. It must be emphasized that early and mid Victorian England was rabidly anti-Catholic.

Because the ritualistic movement was treated with so much suspicion, any dirt associated with it was assiduously collected. For many of the more neurotic supporters of the Middle and Low Church, the ritualistic convents were the last straw, and practices carried out therein were widely publicized, particularly in a rather mad book *The Secret History of the Oxford Movement* by Walter Walsh, published in 1897, which, nevertheless, had gone into four editions totaling 22,000 by 1898, a theological success that more restrained churchmen may have envied. Despite its scurrilous tone, this book is well documented, though the sources from which Walsh drew are often bizarre and betray curious obsessions.

Vows of obedience and chastity were no doubt rigorously carried out, but there are surrealist features of the 'Anglican

Sisters of Mercy' that take the actions out of a strictly religious context. In *A Letter to the Archbishop of Dublin*, 1853, the Reverend W. G. Cookesley wrote:

> One of the Sisters was one day employed in the menial office of lacing Miss Sellon's boots. Whilst she was thus employed with one of the Lady Superior's feet, that dignitary thought fit to bestow her other foot *on the head* of the stooping Sister. Some little disposition to objection and resistance to this disgusting insult being manifested, was immediately checked by the Lady Superior, who remarked that such humiliation *was good* for the Sister.

In 1848 Miss Sellon, the Lady Superior of this odd anecdote, formed her sisterhood in the notorious naval port of Devonport, celebrated for its extraordinarily high rate of venereal disease and its profusion of prostitutes. She was supported by the Bishop of Exeter, though he later withdrew this support. Miss Sellon, and the other Ladies Superior of similar establishments (there were three other principal sisterhoods, at Park Village near Regent's Park, at Wantage, and at Clewer) had civil but hardly religious authority, and the confessions were heard by outsiders, Church of England clergymen. The Reverend Cookesley recorded that on one occasion: 'A Sister who had been hasty with her tongue, and had thrown out some unguarded expression, was commanded by the Rev. Mr Prynne, one of the Confessors to the Institution, *to lie down flat on the floor, and with her tongue to describe the figure of a Cross in the dirt*.' This kind of behaviour is mentioned at length in Victorian pornography though without the ecclesiastical connotations.

These establishments had a high percentage of defectors, one of whom was a Miss Goodman. 'Those who enter Sisterhoods abandon family ties; they acquire peculiar habits; are ignorant of the state of things without their Nunnery gates.' So Miss Goodman told the world. She also said that many of the women were bilked of their money, and this was confirmed by Reverend Cookesley: 'A lady who joined Dr Pusey's establishment, as a Sister, carried into the common stock a capital producing, I believe, so large a sum as £1,200 *per annum*; when she subsequently left the Society, which she did to join the Church of Rome, she did not possess a penny!' A man, whose name was suppressed presumably in the interests of propriety, wrote in 1865 to Tait when he was Bishop of London:

A very near and dear relative of ours, a young lady, unmarried, extremely attractive in every way, and possessed of considerable property in her own right, is very strongly minded to enter the St George's Mission in London, situate within your Lordship's diocese, as a Postulant, with a pre-determination, if the life is what she hopes to find it, to accept the Perpetual Vows which are there administered to ladies disposed to undertake them.[14]

Tait wavered, as he was inclined to do on all questions, taking refuge in a legal quibble – whether or not the imposition of a binding vow or oath was tenable in law. However, Pusey, and the Sisterhoods under his aegis, were, superficially, respectable. This was more than could be said of another closed religious community, the Agapemonites.

Towards the end of 1858, Bishop Tait wrote to Mrs Lancaster, who was concerned with the All Saints Sisterhood: 'Of course there is always danger lest persons (especially females) of strong imagination may persuade themselves that there is some peculiar sanctity in the life these ladies lead, not to be found in the quiet discharge of domestic duties.'[15] The peculiar sanctity of the Agapemonites was always in doubt.

Henry James Prince was born in 1811. He was articled to a doctor but decided his future was in the Church of England, and after due indoctrination he became curate of the tiny parish of Charlinch in Somerset. He gave promise of being a staunch high churchman, though his wandering eye led to scandal, and the Bishop of Bath and Wells forbade Prince to continue preaching. In 1843 he wrote to his brother and explained that the Holy Ghost had settled in his personality, but this did not preclude the Bishops of Salisbury and of Ely from preventing him from taking up a curacy at Stoke-by-Clare, Suffolk. As he had been 'prevented from preaching *within* the pale of the Established Church', Prince proclaimed, he would preach without it. He carried on the *al fresco* traditions of Wesley and his Methodists, preaching in open spaces and in barns, but there the similarity ended. Prince announced that he was the prophet Elijah, which was a thing Wesley would not have done.

Prince made a couple of astute marriages, one of them with the daughter of the vicar of Charlinch, his first curacy, made a good deal of money with religious pamphlets, such as *How You May Know Whether You Do or Do Not Believe in Jesus Christ*, and achieved popular success as a preacher in Brighton. He returned to Somerset with a vast sum of money to set up his new religion. The aim was a closed society cleverly combining the religious with the secular, headed by himself ('the Beloved'), and a clutch of subordinates with titles such as 'the Anointed Ones' and 'the Angel of the Last Trumpet'. Whether Prince was mad or not at this stage is doubtful. His assertion that he was immortal and that his followers would be so may have been astute public relations; certainly he personally had the benefit of another one of his tenets, that copulation between the sexes within this society would be completely innocent.

The Agapemone, or Abode of Love, had, for women, a double charm. It had the appeal of a closed religious sect, and it gave them an opportunity to submit both spiritually and physically to 'the Beloved'. The Abode of Love took two years to complete on the outskirts of Spaxton; it covered two hundred acres, was lavishly landscaped, and it had a chapel that contained sofas, armchairs, and a billiard table. It was on one of these sofas that Prince copulated with a Miss Paterson after prayers in full view of the congregation. He had the pick of the lady believers, and no doubt his followers had his leavings. When Miss Paterson became pregnant, Prince asserted that there would be no birth, and when there was, he satisfied his disciples by proclaiming that this was Satan's final despairing act against God. Those women who came to their senses, who realized that there was something suspect in Prince's *modus operandi*, left the Agapemone. Occasionally, the money they had sunk into their expedition into religious fantasy was more important than subsequent scandal, and one case came up in 1860. The lady disciples were described as 'silly captive women'. The popularity of the Abode of Love reached a peak in the

1850s when there were more than a thousand inhabitants. The court case of 1860 was a thorough exposure, and the Abode of Love began to fall into decline. Prince was also getting older, and his feats of sexual divinity were probably not so welcome as they once were.

There was a revival of interest in the nineties, and the Reverend J. H. Smyth-Pigott took over the role of H. J. Prince. His locale was the lower-middle-class London suburb of Clapton, but he too moved down to Spaxton, where he continued the Prince tradition. His adoring women bore children with names such as Glory and Life. But it was now Edwardian England, and people were less shockable. When in 1909 Smyth-Pigott was found guilty of 'immorality, uncleanness and wickedness of life', very few turned a hair.

A curious feature of the Prince way of life was its way of death. The followers were buried standing up. So was Prince. Despite his boast of immortality, he went to meet his maker at the ripe old age of eighty-eight. The Agapemone is a prime example of the credulity of Victorian woman, the urge to submit to a God figure run riot. For the twentieth century, the Agapemone has a certain kinky charm, and for many of the women it was a golden opportunity for sexual excess with a gilding of religious sanctity. Its most interesting feature was its massive scale; the Agapemone was no scruffy hole-in-the-corner ménage. The motivations of Prince's male followers are pretty easy to discern, but those of his women devotees are less easy to follow. If they were, in Patmore's phrase, 'virginal of thought', copulation with the man they thought a stand-in for God was only a *reductio ad absurdum* of the religious thinking of Patmore and his ilk ('the Highest has found His ultimate and crowning felicity in a marriage of the flesh as well as the Spirit').[16] It may have been, that for the more spiritual of the lady disciples of Prince, union with the Beloved may have been – again it is Patmore's phrase – a 'greatly pangful penance'.

The confusion between real life and religion, the capacity of woman for self-deception, the need to submit to a superior creature, these were capitalized on by Prince, whether he was insane or not, into a kind of sexual Arcadia. There were other odd Victorian sects where religion was bound up with sex. The Walworth Jumpers took the opposite path to Prince. These held meetings under a converted railway arch in Sutherland Street, Walworth Road, and were required to practise celibacy to prepare for the second coming of Christ, traditional marital ties being dissolved and replaced by the concept of brother and sister.[17] It was a subfusc cult; whereas immortality had been guaranteed by Prince on condition that selected women had intercourse with him in private or in public, immortality was promised to the Walworth Jumpers by their founder, a Mrs Girling, only if they remained celibate. Rule 8 of their contract stipulated 'That no undue intimacy, of whatever kind, must exist between brother and sister, and their daily life is to be such as become the Children of God'. Movements run by women had the accent on celibacy; those run by men were more accommodating.

The Predatory Woman

You must either be house-Wives or house-Moths; remember that. In the deep sense, you must either weave men's fortunes, and embroider them; or feed upon, and bring them to decay.

The writer is (who else?) Ruskin (*The Ethics of the Dust*, 1866), and it is one of his most ingenious similes. He does omit another variety – the house-Vulture, woman as predator; when the absence of a wedding ring was a constant shame, a symbolic deprivation, women of a certain robust psyche pursued men with a menacing gusto. 'I constantly hear that I have been "very attentive" to numerous spinsters and widows,' wrote Henry James to his mother in 1880, 'and also that many of my well-wishers think that I should be "so much happier" if I would only marry.'[18] Henry James was well aware of the dangers, and the note of complacency was not smug. He restricted his attentions to the elderly, such as Anne Benson Procter, a great lion hunter who had known everyone of consequence during her long life. She once made a list of her famous friends – two sheets of a closely worded double-column list. In 1879 Thomas Hardy called on her, saw a photograph of Henry James, and made a memo in his diary: 'She says he has made an offer of marriage. Can it be so?' James himself is ironical. 'I expect soon to hear that I am engaged to Mrs Procter *aetat* 82.' Whatever Mrs Procter (christened 'Our Lady of Bitterness' by the historian Kinglake) had in mind, James was too clever. His knowledge, as revealed in his novels, of the predatory woman was extensive.

It was more convenient for the predator woman to strike at men who were psychologically ill-equipped for the onslaught, at those who were uncertain of their sexual roles, those who veered on the edge of queerness, the shy, the timid, the defenceless, and those who had reached a certain age and were confident that they had escaped being barbecued on the spikes of matrimony, proud in a detumescence of the spirit.

William Johnson was a tutor at Eton. He was teaching there during Swinburne's time, though it is said that he did not recall the young poet. Johnson was eccentric, very shortsighted, and was committed to the education and welfare of the young, so much so that his motives – like those of Oscar Browning – were suspect (Browning was also at one time one of his pupils). Extremely clever, Johnson found the drudgery of drumming facts into solid high-born heads tiresome, 'but at Eton in the fifties razors would be used to cut blocks, and there was no way of rising except by seniority'.[19] He was very concerned with the use of the door mat, and no matter who entered his study and pupil room he would yell at them, 'Shoes, Shoes.' When the fifes and drums of the soldiers were heard he would exclaim, 'Brats, the British Army!' and join in the stampede to see them go by. When one of his pupils got a prize, he sacrificed a new hat, and he and the boys kicked it to pieces outside the pupil room. On one occasion he hurled the massive door key at what he imagined was a latecomer, and hit the gout-transfixed tutor Russell Day a sturdy blow on the shoulder. Day complained, thinking that a boy had done it (such was Eton in the fifties), and Johnson promised to look into it. He would spring on his boys unexpected questions, and if they answered correctly he would reward them 'with a new fives ball or a bundle of cedar-wood matches'. At the Eton–Harrow cricket match, Johnson was a conspicuous figure in a huge blue tie, surrounded by empty pint pots. He was in the grand tradition of Eton eccentrics, endearing, and regarded highly by the boys.

He was also a poet, and his verses were treated, especially by ex-pupils, as though they were of great consequence. There are indications that his relationships with his pupils were frequently incautious, as this extract from 'A Separation' hints:

> Though he lies sick and far away
> I play with those that still are here,
> Not honouring him the less for they
> To me by loving him are dear:
> They share, they soothe my fond regret,
> Since neither they nor I forget.
>
> Without him I was weak and coarse
> My soul went droning through the hours,
> His goodness showed a latent force
> That drew from others kindred powers,
> Nor they nor I could think me base,
> When with their prince I had found grace.[20]

He was a master from 1845 to 1872, and left in ambiguous circumstances, which may have been due to politics. Jockeying for position was a favourite pastime of Eton masters, almost as interesting as flogging the boys – on this subject, Johnson took the establishment line ('The squires,' he said, 'wished, no doubt, to have their beefy brats coerced sharply').[21]

It might be supposed that Johnson would repeat the Oscar Browning pattern – retreat to a far-famed place of learning and cultivate the celebrities, to become a male equivalent of the lion-hunting Mrs Procter. But a rather odd thing happened. Johnson changed his name to Cory, for no very clear reason, and with it his way of life. He became acquainted with a young girl, Rosa Guille, who wrote to him, 'I love you very much,' without any advances having been made by Johnson. Johnson, or Cory as he now was, was evidently flattered by the attentions of a girl young enough to be a granddaughter (he was fifty-six, she was twenty), and declared that she was 'a loveable pickle'. Miss Guille amplified her statement. 'I always wanted to marry an *old* clever man, good, tender and true. You are the man.' Against this incredible frontal assault, William Johnson Cory had almost no defence. 'She is as brave as an eaglet and says she will let her feelings be tested till her birthday January 31st, and no longer.' His attitude had turned turtle since his Eton days; when he was forty-five he had said, 'If I had married as other people do, by this time my wife would be pursy, short of breath, addicted to sal volatile, unable to sing, begrimed with frugality.' Now: 'I saw Her yesterday on the road. She looked absolutely a heroine, as I stood above the level of her little pony trap. It was the most admirable satisfactory thing to see her playing the princess before strangers, keeping a face bright and composed, keeping her secret with perfect self-possession.' This scandal of an aged ex-Eton master consorting with this flighty young piece was only partially relieved when the happy couple went to Madeira. Rosa was 'as wholesome as a milkmaid, as merry as an actress, as stylish as a maid of honour'.

After marriage, Cory still had his share of eccentricities. One of them was that he was unable to tolerate the prefix 'Mrs'. His wife must be addressed always as 'Madame', and even 'wife' was frowned upon. The match was materially productive, and a son was born, named Andrew because 'no Monarch or Pope had borne that name'. Cory unquestionably had problems. Mrs Cory was flirtatious and physically attractive. Richard Burton in the course of his travels visited Madeira, and, said Cory complacently, 'his eyes devour Madame'. The rapture of this late love was partly disturbed by Madame becoming neurasthenic. In her prime, Madame was reported as having a magnolia complexion, which sounds pretty ominous.

John Addington Symonds had been given a copy of Cory's poems, and had read between the lines, much as he read between the lines of Edmund Gosse's *With Viol and Flute*. Gosse's early book of verse dates from 1873, and is of a high quality; there is a good deal of erotic imagery, but it would need the slanted imagination of a Symonds to discern much that was overtly homosexual in it. There are passing references to boys' 'white limbs' and one might make what one will of this passage from 'Initum Amoris':

> With sun-kissed face, and body flaming red,
> Down through his luscious Eden Adam went.

Symonds wrote to Cory under the alias 'O. D. X.' but although Cory was sympathetic, it needed more than the advice of an eccentric Eton master to bring Symonds on to an even keel. 'My ship has sailed into a magic sea with tempests of its own,' he wrote in his diary [22] of 29 September 1861. Symonds was involved with a Bristol choir boy, Alfred Brooke, who came to his bedroom. After Brooke had gone, Symonds kissed the spot on the bed where Brooke had sat and sobbed and cursed throughout the night.

Symonds was a fellow of Magdalen College, Oxford. He had an enemy, G. H. Shorting, who had a clutch of Symonds's verses and letters edited so that it seemed as though Symonds's main aim in life was the pursuit of choir boys. In September 1862 a general meeting of the College of Magdalen was convened to consider the dubious material they had received from Shorting, and although Symonds was exonerated it was a near thing, and two letters were strongly censured. Symonds confessed their 'execrable taste'.

After a significant dream in which a weak old man was being beaten to death with clubs, Symonds had a breakdown and went to Switzerland to recover. In Switzerland he met Rosa Engel, fifteen years old, dressed in the local national dress and loaded down with silver chains. Symonds gave her flowers, and kissed her (first time he had kissed a woman), but Miss Engel was suspicious of the attentions of the English milord, and Symonds returned to England *virgo intacta*. His reproductive equipment swelled, and the fashionable doctor Dr Spencer Wells recommended marriage.

The choice settled on Catherine North. It is difficult to decide who was pursuing whom. In the meantime, Symonds had had one or two traumatic sexual experiences, a curious and unresolved encounter with Josephine Butler, and a meeting with the wife of a Norwich clergyman. The wife fancied him, and

Symonds wrote disturbedly of 'voluptuous incitements'. Catherine North was dark, Roman-nosed, with black hair drawn back from the forehead; Symonds had inner conflicts. He wrote to his homosexual friend Dakyns: 'I think only of oné person, and when she is away my mind seems empty. Yet I am not passionately in love.' He asked Miss North, 'Could you manage to be content with me all through life?' They exchanged rings, held hands, married, but the honeymoon in Brighton was a failure, and the marriage was not consummated for several nights. Throughout this match, clamorously ill-starred, Catherine had to adjust herself to the presence, either spiritually or physically, of men and boys whom Symonds fancied, whether it was the Tennyson boys – Lionel, aged ten, and Hallam, aged twelve ('They filled me with a love sadly deep even at first sight'), or the young organist Willie Dyer, or Norman Moor, a young homosexual or pseudo-homosexual on the make ('Norman lives an odd fungoid life on some decaying branch of my soul').

Many of Symonds's homosexual acquaintances came to terms with their tendencies by marrying. Dakyns married the widow of a master at Clifton College near Bristol in 1872; Moor became a master at the same college, married in 1878. Although homosexuals desperately trying to become normal were a relatively easy mark for the more pursuing brand of woman, the theory that marriage would automatically convert them did not rest on a basis of fact.

One of the qualifications for being an efficient predator was a certain physical presence. When this was lacking, then the pursuit became pathetic. As a sonneteer, possibly Samuel Butler was one of the world's worst, but his sonnet on Miss Savage is an effective expression of his guilt at being unable to respond to a woman who hunted him with hand-knitted pot holders.

> She was too kind, wooed too persistently,
> Wrote moving letters to me day by day;
> The more she wrote, the more unmoved was I,
> The more she gave, the less could I repay.
> Therefore I grieve not that I was not loved
> But that, being loved, I could not love again.

I liked; but like and love are far removed;
And though I tried to love I tried in vain.
For she was plain and lame and fat and short,
Forty and over-kind. Hence it befell
That, though I loved her in a certain sort,
Yet did I love too wisely but not well.
Ah! had she been more beauteous or less kind
She might have found me of another mind.

It might be mentioned as a literary tidbit that Butler, notwithstanding the appalling incompetence of this sonnet, considered himself an expert on the sonnet, especially that written by Shakespeare, and his edition of the Shakespeare sonnets, and his 're-arranging' of them, is a salutary illustration of what happens when a minor man of letters gets above himself. Today's writers please note.

Many of the predators had spiderish tendencies. Lady Amberley, daughter-in-law of Lord John Russell, permitted the resident tutor to have sexual intercourse with her as he had tuberculosis and was not likely to marry, and the Countess of Radnor disarmingly, in her *Memoirs*, demonstrated her wiles: 'There was a long frost that winter which was rather distressing to me, as two of our visitors, having nothing better to do I suppose, fell in love with me and were both in the house at the same time. In fact, one of them proposed to me while the other was in the room ... which was very trying, and both the poor dears left the next day.' It took the aristocracy to be really subtle.

Many women chose to start their machinations early. Maria was the youngest daughter of George Beadnell, a London bank manager; pretty, and a performer on that most fetching of Victorian musical instruments, the harp, she captivated the young Charles Dickens, then a mere reporter, so much so that Dickens was driven to try sensuously to improve his station in life. For two years Maria used Dickens as a dancing doll, and when her parents sent her to a finishing school in Paris, he was inconsolable. She 'pervaded every corner and crevice' of his mind, and the experience coloured his subsequent life. His knowledge of the external world was already considerable, but he did not realize that Maria was a tigress trying out her claws. When he found that she was trifling with him, he turned on her, telling her 'whatever of fancy, romance, passion, aspiration, and determination belong to me I never have separated and never shall separate from that hard-hearted little woman – you'.[23] She received her immortality as Dora in *David Copperfield*, while her pet Daphne received the doggy accolade of being transmuted into Dora's petulant little brute, Jip. When they met in later life, Dickens found the enchanting Maria transformed into just another middle-aged woman, out to lionize him as he was rich and famous, and she became the Flora Finching of *Little Dorrit*. Dickens had the ability to use these encounters in his work; others were less fortunate. 'I believe I once had affections as warm as most people; but partly from evil chance, and partly from foolish misplacing of them, they have got tumbled down and broken to pieces.' So wrote Ruskin to Rossetti in 1855. He would have had small change out of Rossetti, whose attitude towards women was sardonic and pragmatic.

It was possible to start scheming at an even earlier age than was young Miss Beadnell. E. W. Benson was a somewhat priggish young man, later to be Archbishop of Canterbury and the father of an extraordinarily talented family of writers. He wrote in his 1852 diary:

I, who from the circumstances of my family am not likely to marry for many years to come, and who find in myself a growing distaste for forming friendships (fit to be so called) among new acquaintances and who am fond indeed (if not too fond) of little endearments, and who also know my weakness for falling suddenly in love, in the common sense of the word, and have already gone too far more than once in these things and have therefore reason to fear that I might on some sudden occasion be led [the diary here goes into a private code] it is not strange that I should have thought first of the possibility that some day dear little Minnie might become my wife.[24]

'Dear little Minnie' is perhaps the clue. Minnie was eleven, Benson was twenty-three. Is this the case of another Lewis Carroll, another man like the Reverend Kilvert, transfixed by the spectacle of Little Girl?

Benson followed this up with dialogue:

Minnie: Edward, how long will it be before I am as tall as if I was standing on that stool?

Edward: I don't know very well, Minnie, five years perhaps . . .

Minnie: When I am twenty I shall be taller than that?

Edward: Yes.

Minnie: When I am twenty, how old shall you be?

Edward: Thirty-two.

Minnie: Thirty-two! Edward, I shan't look so little compared to you, shall I, when I'm twenty, and you're thirty-two, as I do now that I'm eleven and you're twenty-three?

Edward: No, no, you won't, Minnie.

This unexpected close made me blush indeed, and the palms of my hands grew very hot.

Later Benson records, 'Whatever she grows up to be, she is a fine and beautiful bud now.'

Next year, Benson persuaded Minnie's mother, Mrs Sidgwick, to allow him to broach the subject to the child, which seems to be incredibly foolish:

Let me try to recall each circumstance: the arm-chair in which I sat, how she sat as usual on my knee, a little fair girl of twelve with her earnest look, and how I said that I wanted to speak to her of something serious, and then got quietly to the thing, and asked her if she thought it would ever come to pass that we should be married. Instantly, without a word, a rush of tears fell down her cheeks, and I really for the moment was afraid . . .

Although this situation confirms for us the notion that there were differences between the Victorian mentality and ours, fortunately this somewhat creepy rapport between a mature man and a young girl had a fairy tale ending. Benson did wait, and did marry his Minnie, and his son Edward recounts a vignette, 'Grandmamma and her bandoline, the table laid for a dinner party, my mother playing croquet and with poised mallet sending her opponent's ball on to the gravel path, my father's figure in rustling silk gown, the gardener killing an adder with a pair of shears . . .' [25] It is perhaps unfair to include young Minnie Benson *née* Sidgwick in a list of predators, but she is a convenient illustration of the facility with which girls of the tenderest of ages had their eyes on the main chance, their aware-

ness that, in Symonds's phrase, they were for the 'broad onward purposes of life'. One of the occupations of E. W. Benson
and his young friend was the reading aloud of Tennyson's 'The
Princess'. After the 'understanding', the girl flicked through the
pages, saying that there were passages in the poem that she had
not understood until then. There was one particular part she
could say 'almost by heart: she repeated the words "love, children, happiness". "Two of those are mine now," she said.'
This, mark, from a child of twelve.

In any case, the Sidgwick brood were decidedly out of the
usual run. Minnie's brother, Henry, had to tread a constant
moral tightrope; a professional expounder of ethics, he, like
many of his contemporaries, was affected by boyish beauty. His
favourite had 'a face and form of unimaginable beauty, haunted
by thoughts and passions which as yet are undeveloped', but he
was also a man, as George Eliot said of him, 'whose friends
tacitly expected him to conform to moral standards higher than
they themselves cared to maintain', and who, with a great
flourish of metaphysical trumpets, refused to sign the celebrated
Thirty-Nine Articles of the Church of England 26 (when Benjamin Jowett, suspected of heretical tendencies for 'advanced'
contributions to *Essays and Reviews*, was asked to sign this
magical formula, he professed his willingness to sign forty if it
was so desired. On the spur of the moment, no one could
think of a fortieth. So Jowett signed the thirty-nine).

There was a constant vogue for the vampirish type of woman.
Illustrated by Rossetti, copper-haired, slant-eyed, heavy-lipped,
she became for the aesthetes a kind of Mona Lisa. She made an
appearance in poetry, either as a heavy:

> Lady Clara Vere de Vere,
>   There stands a spectre in your hall:
> The guilt of blood is at your door:
>   You changed a wholesome heart to gall.[27]

or as a lightweight in the laborious whimsy of Austin Dobson:

> There was Lucy who 'tiffed' with her first,
>   And who threw me as soon as her third came,
> There was Norah, whose cut was the worst,
>   For she told me to wait till my 'berd' came;

They did not, like the ladies of Elizabeth Browning's *Aurora Leigh* yearn to lose themselves 'and melt like white pearls in another's wine' (what a superb image!). Their aim was the destruction of mate and lover, and their heroine was Salome, whose presence pervades the decadence, in the literary form of Wilde, in the pictorial form of that incredible guide to the passing *erdgeist*, Moreau. Perhaps this is too picturesque; perhaps the destructive tendencies of predatory woman show best in small instances, where she is working within the bounds of a marriage that is passably extant. A very interesting example of this occurred in the marriage of Thomas Hardy. In 1874 he married Emma Gifford. She was thirty-three, past the age when a proposal was a viable proposition, but that she later had regrets is everywhere evident. Harking back to her childhood, she declared, 'My home was a most intellectual one and not only so but one of exquisite home-training and refinement – alas the difference the loss of these amenities and gentlenesses has made to me!'

The simplest way to get at most men, if one is so inclined, is to slip a knife between the ribs. For the wives of literary men who had the urge to destroy there was a better way – get at them through their work. In 1895 Hardy issued *Jude the Obscure*, and this novel shocked the more genteel critics, while from the clergy it produced a predictable conditioned reflex – the Bishop of Wakefield threw it in the fire. Into this battle Mrs Hardy entered on the side of righteousness, throwing aside the pages in disgust, telling her doctor that she would never have anything more to do with any book written by her husband, and, more serious, writing to Richard Garnett, a key man at the British Museum, asking him to use his influence on Hardy to try and get the 'vicious' manuscript suppressed. When Garnett was not interested, Mrs Hardy went to see him, desperate and weeping; the Garnetts were not a particularly close-lipped family, and the story soon went round the learned purlieus of the British Museum, and from thence to the world that lay beyond the imposing portico. 'She leads him a Hell of a life,' said Mrs Brinsley Sheridan, and thought her 'half-cracked'. She disapproved of the social life Hardy led – the women in London society were 'poison' to him, and she was equipped with a train of minor ailments to assist any misanthropic mood she might have. Often, Hardy did not know where his wife was, and she was asked always to 'mention the *town* when you give your address'.

Considering the circumstances, the actions of Mrs Hardy are a fair distance along the road of husband-baiting, the road that begins with petulance, continues with bitchiness, and presumably goes on to jealousy raising, and then mental torment. 'Woman,' said the paper *Bird O' Freedom*, 5 February 1890, 'is an unreasoning creature, who not only pokes the fire over the top bar of the grate, but ruins a half-guinea purse by carrying 7½ pence in bronze therein.' She could also fly off at odd tangents; if a husband proved to be a mouse or crassly insensitive, her hunting instincts could be aroused elsewhere. There was a curious case reported in November 1889, in which suburban sensibilities were used as an excuse for a little sexual feuding.

Mary Jenkins was the wife of a Woolwich hairdresser, and Frederick Anderson, a cheesemonger, kissed her. Even suburban cheesemongers need a certain incentive, but this was not disclosed when Mrs Jenkins summoned him. Somewhat disturbed, Anderson went to stay with his father, who was taken ill and died. Adamant, Mrs Jenkins pursued her charge. On the bench, the magistrate Mr Kennedy was inclined to look upon the whole thing as a peccadillo:

Mrs Jenkins: It was a gross insult, and he ought to be punished.
Mr Kennedy: Yes, but you need not nurse your indignation too long.
Mrs Jenkins: I am a married woman, sir.
Mr Kennedy: Very well; if you cannot excuse him, I cannot. There will be a fine of ten shillings.
Prisoner Anderson: I went to her house twice and apologized to her husband.
Mrs Jenkins: You did not apologize to me.
Mr Kennedy: I think you are too exacting. If he has apologized to your husband that makes a difference. I shall make the fine two and six.

Good for Mr Kennedy, one thinks. Unfortunately his dispassionate attitude was not too common in the legal profession, and insult offered to a respectable woman was considered to need a prison sentence as just expiation, a startling contrast to the way poor women were treated, a good example of which occurred in August 1876, when a zealous do-gooder, R. J. Bodker (who signed his name with an X), thought that Emily Clayton, aged twenty-eight, was a prostitute trying to escape her wicked ways by jumping off Westminster Bridge, chased her when she seemed alarmed, and tried to persuade her to enter a home for unfortunates. Miss Clayton was a dressmaker, and was looking at the ships. Nothing very much happened to Bodker, and it was considered that he had made an understandable mistake, and that he might have better luck next time.

The single woman was frequently predatory because she wanted a husband, she married because she was bored; there was a thin line between the lion hunters, the society hostesses, and those who just wanted fun. One of the latter was the wife of a prosperous distiller in Avenue Road, St John's Wood, a road that was full of gay ladies and superior kept women. This one was 'a lady ... not much turned of thirty, of rich physique, with luminous dark eyes'[28] who liked very much writers and artists. She had scooped up Rossetti for her collection, though Rossetti was usually well provided for in the matter of those who were described in his circle as 'stunners'. She should have been content with addle-brained scholars, who were never so much flattered as when they were ravished by comely women. It was usually a mental ravishment, and one turns to Robinson Ellis, a scholar hypochondriacally preoccupied with his feet, who spent his holidays at dowdy lower-middle-class seaside resorts, and who at a mature age wondered what he ought to do about women. He asked the teenage Grant Richards, later to be a publisher, whether he ought to marry; Richards was delighted that the question should be put to him, when most donnish types looked at him as hardly other than a doughnut-eating urchin, but he was not able to proffer advice. Other acquaintances of Ellis, such as R. W. Raper (the name has no ulterior significance), prodded Ellis with disturbing thoughts. Raper deliberately contrived anecdotes to get Ellis going: 'Yes, there the girl was in her chemise ... and a chemise, I need hardly tell you, Ellis, is the garment which a woman wears next to her skin.' Recording this, Richards in his fascinating *Memories of a Misspent Youth* of 1932 related that 'Robinson Ellis would giggle and disclaim any knowledge of the kind, and would seek an excuse to go off to his own rooms.' Ellis was too dotty and elusive to be pinned down, but one turns to the case of Buckle.

Henry Thomas Buckle, born 1821, was one of the greatest polymaths of the age. Before he was thirty he knew eighteen foreign languages (Richard Burton beat him with twenty-nine languages and six dialects) and had a library of 22,000 volumes to help him write his *History of Civilisation in England*, two volumes of which were completed before his death in 1862 of typhoid fever. Regarded as their peer by the top minds of the day, Buckle appeared to be living a most abstemious and respectable life, loving to his mother, celibate, married only to his books. Upon his death, there was the customary tidying up. Dying as he had done, as it were, off the cuff, Buckle had not been able to sort out a suitable image for posterity, and it was found, by a shocked and adoring female assistant, that Buckle was not quite as he appeared, that when he was journeying in Egypt he had written to a certain Mrs Faunch in terms that led one to suspect his secret life: 'Such favourable offers have been made to me, that it is very likely that I may settle here or in Egypt for a few years. Would you, dear, come out to me if I were to stay here? In such case I should of course make myself responsible for the rent of your house and for every other expense you incurred, either directly or indirectly.'

This Henry Buckle was not the one the world knew. Perhaps it was one of Buckle's landladies (he had a certain inability to look after himself, as one would expect)? Apparently not. No such agreeable construction could be put on the letter. Mrs Faunch, born 1826, was the daughter of a blacksmith, at twenty married a blacksmith, and, had Mr Faunch lived, might have pursued this role till the fullness of time. In 1857, her husband died; three years afterwards she moved to fashionable Wyndham Street, and by 1865 she was at 1 Lodge Place, Regent's Park, even higher up the accommodation scale. How did she get the money? Briefly, Mrs Faunch was a kept woman, one of the high-priced courtesans who favoured the Regent's Park area. It was easier to assume that she had trapped Buckle into a liaison than that he had gone out and got her of his own accord; to be entrapped was the destiny of scholars. Otherwise, what would happen to the image?

The Girl of the Period

The revolt against the tyranny of fashion was part of the pattern of sexual emancipation. This was seen by *Punch* in 1851, with its curious unconscious penchant for putting its finger on basic facts under the guise of heavy facetiousness. In a comic letter purporting to come from 'Bloomer' and apropos of this garment – a kind of pantaloon cum calf-length skirt sponsored by the American Amelia Bloomer *née* Jenks – the 'writer' states: 'Petticoats have been the *Badge of our Slavery to Man*. But the dawn approaches – the hour is *about to strike* – when with one accord we may snap *the Strings of our Yoke*, and stand erect *in the face of our Persecutor*!'

It goes on about the young girl who summons up courage to wear this new-fangled, and to *Punch* disgraceful, outfit:

See her in plumage *for her first flight*! She trips in her *boudoir* in dread and fear. She looks from the window – *her* nest – into the street! With *a beating heart* she trips down stairs – the street door *stands open*! There – there on the other side of the threshold – is a *cold*, a *tyrannous*, a *hungry*, and *insulting* world! This *she knows*; and, if she has the *true soul* of a woman – of a woman fit for *the future destiny* of her sex – she *throws down the guage,* [*sic*] for she crosses the *door-step*!

The readers of *Punch* naturally enjoyed this keen-edged satire. It confirmed in a more literate form their own fumbling perceptions that woman was getting above herself, and it was a tone that was to become a monotonous response whenever woman decided to strive against the dictates of fashion.

The Bloomer Movement was no more ridiculous than any

other of the fashions that were to follow it, but drawing attention to the legs, even when efficiently hidden, and coming from America instead of Paris it was doomed from the outset. The easiest way to finish it was to make it absurd. In a cartoon *Punch* uses two of its most valued props – a pair of unutterably frumpish old maids:

NO 1 (who is looking at the Print of the Bloomer Costume): Well, now, upon my word, I don't see anything ridiculous in it. I shall certainly adopt it.

NO 2: For my part, I so thoroughly despise conventionality, that I have ordered all my new things to be made in that very rational style!

Rational perhaps the Bloomer was not, but it had charm:

The walking-dress consists of a figured silk bodice, purple and white in colour, with muslin wristlets, and a skirt ending six inches below the knees; trousers of the same material as the bodice, just covering the tops of the gaiters, and gathered in with a pretty two inch ruffle; boots of black prunella, with elastic sides, and a straw hat or bonnet, with four-and-a-half inch brim, lined with coloured silk and set off with ribbon and tassels.

The Bloomer had built-in obsolescence, and so had the crinoline. The corset maintained its power. The sociological, even philosophical, implications of the corset were not lost. It kept woman in her place, in every imaginable sense. The corset was the battlefield for reformers and reactionaries alike, and dress reform itself became a cover for emancipationists of every colour. The young women who dared to flout the constrictions of the corset had poured on them a torrent of abuse that only makes sense if one sees the attempt to reform clothing in its context, as an attempt to upgrade woman from a chattel. One of the implications of the corset and of the incredible amount of stuff the well-dressed woman had piled upon her and built around her was that such a woman was certainly incapable of doing work. In 1853 Margaretta Grey wrote in her diary that 'ladies dismissed from the dairy, the confectionary, the store-room, the still-room, the poultry yard, the kitchen-garden, and the

orchard, have hardly yet found themselves a sphere equally useful and important . . .' If the men had anything to do with it,
this was all to the good; their women topped up to the nines
were the best of all status symbols. This was particularly true of
the new rich, especially partial to conspicuous display. Their
predecessors had built themselves Gothic follies to show off
their wealth and taste, or acquired *objets d'art* from the continent. The wife was a far better expression of success.

The rigid shape making of stay and whalebone was also
flattering to women who tended to go to seed rather earlier than
their great-great-great-great-grandchildren, and a little podginess
about the shoulders was all to the good and a flabbiness
around the belly could be corrected by any extra tug by husband
or lady's maid. The rejection by adventurous young women
of this way of life struck at the very roots of middle-class social
life.

The success of what became known as 'The Girl of the
Period' is remarkable when one considers the cards that were
stacked up against her. Her ace was the fact that a pretty girl
can get away with anything. She was also assisted in that ostensible opponents of her new 'fast' ways – fast was an adjective
born of this period – secretly sympathized with her, committed
as they might have been to the continued existence of the corset
régime, and that fashion changed so rapidly in small externals
that at times even the mode makers were confused. The mid
sixties was very productive of such confusion. It was in this
decade that hostile lady journalists woke up to find that there
was a viper in the bosom. 'The Girl of the Period is a creature
who dyes her hair and paints her face,' wrote Mrs Lynn Linton
in the *Saturday Review*, 1868. If she was fast, it was even worse,
as, alongside the impudence to be different, she 'had an inordinate love of gaiety, a bold determined manner, a total absence of respect towards her elders, and sometimes even towards
her parents; a flippant style of conversation and a glaring and
sometimes immodest dress'.

The *Saturday Review*, along with other upholders of the
social order such as the *Queen*, brooded on these manifestations.
In February 1868, it declared sombrely that 'Society has put

maternity out of fashion', and the social upheaval exemplified by the Girl of the Period had even viler implications. What was to become of woman if she carried on in this way? It was best to put it in a kindly way: 'The power of reasoning is so small in woman that they need adventitious help. ... They do not calculate consequences, and they are reckless when they once give way.' [29] Women were in danger of losing their primordial ignorance. 'No woman can or ought to know very much of the mass of meanness and wickedness and misery that is loose in the wide world. She could not learn it without losing the bloom and freshness which it is her mission in life to preserve.' [30]

The focus of disapproval, naturally, was the single girl, who 'must arrange the flowers, help with the house-keeping, pay the family calls, entertain the family visitors, always be at hand, well-dressed, cheerful, and smiling, like household angels, as they are often called, without any personal preferences or pursuits, ready to meet every call, and to contribute to everyone's pleasure but their own'.[31] So wrote the emancipationist Alys Pearsall-Smith in the nineties. What would happen to her once the newfangled ideas of the dress reformers really bit? Would the Girl of the Period turn into a slut, or something worse (as Mrs Linton feared)?

How far would the tolerance of young ladies' eccentricities in dress lead to their taking advantage of the establishment's kindness – in other words, would the rejection of the rigours of tight lacing and unhygienic swaddling lead to the rejection of the idea of woman as naturally inferior to man? In the periodicals in the years subsequent to the first tentative forays by aesthetic or 'new' woman there is a note of hysteria. In August 1875:

The poor girls try to dress in a way which they fondly believe to be artistic, and end in looking like rag dolls. They tie the refuse of Cairo round their waists and wisps of strange fabrics round their necks. Peacocks' feathers eye us from unaccountable situations, and frills of old lace so dirty as to be almost nasty garnish throats which would look much better in clean linen collars.[32]

This thoroughly unpleasant tone was echoed in a poem 'The Girl of the Period':

Her cheeks are painted Babylon red,
With a chignon tall she adorns her head,
Of her bosom the padding's the total sum,
And she wears a bustle instead of a bum.

This pink of fashion, if too soon you call,
You'll find half dressed and not washed at all,
With a bottle of gin (false pride she disregards)
Telling fortunes in the kitchen with a dirty pack of cards.[33]

The Girl of the Period has become a handy scapegoat, a term of reference that has ceased to have any meaning. She caused to be let loose a chorus of hate and envy. William Gaunt has called the 1860s the flashy and morbid decade;[34] it was certainly a make or break point for the future of the century. At the end of it was the first modern European war – the Franco–Prussian; in the middle of it were riots during which the mob invaded the West End and in Hyde Park held civilized society for ransom (quite literally – during a hard winter the Serpentine froze, and well-bred skaters were not permitted off it until they had paid a toll to groups of louts who controlled planks leading on to the lakeside). The *ancien régime* still held on grimly to its preset ideas, defending tight lacing, even in bed ('carries no hardship beyond an occasional fainting fit', reported the *Englishwoman's Domestic Magazine* encouragingly).

Unlike the Bloomer episode, the new spirit of adventure among women was not to be crushed, neither in dress nor in that proud euphemism, women's rights. In 1865 John Stuart Mill had been elected to Parliament on the emancipationist ticket, and tried to get 'man' replaced by 'person' in the Reform Act of 1867 in the unlikely event that woman would get the vote in the near future. Mill had some odd allies, such as: Frances Power Cobbe, Irish, fat, who looked something like Oscar Wilde, and who had passionate interests in antivivisection, friendless girls, and who edited a journal called the *Zoophilist*; the Egyptologist Amelia Edwards and Matilda Edwards, her cousin, prolific novelist of rural England; Annie Keary, author of an Irish novel *Castle Daly*; Harriet Martineau, the deaf eccentric economist with her famous ear trumpet beloved by Victorian reminiscers; the aged Mary Somerville, who at eighty-six had just finished *Molecular and Microscopic Science*; Anna Swanwick, the Hebrew and Greek scholar; Augusta Webster, the daughter of the Chief Constable of Cambridge; Susanna Winkworth, translator from the German; Martha Merrington, first woman Poor Law guardian – a roll call of female intelligentsia. Their train of achievement does much to quell the myth that Victorian woman had no opportunities for advancement. So formidable was one of these, Harriet Martineau, that F. W. Newman once jumped from his window to avoid meeting her.

In Manchester, a stronghold of the women's cause, 5,000 women applied to go on the Parliamentary Register, and thirteen managed it (the situation 'decidedly an odd one' reported *The Times*). These votes were collected by Lydia Becker, who had formed the Manchester Women's Suffrage Committee for just such a freak eventuality. However, the Queen was not amused: 'The Queen is most anxious to enlist everyone who can speak or write or join in checking this mad, wicked folly of "Woman's Rights" with all its attendant horrors, on which her poor feeble sex is bent, forgetting every sense of womanly feeling and propriety.'[35] She added that Lady Amberley, one of the great Russell dynasty, who had dared to read a paper at the Mechanic's Institute at Stroud, should be whipped.

Votes for women was a chimera diligently pursued by this devoted band. It was hardly aided by some of its hangers-on, such as Thomas Anstey 'a malcontent of the highest bore power'. What Mrs Linton – allied against the emancipationists as against the Girl of the Period – called 'The Shrieking Sisterhood' was affably patronized by the aristocracy. 'The real fact,' said Lord Percy, later seventh Duke of Northumberland, 'is that man in the beginning was ordained to rule over the woman, and this is an eternal decree which we have no right and no power to alter,' and so far as he was concerned that was the end of the matter. For such as he it was hardly worthwhile pursuing the idea that woman's suffrage was un-English and Popish (it had been put about that Roman Catholic priests were working for woman's suffrage so as to exert their sinister power). John Bright was concerned about women voters being plied with drink.

The emancipation fever meant that women who for one reason or another got out of line were awarded labels. For born outsiders, the women's rights movement was a natural umbrella. Annie Besant, at various times birth-control propagandist, theosophist, and libertine, was never greatly keen on votes for women, though it proved a handy peg: 'If the Bible and Religion stood in the way of women's rights then the Bible and Religion must go,' she declared.

Most of the women of England stood indifferently by, not caring, happy with the power they already wielded, cynical, or lulled by rhetoric and the pacifications of their chosen journals. 'When I speak of the women of England, I have in my mind those young, pure-minded girls, who are the light and life of their homes: who develop into the wives and mothers of England: who bring up England's children in the fear of God, and in the love of all that is pure and good,' wrote Edward Knatchbull-Hugessen,[36] one of the many otiose little men too well-bred to attack the girls of the period but aware that knocking emancipation was good for the political image.

The girls of the period, who would, surprisingly, be the conformist wives and mothers of the nineties and after, were often negligent of politics, and astonished that they should be associated with the Shrieking Sisterhood (Mrs Linton carried on her feuding into the nineties in the pages of the *Nineteenth Century*, but age had softened her – the Shrieking Sisterhood were now the Wild Women). They were frequently hurt by what they considered to be ill-bred social assassination. 'A pallid face with a protruding upper lip is highly esteemed. Green eyes, a squint, square eyebrows, whitey-brown complexions are not left out in the cold.'[37] So said the bitchy Mrs H. R. Haweis. Margot Tennant, later the wife of Asquith, went to a supper-party dressed thus:

I was wearing a white muslin dress with transparent chemise sleeves, a fichu and a long skirt with a Nattier blue taffeta sash. I had taken a bunch of rose carnations out of a glass and pinned them into my fichu with three diamond ducks. ... I saw several of the ladies eyeing my toilette and, having painfully sharp ears, I heard some of their remarks: 'Do look at Miss Tennant! She is in her night-gown!' [38]

Miss Tennant was not cast down by the scorn of her elders, having the *savoir faire* of an old established family, and therefore not needing to conform. For the genteel daughters of small tradesmen, fashion was an expensive ogre with which it was imperative to keep up. One young lady put it to the anonymous fashion writer of the *Graphic*:

We must give up struggling to dress in the fashion and become dowdies. My quarter's account at Madame B's exceeds my allowance by ten shillings and sixpence; and, as every lady is in duty bound to wear presentable gloves, boots, *lingerie*, and many other minor but necessary details of the toilette, where is the petty cash to come from to supply these necessities for my sisters and self?

Don't worry, said the fashion writer, but remember three rules (a) 'never to buy inferior materials'; (b) 'never to select eccentric colours, however attractive and fashionable'; (c) 'strictly to avoid ... everything which is what the French designate as *chiffoné*, presumably meaning the gauzy and transparent. As one salacious observer put it:

> The ladies they were highly dressed – naked, almost stark,
> Their muslin being thin enough to see the watermark.

This was a phenomenon noted by several, not always disapprovingly.

The Nude

The Victorians were transfixed by feminine beauty. In a sea of changing values, this was something that was permanent; there was a reverence for the naked female body that was reflected in the large number of nudes that were exhibited each year at the Royal Academy, in the engravings of old master nudes that formed the frontispieces of the pornographic magazines, in the comments of the hoary and the respectable when confronted by the naked body (provided that the context was respectable). For many repressed artists, the demand for nude paintings meant that their sexual needs were sublimated in an acceptable and life-enhancing manner. Etty, for example, a great and underestimated painter who died in 1849, was a devout celibate who spent his life painting naked women, in doing so piling up a debt to his brother of £4,000, and who first reached an income of £500 per annum in 1832 when he was forty-five. Gibson, the son of a Welsh market gardener, was a talented and eccentric bachelor, who always carried three packages around with him (the Greeks liked the quantity three), who culled classical knowledge from his brother Benjamin, 'a walking classical dictionary', and whose sexy 'Painted Venus' of 1850 ('rather a grisette than a goddess' said Elizabeth Barrett Browning) created a furore. The sexually potent artists, such as Rossetti, did not create paintings so alluring. In every way, it was a satisfactory equation. The cult of the female form divine in mythological settings formed a sharp contrast to the strict formal sexual ethos proclaimed by the establishment. It was a cult bound up with perfection, with the elimination of the particular, the ruthless excision of grubby inessentials.

Although Etty was a painter of womanly flesh that had the texture of the great Venetians or of Velazquez, he took care not to overstep the limits of propriety. In particular, he conformed to the unwritten code that specified no pubic hair, though his nudes disported themselves in what might be termed suggestive attitudes, provided that the story framework was suitably removed from the epoch in which he and his audience lived. The delineation of pubic hair was the prerogative of the artists who specialized in pornography or studies direct from the model and not for further promulgation, though occasionally there is a certain ambiguity when mythical creatures half-woman half-animal were recruited for the pictorial enactment of a classical scenario.

The power of art in Victorian Britain can hardly be overestimated, and Oscar Wilde's paradox that nature follows art rather than the other way about would seem to be confirmed. In particular, towards the end of the century a type of beauty appeared that owed its genesis to Dante Gabriel Rossetti, a painter of inadequate skills but impelling directness.

Just as the twentieth-century adman creates a type of beauty to appear in magazines or in television ads, so did the painters of the nineteenth century force their images of the perfect woman onto the consciousness of the observer, and these painters were so proficient in their craft that they have continued to force their images of the perfect woman of their period onto the consciousnesses of twentieth-century spectators.

After Etty, there is little in English nineteenth-century painting of the nude that has the casual robust sensuality of Renoir's buxom women, a casual sensuality that has the effect of rendering one Renoir painting very much like another. (Renoir, it might be added, was born in 1841, and is therefore a contemporary of the great English academic painters of the century, Lord Leighton and Lawrence Alma-Tadema.) The inhibitions under which the English artists operated turned in a curious way to their advantage, and straightforward historical and mythological scenes were given a piquancy that strangely forms them into quasi-erotic paintings. Whereas 'respectable' writing was often shackled by the chains of a critical machine, and any deviation outside a circumscribed vocabulary and range of descriptions was dealt with harshly, the painter had much more freedom and could depict what he felt about legs, breasts, and any other primary or secondary sexual characteristic with a precision that was denied his literary brethren. Many painters had their favourite types, and for the extremely repressed, their work, overtly mythological, was a sex substitute, a kind of masturbation in paint. The sexuality of many of the paintings exhibited at the Royal Academy was not overlooked by spectators, especially those who were themselves sexually repressed.

Of these painters, one of the greatest was Frederick, Lord Leighton, who died in 1896, unmarried. Perfection of the female form was his close and endless study. As President of the Royal Academy, he said in his Academy Address of 1883, 'In the Art of the Periclean Age of which the high truthfulness was one of its noblest attributes ... we find a new ideal of balanced form,

wholly Aryan and which the only parallel I know is something
found in the women of another Aryan race – your own,' and
this race he painted diligently from the early 1850s until his
death, even though his models were usually set in a never-
never land where it was considered *de rigueur* for women to dis-
port themselves in the nude. It was the never-never land of
'Venus Disrobing for the Bath' (1867), 'Ariadne Abandoned by
Theseus' (1868), 'Phryne' – a nude figure merely standing in
the sun (1882), and that very handy mythological present for
artists and spectators who liked to see a naked woman bound
with chains to a post or to a rock, 'Andromeda' (1891).[39]

Not that the Royal Academy was just a repository of nude
paintings. Anecdotal and genre paintings formed perhaps the
bulk, with a steady leavening of straightforward portraits, and,
indeed, Leighton provided his share of these. In 1868, the year
of Leighton's 'Ariadne', Carroll visited the Royal Academy and
noted the pictures that most interested him; being in particular
charmed by little girls, whom he delighted to photograph,
naturally pictures on this theme attracted him most. He was
pleased by Hughes' 'Sigh No More, Ladies', depicting a 'dreamy
melancholy young lady with hands clasped round one knee
looking into vacancy'; Westmacott's 'Foolish Virgin', to which
Carroll gave his own title, 'While the Bridegroom Tarried';
Mrs Anderson's 'Red Riding Hood'; and a pair of pictures by
Schlesinger, 'The Tedious Task' and 'In Disgrace' (a child
'locked up in a garret with bread and water; she sits clasping
her hands round one knee, looking up, with tears standing on
her cheeks'). Such paintings of easy sentiment – and why should
they be any the worse for that? – formed the staple diet of the
gallery-goers.

The sexual content of many Royal Academy paintings did not
go unreproved by churchmen. The Bishop of Carlisle wrote to
the portrait painter George Richmond (not a great exponent of
the nude):

My mind has been considerably exercised this season by the exhibition of Alma-Tadema's nude Venus ... [there might] be artistic reasons which justify such public exposure of the female form. ... In
the case of the nude of an Old Master, much allowance can be made,

but for a living artist to exhibit a life-size life-like almost photographic representation of a beautiful naked woman strikes my inartistic mind as somewhat if not very mischievous.

People such as this bishop did not overlook, either, the extravagant style in which the top painters lived; and when they were bachelors, like Leighton, and had decor that included a stuffed peacock on a mother-of-pearl cabinet, and an 'Arabian Court' that was considered by Sir Caspar Purdon Clarke, a director of what is now the Victoria and Albert Museum 'the most beautiful structure which has been erected since the sixteenth century', then there were even more grounds to cavil. Even G. F. Watts, one-time husband of Ellen Terry and the prime parasite of the century (his hostess, Mrs Prinsep, said that 'he came to stay three days, he stayed thirty years'), a painter of murky 'sublime' pictures, did not turn his head from his painter contemporaries' dream of fair women. He said: 'The modern young lady is often of splendid growth and form such as probably the ancient Greek never saw,' though some artists considered English models to be awkward, and preferred Italian girls. Such was the demand, so opulent were the drawing-room painters, that a colony of Italians grew up in the Holland Park–Kensington area where many of the wealthier artists lived. There were hazards, of course; the models had a strange propensity for getting into trouble or otherwise disappearing from the aesthetic scene (one of them married an ice-cream man).

The degree of immortality, real or imagined, of personages of the second half of the nineteenth century, can usually be judged by reference to Ruskin, and the adjectives he applied to the paintings of Alma-Tadema likewise tell us more about Ruskin and people who thought along his lines than they tell us about Alma-Tadema's paintings (they were, said Ruskin, 'gloomy' 'crouching' and 'dastardly' [40] – any readers who came across these aesthetic judgements in contemporary art criticism would rub their eyes in wonder not unmixed with alarm).

The nude adolescent girl was considered less heinous than the nude woman, if only for the absence of voluptuousness and pubic hair, which was a constant cause of affront to the respectable; a thesis could be written on the effect of pubic hair on Victorian sexual thinking. Pubic hair was the omnipresent reminder of the animal in man, the hairy beast brought to the knowledge of the shocked middle classes by Darwin in *The Origin of the Species by means of Natural Selection* (1859). It has been speculated that Ruskin, conditioned as an art critic by the smooth hairless female bodies he had viewed on countless canvases, was unable to consummate his marriage with Effie Gray because of the shock he received on the bridal night, the shock of finding that his wife had acquired the natural attributes of puberty – a growth of hair about the pubis. In 1858 in Turin, ten years after his marriage, and a year or two after the annulment of this marriage, Ruskin was transfixed by a young girl, 'half naked, bare-limbed to above the knees, and beautifully limbed ... her little breasts, scarce dimpled yet – white – marble-like ...' This was as much sex as Ruskin, or Carroll, could cope with, or even John Gibson, sculptor of the 'Painted Venus' as he was.

Artists during the early and mid Victorian period were not great respecters of persons. In their quest for knowledge of anatomy, a group of artists including Gibson went grave robbing. They came across, recorded Gibson, a 'very beautiful girl about sixteen; her face was full and round. How sweet and innocent she looked in death! She was shrouded in white linen and sprinkled over with bits of red wool like flowers.' [41] The artist's life, it is clear, was not all drawing from the nude in the 'pepper-pot', the cupola of the National Gallery, or starving in attics.

The attitude of Victorian England towards the nude model was not ambiguous. Little less than a tart to those who did not know very much about it, she was forbidden fruit to the hot-blooded student fraternity. Students at the Royal Academy could not, at one time, draw from the nude model unless they were married. The model got what was then a lavish three guineas a week; some of them sat under economic duress.

During the time when W. P. Frith – whose 'Derby Day', now in the national collection, he sold for £5,250 – was at the school, he noted that the model was quietly sobbing. He drew this to the attention of the 'visitor' (i.e., a visiting teacher-celebrity), who happened to be George Jones, known as 'Liquorice' Jones because of the colour of his sepia drawings. He prided himself on his resemblance to the Duke of Wellington, for whom he was often mistaken. 'Dear me,' the Duke is said to have declared. 'Mistaken for me, is he? That's strange, for no one mistakes me for Mr Jones.' [42] Frith thought the model might be in pain. 'Oh no!' he reports Jones as saying, 'she can't be in pain; no, I think I know what distresses her. Take no notice. Go on with your work.' Later Frith was employing a model and after two or three sittings he realized that this was the same girl. He questioned her about it, and she blushed, and began crying again. Her father was a tailor who owed three pounds ten, and to get him out of the dilemma, she agreed to submit to the supreme indignity – sitting naked for the edification of young students. 'I never sat in that way before,' she told Frith, 'and I never will again.' Frith pontificated on this:

She is a mother and a grandmother, and no one has any idea that she sat for the nude figure to save her father from prison. I desire to say as little as possible on a disagreeable subject; but attempts have been made now and again to prevent the study of the female nude. If the well-meaning objectors knew half as much as I do of the subject, they would hesitate before they charge a small section of the community with immorality, which exists only in the imagination of the accusers. I declare I have known numbers of *perfectly respectable* women who have sat constantly, and habitually, for the nude...

Frith, whose excellent *My Autobiography and Reminiscences* (1887) demonstrates a lively mind and an inquiring spirit, could countenance the view that by and large the profession of model was an unholy one; how much greater was the suspicion of those who knew nothing of the subject. Even as late as 1894, the fact that the heroine of Du Maurier's *Trilby* was a model was sufficient to shock.

One is not surprised that, as Frith tells us, there were many attempts to prevent the study of the nude in art schools; in most of the private art schools, in any case, drawing from the nude was out, and innocuous plaster casts, or drab bric-à-brac, were in. It was fortunate for the career of the model that reverence for Greek sculpture, with its strong emphasis on the beauty of the human form, male and female, never suffered any reverses. The extended love affair with the classical age, consummated both in art and literature, guaranteed the status of the nude. There were several reasons why the Greeks and Romans exercised this spell over the barbarians of the north; in 1812 Lord Elgin had piloted his shipload of Greek antiquities to alien shores; execrably housed as they were, the Elgin Marbles were a *ne plus ultra* for sculptors. The establishment, educated as most of its personages were at the public schools, was orientated to Greek and Latin and their ethos. Even those who tried to break away were catapulted back, as if on a piece of elastic; no one could have been more against the established order of things than Samuel Butler, but he spent no inconsiderable time trying to prove that Homer was a woman. Statesmen and politicians of every kidney took refuge in times of stress with the ancients; in quiet moments, Gladstone sought consolation with Homer. To conform to the wishes of the enlarging and powerful middle classes – a proportion of which had had no public school education and was therefore unaware of the attractions of Horace and Ovid – and suppress the nude would have savoured of giving in to the new barbarism of the industrial revolution.

It was not only the votary of the middle class who resented the way the Greeks and the Romans permeated the thought of the upper crust, carrying in their wake the naughtiness of Plato and the frank immorality of Martial; also against the cult of the ancients, especially in art, were the votaries of the prime Victorian aesthetic style, the Gothic. 'It is quite right,' lectured Ruskin reluctantly in May 1883, 'that the British public should see the Elgin marbles to the best advantage; but not that they should be unable to see any example of the sculpture of Chartres or Wells, unless they go to the miscellaneous collection at Kensington, when Gothic saints and sinners are confounded alike among steam thrashing-machines and dynamite-proof ships of war.' Furthermore, so far as Ruskin was concerned, the Greeks had committed the gross aesthetic sin – 'the singular defect in Greek art, that it never gives you any conception of Greek children.' [43]

The nude in high art was something that slipped through the clutches of middle-class morality, argue as they might that calling a naked woman Andromeda or Psyche did not make her any the less a naked woman. The notion that mythological art was, if not respectable, sanctified, meant that naked women were usually somewhere on gallery walls or enmarbled in superior foyers. In 1820 a Venus was discovered at Milo; in 1834 it was put in the Louvre; the French bourgeoisie were, too, placed in precisely the same position as the great English middle class. The quantity of erotic art in the guise of mythology was massive; unfortunately time has dealt meanly with this art. Most of the products of these extremely proficient craftsmen were stuck in attics and in damp basements; at the very best they form part of the vast English schools collection that the Tate Gallery owns but cannot display because of lack of space; at the worst they were unceremoniously destroyed.

The painter with the itch to draw naked women had a seller's market if he was well connected and could cloak his nudes with mythology. The sculptor, too, if he knew where to stop. In his novel *Lothair* of 1870, Disraeli describes one typical success:

When the curtain was withdrawn they beheld a life size figure exhibiting in undisguised completeness the perfection of the female form, and yet the painter had so skilfully availed himself of the shadowy and mystic hour and of some gauze-like drapery which veiled without concealing his design that the chastest eye might gaze on his heroine with impunity.

High Victorian art is a story of undiminished success. Leighton sold his 'Daphnephoria' to a private buyer without much effort for £1,500; his money he wisely put in Eastern Counties Railway Debentures at 4½ per cent. Painters with a talent for portraying pretty women in a state of undress, partial or complete, and who did not reach the summit of this parochial Mount Olympus had only themselves to blame. Albert Moore was one of these. Born in 1841, he, like Lord Leighton, was a bachelor, but unlike the one-time president of the Royal Academy, he lived in squalor and disorder. Whistler visited him, found an array of handleless jugs to catch the rain streaming through the roof and Moore wearing a big ulster and a broad-brimmed straw hat (without a crown). He might have a dachshund 'Fritz' who 'sat up and did George Eliot', he might like painting beautiful girls, but he did not live in Holland Park, he did not entertain lavishly, he did not have an Arabian Court, and he did not call his pictures 'Psyche' or 'Clytie Reading' but 'Lightning and Light', 'An Idyll', 'Blossoms', and 'Dreaming'. He also did super-fine nude studies in black and white chalk on brown paper. He painted for himself; after the flamboyance of Leighton, Alma-Tadema, and, in later life, Millais (who spent £6,000 furnishing a house), Moore's quiet dedicated life comes as something of a relief.

Dress

After the King of Sardinia had visited the French Empress, and, seeing a lady-in-waiting trip over her crinoline, observed that the gates of paradise were always open, he came to England, where, reported Henry Greville, 'the Queen has been a good deal amused on her part by anything so new and strange to her as his conversation, which is certainly very original and often droll, though to the last degree brusque and *soldatesque*'.[44] He was very popular during his stay in Britain. He had the figure of a circus strong man and was the only Knight of the Garter – he dressed in white shorts 'which in combination with a very short tunic looked exactly like drawers' so that the Garter would show – 'who looks as if he certainly would have the best of it with the Dragon'. The King of Sardinia had been pleased that the French ladies did not wear drawers, and no doubt when in England he saw, licentious soldier as he was, a good many more bare rumps. He would no doubt have been puzzled by the way the

English looked embarrassed when the word drawers was mentioned. Clues to the inhibitions can be found in the nineteenth-century sex joke:

A young lady was taking an air on horseback near Bristol with her footman behind, unluckily her horse threw her, when she called out, 'John, did you ever see the like?' 'Yes, Madam,' says John, 'your sister has just such another backside.'

Miss ——, the celebrated Diana, one day fell topsy turvy in a fox chase, when a countryman immediately flew to her assistance, she asked him if he had been a married man she would have given him a crown, but as he was a batchelor [*sic*], the treat was quite sufficient.

Similarly, the Duchess of Manchester came off her horse when out hunting, and, bottom up in *déshabillé*, disclosed that she was wearing drawers of a bright tartan. Like her paramour, Lord Hartington, the Duchess of Manchester liked to be different in her dress. *The Handbook of the Toilet* of 1841 is an interesting guide to the pressure being put on women to take care of their nether regions. The undergarments of the average upper-class woman worn 'over her vital organs are totally inadequate, and bare shoulders in evening dress is largely instrumental in starting consumption ... flannel should be worn next the skin all the year over the whole body and arms, and as low as the middle of the thighs ...' From time immemorial, the basic undergarment of both man and woman had been the shift, an article renamed 'chemise' by fashion-conscious Victorians.

The first drawers were made of flannel, angola, calico and stocking-web. In the sixties coloured underwear came in, a favourite colour being magenta ('the queen of colours'). Drawers of this period were of lace, silk and flannel, and for the more exotic ladies there were plush drawers. In 1877 the hybrid combinations were introduced, 'a new style of combining chemise and drawers', which were pretty in pink and cream, but inconvenient, and this decade saw that curious anomaly, the chamois leather combinations worn over ordinary underclothes.

The age of conspicuous waste was at its most revealing in

underwear. A trousseau in the sixties for lingerie was expected to cost £100:

12 chemises
12 nightdresses
12 drawers
 4 petticoats
 1 dress petticoat
 6 camisoles
 6 vests
 4 flannel petticoats
 2 pr French corsets
 2 crinolines

The young lady not only had to persuade her mother to spend this large sum of money on her underwear, but was expected to engross herself in making her underwear custom-built. 'A young lady spent a month in hemstitching and embroidering a garment which it was scarcely possible that any other human being, except her laundress, would ever see,' stated the *Englishwoman's Domestic Magazine* coyly in 1866.

Drawers had moral as well as health overtones. The unknown author [45] of *The Mysteries of Verbena House or Miss Bellasis Birched for Thieving* (1882,) one of the flagellation sagas, declared:

The greatest enemy to a woman's chastity is contact. Let her wear her things loose and she may keep her blood cool. Nuns – continental ones at least – don't wear drawers. Peasant women, who are chaste enough as times go, don't wear drawers; and when they stoop you may see the bare flesh of their thighs above their ungartered stockings. But the bigger the whore – professional or otherwise – the nicer will be the drawers she wears, while the prude or the cantankerous old maid will either wear the most hideous breeches imaginable, or none at all ... let the graces be stark naked, or vest them only with flowing drapery, and they may be as chaste as Susannah. Put them in drawers or tights and they become prostitutes.

The early drawers were two split legs, anchored at the waist. In the age of the crinoline these were replaced by the long white pantaloons, edged with lace, ankle length. Little girls of the time were treated as miniature women, though miniature women who tended to get dirtier than the mature model, and who therefore had to wear pantalettes, an idiotic article that reached from ankle to knee. The crinoline itself must be surely one of the most charming inventions ever, replacing the incredibly uncharming bustles, the invention of which precedes the Victorian age by a few years. The bustle, ugly in its upper-class form, was ludicrous when adopted by the lower orders, who improvised. Not infrequently, the bustles of servant women looked like domestic utensils slipped under the dress, and the down which had stuffed ladies' bustles was replaced by kitchen dusters in great quantitites. Like the corset, the bustle altered the external shape of woman, for the purpose of which it is not clear to see.

Unlike the bustles, crinolines were intriguing and sexually attractive. They were light, easily manoeuvrable, took up a lot of space, kept men at arms' length, and expressed the untouchable essence of chaste womanhood. They were intriguing in that they hinted more than they showed; the cult of the ankle and the calf can be dated from the crinoline boom. Crinolines swayed about like captive balloons. In their essentials, they were a series of circular hoops of increasing size affixed to an underskirt, and for a time they rendered the petticoat obsolete. The crinoline, one of the most characteristic and aesthetically pleasing of nineteenth-century women's fashions, were relatively short-lived. It plunged into decline in 1866, to make way in 1868 for the 'tournure' or 'dress improver', another form of bustle, that in one way or another held sway along with the corset for the rest of the century, though it foretold new gimmicks, such as steels in the petticoats of 1882. The crinoline was a piece of adorable extravagance, but was ridiculously out of place in the drawing rooms crammed with bric-à-brac, in the railway carriages, in the crowded streets of omnibuses and cabs. It has left its legacy in buildings built during the sixties, in the unnaturally wide staircases, and curious articles of furniture that turn up in the sales room owe their genesis to the space-consuming frolics of the crinoline. For naturally amorous men, it was a daunting phenomenon; it put an end to the *tête-à-*

tête, and only the most reckless essayed an embrace. Although it did not last long, it is perhaps surprising that it lasted as long as it did, when one considers the handicap to the women who wore it; clearly the mere act of sitting down was an operation of some magnitude. Urinating and defecating must have been thwart with disillusion, especially when one views the minute lavatories of many nineteenth-century houses. The reign of the crinoline was a mere ten years, and its death was forecast many times during this decade. After about five years, the *English-woman's Domestic Magazine* announced its probable demise: 'The reign of the crinoline is not yet over, although it is doubtful whether the fashion will last more than a few months longer.' During its prime, the crinoline competed with a host of new ideas – matching skirts and jackets with a broad belt, crepes, alpaca, new aniline dyes, epaulettes in quasi-military style (reminiscences of the Crimean War).

Historians of fashion note permutations of sleeves, new materials coming into general use (poplin, satin, velvet), the long train of the skirt, the mannish look of the eighties, the introduction of the jersey in 1879, open-air styles for tennis and semi-open-air styles for the new rage, roller skating. Exotic fabrics from India and all points east were part of the armoury of every well-dressed woman. After the death of the crinoline, the fashion journals announced the 'style of the Empire'. Some of the more lush fabrics, the velvets and the satins, spread themselves almost uncontrollably over womankind, and tapes were used for drawing and controlling this overflow of skirt and dress – the woman, in fact, as kite. Some of these styles were unquestionably very fetching; the curious correlation between women and horses – a wife, said Tennyson, was 'a little dearer than his dog, a little nobler than his horse' – led to a preoccupation with woman as a horse-riding animal, and this was partly responsible for what the *Queen* called 'the mannish effect', not much liked by this most snobbish of journals ('unhappily the prevailing taste' in 1883.) It had been more enthusiastic with French-inspired fashions of three years earlier ('very effective on the green grass are the Pompadour cottons over plain coloured petticoats ... the tunic sometimes a Watteau'). The *Queen* at this time had one of the most hideous mastheads of all the periodicals, for all the good taste it tried so desperately to inculcate. The mannish look had its defenders in *haute couture*. The *Ladies' Gazette of Fashion* spoke approvingly of 'neat tailor-clad figures that flit along our busy streets'. The military aspect of woman was reinforced by the 'Langtry busque', a tight bodice fastened with two rows of military buttons. This was popular in America especially. Lillie Langtry was a great sponsor of commercial products, from a head band of velvet, through shoes, parasols and toothpaste (a brand called 'Odontobaph', which she described as 'excellent and most pleasant to use').

The rapid transformation of the exterior of woman more than compenssated for the drab garb of man, occasionally lit by brief episodes of inspiration – the bright-hued waistcoats of one period, the frilly shirts of the fifties, and hand-tooled braces (gentlemen, said the *Englishwoman's Domestic Magazine*, were 'generally pleased to have them prettily worked'). The aesthetic gentlemen did their best to bring in a touch of colour. Oscar Wilde, despite his paunch and his green teeth, was one of these. So did the sporting gentry, such as the Duke of Hamilton, 'The Butcher', named not for any violent traits in his nature, but for what were termed butcher-blue shirts and ties. He also had a *penchant* for coral studs, a brown billycock hat and coloured spats. Wilde's friend, the publisher Smithers, dressed like a bookmaker, though even in these decadent circles, traditional modes of dress held sway – Aubrey Beardsley dressed, it was said, like an insurance man.

Biologically, and universally until the nineteenth century, man was the bird of paradise with his gay hues. It might be that he abdicated this role for the purpose of allowing women to express themselves with the wide ranges of colours and materials provided by the accumulating technology wrought by the industrial revolution. It may be that the nineteenth century was a turning point in the evolutionary pattern, and the respective sartorial fashions of man and woman are an obscure indication of this, not, as Wilde flippantly put it, 'a form of ugliness so intolerable that it had to be changed every six months'.

Presumably one of the aims of a rapid change of fashion is to recaptivate the interest of a jaded opposite sex. If this is true, some of the changes had self-defeating modifications built in. If one sees the corset as a device to uplift the breasts, the effect was partially nullified by the day-time costume that was especially prevalent amongst the rising working class and the artisan lower middle class, the high necked dress, presented to us in many hundreds of thousands of studio photographs. This makes late Victorian attire seem very unexciting and dowdy; no wonder the men made such a fuss about the accessories, the shoes that peeped in and out like mice, the gaily coloured parasols, the delectable straw boater hats.

In 1843, the venerable *Blackwood's Magazine* ventured into art criticism, sampling the nude paintings of Etty, and criticizing his Graces for looking as though they had worn stays. It would have been surprising if the models who had served Etty's turn had not. Half a century earlier, the waist had been located just beneath the breasts, but gradually the waist dropped to its normal level, and thus needed the constrictions of stays to keep it there, and keep it neat.

The primitive corset was barbaric. One of the Medici women was said to have acquired a waist of thirteen inches by using a corset of iron, and materials used at the opening of the nineteenth century included half-inch-thick leather. In 1828 occurred a technological breakthrough that was to make the corset the most prominent article of womanly equipment – the metal eyelet hole was invented in France. Previously, the holes for the lacing cord had merely been reinforced with buttonhole stitching, and this had laid stringent limits on the force exerted on the wearer's figure, though some women managed to overcome this. In 1826 someone wrote, the figure 'resembles an ant with a slender tube uniting the bust to the haunches'.

This new dimension in shape was received rapturously by womankind. The metal eyelet hole was supplemented in 1830 by advances in metalwork. The year 1836 saw the 'patent caoutchouc [i.e., india rubber] instantaneous closing corsets'. Troubles were already starting, and Mrs Walker in *Female*

Beauty (1837) reported that 'women who wear very tight stays complain that they cannot sit upright without them, nay are compelled to wear night stays in bed'. The corset rage spread through all levels of society, the poor having the cast-offs of their betters, and no doubt, due to the ramifications of supply and demand in the old clothes markets, they were even more uncomfortable than the rich.

The cultivation of a small waist was a phenomenon that brooks no explanation;[46] the small waist was an aesthetic attraction to men, but its sexual potential was limited. However, the corset did two subsidiary jobs that might be termed sexually useful – it kept the size of the waist within limits (necessary when there were endless crinolines, and/or yards and yards of material; in 1842 Lady Aylesbury wore a gown containing forty-eight yards of material), and it forced the breasts up until they were at one time or another nestling immediately beneath the chin. The cult of the corset was a self-imposed trial. It caused innumerable ailments, and autopsies often confirmed that livers were nearly sliced in two by over-tight lacing. Tight lacing also produced a very close simulacrum of hysteria, and could result in certain erotic sensations. To those who cared to think about the subject, tight lacing was not only a health problem, but a moral problem as well.

Where these two factors are in conjunction, there is a tendency to overstate the dangers. In the *Ladies' Pocket Magazine* of 1837 appeared a review of William Coulson's *Deformities of the Chest and Spine*:

We would earnestly recommend the perusal of a work under the above title to that portion of our readers which have a rising family of daughters. It presents a faithful but melancholy portrait of the organic evils which result from the injurious practice of tight stay-lacing. Among the frightful complaints which this system is the source, are enumerated cancer and consumption. . . . His book is illustrated with plates of the human structure, which at once show the superior symmetry of the form which has not been compressed by stays, to that of the deluded votary of a vain and destructive habit. . . . To use means for contracting the space necessary for containing the machinery of the human frame is very like presumption; and we hope yet to see the period when fashion will expel the folly of tight-lacing.

Twenty years later, the medical profession was still trying valiantly to stem the flow of corsets on to the market. 'The injurious influence of stays on the female economy, as respects not only diseases of the spinal cloumn but also the disorder of the uterine organs, is manifest to all who consider the subject,' wrote Dr Copeland in his *Medical Dictionary (circa* 1850). Dr Spencer Thomson (1856) resorts to irony: 'It seems as if people imagined that the Creator had made the body of the adult female so weak, that it cannot support its own weight; for either on this account, or without reason, they case it up in artificial supports.' Particularly heinous was the practice of fixing growing schoolgirls into corsets (though the Victorians had not gone to the length of twentieth-century manufacturers in providing eight-year-old girls with bras, probably because they did not have bras).

Dr John Forbes, in his *Cyclopaedia of Practical Medicine*, reported: 'We lately visited in a large town, a boarding-school containing forty girls; and we learnt on close and accurate inquiry, that there was *not one* of the girls who had been at the school two years – and the majority had been as long – that was not, more or less, *crooked*!' Most doctors asserted that the most a growing child should wear was a close-fitting bodice.

The Great Exhibition in the Crystal Palace in 1851 emphasized British wares, and these included a variety of corsets. The manufacturers, with splendid mock-humility, had pretended to have taken note of the strictures of medical men, and were insistent that they were now producing corsets to suit every kind and condition of woman. There was the *'Corset Amazone'* which was 'quite a triumph of invention. By aid of elastic lacings, it yields to every respiration or movement of the equestrian and may be worn long or short at pleasure. The touch of a silken cord curtails by about three inches the length of the corset, and thus reduces the ordinary stay to a riding one in a moment.' Of no less interest was *'The Corset à la Nourrice'* for ladies who are fulfilling the dearest offices of maternity, and by a simple arrangement obviates every usual annoyance and inconvenience. It is not very easy to describe this corset, but we may observe that by the withdrawal of two slender bones, an entire gusset is removed – but may be replaced with equal expedition. For obvious reasons it is an advantage to be provided with an extra pair of gussets.

Many women in childbirth had a touching loyalty towards their corsets, and frequently wore them throughout the entire process.

The first glimmerings of the whole of foundation garment advertising can be found in the 1850s, including a soothing soft-sell approach. 'Nature has taken care to suit the external envelope to the internal organs of the frame – has made even the bones so yielding that the soft and delicate organs which are encased in them may have a free development.' So runs a paragraph in *Health and Beauty or Corsets and Clothing* by Madame Roxey A. Caplin. This hard-cover book proclaimed the merits of the superior corsets that Madame Caplin advocated, and exemplified the fact that the corset industry was out of its infancy.

Amongst the products were:

Hygienic Corset
Hygienic Corset – Elastic Front
Self-Regulating Gestation
Self-Regulating Semi-Corset
Self-Regulating Corporiform (for fat women)
Self-Adjusting Corporiform   (the distinction is not explained)
Self-Adjusting Corporiform with invisible props
Self-Adjusting-Symmetrico-Restorator Corporiform (for fat women with a curved spine)
Original Elastic Bodice (for youngsters)
Juvenile Elastic Corset (for young ladies growing too rapidly)
Riverso-Tractor Hygienic Corset (for sloppy children standing on one leg')
Young Lady's Riding Belt ('to prevent concussion taking place in the lower region of the spine during horse riding exercise')
Abdominal Supporter Belt
Elastic Compressing Belt
Gestation Compressing Belt

Contracting Compressing Belt
Dropsical Compressing Belt
Medical Compressing Belt
Dorso-Abdominal Support   (to maintain centre of gravity)
Invisible Scapula Contractor   (to develop chest)

'Your corset,' stated Madame Caplin blandly, 'is more like a new layer of muscles than an artificial extraneous article of dress.' Then more ominously she drew attention to the disadvantages of not wearing one of her delectable garments, pointing out the African negress 'whose breasts hang down to an inordinate length', and quoting the explorer, James Bruce ('this part being of such a length as, in some cases, to reach almost to the knee'). Bruce could have done with the Dorso-Abdominal Support ('to maintain centre of gravity'). He fell downstairs in 1794 and died. Bruce's findings were confirmed by a Captain Tuckey, who told of the 'pendent flaccidity of bosom' of African woman.

One of the first of the 'named' corsets was Mrs Geary's 'New invented Anatomical Stay' of early 1840. These 'present a new and rational principle in the construction of these most important portions of dress. The formation of the bosom, and of all parts adapted to prominences, is a matter of great ingenuity, and of extraordinary beauty.' Occasionally, these 'prominences' were treated with brusque incivility. Infants at the breast discovered frequently that the nipple had been pressed back into the teat by their mother's conforming to fashion. Some doctors did not reject the corset movement out of hand, and some were not averse to a little discreet advertising. Thus Dr James Johnson in the *Medico-Chirurgical Review* of January 1840, a journal that often was, in its reactionary attitude, the medical equivalent to the *Saturday Review*: 'The problem to be solved was to support the figure, yet not to diminish freedom of motion, and to conceal the size of the abdomen when too large.' He was writing nearly two decades earlier than Madame Caplin. She would not have expressed it quite so keenly.

There was little need for the strenuous espousing of the cause of lacing. The corset, elasticated, with metal eye holes, often moulded by steam power and coloured scarlet, was here to stay. The year 1873 saw the emergence of the *cuirasse* corset, with a 'spoon busk'. The cords for lacing gave way to two steel strips, one with knobs or catches, the other with buttonholes. This made the request to husbands to 'do me up' a simpler matter than had been the case with cord.

That the corset was one of the key articles of clothing of the epoch was affirmed by the Pompadour corset, which was worn over the skirt. This was pointed in front and behind, but the form apparently did not make men's pulses beat any faster – the pointed woman was a novelty that had no sexual charm – and it died a natural death in 1885. In 1889 a more exciting variant appeared, with the shape curving inwards over the waist and outwards over the lower belly, and in the nineties the cut-away corset made its entrance. The breasts, which in earlier years had been an amorphous mass, were now divided by groups of short bones known as 'divorces'.

Women with good figures managed to survive the curious postures into which they had been forced by fashion, but older women and those ill-equipped by nature were not so fortunate. 'There is Lady Flabbyson,' wrote a journalist in the *Tomahawk* of 1868, 'whose shoulder blades appear midway above her *corsage*, and in whose back you may count ten vertebrae when she is not even stooping.' 'The upper part of a ball dress,' said the *Queen* reprovingly, 'should be both modest and picturesque.'

For many aestheticians and artists, the corset was an instrument of the devil. 'Right dress,' said Ruskin in his eccentric *Arrows of the Chace* 'is therefore strong – simple – radiantly clean – carefully put on – carefully kept,' though there is no evidence that he joined the Anti-Tight-Lacing League, as G. F. Watts, a painter Ruskin admired to excess, did. Watts was one of the many artists who regarded Greek dress as the extreme in rationality (though contemporaries of the ancient Greeks, the Cretan women, used some kind of tight lacing). One of Watts' colleagues in this crusade was Edward William Godwin, architect, stage designer, and a sharer with Watts of the charms of Ellen Terry. Godwin, who possessed as a token of his affiliations a life size statue of the Venus de Milo, had been most impressed by a health exhibition in Kensington, where young

women had cavorted with dumb bells. A Greek woman, declared John Collier, a pupil of one of the leaders of high art,
Edward Poynter, 'never supposed she had a waist. She often
for convenience tied a string round her body, but only just
tightly enough to keep the clothes in place, and then let folds
of drapery fall over and hide the unsightly line.' The aesthetic
movement satirized by *Punch* ('Are you *intense*?' asked a lanky
young woman in a smooth-flowing vaguely Greek robe of a
bored paunchy man) was involved in a dilettante way with the
cause of the anti-lacers including Constance Wilde, Oscar
Wilde's wife, who edited the *Rational Dress Gazette*; but it
was never a threat to the corset manufacturers.

In 1890 a paper appeared in the *British Medical Journal* by
Dr Wilberforce Smith, *On the Alleged Difference Between
Male and Female Respiratory Movements*, and medical objections to corsets were revived. It did seem that tight lacing was
producing a change in secondary female characteristics. There
are two kinds of breathing, from the chest and from the
abdomen; it was observed that women breathed primarily from
the chest, and it was believed that this is the way it always had
been. However, argued Smith, comparisons 'tended to confirm
the belief . . . that the alleged difference is chiefly or wholly due
to the effects of woman's conventional dress'.

Amplification came from Dr Mays of Philadelphia, who had
had the opportunity to compare full-bloodied Indians with those
who had adopted civilized dress. He discovered that the vast
proportion of the reservation Indians 'showed a decided abdominal type of breathing'. This was confirmed by Dr J. H. Kellogg,
who did his own researches with the aid of what he described
as 'a Marey's stethograph and rotating cylinder', which must
have impressed his more uncivilized subjects no end. The hypothesis that costal (chest) breathing and abdominal breathing
was a race thing was dispelled by examining Cherokee women,
both those who lived a natural life and those who lived in
corsets and tight dresses, and again the difference was borne out.
From this it was only a short step to the idea that abdominal
breathing was good and costal breathing bad, only a short step
to the notion that the natural life was the better, a short step

to the resurrected myth of the noble savage. Kellogg wrote a pamphlet *The Influence of Dress*, illustrated with line drawings of a German peasant woman aged twenty-nine who had been accustomed to carry heavy weights on her head (good) and an American woman with sagging breasts, protruding abdomen, and inset waist (bad). To make sure that his message would go home, Kellogg's illustrator gives the German woman a pleasant, somewhat arrogant, expression, and the America woman a downtrodden 'spinster-aunt' expression.

The continued and irrational use of this curious instrument, the corset, fostered by fashion, encouraged by devotees of fashion – the women's magazines – was a new and benign fact of life for whalers. In May 1888, one of those assiduous observers of the social scene with which the age was crammed, A. G. C. Liddell, was in conversation with the explorer Sir Allen Young. 'He went on about whales. The price of whales had increased so much on account of the demand for whalebone for women's dresses that it made up for the immense falling off in the value of oil. A good whale was now worth about £2,000.' [47]

It might be speculated that during the nineteenth century woman was working her way towards some new modification of her species, as expounded by Charles Darwin. The ostensible regard for a tiny waist was actually incidental to the main purpose of the corset, which was to accentuate bosom and hips. The second half of the nineteenth century was a breast-orientated age. Because legs were forbidden articles except in private, the sexual attentions were focused on the breasts. The celebrated beauties were chesty women; their pumpkin-like breasts were partly the product of constant upward pressure since before puberty, and their measurements were psychologically augmented by clothes fashioned for the small waist. In a letter to Havelock Ellis, Dr Louis Robinson made an honest assessment of the corset syndrome: 'I think it very likely one of the reasons (and there must be strong ones) for the persistent habit of tightening up the belly-girth among Christian damsels is that such constriction renders the breathing thoracic, and so advertises the alluring bosom by keeping it in constant and manifest movement.' [48]

The corset was legislated against at a government level by Russia, Germany, and Rumania, especially the corset for growing girls. The reaction against the extravagant distortions of womanly shape began to have an effect on fashions about 1910, when corsets became lower, leaving the breasts free for the manipulation of a new industry – the brassiere – though *Punch's* fantasy of a 'spat corset' to be fastened beneath the instep remained just that, mercifully.

To the more picturesque, the corset was a man-made self-perpetuating monster, that 'pretending to be a servant is, in fact, a tyrant – that, aspiring to embrace, hugs like a bear – crushing in the ribs, injuring the lungs and heart, the stomach, and many other internal organs'. Thus wrote Mrs H. R. Haweis in *The Art of Beauty* of 1878. Nevertheless, the corset was not wholly useless,[49] as it served to spark off the genesis of a novel aphrodisiac – the suspender. When the plain white stockings of the early years of the reign gave way to the long black stockings of the nineties, via pale mauve, and gay stripes to match the petticoats of the sixties, the added sophistication of a suspender made the thigh an erogenous area of rare impact, especially to those men who had been captivated by gartered thighs of the Parisian can-can dancers. No doubt the suspender had its detractors, but they have been lost in the columns of long dead periodicals.

4
Courtship, Love and Marriage

The Courtship Ritual

'I T H I N K that you ought to be A little more cairfuel I houffering you hand and heart to A young man that you know nothing about nor never seen before. Now that the way A grate meney you womean gets into trouble thro being free with young men they now nothing about.'

This letter was written in March 1866 to a young lady by Police Constable 351, James W. Mitchell, attached to the Ladywood police station of Birmingham. The young lady had been courted in whirlwind fashion by a man who purported to be Mitchell, but who turned out to be no one of the kind. The second half of the nineteenth century was a succession of field days for the young man who could persuade the working-class girl that he was single and ready to marry, and the etiquette of courtship as laid down in the manuals of behaviour applied to a minority of the population, except for such books as *How to Woo* (Ward Lock, sixpence), which offered advice that was not only unpalatable but singularly inappropriate: Young women were advised that 'matrimony should be considered as an incident in life which, if it comes at all, must come without any contrivance of yours'. On the contrary, for working girls matrimony was the prime object of life, to be pursued intensely and from an early age – as it could be when the age of consent was twelve.

The whimsy of humorous writers – men, of course – on courtship had no relevance at all to the frenzied efforts of the women to get themselves a husband, and there was a good deal of mock indignation by such writers at the insufferable way in which young men were taken advantage of (if he but looked at a lady he was 'smitten', if he spent an hour with her it was 'courtship', if he gave her his arm he was 'engaged'). People do not change much in a hundred years, and courtship was in Victorian times as much a rough and ready affair as it is today, with as many kinds of courtship as there were kinds of people. The ideal was set forth by Robert Louis Stevenson – 'two people who go into love step by step, with a fluttered consciousness, like a pair of children venturing together into a dark room'. In such a sentimental age this released echoes in the educated readers of Stevenson's essays – such as the collection *Virginibus Puerisque* of 1881 from which the extract is taken – and who a couple of years later were to be disconcerted when Stevenson turned to children's stories (*Treasure Island*, 1883). For many couples, the dark room of Stevenson's pretty parable was one that had been entered several times before. No hysterics by committed writers of the time can gloss over the fact that the chaste courtship and the passionless marriage of myth were exceptions rather than the rule.

The courtship ritual was a formalized procedure that was more applicable to lyre birds than people, and it was fostered by a good many well-meaning people, not least important being the 'shamelessly avaricious bawds' who palmed off their daughters on the not altogether willing, and for whom the courtship etiquette was a handy shoehorn for sliding their daughters into matrimony. In particular, the essence of courtship etiquette was time. Nothing was precipitatd, and a rush of blood to the head could often be dealt with by a few days' seclusion. At a time when young men planned their careers as if they were climbing ladders, and were reluctant to undergo an early marriage, the courtship procedure was a buffer, and it was not difficult to spin out an engagement for five years or more.

This procedure was especially favoured by the industrial middle classes who had acquired wealth and power at the expense of their birthright, and who did not quite know how to cope with new situations. Many of them had jumped clean out of their class, and men whose sisters had been turned out to service or into factories when they were young women were at a loss when their own daughters reached such an age. Naturally such daughters could not do anything useful – governessing was the prerogative of daughters of the clergy and the professional classes – and their lives had to be arranged in an artificial way. An aspect of this life was love, and men who controlled hundreds in the sweatboxes that were the factories of the era considered that love was subject to control, just as employees were. Many of the constrictions of the courtship ritual must be laid at the door of the new middle classes who found themselves in a strange territory, a territory newly carved by the aftermath of the industrial revolution.

The lower orders were far too busy working, drinking and sleeping to bother much about the precise manner in which sons and daughters would get themselves married off. The upper classes had found over the centuries that these things arrange themselves and had no need to formalize a courtship pattern. The middle classes took as their model what they imagined was the high ideal of upper-class courtship; in many cases, this was a representation by poets and novelists of what *they* imagined upper-class courtship to be, with all the unsavoury bits discreetly omitted. No one could be more upper-class than Byron, but his courtship and marriage partake little of the image. 'What an odd situation and friendship is ours!' [1] he wrote in his *Journal*, 'without one spark of love on either side, and produced by circumstances which in general lead to coldness on one side, and aversion on the other.'

The courtship manuals that were deferred to as if they were holy script were characteristic of an important and growing class, but they were not characteristic of an age. The tone of these manuals was usually genteel, and often simpering. For example, when a young girl saw a young man whom she admired, if 'by the expression of his countenance you perceive he recognises you, if his company has been agreeable, his connections are respectable and you have no objection to his acquaintance, it is your province to salute him; for if he be a decidedly well-bred man and believe you equally a gentlewoman, he will not salute you first'. Such a situation could not arise where people were sure of their social positions, and when it did it created all kinds of embarrassing, ridiculous, and often cruel side effects. Young men and women were badgered into playing this game, and the business of behaving naturally became encrusted over with this mock-genteel rust. The unnecessary ceremony with which in this idyllic no man's land the sexes came together was taken over by the aspiring working class, and there issued in the last quarter of the century an uneasy compromise between the free and easy ways of the libidinous old days, and the correct code of behaviour that had filtered through from the middle class, that target of emulation.

In this never-never land, to be perpetuated in that most middle-class comedy *The Importance of Being Earnest*, it was all right for a man to find out where a girl lived if he liked the look of her, but he could not mention her name in such a search. If he could not find out where she lived he might be able to find out her place of worship. If not, he would just have to hang around the streets (and have his motives possibly misunderstood) until the girl appeared. Even then, his anxiety was not at an end, because he could not speak to her until she blushed or brought out of her ragbag of womanly tricks, 'a smile lurking in the half-dropped eye'.

After he had spoken to her, and he had received her assurances that she did not think he would rape her there and then, he was, under this honourable code, permitted to write to her father for permission to woo the girl. Secret meetings were out, naturally, since the whole of courtship etiquette was a device of parents; to make secret meetings more heinous they were renamed 'clandestine intercourse'. Calls on the girl should not be too frequent, and 'anything like a fondling behaviour' was likewise out; it was the girl's duty 'to repress excess of ardour, whether in her own case or in that of her lover'.

In such circumstances, misunderstandings must be bound to

occur, especially when one considers the constant struggle between the edicts of the ritual and the edicts of the heart. A spontaneous coming together that is characteristic of the popular romantic fiction of the twentieth century was more difficult, both physically – the crinoline and bustles and half-bustles made the embrace a hazardous project – and mentally. The misunderstanding became a focus of attention of writers eager to tap the vein of easy sentiment. There is the young man who finds the courtship ritual tongue-tying. An anonymous poet in *Chambers's Journal* of 1871 puts it succinctly. The long-suffering narrator is typical of the period:

> Maybe 'twould pain her to despise
> A lover in this humble guise;
>   I bear my lot;
> I feel her presence in the air,
> I know an angel has been there,
>   And murmur not.

This verse from a long poem 'Reverence in Love' depicts the situation of the person who 'never told her love'. There is a compensation:

> Though now, perchance, for aye we part,
> Her form is printed on my heart;
>   I still can pray;
> Who knows but He will hear, and shed
> Unnumbered blessings on her head
>   From day to day!

Courtship as a biological prelude to marriage often ceded preference to courtship as an emotional and quasi-religious situation complete in itself. Courtship blighted by misunderstanding was a circumstance that poet, novelist and song writer returned to time and time again, a ready surety for the easy tear. The perfect example of this for the mass audience is the song 'After the Ball' by Charles K. Harris, a song from the eighties that is still sung at urban weddings when the endless pints of bitter beer have opened the floodgates of memory:

A little maiden climbed an old man's knees
Begged for a story 'Do, Uncle, please,
Why are you single, why live alone?
Have you no babies? Have you no home?'
'I had a sweetheart, years, years, ago,
Where she is now, pet, you will soon know.
List to the story, I'll tell it all,
I believed her faithless, after the ball.

CHORUS: After the ball is over, after the break of morn,
After the dancers leaving, after the stars are gone,
Many a heart is aching if you could read them all . . .
Many the hopes have vanished after the ball.

'Bright lights were flashing in the grand ball-room
Softly the music, playing sweet tune,
There came my sweetheart, my love – my own –
"I wish some water; leave me alone!"
When I returned, dear, there stood a man,
Kissing my sweetheart as lovers can,
Down fell the glass, pet, broken – that's all,
Just as my heart was, after the ball.

'Long years have passed, child, I've never wed,
True to my lost love, though she is dead –
She tried to tell me, tried to explain
I would not listen, pleadings were vain.
One day a letter came from that man
It was her brother, the letter ran.
That's why I'm lonely, no home at all,
I broke her heart, pet, after the ball.'

This immensely popular song tugged at the heart-strings of the late Victorians for any number of reasons. It illustrated how fragile was the courtship situation, how lucky the auditors were that their own humdrum love affairs had gone so well, and how fickle were the workings of fate. It might have occurred to a few cynical listeners to wonder why no one ever told the narrator who the man was.

The blameless tone of such a song would have been guffawed off the music hall stage a few decades earlier, and its popularity parallels the growing respectability and middle-class attitudes of the working classes. In the earlier days the sentiment was direct and forthright:

Come all you single fellows, if you want to change your life
I want a loving husband, if you want a loving wife,
He must be very handsome, not short, not very stout,
That would roll me in his arms at night, and blow the candle out.

Then I shall want a parasol, a mantle and a veil,
And I shall want a hairy thing just like a donkey's tail,
I shall want a tidy bustle to put upon my bum,
I shall want a little daughter and a pretty son.

I shall want a dandy cap with flowers in full bloom,
I shall want a looking-glass to view me in the room,
I shall want a dandy feather stuck in a Russian hat,
And I shall want a parrot, and a pretty cat.

The devices regulating the conduct and the relationship between the sexes reached a peak towards the end of the century, in a desperate attempt to choke what was thought of as the advance of libertinism. The influx of young girls into the man's world, the introduction of the 'typewriter' – not a machine but a stenographer – and the influence of what was known sardonically as The Girl of the Period, not only replaced the time-honoured coffee-house by the teashop but tended to reduce formalities between strange men and strange women. The manuals of etiquette that had been conned with such assiduity a couple of decades earlier were now treated with less respect, even by those who had been responsible for the widespread vogue for such manuals. *Punch*, which had for some years cruised along on its patronizing jokes about breaches of social etiquette, found itself increasingly passé. The handbooks of behaviour, such as the widely popular *Manners and Tone of Good Society* or *Solecisms to be Avoided* by 'A Member of the Aristocracy', which had gone into twelve editions by 1895, began to be treated as humorous social documents ('The lady ... like a stately flower, does not care to descend from her *parterre*, to mingle with the flowers of either field or forest; but a gentleman possesses the freedom of a butterfly, and can wander from garden to field and from field to forest *sans se déroger*').

The philosophy of the courtship game was put into the most clear-headed form by John Stuart Mill, whose own pet philosophy *Utilitarianism* ('the greatest happiness of the greatest number') has triumphed sufficiently despite uplifted hands of horror for one to regard his slightest dictum with respect. In his *On Liberty* of 1859 he speculates wisely: '... the individual or the family do not ask themselves – what do I prefer? Or what would suit my character and disposition? – They ask themselves, what is suitable in my position? What is usually done by persons of my station and pecuniary circumstances? or (worse still) what is usually done by persons of a station and circumstances superior to mine? ... Even in what people do for pleasure, conformity is the first thing thought of ... peculiarity of taste, eccentricity of conduct, are shunned equally with crimes.' This was not to Mill's taste, as he was one of the few philosophers who lived openly with a woman without concerning himself overmuch with marriage; however, as applied to courtship generally it clicks irrevocably into place. The courtship pattern of the nineteenth century was one stamped from above. It was arbitrary, designed for a middle class that was not professional or rustic, for girls who achieved puberty at a late age, for young men who were forced to marry later than had hitherto been the case. Before matrimony they 'had to make their way in the world', and a kept mistress was better than an imprudent match; to fathers 'in trade' and wanting their sons 'to get on', an imprudent match was an imprudent match.

The notion that young women did not *mind* waiting to get married was one that was widely held, especially by the celibates who normally pontificated on this theme, and who were not usually acquainted with the condiments of this proscription, e.g., masturbation and nervous disorders (and who usually did not *want* to be acquainted with *these*). Even the men had to be content with an enforced virginity. 'Is it not certain,' wrote W. R. Greg in the *Westminster Review* (1850), 'that all of delicate and chivalric which still pervades our sentiments towards women, may be traced to *repressed*, and therefore hallowed and elevated passion? ... And what, in these days, can preserve chastity, save some relic of chivalrous devotion?'

The artificial slowing down of the courtship routine by ritual and precept that were so characteristic of the up-and-coming middle classes was lacking among the aristocracy where the rhythm was a gentle *andante* anyway. Without pressures, where the right man and the right woman were bound to come along – if only for the reason that the major families were always inter-marrying and were interlocked like Chinese puzzles and therefore possible fiancés and fiancées would turn up in the ordinary course of visits and parties – the passing of the seasons did not convey the panic that was elsewhere evident, both among the parents of marriageable girls and the girls themselves. If a personable man appeared on the scene, either interested parties would do something about it, or God would, and the days, weeks, and even years were irrelevancies.

Clarissa Trant was quite willing to wait for four years for a man she had met once to return and claim her, a man 'who for the last three years has haunted me thro' the speculation of our mutual friends. He is much too amiable for such a faultfull wife as I should make. ... However of this I feel assured that if it is *His Will* that we should be better acquainted ...' [2] Miss Trant was then past thirty; had she been on a slightly lower social plain, this acquiescence would have been well nigh impossible.

The patience of the aristocratic daughter was commensurate with the education she had received. Just as Penelope had waited for Ulysses while he had been roaming the world (the girls were soaked in the classics), so would they wait for their chosen, from whichever direction he was wheeled, and wheeled he usually was – the machinations of the families were subtle, but none-theless efficient for that. Lucy Lyttelton's loved one was, for instance, a third cousin, and it was not by accident that she met and married him. Marriages might be made in heaven for some, but there was nothing quite like interlinking two great houses that might otherwise be inflicted with interlopers (one could never tell with the new rich). Occasionally this régime became manifest. In 1842 the Nightingale family was invited to Chatsworth, the seat of the Duke of Devonshire. It was loaded with 'Howards, Cavendishes, Percys, Greys, all in gala dress with stars, garters, diamonds and velvets'.[3] Even when no such meetings took place, the interrelationships of the classical families were always evident, as the briefest glance through nineteenth-century memoirs and diaries makes plain – a trade unionship of the elect.

After the engagement of Lucy Lyttelton to Lord Frederick Cavendish, the family disports itself like eager dolphins welcoming a new entrant into their exclusive school. ('I also saw Ly. Fanny and Margaret Howard,' wrote Lucy in her diary. 'Ld. Hartington, Ld. Edward; and Ly. Louisa gave me a photogr. of the Duke, and one of Lady Burlington, who must have had a look of Mamma. At 4½ I went with him and Ly. Louisa to Ly. Caroline Lascelles' where I saw her daughter May, Lord and Ly. Chesham, and Ly. George Cavendish, who were all most kind.'[4]

This awareness of belonging to an unalterable and indivisible elite often produced a smugness and an arrogance in the pursuit of the game of love, an arrogance that was recognized, hated, and yet envied, by the middle classes, the daughters of which were often enmeshed in a cobweb of misunderstanding and unrequited affection due to the etiquette enforced upon them.

To the lower echelons of society, there was something of a juggernaut in the spectacle of the aristocratic lady preparing herself for the matrimonial stakes. As the professional invalid Elizabeth Barret Browning put it:

There's a lady, an earl's daughter, – she is proud and she is noble,
And she treads the crimson carpet and she breathes the perfumed air,
And a kingly blood sends glances up, her princely eye to trouble,
And the shadow of a monarch's crown is softened in her hair.[5]

To the *bourgeoisie*, the insouciance of the aristocracy in their dealings with sex and marriage was something that could not be emulated, and the image they adopted for their own purposes was radically different to the reality.

Over the upper-class marriage, love match or not, loomed the shadow of the marriage settlement. Before the Married

Women's Property Act, which came into force in 1870, lawyers were kept busy building into marriage settlements protection for the woman. Perhaps, like Elizabeth Barret Browning's Lady Geraldine.

> She has voters in the Commons, she has lovers in the palace,
> And, of all the fair court-ladies, few have jewels half as fine.

Nevertheless, as soon as she was married, her basic situation was the same, during the earlier part of Victoria's reign, as any Drury Lane drab. What Blackstone stated in 1765 in his *Commentaries on the Laws of England* was still operative: 'By marriage, the very being or legal existence of a woman is suspended, or at least it is incorporated or consolidated into that of the husband, under whose wing, protection or cover she performs everything, and she is therefore called in our law a feme covert.'

For many high-spirited and independent aristocratic ladies it was no comforting thing to be a 'feme covert'. For those who had indulgent parents who cared more for the happiness of their daughter than for the financial and social gain possible through an adroit match, the days of playing the field were over.

As for the women's spouses, virtue had not consisted solely of celibacy. Oxford undergrduates had avowed that 'adultery, seduction, were utter scoundrelism', but the voice that counted was that of the headmaster of Eton, who, in *Training of the Young in the Laws of Sex*, of 1901, declared that 'a thoroughly conventional man in good society would sooner that his son should consort with prostitutes than should marry a respectable girl of a distinctly lower station than his own'. It was an opinion that had been widely held, but rarely had it been put in such an uncompromising form.

The aristocratic girl went into marriage more often than not *virgo intacta*; that is the impression that was meant to be projected, and it is probably true. As for the men, there is more doubt, though probably the more intelligent of the ducal sons turned their attentions to the large servant class or the daughters of the small farmers on the family estate. The wicked squire of the Victorian melodrama had his counterpart in real life, but it is less likely that the fallen girl would have been thrown out.

The prostitutes, with their high ration of 'speck'd uns', would have presented a challenge rather than a promise. The men, clever and stupid, who were eventually to acquire a dukedom or something less noble would know that there would always be some nubile maiden eager to sacrifice herself on the nuptial bed.

In the early forties, *Punch* gave its advice to lady readers: 'Between ourselves, my dear, almost every young woman is either married or intends to be. It is what we have to look to, poor things!' Perhaps for every gallant Albert from over the seas, there were a hundred mumbling drunken younger sons of minor barons. Everyone loves a lord, it has been mooted; and at no time was this truer than between 1837 and 1901.

Courtship, love, and marriage among the nobs had the same casualty rate as among the lesser in fortune. The same tragedies occurred, only sharper and brighter. Courtship for the upper classes was elegiac, literary, comfortable, nor weighed down with the prohibitions and proscriptions, the embarrassments and the formalities, that made courtship for the anxiety-prone middle classes something of a cakewalk. But gay or sombre, courtship was a prelude to a dangerous condition – marriage.

Marriage

Marriage, for every couple that ventures into it, is a special case and can be viewed in many lights: as a social contract; as a religious compact; as a means of restoring health, gaining a fortune, proving virility, getting away from uncongenial parents. It can be an adventure or it can be a sacrifice. It is the social condition under which one may have children, it is the formula that turns copulation (socially acceptable) into fornication (socially unacceptable); 'The law that springs from this source is not pleasant to read,' wrote F. Pollock and F. W. Maitland in their authoritative *The History of English Law* (1898).

Marriage, stated *Haydn's Dictionary of Dates* of 1898, 'was instituted by God (Genesis ii) and confirmed by Christ (Mark x)'.

As such it could be a sombre prospect, especially to clerics, for whom marriage was an institution to which they had a special relationship. In May 1850, the well-known hymn writer John Bacchus Dykes moved into the cottage that was to serve in two months as the bridal home. He wrote to his fiancée, Susan Kingston, in lugubrious tones:

I cannot go to bed on this the very first night at the Cottage, without entreating you to join in the earnest prayer that the Divine Blessing may rest upon me in this house, to which, by His Good Providence, I have at last arrived. That I may acknowledge Him and seek His heavenly guidance in all my ways and doings; and that He may in mercy direct my paths, that this house may be, (as it were) – a little Temple devoted to His service, and hallowed by His Blessed Presence. . .[6]

Marriage for Miss Kingston cannot have been visualized as a very lubricous state, and certainly not the perpetual honeymoon promised by romantic writers.

The seriousness of marriage was brought home to the daughter of a Chelsea doctor, who was marrying in 1859. Jane Welsh Carlyle wrote to her in a detached rather forbidding tone:

You are marrying under good auspices, since your father approves of the marriage. But congratulations on such occasions seem to me a tempting of Providence. The triumphal-procession-air which, in our manners and customs, is given to marriage at the outset – that singing of *Te Deum* before the battle has begun – has, ever since I could reflect, struck me as somewhat senseless and somewhat impious. If ever one is to feel grave and anxious – if ever one is to shrink from vain show and vain babble – surely it is just on the occasion of two human beings binding themselves to one another, for better and for worse, till death part them, just on that occasion which it is customary to celebrate only with rejoicings, and congratulations, and *trousseaux*, and white ribbon? Good God![7]

Another person who tried to see the marriage state objectively was Charles Darwin, who diligently penned the pros and cons. The pros – children, a constant companion and friend in old age, and the charms of music and female chit-chat. The cons –

the loss of time that marriage assuredly meant. For Darwin, the pros won. The philosopher Herbert Spencer viewed marriage in an appropriately abstract way. Writing to a friend, he speculated that, 'You agree I believe with Emerson that the true sentiment of love between man and woman arises from each serving as the representative of the other's ideal. From this position I think we may deduce the corollary that the first condition to happiness in the married state is continuance of that *representation of the ideal ...*' [8] Wistfully he looked at the condition at the age of twenty-four: 'I often feel melancholy enough at not having yet found any one to serve for the type of my ideal, and were it not that I make up the deficiency as well as I can by anticipations of future happiness, I should scarcely think existence worth having.' Nevertheless, Spencer never married.

The scientists and the intellectuals were often the most starry-eyed on the subject of marriage. T. H. Huxley, as cool a mind as the nineteenth century produced, kept a red camellia amongst his papers from his early love life. These scientists and intellectuals were a good deal more sentimental than the literary men, disguise it as they may. Disaster stalked the marriages and loves of the literary fraternity. No one can flip through any list of Victorian writers without reflecting on their crass choice of mates. 'Women can occasionally be fine creatures if they fall into good hands,' wrote George Meredith cynically. His own marriage fondered on the rocks.

Some expected too much of marriage. Certainly the poor approached wedlock with a breeziness and a realism that was refreshing. 'Their lives are an unending struggle,' wrote the sociologist Charles Booth benignly, 'and lack comfort, but I do not know that they lack happiness.' [9] Working class marriage was summed up in a music hall monologue, 'Wedlock's Joys', printed in Birmingham:

Marriage is a most delightful thing, in the beginning so very sweet, all love, sugar and honey, but in a short time after the matter changes amazingly, then there is a great deal of mustard, pepper, and vinegar, then the man has to buy every thing to go into housekeeping, beds, chairs, tables, kettles, and a cradle, then if the man wants to go out he as [*sic*] to take his wife with him, there she is chattering in his ears, treading on his heels like a dog with a kettle tied to his tail, he is twitched for life.

and in the words of a music hall song:

> Don't be too particular
> When you come to woo.
> Lay aside your spectacles
> Worthy bachelors, do!
> When wives are young and dutiful
> Honeymoon's pleasure abound;
> But who would wish for a beautiful
> Honeymoon all the year round?
> Then don't be too particular,
> But be kind and true;
> Don't *look* out for miracles,
> Very few wise men do.

The poor were speedily conditioned out of a beautiful honeymoon all the year round. Reality soon jerked them back to the common run of life; even if a bedroom could be furnished for ten pounds, ten pounds for the labourer was a vast sum in the hungry forties, when this kind of bargain was advertised: 'French bedstead, paillasse or mattress goose feather bed, bolster and pillow, linen ticks, three blankets, white counterpanes, two pair linen sheets, two pair pillow cases, wash stand, jug and basin, soap, brush, tray, toilet table, double towel airer, chest of drawers, two chairs, British plate, tray, glass, Kidderminster carpet, double-handed three-quart po-de-chambre.'[10] It must be remembered that as late as 1889 the dockers struck for a sixpence-an-hour wage.

It is doubtful whether the poor shared in any of the modifications that were made to marriage during Victoria's time on the throne. Possibly some benefited by the 1836 Marriage Act. This permitted religious ceremonies in Roman Catholic or Nonconformist places of worship to be legally binding. Before this date, on account of Lord Hardwick's notorious Marriage Act of 1753, no one could be legally married except by a parson of the Church of England. The 1836 act established civil officers called Registrars of Births, Deaths, and Marriages, and helped redefine marriage as a social condition as well as a religious union.

It is doubtful whether the poor gained much from the epoch-making Divorce Act of 1857, which made divorce possible without the need for a special bill through Parliament, or the Married Women's Property Act of 1870. For the first time, legally, a married woman was not an appendage to her lord and master, and although unscrupulous men still married for money, it was no longer a question of what's yours is mine, and what's mine is my own. A minor result of this important and hardly to be overestimated act was that lawyers were deprived of a time- and money-consuming job – building into marriage settlements safeguards for the wives.

The Married Women's Property Act also raised controversial issues for those engaged in the vexing question of women's suffrage. 'The grant of Women's Suffrage cannot be confined to spinsters,' declared the Earl of Shaftesbury. 'In the alterations at hand in respect to woman's property, it must be extended to wives; and this, conjoined with certain changes in the laws of marriage, now apparently inevitable, will remodel, as it were, the entire system of domestic life.'[11] The assumption that the new freedom extended to the wife would lead to new marriage legislation was one shared by many. It is astounding that so many reasonable men should have thought that votes for single women, but no votes for married women, was an acceptable compromise, though on the subject of votes for the masses, Shaftesbury was never other than reactionary; universal suffrage, he maintained, was 'creeping socialism'.

The Married Women's Property Act was the culmination of decades of hard work. Barbara Leigh Smith, a cousin of Florence Nightingale, was fortunate in that she had an enlightened father, who gave all his children, male and female, £300 a year on their coming of age. Independent in a way that was rare even amongst affluent young ladies of the fifties, Barbara Smith decided that it was her mission in life to alter and amend the laws of property, and to this end drew up and published, a *Brief Summary in plain Language of the most important Laws concerning Women*. This pamphlet was placed before a friend, Davenport Hill, recorder of Birmingham, and he in turn submitted it to the Law Amendment Society, which was obliged to examine it if only for the reason that Hill had helped found the Society. The Society gave the matter its attention and its approval, and in due course a giant petition was organized with 26,000 signatures. A bill was introduced in May 1857, but unfortunately it competed for parliamentary time with the Divorce Act, which had much more power to excite. The property act bill had two main purposes (a) to allow a woman to own property; (b) to allow her to make out a will. The *Saturday Review*, always there to uphold feudal rights, declared that the bill would 'set at defiance the common sense of mankind, and would revolutionise society. There is besides a smack of selfish independence about it which jars with poetical notions of wedlock.' It was a theme on which the *Saturday Review* perpetually evolved variations, a subject always good for a half-column. Apropos of pretty well nothing, it returned to the motif when the battle for woman's ownership of property was lost: 'Married life is a woman's profession . . . to this life her training – that of dependance – is modelled' (12 November 1859). The battle was lost because the battle for divorce was won; the Divorce Act had provision for legal separation that would permit of maintenance for an injured wife and the right to possess any future earnings or inheritance. If the divorced and separated woman had her own property, why should the happily married woman want her own property?

Although the 1870 Married Women's Property Act was incomplete and inadequate – it was not until 1882 that it covered all the areas commonly understood as property – it was a first sprouting of the seed of suffrage. The House of Lords had cut at the 1870 act until it was a vestige of the act that the House of Commons had had in mind when it had sent it across to their lordships. This vestige, however, was of prime importance – the right for women to keep their earnings; no longer could the drunk, the unemployable, or the profligate ransack the purses of their spouses with the confident knowledge that their actions were well within the law of the land. Of course, the class for whom this knowledge would have been most valuable – the poor – were usually not aware of the new freedoms of their womankind.

The cause of woman's property had a hidden caucus of support – trade. The twentieth century has seen the commercial exploitation of the teenager; the nineteenth was anxious to do the same with women. An expanding economy needed the purchasing power of woman. As it was, the law was so confusing, possibilities of fraud so great, the ability of men to renounce their wives' debts so universal, that trade was in despair. The Mercantile Law Conference was not, it admitted, bothered about 'the hardship sustained by married women'. The conference was interested only in traders and their profits. A solicitor of the Law Association for the Protection of Trades said: 'This state of law is a constant source of loss and annoyance to tradesmen, and such an alteration as would make women the owners of their own property, responsible for their own debts, would greatly increase the safety of trade transactions.' Naturally, in most cases, women were free to spend what they wanted; the money in their purses was, in practice if not in law, their own. If anything, their housekeeping money was more sacrosanct than the housekeeping money of their great-great-grand-daughters, if only for the reason that the Victorian household was a tiny empire, with its own minions and chain of command – the lower-middle-class house without at least one servant was very lowly indeed.

Reason and the conditions of industrial society were against the constrictions of outdated laws, but reaction was strongly entrenched. 'The protection which has been thrown around a married woman already is sufficient,' declared Lord Fraser in 1881, 'and why she should be allowed to have money in her pocket to deal with as she thinks fit I cannot understand.' Those who could understand, nevertheless, triumphed.

One of the most fascinating aspects of nineteenth-century marriage law was the crusade to legalize marriage with a deceased wife's sister. That this should be allowed was mooted early in Victorian England without anything coming of it, and the proposal came before the legislature subsequently in 1850, 1855, 1856, 1858, 1859, 1861, 1862 1866, 1869, 1870, 1871, 1872, 1873, 1875, 1877, 1878, 1879, 1880, 1882, 1883, 1884, 1886, 1888, 1889, 1890, 1891, 1896, 1898 and 1900. That someone, unaccountably long-lived, had a vested interest in the subject was plain to see. What is more difficult to discern is the reason for the strenuous opposition. It was a topic that engaged the highest interests in the land – in the 1879 session the Prince of Wales and the Duke of Edinburgh actually voted for it in the House of Lords. Gladstone had in earlier years taken a stand against it, but after a couple of decades he withdrew his opposition. Similarly the Earl of Shaftesbury, who, in response to the plea of Thomas Chambers who was sponsoring the bill for Shaftesbury's neutrality, wrote that in future, 'the people can have what they wish, and they, probably, will have it. I, for one, shall henceforward think it my duty to accept the measure and submit to the deliberate decision of the country,'[12] a charitable decision that went against his inclinations. More than a decade later he wrote to a friend that his personal opinion had 'remained the same ever since 1842, when he spoke against it in the House of Commons'. It was now 1883.

The attraction of this doomed and forlorn bill was that it went through the House of Commons quite easily but was blocked at every turn by the House of Lords, aided and abetted by the churches. In June, 1883, when it seemed as though the Lords might give in, Shaftesbury, conveniently forgetting his earlier resolution to let the mass of the people have their say, presided at a combined meeting of Church of England clerics, Presbyterians, Roman Catholics, and others, convened by the High Ritualistic Society, against the Deceased Wife's Sister Bill.

Why should there have been this opposition, why was it not until 1907 that the Deceased Wife's Sister Marriage Act was finally passed?

Briefly, the shadow of incest. Even the 1907 act permitted a clergyman to refuse to officiate, and it preserved as a quaint reminder of the 1857 act the view that adultery with a wife's sister was incestuous.

In 1882 Lord Dalhousie was trying to guide the bill through. He wrote to the aged relic of the Oxford movement, Edward Bouverie Pusey, for the theological implications of such a bill. Pusey had no doubts about the matter as he expounded in a uniquely ridiculous dogma:

Things are very much changed, since forty years ago a firm was employed to solicit signatures to petitions in favour of legalizing those marriages. The agitation was then, in favour of this particular marriage, from some known individuals who wished to marry their deceased wives' sisters. Now it has spread (as all such questions do spread) consistently, to the whole subject of affinity. Now the question is raised whether *any* affinity is a hindrance to marriage. If marriage with the deceased wife's sister is legalized, I do not see how any other marriage with one connected by affinity can be consistently maintained to be illegal . . .[13]

Pusey did not push a papier-mâché replica of Oedipus into the arena, but the implications are clear, thus: 'The principle is one, and as the question has been discussed, people have come to see that the whole subject of affinity is one, that the sisters, mothers, daughters (if there be any by a former marriage), are sisters, mothers, daughters to him, with whom the wife is become one flesh.'

Pusey pointed out, 'The social effects of the permission in Protestant Germany were said to be frightful,' and, while marriage was being discussed, it was worth mentioning divorce. 'We are already suffering so fearfully from the new Divorce Court, in which it is said to be notorious that every undefended suit is a case of collusion.' To return to the matter of deceased wives' sisters, there was no question that it was forbidden by Holy Writ (Leviticus xviii 6: 'None of you shall approach to any flesh of his flesh to uncover their nakedness, I am the Lord').

What was the clergy to do when it came to their notice that someone had committed the unforgivable, had, in fact, married a deceased wife's sister? If it was possible, of course, overlook it, or avert the eyes. Unfortunately there were some worthies who, having done this dastardly deed, had not realized the enormity of their offence, and, incestuous blackguards as they were, were rubbing salt into ecclesiastical wounds by requesting Holy Communion. Mandell Creighton, one-time Bishop of London, was confronted with this dilemma:

The question which you refer to me about admitting to Holy Communion persons not legally married is a serious one. I have had some difficulty in deciding what answer to give. But it seems to me that, so long as two persons *continue to live together unlawfully*, it is impossible to treat them as pious Christian people. If they pledge their word that they do not cohabit, but only live under the same roof, that alters the case. But so long as illicit cohabitation continues, the offence continues.[14]

There was one thing that *all* churchmen were agreed upon. Sin was bad. There was another thing that most of them were agreed upon. Marriage was a subject upon which they had the last word. No one else was equipped to deal with the matter. The notion that marriage was a means of regulating the sexual appetite of man and woman in society was beastly. Admittedly, there was some difficulty in reconciling sex and the soul, but diligent inquiry would reveal the answer.

The more adventurous went back to Swedenborg, the Swedish mystic for whom 'all knowledge is nuptial knowledge' and who proclaimed in the most unexceptional terms that sexual duality was the basis of all being. The clergy who found Swedenborg difficult had the aid of a layman, Coventry Patmore, for whom coitus was the supreme religious ecstasy, and who could rationalize in the most ultra-Swedenborgian style. The sexual embrace was a transcendental experience that paralleled the love from Christ: 'The relationship of the soul to Christ *as his betrothed wife* is the key to the feeling with which prayer and love and honour should be offered to Him. In this relation is a mine of undiscovered joy and power.'[15] Perhaps it was a disadvantage that Patmore was a Catholic, but one was not to worry, as this might be a transitory stage – 'Patmore,' wrote William Michael Rossetti in *Pre-Raphaelite Diaries and Letters* (1900), 'who became a fervent Roman Catholic toward 1863, was in 1849 a strict and indeed prejudiced Protestant.' In any case, should Patmore prove unacceptable, there were other theologians providing connecting links among Christ, the betrothed wife, and sex. To non-theologians, some of this identification can be torturous. One of the most lugubrious of nineteenth-century churchmen was the famous F. W. Robertson of Brighton, for whom beautiful woman was unattainable. A Swedish girl he met when he was eighteen gave him 'hair, lines, books', and he 'worshipped her only as I should have done a living rainbow, with no further feeling ... she was to me for years nothing more than a calm, clear, untroubled fiord of beauty, glassing heaven, deep, deep below, so deep that I never dreamed of an attempt to reach the heaven'.[16] He soon, reported his biographer, Stopford Brooke, incorporated these entirely unexceptional adolescent feelings into his religion. 'To Christ also, as the spotless Purity, he transferred his young belief in the entire stainlessness of womanhood. He saw in Him not only perfect manhood, but perfect womanhood.' Robertson and his ilk were the kind of people reckoned to be the ultimate authorities on the institutions of marriage. It was small wonder that when adaptations were made to the mechanisms of marriage – such as the Divorce Act of 1857 – the voluble protests of elements of the church were treated by the lawmakers not so much with anger as with contempt.

The family unit was believed by many to persist after death. That marriages were made in heaven, and presumably must continue there for otherwise why make them, was a self-evident proposition. Marriage as a mystical religious state was laid down for the reading public by Coventry Patmore in *The Angel in the House* (1854–66), and this sold 250,000 copies. The pursuers of this chimera – marriage and its corollaries in the hereafter – were therefore not an inconspicuous lunatic fringe.

Belief in a particular theory frequently does not depend on the amount of data available. Of the 250,000 readers who bought Patmore's book, many no doubt were alienated by the spiritualist movement, by its wagon train of crooks, by its mixture of credulity and pseudo-science, by the recantations of many formerly in its ranks, and by the human frailties of those key figures who clearly were out of the ordinary run. For example, D. D. Home, a medium of powers that are still inexplicable, forfeited much good will by marrying two Russian ladies in, some thought, over-rapid succession, and enticing from a rich woman £60,000 (the woman reclaimed it, successfully).

Like all movements that originated in Victorian times, the spiritualist movement is loaded with data that has never been evaluated. The *Proceedings* of the Society for Psychical Research contain material that is amply documented, fully substantiated by independent witnesses. Cases of what were known as 'phantasms of the living' exist in their hundreds, with names, addresses, and hard evidence. Victorian spiritualism was not just trumpets in the night, crystal gazing in Bayswater salons, and fake ghost photography by using two negatives or fancy processing.

Many devotees were unquestionably secretly ashamed of their devotion to spiritualism. There were others who were embarrassed by the necessity to cloak this belief in self-justification. F. W. H. Myers' apologia is more literate than most, but still does not disguise the egocentric springs of his belief:

I find that love in its highest – in its most spiritual-form is a passion so grossly out of proportion to the dimensions of life that it can only be defined, as Plato says, as 'a desire for the eternal possession' of the beloved object, – for his or her ever-growing perfection and bliss; while removal by death, if no reunion be looked for, at once reduces this life to an act of endurance alone.[17]

And why not, indeed?

'And who is your lean young friend with the frayed coat-cuffs?' Monckton Milnes was asked. The answer was Coventry Patmore. For many years Patmore has been of more interest as a character than as a poet, and numerous attempts to re-evaluate him from Clifford Bax in 1932 ('the most neglected of our notable poets')[18] onwards have met with scant response from a public never much interested in Victorian verse any way. The seal was set by Edmund Gosse's memorable dismissal in the *Athenaeum* in 1886 – 'this laureate of the tea-table, with his humdrum stories of girls that smell of bread and butter'.

Patmore is more amusing to write about than read. He is an authentic Janus-like man of the period. Arrogance and a savagery that could lead him to pen 'His leprosy's so perfect, men call him clean' of Gladstone was combined with the ability to fawn and kowtow at the drop of a hat. Colloquial domestic verse and high-sounding mysticism came forth with great fluency.

His background was unfortunate. His father, P. G. Patmore, speculated in railway shares during the boom (in November 1845 *The Times* reported that £500,000,000 was needed for 1,200 projected railway lines) and like so many of his contemporaries came a cropper. Finding himself in debt, he fled to France in 1845 to evade his creditors. Coventry Patmore's mother was undemonstrative and unsympathetic. It was not surprising that he early acquired a sense of inferiority. Richard Monckton Milnes, recognizing the promise of this young man, got him a job in the Reading Room of the British Museum, and used him when writing his *Life of Keats*.

Patmore married three times, first of all to Emily Augusta Andrews in 1847 ('Her Norman face; Her large sweet eyes, clear lakes of love'),[19] then to Marianne Byles, an invalid, and, finally, Harriet Robson in 1881. In addition, he had a 'passionate friendship' in 1892 with the poetess Alice Meynell (He disappointed her, she burned nearly all his letters, and turned her attentions towards George Meredith). When it is not ambling amiably among the tea cups, Patmore's *The Angel in the House* has a surprising zest and an even more astonishing sexuality. Patmore can pass from:

> He hoped the business was not bad
> I came about: then the wine pass'd.
> A full glass prefaced my reply:
> I loved his daughter, Honor; he knew
> My estate and prospects; might I try
> To win her? To mine eyes tears flew.

to

> She approach'd, all mildness and young trust,
> And ever her chaste and noble air
> Gave to love's feast its choicest gust,
> A vague, faint augry of despair.

and, rare in poetry, he could write of woman as the pursuer and not the pursued:

> Without his knowledge he was won;
> Against his nature kept devout;
> She'll never tell him how 'twas done,
> And he will never find it out.

> If, sudden, he suspects her wiles,
>   And hears her forging chain and trap,
> And looks, she sits in simple smiles,
>   Her two hands lying in her lap.

Tennyson said that some of Patmore's lines seemed 'hammered out of old nails'; Swinburne, contemptuous of Patmore's lack of 'ear', wrote a parody on *The Angel in the House* (though he, too, would have liked to have sold 250,000 copies of his *Poems and Ballads*). The appeal of *The Angel in the House* lay in the affirmation that domestic bliss was best, and that it could persist into the great unknown – occasionally Patmore was conscious that he had not spelled out the implications enough. Of the hero and heroine of his saga, he wrote in a notebook of 1861: 'It must be impressively shown that Felix and Honoria also look to Heaven for the fruition of their love.' He contemplated *The Wife in Heaven*, but it remains in skeleton only. At best, his conviction that the consummation of love is reserved in its most crystalline form for the hereafter is declared with a power that reminds one of Blake. In his ode, 'To the Body' (1877), the erotic imagery is also striking:

> Thou needs must, for a season, lie
> In the grave's arms, foul and unshriven
> Albeit, in Heaven,
> Thy crimson-throbbing Glow
> Into its old abode aye pants to go.

In *Religio Poetae* (1893), Patmore wrote: 'The whole of after-life depends very much upon how life's transient transfiguration in youth by love is subsequently regarded.' That he was not at all sure how far he could go – remembering that he was now a Catholic – is evident by the fact that he destroyed what was described by Herbert Read as 'a lost masterpiece': 'Sponsa Dei', which, said Edmund Gosse who read the manuscript, 'was not more or less than an interpretation of the love between the soul and God by an analogy of the love between a woman and a man; it was, indeed, a transcendental treatise on divine desire seen through the veil of human desire'. 'Nuptial love,' wrote Patmore (*Religio Poetae*) 'bears the clearest marks of being nothing other than the rehearsal of a communion of a higher nature.'

Even so, Patmore found it difficult to reconcile vision with reality. His first wife was malleable, a writer of children's verse, *Nursery Rhymes by Mrs Motherly*, whose role was 'instant submission' to her husband's 'slightest wish'. Her fears that Coventry would turn Catholic were justified. To the end of his life, Patmore devoted the anniversary of her death to prayer and seclusion. It has been speculated that the second Mrs Patmore's invalidism made sexual intercourse a doubtful proposition. It it certain that the third Mrs Patmore was, compared with the previous two, something of a cipher. It was also apparent to Patmore that outside the marriage bonds, too, girls did not necessarily smell of bread and butter and that the puppy dog admiration he succeeded in purveying so admirably in poetry for Woman was not altogether suitable. The divine sanctity of the female vagina was not always implacable, as shown by this passage:

A man, however degraded he may be, has a secret horror of an innocent young woman allowing the last intimacies to a man whom she does not passionately love; but the innocent young woman, with full knowledge, usually yields, without remorse, the sanctities of her person to any man, whose companionship is not actually repulsive, in order to 'improve her station' and to get a house and babies of her own. The man she regards as an *accident*. This proves that she has really no consciousness of personal sanctity which is indeed so horribly outraged, if only she could see it, by bodily conjunction without mutually passionate love, that though it would not do to preach such a doctrine – it is absolutely true that adultery, with such love, is far less essentially immoral than the most exemplary marriage without it.

One need hardly add that this memorandum of Patmore's was not published.

At its lowest level, Patmore's writings made sex in marriage respectable. 'In vulgar minds the idea of passion is inseparable from that of disorder,' he wrote in *Rod, Root and Flower* (1895), and, in *Principle in Art* (1879), 'The best use of the supremely useful intercourse of man and woman is not the begetting of children, but the increase of contrasted personal consciousness.' When one penetrates the studied and not too elegant prose style of Patmore, one is suprised by what exactly he is saying. Without being air-fairy or too prosaic, he made sex in the hereafter a proposition not inherently absurd; wisely he did not pay too much attention to the mechanics of it.

The Wedding Ceremony

The wedding ceremony could be used for a variety of purposes, several of which only peripherally concerned the happy couple. It could be an instrument of *Realpolitik*, it could be a nostalgic ritual, and it could be a means of flaunting wealth and social position. It could also be a wildly amusing farce, in which the disparate elements of Victorian life resolutely refused to jell. It could be an opportunity among the lower orders for a gigantic party, while for the rich a society wedding could provide a setting for some Draconian one-upmanship.

For the rich, there were two styles of wedding – the town wedding, and the country wedding. Where there were estates involved, and bridegroom's parents wanted to impress bride's parents, or vice versa, there was nothing quite like a country wedding. Lady Dorothy Nevill was married in 1847. 'We were married in the old English style – the tenantry drawn up at the gate, and all the neighbourhood jolly and gay with that robust happiness once the characteristic of English country life.' She admitted that she went through the ceremony without the *sang-froid* of her sister who 'at her wedding announced that she was not at all nervous or upset, as she saw nothing to be ashamed of in being married'.[20] Richard Monckton Milnes, ace of pornography collectors, was married in 1851 to the sister of Lord Crewe, and this wedding, too, was in the old English tradition. At the 'Crewe Arms' 120 of the tenantry dined, the celebrations lasted for three days, and meat and ale was given to the poor, and presents to the bride included Oriental pearls, a ruby and diamond locket, a massive gold bracelet, three brooches of blue enamel, diamonds to go down her gown, a dressing-case, a 'blotting-book with electro-silver embossed figures' (after all, it was the year of the Great Exhibition), and a gold penholder set with stones. Small wonder that Monckton Milnes, now in his early forties and decidedly podgy and faded, thought that he was marrying into the right circles, though he must have wished that his father was not so outright and blunt when he engaged his new wife in conversation thus: 'Are you aware, in Protestant Germany, how easily you may be divorc'd? They don't require, as with us, any thing serious – only some incompatibility and almost any will do. A difference between you and Richard about your white dog would be quite enough.'

Of all the traditions that have seeped from the nineteenth into the twentieth century, the church wedding has changed less than most. The basic wedding dress is still made of lace, irrespective of the fact that the ability to buy lace is no longer indicative of a certain *ton* (before machine-made lace, this material was, weight for weight, more expensive than gold). The formula of the wedding service is basically unchanged, though the trips and snares of wedding etiquette are less in evidence. By the end of the nineteenth century, certain forms were being dropped. Groomsmen – male equivalent of the bridesmaid – were no longer necessary, and sending wedding cake around to friends who could not turn up at the ceremony was beginning to be considered vulgar. It remained the bridegroom's job to furnish the wedding ring; it was also his duty to equip bride and bridesmaids with bouquets, and the bridesmaids with presents. It was a great solecism to omit doing this. The chief bridesmaid was almost certain to be the bride's eldest unmarried sister. The nineteenth-century wedding included the donations of wedding favours by bridesmaids to the guests – sprigs of orange blossom with silver leaves and a white satin ribbon for the women, silver oak leaves and acorns for the men.

It was difficult, but not impossible, for some *faux pas* to be committed in the church, as there were a sufficient number of experts among the officiating clergy to prevent anything frightful happening. It was considered bad form for the bride and groom to hurry out; a leisurely mode of procedure along the centre aisle was much preferred. There were, of course, certain 'in' churches, and if one could get some high-ranking cleric to do the honours, then so much the better. Yet even the most fashionable churches had their disadvantages:

A wedding dress – all white satin, lace, and silver sprigs. Methinks I can see it now, glistening and sparkling in the August sun, and rustling and crumpling in the August season, its beautiful wearer descends that ugly narrow little staircase, which has been a ladder of delight to so many, a *via dolorosa* to so many more, and which leads from the vestry-room of St George's, Hanover Square, into Maddox Street.

Any disasters in the church had usually a comic opera quality:

Fourteen young bridesmaids in white have wept at the responses. Two have fainted, and one has been carried into the vestry, to be sal-volatilised. A nervous clergyman has addressed the bride-expectant as 'Thomas, wilt thou have this man to be thy wedded wife?' The bridegroom has been seized with the usual deadly perturbation, and offers to place the ring on the finger of the pew-opener.

A certain cachet could be obtained by the manner in which one inscribed one's name in the register; for example: '. . . by the bridegroom in a character meant to be very valiant and decided, but in reality very timorous and indistinct; by the bride with no pretence or compromise, but in a simply imbecile and hysterical manner; by the father of the bride in a neat hand I should like to see at the bottom of a cheque'.[21]

Characteristically nineteenth-century etiquette considered the widow to be a second-class citizen when it came to marriage. As for the divorced, they were unmentionable species. The widow going into matrimony for a second time was not allowed to wear a favour, nor orange blossom, nor a veil, nor white. White was the prerogative of the virgin, even when the virgin was getting on a little in years, as was Augusta, the bride-to-be of Dean Stanley. There is a certain ambience about the congratulations of the young Princess Beatrice (the one who was shocked at seeing corsets on open sale in royal Windsor): 'I hope you are quite well dear Guska. I find it very extraordinary that you are going to be married [many others found it equally so]. Are you going to marry here, and when are you going to marry? Is it this year? I suppose you are going to dress in a low white gown, or are you going to have a high white gown?' [22]

Outside the church, it was possible to impress by a display of carriages. If one had coats of arms on them, these could be refurbished and tarted up for the occasion. At the wedding breakfast, the presents could be displayed. 'It is a pretty fashion to surround the presents with flowers, notably roses, and this is often done by persons of artistic tastes.' So 'A Member of the Aristocracy' wrote in her book on etiquette. At the wedding breakfast, the unwritten laws of class could strike down the ignorant; a lady who took off her bonnet or hat was immediately recognized as an outsider.

There were two kinds of wedding breakfast, the standing-up and the sitting-down. The ladies and gentlemen went in two by two, to sip the champagne and other wines. If they were confronted by tea or coffee, they would know that someone was not well versed in wedding ceremonials – these drinks were absolutely forbidden. One could take soup, entrées, chicken, game, mayonnaises, salads, jellies, creams; the soup could be discovered in covered soup cups spread along the length of the table(s). Sherry was OK at standing-up breakfasts, but out at sitting-down. Beef and mutton were considered beneath the occasion. Table napkins were the thing for sitting-down breakfasts, but it was considered bad form to supply these for the standing-up variety. At class-conscious wedding breakfasts there would be a good deal of fuss over who was the person of highest rank, as there was a good chance that he might be called upon to propose the health of the bridesmaids.

After the breakfast came the going away. Confetti was considered decidedly ill-bred, and rice was not much better, though the satin slipper slung at the departing couple was still in order. Woe betide unmarried girls who participated in the rice throwing; this was a job reserved for the married ladies. The presents would be sent to the couple's home. It was bad form to put them on show, but it was even worse to place the wedding-cake ornaments under a glass dome as if they were stuffed birds or trophies, and only a shade less vulgar to similarly deify the bridal bouquet.

In the country there would no doubt be some village chil-dren who would throw flowers on the path for the bride to walk over, and unquestionably the peasants would want to show their respects. At the return home of the Nevills, the tenantry in-cluded in their presents 'bowls of beautiful rich cream, the re-membrance of which is still implanted upon my memory. The cream looked delicious, but it was so infected with the taste and smell of turnips that it quite overpowered one ...' [23] Yes, even the well-to-do had their problems.

The wedding as an instrument of state policy was well under-stood by the nineteenth century. In 1863 the wedding of the Prince of Wales and Alexandra of Denmark was used by Queen Victoria as a means of conveying to her people her grief at the death of her husband two years before, by the City as a means of demonstrating their loyalty, and by the people as a means of forgetting their multitude of troubles. The arrival of Princess Alexandra in London on 7 March (three days before the wed-ding) was also a great event, though it was bungled and badly managed. Around St Paul's tiers of seats had been erected to seat 10,000 people, and they watched the dignitaries in their finery marching by. The diarist William Hardman found these minor figures tiresome : 'I thought they would never cease dribbling along, and began to think we were doomed to see Common Councilmen for the rest of our days.' [24] During the procession, the rain came. The police in their top hats lost control, and the cortège was stuck for half an hour on London Bridge.

For the wedding, the arrangements were even more spectacu-lar. Statues and portraits of obscure Danish kings lined routes, and there were triumphal arches of white, gold, and purple. Temple Bar had not yet been carted away to its new rural home, and was covered by a cloth of gold covered with hearts. In the immediate vicinity of St Paul's there were said to be 2,000,000 people taking a preview of the scene. For the occasion, electric lighting was to be used to illumine St Paul's, but this proved a failure. No one had anticipated the interest of the populace. Six people were killed in the crush.

It was a time for fun and frolic. Ten days before the wedding, someone hoaxed *The Times*: 'ROYAL PROCESSION. First floor, with two large widows, to be let, in the best part of Cockspur Street, with entrance accessible behind. For cards apply to Mr Lindley, No. 19 Catherine Street, Strand, W.C.' Nineteen Catherine Street happened to be a house 'of evil repute'. Londoners were tickled to death by this lapse on the part of 'The Thunderer', and a copy of this particular issue was soon fetching seven shillings and sixpence.

Generally speaking, the English are pretty good at spectacular turnouts, but something went decidedly wrong with the Prince of Wales's wedding. Lord Malmesbury (a Foreign Secretary for a couple of years in the fifties) wrote: 'I was never more surprised and disappointed. The carriages looked old and shabby and the horses very poor, with no trappings, not even rosettes, and no outriders. In short, the shabbiness of the whole cortège was beyond anything one could imagine.' *The Times* was even severer:

Our Queen's equipages have not of late years been remarkable either for their beauty or for the taste and finish with which they are turned out, and certainly the servants, carriages, and cattle selected to convey the Danish Princess through joyful London attired in its holiday clothing must have been the very dregs of that singularly ill-appointed establishment known as the Royal Mews of Pimlico.

It was construed that Queen Victoria was getting back at her eldest son for the trouble he had caused her husband during his last years and that she resented anyone being happy when she was still wallowing in grief. The ceremony was not performed in London at all, but at St George's Chapel, Windsor. The Queen herself was hardly radiant in black crepe, though, recorded by Lady Augusta Bruce (later Stanley), 'Most beautiful Her expression was, tho' more drawn and pinched than usual.' A Mrs Wellesley even speculated that the Queen was 'cheery', though 'the trumpets, which were too much for any of us, almost overcame Her'. The doleful mien of the Queen affected the bevy of princesses, who 'wept as they saw their Brother's advance without his Father, and presently *a Person* wept also, but when cross-examined, did not know why, and was *indignant* at the idea of its being because she saw the others weep!'

The ceremony was lugubrious. 'The Queen,' wrote Mary Stanley, the sister of Dean Stanley, 'was agitated and restless, moving her chair, putting back her long streamers.' Young Prince William of Prussia (later Kaiser William of World War I fame) created an incident by throwing something across the chapel to relieve the monotony. The music, predictably, was composed by the Prince Consort, and this further affected the Queen. She 'raised her eyes upwards and sat as if transfixed'. Prince William of Prussia proved to be intractable and unmoved by the occasion; when the Queen later asked a companion of his if he had been good, the answer was, 'Oh no, he was *biting* us all the time.'

The assorted nobility and aristocracy used the wedding to show off their finery. Lady Augusta Bruce clearly fancied herself ('the mauve silk with petticoat of tulle mauve *bouillonne* and upper skirt of silk *en châle*, trimmed with Mechlin lace, mauve and white Rhododendron wreath, flowers and lappets. Dressmaker £42 13s'[25]) though she had to compete with the younger and the prettier, such as Lady Spencer in a cerulean blue gown with magnificent lace that had once belonged to Marie Antoinette. There was dissatisfaction among the noble ranks; many of their number had been excluded. After a totting up of essential personages, it had been found that there were just four places left in the chapel, and the Queen had donated two of these to Disraeli and his wife in preference to the batch of bluebloods clamouring for entrance.

After the wedding was all over, and it was time for the privileged to go back to London, there was more bad management at the station. A mob had disrupted everything, the station was closed, and the aristocracy were forbidden the platform. They had to climb through windows to get into the station, and when the train came in there was a mad rush for compartments (travellers on the London Underground railway will know how they felt, but it was a novel experience for the upper classes). Lady

Westminster found herself, loaded with diamonds, among a rough crowd, and 'the great ones of the land were too thankful to find themselves safe in a 3rd class' carriage to worry about the proprieties of being there. The Archbishop of Canterbury had an especially tough time; he was suddenly lost in the crowd, shouting 'Policeman, what can I do?' The policeman replied, 'Hold on to the next carriage, your grace, it's your only chance.' Back in London, Bishop Tait of London was baited by the mob. It had not been a particularly happy time for the high ecclesiastics. *Punch* had suggested that as the wedding was to be in an obscure Berkshire village noted only for its old castle and with no sanitary arrangements, the greatest secrecy should be observed, and that the only token to the outside world should be an announcement in the marriage column of *The Times*. 'On the 10th inst., at Windsor, by Dr Longley, assisted by Dr Thomson, Albert Edward England, K.G., to Alexandra Denmark. No cards.' Many of the guests who had suffered at the ceremony and afterwards, no doubt wished that this had been the case.

Conceivably only two people merge with credit from this 1863 *débâcle* – the Prince of Wales and Princess Alexandra. There was an honesty about the Princess that contrasts strikingly with the conspicuous display of her adopted country's top ten thousand. When she visited the Queen, during the engagement, Victoria asked her why she always wore a jacket. 'Oh, I wear it because it is so economical. You can wear it with any sort of gown; and you know I have always had to *make* my own gowns. I have never had a lady's maid, and my sisters and I all made our own clothes.'[26] A 'lady residing at Windsor' said 'she was sure the Prince was a person of no mind at all, as he had gone up to the bookstall and bought a copy of *Punch* and actually paid for it himself'. The royal couple got through the ordeal with almost somnambulistic tact, though no doubt they were glad eventually to shake off the gloom of Windsor, then something of a living tomb.

Swank also played a large part in the weddings of lesser folk, and the middle classes spent more than they could afford. A writer in *Chambers's Journal* of 1881 summed up the predicament: 'It is undoubtedly immoral to make marriage difficult and imprudent by artificial means, but this is really what ostentatious weddings often do. They give a false start to people with small incomes.'

It was easy for the anonymous journalist to give advice, and easier still to be smug:

No doubt it requires some resolution to make a dead set against the follies of the age; and a dread of singularity is often conspicuous in the young. It is amusing sometimes to notice how frightened a young girl is – frightened is really not too strong a word – lest her dress should not be 'what is worn'. No doubt the dread of singularity – a dread which is sometimes akin to modesty – in a great measure actuates the feeling.

The writer went on to suggest that the upper classes could provide a good example by cutting down on their own weddings, a fatuous suggestion that could only have been made in the nineteenth century. What was station for if not to reduce the lower orders to a quivering obsequious pulp?

The wedding customs of the masses were always good for a laugh. Chatty little articles appeared in middle-class journals written by clergymen who had been convulsed by the ignorance of their flock. At one provincial wedding, the only other person present beyond bride, groom, best man, and bridesmaid, was a stout elderly woman who stationed herself at the back of the church. On occasions it seemed as if she would interpose, especially where the hostile are requested to 'Speak, or else hereafter for ever hold their peace'. After the service, the clergyman cornered her and asked who she was. 'I am the girl's mother, and I came to prevent the business.' Asked why she had not, she said that the thought had struck her that they 'might do worse than get married after all'. There were always yarns to be told about the wedding ring that slipped down a grating, while 'marrying a couple one or both of whom are deaf is a funny experience'. When one of them was feeble-minded, and could not escape from the conviction that he was the M. of 'I, M., take thee, N., to be my wedded wife', that M. was his name, a sort of religious pseudonym, then hilarity knew no bounds. It was also considered amusing when a couple who wanted to get married by licence thought that the clergyman could make one out on the spot. In the more rustic parts, unwilling girls were pressurized into marriage by cunning men telling them that as the man had put up the banns, the girl would have to get married any way, irrespective of her own wishes or those of her parents. One mother: 'Oh, she doesn't want to marry him; but I s'pose she must now, 'cause the banns are put up.' (The clergyman [27] who wrote this anecdote had evidently been influenced by the speech patterns of Little Eva in *Uncle Tom's Cabin*). At one wedding, the couple went to church in the local fly. On arrival there, the groom told the driver that he was to act as 'his man' and that being best man was part of the job.

In the domestic novels of the period, the weddings are invariably punctuated by the mysterious young man who rises up in the middle of the ceremony and objects. This was a convenient fiction taken over *en bloc* by the movie-makers. In fact, this was quite a rare occurrence. Fear of being conspicuous countermanded the desire to prevent a marriage; life does not have such neat plots as fiction.

Francis Anstey (real name Thomas Anstey Guthrie) is best known today for his amusing farce *Vice Versa* (1882). In his day, he was a prolific contributor of little playlets to *Punch*. His *At a Wedding* includes in its *dramatis personae* the young man who considers that he has been treated badly:

Bride and Bridegroom pass slowly down central passage, recognizing their friends at hazard; several are left unnoticed with their elaborately prepared smile wasting its sweetness on the bride's brothers. A young man, rather negligently dressed, who has been standing behind *Mrs Ripplebrook* the whole time forces his way to the front.
The Y.M. (to himself). She *shall* see me – if she has the courage to meet my eye after her conduct!
The Bride. What, Mr Oldglove? I'd no idea you were in town! We shall see you presently, I hope.

Temporarily, Mr Oldglove stands on his dignity, but turns up at the reception.

Mr Oldglove (who has come on after all – bitterly to the *Bride*). All I can wish you, Mrs – (choking) – Mrs Pilbergilt, is that you may be as happy as – as you *deserve*!

The Bride (sweetly). Thanks awfully. That's the prettiest thing I've had said to me yet. (To neighbour). Oh, Mr Cashley, how *am* I to thank you? – that *lovely* plate-warmer!

(Mr O. retires baffled, and contemplates committing suicide with a piece of wedding-cake.)

So could a melodramatic situation be turned into farce by a cool observer. For what it is worth, Anstey's collected pieces from Punch, published in 1892 as *Voces Populi*, are as superbly evocative of the period as that masterpiece of Victorian humour, Grossmith's *Diary of a Nobody*.

The laconic wedding is well worth a mention. Sir John Astley was a man who devoted his entire life to sport. 'As my 30th birthday came off on February 19th, 1858, I had pretty well made up my mind it was about time I got wed, and changed the cinder-path and spiked shoe for the polished floor and varnished pump.' Two pages of his autobiography pass. 'On the Saturday of the Derby week, May 22nd, 1858, we were married at St James's Church, and all agreed that it was a right jolly wedding.' [28] When Sidney Webb got married in the early nineties, the organ of his brand of socialism, the *Fabian News*, was even more prosaic; it waited six months, and then announced, 'Sidney Webb and Beatrice Potter have married one another'. Then there was the romantic elopement; these marriages had a high failure rate, and Lady Florence Paget, known as the 'Pocket Venus', made a bad bargain when she jilted Harry Chaplin in favour of the Marquis of Hastings, who was something of a cad. The wedding date with Mr Chaplin had been fixed, the presents were rolling in in their aristocratic profusion. A few days before the date, Lady Florence went shopping in the West End. She went into Marshall and Snelgrove's by a minor entrance, went through the store, and left by the Oxford Street way, where the Marquis of Hastings was waiting for her with a licence. It is an interesting facet of psychology that one tends to hate those one has injured, and the attitude of the marquis towards his wife's erstwhile lover was little less than malevolent. Chaplin and the Marquis of Hastings were both passionately concerned with horse racing. In 1865, Chaplin bought a colt named Hermit, which he entered for the 1867 Derby, and in pique, Hastings bet heavily against the horse; it would seem that he was on a good thing, for Hermit had a severe haemorrhage, and although Chaplin continued to believe in the capabilities of his horse, the news of the misfortune got around, the price went down to 66-to-1, Hastings continued to bet against him, the day was cold and snowy, and it appeared that Chaplin was courting disaster. Nevertheless, Hermit won by a neck, Chaplin cleaned up £140,000, and the Marquis of Hastings lost £120,000, two thirds of this sum to Chaplin, though it took him several months to pay up, with Chaplin waiting with seraphic benevolence. The stealing of other men's fiancées did not always meet with such graphically providential intervention.

Romantic Love and Marriage

'Who, without agonies of desire, could see breasts round and hard as an apple; a skin whiter than the driven snow, suffused with a glowing warmth, that brightened the colour and heightened the temptation, softer than the down of swans and sweeter than all the balmy spices of Arabia?' The question is posed by the anonymous pornographic author of *The New Metamorphosis* (*circa* 1843). The answer, so far as men were concerned, was – more than one might imagine. It was better to marry than burn, said St Paul, with the complacent implication that he was himself equipped with the self-restraint to do neither one, but in the nineteenth century there was a considerable portion of the male population who could vie with St Paul in his ability to remain celibate. It was not considered odd for men to remain outside the sparring ring of marriage, and there was no shortage of non-combatants.

There were many who were forced to eschew marriage on financial and family grounds, to find, as they reached their forties, that the bloom had disappeared from the peach, both literally and figuratively. Fiancées who had remained true to them over the years were no longer so comely. Honour being what it was, some men made the sacrifice and went despairingly into a middle-aged marriage.

However, for many men not particularly ardent nor captivated by marriage as an institution, there were family pressures. If there was not to be a marriage through love, then there was marriage as a therapeutic. For women, marriage was reckoned to be a sure cure for hysteria, and even madness, as well as an antidote to heartless playing about by previous suitors or imaginary suitors. The formal etiquette of the nineteenth century often misled ladies. 'It is not usual to ascertain a gentleman's wishes as to whether he will be introduced to a lady or not,' wrote 'A Member of the Aristocracy', but ladies who were introduced willy-nilly to acceptable men assumed that this was because they were destined to be soul mates. Arbitrary introductions could lead to far-reaching and uncomfortable misunderstandings, for example, this excerpt from the *Pink 'Un*, 5 February 1890:

> Men are usually ignorant how girls note and weigh the attentions they received, and they impart the details of such homage to sympathetic – if envious – feminine ears, thus giving body to vague nothings, and brooding over trifles till they gather shape. Meanwhile the man having said the pretty things his idea of politeness has prompted, goes away, forgetting them and their recipient, while she is expecting a declaration as the result of a few soft nothings, a squeeze of the hand, or some tender glances.

So far as marriage was concerned, it was a man's world. He could marry or not marry as he chose. Until the Married Women's Property Act (1870) was passed, and even then, he could sacrifice himself for someone for whom he did not care with the certain knowledge that as soon as the rites were performed he would be at liberty to run through any money his wife had. When a marriage was decided upon by a girl's parents as a therapeutic measure, a man could be bribed to take her. In, for example, the Peaty case of 1867, the husband was hardly more than a paid gigolo, though in this case he got more than he perhaps anticipated, in disillusion if not in money.

The future Mrs Peaty had been diagnosed by a Dr Lee as a

case of hysteria, for which the remedy was marriage. He did not think her condition was very serious, though she was under the impression that she was Princess Charlotte, and was in a 'wild and excited condition' on her wedding day, walking into church alone to the surprise of the congregation. Her husband was a £200-a-year clerk at the Bank of England, and no doubt he thought that he was on to a good thing as his wife-to-be had £3,000, nominally tied up as it was by that bugbear of every young man on the make, trustees. He found to his surprise that life at home was every bit as hectic as life at the bank (the Bank of England was not the sedate establishment it is now; fighting dogs were chained to the clerks' desks so that they could be matched against each other in the lavatories, and ledgers and customers' passbooks were used as missiles). He found that his wife got up in the night, nude, and rang all the bells in the house. He might well have had qualms at the wedding break-fast, when his wife kissed a young man, telling him that it was his 'own fault he was not the bridegroom'. Mrs Peaty also wore rags around her wrists, believing them to be bracelets, and did not wash for several days at a time, considering that she was 'too pure'. She instructed her husband to read the communion ser-vice every night to her, and a month after marriage she walked through the streets in her wedding dress and a nightdress, a cash box under each arm. It was clear that she was mad; a doctor named Baker Brown performed a mysterious operation on her, unknown to her husband. Marriage had not worked its miracle, and a divorce was set in motion. The husband was not too happy about this. If she was mad, he declared, it was through extreme love for him (the husband).

The participants of marriage, even those engaged in such an ill-starred matched as Mr and Mrs Peaty, were in no position to see the marriage state objectively. Dazed by love and anticip-ation, they read into a pragmatic social arrangement for the rear-ing of children and the satisfaction of the sexual instinct factors that were not there. In April 1871 a promising young clergyman wrote:

Copleston made a profound remark the other day, that everyone thought their own love story exceedingly romantic. I think it is a true statement, but I never thought that of ours; its genuineness and sincerity struck me more: two human souls absolutely rushed together because they saw there was nothing else to do consistently with continuing to exist. That was something better than romantic, was it not? [29]

This statement is interesting, in that the writer, Mandell Creighton, could state what he considered a truth, and then immediately contradict himself by making a personal exception, thus affirming more than ever the truth of the initial statement. 'Two human souls absolutely rushed together' is, however, the essence of the romantic view.

It is a commonplace that love has always been the prime spur to poets; it is also a commonplace that for poets marriage has been the funereal baked meat of love. Auto-intoxicated by love, writers have frequently rushed into print with a passion that they were afterwards to regret. The young Disraeli in his novel *Henrietta Temple* (1837) put into the mouth of one of the characters the conventional view of sensitive adolescence:

The gratification of the senses soon becomes a very small part of that profound and complicated sentiment, which we call love. Love, on the contrary, is an universal thirst for a communion, not merely of the senses, but of our whole nature, intellectual, imaginative, and sensitive. He who finds his antitype, enjoys a love perfect and enduring; time cannot change it, distance cannot remove it; the sympathy is complete.

Disraeli confirmed this in another early novel, *Contarini Fleming* (1832): 'Talk of fame and romance, all the glory and adventure of the world are not worth one single hour of domestic bliss.' Devious and sharp, the reality of Disraeli was not quite of the immaculate order of his theory: 'Dizzy married me for my money, but if he had the chance again he would marry me for love,' wrote his wife. She might have added in parenthesis, 'I hope.' Heavily in debt, a dandy, a parliamentary meteor, Disraeli was captivated by this widow of forty-five, with a grand house in Park Lane, and an income of around £4,000 a year. 'I am mad with love,' he wrote to her. 'My passion is frenzy. The prospect of our immediate meeting overwhelms and entrances me. I pass my nights and days in scenes of strange and fascinating rapture . . .' His bride-to-be, Mrs Wyndham Lewis, had confided to her friend Mrs Duncan Stewart that after her husband's death she had had many offerss, but they were all after her money, with the exception of Disraeli, whom she knew loved her and not her prospects 'because he showed his affection and love to me while my first husband was alive'. In the end, she proposed to him: 'I brought the matter to a head by laying my hand on his and saying, "Why should not we two put our two fortunes together?" and thus it came about that we were engaged.'

The Disraeli–Mrs Lewis match demonstrates very clearly the complex factors that go to make up a marriage. To do Disraeli justice, he did admit to his fiancée that he had made up to her on account of her money, but had discovered that he loved her. During the honeymoon on the continent, she dressed in a manner that reminded him of Madame de Pompadour, but as the honeymoon lasted three months no doubt Disraeli managed to accustom himself to such foibles.

What Disraeli called the universal thirst for communion was a multi-purpose switch that activated the most diverse of characters. In his sentimental poem 'Remembrance' (1827) John Ruskin, then aged eighteen, penned his recollections of the young daughter of his father's partner in the successful sherry firm, the firm that was to make him always financially self-sufficient. Ruskin began the verse by saying that he ought to be joyful, what with the fond memories of jest, song, smile, and tone of voice of beloved. But he was now alone. Adele had returned to France.

> Alone, said I, dearest? Oh, never we part –
> For ever, for ever, thou'rt here in my heart;
> Sleeping or waking, where'er I may be,
> I have but one thought, and that thought is of thee.

Self-immolation on the spokes of memory was ever to be Ruskin's lot. As with all failed and disappointed lovers, memory was subject to distortion and rationalization. After his marriage, unconsummated, disastrous, he was again alone. Long before John Millais took his wife off his hands, he was temporarily parted from her. He wrote to her:

> I expect a line from my dearest love tomorrow at Sens. Do you know, pet, it seems almost a dream to me that we have been married? I look forward to meeting you; and to your *next* bridal night; and to the time when I shall again draw your dress from your snowy shoulders; and lean my cheek against them, as if you were still my betrothed only; and I had never held you in my arms.

If this statement were true, it would make hay of every theory relating to Ruskin's love life. It would raise the questions: Was the marriage consummated after all? Was the nullity suit a put-up job? Was there – against the views held by Ruskin scholars – a considerable degree of love play that stopped short of copulation? Or did Ruskin's sexual proclivities not include copulation but include various other facets of sexual pleasure? Idle speculation, of course. Ruskin's amorous declaration means little, affirming rather that men – and women – are not to be trusted to adhere strictly to the truth when they are discussing their own love life, that the relationship between a man and a woman being the most personal of all relationships is the one more subject to distortion, deliberate or involuntary. Add to this the mystique of Victorian marriage, that it was made in heaven, and one has a situation open to almost any interpretation.

Poets of the period, especially those appealing to the more sensitive lower middle classes, were in love with love. Mrs Felicia Hemans (1793-1835) belongs strictly to the Regency period, dying during the reign of William IV, but she was widely popular during Victoria's time. Although her marriage was inauspicious – her soldier husband left her within a few years – love triumphant was a constantly occurring theme in her verse (there are seven hundred pages of double columns of it), even in situations that are ludicrous or macabre. In her *Records of Woman* (1828) there is a poem entitled 'Gertrude: or Fidelity Till Death'. One verse runs:

> Her hands were clasped, her dark eyes raised,
> The breeze threw back her hair;

Up to the fearful wheel she gazed –
  All that she loved was there.
The night was round her clear and cold,
  The holy heaven above,
Its pale stars watching to behold
  The might of earthly love.

If this were couched in a less insipid format, this would be
poetry of an extreme situation, for the husband is being tortured
to death on the wheel. If poetesses could be thrown into a tizzy
by the very mention of love, so were their readers, a class who
would today be catered for by middle-brow romantic fiction.
True, they had their own periodicals, such as the *Family Herald*,
started in 1842 by George Biggs to use the first composing
machine, and which was fit to be read by children; and they had
their own fiction. For high-flown romance, however, there was
nothing quite like verse; popular fiction had a quaint tendency
to portray life as it really was, as the writer Mrs E. C. Grey complained in her *The Little Wife* of 1841: 'Novel-writing has
completely changed its character. From its high-flown, elaborate
style, it is now fallen into its opposite extreme; from improba-
bilities, always impalpable, sometimes gross, now, in their place,
we find nothing but the hum-drummeries of reality.'

A contemporary novelist, J. M. Rymer, saw the scene differently. In his 1846 *Jane Brightwell* he refers to 'the maudlin
sickly fashion of the present day. ... All this clinging affection,
about which so much romantic nonsense is continually written
by ladies' maids, and lovesick boys, merely arises from habit and
a weak intellect.' The romantic nonsense, despite these strictures, was more likely to have been written by hardboiled professionals, who made their heroines pure as driven snow, and
whose heroes had 'light hazel tigerish eyes, of great depth and
brilliancy'.[30] The hacks had a potent effect on Victorian behaviour, especially on the respectable working class and the not-
very-bright lower middle class, spreading a gospel of virtue and
light, the admen of a love free from all gross appurtenances;
and, as with the admen of our own day, the ultimate result was
confusion and bamboozlement. Love became romance, a state
that is defined by one dictionary as 'a fictitious narrative in prose

or verse which passes beyond the limits of real life'. As an expression of a love that never was on land or sea, there was no doubt a niche for the more specious romantic fiction; honest escapism ever has its devotees. However, many readers took the standards of hack fiction as their norm and were distressed when ordinary behaviour – their own as well as others' – failed to match up to the image. No one is more extravagantly shocked than the lower middle class when one of their number goes off the rails, no one is more bemused when one of their number does not present a sexually conformist front, no one is more mystified by perversions such as homosexuality. This was true a century ago, when the lower middle class was additionally trying to emulate what it thought was a hermetically sealed inviolate class, the upper middle. The father who said in melodrama to his unmarried daughter with child, 'Do not darken my doorstep,' was not a figure of fun, but a viable figure. The daughter had run foul of the love mystique and had to be made to suffer.

The stripping of love of its baser attributes was a project especially suited to the Victorian mind. It was emarginated, leaving a text that was curiously amorphous, open to any number of picturesque interpretations. Love as a concept led to ridiculous concentric projects such as the 789-page *The Lovers' Dictionary*, published by Cassell in 1867, 'A Poetical Treasury of Lovers' Thoughts, Fancies, Addresses and Dilemmas – Indexed with Nearly Ten Thousand References as a Dictionary of Compliments and Guide to the Study of the Tender Science.' The quintessence of love into marriage as seen by the middle-brow Victorian is contained in *Verses Written Before Marriage* by 'A Clergyman', a coy anonymity that was respected by the compilers of this thesaurus:

> Hence, every gloomy care away!
> Hence, every secret fear.
> With joy I see th' approaching day
> Which gives me all that's dear.
>
> What though no jewels grace my bride,
> (She owes no charms to them),
> Yet virtue in her bosom dwells –
> There glows the brightest gem.

There white rob'd innocence appears,
Fair Peace in smiles array'd,
And sweet Content in humble guise,
Adorn the lovely maid.

Oh! born to bless me with thy love,
My dear, my joy, my life –
Soon will those tender names unite
In that dear name of wife.

Thee meek-eyed gentleness adorns,
With modest virtue join'd,
Thy decent form, and humble mien,
Bespeak a spotless mind.

On these I build my hopes of peace,
On these bright charms of thine:
How shall I bless that happy hour
That makes thee ever mine.

This is more revealing than 'A Clergyman' ever imagined it would be. It sums up to perfection the chaste courtship and passionless marriage of Victorian legend. Marriage was a panacea to 'gloomy care' and 'secret fear'; one's own marriage differed from all other marriages in that it was 'special', the spouse being particularly and uniquely matched to one (i.e., 'born to bless me with thy love'). The 'decent form, and humble mien' would no doubt help to tame any less noble impulses. The respectable and naïve accepted the formula of love's young dream as it was the stuff from which domestic romance was made, and the slightly higher-class clergy used it also as it was a convenient compromise.

Love in its more ethereal form was highly rated by poetesses, as it was a self-evident fact (to them) that women's capacity for unphysical rapture was far greater than man's. Letitia Elizabeth Landon, who wrote under the initials 'L. E. L.', was a contemporary of Felicia Hemans. Born in 1802, she languished in repressed spinsterdom until in 1838 she married a Mr Maclean, pouring out frantic expositions of womanhood's superior qualities:

> It is a fearful thing
> To love as I love thee; to feel the world –
> The bright, the beautiful, the joy-giving world –
> A blank without thee . . .

Mr Maclean was a minor colonial governor; two months after
Miss Landon went to join him, she died from prussic acid, taken
to counter what were described as spasms.

Humankind, as T. S. Eliot reminded us, cannot bear very
much reality. Love in the abstract was best treated by those for
whom love in the concrete was lacking, or those who volun-
tarily relinquished physical love on religious or philosophical
grounds, who could study the 'brow/Of innocence ineffable' on
which 'The laughing bridal roses blow' (Coventry Patmore).
It was easier to be constant when there was no real man or
woman to be constant to; constancy against all the odds features
continually in the verse of that supremely spinsterly poetess
Christina Rossetti, who could create a well-turned stanza every
time she pondered on the theme, on man's ingratitude, on love
that was interrrupted by death, on the superiority of woman
when faced with double-dealing and male iniquity.

> I did not chide him, though I knew
> That he was false to me. . .

Naturally the disposition of ultra-innocent lady versifies to
get steamed up about love was noted by outsiders. 'L. E. L.' was
a model for Thackeray for his Miss Bunion, and Max Beerbohm
did a notably acrid cartoon of Miss Rossetti. Love as seen by the
lady poets was an inchoate condition, indefinable but omniform.
Thus Miss Rossetti:

> Love is all happiness, love is all beauty,
> Love is the crown of flaxen heads and hoary;
> Love is the only everlasting duty;
> And love is chronicled in endless story,
> And kindles endless glory.

This was written in her teens, just before she became attached
to the Pre-Raphaelite painter James Collinson. Before he had
met her, he had turned Catholic; he proposed to her, but be-

cause of religious differences she felt obliged to deny him. He changed his religion to the more suitable Church of England, proposed again, and was accepted. After a time he found that Rome had claimed him for her own, and defected once again to the alien faith. Upon this, Christina Rossetti broke off the engagement. Her brother, William, said that this 'struck a staggering blow at Christina Rossetti's peace of mind on the very threshold of womanly life, and a blow from which she did not fully recover'. A blighted love life seems to have been an essential ingredient in the Victorian poetess.

Certain characteristics recurred in the poetic treatment of polite love. There is the assumption that there was a Destined One:

> Faces that fled me like a haunted fawn
> I followed singing, deeming it was Thou.
>> Richard le Galliene

The assumption that the Destined One was out of reach forever:

> O were I a cross on thy snowy breast,
> O were I a gem in thy raven hair;
> O were I the soft-blowing wind of the west,
> To play round thy bosom with cooling air.
>> Anonymous from the
>> *Eton Magazine* of 1848

The assumption that the Destined One will have problems deciding between God and the narrator:

> In the merry hay-time we raked side by side,
> In the harvest he whispered – Wilt thou be my bride?
> And my girl-heart bounded – Forgive, God, the crime,
> If I loved him more than Thee in the merry hay-time.
>> C. K. Paul

> A prudent, gentle, loving wife,
> The boon most precious to the life
> Of him to whom her all is given,
> Save love of God, and hope of heaven.
>> Janet Hamilton

The assumption is that an adolescent conception of love is consistently valid, that an unreciprocated love can only be responded to by: (a) unutterable despair; or (b) death, preferably tragic and speedy. The theme of the wife dying between the wedding and the bridal night is also used with a frequency verging on the obsessional. The poets of the spinster school are especially prone to this indulgence, and one suspects that behind the flowery sentiment there is a touch of the vengeful.

It is difficult for the twentieth century to appreciate that poetry was read by all kinds and conditions of men, and the mass of the people today have lost more than they realize when they dismiss poetry *en bloc* as effeminate. The Victorians were aware that poetry was life-enhancing and obtained something tangible from it. Of course, the verse was easy in the main, and not essays in clever tricky exhibitionism. On the second day of her honeymoon, Lady Frederick Cavendish could write quite naturally in her diary '... also I spouted to Fred the "Allegro" and the "Penseroso", and other bits of poetry; and I don't find him entirely unworthy.' It is necessary to emphasize that poetry was best-selling, not the prerogative of a rather precious clique, and that its effect was on a very broad segment of society who found their unformulated views on the cosmic power of their own particular love echoed in the masters and mistresses of line and meter.

The sophisticated used the material fed to them by the poets. It sharpened their own perceptions, and they could discard the airy-fairy stuff – the macabre imaginings of Mrs Hemans with lover being tortured on the wheel, and child brides dying of grief by the cartload. There was always an impressive body of readers who took the poetry at its face value. The love that was for them alone, the union of kindred spirits, two souls mingled in one exotic whole – these, they found, did not last; the working-class songsters of the music hall spoke contemptuously, if wistfully, of a honeymoon all the year round. Readers of domestic poetry and romantic fiction expected it, and were disillusioned. So were writers. George Meredith could strike a conventional tone with 'Angelic Love':

> Angelic love that stoops with heavenly lips
> To meet its earthly mate ...

He could also reject the poetical marriage in favour of the marriage that had failed:

> By this he knew she wept with waking eyes:
> That, at his hand's light quiver by her head,
> The strange low sobs that shook their common bed
> Were called into her with a sharp surprise,
> And strangled mute, like little gaping snakes,
> Dreadfully venomous to him. She lay
> Stone-still, and the long darkness flowed away
> With muffled pauses...

Meredith, in his superb sonnet sequence 'Married Love', struck a plangent chord, but it was not the kind of poetry the readers of 1862 wanted, though the critics recognized its worth (these included Swinburne).

In a century of swiftly changing values, many clung to the notion of romantic love as a permanent reality in the midst of chaos, in the same way as there existed the conventional idea that basically England was still a rural and idyllic place, and that cotton mills, iron works and coal mines were accidental excrescences that would soon pass away. Romantic love was also a convenient smoke screen to hide the fact that woman was a second-class citizen who, when she was married, had few rights and was subject to inexorable male law. During courtship and, in theory, marriage, romance decreed that the man could be submissive without loss of face, that he could grovel and kowtow without feeling that his manhood was in danger of emasculation. In his ineffable way, Ruskin put this in *Sesame and Lilies*:

> In all Christian ages which have been remarkable for their purity or progress, there has been absolute yielding of obedient devotion, by the lover, to his mistress. I say *obedient*; – not merely enthusiastic and worshipping in imagination, but entirely subject, receiving from the beloved woman, however young, not only the encouragement, the praise, and the reward of all toil, but so far as any choice is open, or any question difficult of decision, the *direction* of all toil.

Similarly, Elizabeth Barrett Browning in *Lady Geraldine's Courtship* (1944):

> I was only a poor poet, made for singing at her casement,
>   As the finches or the thrushes, while she thought of other things.

The dominance of a woman in the world of romantic love could extend to sexual fun and games. Again, it is Mrs Browning, this time in her novel in verse *Aurora Leigh*:

> When he tried in vain
> To raise her to his embrace, escaping thence
> As any leaping fawn from a huntsman's grasp,
> She bounded off and 'lighted beyond reach,
> Before him, with a staglike majesty
> Of soft, serene defiance, – as she knew
> He could not touch her, so was tolerant
> He had cared to try...

Here, as in many other instances, romantic love was used as an *hors d'œuvre* to sexual union. Robbed of its cosmic and wide-blue-yonder implications, the massive universe of poetic love can be regarded as a convenient addendum to the sexual instinct.

Divorce

IN 1857 modern divorce was born.

The situation prior to this Divorce Bill was admirably expounded by Mr Justice Maule to a hawker who had been convicted of bigamy:

I will tell you what you ought to have done under the circumstances, and if you say you did not know, I must tell you that the law conclusively presumes that you did. You should have instructed your attorney to bring an action against the seducer of your wife for damages; that would have cost you about £100. Having proceeded thus far, you should have employed a proctor and instituted a suit in the Ecclesiastical Courts for a divorce *a mensa et thoro*; that would have cost you £200 or £300 more. When you had obtained a divorce *a mensa et thoro*, you had only to obtain a private Act for a divorce *a vinculo matrimonii*. The Bill might possibly have been opposed in all its stages in both Houses of Parliament, and altogether these proceedings would cost you £1,000. You will probably tell me that you never had a tenth of that sum, but that makes no difference. Sitting here as an English judge it is my duty to tell you that this is not a country in which there is one law for the rich and another for the poor. You will be imprisoned for one day.[31]

This ironical summary of the law did much to create a favourable climate for a new look at marriage and divorce. It matters not that every reference to Mr Justice Maule's pronouncement quotes him differently. Royal Commissions had reported that a special court to deal with divorce was long overdue, and from 1850 there had been strenuous efforts to push through a bill to this effect. The Report of the Royal Commission of 1853 declared

that the total cost, under the most favourable circumstances, of obtaining a divorce *a vinculo matrimonii* [that is, absolute divorce] can hardly be less than £700 or £800, and when the matter is much litigated, it would probably reach some thousands. In Scotland, the average cost of rescinding a marriage is said to be £30, and that when there is no opposition, £20 will suffice.

One of the disadvantages of formulating a divorce bill was the fact that the law relating to marriage was an utter shambles. That this was the fault of the church was admitted by Mandell Creighton:

It seems to me that there is no point upon which the Western Church displayed such incompetence, for I can call it by no other name, than in its dealing with the question of marriage. Marriage was a matter which was left entirely in the hands of the Church. Ultimately, as a matter of fact, the State had to interpose, because the Church had reduced matters to such extraordinary confusion. . . it is a matter of fact that the Church found exceeding difficulty, and showed exceeding reluctance, in defining what marriage was. Therefore, while it is perfectly true to say that a valid marriage properly contracted was indissoluble, yet during the greater part of the Middle Ages it was almost impossible to say what a valid marriage was and how a valid marriage could be contracted. . .[32]

The difficulty of laying down exactly what a marriage was

also penetrated the legal profession. What was one to do about the 'irregular marriage'? Lord Stowell retired in 1828, but his poetic treatment of the irregular marriage was a comfort to Victorian legal luminaries: 'The woman carried her virgin honours to the private nuptial bed, with as much purity of mind and of person, with as little violation of delicacy, and with as little loss of reputation as if the matter was graced with all the sanctities of religion.'

The problems of defining the married state were manifest. Divorce had its own train of difficulties. In the first place, marriage was a private affair; by its very nature, divorce law must be subjective. Despite this, it borrowed concepts from criminal law, inappropriate as this was. Many of the act's supporters underestimated the difficulties; desertion and adultery were facts that could be checked, but how about cruelty? Cruelty was a matrimonial offence against which few lawyers did not bark their shins. The contrast between divorce law, concerning two and only two people, and criminal law, concerning everyone, was exemplified by the situation in which a spouse might forgive an act of adultery even though he or she could petition for divorce on that ground. In criminal law, this acquiescence would itself be an offence – it would be compounding a felony. Divorce in many ways was like breach of promise. There was no obligation to act. But all this was in the future – first of all there was the necessity of getting the bill through Parliament. The year 1857 saw a determination by the government under Palmerston to do something at last, despite the frenetic opposition of a powerful minority, led by Gladstone, and aided by Bishop ('Soapy Sam') Wilberforce.

The Matrimonial Causes Act (20 & 21 Vict., c. 85) came into operation on 1 January, 1858. Gladstone had failed in his mission. He apologized for any hasty words during the debate, his own opinion, apparently, he admitted later, was 'isolated and peculiar'. One of his objections was rapidly proved wrong. He had maintained that the public did not want the act. It was supposed that there would be twenty or thirty cases a year, but clearly politicians had no idea about the way the other half lived. The number of divorces were as follows:

1858	326	*1869*	351	*1880*	615	*1891*	632
1859	291	*1870*	351	*1881*	589	*1892*	629
1860	272	*1871*	384	*1882*	481	*1893*	645
1861	236	*1872*	374	*1883*	561	*1894*	652
1862	248	*1873*	416	*1884*	647	*1895*	683
1863	298	*1874*	469	*1885*	541	*1896*	772
1864	297	*1875*	451	*1886*	708	*1897*	781
1865	284	*1876*	536	*1887*	662	*1898*	750
1866	279	*1877*	551	*1888*	680	*1899*	727
1867	294	*1878*	632	*1889*	654	*1900*	698
1868	303	*1879*	555	*1890*	644	*1901*	848

To give these figures some kind of reality, it might be mentioned that in one typical year (1886), there were more than 25,000 divorces in the United States, which had then approximately twice the population of Great Britain. Clearly those who thought that the new relative ease of divorce would lead to a mad stampede to the courts were just as mistaken as the politicians who had optimistically predicted a turnover up to thirty couples a year. It was also thought that the changes in divorce procedure would lead to a weakening in the structure of marriage, and an increase in adultery. This was illustrated by a verse from *The Pearl* 1879–80:

> A virgin coy with sidelong eye
> Your mere approach, at once will fly,
> Abhors your nasty hot desires,
> Nought less than marriage she requires.
>> Such maidenheads the wise detest,
>> The adultery maidenhead's the best

> The genial flame I've oft allayed,
> With buxom Kate, my chambermaid,
> And dozens such as her, but found
> Such sports with ills beset around;
>> He who at liberty would feast
>> Will find another's wife the best.

> A mistress kept at first is sweet,
> And joys to do the merry feat;
>> But bastards come and hundreds gone,

> You'll wish you'd left her charms alone,
> Such breeding hussies are a pest,
> A neighbour's wife is far the best.

The bill needed constant amendments over the years. Its biggest flaw was that it enshrined the double standards of morality. As the *Saturday Review* put it in 1869:

> Whether women can understand it or not, as long as society exists, incontinence on man's part will be compared with incontinence on woman's part, not as a matter solely of personal right, which here means personal wrong, but as a matter of public policy. On ethical grounds it is the same in one case as the other: on social consideration, the adultery of the wife is, and always will be, a more serious matter than the infidelity of the husband.

The 1857 act made adultery by the wife grounds for divorce, but adultery by the man had to be allied to some other matrimonial offence if the woman was to obtain a decree. Thus section 27:

> It shall be lawful for any husband to present a petition to the said court, praying that his marriage may be dissolved, on the ground that his wife has, since the celebration thereof, been guilty of adultery; and it shall be lawful for any wife to present a petition to the said court, praying that her marriage may be dissolved, on the ground that since the celebration thereof, her husband has been guilty of incestuous adultery, or of bigamy with adultery, or of rape, or of sodomy or bestiality, or of adultery coupled with such cruelty as without adultery would have entitled her to a divorce *a mensa et thoro*, or of adultery coupled with desertion, without reasonable excuse, for two years and upwards. . .

Operating the new divorce laws was no sinecure. In a case Scott versus Scott of 1863, Judge Ordinary Wilde pointed out the difficulty of getting agreement on what constituted cruelty:

> The domestic history of years is poured forth by husband and wife in alternate streams of opposite colours; the memory of each is ransacked for the most trivial details, the posture of each mind is antagonistic in the extreme, drawing memory and sometimes imagination after it in the attack or defence. Events are often misplaced in date, and always exaggerated in aspect. Unqualified accusations

serve only to elicit absolute denials, and amidst a volume of evidence and at the end of a protracted investigation, the truth, obscured, disfigured, and transformed by prejudice and passion, is indeed hard to find.

The extent of the demand for divorce had been under-estimated. So had the problems of the lawyers. So had the interest of the general public in divorce, a subject that was to prove staple diet for the more sensational papers, so much so that Queen Victoria tried to cry halt:

The Queen wishes to ask the Lord Chancellor whether no steps can be taken to prevent the present publicity of the proceedings before the new Divorce Court. These cases, which must necessarily increase when the new law becomes more and more known, fill now almost daily a large portion of the newspapers, and are of so scandalous a character that it makes it almost impossible for a paper to be trusted in the hands of a young lady or boy. None of the worst French novels from which careful parents would try to protect their children can be as bad as what is daily brought and laid upon the breakfast-table of every educated family in England, and its effect must be most pernicious to the public morals of the country.[33]

Queen Victoria, indeed, was not amused. The Lord Chancellor replied that he had attempted in the last session of Parliament to introduce measures to try to muzzle the news hawks, but he had failed, and therefore, Britain being a democracy, his hands were tied. The interest of the newspaper-reading public in divorce was not solely prurient. There was also a search for information, curiosity in the details of one particular marriage that had gone astray. Marriage, in its pre-packaged hygienic state as defined with crass presumption by church and the law, did not coincide with marriage as it was widely experienced by such readers. Marriage, apparently unbeknown to parson and judge, was a unique state, a private pact between two people for whom, if the auspices were right, anything went. For outsiders it was a mystery, a possible fulfilment, a health-giving elixir, impressions that were fostered when the puzzled and the ignorant wrote to periodicals and magazines and received the words of wisdom of the editors, in the form of tantalizingly enigmatic messages. For example, in the *Family Doctor* of 11 September, 1886:

J. Lincroft: You are quite well; marriage is quite another thing from experiments.

A Worried One: Marriage is the best cure. Seidlitz powders will be an auxiliary.

With a somewhat bland complacency, the lawgivers tried to project their purified vision of the true married state on to the real world. For many, the married state was a coupled steam engine; if anything went wrong, it was a mechanical failure, and the trouble could be located, rectified, put right. If a wife had an arm broken and a succession of black eyes, the court was willing to accept that this constituted cruelty on the part of a husband, and if he made a practice of beating her savagely this might also be a ground (though he had the right of chastisement) for divorce. Yet even here there were random factors. What was one to make of the fervent letter in the magazine *Society* (*circa* 1870)?

With my whole heart I endorse the opinion of your correspondent with regard to the reciprocal punishment of man and wife; family discords of many sort can be easily avoided thereby, and I think it is a wonderful excuse for the renewal of old healing remedies – the kissing habit, etc. There is a unique attraction in whipping one's own wife or in being whipped by her hand. I hope that a time will come when all quarrels will be settled by the rod.

An extreme example of marital fun and games, perhaps, but the writer was no freak, and was only unusual in that he realized himself that he was no freak, being willing to try his arm against the establishment view of marriage as something rather dull. Clearly in this mutual whipping situation, cruelty was not a factor. What was allowed in marriage? What was allowed in *Victorian* marriage? It depended mainly on the disposition of the courts. At rock bottom, it often depended on the whims or the sex life of the gentlemen dispensing justice.

Smallwood *versus* Smallwood was a case from 1861. Mr Smallwood took his wife viciously by the throat and threw her to the floor. This was not considered sufficiently serious to be called cruel, though in the following year, in the case of Waddell *versus* Waddell, a husband who drank heavily, who spat at his wife, who threw cold water over her, and indulged in 'minor' violence overstepped the wavering line hesitantly drawn by the law. Scott *versus* Scott of 1860 had the shoe on the other foot; Mrs Scott was accustomed to striking her husband with a poker, and when he protested, she threatened him with a knife (the Mrs Scotts of the nineteenth century were more plentiful than one is often led to believe). The unfortunate Mr Scott did not get his freedom. This case proved that the law was flexible, true, but it also indicated that it was erratic. It was perhaps a pity that so much attention was paid to pre-1857 divorce cases; the rich and pampered protagonists in the early cases were served up again in circumstances and at social levels that had no relevance to such often quoted cases as Evans *versus* Evans of 1790. Nor did Lord Stowell, who was so poetic on irregular marriages, seem a startlingly suitable personage to lay down the law for the 1860s and 1870s, precedent is all).

'To amount to cruelty there must be personal violence, or manifest danger of it'; so related Sir John Nicholl in Barlee *versus* Barlee in 1822. 'Threats of personal ill-usage have been deemed sufficient to justify a separation,' declared Dr Lushington in 1847. Nicholl changed his mind, evidently, in 1828, when a Mr Bray accused his wife of incestuous adultery ('It is not, I think, possible to conceive cruelty of a more grievous character').

Seven years before the Matrimonial Causes Act (1857), that personality who seems to crop up in every aspect of Victorian life, Lord Brougham, was accountable for the decision *vis-à-vis* the Patersons. Admirably refusing to play God, he called on the expert, a Dr Harding, to expound the law relating to cruelty. Harding said plainly that, 'there is no code, or canon, or statute regulating the law of separation by reason of cruelty. That law is only to be collected from the decisions.' The decisions were made by men no less fallible than others. Lord Brougham, with that carelessness that led him later to start a chain of scandals, chose to misinterpret Dr Harding, and Paterson *versus* Paterson was a nut on which subsequent jurisprudence choked: it could 'hardly be regarded as conclusive upon any legal point', declared Lord Ashbourne (and this was forty-seven years later, the long arm of the law extending in time as well as in space).

One violent act under excitement did not constitute cruelty. This was not accepted by Sir Cresswell Cresswell who as Judge Ordinary let a wife have a divorce in 1861 because her husband had treated her in such a way that passers-by believed her to be a prostitute (passers-by were always ready to believe this kind of thing, anyway). He had also committed adultery, but that was by the way. Sir Cresswell Cresswell did not have much more time to effect any further curious decisions, which, of course, would then become precedents, for he was killed soon afterward in a carriage accident. Nevertheless, wives who felt that they had been treated as prostitutes might well have felt, had they concerned themselves with legal frivolities, that it was worth a try if the husband was otherwise guiltless but unacceptable.

On Cresswell's death, his province was taken over by Lord Penzance. Later, Lord Penzance was to acquire a permanent black mark in the eyes of the right wing of the Church of England, as it was he who found against the unfortunate pseudo-martyr, the Reverend A. Tooth, vicar of St James's, Hatcham, for practicing 'ritualistic' rites, and for which, in due course, Tooth found himself languishing in prison. As a successor to Cresswell, Lord Penzance had the same penchant for quirkish decisions, but he too had to make the best of a bad job, a bill inadequately drafted and reflecting an upper-class view that preferably reproduction should take place by parthenogenesis. Brown *versus* Brown of 1865 presented him with a split problem, concerning Mr Brown's cruelty in: (a) wilfully communicating venereal disease to Mrs Brown; (b) being customarily drunk. Penzance accepted (a) but not (b) as he felt that he was unable to 'break with the decided cases to sympathise with the petitioner's misfortunes'. Nevertheless, Lord Penzance was a humanist, and the superciliousness that Cresswell had in abundance was largely lacking (in so far as legal considerations allowed). In the same year, 1865, he treated non-violent conduct as constituting cruelty (Knight *versus* Knight), and one can discern a whiff of the twentieth century in his handling of Mr Swatman, who was an adulterer but not a wife-beater. Mrs

Swatman obtained her divorce; the burden she bore – frequently her husband had this woman in the marital home – was such that 'she could not be expected to discharge the duties of married life'. This view that a threat of cruelty was as potent as cruelty itself Lord Penzance confirmed in his decision in Kelly *versus* Kelly of 1870. Lord Penzance's influence in the divorce court was liberalizing, reflecting a pragmatic view of marriage that had been sadly lacking.

How important was the 1857 Matrimonial Causes Act? If it had just been that, it would have had scant effect on British life. But it was an indication of the future. It confirmed that marriage once and for all was being taken out of the hands of the clergy, who were swamped by contradicting dogma frequently laid down by men who had the least knowledge of the married state – the celibates of yesteryear. The act was a rock on which future legislation could be raised, and as the years went by, the absurdities were clearly recognized for what they were, were eliminated or amended, though it took the most manifest anomaly – the different treatment meted out to wife and husband in respect of adultery – a long time to be seen as such. It is easy to be ironical about the way in which the law wavered and shilly-shallied regarding cruelty, but cruelty in marriage was not a phenomenon confined to nineteenth-century marriage, and the questions must still be asked: (a) how far can sexual fun at one time be treated at a later date as cruelty? (b) who is to be believed?

The nineteenth century, sentimental and often fitfully blind, took a long time to let go its concept of a chaste marriage. The bridal night was frequently an occasion of what in other contexts was cruelty, i.e., rape (a husband cannot commit rape on his wife). In 1889, Dr Neugebauer reported that he had dealt with 150 injuries to women occasioned by their experiences of the bridal night. Although sex practices that were unusual were unquestionably on a much smaller scale than presently is the case, unreliable statistics, inadequate sampling by sociologists, and inhibitions upon publishing details must not lead one to believe that such practices were little known and used. People do not alter much over a hundred years, and the techniques of sex, including foreplay, do not need the manuals of the twentieth century to ensure their being carried out. What happens in a marriage has been amply recorded by Dr Kinsey and his associates, and there is no evidence to suggest that marital behaviour so admirably documented is special to our own time.

The changes of attitudes towards 'abnormal marital relations' have made divorce on grounds other than straightforward adultery, desertion, or a beating a curious reflection of social *mores*. For instance, regarding sodomy, how much does consent regularize this crime? Although it falls out of the period, a case of 1929 is worth mentioning in this respect. In this case, Lord Justice Russell declared that the wife's

evidence makes it clear (1) that her husband explained to her quite plainly the exact physical act which he wished to do upon her; (2) that she assented and placed her body at his disposal for the purpose of that act being committed; (3) that no compulsion of any kind was brought to bear upon her; and (4) that the only reason given by her for refusing subsequent invitations to a similar act was fear of pain.

The decree was not granted, as she was a consenting party.

Sodomy was one of the ambiguities of the 1857 act. Under section 27, sodomy by the husband was in itself a ground for divorce. But the act did not specify further whether sodomy with a third person was meant or whether sodomy with the wife was included. The courts were left to make the decision; the section included sodomy with a wife. This being so, wives who employed sodomy as a regular means of birth control unknowingly could have had their freedom at any time of asking.

The difficulties of enforcing the 1857 Matrimonial Causes Act must have led many supporters to have had second thoughts – e.g., Bishop Tait, who voted for the act out of convenience, and because he thought that if this act was defeated, another one would arise like a phoenix out of the ashes and give the clergy a rougher deal. 'I fear my votes on this bill have given great offence to many, but I have acted according to my conscience, and I pray God that all may go right,' declared Bishop Tait.

The 1857 act demonstrated many of the shortcomings of the Victorian way of thinking, in that it attempted to solve a complex problem by relatively simple means, in that insufficient attention had been given to finding out the public demand for such a bill, and in that the act was not simply a transference of power from the ecclesiastical courts to the new divorce court. The interest of the public in divorce was grossly underestimated, and the crabbed world of Dickensian law was invaded by sensation-hunting journalists.

The lurid cases, such as the Dilke case in the eighties, created an appetite among the general public that was difficult to satisfy, a general public that was still too poor to petition for its own divorces. As late as 1909, the County Courts Committee reported that the 'Divorce Court in London [was] outside reach of poor'. Not surprisingly, the more extravagant cases caused reactions in the lawyers that were not solely governed by legal technicalities. Everyone speaks on sex with authority and prejudice. In the case of Sir Charles Dilke, Mrs Crawford said that Dilke 'taught me every French vice. He used to say that I knew more than most women of thirty. ... I believed I should have to do whatever he pleased,' and such statements aroused the wrath of her counsel. Henry Matthews declared that Dilke's actions represented 'ruthless adultery unredeemed by love or affection – he was charged with coarse brutal adultery more befitting a beast than a man, he was charged with having done with an English lady what any man of proper feeling would shrink from doing with a prostitute in a French brothel, and yet he was silent'. The probability that Dilke was innocent is by the way. Specialists in divorce found that they had a wonderful platform for airing their views and indulging in oratory, and, with wide newspaper reportage, who could not say where such orations might not lead?

For the less well-to-do, Lord Penzance in 1878 provided a further Matrimonial Causes Act, in which magistrates had the power to grant a separation order and maintenance to a wife on the ground of aggravated assault, and the Maintenance of Wives (Desertion) Act of 1886 also helped the most needy of classes, in that the runaway husband could be summoned to pay £2 a week. The 1857 act was a preview of things to come, and the subsequent years of the century were dotted with statutes that tried to make the break-up of a partnership a civilized procedure. Divorce, said Coventry Patmore, was a 'vulgar solution' to the unhappy marriage, but he was in a minority.

It cannot be stressed too frequently that newspapers reported sensational court cases with a freedom that would be considered rare today. It is not from respectable fiction, nor is it from pornography, nor is it from the 'penny dreadfuls', that one gets glimpses of what the Victorians got up to. The mirror of events behind closely curtained bedroom windows is held up by the staff journalist, haunting the echoing Gothic corridors of the new law courts.

Not that every divorce case was expected to make the readers of *The Times* lick their lips. Much of the time was devoted to the judges, many of whom, without precedent to guide them, were helpless, especially when faced with the difficulties of property in relation to divorce. The Divorce Act had been in operation for more than three years when Gurney *versus* Gurney and Taylor turned up before the justices; this case had considerable property complications, and his lordship waxed poetic on the theme. He was, he declared, 'navigating a new sea without either chart or compass'. Many judges were also uncertain in their own minds whether or not divorce was a criminal offence. They had all the tools of their trade at their finger tips, but did not know whether they ought to use them.

What about the man or woman who was trying it on, who was trying for a divorce, and was willing to proffer false evidence, usually with accomplices? Would it not be nice to slam these naughty people with perjury suits? Unfortunately, they were not able to do this too often; the most they could do was to turn the suit down. In this respect, a most interesting case occurred during the formative years of the act. It came to court on 30 April, 1860, Alexander *versus* Alexander and Amos.

Mr Alexander was a man of substance, who had married beneath him. He decided that he would like a divorce, and the machinery was brought into operation. His witness was a farm labourer, Patrick Sullivan, who claimed that he had on many occasions seen Mrs Alexander with the groom, Amos. It would seem from Sullivan's statements that he spent more time as a voyeur than harvesting. On one occasion, 'He heard them go into another room, and went round to a stable upon which he climbed, and looked through the window of that room. It was a bedroom on the same floor. He gave evidence of an act of adultery which he then witnessed.' At another time, Sullivan entered an outhouse: 'He went in and saw them in an indecent attitude.' He told Alexander, who would not listen, but Amos was most indignant. He 'struck him and kicked him and knocked him about'. Both Mrs Alexander and Amos, commented Sullivan superciliously, were usually three parts drunk. Unfortunately for Alexander, Sullivan was not of the class to command much respect in the divorce court. The judge made a few sardonic remarks on the improbability of Mrs Alexander and her lover failing to draw curtains or shut the doors of outhouses when indulging, and dismissed the suit.

Mr Thompson, when his case came up on 14 January, 1861, was also out of luck. His wife had petitioned, so he countered with his own tale of woe. A clerk to a wine merchant, he had married in 1858 and had already acquired three children. His wife

threw three flower-pots full of mould at him, one of which struck him on the head, and another on the shoulder. She then went upstairs and threw a jug wth some bran in it out of the window at him, and also a stone bottle and the legs of a chest of drawers, but he got out of the way. A day or two afterwards he asked her to show him a letter she was reading, and she refused and swallowed it that he might not see it.

Ludicrous as it is, this catalogue has the ring of truth about it, but it was not sufficient to earn Mr Thompson his release.

Like breach-of-promise cases, divorces were always good for laughs, and the audience was frequently given its head. Owen *versus* Owen and Brooks was even funnier than usual, because Owen was a publican, a traditional humorous figure, and mine host as cuckold is a sure-fire winner. The case came to court on 5 May, 1860, and already the demand for cheap divorce was outpacing the expedition of justice – there was a total of 153 divorces pending. The villain in the piece was Brooks, a waiter.

For the lower middle class and tradesmen, extramarital games were difficult to keep quiet on account of the servants they were obliged to have. If Mrs Owen had made her own beds, incriminating evidence would not have come to light. 'A nightcap of his was once found in her bedroom, and a hat-pin was once found in his bed.' Also, 'various instances of familiarity were spoken of by the servants who had been in Mr Owen's employment at the same time as Brooks, and a coachman named Allison proved that on one Sunday in June, 1858 he went downstairs to see whether his dinner was ready, and he caught Mrs Owen and Brooks in a dark passage, leading to the kitchen, in an indecent position.'

The case of Stohwasser and Mrs Welzenstein, also of 1860, was not divorce, but it had the basic elements, risibility and naughtiness, to amuse the populace. Stohwasser was a tailor, and naturally it made him even more comical being of continental descent. He was around fifty or sixty, and Mrs Welzenstein was twenty-eight; she was accused with two accomplices of having milked Stohwasser of £300.

He was on very friendly terms with Mrs Welzenstein and frequently visited her when she was in bed [a laugh]. He generally visited her at night, and once he gave her a cup of soup; but he did not put his arm round her to hold her up at the same time [a laugh]. ... She used to talk to him about her misfortunes and she never exhausted the story, but always had something fresh to tell him [laughter]. They never sat together in the dark. There were two sofas in the room, but they were not sitting near either of them. ... There was a sofa in the room but he never sat upon it [a laugh].

Stohwasser was a victim, though he did not know it as the term was yet to be invented, of the badger game, and in due course Mr Welzenstein turned up to put the bite on him. 'The sum he wanted was £50 or £60; he was not particular which.' There were, and are, poor Mr Stohwassers in their hundreds, but what is interesting in this case is what was activating the audience. They were laughing exactly as they did during the divorce cases; they found extra-marital sex hilarious, and reacted to the various key properties as they did in the music hall. For them, there was only one purpose in this context for a sofa – to have intercourse upon. Poor Stohwasser discerned this, and was at great pains to disown any such ignoble connection. This, of course, made the tableau even funnier. It was small wonder that respectability, from Queen Victoria downwards, found the newspaper reports of divorce and similar cases distasteful.

Those divorce cases that lacked humour were sure to be plentifully supplied with pathos. On 13 December 1859, Mrs Gurney left her husband for a former footman, Taylor, long since dismissed. The court, when the case came up in January 1861, was puzzled by Taylor's heinous behaviour, for although the son of a small farmer he had had a decent education. It also made it worse when Mrs Gurney's letter to her husband was read out in court:

My poor Husband – I have, indeed, left you and our poor children, but you know my heart has been long another's, and therefore I could not be happy with you any more. Please send my luggage and Dick to 216, Marylebone-road. Also the small books I bought from Catton, and my work.

Your miserable wife

Mary Jane Gurney.

I pray God to forgive me, and to preserve you and the children.

The inner contradictions in tone of this letter did not escape her husband, though he did, indeed, send her luggage as requested, together with Dick, who happened to be a small dog. He also sent a 'person named Simpson' who was employed by ex-detective Fields as a private investigator, an easy task, as Mrs Gurney herself had kindly supplied her new address, and it was no difficult matter to find out that she had taken three rooms at 216 Marylebone Road. Somewhat surprisingly, her lover was occupying a room in the upper part of the house. No doubt Simpson, an early exponent of his seamy trade, was put out by this, though the couple 'had opportunities for criminal intercourse if they chose to avail themselves of them'. In due course, they moved off to the Pavilion Hotel, Folkestone, where they lived as man and wife.

The pattern established, the 'person named Simpson' was

happy. The increased facilities for divorce offered employment to such as Simpson, as well as young lawyers anxious to get their feet in the doorway of success, and thirty years later it is amusing to notice that among the advertisers in the newly formed magazine *Woman* was the National Detective Agency of 41 Wych Street, run by the ex-chief of police of Jersey. To reassure his readers, the telegraphic address was 'Sleepless London'.

Improved as was the situation of woman in respect of divorce, the progressives were still dissatisfied, as well they might be. In 1882 Annie Besant published her excellent little booklet *Marriage*. Her observations on divorce were particularly acute:

The first reform here needed is that husband and wife should be placed on a perfect equality in asking for a divorce: at present if husband and wife be living apart, no amount of adultery on the husband's part can release the wife; if they be living together, a husband may keep as many mistresses as he will, and, provided that he carefully avoid any roughness which can be construed into legal cruelty, he is perfectly safe from any suit for dissolution of marriage.

Mrs Besant believed 'that the system of judicial separation should be entirely swept away. Wherever divorce is granted at all, the divorce should be absolute.' She went on to say that 'Judicial separation is a direct incentive to licentiousness and secret sexual intercourse.' She believed that there were three logical grounds for divorce: (a) adultery; (b) cruelty; (c) habitual drunkenness. She protested against the unfair way in which access to the children of the marriage favoured the man, quoting from Broom's *Commentaries*: 'In the case of a mother who is proved guilty of adultery, she is usually debarred from such access, though it has not been the practice to treat the offending father with the same rigour.'

It is quite true that when progressives did not know what to write about, they wrote about marriage, but Annie Besant was unusual in that she was thoroughly sound. True, her quotations are restricted to Broom and Blackstone, with an extended episode from Owen, but she does not seek refuge in a private language, as did Edward Carpenter (from *Marriage*, 1894, on the hasty marriage: 'A brief burst of satisfaction, accompanied, probably through sheer ignorance, by gross neglect of the law of trans-mutation. . . .'). Annie Besant also focused her attention on a little reviewed aspect of marriage law – the restitution of con-jugal rights. When a couple were living apart, it was open to one of the parties to bring a suit; the court would then order the offending party to return home. 'It is difficult to understand how any man or woman, endued with the most rudimentary sense of decency, can bring such a suit, and, after having suc-ceeded, can enforce the decision,' speculated Mrs Besant. Such a suit is similar to breach of promise, in that one of the partici-pants in a bilateral agreement is willing to let the outside world in on their mutual secrecy. It is a good deal less amusing. Primarily, it was a man's weapon, activated by two elements: (a) revenge; (b) failure. The restitution of conjugal rights was legalized rapine. The courts, being mostly made up of men, usually supported the man. When a woman left her husband, justice was more than willing to hound the woman. In a case in 1885, Ruthven *versus* Ruthven, there is an instance of revenge on a childish, yet exceptionally revealing, plane: 'She took a little house at Wells, Norfolk, and on one occasion he came there very drunk, and she would not let him in. He remained in the front garden all night and amused himself by pulling up all the plants.'

No progressive writing on marriage could forfeit the oppor-tunity of postulating the ideal marriage contract. 'Husband and wife bound in closest, most durable and yet most eager union, children springing as flowers from the dual stem of love,' wrote Mrs Besant enthusiastically. She went on:

The loathsome details of the Divorce Court will no longer pollute our papers; the public will no longer be called in to gloat over the ruins of desecrated love; society will be purified from sexual vice; men and women will rise to the full royalty of their humanity, and hand in hand tread life's pathways, trustful instead of suspicious, free instead of enslaved, bound by love instead of law.

This was the burden of a song often sung, and no doubt at the end of the present century love's young dream will have equally fervent supporters.

Adultery

The Victorians had an extravagant sense of sin, especially when it affected other people, and in few societies have people been more eager to throw the first stone. What constituted sin was framed with a breezy inconsequence in law, and offences against property were regarded as prime elements to the old Adam in man. Throughout the century law was in the process of being reformed, but this was a long and complex operation; in earlier days, before urban and rural Britain had reached parity, the instruments of law enforcement – the magistrates, the justices – had used their discretion, but a country that was rapidly going over to industry had created a new race of administrator – the middle-class man who had made good. On the bench he was anxious, indeed, over-anxious, to exert his authority, and he adhered to the letter of the law, regardless of how cruel this could be, ignoring any social consequences. In 1871, for instance, a cook named Sarah Graves was sent to prison for stealing a penny stamp from her employer a Mr Holland who not only put the police onto her, but declared that she was guilty of previous crimes and made it his business to inform Miss Grave's young man. As it happened, she was not guilty of this heinous crime, nor had she been of any previous ones, but the humiliation was so great that she committed suicide with Battle's Vermin Killer.

There is a curious connection between the offences against property and adultery. Adultery of the man was, of course, of no consequence; however, adultery of a married woman was different. The co-respondent was treated as if he had, indeed, committed an offence against property, a wife (a 'feme covet') being in law a possession of the wronged husband. Despite this, the law could not punish; reform had meant something, and ducking stools for adulterous women were now very much things of the past. In 1857, the Matrimonial Causes Act had eliminated the offence of 'criminal conversation', which had allowed the injured husband to take out a civil action against the offending male, whereupon he could, if he was successful, get monetary compensation for his wife's loss of virtue. How different this was, considered atavistic magistrates and the like, from the halcyon days when adultery really was punished – death under the law of Moses, burning of the adulteress and hanging of the adulterer by the early Saxons, ears and nose cut off under a statute of Canute (A.D. 1031), while as recently as 1650 the Cromwell régime considered it a crime worthy of death, though there is no record of this having been inflicted. Compared to these violent remedies, adultery in Victorian England was hardly more than a misdemeanour. It was a spiritual crime at which the affronted could do little more than froth at the mouth.

Nevertheless, it was found that adultery on the part of a married woman carried with it an extraordinary sense of guilt, and this could be played upon, especially if it was followed by court action. What had been mad passionate drama could be made, by journalists, to appear ludicrous, and a woman's pride could be submerged in the columns of the more salacious periodicals, which took time off from expounding the delights and charms of the fashionable whores of the period to indulge in some pseudo-indignation that could have the effect of acid.

In 1837, Mrs Charlotte Trevanion *née* Brereton, of Cornwall, was accused of having criminal conversation with a man named Daubuz. The weekly the *Town* wrote it up:

The sinful pair chose hayfields for their ramblings, and hay-cocks for the indulgence in their illicit recreations; they floundered about in the broad glare of day, with nought but the wide canopy of heaven for their coverlid; and there is little doubt but that, like the Aborgines [*sic*] of our land, they performed the functions of procreation in the open air, with a most shameful disregard either to rite or licence.

Serjeant (barrister) Wilde declared that 'they advanced from boldness to a licentiousness almost unknown to persons in their rank of life'. The affronted husband got one shilling's damages, but there is no question that Mrs Trevanion was socially ruined by such an exposé, irrespective of the improbability of this urban rag being on sale in far off Cornwall.

The relish with which scabrous publications adopted the establishment line relating to adultery is odd. *Annals of Fashionable Gallantry* of 1885 was one of those boring late Victorian books that pretend to be naughtier than they are. It consists of a number of court cases, crim-con [34] and divorce, written up in a knowing but blameless manner. Occasionally the book halted in its browsings through long-forgotten newspaper files for a homily:

When a woman (especially of the superior class) has lost that inestimable jewel, virtue: alas! how is she fallen? Her nobility no longer claims our reverence; her coronet ceases to be enviable; her birth (which she has disgraced) but adds to her offence, as, from her situation, it was incumbent on her to have been an example of purity to the rest of her sex.

This is an interesting statement from a pornographic source. It emphasizes that adultery is a class thing, and that it is worse in that it sets a bad example to the lower orders. Much of the popularity of adultery as a subject for entertainment lies in envy. How the mighty are felled, not, as *Samuel* has it, in the midst of battle, but with all the advantages that class had in the day-to-day business of life. Agreeably unedifying as misconduct in high places was (and is) to the lower classes, to adulteresses' equals it was an affront, the letting down of their side. The underprivileged, it was believed, would get above themselves if they saw their betters kicking over the traces in the manner reported in the newspapers with such depressing glee. It was an attitude exemplified by a comment by Mrs Clough, widow of the poet, when she went with Miss Katharine Loring (companion to Henry James's dying sister) to see the play *The Dancing Girl* by Henry Arthur Jones. The villain in this play says how much better the lower orders are. 'I'm so sorry to hear him say that,' said Mrs Clough, 'it is hard enough as it is to keep people in their place, and it does them a great deal of harm to hear that kind of talk.'

If publicity was a guide, the strictures of this play villain were correct. But the lesser folk did not go in for divorce, nor had they gone in for criminal conversation actions. What a provincial report in 1837 had stigmatized as 'the overwhelming mass of ignorance, indifference, immorality and openly avowed infidelity' (Report of the City Mission, Bath) was only slightly less true in 1887. Adultery was a condition peculiar to moneyed people, and its concomitants – humiliation, guilt, social disgrace – were only applicable to those for whom these were real states.

Adultery has never been a particularly uncommon state, save possibly in those centuries when it was a mortal crime. Among the upper crust of the nineteenth century it was skated over – provided it was not discovered. On 7 May 1857 *The Times* reported that thousands were 'living in sin ... almost without a thought of the misery they are causing, and the curse they are laying up for themselves'. Adultery made public was the condition nineteenth-century offenders considered 'it might happen to others but not to me', a state of mind that is now applied to being killed in a motor accident. For high-class devotees, it was the only situation that could get them a bad press. An aristocratic woman was exempted from any of the trials and tribulations that lesser mortals were prone to; a woman who had married well was not likely to be hauled over the coals for anything she might do, whether it was squandering the housekeeping money, ill-treating servants, beating children; if she was a kleptomaniac, store managers would be accommodating. She could get away with anything less than murder – or adultery. The bane of being a possession of her husband had its advantages; she did not belong to the culpable class – in a million years the well-bred woman would not find herself in prison for stealing a penny stamp.

Adultery exposed altered all this, and guilty women found themselves in a nightmare world where the old frames of references no longer applied. They were outside the pale. A servile press, diligent in reporting their presence at this or that function, proved to be something of a Janus. What for the woman was a tragic situation could be treated as 'Amusing Divorce Case', and an eternal triangle could be an infernal triangle, with conversations rehashed by blasé journalists to fit an accepted formula, moments of passion reduced to 'committing misconduct'. The language of adultery is a curiously formalistic one. The notion that the nineteenth century talked differently from the way we talk dies hard – we are inclined to take self-conscious archaisms such as the 'thee' and 'thou' of Victorian poets as representing vernacular – but the material presented in the divorce courts might lead one to suppose that adultery encouraged high-flown verbiage left over somehow from the world of the Jacobean playwright.

One of the most famous of late nineteenth-century divorce cases was the Dilke case. Charles Dilke was a politician of great talents. A radical, and at one time a professed republican, he nevertheless found a niche in Gladstone's government. He was forty-two when he married the widow of the legendary Oxford don, Mark Pattison; a man of the world, efficient, Dilke represented the managerial concept of government as its best. He exasperated some. In 1898 Oscar Wilde declared, 'I've only one fault to find with Dilke; he knows too much about everything. It is hard to have a good story interrupted by a fact. I admit accuracy up to a certain point but Dilke's accuracy is almost a vice.' Accuracy was a quality the nineteenth-century political scene could not have too much of, replete as it was with double-dealing, insincerity and jerrymandering.

Three years before Dilke's marriage, a Mr Crawford had received an anonymous letter, telling him that his wife had 'been carrying on flirtations' with students. He was additionally advised to 'Beware of the member for Chelsea'. In 1885, Mr Crawford received further information: 'Fool, looking for the cuckoo when he has flown, having defiled your nest. You have been vilely deceived, but you dare not touch the real traitor.' Crawford took his wife to task, reported in the following terms:

'Virginia, is it true that you have defiled my bed? I have been a faithful husband to you.'

'Yes, it is true, it is time you should know the truth. You have always been on the wrong track, suspecting people who are innocent, and you have never suspected the person who is guilty.'

'I have never suspected anybody except Captain Forster.'

'It was not Captain Forster. The man who ruined me was Charles Dilke.'

This is the language of second-rate melodrama, but, whether or not the Dilke case was a put-up job – as many believe (Mrs Crawford's mother was once Dilke's mistress; could motives be envy and jealousy?) – Grand Guignol stalks the confessions of women who have been so sensationally ruined.

In 1872, Henry Cavendish Cavendish, a country gentleman living in the county of Shropshire, was wronged by Captain W. H. Moseley, a £30,000-a-year man who could afford to keep Mrs Selina Cavendish in the condition to which she had been accustomed, installing her at 39 Upper Berkeley Street. It was from this address that Mrs Cavendish wrote to her husband:

I think it is doubtful if you will ever read these lines. They are not written to ask you for mercy and even for pity. Too deeply have I sinned to deserve either, and yet I think you might, perchance, pity me if you knew the utter loneliness of spirit in which I write. I have lost home and reputation and children for ever; but all this is as nothing in comparison with having lost you. Oh, if I could be with you again as I used to be. I should care for nothing else night and day. I grieve in agony that I shall see you no more.

The same literary conventions are respected in a divorce case reported in the following week. Louisa, the wife of a vice-admiral, had committed adultery with Baron de Billing, who was attached to the French embassy. One evening she broke into her husband's bedroom while he was asleep, asking him, 'Am I your wife or am I not? I own I have wronged you. I have done you the greatest injury which it is possible for a woman to inflict upon a man. What are you going to do with me? I am willing to come back to you, and I will not leave until you tell me what you are going to do with me.' The admiral was not interested. Sinning in haste and repenting at leisure were circumstances that he could not forgive. If husbands were rigid and doctrinaire in their attitudes, so were the clergy, for whom the marriage state was considerably more than a social convention. 'It is not a happy accident,' wrote Archbishop Trench, 'that has yielded so wondrous an analogy as that of husband and wife to set forth the mystery of Christ's relation to his Church. There is far more in it than this: the earthly relation is indeed but a lower form of the heavenly on which it rests and of which it is the utterance.' This was the kind of reasoning that a millennium earlier had led to death for adulterers. Adultery was spitting in the face of God, thought the churchmen.

A marriage therefore that had come adrift was not something to sympathize with, adultery was not an unfortunate *contretemps* that was always on the cards when a marriage had not proved so auspicious as was once hoped, nor was it a natural consequence of conflicting sexual demands. It was necessary to see something metaphysical in the breakup of a marriage, just as in the institution itself. 'Verily, sex, love and marriage are eternal,' said William Holcombe (*The Sexes – Here and Hereafter*), and although this theological dogma was not wholly shared by the doyens of the established church, Holcombe was presenting in handy capsule form an assumption muzzily made by generations of parsons. Although religious belief became gradually less important to the bulk of the population, unquestionably many adulterers felt that there was something irreligious as well as 'wrong' in their pursuits. In this setting, guilt was fostered, and frequently it festered, objectivity was lost, and a single lapse could ruin a life. A stereotyped image of a married woman irrevocably finished as a social being was projected by novelists, many of whom were ill-equipped to point an accusing finger.

The double standard of morality enshrined in the 1857 Matrimonial Causes Act (a husband could only be divorced if adultery was combined with something else or unless it was adultery in the highest, i.e. incestuous adultery, a woman could be divorced for adultery alone) also operated in the aftermath of an action at law (whatever the result). After the Dilke case, Granville said to Dilke: 'After all, you are not the Archbishop of Canterbury and continuous action on public affairs will soon cause a nine-day wonder to be forgotten.' Dilke, like Parnell, was unfortunate in that he was an exception that proved the rule. Political capital had been made of his escapades, and he was not allowed to drop so easily from the limelight. Gladstone was more accurate than Granville: 'But you will perceive that the judgements of the world are in certain cases irresistible as well as inexorable, and must be treated as if they were infallible.' Dilke redeemed himself through work, though high political posts were out of his range for ever. For women, judgements of the word were irresistible, inexorable and infallible. For newspaper readers of the middle and lower orders of humanity, divorce cases were 'amusing' and 'droll' (daughter of correspondent: 'Oh mother! mother! father is in bed with Mrs Fisher' – a case reported on 10 February 1872). For the timid readers of under-the-counter pornography adultery was hilarious:

> When we were boys the world was good
> But that is long ago:
> Now all the wisest folks are lewd,
> For Adultery's the go,
>   The go, the go,
>   Adultery's the go.
>
> Quite tired of leading virtuous lives,
> Though spotless as the snow,
> Among the chaste and pious wives,
> Adultery's the go,
>   The go, the go,
>   Adultery's the go.
>
> Long life then to the House of Lords
> They know a thing or two;
> You see from all their grand awards,
> That Adultery's the go,
>   The go, the go,
>   Adultery's the go.
>
> And Lady Barlow, Mrs Hare,
> Case, Clarke and Bolders,
> Teed, Ashton, James, and all declare
> Adultery's the go,
>   The go, the go,
>   Adultery's the go.

Some husbands still are jealous
And guard the furbelow,
But spite such prudish fellows,
Adultery's the go,
 The go, the go,
 Adultery's the go.

Horn'd cuckolds were mad raging bulls
A century ago;
Now, they're tame oxen, silly fools,
For Adultery's the go,
 The go, the go,
 Adultery's the go.

Then, hey, for Doctors' Commons,
With horned beasts arow [*sic*]
For man's delight and woman's,
Adultery's the go,
 The go, the go,
 Adultery's the go.

It was not so funny for the women themselves. They had a lifetime to wonder whether the game was worth the candle.

The Free Love Movement

The free love movement was a curious mixture of genteel left-wing idealism, women's emancipation, theatrical goings-on and, its least important aspect, a genuine libertinism. Its philosophers had as much capacity for exciting sexual passion as the Albert Memorial, and its advocates were either sexually neuter (what Bernard Shaw called the 'sandal making village set') or homosexuals intent on improving their own positions by proselytizing on the advantages of a love free and untrammeled by matrimony. It was a movement in which words were more important than deeds, in which even its most ardent disciples used a language that was hardly less than coy, and it reached its apotheosis in the nineties, when the doors of the twentieth century were thrown open with a bang.

At its most negative, the movement was a plea against marriage. The Married Women's Property Act had taken much of the magic out of marriage and had enabled it to be seen as primarily a social institution to cater to the animal in man and as a pragmatic solution to the rearing of children. In 1882 Tennyson in his play *The Promise of May* had one of the characters mouthing the new view of matrimony:

Marriage! That feeble institution! Child, it will pass away with priestcraft from the pulpit into the crypt, into the abyss. For does not Nature herself teach us that marriage is against nature. Look at the birds – they pair for the season and part; but how merrily they sing! While marrying is like chaining two dogs together by the collar. They snarl and bite each other because there is no hope of parting.

The personages in the free love drama are endlessly self-important and have been rewarded by utter oblivion. One of the most important (at the time) was James Hinton, who was for Mrs Havelock Ellis, (a Lesbian who doted on Lily, an amateur artist of St Ives, Cornwall), one of the great heroes of the movement. He was a hero because he hacked at the crumbling framework of the established church and dared to stand against the respectable view of marriage. 'Christ was the Saviour of men,' he declared, 'but I am the saviour of women, and I don't envy Him a bit.' This remark was thought to be very risqué, verging on the blasphemous.

Like many of his colleagues, Hinton was the son of a minister. He was born in 1822, the third in a sequence of thirteen children, and he speedily made himself a foundation member of the 'sandal making village set', dressing as a tramp and walking barefoot down Fleet Street to ascertain how it felt, and getting drunk to see if he was inclined to beat his wife. Wrote Mrs Havelock Ellis without intentional irony:

The friend who came to see him, and found him eating a mutton chop and dissecting a human ear at the same time, would have found it difficult to place this intense, enthusiastic, unconventional, and in many ways uncontrolled nature under the banner of 'good form' and 'balance' to which the world gives it favour. . . . This seer, with the almond-shaped blue eyes, liquid as a woman's, soft skin, brown hair, long and high forehead, narrow, pallid and hollow cheeks, large quivering nostrils, and curved mouth betokening the ascetic and the sensualist alike – the upper lip being thin, and the lower full and sensitive – this quivering, vibrating creature, dreadfully thin, not with illness, but through the fire which consumed him, this muscularly strong man with the tenderness of a woman.[35]

This was the pattern of the free lover, though Hinton died too soon (in 1875) to see his doctines brought to the masses. He was also characteristic in that his opinions masked an almost psychotic shyness with women, which he rationalized by excessive self-abasement. 'I look upon myself as a sort of conglomeration of faults, a kind of aggregate of defects put into a bodily shape,' he wrote, mock-tongue in cheek. Ruskin had the same attitude when confronted by mature woman, 'looking like nothing so much as a skate in an Aquarium trying to get up the glass. . . . In my social behaviour and mind I was curious combination of Mr Traddles, Mr Toots and Mr Winkle.' [36]

Hinton fell in love at nineteen, but was handicapped because when he was with the girl he turned white with apprehension. His proclivities for dissecting human ears came from his time at St Bartholomew's Hospital, whence he went to practise as an assistant surgeon. He had traditional religious doubts, went to Jamaica as a medical officer on board an emigrant ship, returned, got married, began to breed, and took an interest in homeopathy, where he discovered that 'anything that acts on the emotions will cause or cure disease, because of the simple fact that all the emotions produce a specific effect upon the small vessels, the capillaries, which expand under exciting and pleasing emotions and contract under depressing ones'.[37] His erstwhile instructors at the hospital would have despaired had they heard these doctrines. It was an early example of Hinton's tendency to wrap up things in a convenient capsule for easy assimilation. He became an ear specialist at Guy's Hospital, but his main attentions were devoted to ethics, the problem of pain and pleasure, marriage and sex. To this end, he wrote a series of books, full of muddled thinking, that because for his followers a kind of holy writ.

He considered a fixed system of morality as somehow indecent. He used words such as 'passion,' 'love' and 'pleasure' as counters in a Hinton-orientated parcheesi. 'The evil is not in indulging passion, but in not following good; not in putting away indulgence, but in having no reason to put it away.' One of his favourite terms was 'service', which he uses in a way that is incomprehensible to those without special training in semantics:

Woman's relation to man has been mixed up with the problem of pleasure: she has been sacrificed for that. So long as man either pursues or refuses pleasure, he does, and must, muddle his relations with women, and cannot get them right; that is, true to service. We do not ask even what woman needs, but what suits us. Those who love and honour her most are even more intent upon treating her with that utter disregard and practical cruelty (for it is so), intenser, more exquisite, than can be conceived.[38]

Love was 'a telescope given us, just for once, by God, to reveal to us wonders and glories hidden indeed from the unaided eye, but none the less real and glorious for that'. Man must pass through licence to restraint. Actions become acceptable or unacceptable depending on the purity of the participants. Ethics must be self-imposed, not handed down from above. 'The law is, have no law, and this is expressed and made intelligent merely by that physical condition, a constant change. Hold to nothing. Be ready for anything. Let right change as nature changes, but have absolute regard to claims.' Whose claims? What claims? The contradictions and fuddle that permeate Hinton's thought are the bastard issue of the mystical doctines of Patmore; Hinton can be seen as a rather squalid secular version of Patmore, and he surely would not have disowned Patmore's 'Purity ends by finding a goddess where impurity concludes by confessing carrion'.[39] Hinton acted as though he had a special relationship with Eros, as though only he had been vouchsafed nuptial delight. He wanted to be remembered as 'the man who said, "Man is made that he can rise above the sexual passion and subordinate it to use." ' He was thrown into a perpetual tizzy by sex, a favourite synonym for which was 'pleasure'. 'Let pleasure be no more a power to ruin and destroy. Learn to be able to use it and not to be crushed by it.' Although 'the embracing of a woman is the most spiritual of all things ... lust is that distortion of one or some desires that comes by absence of desires that ought to be present.' Hinton used language in a peculiar way. At times he indicates that there is more pleasure in restraining oneself from sex, at other times his message is go to it (preferably the woman should enjoy it too). 'Is it more shame or wonder that of all the thoughts man has had respecting his passion for woman and joy in her, he has never had the thought of its good for her?' Sex on the mind has frequently given rise to such vague generalizations. His notion, as Mrs Ellis put it, 'that sexual pleasure, rightly understood, is the most spiritual thing, sublimer, purer, more noble and ennobling than any prayer' was, he thought, a wonderful discovery that he, and only he, had made. As an exponent of parish-pump sex, Hinton has his own small niche, but though his words frequently sent the blood coursing through the veins of his disciples, his own actions were that of an uxorious conformist. He did not taste the pleasures of beds other than his wife's. Not so his son, Howard, brought up in this mock-emancipationist atmosphere. He practiced what his father preached and became an authentic martyr of the free love movement. In 1886 he was tried at the Old Bailey for bigamously marrying Maude Welden. A week of free love at King's Cross Hotel (of all places) proved to be more expensive than Howard Hinton believed at the time.

If Hinton was a booby, so was Edward Carpenter, socialist, vegetarian, and, for Bernard Shaw, the key man in the set. Born in 1844, he was clearly cannon fodder for the established church, especially that branch of it labelled 'broad'. He became curate to the socialist do-gooder F. D. Maurice, but in 1883 he bought land near Sheffield and lived the life of a market gardener. His affirmations of a love free from chains have the same lordly ring as those of Hinton, and behind these statements Carpenter lived a timid life. 'Now understand me well,' he wrote peremptorily – he was not an admirer of Walt Whitman for nothing, 'there is no desire or indulgence that is forbidden;

there is not one good and another evil. All are alike in this respect. In place all are to be used.' Unequivocal, one would think.
But Carpenter, like Hinton, was using the specialized vocabulary of his calling. He did not mean *quite* what he said. 'When
thy body, as needs must happen at times, is carried along on
the wind of passion, say not thou, "I desire this or that." For
the "I" neither desires nor fears anything, but is free and in
everlasting glory, dwelling in heaven and pouring out joy like the
sun on all sides. Let not that precious thing by any confusion
be drawn down and entangled in the world of opposites, and of
death and suffering.' [40] The coloured counters that figured as
words in the Carpenter mind might produce any effect in the
mind of a receptive reader. The ambiguity of his statements
might be supposed to have had relevance only to his contemporaries, and it is perhaps shocking to learn that Carpenter's
Love's Coming of Age (1896) still has a wide circulation among
thoughtful working-class socialists of the Fabian persuasion.

Carpenter echoes Hinton in his exhortations that sex is a
mystic state, and also in his trepidation that it may be trans-
mogrified into a hammer that could hit him on the head: 'But
ever when desire knocks at thy door, though thou grant it admission and entreat it hospitably, as in duty bound – fence it
yet gently off from thy true self, lest it should tear and rend
thee.' The use of the second person singular, that most unscrupulous of nineteenth-century mechanisms for establishing a
coy empathy with the reader, is combined with the device of
chopping up the lines into fragments, like 'thoughts'. Not that
it was likely that desire would tear and rend Carpenter. In his
thatched hut at Millthorpe, Carpenter was effectively insulated
from such temptation; he had drawn a cheque on the free love
account, but had not bothered to cash it, being content to wave
it around in the air.

The fuzzy outlines and the ambiguities of Hinton's and Carpenter's theoretical free love failed to state the nature of such
freedom. This was left to the feet-on-the-ground philosopher
Herbert Spencer:

Freedom in its absolute form is the absence of all external checks
to whatever actions the will prompts; and freedom in its socially-

restricted form is the absence of any other external checks than those arising from the presence of other men who have like claims to do what their wills prompt. The mutual checks hence resulting are the only checks which freedom, in the true sense of the word, permits. The sphere within each may act without trespassing on the like spheres of others, cannot be intruded upon by any agency, private or public, without an equivalent loss of freedom.[41]

This classic definition of freedom is particularly well suited to the sphere of sexual morals. Free love in theory was all very well; but in practice, who would suffer, if anyone?

Until he was trapped in a slough of sentimentality by Ellen Terry about his fortieth year, Bernard Shaw was one of the most rational stars in the firmament. Although a vegetarian and a Fabian socialist, under whose banner the lunatic fringe circulated, Shaw could view the caprices of his colleagues with a cool detachment that does him credit. He had his own foibles, in particular his attachment to Dr Gustav Jaeger's 'sanitary woollen system', which advocated the use of wool, and only wool, in clothing. Shaw's one-piece woollen suit was an omniscient advertisement for Jaegerism. Shaw was not averse to free love, and he cynically exploited the ageing widow Jenny Patterson, to whom he lost his virginity at the age of twenty-nine. He was not wholly lacking in the timidity that made Carpenter a non-starter. She and a friend 'have about as much reason to be frightened as a pair of vigorous and experienced cats have to recoil before an exceptionally nervous mouse',[42] Shaw wrote to Jenny Patterson in 1886.

On the subject of marriage he took the party line:

I strenuously object to the marriage laws as they stand today, and am for granting divorce where both parties consent to it, on sufficient guarantees being given as to children &c. I also object to the family as a legal institution on the ground that the equality of the wife and child is destroyed by making the husband the unit of the State, with powers over them which are often grossly abused. These views get stigmatized as mere libertinage.

Such views would have got even shorter shrift twenty years earlier, but he was writing in December 1890, and a new pat-

tern of free thinking was being played out. The iron hold of the
Victorian middle classes was loosening. This was compensated
by fanatical tirades by journalists and critics who saw the humdrum respectability that had marked their formative years coming apart at the seams. In 1891 Ibsen's *Ghosts*, dealing with
veneral disease, was put on the stage. It was, said Clement
Scott, the hoary critic of the *Daily Telegraph*, one of those who
drivelled over the rubbish that forms ninety-nine per cent of
Victorian drama, 'A dirty act done publicly'. In 1893 the conformist Arthur Wing Pinero, darling of the Clement Scott
school, ventured into this new territory with *The Second Mrs
Tanqueray*. One of the characters in this lively melodrama says:
'I believe she kept a thermometer in her stays, and always registered ten degrees below zero.' That the fashionable ladies in
the dress circle did not faint by the cabload said much for the
change in the social climate. The second Mrs Tanqueray was a
prostitute. Shaw opened up this vein with *Mrs Warren's Profession* – Mrs Warren was a brothel keeper. In this play, related Shaw to an up-and-coming young critic, R. Golding
Bright:

I have sought to put on the stage for the first time (as far as I know)
the highly educated, capable, independent young woman of the
governing class as we know her today, working, smoking, preferring
the society of men to that of women simply because men talk about
the questions that interest her and not about servants and babies,
making no pretence of caring much about art or romance, respectable
through sheer usefulness and strength, and playing the part of the
charming woman only as the amusement of her life, not as its serious
occupation.[43]

Shaw had experience of such women, for they thronged through
the Fabian circles, eager for life, not averse to sexual experiment, the second generation of free lovers. Shaw could have had
a succession of such girls had he been so inclined, but he came
up against the barbed wire of finding that, despite his shabby
treatment of Mrs Patterson, he was by and large an honourable
man. 'Unless a man is a rascal who seduces his friends' wives
and is prepared to practise on the credulity of innocent young

enthusiasts who take every socialist for a saint, he cannot lead a very wild career,'[44] he wrote to a friend ironically.

Being a socialist and having brave new ideas about sexual freedom did not, then, necessarily mean endless high jinks, and Shaw frequently had to calm down girls anxious to lose their virginities in the cause of emancipation ('the provocative, the mischievous, the risky, the dramatic have no charms for me'). Similarly, girls who considered that free love was theirs for the asking found that when the chips were down their bourgeois upbringing placed a veto on any uninhibited behaviour. Shaw recounted a tea party in which the hostess, professedly forward-looking and modern, was thrown into confusion by the departure of a third party:

> She hurried up the tea, and then, before we could intervene, nodded at us in a 'I know you want to get rid of me' way, snatched up her things; and deserted her hostess, leaving us in the most miserable confusion and consciousness. . . . I tried hard to behave myself, although the breaking off of the end of the sofa reminded me rudely that I had lapsed into my habit of sprawling and lolling.[45]

The tea party took place in Manresa Road, Chelsea, then achieving its reputation as the place for smart people to live, and the hostess was a young artist, Nelly Erichsen, a versatile girl who later turned her attention to translating Strindberg and who died young in 1918.

Fashionable left-wing activity in the last two decades of the nineteenth century had two main strands. In 1881 H. M. Hyndman, an adventurer on the make, formed the Democratic Federation; he changed the name in 1884 to the Social-Democratic Federation and gathered around him a weird group of intellectuals who found Hyndman's half-baked interpretation of Marxism compelling and exciting. In 1885 there was a comic opera sequence in which Hyndman put up for the general election three socialist candidates backed with conservative money, and several adherents, including William Morris, left to form the Socialist League, which fell apart because of anarchists in their midst. The Fabian Society was formed in 1884. They talked more and did less than the Social-

Democratic Federation; whereas Hyndman and his crew were all for bloody revolution, the Fabians favoured a gradual transfer of power, the gradual permeation of the ruling orders.

For the more extreme of the members of these two groups, marriage was a relic of a bygone age; speculated Shaw:

What will happen about marriage is probably this. As soon as it is realized that people are learning how to do without it, it will be considerably modified, as in America, by a great extension of divorce. The English will never abolish marriage. They never abolish things; but they circumvent them more unscrupulously than any other nation. At present it is far better for two people who do not mean to devote themselves to a regular domestic, nursery career to maintain a clandestine connection than to run the risks of marriage.

The two movements were interpenetrated by other groups, the vaguely progressive, the outsiders who wanted a convenient umbrella, and vestiges of the village guru set, as well as those who wanted to do something for the lot of the masses, such as Belfort Bax,[46] whose intentions were good, but who was terrified of the workers on whose behalf he was struggling, and a couple of fervent believers in land nationalization, who got their comeuppance in a curious way – one of them married a washerwoman's daughter who was posing as a great lady, and the other went to Australia where he died of venereal disease. Circling the arena were the weirdies, such as Howard Hinton, who was known as 'The Wizard'. Sexual freedom was part of the manifesto. Novelists in sympathy propagated this in their books. 'I like to experience, I like to try,' declared the heroine in Olive Schreiner's *The Story of an African Farm* (1883), 'I cannot marry you because I cannot be tied; but, if you wish, you may take me away with you, and take care of me; then when we do not love any more we can say goodbye.' Miss Schreiner plunged into this freedom with zest, was alarmed when she missed a period, and even more so when she found that she was becoming a nymphomaniac. She took potassium bromide to curb her desire, acquired psychosomatic asthma, and fell in love with a sadist. Havelock Ellis, a believer in all kinds of freedom, took her on holiday in Derbyshire. Despite this, Ellis related delicately, 'We were not what can be technically, or even ordinarily, called lovers.'

There were two diametrically opposed groups endeavouring to abolish marriage. One consisted of the more extreme emancipationists who nurtured a profound contempt for man; free love, love between equals, was furthest from their thoughts. In an article 'What Shall We Do With Our Old Maids?' in *Frazer's Magazine* (November 1862), Frances Power Cobbe maintained that 'when we have made it *less* women's interest to marry, we shall indeed have less and fewer interested marriages, with all their train of miseries and evils, but we shall have more loving ones, more marriages founded on free choice and free affection'. Governesses who had married to avoid the indignity of being out of work, daughters of the country clergy who had married to get away from the suffocating environment – these were a self-perpetuating species that became a close-lipped adamantine tribunal passing judgement on their daughters who wanted to be free from the chains that society had forced on their weary mothers. They joined with the professional squeakers trying to support the *status quo*. 'Freethought has made havoc of the sanctity of marriage,' declared Elizabeth Chapman in *Married Questions in Modern Fiction and Other Essays* (1897). 'Nothing savouring of sacerdotalism, nothing smacking of superstition, nothing attaching in any manner to discarded sanctions or exploded dogmas, can weigh seriously with the enlightened thinker of the nineteenth century, who is essentially a law unto himself, and recognises no superior, human or divine.' The free love people would have seen a true outline of their faith in this; the irony would have escaped them.

Enthusiasts for free love were frequently shocked to find that they were pigeonholed with the free thinkers. Elizabeth Chapman clearly considered that the two terms were synonymous. Free thought was a not too distasteful substitute for atheism, and free lovers did not relish the confusion, even those whose faith rested on a vague deism. Many free lovers were committed to a saintly way of life, if only because it side-tracked the difficulties inherent in their calling. 'Formerly it may have been difficult to live in a modernized Jesus Christ style,' wrote Shaw, in an essay dealing with his favourite hobbyhorse, Ibsen, 'but now it is easy, convenient and cheap; and if a man makes a merit of it he is pretty sure to be a humbug.' Tripping through the daisies in the buff, admiring the sunset, and sex among the haystacks – these were often mutually inclusive. Again it is Shaw who lifts a flap and shows us the other side of this idyllic existence:

I wonder what you would think of our life – our eternal political shop; our mornings of dogged writing, all in separate rooms; our ravenous plain meals; our tricycling; the Webbs incorrigible spooning over the industrial and political science; Miss P. T. [i.e., Miss Townshend whom Shaw later married] Irish, shrewd and green eyed, finding everything 'very interesting.'[47]

The back-to-nature movement was often allied to this amiable Fabian socialism, and the advanced political views frequently went with advanced sexual morals. There was one great snag; even the most forward-looking had been conditioned by education, precept, and upbringing. 'Man for the field and woman for the hearth. ... All else confusion,'[48] Tennyson had written half a century earlier. Beneath every emancipated cigarette-smoking woman with freewheeling sexual views there was a lily of the field, a girlish, plaything, embryo wife and mother, a rooted conservative, depository of inconsistency and irrationality. Patmore put this in an uncharacteristic avuncular tone: despite

absolute outrages against nature – such as divided skirts, free-thinking, tricycles and Radicalism [for free-thinking read 'free love', for Radicalism read 'socialism'] – neither Greek nor conic sections, nor political economy, nor cigarettes, nor athletics can ever really do other than enhance the charm of that sweet unreasonableness which humbles the gods to the dust and compels them to adore the lace below the last hem of her brocade![49]

Those who talked most about free love did least; the spirit was willing, but the flesh was weak. After flaunting their freedom, the women relapsed into a cosy domesticity, and their men capitulated, sometimes with a disarming duplicity. In 1898 the assistant editor of *Hearth and Home*, J. S. Nolan, drew attention to the practicality of the Fabian socialists. 'Every few years some prominent member of the Fabian Society contrived to marry an heiress whose wealth and energies were subsequently devoted wholly to the cause. Thus Sidney Webb married Beatrice Potter; B. F. Costelloe married Miss Pearsall Smith; and J. R. MacDonald married Miss M. E. Gladstone.'[50] And, of course, Bernard Shaw married Miss Payne Townshend. Had there been some viable alternative to marriage, then these pioneers of the Labour Party (the ideas and ideals of the present Labour Party derive from this tiny Fabian movement) might well have tried that. Unfortunately, alternatives were few and unworkable. The Legitimation League, in which marriage would be replaced by a 'formal acknowledgement of union' was a promising outsider, but one of its chief sponsors was a rascal – Roland de Villiers, alias Goerg von Weissenfeld, ex-jailbird (twelve months for forgery), seller of other peoples' vineyards, and possessor of thirty banking accounts in London alone. He was one of the crosses the free lovers had to bear. With such dangerous allies in the field, it was better to surrender to marriage, eventually to indulge in diatribes against their children when they in their turn discovered the delights of unrestrained love in the 1920s.

5

The Facts of Life

Childbirth and Women's Diseases

O the pain about my belly,
    O the pain about my back;
How shall I ever get o'er it,
    Faith my aching head will crack.
Her mother was stuck in a corner,
    With a big drop in her eye;
Hush my dear and darling creature,
    You'll be better bye-and-bye.

E v e n in the seventies and eighties childbirth was still a great social occasion. The dangers had been lessened, but childbearing remained a hazardous occupation, and the principal character etched in the above verse of a music hall song of the period was fortunate that she was having a baby at home, where, despite the manifest discomfort and the folk traditions taken over from generation to generation, it was generally safer than a lying-in hospital, where there was a dreadul death rate from the ravages of what was called childbed fever, lying-in fever, or puerperal fever. 'Within the first few hours or days after delivery,' wrote Dr Spencer Thomson (*A Dictionary of Domestic Medicine*, 1856), 'the woman may be attacked with shivering, or rather shaking so severe as to shake the bed, succeeded by heat of skin, thirst, delirium, and with or without severe pain in the bowels;

she is attacked with child-bed fever, and cannot too quickly [be] seen by a medical man.'

Alas, the medical man too often was unable to do anything beyond prescribe a pill composed of one grain of opium and five grains of calomel and apply leeches, frequently in batches of sixteen dozen at a time, to the abdomen. Puerperal fever was a killer infection that haunted the dreams of brides, a mysterious disease that came from no one knew what. There were not wanting speculations. Dr George Johnston thought that puerperal fever might follow from 'constitutional disorders' that succeeded 'seduction, remorse, fretting'. Others considered that it rose from infection from cases of typhoid. The more advanced doctors thought that the doctors themselves were to blame, that they transferred bacteria from dead bodies to living women.

The Boston poet-doctor, Oliver Wendell Holmes, proposed this with his paper 'On the Contagiousness of Puerperal Fever' (1843), and the Vienna specialist Dr Ignaz Semmelweis confirmed this in 1847 when he wrote that 'Puerperal Fever is caused by conveyance to the pregnant woman of putrid particles derived from living organisms, through the agency of the examining fingers'. This theory was not liked by many in the profession, who thought that a slur was being cast on them by this wild talk, and who considered that the sensible advice offered to them by Holmes and Semmelweis to thoroughly wash their hands in chloride of lime before delivering babies savoured of impertinence.

In Britain, these continental and American ideas were slow in being taken up. Complications during gestation could not be dealt with. There is a sad little sentence in Lady Frederick Cavendish's *Diary* of 25 February 1859: 'Aunt Emmy came, and we talked parish matters, which are unusually exciting with illness; 6 people prayed for, 4 expecting babies, 3 of whom are anxious cases,' and in the letter that Charlotte Nicholls née Brontë wrote to her friend Ellen Nussey on 19 January 1855:

My health has been really very good since my return from Ireland till about ten days ago, when the stomach seemed quite suddenly to lose its tone; indigestion and continual faint sickness have been my portion ever since. Don't conjecture, dear Nell, for it is too soon yet, though I certainly never before felt as I have done lately. But keep the matter wholly to yourself, for I can come to no decided opinion at present. I am rather mortified to lose my good looks and grow thin. . .

For cases in which the normal channels of delivery were not available the prognosis was not favourable. Although Caesarian operations had been carried out for centuries, in the first half of the nineteenth century each attempt had a seventy-five per cent chance of death, and in 1870 Dr R. Virchow (1821–1902) noted that of forty Caesarian cases he had encountered, all proved fatal to the mother. It was not until the last quarter of the century that any great advances were made in specialized gynaecology, though in 1851 Dr Reynale incised a woman's cervix to facilitate the vaginal route, much in front of his time.

The high death rate that permeated the lying-in wards of general hospitals was brought to the attention of the influential mainly by accident. In 1867 Florence Nightingale – the 'Lady with the Lamp', the heroine of the Crimean War – entered the arena. A training school for midwives had been opened in King's College Hospital with the financial backing of Miss Nightingale and her associates. Puerperal fever struck the lying-in ward and spread until the school was closed. Shocked and troubled, Miss Nightingale decided to investigate and found to her astonishment that no reliable statistics existed relating to deaths by puerperal fever. 'There appears to have been no uniform system of record of deaths,' she wrote, 'or the causes of death, in many institutions, and no common agreement as to the period after delivery during which deaths should be counted as due to the puerperal condition.'

It was fortunate that the prestige of Florence Nightingale had never been dimmed in the decade that had passed since the Crimean War, for otherwise she would have found it doubly difficult to get hold of any reliable figures. As it was, many institutions refused to divulge their secrets.

Three years were spent carrying out researches, and it was soon evident that confinement at home was much safer than delivery in hospital. Not only that – the bigger the hospital, the greater were the chances of death. By 1871 there was enough data for Dr John Sutherland to put a book together at the behest of Miss Nightingale – *Introductory Notes on Lying-in Institutions*. In London workhouses, the death rate was dependent upon the number of deliveries; thirteen infirmaries without deaths for five years had hardly more than one delivery a month. The Military Female Hospital at Shorncliffe was an old wooden hut, but it was safer to have a baby there, with its one attendant and rarely more than one bed occupied at a time, than in the most lavishly endowed hospital in the metropolis. 'Not a single lying-in woman should ever pass the doors of a general hospital,' declared Miss Nightingale.

She saw part of the reason for the high casualty rate in ignorance, carelessness and the general inferior quality of midwives; and she set to work to encourage the recruitment of educated women for midwifery, to replace the Mrs Gamp type, far too long the image of the average midwife. However, even the clarion call of Florence Nightingale fell on ears that were tuned in to higher things – the emancipated women of the period wanted to be doctors, not midwives. 'The more chattering and noise there is about Women's Mission,' she had written in 1865, 'the less of efficient women can we find. It makes me mad to hear people talk about unemployed women. If they are unemployed it is because they won't work. The highest salaries given to women at all we can secure to women trained by us. But we can't find the women. They won't come.' Those women who would have made ideal nurses and midwives were 'trying to come over the doctors by all kinds of feminine dodges' – so Elizabeth Garrett wrote to a friend.

Miss Garrett had insinuated herself at Middlesex Hospital to the contempt of the doctors and male students, but she was foolish enough to win top marks at an examination, upon which the wrath of her fellow students knew no end, and she was barred from future forays into this man's world. She cleverly sidetracked the forces of reaction by passing the easy apothecaries' examination so that she could practise as a doctor – the Society of Apothecaries was legally bound to accept her on her merits and not on her sex. As for Miss Nightingale's problem – persuading intelligent girls that there was a future in midwifery – this was unsolved so long as anyone could venture into this field without qualifications, without talent, and with only the vaguest idea of what to do if things went wrong. It was not until 1902 that the profession of midwife became respectable. During the Nightingale period, it is a pity that the many thousands of girls deflected from being governesses by lack of situations vacant were not encouraged into midwifery by improving the image with legislation, or by removing the stigma that Dickens had inadvertently given to the calling by the invention of the comical Mrs Gamp.

If childbearing was marginally safer, so during the second half of the nineteenth century was it considerably less painful. In his student days, Dr James Young Simpson had undergone a traumatic experience when watching, in the surgery class of Professor Liston, the agony of a woman having a breast amputated. After he had decided to specialize in obstetrics, Simpson made it his aim to make childbearing as painless as possible by the use of anaesthetics; there was a choice of two—ether and chloroform. Chloroform was better as it did not need the cumbersome machinery necessary for the manipulation of ether.

His first dramatic use of chloroform as a prime agent in obstetrics on 17 January 1847, was described by Simpson. 'I placed her under the influence of the chloroform by moistening, with half a tea-spoonful of the liquid, a pocket handkerchief, rolled up into a funnel shape, and with the broad or open end of the funnel placed over her mouth and nostrils.' As if on cue, the woman, after giving birth to a child, awoke and said that she had 'enjoyed a very comfortable sleep, and indeed required it as she was so tired, but would now be more able for the work before her'. In March of the same year, Simpson communicated his feelings about chloroform to an Edinburgh medical society, outlining the brief history – discovered and described in 1831 – and its properties, 'a dense, limpid, colourless liquid, readily evaporating, and possessing an agreeable, fragrant, fruit-like odour, and a saccharine pleasant taste'.

That this new dimension in healing should not go unreproved, the *Lancet* in 1848 launched into an attack: 'I have long inculcated at Guy's Hospital,' wrote Dr Ashwell, the obstetrician, 'that unnecessary interference with the providentially arranged process of healthy labour is sure, sooner or later, to be followed by injurious and fatal consequences. I think chloroform will be no exception to these precepts.' In 1866 the *Lancet* changed its tune – Dr Simpson had been given a baronetcy, and, besides, the Queen had had chloroform administered during her own confinements, and 'was greatly pleased with the effect'. 'Sir James,' declared the *Lancet*, 'has long been foremost in his department of practice, and his name is associated with the discovery of that invaluable boon to suffering humanity – chloroform.'

The very ease with which chloroform was administered carried with it its attendant dangers, and old prejudice returned when a woman named Hannah Greener of Newcastle who had been in great fear of chloroform but who had been persuaded to give it a try died in two minutes. This was given more than its due publicity. Nevertheless, in surgery there was no question that chloroform was a life-saver – in the amputation of the thigh, where death through shock ran at sixty-nine per cent in Paris and forty-nine per cent in Edinburgh, chloroform had reduced the mortality rate to twenty-five per cent.

For Simpson – as a hero-worshipping medical officer in the Indian Army wrote to the *Bombay Telegraph and Courier*, 'ether and chlorofrom ... seem like invisible intelligences, doomed to obey his bidding – familiars who do his work because they must never venture to produce effects one iota greater or less than he desires. While other men measure out the liquids, fumble about and make a fuss, Simpson, in what an Irishman would call the most promiscuous manner possible, does the job in a minute or two.' Whatever the Irishman might think, such cavalier treatment would hardly comfort the nervous. Whether or not Simpson was approved of by royalty for 'his high character and abilities' – as the Queen wrote to the Duchess of Sutherland – an off-hand attitude towards the wonder drug of the age was not wanted by his patients. 'Chlory', as Simpson's butler Clarke called it, was in danger of being treated like the household pet, and many women preferred to take their chances, labour pains or not, with the *Lancet's* 'providentially arranged process.'

To women of the twentieth century, there might well be a number of viable reasons for a belief that to them the Victorian age was not a good one to live in. The women of the era had more influence and power than is often accorded to them – they were not always just breeding animals and playthings any more than they are now – but in one respect they were certainly not to be envied. If anything went wrong with the delicate mechanism of reproduction they were left to the mercy of a profession that was inclined to drag its feet – the medical. As discovery succeeded discovery, the doctors stood by and watched with often an unbecoming cynicism, and for even the specialists the inside of woman was a place of magic and of mystery. Among the more reactionary the myths of ancient Greece still held sway. Aretaeus, who flourished about A.D. 100, was regarded as a fount of knowledge, and the edition of his works that came out in 1856 was no mere historical curiosity. As a doctor he had stood second only to Hippocrates, and to the doctors of 1856 there was little cause to reverse this decision. His description of the uterus was still worthy of consideration as a working hypothesis: 'The uterus greatly resembles an animal. It moves itself to various parts of the body, sometimes upwards in the throat, then to the sides, causing oppression in the lungs, the heart, the diaphragm, the liver, and the intestines.' It was worthy of consideration as this was the classical etiology of hysteria.

If anything, doctors of the nineteenth century took a step backward in the treatment of hysteria and its allies – nervousness, anxiety and hypochondria. In the eighteenth century, doctors were inclined to look upon psychosomatic disorders with more sympathy than was later to be shown; in their dealings with diseases associated with the female reproductive system, Victorian doctors were hardly more understanding, and there was an unsatisfactory shift of emphasis, from doctor as healer to doctor as preacher. There was frequently an air of self-righteousness and indignation when doctors encountered cancer of the womb. Dr F. W. Scanzoni (1821–91) promulgated the views of many when he declared that 'immoderate coitus and excessive sexual excitation are not without importance in the aetiology of cancer ... it is not the frequency of the coitus but the moral excitation which accompanies it which seems here to be the important point.' Doctors were even more affronted when they encountered nymphomania under its various headings, *furor uterinus*, 'metromania', 'andromania', 'erotomania', 'clitorimania', or 'lypatia', and their cures were symbolic rather than efficacious – the use of a straw mattress and the washing of the genitals.

The discharge of a white liquid from the vagina led to puzzlement and it was easier to affix a cause for this disability than to assign a cure. *Fleurs-blanches* ('white flowers', flowers being the colloquial expression for the menses) were caused by erotic reading, the establishment of an early and artificial puberty, masturbation, and 'the concentration of the sentiments and thoughts on objects which keep the genital organs in a sort of permanent turgescence and excitation'. Also of account were bad weather, low marshy regions, too much coffee, and foot-warmers. As for inflammation of the womb – metritis – this could be caused by masturbation, coitus, abstinence, ice cream, tea, alcohol and 'tight corsets worn while reading French novels.'

Yet despite the mumblings and fantasies the technicians of the medical profession were providing a vast new range of equipment for the treatment of diseases of the reproductive system. In 1877 the axistraction forceps for difficult deliveries was invented, and H. L. Hodge evolved a pessary to correct displacement of the womb, an innovation that was prompted by the design of a stand to hold shovel and tongs that stood by his fireplace. Specialists found that the prohibitions of early nineteenth-century doctors to leave the interior of woman well alone no longer applied. The removal of the ovaries remained a hazardous operation, but it no longer meant almost certain death to the unfortunate woman. During the course of his long career, Dr Charles Clay of Manchester performed 395 ovariotomies, of which only 101 resulted in death.

Another doctor who made something of a speciality of ovariotomy was Dr Lawson Tait, who opened a private hospital in The Crescent, Birmingham. Although Tait did not enter the field until 1872, he used no antiseptics, preferring to clean his instruments with boiling water, soap, washing soda and turpentine. In the room where he operated – he had no operating theatre – there was an open fire. Tait operated on a board seven by two feet, supported on two wooden trestles and covered by a piece of mackintosh sheeting. The patient (or victim) was secured to this board by iron bands encircling wrists and legs. An American surgeon saw this set-up, and afterwards commented, 'Mr Tait used three drugs, the chief of them is water, and the other two are the nearest approach to water as possible.' In his frockcoat with cuffs rolled back, with his huge paunch and his cavalier contempt for what Oliver Wendell Holmes called 'the little army of microbes', Dr Lawson Tait might be seen as a throwback to the age of merciless medicine. It was fortunate that he was a type gradually becoming obsolescent, and a new race of doctors was coming to the fore in whose codex the qualities of gentleness and consideration were contained.

Menstruation

More was discovered in the nineteenth century than in any previous batch of five centuries, and it is not to be wondered at that pioneers were striding ahead while the journeymen were still trying to assimilate material that the discoverers now took for granted. This was particularly true in the field of medicine, where quaint survivals from the age of Galen rubbed shoulders with a technology that was truly astonishing. In medicine, the tendency for practitioners to dig in their heels and refuse to listen to the prophets of the new order was particularly widespread; occasionally the forces of reaction were right. Sometimes it was advisable to treat new *outré* theories and methods of treatment with suspicion, and if the enthusiasm with which forward-looking pharmacists greeted new preparations had been echoed by practising doctors, the mortuaries would have been filled with overconfident patients who had dosed themselves with, for example, strychnine and digitalis.

Hindsight enables us to be appalled at the cavalier attitude of Dr Lawson Tait with regard to hygiene, his frock-coat, his open fires, and his gallons of water for sluicing out his patients. It is easy to make out that he was a kind of a crank battening on the rich and easy to forget that in 1883 he carried out the first operation for ruptured ectopic gestation (a pregnancy outside the womb). Similarly what is common knowledge today was then a subject for speculation or distrust, even when the correct facts were known and in print. The discarding of centuries of instinctive belief in favour of truth was often difficult.

Because, in medicine, many of the factors are complex and specialized, transitions from error to truth are observable only to medical historians – though there are dramatic cases, such as the use of carbolic acid to facilitate germless childbirth – and where the opposition of doctors in power does seem to be needlessly obscurantist. The myth that childbirth was a natural process that could not be aided or interfered with in any way died hard.

A greater myth was in the course of being dissolved, the myth of menstruation. The discharge of from four to six ounces of blood and mucous matter every month had been a source of wonder and disgust for thousands of years. This was Queen Victoria's 'poorly time'; the menses were known as the curse, or as the flowers, and most people believed that menstruation had something to do with the moon, giving it, for the primitive, a cosmic significance. Havelock Ellis pointed out, 'the fact that women are thus, as it were, periodically wounded in the most sensitive spot in their organism, and subjected to a monthly loss of blood, is familiar, and has been used, legitimately or illegitimately ... to explain numerous phenomena'. Ellis also suggested that men, too, possess some traces of a rudimentary menstrual cycle, affecting the entire organism. Surprisingly this suggestion has never been followed up with the assiduity that it surely merits.

This monthly incapacitation led to the idea that women were natural invalids, but it was a subterranean idea in England. On the continent, opera singers had a clause built into their contract so that during their periods they could back down; in Britain such a disgusting idea was not to be mooted.

The ability to ignore this prime fact of female life was especially sacred to the Victorians, both male and female. Women were averse to passing on information to their daughters of thirteen and fourteen. 'The development of the function is checked by imprudences which a little information might have prevented,' commented a medical manual of 1856 severely. Where the first menstruation coincided with the discovery of sex and possibly auto-erotic activities, then alarm combined with guilt feelings often created a climate for all kinds of neuroses.

The notion that woman was a basic invalid was promulgated by generations of medical men, especially in the years before they knew what menstruation was. Galiani in his *Dialogue sur les Femmes* is very brusque:

At first she is an invalid, as all animals are until they have attained their full growth; then come the symptoms so well known in every race of man, and which made her an invalid for six days during every month on an average – [unless the woman was a Red Indian when the norm was two days] – which makes at least a fifth part of her life; then comes pregnancies and lactations which, properly considered, are two troublesome disorders...

Jules Michelet, a historian whose energy does not quite key in with his fallibility, a mock-scientist who wrote what he thought were definitive works on *The Bird* (1856), *The Insect* (1857) and *The Sea* (1861), also weighed in with *L'Amour* (1859), in which he states, 'woman is for ever suffering from the cicatrisation of an interior wound which is the cause of a whole drama. So that in reality for fifteen or twenty days [!] out of twenty-eight – one may also say always – woman is not only invalided but wounded. She suffers incessantly the eternal wound of love.'

For those who believed in the emancipation of woman, menstruation was a hurdle that was difficult to cross, and those enthusiasts on the extreme fringe believed that when woman had the vote menstruation, which they blamed in an inexplicable way on the brutality of man, would miraculously cease.

Dame Millicent Fawcett, one of the leaders of the movement, had a better way out, by denying that woman was at all inconvenienced by menstruation. 'The actual period of childbirth apart, the ordinarily healthy woman is as fit for work every day of her life as the ordinarily healthy man,' she declared. While the English were hiding their blushes, while the French were sneering at woman as invalid, the Americans were collecting data. At the same time as Dr Goodman was publishing his 'The Cyclical Theory of Menstruation' in the *American Journal of Obstetrics* in 1878, English doctors were still debating which of the two alternate theories of menstruation they should adopt, and whether there were grounds for the well-bred Englishman's instinctive disgust at the very concept of menstruation. For the benefit of posterity, they permitted their debates to take place in the letter columns of the *British Medical Journal*.

The ovum was discovered in 1832; the theory that menstruation depends upon ovulation was posed in the forties; in 1863, Dr Pflüger comprehensively sewed up the facts. This was a fact of life that had been rationally explained, but it was not accepted. In the authoritative medical paper the *Lancet* of 9 March 1878, there was a paper, 'The Rationale of the Menstrual Flow' by G. Aldridge George LRCP, MRCS. 'The occurrence of the menstrual flow, although a phenomenon that has excited much interest and been the subject of numerous speculations, is still, I believe, without an accepted explanation.' George's theory was the 'other' one, one that was widely held. The growth of the girl before puberty was more rapid than the growth of the boy, and consequently more blood was being produced. At puberty the rate of growth slowed dramatically, and there was increased tension in the blood vessels, leading to headache, a sense of fullness, hot sensations in the loins, and tense breast.

Now in these young women who are making blood rapidly the lining mucous membrane of the uterus, considering its functions and its recent increased development, may be supposed to be the weakest spot of the vascular system. When the blood-tension reaches a certain limit, the delicate capillaries rupture, the tension and local congestion are relieved, and a few ounces of blood are lost, the proper equilibrium is restored, which restoration is synchronous with the disappearance of the unpleasant symptoms before mentioned.

Were the girl at puberty to have just one period, then this explanation would be cunningly viable. Surely when the period occurs in a regular pattern except during pregnancy and lactation this theory is seen to collapse. But apparently not. The excess of blood that was spilled at puberty is used during pregnancy for the building of the foetus. 'When conception has taken place there is an outlet for the surplus of nutritive income over expenditure in the growth of the foetus and uterus, and a similar outlet also exists during lactation, so the occurrence of menses during lactation is a comparatively rare event.' The drawing of incorrect inferences from correctly observed phenomena can be seen to be very logical.

If this was believed by the unquestionably competent Dr George – after all, being a member of the Royal College of Surgeons carried some weight – it was assuredly believed by women, for whom the discharge of blood every month was evidence of their failure to conceive a child. It must have been more potent psychologically to see this blood as blood that might have been building a child; it did not escape the notice of theorists that menstruation per se was an unnatural activity; in the primitive state of man, woman was constantly conceiving and menstruation was therefore rare.

Dr George had been preceded two years earlier by a woman doctor, Dr Mary Putnam-Jacobi, who confirmed that this was the theory most likely to be true. Menstruation was 'an excess of nutritive force in the sex upon whom devolves the greatest cost of reproduction'. She also explained, to her own satisfaction, the phenomenon of amenorrhoea – absence of flow. This was 'often a piece of conservative economy when the system cannot afford the loss, and that its real treatment is that of the system generally; and that the reappearance of the menses is but the evidence of the general improvement'. She pointedly refuted the ludicrous idea that menstruation had anything to do with ovulation. Although she was wrong, Dr Putnam-Jacobi did carry out one of the first researches into pain and menstruation in Britain. She sent out 1,000 questionnaires (she called them tables), and received 268 answers. 35 per cent suffered no pain, discomfort, or weakness, 18 per cent suffered slightly, and 47 per cent found their periods seriously painful. After backache, menstrual troubles were an indication of a breakdown.

'My mind,' Charles Darwin tells us in his *Autobiography*, 'seems to have become a kind of machine for grinding general laws out of large collections of facts.' Darwin was a genius, and his general laws have turned out to be more or less right, but his propensities were shared by others, for whom any general law was better than no general law. The self-fulfilling prophecy so distinctively defined by Daniel J. Boorstin (*The Image*, 1962) was no stranger to nineteenth-century thought; prophets who took themselves seriously were taken seriously. Deflation was a hazardous art. The *ancien régime* who refused to review their theories in the light of new discoveries were often puncture proof, even when their notions were ridiculous and sometimes vicious. In the medical world, there held on to authority a considerable number of men for whom Hippocrates was still a living model and who eschewed all the advantages of progress. Some were stuck fast in medieval medicine and absurd folk wisdom, and contentedly sucked on hypotheses that would have been adequate in fourteenth-century Basle.

Of all these hypotheses, one of the most astounding is the view of menstruation as an immoral event. Dr Milne of Edinburgh in his *Principle and Practice of Midwifery* includes a couplet of his own:

> Oh! Menstruating women, thou'rt a fiend
> From which all nature should be closely screened.

Other doctors considered menstruation to be the female equivalent of the erection in the male. Others suppressed their inborn feeling that somehow menstruation was nasty and dirty, and it needed an amazing series of letters in the *British Medical Journal* to bring this to light.

A glance into the *British Medical Journal* of 1878 reveals a frightening world. For those who hark back to this golden prepetroleum age, such a glance can be a salutary experience. The engravings are mean and not very competent, and the close columns of print are crammed with do-it-yourself medicine. The news items are the kind of thing one sees in popular 'Did You Know?' features. This was the year in which a man burst, literally, after eating four plates of potato soup, 'numerous' cups of tea and milk, and after taking a large dose of bicarbonate of soda. This was the year when a boy of ten was discovered who 'bleats like a sheep ... sea-baths during four months at the seaside reduced the bleating to once a day'. Vital statistics for 1877 were being totted up. Seventy-one people in London, the richest city the world had ever known, had died of starvation. The *British Medical Journal* had not had a bad year – they had made a profit of £1,207. They had even managed to make a special grant of £100 to look into the question of hydrophobia and rabies.

The correspondence columns were full of all kinds of odds and ends – scraps of folk medicine and descriptions of gruesome autopsies. In the issue of 2 March 'A Member' posed this problem:

It is a very prevalent belief amongst females (both rich and poor) that in curing hams, women should not rub the legs of pork with the brine pickle at the time they are menstruating, or the hams will go bad. I shall be glad if any of your readers can tell me if this be mere imagination, or if such be really the case, and if so, how it is to be explained. I have seen it twice tried, and both times the hams did go bad; but whether this was in any way due to the menstruation I cannot tell.

The following week, 'FRCP' joined in. He kept pigs himself, but believed that hams only went bad when the sows were menstruating, or 'hogging'. He had not heard that women who were menstruating caused hams to go bad. However, other doctors had, much to the disgust of 'Surgeon', who in the issue of 20 April declared:

There have been some interesting letters on the above subject in the Journal, and the following question, which could readily be answered by any of the female members of our profession naturally arises. If such bad results accrue from a woman curing dead meat whilst she is menstruating, what would result, under similar conditions, from her attempt to cure living flesh in her midwifery or surgical practice?

Nevertheless, 'Surgeon' was flying in the face of reaction. 'A Member' had his myrmidons, such as 'Another Member':

Some time ago, a pig was killed and cured, and the hams went bad. Two months afterwards, a second supply of pigs' legs was obtained, cured, and verified yesterday as perfectly good. On questioning my housekeeper, who cured both lots, I find she was menstruating on the former occasion, and not so on the latter. I also should be glad to hear of an explanation for so singular a circumstance.

The following week, 'R. B.' entered the arena:

Last week I ordered a pig to be killed, but the cook demurred, and made excuses about not being able to attend to the curing. My wife afterwards informed me that she objected because she was in a 'certain way'. The killing was therefore postponed. This was a *hog* pig. The next day, my men remarked that I must not think of killing the sow, as she was 'bremming', and therefore would not take the salt. I have, then, in my establishment two persons firmly asserting two distinct facts – that the hams and bacon will not cure if the rubber be menstruating, and that if a sow be killed when 'bremming' it will not take the salt. During the past few days, I have spoken to several matrons about the opinion, who all believe firmly in it. One person had a number of hams spoiled through the carelessness of the cook; and since then she has had them rubbed by a man. I may say that this belief is not peculiar to a locality. I knew it to be held in the north and south of England. I have only heard one explanation – the moisture that is on the hands and body during the catamenial period. This matter might be decided by experiments made in lunatic asylums or prisons, under the direction of the medical officers.

This letter is worth including if only on account of the astonishing sentiments contained in the last sentence. It is also interesting in that 'R. B.', presumably a medical man, was quite happy to take the word of local matrons – 'matrons' merely being a fancy word for married women – that this folk belief was indeed still in operation. As for the cook, who spoiled the hams through 'carelessness', one wonders what happened to her.

The next writer to take up the theme is William Story, who

was something of a crank, proud of his ability to get letters printed in the medical journals. He boastfully refers to a letter in the *Lancet* of ten years earlier as though this would tie up the whole question, though when this letter is in fact referred to, it has nothing to do with menstruation, but with hydrophobia. 'Perhaps the fact is not so generally known,' he wrote, adding a further element of mystification, 'that meat cured by men suffering from gonorrhoea or syphilis will also be spoilt. Whatever the *rationale* may be, I can speak positively to the fact.'

Six months later, the letters continued to roll up to the *British Medical Journal*, but 'A Member' and his associates were not having it all their own way. One doctor who believed in investigating theories bought two hams from the same pig, and had them cured, one by his cook, who was menstruating, and one by his housekeeper, who was not. Both hams turned out well, 'My own opinion,' the writer summed up, 'is, that when hams turn bad, they were probably from a sow-pig killed during the period of the oestrum at which time the meat is spongy, and does not take the pickle so well, and always tastes strong. I believe this to be the entire secret.'

Over all this, the editor presided benignly. One can hardly call the flow of letters a controversy, for it was only towards the end of the spate that common sense began to get a look-in. Eventually, the editor spoke, and he spoke thus:

We have received other letters giving even stronger evidence of the same sort (i.e., the pig was to blame not the woman). It is time to close this correspondence, which we have indulged chiefly as an experimental example of the astonishing facility with which, even among educated men, superstitions in themselves irrational and capable of easy disproof retain the hold once acquired, and the readiness with which by many in a series of even slightly complex phenomena, *post hoc* is confounded with *propter hoc*.

This note of acerbity is not rare among journalists of the period, though professional journals did manage to preserve a note of bland unconcern, probably because they did not exactly overpay their minions. Although the editor of the *British Medi-*

cal Journal received a lordly £500 a year, his amanuensis, the sub-editor, got £150 a year, and the boy, the third and final member of the staff, received £26 6s. a year.

To men, menstruation was often a subject of disgust or hilarity. It was possible to award marks on whether it was easy or difficult; dysmenorrhea, or painful menstruation, was a consequence of 'an irritable constitution, and of indolent habits'. Treatment for amenorrhoea, suppressed menstruation, was similar to that for anaemia – keeping the bowels open with compound rhubarb or colocynth pills, ten drops of tincture of iron; stimulating the appetite with tonic bitter or quinine; building up the diet with cold liver oil, meat twice a day, and bread substituted for vegetables, plus a pint of beer a day, or, if this disagreed, a couple of glasses of port wine. It was partly a moral problem, so a hair mattress was preferable. There was nothing quite like a hot bath, hot enough to make the sufferer faint, and this was useful for cases of dysmenorrhoea. The psychological effects that often accompanied the menstrual period were generally overlooked, save in books on insanity where it was pointed out that quirks of behaviour in consequence of menstruation could lead to madness.

For the sexual savages who thronged through nineteenth-century England, the prime result of menstruation was that it made women for a few days *hors de combat*. In the parody on Charles Kingsley's 'The Three Fishers' published in Oxford in 1870 there is the couplet:

> They longed for a prick, but they thought of the flowers,
> And the clap-rag they rolled it up, ragged and brown.

The makers of sanitary towels were faced with the problem of how to advertise them. The principal manufacturers, Southall Brothers and Barclay of Birmingham, often selected the oddest sites for their advertisements; the desire to avoid offending sensibilities had run riot. Surely there can have been few more unlikely spots than the *Antiquary* of July 1888, in which Southall Brothers took a third of the back cover. The advertisement was addressed in large sans serif letters to 'Ladies Travelling by Land or Sea' and the items were 'patented Articles of Underclothing, Indispensable to Ladies Travelling. Sold at Cost of Washing Only! To burn when done with. Of Drapers and Ladies' Outfitters Everywhere.' The price of these disposable sanitary towels was a shilling and two shillings a dozen. The disposable sanitary towel replaced the 'monthly napkin'. The advertiser assured the reader, who had just been perusing an advertisement for the book *Old Southwark and Its People* and one entitled 'Is Rupture Curable?' (it was, through electricity), that 'private parcels' were 'quite free from anything to attract observation', and the smitten were requested to write to the Lady Manager – 'this Department being managed by Ladies'.

All speculation about menstruation, the whys and the where-fores, should have ceased in 1896, when theories that had been in existence for half a century were finally and completely vin-dicated. Dr E. Knauer found that excising the ovaries abolished menstruation; more to the point, transplanting ovaries re-estab-lished it. Even the most reactionary vestiges of medieval opinion could not rationalize this.

Birth Control

There is no neat picture of nineteenth-century birth control, no easy pattern. The extent to which contraceptive devices were used is uncertain. Certainly more than a million tracts were sold on contraception, and many more were distributed free door to door by bands of do-gooders who frequently faced prosecu-tion and disgrace in taking the good news to the masses. Other people used contraception as a means of advancing their own revolutionary or radical views, and others made a good deal of money by advocating certain methods and then selling them surreptitiously.

The base of those who believed that it was the nation's duty to limit population was firmly affixed on Thomas Malthus, a mild benevolent man, fellow of Jesus College, Cambridge, and an obscure curate at Albury, Surrey. A year after he took up this modest post he published in 1798 *Essay on the Principle of*

Population; for a man just turned thirty it was an astonishing and prophetic production. It maintained that there is a natural tendency for population to increase faster than the means of sustenance, that the only barriers are limited food and limited space. True, there are natural checks – disease, famine, plague and war. Man must exercise his reason, must copulate only when it was necessary to produce the bare minimum of off-spring. Malthus was reluctant to specify ways and means if reason proved an insufficient incentive. He has been described as a timid bird in the sociological aviary and was an inappropriate person to have a euphemism for birth control – Malthusianism or neo-Malthusianism – fathered on him.

He provided a philosophical as opposed to a selfish reason for birth control, and his *Essay* convinced those who were badgered and harassed by the authorities that they were on the side of the angels, a conviction inexorably driven in by the stupidity and insensitivity of vested authority, which, as always, was convinced that it knew best what was good for the nation. The manic opposition to the propagation of birth control information had its obvious results – respectable literature was driven underground and had to be distributed in a clandestine manner, and the way was open for all sorts of crank pamphlets and booklets, setting forth methods of birth control that were dangerous.

Contraception was not new, though during the nineteenth century the emphasis changed. It was no longer the young man about town who was the target for the propaganda, but the respectable married man. In a handbill of 1776, Mrs Philips, over whose door was the sign of 'the Golden Fan and Rising Sun', proclaimed:

> To guard yourself from shame or fear,
> Votaries to Venus, hasten here;
> None in my wares e'er found a flaw,
> Self preservation's nature's law.

Her wares were 'machines, commonly called instruments of safety' or 'bladder policies' or, more prosaically, 'French letters', then called 'condoms'. Condom was a dirty word, and invariably spelled even in the most salacious context c—m. As the handbill indicates, her market was a small segment of society. The French letters were made of sheep's intestines and were apparently very reliable. Vulcanization of rubber by Goodyear and Hancock in 1843–44 made the present-day sheath possible, but it was many years before the rubber sheath was produced. It was possibly introduced to Europe after the World Exposition of Philadelphia in 1876.

There were two main channels of information in the period immediately prior to the ascension of Queen Victoria to the throne – America and London. In 1832 Charles Knowlton's *The Fruits of Philosophy* was published, containing contraceptive advice a good deal more sophisticated than that of Mrs Philips. Knowlton advised the use of the douche within five minutes of coitus. The mixture could be a chestnut-sized lump of alum dissolved in a pint of water, a large thimbleful of sulphate of zinc in a pint of water, two teaspoonsful of sal eratus (i.e., sodium bicarbonate as used in baking powders) to a pint of water, four or five 'greatspoonsful' (i.e., tablespoons) of vinegar to a pint of water, or four or five greatspoonsful of liquid chloride of soda to a pint. Knowlton was an American; by 1839 his book had sold 10,000 copies in the United States. Within two years of its American publication it was taken up by an English publisher, James Watson, and between 1834 and 1876 it had sold 42,000 copies.

In England, there were earlier excursions into the field of birth control for all. Two pioneers were Francis Place, a London tailor, and Richard Carlile. In 1822 Place published *The Principle of Population*; it was a subject on which he was something of an authority, as he had fifteen children. He had read Malthus who, he wrote, 'seems to shrink from discussing the propriety of preventing conception'. In 1826 Carlile published *Practical Hints on How to Enjoy Life and Pleasure without Harm to Either Sex*. Place recognized that birth control was a class thing, and produced three pamphlets, with contraceptive methods suited to the various stations in life. *To the Married in Genteel Life* the advocated method was a soft sponge in the shape of a small ball, attached to a narrow ribbon, and moistened. This was a 'cleanly and not indelicate method', and 'accoucheurs of the first respectability and surgeons of great eminence have in some peculiar cases recommended it'; *To the Married of Both Sexes* did not mention these testimonies. And the sponge was to be one inch square, attached to a double twisted thread or bobbin (this inferior class obviously is not up to the ribbon standard). The sponge for the 'Working People' was to be of the size of a green walnut or a small apple. 'No injurious consequences can in any way result from its use, neither does it diminish the enjoyment of either party,' declared Place. The mere idea that woman could have enjoyment in sex was tantamount to treason, and the vengeful attacked. A magazine, the *Bull Dog*, was produced to persecute Place and his associates, one of whom was Carlile, but Place was, said the *Bull Dog*, 'the master spring that moves the whole infernal machine'.

It was always possible that a sponge was not available at the crucial time. In that case, advised Place, 'lint, fine wool, cotton, flax, or what may be at hand', could be used. What would be the results of using the sponge contraceptive? 'Debauchery will diminish – while good morals and religious duties will be promoted.' This view was decidedly not that of the church. Or the medical profession. Or the more high-flown journalists, including the ubiquitous F. W. Newman, who wrote of 'the Corruption now call Neo-Malthusianism' that woman's 'internal structure fights against the success of unnatural acts; her tissues imbibe any poisonous drug, and resent the absence of what is natural.' The tendency of outsiders to make broad pronouncements about something they know nothing at all about was never so evident as in the birth control furore.

Book and pamphlets poured from the presses. George Drysdale introduced the concept of 'preventive intercourse'. His *Elements of Social Science: or Physical Sexual and Natural Religion* went into thirty-five editions by 1904 – 600 pages of it. He had no new message, advising the combination of sponge with douche, and the utilization of his interpretation of the 'safe period', which he reckoned as two or three days before menstruation to eight days afterwards. He considered that water by itself was sufficient as a douche.

The objections to birth control were many and various. According to the Manchester Church Congress that met in 1888, contraception was 'the awful heresy which is prevailing throughout the country as to restraining the growth of population by artificial means'. One of the most powerful voices was that of Elizabeth Blackwell, the first woman to obtain a medical diploma in the United States, who settled in Britain in 1868. She claimed that 'artifices to indulge a husband's sensuality while counteracting Nature is on the one hand most uncertain of success, on the other hand is eminently noxious to the woman'. Another American, W. D. Buck of New Hampshire, was more prosaic and laconic: 'I do think that this filling of the vagina with traps making a Chinese toyshop of it is outrageous.' Many doctors were profoundly disturbed at the more amateurish concoctions. *Notes on the Population Question* (anonymous, 1831), advised corrosive sublimate, which could cause death. As recently as 1918 this was used, and killed a thirty-two-year-old woman, who had heard of this method as a form of contraceptive and who had inserted an 8.75-grain tablet of corrosive sublimate into her vagina. Similarly, the colleagues of Dr Soule would not have been happy about the recommendations he makes in *The Science of Reproduction and Reproductive Control* – strychnine and iodine taken internally.

As the accent became more and more stressed on mechanical methods, exponents of the old way of life proclaimed the virtues of self-restraint. 'The first safeguard against impurity is to believe in the possibility of self-restraint,' wrote A. S. Dyer in 1884. A middle school of thought was evidenced by *The Power and Duty of Parents to Limit the Number of their Children* (anonymous, 1868), where contraceptive measures included use of the safe period, coughing, sneezing, jumping, and violent exercise immediately after coitus.

One of the most popular of the smaller handbooks was by Dr H. A. Allbutt, who underwent the humiliation of being crossed off the medical register on account of his 'indecent publication' *The Wife's Handbook*, price sixpence. This was selling well far into the present century. Allbutt made the point that the safe period could fail in five per cent of cases, that douching was not necessarily a hundred per cent reliable. His handbook of 1887 had the advantage that it included new technological developments. In 1886 Mr W. J. Rendell of 26 Great Bath Street, Farringdon, London, had perfected the soluble quinine pessary. 'My opinion,' declared Allbutt, 'is that [it] will do all their inventor claims for [it].' He also mentioned sponges, tampons and Dutch cap, then made in three sizes. The sheath, now of rubber, was a 'very certain check'. 'Malthus' sheaths were selling at three shillings a dozen, W. J. Rendell's soluble pessaries at two shillings a dozen. Dutch caps of India rubber were two shillings and threepence; two shillings and sixpence; and three shillings each. The indestructible French letter was introduced about this time, 'Lambert's Paragon Sheath', and cost four shillings each. Dr Allbutt left himself open to all kinds of disciplinary action even had he not been ejected from the medical register; he invented an 'Introducer' for obdurate pessaries, and advertised it.

Industrial progress had succeeded in making contraception a fairly sure operation, though older methods, such as the safe period, kept their place in families who were Catholic or who had heeded the strictures of the established church and the medical profession. The safe period was still of dubious merit, as the experts were inclined to chart it differently. One 'authority' – an authority only because she benefited from the state of affairs that made all contraceptive literature seizable and therefore compulsive reading – was Mrs Ida Ellis (*Essentials of Contraception*, 1891) and her interpretation of the safe period was wide indeed, so much so that husbands who yielded to her persuasive pen were *hors de combat* for fully half the month. Vulcanized rubber had made the sheath a more hygienic object than was the case when it was an animal's gut, and, to facilitate the injection of the various mixtures into the vagina, syringes were available at low cost (one firm advertised three kinds – three shillings and sixpence; four shillings and sixpence; and five shillings and sixpence.) The mixtures were inherited from the early writers on the subject – vinegar, alum. Because of the readiness of the law to prosecute – one man got two years' imprisonment for issuing a book on birth control (though illustrated with dirty pictures) – birth control literature was a subject that could not be discussed openly, and the methods could not be compared. The public could not know which was the best buy, unless they had a good deal of ingenuity in acquiring numbers of the pamphlets and books. If in doubt they could write to those disciples of the movement who were not averse to publicity, such as Annie Besant. She was written to by a Mr Cole, but she replied to the wife: 'In reply to your husband's letter, I advise you to write to Mr Rendell ... He is a respectable reliable chemist, and will give you all directions.'

One of the objections to contraception was that it was unaesthetic. At its crudest, this was put in the pornographic magazines after the Bradlaugh–Besant case:

> Said good Mrs Besant
> To make things all pleasant,
> If of children you wish to be rid,
> Just after coition,
> Prevent all fruition,
> And corpse the incipient kid.
>
> To do this completely,
> Securely and neatly,
> That your conscience may suffer no twinge,
> Before having connexion,
> Procure an injection,
> Likewise an elastic syringe.
>
> Then after the 'coup'
> All the ladies need do,
> Is to jump out of bed on the spot,
> Fill the squirt to the brim,
> Pump it well up her quim,
> And the kid trickles into the pot.

At its most genteel, in *Neo-Malthusianism* of 1897, by R. Ussher, who claimed that contraception must 'degrade the finest moral instincts of both men and women, especially, of course, the latter; in them it cannot have any other effect than to bring about a bestial sensuality and indifference to all morality'. There are hints here of a further reason, propounded by the *Liverpool Mail* two decades earlier. General contraceptive knowledge would 'tear down one of the greatest protections public morality has' – fear of conception outside marriage. The *British Medical Journal* (January 1878) tore a sheet out of Coventry Patmore's concept of mystic marriage in its view that in some way the relationship between man and woman was programmed for decency; contraceptive doctrines were 'contrary to the purity of thought and manliness of life which are the characteristics of this nation'. The *British Medical Journal* may have thought that it had its finger on the pulse of the nation, but the evidence would seem to indicate that, as always in any area of Victorian sexuality, there was a wide discrepancy between what was written and what was done. The link – what is said – has been broken by time.

The hush and the secrecy surrounding contraception was broken in a melodramatic manner by two people of startling energies and unlimited enthusiasms, Annie Besant and Charles Bradlaugh. Annie Besant was born in 1847. Her father died when she was five, and her mother considered herself psychic, traits she transmitted to Annie. Annie had a conventional enough upbringing; as a teenager she played croquet and the piano and was influenced by the ritualist aspect of the established church. At a ritualist church in Chelsea she met Frank Besant, a new curate, flirted with him, upon which he assumed that she was his beloved, and asked permission of Annie's mother to marry the girl, permission that was withheld. This created a block between mother and daughter, and Annie, though not in love with Besant, married him through pique, had three children in fairly rapid succession, and left him after less than six years, obtaining a formal separation that allowed her £110 a year from his money. Cheltenham, where they had lived, had not proved the ideal venue for this ill-starred marriage. Its intellectual appeal for Annie was minimal; it was replete with

ladies who talked to me only about babies and servants – troubles of which I knew nothing and which bored me unutterably – and who were as uninterested in all that had filled my life, in theology, in politics, in science, as I was uninterested in the discussion on the housemaid's young man, and on the cook's extravagance in using butter 'when dripping would have done perfectly well, my dear!'

Annie Besant had clearly the makings of a young prig.

She obtained a job as a governess, her mother died, she did research for a Mr Thomas Scott at the British Museum, in the course of which she encountered a periodical called the *National Reformer*, in which was announced a lecture to be given in the Hall of Science in unfashionable Hoxton, a dilapidated district nudging the East End of London. The lecturer was to be Charles Bradlaugh.

Bradlaugh was a professional malcontent. His father had been a £2-a-week clerk (for twenty-two years) who was rewarded for his diligence upon his death by thanks in *The Times*, and his son began to operate the same sort of treadmill — a timekeeping job with a Fulham builder at £1 a week, errand boy for a solicitor at ten shillings a week. He made an early rash marriage — his wife proved to be a dipsomaniac — and almost obsessively Bradlaugh set out to have humiliations piled upon him, lecturing on subjects with which he was ill-equipped to deal. In 1860 a man named Grant put out his tongue at Bradlaugh, and the audience roared, 'Shame!' To the working classes, anxious for the parboiled education Bradlaugh was only able to promote, Bradlaugh was 'our Charlie', but to the Reverend D. Brindley, a drunkard and a bankrupt who was buried in a pauper's grave in New York, he was 'an incendiary, a story-teller, a nuisance, who would make a rumpus and make everybody miserable, even in the Garden of Eden'. This view was echoed by the newspapers whenever Bradlaugh lectured on his pet subject, the necessity of atheism. In obscure Dewsbury, a bill was pasted up in February 1862: 'Grand discovery! To be seen tomorrow, Sunday, not one hundred miles from the Public Hall, a fine specimen of the gorilla tribe, standing seven feet six inches in height, imported into England from Sheffield, the capital of the Hollycock settlement, in the interior of Africa ...' Being a professed atheist, Bradlaugh was an outsider, a scapegoat, for whom no insult was inappropriate. Lectures were all very well, but books were better. Bradlaugh's friend Austin Holyoake set out to raise £650 to buy a printing and publishing business.

In 1874, when Annie Besant and Charles Bradlaugh came together at the Hall of Science in Hoxton, Bradlaugh was in his early forties, a big man (forty-six-inch chest at death) now running to seed. The fact that at the hall Bradlaugh went up to her with the query, 'Mrs Besant?' was later taken by her to have cosmic implications. This meeting of minds was auspicious; also Mrs Besant was a ravishing beauty. She stares out of photographs of the period with a saucy arrogance that is wholly modern, with short shingled hair, wide-spaced eyes. Not surprisingly, Bradlaugh invited her to his lodgings in Whitechapel, where she insisted on reading to him parts of a pamphlet on the existence of God. He employed her on his freethinking organ, the *National Reformer*, at a guinea a week, and she gave her first lecture at a Cooperative Society hall, the subject being 'The Political Status of Women'. She joined the National Secular Society, and when Bradlaugh went to America to lecture, she became the number one star, to the chagrin of other freethinkers without her dynamic personality (or her looks).

To many freethinkers, religion was a subject that was stoned to death. Socialism was making its inroads into their ranks. The condition of man was more to their taste than the existence or nonexistence of God. Philanthropists were looking after the dwellings of the poor; by 1874, the American philanthropist George Peabody had given £500,000 to 'ameliorate the condition and augment the comforts of the poor', and the barrack-like buildings promoted by such as Waterlow were settled landmarks. But the poor would always be poor while they continued to breed like rabbits. The middle and upper classes were already beginning to make use of the surreptitious information of birth control literature, and that article of furniture dear to the heart of the wife who was expecting, the chaise-longue, was being demoted to the attic or the servants' quarters.

The emancipation of birth control was as important as the emancipation of woman. What would promote it? It was decided to republish Knowlton's creakingly antiquated *The Fruits of Philosophy* of 1832. Bradlaugh persuaded a publisher named Watts to declare responsibility for the Knowlton reissue, and speedily (in January 1877) Watts was committed to the Central Criminal Court, swift sharp action that encouraged him to change his plea from not guilty to guilty. Bradlaugh was sardonic: 'If the pamphlet now prosecuted had been brought to me for publication I should probably have declined to publish it, not because of the subject matter, but because I do not like its style. If I had once published it, I should have defended it until the very last.'

The court decided that it was 'unlawful to publish such physiological details' as were contained in Knowlton, but nevertheless Mrs Besant and Bradlaugh republished the book, and in March they went together to the Guildhall to deliver the earliest copy of the new edition to the chief clerk, notifying him that they would reappear the following day to sell the pamphlet. Making certain that the enemy would take notice, they also informed the chief office of the detective department of the police, and the city solicitor.

The following day the street was thronged with eager spectators, including detectives, and Mrs Besant and Bradlaugh were arrested on warrant and searched for compromising literature. Bradlaugh was accustomed to being hounded by the police, but for Mrs Besant, vilified as she had been at her lectures, it was a novel experience. The big guns were brought to bear. Lord Chief Justice Cockburn said it was a 'fair question as to whether it is a scientific production for legitimate purposes, or whether it is what the indictment alleged it to be, an obscene publication'. In the background, the police probed; they seized book packets containing *The Freethinker's Text Book* and *Jesus, Shelley, and Malthus*, and they raided the bookseller, Truelove, confiscating R. D. Owen's *Individual Family and National Poverty*. Truelove was also foolhardy enough to have 650 copies of Knowlton; Bradlaugh and Mrs Besant were more cautious. They had their copies hidden in Bradlaugh's establishment at 10 Portland Place, Circus Road, St John's Wood, in the garden, under the floor, behind the cistern in the lavatory.

The trial was fixed for 18 June 1877. The Solicitor General, Sir Hardinge Giffard, would lead for the crown. Mrs Besant was 'light, jesting', but inwardly it was a traumatic experience, as she recorded herself in her *Autobiogrpahy* (1908): 'To me it meant the loss of the pure reputation I prized, the good name I

had guarded — scandal the most horrible a woman could face.'
Bradlaugh, who fancied himself as a lawyer, subpoenaed emancipationist and reformer Professor Henry Fawcett and his wife,
Charles Darwin, the chaplain of Clerkenwell House of Correction, and a Reverend S. D. Headlam, an expert on overcrowding. Fawcett was shocked and declared that he would send his
wife abroad rather than that she should undergo this humiliation. Darwin, who had recognized the truths of the Malthus
theory in his early days, was now more concerned with fertilization in plants rather than people (his *Fertilisation of Orchids*
was published in this year). Darwin, the scientist whose writings conceivably did more to wrench the nineteenth century into
modern times than any other man, was timid, nervous and
retiring. He wrote:

I have been for many years much out of health, and have been
forced to give up all society or public meetings; and it would be great
suffering to me to be a witness in Court. It is, indeed, not improbable that I may be unable to attend. Therefore, I hope that, if in your
power, you will excuse my attendance. . . . If it is not asking too great
a favour, I should be greatly obliged if you would inform me what
you decide, as apprehension of the coming exertion would prevent
the rest which I require doing me much good.

Bradlaugh's band of hawks were turning before his eyes into
doves, though there were extra volunteers for his side — H. G.
Bohn of the Bohn Library, and Dr Drysdale, who, as a writer
on contraception, had a vested interest in the outcome of the
trial.

The trial turned against Bradlaugh. The jury announced that
'we are unanimously of the opinion that the book in question is
calculated to deprave public morals, but at the same time we
entirely exonerate the defendant from any corrupt motives in
publishing it'. British compromise had worked again. One juryman said that six of them did not assent to the guilty verdict; it
was discussed so loud that it was heard outside the jury room.
Two jurymen returned their guinea fee for the use of the defence.

Bradlaugh wanted to quash the indictment, have the judgement arrested, and a new trial. Before judgement Bradlaugh and Mrs Besant were set loose, and immediately they began selling the pamphlet again. This was 'a grave and aggravated offence'. Judgement was passed of six months' imprisonment, and a £200 fine each, but it was quashed on appeal and no one went to prison. When it came to true martyrdom, Bradlaugh was weighed in the balance and found wanting. Karl Marx may well have been right when he said of Bradlaugh that he was a 'huge self-idolator'. The people who suffered were Mrs Besant, who had her child Mabel taken from her and given into the custody of her estranged husband, and the bookseller Truelove, who, although nearly seventy, was fined £50 and sent to prison for four months, where he picked oakum and slept on a plank bed.

It was a trial that did not mean what it ostensibly said. The cumbrous machinery of the law had come out with punishment that it did not inflict. It was an expensive show of fist-shaking. Bradlaugh went on to become the Member of Parliament who could not take his seat because he would not take the requisite oath, and who was ejected by force from the House of Commons. 'Mr Bradlaugh's real offence is not his Atheism, but the coarseness which accompanies it,' wrote Henry Parry Liddon, religious apologist of the high churchmen, 'Mr Bradlaugh's presence in the House will not really add much to the Anti-Christian and Anti-Theistic elements of it.' However, Liddon did not need to worry. It was six years – after being successively re-elected by his constituents in Northampton – before he managed to take his seat without being thrown out by the burly men who officiate at these un-English ceremonies. In 1886 Mrs Besant defected, according to Bradlaugh's lights. She joined the Socialists; she already had her own paper. – few indeed were those who did not – *Our Corner*, and she published Bernard Shaw, with whom she had some kind of an affair. In 1888 she started a new paper, the *Link*, and publicized the tragedies of the match girls, dying from 'fossy-jaw' and earning eight or nine shillings a week. In characteristically callous vein, our own age has made a musical on this theme. Mrs Besant took to the occult, met Madame Blavatsky, the leader of the Theosophist

Movement with 'her heavy white face, as deeply pitted with smallpox as a solitaire board', resigned from the Secular Society, the Fabians, and the other interests of that kind, and transferred her entire attentions to the other-worldly. 'She has always shown height and prominence of the forehead in the region of Human Nature,' wrote the phrenologist J. Millott Severn brightly, 'but more so since she has taken up occult thought and study.' Fortunately for his peace of mind, Bradlaugh was not alive to see this treachery on the part of his one-time *alter ego*. He died in 1891, almost respectable. 'A distinguished man and admirable member of this House was laid yesterday in his mother-earth.' The speaker, most improbably, was Gladstone.

Venereal Disease

Venereal disease was the Russian roulette of Victorian sex. For the pure, it was a subject of dread, to be shunned; and for the licentious it was a chance one took, no more predictable than rain in an English summer; and the more phlegmatic approached it in a stoical mood. To persist with the metaphor of Russian roulette, this particular revolver contained not one, but two bullets – syphilis and gonorrohea, of which the latter was virtually a blank. Gonorrhea, said Dr Grandin, had little more significance than a cold in the nose. It was believed to account for ninety per cent of sterile marriages – the nineteenth-century libertines were nothing if not selfish, though this figure was always in dispute (Dr A. Neisser (1855–1914) suggested fifty per cent). The Committee of the Ophthalmological Society of 1884 investigated four lunatic asylums, and they found that up to forty-one per cent of the blind patients were blind because of gonorrhoea. Dr W. H. Erb (1840–1921) of Heidelberg discovered that of 2,200 patients in an asylum, 48.5 per cent had gonorrhoea.

In England, statistics, as we have seen, can be made to spell out almost anything. Fear made accurate estimates of the numbers of people suffering from the venereal diseases even more unreliable than they would have been anyway. For many medical men, syphilis *was* venereal disease, 'contracted in consequence of impure connexion', wrote Dr Spencer Thomson in 1856. He goes on to paint the picture:

The fearful constitutional consequences which may result from this affection; consequences, the fear of which may haunt the mind for years, which may taint the whole springs of health, and be transmitted to circulate in the young blood of innocent offspring are indeed terrible considerations, too terrible not to render the disease one of those which must unhesitatingly be placed under medical care.

This was all very well, but the medical men could do little. The sores should be touched with caustic – nitrate of silver and strong acetic acid were recommended at this time, the diet should be reduced, the bowels kept open, and violent exercise avoided. A favoured remedy was mercury, which probably killed more people in the nineteenth century than any other drug. As quicksilver it was used as a purge – as much as a pound was taken at a time, the idea being that the weight would press down on any stoppage in the bowels. The celebrated blue pills and grey pills that are constantly being referred to in Victorian times were fairly harmless preparations of mercury. More dangerous was calomel, a compound of mercury and chlorine; this was known as chloride of mercury. The combination of mercury and chlorine was also responsible for another killer, corrosive sublimate (bichloride), in which the percentage of chlorine was higher. This was used as a contraceptive as well as a 'cure' for syphilis.

Morbid fear of syphilis was so widespread as to give currency to its own name – syphilophobia. This trepidation also included the fear of mercury poisoning subsequent to treatment, and mercury poisoning was frightening indeed – the teeth felt as though they were being stretched, the breath took on a characteristic foetid odour, and the gums turned purple. All this was accompanied by excessive salivation. The antidote to mercury poisoning was the white of egg mixed with water (flour and water if no eggs were available), plus a dose of ipecacuanha and the tickling of the throat with a feather to help vomiting.

Many people who had left the straight and narrow imagined that they had syphilis, and this produced a widespread form of hypochondria known as *syphilis imaginaria*, which had its own battery of pseudosymptoms, though the sores and scabs of syphilis were not easy to recapitulate via the imagination. This fact was not a comfort, however, as it was well known that syphilis could remain dormant for long periods. Many believed that the contraceptive sheath would save them from syphilis; the French letter was used primarily – outside the family – not as a means of preventing conception but of preserving the private parts from infection. The man of pleasure was not particularly interested in whether or not he sponsored gestation.

The nineteenth-century libertime who went out on the town had to make the decision for himself whether the game was worth the candle. The pocketbooks and handbooks often had a wallet at the end containing a French letter, and also usually a chapter telling the reader what to do if he caught syphilis. The tone of such a chapter was usually jolly, a tradition taken over from the eighteenth century. Until 1793 gonorrhoea and syphilis were thought to be two facets of the same disease, and the well-known surgeon John Hunter had helped to sustain this illusion. A true hero, he had infected himself from a patient so that he could try his wiles on himself, but the patient he had selected had both syphilis and gonorrhoea.

'It is hardly one in ten that a Town Spark of that age has not been clapt,' wrote the author of *The Laws of Chance* in 1738. For some men, bizarre as it might seem, the chance of catching syphilis was amusing rather than worrying. One aristocrat caught syphilis for a bet, giving Charlotte Hayes, a procuress, £30 to find him a diseased whore, no difficult task. Naturally enough, such eccentrics formed a minority. Those who were not deterred would rather not catch syphilis, and their morale was given a lift in 1836, when William Wallace of Dublin cured 142 cases of syphilis with iodine of potassium, a method that is still used in certain suitable cases. Iodine of potassium and mercury were the only substances that did anything to counter the ravages of pox, though the quacks never tired of pushing their own placebos. There was another 'cure' that nineteenth-century gentlemen were partial to – the raping of a virgin was believed to cure syphilis.

That venereal disease was amusing – especially when caught by someone else – is clear from the large number of pornographic poems that exist on this theme:

> But ah! my luck! for in three weeks
> (Oh how it made me cuss),
> Three chancres did appear upon
> My tolly-waggy-buss.
>
> Thy genitals I used to bore
> Are clapped, and damp and grey,
> Ah! finger 'midst those lips once more,
> And hum thy farting lay.
>
> But when your chances are touched up with caustic,
> It makes a man roar, let him do what he may,
> And a second edition's a certain prognostic
> He'll soon have no frenum to his fol-de-rol-lay.
>
> But from a chance venereal go,
> When once the Rector was erected,
> He was unlucky down below,
> And with disease he got infected.
>
> He was afflicted with this blow
> So badly in his manliest quarter,
> That all fell off into the po
> One day as he was making water.
>
> This virgin she did prove
> A trap, a trap;
> The end of all her love
> The clap, the clap.
> Since I that cursed whore
> Did meet, did meet,
> Captivi cannot cure
> My gleet, my gleet.
>
> I kept on going this maid to see,
> Until I found I couldn't pee,
> For I had got a damned chordee
> From fucking little Sally.

It was a field also entered by the limerick:

> There was a young lady of Hadley
> Who would with an omnibus cad lie,
> He gave her the crabs,
> And besides minor scabs,
> The pox too she got very badly.

> There was an old party of Fife,
> Who suspected a clap in his wife,
> So he bought an injection
> To cure the infection,
> Which gave him a stricture for life.

Where there exists this curious lighthearted attitude one suspects whistling in the dark or an ignorance of the consequences. Disfigurement and the erosion of the genitalia were regarded as the terminal stages of syphilis. The Victorian was accustomed to facial disfigurement in the form of smallpox. The composers of these gay verses may not have suspected that beyond the inconveniences described therein there lurked that spectre of what Havelock Ellis described as the *maladie du siècle*, 'the disease of excess, of vice, of prolonged worry' – general paralysis of the insane. It was particularly prominent in 'such urban centres as Newcastle and Cardiff', Ellis stated, though there is no clear reason why he should have picked on these two places. Ellis was also being less than objective – prolonged worry does not figure in general paralysis, which is the terminal stage of syphilis.

The syphilitic basis of this malady was suspected by Dr J. F. von Esmarch (1823–1908) and Dr F. Jessen (1859–1933), and conclusive proof was offered by Dr H. Noguchi (1876–1928) in 1913. General paralysis develops usually about ten years after infection, but it can vary between three and thirty years. Death usually occurs within three years of the onset of the symptoms. It is today very rare (twenty-six deaths in Britain in 1964) thanks to the use of penicillin in the early stages of syphilis (penicillin was first used in Britain in 1943). In the nineteenth century when syphilis once caught was rarely dispersed, cases of general paralysis were unquestionably numerous (though they always formed a small proportion of total syphilitic cases). General paralysis of the insane is a general run-down of the entire organism, the progressive destruction of the whole nervous system. The memory goes, muscular coordination falters, there are delusions and hallucinations. An odd feature of this terrible disease is the inability of the patient to do simple arithmetic; he adds or multiplies from left to right. Asked to multiply, say, 35 by 5, he will begin 'Five fives are twenty-five,' putting this down on the answer line, then 'Three fives are fifteen,' putting this down as well, the sum appearing:

$$
\begin{array}{r}
35 \\
\times 5 \\
\hline
1525
\end{array}
$$

The approach of the disease is stealthy. The man (there are three or four men to one woman) becomes sluggish, fat, the muscles lose tone, the instincts get out of hand, especially the sexual, and he can fall into the hands of the police, having lost all insight into his condition. He may make ludicrous collections of old newspapers, buttons, pebbles; eating habits get out of control, and if he has not by this time been put away, meal may follow meal without cease. He may proclaim that he is an onion or a poached egg, in a spirit of fun, and he is given to reckless practical jokes. He has delusions of grandeur, thinks up vast schemes, is emotionally chaotic. This is a transitional stage. As the nervous system crumples, the patient reverts to childishness, crawls about on the floor, cannot control his evacuations, eventually subsides into mindlessness, followed remorselessly by death. General paralysis of the insane was the Queen of Spades in the pack of the man about town or the East End whoremonger. It was estimated towards the end of the nineteenth century that sixty-six per cent of the prostitutes in western Europe had syphilis.

It is difficult to estimate how much syphilis existed in Victorian England, or how many cases led to general paralysis and death. The brave attempt of the government to control its effect on the army and navy (the Contagious Diseases Acts 1869) failed because prostitutes preferred money to the welfare of their customers. Prostitutes undergoing treatment for syphilis at the seaports left the hospitals when a promising ship came in. In Devonport between 3 December 1863 and 31 March 1865 (just prior to the acts) 'forty-eight syphilitic patients and twenty cases of gonorrhoea were discharged uncured at their own request'.

Syphilis was widely regarded as a corollary of prostitution. Clergymen saw it as a just reward of sin. During the agitation to repeal the Contagious Diseases Acts of 1869, there were innumerable meetings. At one, reported *The Times*, 'a large number of persons, many of them apparently clergymen, had come to the meeting with the express purpose of protesting against the acts, and did so with the enthusiasm of those who fancied they saw in physical disease a Divine Judgement against moral transgression'. Josephine Butler thought that she had a better way of dealing with prostitution and disease: 'I would sit on the steps of the brothel and pray the people out.' Josephine Butler and her colleagues — 'persons of serious and thoughtful habits' said the Home Secretary, H. Austin Bruce, later Lord Aberdare — dealt in exaggerations and emotional appeals. Among these persons of serious and thoughtful habits were the Trades Union Congress, and Cardinal Manning, who said that 'No Catholic who fears God can refuse to give his allegiance to the sacred cause which [Mrs Butler] has espoused.' Syphilis was a counter in a social game, and, for Gladstone, a political game: 'Among other things, if the Acts can be shown to be immoral in their principles and tendencies, no supposed physical advantages can justify their continuance.' They could also lose him votes.

In treating syphilis as a social matter, the fact was frequently over-looked that it could be contracted innocently. A child who was kissed by a prostitute out of the goodness of her heart infected both her mother and her grandmother. Similarly, the wife who was infected by a diseased husband. 'A husband knowingly and wilfully infecting his wife with the venereal disease cannot be convicted criminally either under a charge of assault or of inflicting grievous bodily harm.' And this, it might be noted, is 'knowingly and wilfully' (*Law of Marriage*, Sir W. Nevill Geary, 1892).

Nothing kept the nineteenth-century citizen to the thorny

path of righteousness so effectively as the fear of contracting venereal disease, and many were pretending to be virtuous when they were only being careful. The medical dictionaries are never less than lurid on this topic, with good reason.

The Facts of Life

The nineteenth century saw the frontiers of sexual knowledge pushed ever forward so rapidly that age-old myths existed side by side with most sophisticated reasoning. This is the sex act seen in 1843:

The penis on the part of the man, being erected by a conflux of blood to that part, the glans tumefied, rubbed, and highly excited *in coitu*, an ejaculatory contraction follows, by which the seed is pressed out of the *vesiculae seminales*, and injected into the uterus of the female with some force: at the same time, the *clitoris* of the female being erected, and the parts adjacent swelled, the better to embrace the penis and a viscous liquid being compressed from the glands, the better to lubricate the passage, in the instant of the male injection, the fallopian tubes grow stiff, and closely embracing the *ovaria*, squeeze off some of the ripest of them; these meeting the male seed, either in the uterus, or the tubes themselves, are impregnated by the animalculae, and conveyed into the womb, the mouth of which, at other times close shut, is now by the contraction of its fibres, open for the reception of its new guest.

Many laymen of today would be hard put to it to improve upon this. Similarly, they might well echo the doubts of these early Victorian erotologists:

But what revolts against reason is the strange disproportion found between the number of these little beings contained in a drop of the seminal fluid and that of the individuals which come into the world . . . of this prodigious multitude of little animals that swim in the seminal liquor, there comes but one only to humanity; for the most fecund woman rarely brings two children to the world, hardly ever three.

These amateurs were often better versed in the psychology of sex than the professionals, especially regarding sexual pleasure in woman. *Rees's Cyclopaedia*, which expressed the establishment view, declared, 'that a mucous fluid is sometimes found in coition from the internal organs and vagina is undoubted; but this only happens in lascivious women, or such as live luxuriously'.

Michael Ryan, however, in his *Philosophy of Marriage* of 1837, maintained that sexual enjoyment was 'more delicious and protracted' for women, for which there were four basic reasons: (a) a more sensitive nervous system; (b) finer and more delicate skin; (c) acuter feelings; and (d) a mystic sympathy between the breasts and the womb (the concept of erogenous zones had not yet been evolved). Shortly afterwards another writer put the same thing forward in slightly different language: 'the delicacy of their constitutions and even their weakness procure them some benefits of which men are deprived. The parts which concur to excite voluptuousness are more numerous than in men; and the agitation of some of these suffice for communicating sensation to all the others.'

This was a question about which one could have various opinions. Regarding tumescence in men, 'indeed, the long vessels, folded so many times on each other, and through which the seminal liquor is compelled to take its course, for the purpose of discharging itself, present advantages which are not discoverable in woman'.

One of the great staples of writers on sexuality, especially those who were committed to the view that women were as lascivious as men, was that women had orgasms in precisely the same way as men. To medical men this idea was heresy; it rendered the ideal of woman as a pure creature compelled to suffer the animal nature of her husband difficult to uphold. A great advantage to both schisms was that there were masses of facts that could be made to support anything. In 1891 Harry Campbell in his *Differences in the Nervous Organization of Man and Woman* investigated 52 working-class women. Before marriage, he found out, 12 had sexual instincts; 40 had not. Out of these 40, 13 claimed that they had never acquired any. This would seem to confirm what Dr Lawson Tait wrote in the same year in the *Provincial Medical Journal*: 'When the question is carefully inquired into and without prejudice, it is found that women have their sexual appetites far less developed than men.' Yet five years earlier, the celebrated German specialist E. H. Kisch maintained that 'sexual excitement on the woman's part is a necessary link in the chain of conditions producing impregnation'. This contradicts the earlier expert, Dr William Acton (1857): 'Now, as all that we have read and heard tends to prove that a reciprocity of desire, is, to a great extent, necessary to excite the male, we must not be surprised if we learn that excesses in fertile married life are comparatively rare, and that sensual feelings in the man become gradually sobered down.'

In no other area is the desire so manifest to produce general laws out of collection of facts. Whatever view one takes, there is sure to be a quantity of contradictory evidence. He who generalizes, said Bertrand Russell, generally lies. This was certainly true of doctors trying to preserve the image of demure matronhood; admirable as they were when investigating subjects they could regard objectively – Acton on prostitution, for instance – their hectoring attitude when it comes to sexual behaviour in the respectable gives their writings a note of rather displeasing hysteria. Most of them refuse to admit that the evidence they receive from the protagonists is suspect – many present-day investigators into sexuality have the same inhibitions. Dr Tait (*Diseases of Women*, 1889) admitted this in a wry manner in respect of female masturbation, especially that mode in which the woman excites herself by means of a hairpin manipulated in the urethra: 'I have removed hair-pins encrusted with phosphates from ten different female bladders, and not one of the owners of these bladders would give any account of the incident.'

It was widely held that man had only a certain quantity of semen to use up, or as it was put, 'spend'. This quantity depended on the amount of food and the kind of food ingested. 'Some physicians, for example, give it as their opinion that a man should not caress his consort immediately after the use of food, because the semence can produce at that time no other than badly constituted children.' If one ate too much, there would be an overflow of semen. 'When the seminal vesicles are filled with the liquor to which they serve as reservoirs, like the other receptacles of our body they tend to disburden themselves (even in men whose imagination is the least inclined to voluptuousness).' Certain foods were believed to add extra potency to the semen, such as chocolate. Coffee, 'far from weakening the power of those who have a vivid and robust temperament, whose parts of generation are in a good state, tends, on the contrary to excite them to love'. There was a cult of aphrodisiacs and anti-aphrodisiacs. Opium could serve 'as a lustful provocative'; on the other hand, it was a help to simmer down 'persons of a hot temperament, nocturnal pollutions, and continual priapism'. Other favoured items were water lily, lettuce, camphor (used as a 'refrigerent' by monks), and mint, mainly because these were mentioned by classical writers such as Pliny. The myths of legend were being incorporated into modern thinking. Two guaranteed aphrodisiacs of the early forties were:

Take 4 eggs, beat well with ½ glass of snail froth from shells. Add a pinch of salt and a pinch of powdered ginger, with 20 grains of pulverised ginseng.

1 oz ox-marrow, 2 yolks of fresh eggs, beat together and add 4 grains of ambergris (or 2 drachms i.e. 144 grains) a pinch of ginger. These were baked 'to the consistence of omelet'. Take a glass of Canary wine. Repeat in 8 days.

Ginger was also used as an aphrodisiac applied externally. Nevertheless, although these curious mixtures may have had psychological value to those not of a particularly robust or sceptical disposition, the main questions regarding sex were when, how, and where.

The ancient doctrine of temperaments was of use here: 'It is not impossible for the man of a bilious temperament to surpass the number of five embraces during one night; but it is certainly beyond the power of a phlegmatic man to attain that number.'

This estimate of 1843 would have shocked Acton (once a week, but then twice in the night to ensure a thorough 'emptying');

Dr W. A. Hammond (whose *Sexual Impotence*, 1887, advocates once a week); Dr A. von Haller (twice a week, though his *Elementa Physiologia* dates from 1778); and even Dr A. Forel (*Die Sexuelle Frage*, 1905) two or three times a week (though not to worry if once a month is more acceptable); Guyet (*Bréviare de l'Amour Expérimental* – indeed! three times a week) or Dr P. Mantegazza (1831–1910), whose *Hygiene of Love* recommends two or three times a week for the twenty-to-thirty age group, twice a week for the thirty-to-forty-five age group. Presumably it is hard luck for those past forty-five.

How far were these figures arbitrary, depending on the personal caprices of the writers and certain stock ideas? In the annals of sexology, there are indications that these figures are, briefly, out of a hat. Robust elderly people have related that they have had intercourse every night of their married life without adverse effect; spinsters in their forties and fifties have admitted that masturbation has been their daily rite; in certain marriages, men have had orgasms five and six times a night, performances continued for long periods. These cases usually came to light when it dawned on the participants that there was something excessive in the demand of the woman upon her man.

Regarding times for sex, there were, naturally, two schools of thought. The romantic school considered that marriage should not be necessarily consummated at night, and that daytime was preferable; they pointed out that sex was not a deed of darkness, despite evidence to the contrary. However, from the early forties, 'pleasures taken during the day are more hurtful than those of the night; and it must be acknowledged that, when we have been exhausted by love, there is nothing better calculated to repair our strength than tranquillity and sleep'. It was also worth bearing in mind, 'the importance of the seminal liquor in supporting vigorous health announces the constant necessity for returning a part of this precious fluid to the mass of blood, after it has attained all its perfection'. Naturally this procedure was more easily accommodated during the sleeping hours.

Most lubricous writing dealt with the penis as an instrument of punishment rather than of pleasure. Just as the clitoris was considered to be quite adequate in the dealing out of pleasure to Lesbian women, as a general rule and not as a peculiar pathological state (norm was one inch, distended 1½ inches), so the penis was invested with majesty. In an auction in March 1840, 'curiosities and articles of vertu' from the collection of an anatomical lecturer included the penis of Captain Nicholls who died in Horsemonger Lane jail in 1835 and that of a private in the Blues, bottled in a glass twelve inches long, and was in, said the auctioneer, 'a beautiful state of preservation'. There was also the unnamed portion of the late Lady Barrymore which went into the possession of Sam Israels. Among the audience for this curious sale were medical students and a mystery woman described as Old Leah of Theobalds Road, London.

The pornographic prints give great play to the penis of great length, as do the stories. In the *Cremorne*, of the eighties, there was a serial *Lady Hamilton*; Lady Hamilton has to undergo numerous ordeals. 'Stooping over her prostrate form the brawny brute drew out a monstrous prick ... with brutal hideous laughs the monster drove his trenchant weapon to the hilt in her gaping quim.' For unsatisfied women there were two main ethnic groups with the wherewithal to satisfy them: (a) soldiers; (b) Negroes. The latter were highly thought of, and some were introduced into free and easy establishments that catered for the unsatiated or unsatiable. In the nineteenth century, where sex was concerned, there was no expense spared. So lucrative was this business that Lord Frankfort de Montmorency surpassed himself, sending printed letters offering to keep husbands 'insensibly asleep' while wives and lovers cavorted in the drawing room. He was remiss enough to send one to the vicar of St Martin-in-the-Fields. This was a case where organized adultery did not pay – Lord Frankfort received twelve months' imprisonment for indecent libel.

Whereas the vulva was a favoured subject for poetic and picturesque metaphor-making, the penis was neglected – again for the reason that lewd literature was directed at lewd men. One interesting example occurs in the *Exquisite* (1842):

The Tree of Life, then, is a succulent plant, consisting of one only straight stem, on the top of which is a *pistillm* or *apex*, sometimes of a glandiform appearance, and not unlike a May-cherry, though, at other seasons more resembling the Avellana or filbeard tree. Its fruits, contrary to most others, grow near the root; they are usually two in number; in size somewhat exceeding that of an ordinary nutmeg, and are both contained in one Siliqua, or purse, which, together with the whole root of the plant, is commonly beset with innumerable fibrilla, or capillary, tendrils.

Women who could not be satisfied was a subject fraught with much winking and nudging. As the poet has it:

> Blest enjoyment, oft repeated,
> Gaping quims cessation fear.

The ancients were drawn upon as authorities. Cleopatra was said to have had twenty-five lovers in twenty-four hours, and Messalina, wife of the emperor Claudius, 106 overnight. On account of her excesses of various kinds she was executed in A.D. 48. In more recent times, Catherine the Great was referred to as the ultimate in the insatiable, and there were sufficient nymphomaniacs in the extensive medical annals of the nineteenth century to satisfy the most incredulous. Extent and capacity of the vagina were agreed to vary. Less attention was paid to the urethra; in 1897, Dr H. van den Bergh published figures which announced that six per cent of urethras examined admitted the tip of the little finger. There were also the myths of pubic hair; it was held by sexologists that the pubic hair of women who masturbated was straighter. Havelock Ellis in his early days acted as midwife. Of a hundred women delivered he stated that only in one case did pubic hair inconvenience him. The case recorded by Dr F. L. Jahn (1778–1852) – pubic hair was longer than the woman's ordinary hair; Paulini – pubic hair reached knees; and Bartholio – pubic hair was plaited behind the woman's back, are unquestionably freakish.

If one accepted that woman was basically cold – even the Latin temperament came up with this: 'Woman is naturally and organically frigid' (*La Donna Delinquente* by Lombroso and Ferrerio, 1893) – then one accepted that attentions of men were not greatly welcome in excess, and those who did make unacceptable demands clearly had some psychological defect, known as temperamental emotion or the sexual temperament, caused by 'idleness, inaction, too much sleep, a soft bed, succulent, aromatic, salt and vinous diet, suspicious friends, licentious publications'. Furthermore, 'those men who languish in repose and effeminacy are always impelled to the same object – pleasure; but the weakness of their constitution not permitting its enjoyment in reality, they taste imaginary transports: and relative to this are their discourses, their readings, their ailments, and, in short, everything'. For those men who tasted real transports and not imaginary ones, there was the curious condition called marasmus: 'The whole body, in this disease, grows lean and consumes. This state is sometimes frightful: in the last stage the body resembles a skeleton: the skin clings to the bones, the belly sinks on the back, the visage is pale and frightful, the eyes sink, the temples fall in &c. &c.' &c. &c. indeed. Such was the penalty, it was held out, for too much indulgence or self-abuse – a penalty held out, it might be remarked, by the pornographic magazine the *Exquisite* which elsewhere in its pages was drumming up the excitements it here tried to quell. 'Very different,' added the writer, 'from a robust artisan, the indolent man is excited by a thousand objects, that press and accelerate the hour of pleasure.'

The *via media* was the only road for Victorian man. Supposing that the husband kept to the timetable laid down by the medical men, it is reasonable to assume that he would, to use the jargon of the time, mark these days with a white stone. But he must curb his enthusiasm. 'Another cause of sterility arises in the violence of the transports that agitate spouses. This cause exists by vivid and ardent persons, who precipitate the flashes of enjoyment, without attaching themselves to the favourable instant.' Thus nineteenth-century husbands were beset with difficulties.

There was also the unspeakable question of positions. Among the *cognoscenti* nurtured on the recent translations by Sir Richard Burton of the *Kama Sutra* and other works this subject was of great interest. It was a subject also of confusion. Any attitude that facilitated conception had the blessing of many theologians, though those against intercourse except in the officially approved manner could point to theologians of the past who took diametrically opposed attitudes (figuratively, not literally). To the seventh-century theologian Theodore, copulation *a posteriori* was worth forty penances; it was a sin that vied with masturbation (also forty penances). However, if copulation *a posteriori* was habitual, there must be three years of penance. Towards the end of the century, encouraged by the objective appraisals of their continental colleagues, British writers on sex matters proffered the theory that copulation *a posteriori* was the natural way. There were two grounds for this belief (a) the sexual proclivities of other anthropoids; and (b) the position of the clitoris.

Regarding the various postures to be adopted, Romano, a pupil of Raphael, drew twenty-six. F. K. Forberg accounted for ninety. The general consensus of opinion was for forty-eight positions.

Even more vexing was the question of anomalies and perversions. Dr C. S. Féré, a little-known but reliable writer on sex matters, maintained in his *The Sexual Instinct* (1904) that masturbatory habits were so universal as to be considered normal. Similarly, *fellatio* and *cunnilinctus* were so often demanded as to be scarcely an aberration. Max Dessoir reported in 1894 that Berlin prostitutes were frequently asked to provide this service – twenty-five per cent of them. The wide use of prostitutes in Britain unquestionably arises from unusual demands made upon them – the 'disgusting practices' noted by Henry Mayhew. The sly hints in the handbooks for men about town add substance to this. Naturally there are no references to such anomalies in high literature of the period, but pornographic literature is replete with them, as is the rare I-tell-everything autobiography, such as Frank Harris's. Exceptions exist in French high literature, such as Zola's *Nana*. A characteristic description of *cunnilinctus* occurs in *The Three Chums* of 1860: 'She inclined her body backwards, and gave up her person entirely to his tonguing caresses, both her hands lovingly pressing the top of his head, as he ravenously sucked the very essence of her life, which she constantly distilled in thick ambrosial drops under the voluptuous evolutions of his busy tongue.'

So often looked upon as an instrument of prudery and repression, the church, especially the Roman Catholic Church, has often shown more honesty than the lay authorities. The Jesuit Gury maintained that wives could masturbate; though Aquinas was against this, matters were, after a fashion, discussed. The pretence that widely varied sexual activities did not exist was so overpowering during the nineteenth century that many fell into mental confusion when persuading themselves that impulses they well knew they had did not exist. Ruskin's madness was almost certainly due to sexual repression. In his diaries there are guarded references to this: 'The quantity of love which we betray by our vices,' he wrote in September 1867, 'or leave desolate by our death – self-wrought – for such suicide differs only from sudden suicide by its deliberation. It is suicide committed daily.' This could be seen as a reference to his masturbation, and his perplexity is mirrored in a letter he wrote in 1870 to his friend Mrs Cowper: 'My mind is getting so mixed up now of desire for revenge – and a kind of hatred which the love is changing into – that my whole life is getting distorted and I don't well understand anything, besides a shame and anger at myself – increasing day by day – which checks me and lowers me fatally.'

Had the nineteenth century shown the same courage in facing the facts of sexual and reproductive life as it had in facing the new elements in industrial life – in the honest endeavour to clear up poverty, in the acceptance of a decline in religious faith, in the awareness of the barbarity and cruelty of much of modern life – then much guilt and heartache would have been avoided. The classic monument to progressive thought on sexual matters is unquestionably Havelock Ellis' *Studies in the Psychology of Sex* (1901–10), which had all the virtues of Victorian scholarship. 'When the rigid secrecy is once swept away a sane and natural reticence becomes for the first time possible,' wrote Ellis in the general preface. This monumental work was preceded by works on a smaller scale, such as his *Sexual Inversion* (1898), an effort to obtain a reasoned hearing for homosexuality.

The fate of this pioneering book demonstrates the difficulties that dogged writers anxious to disturb Victorian complacency, to substitute prurience by scientific investigation. *Studies in the*

Psychology of Sex was burnt by Dean Inge as 'too unwholesome', and it made Margaret Sanger 'spiritually ill' with its 'mountainous array of abnormalities'. Gentility got in the way of its acceptance. *Sexual Inversion* had had an even rougher ride. Havelock Ellis, knowing that reputable publishers would not touch it, was foolish enough to let the book come out under the aegis of Roland de Villiers, whose imprint was the farcical 'Watford University Press'. De Villiers was a believer in the Legitimation League, which sought to replace marriage by a formal acknowledgement of union, and was a clover for all kinds of outsiders including anarchists. Chief Inspector Melville used a double-agent John Sweeney to get something on the League. De Villiers was pushing *Sexual Inversions* on the sly; it was pounced upon as an obscene libel, and the case came to Bow Street court in June, 1898. Nobly to its defence came a mixed bag of freethinkers and left-wing agitators and heroes *manqué*, not to mention the odd nut – the Free Press Defence Committee. They included Walter Crane, a pretty-pretty illustrator; Bernard Shaw; Edward Carpenter, the rather prissy wide-blue-yonder writer on marriage; Gant Allen, author of *The Woman Who Did*; Belfort Bax; the socialist H. M. Hyndman; George Moore, the poor man's Frank Harris; and William Sharp, the Celtic twilighter who wrote under the name of 'Fiona Macleod'. So was earnest and authoritative sexology represented in the lists. The indictment made out that *Sexual Inversion* was 'lewd, wicked, bawdy, scandalous and obscene libel'. Few doubted it. Such was the climate of 1898.

The fate that had been meted out to advocates of birth control information for the masses was reserved also for serious writers, whose only outlets were through the dirt distributors. The unwillingness of reputable publishers to become involved with the police and the umbrella-wielding purveyors of public morality was well nigh total. The way was clear to under-the-counter writers such as Mrs Ida Ellis, a phrenologist of Batley, Yorkshire, whose *Essentials of Conception* (1891), price sixpence, was for 'Married Persons only' and no doubt sent under plain cover. Besides a lot of misleading information it advertised the wares of, presumably, a husband, J. Ellis, a photographer, of Canterbury, and her own trade (character from handwriting one shilling and sixpence, character from photograph five shillings and sixpence, character from physical description one shilling and sixpence – character from photograph included '*a first-class* chart fully marked, including profession, marriage, health and diet').

The prize plum from *Essentials of Conception* was this:

It is the male who can progenate a male or female child at will, by putting an elastic band round the testicle not required. The semen from the right testicle progenates male, whilst that from the left female children; Men who have only one testicle can only beget one gender, but sometimes they do not descend, remaining in the body, in which case a child of either gender may appear.

So are the anxious, the ignorant and the puzzled served when conditions prevent rational and expert information being published.

Part Two
The Victorian Buried Life

Alas! is even love too weak
To unlock the heart, and let it speak?
Are even lovers powerless to reveal
To one another what indeed they feel?
I knew the mass of men concealed
Their thoughts, for fear that if revealed
They would by other men be met
With blank indifference, or with blame reproved;
I knew they lived and moved
Tricked in disguises, alien to the rest
Of men, and alien to themselves—and yet
The same heart beats in every human breast!

But we, my love! — doth a like spell benumb
Our hearts, our voices? must we too be dumb?

Ah! well for us, if even we,
Even for a moment, can get free
Our heart, and have our lips unchained;
For that which seals them hath been deep-ordained!

Fate, which foresaw
How frivolous a baby man would be
By what distractions he would be possessed,
How he would pour himself in every strife,
And well-nigh change his own identity —

That it might keep from his capricious play
His genuine self, and force him to obey
Even in his own despite his being's law,
Bade through the deep recesses of our breast
The unregarded river of our life
Pursue with indiscernible flow its way;
And that we should not see
The buried stream, and seem to be
Eddying at large in blind uncertainty,
Though driving on with it eternally.

But often, in the world's most crowded streets,
But often, in the din of strife,
There rises an unspeakable desire
After the knowledge of our buried life;
A thirst to spend our fire and restless force
In tracking out our true, original course;
A longing to inquire
Into the mystery of this heart which beats
So wild, so deep in us—to know.

Whence our thoughts come and where they go.
And many a man in his own breast then delves,
But deep enough, alas! none ever mines.
And we have been on many thousand lines,
And we have shown on each talent and power;
But hardly have we, for one little hour,
Been on our own line, have we been ourselves —
Hardly had skill to utter one of all
The nameless feelings that course through our breast,
But they course on for ever unexpressed.
And long we try in vain to speak and act
Our hidden self, and what we say and do
Is eloquent, is well — but 'tis not true!
And then we will no more be racked
With inward striving, and demand
Of all the thousand nothings of the hour
Their stupefying power;
Ah yes, and they benumb us at our call!
Yet still, from time to time, vague and forlorn,
From the soul's subterranean depth upborne
As from an infinitely distant land,
Come airs, and floating echoes, and convey
A melancholy into all our day.

6

Prostitution

Aristocratic Fun

HENRY MAYHEW, whose *London Labour and the London Poor* (1851–62) is the great sociological masterpiece of the century, divided prostitutes into six categories:

1. kept mistresses
   prima donnas

2. convives

2a. independent

2b. subject to mistress
   i 'board lodgers' (given board)
   ii 'dress lodgers' (given board & dress)

3. low lodging houses women

4. sailors' and soldiers' women

5. park women

6. thieves' women

From their behaviour, many ladies of the aristocracy were hardly more than kept mistresses, and no doubt Mayhew had his own private opinions on them. However, they were outside the scope of his survey, though hardly more than the kept mistresses and the 'prima donnas' whom no one would have called poor.

The kept mistresses and the prima donnas had a life that was envied by ostensibly more respectable ladies. 'I am not tired of what I am doing. I rather like it. I have all I want, and my friend loves me to excess.' So one happy whore told Mayhew. As for the sanction of her parents, 'Oh, yes! they know I am alive, for I keep them pleasantly aware of my existence by occasionally sending them money.' And money there was in plenty for those ladies who managed to entice the upper crust, who did not succumb to the prime temptation of prostitutes, 'satin' (i.e., gin), and who managed to avoid having their features eaten away by syphilis. Dr Michael Ryan, one of the period's authorities on prostitution, believed that £8,000,000 were spent each year on prostitutes; he also had the idea that the average duration of life after a woman became a prostitute was four years, so rapidly did their looks go, so rampant was syphilis, so merciless was this way of life.

The *demi-mondaines* were contemptuous of this way of life, and, as if to prove the foolishness of Dr Ryan's pronouncements, the most famous one of them all, Catherine (Skittles) Walters, lived to the age of eighty-one, dying as recently as 1920. During her last years she was a familiar figure in Hyde Park, trundling along amiably in her bath chair. Among her friends she numbered the Prince of Wales (who else?) as well as, more surprisingly, Lord Kitchener, hero of the First World War, and Gladstone, who tried to reclaim her in his chivalrous way. It was not surprising that he selected Miss Walters. As his parliamentary colleague, Henry Labouchere, said, 'Gladstone manages to combine his missionary meddling with a keen appreciation of a pretty face. He has never been known to rescue any of our East End whores, nor for that matter is it easy to contemplate his rescuing any ugly woman, and I am quite sure his conception of the Magdalen is of an incomparable example of pulchritude with a superb figure and carriage.' However, as A. Tilney Bassett announced when editing Gladstone's letters to his wife, 'none dare now question the fearless rectitude and purity of Gladstone's motives'. Gladstone's contemporaries were not so generous; Lord Milner's sardonic reference to 'Mr Gladstone's seraglio' found its echoes elsewhere, and when Gladstone was once caught kissing Mrs Cornwallis West [1] the news was soon circulated among those who found Gladstone's efforts at reclamation hilarious.

Skittles Walters must be proclaimed as one of Gladstone's failures, even though he had tea with her, presenting her beforehand with twelve pounds of Russian tea, and taking her for a conducted tour of St Paul's Cathedral. In return, Skittles confessed that Gladstone was 'the living monument of nobility of thought'.

Catherine Walters made her first London appearance, according to *The Times*, in 1861, and transfixed the men about town. Along with other members of the superior echelons of the profession, she made her appearance at the fashionable hours in Hyde Park, riding in Rotten Row. There were ballads about them:

> The young swells in Rotten Row
>   All cut it mighty fine,
> And quiz the fair sex, you know,
>   And say it is divine.
> The pretty little horse-breakers
>   Are breaking hearts like fun,
> For in Rotten Row they all must go
>   The whole hog or none.
>
> Oh! dear girls, I love you more than honey,
>   London is a funny place,
> But costs a lot of money.
>   Yes, London is a funny place
> Where rummy things are done,
>   For in London Town they all must go
> The whole hog or none.

Not only the song writers were using the girls in the Row. The 'real' poets were also exercising their talents. Wilfrid Scawen Blunt,[2] now more interesting as a period figure than as a poet, wrote of 'Skittles' Walters that she was:

> A woman most complete
>   In all her ways of loving,
> And prodigal of love as one
>   Who careless of deceit
> And rich in all things is of all things free

This does not seem to say very much, except that Miss Walters was evidently a most unusual whore. Labouchere – the man

responsible for the Labouchere Amendment of 1885 that landed
Oscar Wilde in Reading Gaol – wrote that 'she had the most
capacious heart I know' and 'must be the only whore in history
to retain her heart intact'. In 1862 she was such a draw that
crowds assembled to look at her, seriously upsetting the traffic
arrangements for the great exhibition at South Kensington a
short distance away. She had all the qualities for the prurient
Victorians – she was notorious, yet she was beautiful, and for the
henpecked lower-middle-class husbands who formed a fair percentage of the 6,117,450 visitors to the Great Exhibition
of 1862, there was always the chance that when eventually they
had made their pile, they, too, could enjoy the favours of the
adorable 'Skittles'. She was the centre of a cult, and books were
written about and around her – *Skittles, a Biography of a Fascinating Woman; Skittles in Paris; Anonyma, Fair but Frail;
Mémoires d'une Biche Anglaise* (hardly chivalrous).

The cult of the lady riders in Hyde Park also fostered a certain creeping sadism and masochism, sponsored with becoming
innocence by the *Englishwoman's Domestic Magazine*.[3] The
tight lacing that went with the trim figures cut by lady riders
produced a 'delightful sensation', and riding trousers for women
were evolved in chamois leather with black feet. There was a
good deal of technical stuff about spurs, and a rather coy admission that 'the secret stimulus of the hidden steel is more frequently resorted to than some of the fair ladies would like to
admit'. The journalist G. A. Sala was intrigued by this, noting
inferences no one had drawn, and wrote fetching letters to the
ladies' magazines purporting to come from a lady undergoing
all these strange new experiences – the tight lacing, the spurring
of a horse, and displaying 'a tiny coquettish brilliant little
boot ...'

Riding in Hyde Park was a pursuit in which everyone joined.
One of the most celebrated of the respectable ladies was the
beautiful Lady Florence Paget,[4] with her light blue riding habit
and golden hair. A foreign visitor to London was surprised and
slightly shocked when, visiting an acquaintance, he was urged
to take the daughter of the house unchaperoned for a spin in the
park in the family carriage. The massed hordes of riders, horses,

and carriages, that trampled and rolled over what had once been known as 'The King's Private Road' had found a way to break through the uneven fences of nineteenth-century convention.

Laura Bell belongs to a slightly earlier set of *demi-mondaines*. She was born in 1829, ten years earlier than Skittles Walters, making her London debut in 1850. Her reputation as a high-priced whore had been established in Dublin, after a short hectic period as a streetwalker in Belfast. She was the daughter of the bailiff on the Irish estates of Lord Hertford. In Dublin she had reached the stage of having a barouche of her own (a barouche was a two-seat four-wheeled carriage with a folding top) plus the inevitable pair of white horses.

In London she established herself in fashionable Wilton Crescent and rapidly became one of the favourites of the 'swells' with money to burn. Unlike Skittles, who never got married though she called herself Mrs Baillie in later life, Laura Bell decided upon Augustus Thistlethwayte as a husband a mere two years after she set up in London. Gladstone once observed, 'I know from personal experience that these women dread, yes, actually dread going back into the kind of ordered, decent world they have left behind.' Possibly because Laura had never known an ordered decent world, she had no problem, and became an evangelical preacher, beginning this unusual career in an out-of-the-way spot in Scotland. After a certain success – her address was 'impassioned ... not eloquent nor convincing, but certainly effective' – she moved into town, where her past reputation resulted in a large audience. One observer saw her preach in 1874. 'She was getting on in years then, and inclining to be obese ...' Laura Thistlethwayte was then a mere forty-five; the autumn leaves certainly fell early in the nineteenth century.

It might be supposed that her husband (whose mother was the daughter of a bishop) was delighted by this reformation, but the moral fervour of his wife's newly found vocation was not matched by a corresponding change in worldly values. She was wildly extravagant – after all, had she not been the mistress of an Indian prince? – and Thistlethwayte had to announce that he would not be responsible for any debts she incurred. Thistlethwayte came to a mysterious end; he had a habit of keeping a loaded revolver by his bedside, and it is 'supposed' that on 9 August 1887, he was seized with a fainting fit, fell, knocking over the small table on which the revolver lay. The revolver most improbably went off, and, even more improbably, killed Mr Thistlethwayte. These odd happenings at 15 Grosvenor Square might well be deserving of a closer scrutiny.

The kept women of the early Victorian period, the professional mistresses, were a numerous class. Were they prostitutes, in the strict sense of the word? Henry Mayhew thought so – 'prostitution does not consist solely in promiscuous intercourse, for she who confines her favours to one may still be a prostitute.' The rich men who had a prima donna were also in a dilemma. The top girls who had come through all the vicissitudes of frailty might always be tempted by: (a) more money elsewhere; (b) a more impressive title – the eldest son of a duke of Blood Royal was better than a marquis, a duke's younger son was better than an earl's elder son, while a baronet's eldest son was no better than a Master in Lunacy or Serjeant at Law; and (c) better performers.

It was often the case that men were getting on in years before they came into their titles (and their money). As younger sons, or even elder sons, their pleasures might well have to be taken with the cheaper prostitutes; it was one of the lordly ambitions to have a quality mistress in one of the elegant West End squares. However, these aged lords and dukes did not often give satisfaction, and it has been noticed, 'that sexual desire, once aroused, does exercise a potent influence on the female organization'.[5] The Victorian sexologists – and they were many – did not need a Kinsey report to give them information.

Similarly, to be a kept woman was every intelligent prostitute's ambition, if only to escape the hazards of the street. Some of the data supplied by Victorian doctors and authorities is suspect; too often moral judgements are allowed to interfere with hard fact. Dr Tait was one of the self-styled experts on prostitution, and some of his conclusions are lurid in the extreme. 'In less than one year from the commencement of their wicked career, these females bear evident marks of their approaching decay,' he wrote. In three years, they could not be recognized, not above one in eleven survives twenty-five years, and a fifth or sixth of prostitutes die regularly. The population of London at this time was 2,362,000. To cater for this, three of the most reliable doctors (Ryan, Campbell and Talbot) reckoned that there were 80,000 prostitutes. William Acton, surgeon to Islington Dispensary, went further: 'Were there any possibility of reckoning all those in London who would come within the definition of prostitutes, I am inclined to think that the estimates of the boldest who have preceded me would be thrown into the shade.' A journalist who moved exclusively among low life, and who often wrote editorials from prison, Renton Nicholson, put the figure at 120,000.

Competition to be in the top flight of prostitutes was therefore fierce, though few of the aspirants had the qualities to make it. The successful had not only to perform well, but had to look well, talk intelligently, and if possible possess additional talents; a good singing voice was highly prized. For those who had these qualities and who were set up in an establishment there were two subsequent disasters that might befall them: (a) disease; and (b) children. In Britain in 1851 there were 42,000 illegitimate children born.[6] Thousands more, many thousands more, were killed, and dead babies in the Thames were so common that attention was not drawn to them. Every whore was supposed to have a tender heart, and unquestionably many thousands of babies were farmed out by those prostitutes who accepted their misfortune. In the highest ranks of kept mistresses, where there was little question as to the father, the children often had the same opportunities as legitimate half-brothers and half-sisters.

Prostitution, from the 'mott' to the prima donna, was a pursuit reasonably free from police interference. The police divided the whores into three basic kinds — well-dressed prostitutes in brothels, prostitutes walking streets, and prostitutes in low neighbourhoods (the 'motts'). Arrests were infrequent. In the London area in 1841 the total was 9,409, more than half of which were 'motts'. There was a good deal of interesting etymological controversy carried out by scholars about the derivation of 'mott', and there were two basic schools of thought – one stating that it was a cant word for the vulva, the other that it was an older reading of moth (possibly because of their brief lives and their diverse protective colouring).

When prostitutes had got to the top of the tree they were in an unassailable position. Success breeds success. Girls of the sterling quality of Skittles Walters and Laura Bell could change protectors as it suited them, and the only hazard was the possibility of turning moral, as Miss Bell did. This was a consummation devoutly to be wished not only by Gladstone, but by the Religious Tract Society which, up to the accession of Queen Victoria, had issued 500,000,000 tracts directed at bringing prostitutes back to the straight and narrow (whether they succeeded with Skittles Walters is a moot point – she died in the Roman Catholic faith).

The do-gooders of the Gladstone type were suspected by the prostitutes (they called him 'Old Glad-eye') but detested by those who profited from the prostitutes. Gladstone had a continuous running battle with Mrs Jeffries, who ran a chain of brothels in Windmill Street and Queen Street, though he deplored procurers and procuring houses more than brothels. His eager beaver interest in an 'introducing house' in St George's Road, near Lupus Street, was particularly resented by his colleagues as it catered almost exclusively to Members of Parliament.

The efforts of Gladstone to rehabilitate fallen women – provided that they were pretty and perambulated in the better parts of London – were not outstandingly successful. In three years he managed to reclaim a dozen 'persons to his complete satisfaction'. One of his successes was a girl whom he described as 'at the top of the tree'. Although only twenty, she had been in the game for some time (married at fifteen), had a place in Brompton Square, and kept a carriage and pair at the stables in Cheval Place. After Gladstone had worked his wiles on her, and she had been added to the small number of the reclaimed, the proprietor of the stables wrote to Gladstone, 'I feel justified in asking you to pay the heavy account.'

Gladstone unquestionably got a great kick out of his relationships with these girls, and many were awed by his presence. One of these was Sweet Nelly Fowler, of whom D. Shaw in *London in the Sixties* said: 'This beautiful girl had a natural perfume so delicate, so universally admitted, that love-sick swains paid large sums for the privilege of having their handkerchiefs placed under the Goddess's pillow, and sweet Nelly pervaded – in spirit, if not in the flesh – half the clubs and drawing-rooms of London.' A Tennysonian spirit that does credit to the sentiments of the author.

'The Prime Minister,' Nelly Fowler wrote, 'actually called to see me. He is not at all as stern as they all say he is, but most well-mannered, kind and considerate, and, indeed, a wonderful figure of a man, so very, very handsome, that one longs to stroke that magnificent head.'

The interrelated worlds of high and low, moral and immoral, are surprising to those who look on the Victorians as being secreted in watertight compartments of class. In theory, it should have been an impossibility for the rich heiress Miss Burdett-Coutts (who had had a schoolgirlish crush on the ancient Duke of Wellington and who married a man young enough to be her grandson) to take Skittles Walters to the pantomime. In fact, these kinds of relationships were as common as they are today. The cult of low life was as fascinating then as it is now provided that it was not too low, and the specimens of low life were presentable; one could not imagine Miss Burdett-Coutts cultivating the dockside whores – Black Sarah, Cocoa Bet, Bet Moses, the Mouth of the Nile, Salmony-faced Mary Anne, Peg Mitchell, Poll Sellars, or Long Nance Taylor. And as for the pimp Vampire Tom, why, even the Prince of Wales in one of his self-conscious slumming expeditions would have given him a wide berth.

It was not uncommon for the more superior type of prostitute to be recruited from the ranks of cast-off mistresses. As one plaintive writer in the *Town* put it in 1837, 'Years back, if a man of property wanted to provide for a discarded mistress, it was the fashion to look out for some bloodless sappy, to whom was given a sum of money to marry her.' The only disadvantage to such an entry into the profession was age; prostitutes were a short-lived breed, though the Germans resolutely maintained that it was a healthy life.

Louisa Turner was one who went into prostitution via the stage. The daughter of a glove-shop owner in Carlton Street, she studied music and went into Italian opera, which was known as 'the hot-bed of seduction'. The girls in the cast took her to a brothel in Tichfield Street, near Oxford Street, and she decided that this was easier work than flying through the air as a sylph. Lord Yarmouth took a fancy to her, and his love took the usual form of a horse (this one was worth £200) and, a curious luxury of the time, a plume of ostrich feathers.[9] She now saw opera, rather than participated in it, but the boxes at the opera were as much a hotbed of seduction as the stage, and when a man bowed to her, she told Lord Yarmouth to 'go out of the box for a little while, love'. Characteristically she took to the favourite beverage of whoredom – gin.

At one time she was in competition with Ellen Clarke for the affections of the exiled Duke of Brunswick, whom no one particularly wanted as ruler. Ellen Clarke, referred to as 'the flashest of the frail ... up, down, and fly', is supposed to have addressed a little poem to her rival :

> Now, Miss Louisa, rest assured,
> That never unto thee
> Shall come again my only love,
> The frisky Duke of B.

At one time the Duke of Brunswick was on the list as a possible suitor of Victoria. It is certain that he fascinated her, especially the way he did his hair, 'it is divided all down the head (parted in the middle) and hangs I should say about two inches below the ear all round. It may not suit ugly people, that's true, but it certainly becomes these handsome ones.'[10] Princess Victoria discussed the mysterious duke with her ladies, who confided that they had seen him close to. His expression was 'dreadful, so very fierce, and desperate'.[11] He had the *outré* touch Victoria later admired in Napoleon III who had the foresight to remember the dresses Victoria wore. Not over-used to gallantry, Victoria had mentioned to Lord Clarendon, then her Foreign Secretary, 'Isn't it odd, Lord Clarendon, the Emperor remembers every frock he has ever seen me in!' Clarendon, a cynical man of the world, had put down the Queen's interest in the amorous approaches of Napoleon to deficiencies in the ardour of Albert (he seems to have been wrong). As for the Duke of Brunswick, he never came near enough to the Queen to achieve the response he conjured up in Ellen Clarke and Louisa Turner.

Louisa Turner was also associated with Prince Esterhazy, who later married one of Queen Victoria's bridesmaids, Lady Sarah Villiers. Prince Esterhazy belonged to an old Hungarian family noted for their extravagance, and he represented Austria in London, a career that apparently was not over-arduous.

These high-powered ladies were adept at getting through a fortune. In 1862 Skittles Walters ran off with Aubrey de Vere Beauclerk. 'This wretched fool has left a charming wife, and, I believe, young children,' wrote Sir William Hardman, lawyer and dilettante, 'he has some four thousand pounds a year, which will be even as fourpence halfpenny to such a woman.' [12]

Amy Johnson, alias Hope, alias Scott, was the daughter of an army officer, and was small, plump, 'a damned desirable little creature'. She soon found a protector, Charles Dowell, who most fortunately had come into a fortune of £15,000. This was gone within two years, and instead of being an affluent 'swell' and man about town, Dowell found himself doing six years in King's Bench Prison. He died at the age of twenty-nine. Amy Johnson went on from success to success. She had a red four-horse carriage, and two establishments, in Connaught Terrace, Edgware Road, in newly fashionable Bayswater, and at Brighton, a place that still had the kudos it had won as the play centre of the Prince Regent. However, Amy also found herself in prison, but was discharged after two or three months; she became a streetwalker in York Street, Bryanston Square, and ended her life in obscurity.

An even more expensive form of sexual entertainment than

the high-class prostitute was the private brothel. 'In York Street we find a brothel kept, positively, for the sole accommodation of a noble duke, and he far advanced in years.' The private brothels usually contained three or four women, with a lady 'abbess' to look after them and see that the facilities of the establishment were not abused by strangers. The more shy or eccentric or perverted aristocrats preferred to have their vice organized for them, by the 'abbesses' or by operators of a string of prostitutes, such as the redoubtable Mrs Emerson – known to favoured clients as 'Mother' – with whom it was a privilege to drink, and who habitually wore jewellery 'worth a cool thousand'. One of the aristocrats who patronized Mrs Emerson was the Marquis of Waterford.

The Marquis of Waterford, the 'mad marquis', was one of the most colourful figures of the period. At one time he, too, was connected with the ubiquitous Louisa Turner, and once, when it was suggested that his sister, Lady Sarah Ingestre, had hissed the Queen at Ascot, the *Argus* urged the marquis to go to the palace and use his horsewhip, preferably on Lord Melbourne. (Before she was married, it was often scouted that the Queen and Melbourne were lovers – indeed, at Ascot people dared to call out 'Mrs Melbourne'.)

When in London, the marquis and his friends would wander through the streets looking for fights with rougher elements from the lower orders.[13] A certain Policeman Ellis dared to arrest the marquis at five o'clock in the morning one morning in Piccadilly for driving along the pavement in his carriage, accompanied by two or three men and a woman. The carriage hit a post, the lady was thrown half a dozen yards; the marquis was collected, drunk, taken to the police station, and later fined £2. At Crockford's, the celebrated gaming club, the marquis smashed a handsome French clock on the staircase with one blow of his fist; he used family portraits as targets with the eyes as the favourite focus of attention; he introduced a donkey into the bed of a stranger at an inn; he doctored the hoofs of a clergyman's mount with anis-seed and hunted him with bloodhounds; and near his estate at Melton Mowbray he and three companions (including Sir Frederick Johnstone, co-respondent in the Mordaunt case) upturned a constable and painted him red (this fun cost the marquis a £100 fine). He was also one of the leading figures in that curious atavism, the Eglinton Tournament, in which Lord Eglinton tried to revive the spirit of the Middle Ages, with joustings in suits of armour, a lunatic venture that cost Eglinton £40,000 and was rendered ludicrous by typically heavy English rain. The Marquis was the Knight of the Dragon, and in an off-court argument with Lord Alford, Knight of the Black Lion, tempers were lost, and they laid into each other with all the vigour of a medieval fight to the death. Knowing the marquis's violent inclinations, no doubt the marshals parted them with some anxiety. The Eglinton Tournament collected together in one place most of the rakes of the period, including Prince Esterhazy and Lord Ossulston,[14] who figure in many of the anecdotes of the period.

The Marquis of Waterford, almost if not quite mad, was the kind of person the procuresses of early Victorian London had to deal with. It is hardly to be wondered at that the life of a prostitute was hazardous. No doubt the marquis would have been enrolled in the Prince of Wales's band of brothers had he lived long enough, but he died as he lived, excitingly — crushed beneath his falling horse.

Men About Town

When the rich young men arrived from the country, whoring was the favourite pastime. It was something they were expected to do. There was much more of the country then, and in 1851 the proportions of people who lived in town and in the country were nearly equal (there was a rural population of 8,772,000, an urban population of 9,156,000). These sprigs of nobility, these refugees from the rising middle classes, did not have to mill around London in an aimless way, wondering whom to accost and which was the best way to find a whore; there were handbooks for them.

There were probably as many amusements in London in the

middle years of the nineteenth century as, allowing for population growth, there are today. There were two great opera houses – Covent Garden and Her Majesty's – and, for ordinary drama, the Drury Lane, the Princess', the Haymarket, the Lyceum, the Adelphi, the Olympic and the Sadler's Wells. On a slightly lower level were Astley's Amphitheatre, and the Surrey Theatre. For the poor there were 'penny gaffs' (the celebrated Effingham in Whitechapel could accommodate 2,000).

In the West End, there were respectable treats such as massive panoramas, which were very popular (Risley's Panorama of the Mississippi, Gompartz's Panorama of the Arctic Regions, Cambon's Panorama of Paris, Versailles, and St Cloud – all three lavish productions put on between 1849 and 1851). There were freak shows – Joseph Gantonio, the Italian giant, seven feet, seven inches tall; five feet, five inches around waist; span fourteen and three-quarters inches; and his companion, the Lapland Giantess, seven feet, two inches tall. Equally respectable were Reinhamis's 'Industrious fleas' and a 'black opera bouffe from cotton-picking negroes'. His troupe of a hundred fleas, claimed Mr Reinhamis, had 'unwearied perseverance', a quality shared by the culture-hungry Victorian paterfamilias, quite willing to pay to see a globe sixty feet, four inches in diameter, diligently made from 1,000 plaster castings to represent the earth at a ratio of ten miles to the inch (this globe, costing £3,000, lasted ten years as an entertainment in Leicester Square).

The blades had none of this. There was mid-Victorian striptease, the 'unequalled *Tableaux Vivants'* and the *'Poses Plastiques'* in which there was 'a great parade of art ... and a studious avoidance of all indecency of phrase' (at least, that was the original intention). The Hall of Rome prided itself on its representations of 'mythological divinities' and its *'corps dramatique'* and charged a shilling for admission (reserved seats two shillings). There were concert rooms, sporting houses ('sparring', rat killing and man against dog), and the public houses, which sometimes were useful as accommodation houses (at The Cross Keys, Gracechruch Street, 'private rooms can be had here either by day or night; the charge for a sleeping room for self and lady is four shillings, but for a short visit the mere calling for wine is deemed sufficient'). However, the 'calling for wine' could be an expensive proposition. At the famous night house of Kate Hamilton, who wobbled like a blancmange when she laughed, a bottle of Moselle cost twelve shillings.

The handbooks for novice men about town related all this, pointing out that the White Hart in Catherine Street, Strand, contained 'some very questionable characters in the way of pugilists, &c.' and that the Surrey Saloon was frequented 'by the better sort of girls'. This was interesting information, but hardly what the books were for. *Hints to Men About Town or Water Fordiana* was advertised as having 'a notice of the celebrated seraglios, temples devoted to "wit, pleasure and wine"; with hints to "yokels" to prevent their being kidded, grabbed, and flabbergasted, and eased of their tin and their health by —. To which is added hints to prevent infection, remedies to cure, and a fund of useful information by a sporting surgeon.' The sporting surgeon, knowing that his cures were well nigh useless, also took the precaution of equipping these handbooks with a pocket for French letters made of animals' intestine.

The principal purpose of the handbook or the pocket book was as a directory of whores, with addresses, descriptions and, occasionally, prices. Jane Fowler 'is tall, slender, of graceful form and carriage; light hair, with a surprisingly fair and transparent complexion; a full blue eye, fringed with beautiful silken lashes, through which her luscious orbs dart a thousand killing shafts. Jane has a beautiful leg ...' This is the kind of description one meets in the hack fiction of the time, except for the 'beautiful leg', that prohibited article. The description goes on, 'In the chamber, Jane has a peculiar method of disrobing, and possesses excellent tact in managing a charming repulse to the eager advance of a vigorous gallant for the purpose of enhancing the enjoyment, which she well understands how to take share of.' Miss Newman was 'tall and genteel, with a divine face and neck', Miss Merton had 'sister hills' that were 'prominent, firm, and elastic'. The use of Miss Merton cost a guinea. Miss Jane Wilmott had a mouth that 'looks when closed like a rose when it begins to bud', but her eyes were small and gray, while Miss Tibby Leighton was a red-haired whore of 'middling stature ...

rather pale and delicate' and her adman advised her to rouge her face (she cost £2).

Miss Maria Bolton was a six-foot Amazonian, with firm, plump, and white breasts, which, curiously, when they 'rise and fall, paint the exuberance of the soil in the most expressive terms' (could soil be a misprint for soul?). She walked 'singularly genteel', and was 'supported' by beautiful legs. Miss Parks lived in a house which had the Venetian blinds generally drawn down. She cost a fiver, and almost certainly catered to perverts, though the language that describes her in her blurb is so ambiguous that one wonders if the swells of the 1850s had a recondite language to which we are ever to remain ignorant: 'In duets she employs her *tongue* and *voice* full as satisfactory as when it emits the shrillest note. She performs her part with skill and dexterity, and in such cases chooses the *lowest* part.' Knowing as we do the fondness of Victorian writers for italics, perhaps it is just the case of a propagandist laying on a little mystery for the sake of the yokels.

It is apparent that the Victorian 'swell' looked for qualities in their prostitutes that would be inconceivable nowadays. The handbooks time after time hammered away at the genteel behaviour of such and such a woman, and expressive eyes were highly thought of; everyone went into a tizzy when legs are mentioned, though the days of high Victorianism had not yet come when 'legs' was a dirty word, and had to be replaced by the euphemism 'limbs' or even 'unmentionables'. Tallness was also a valued commodity, as were lustiness and energy. Miss Moriella's fee was £1, but if two were proffered, it would 'give her such a flow of spirits as induce her to make uncommon exertions, which have produced incredible effects'.

Mrs Woolford aroused enthusiasm above the average. Her breasts were 'rather small, but as plump and hard as an untouched virgin's … her leg and thigh are (without exception) the most perfect pieces of work nature ever formed'. She also possessed a ready wit, vivacity, and could write a fair hand, another quality that has few captivating charms today. The handbooks did not, unfortunately, give specimens of the wit; for that one has to go to the indefatigable Henry Mayhew. The whore's humour could be slightly black ('Strange things happen to us sometimes; we may now and then die of consumption') or mocking ('When I am sad I drink. I'm very often sad, although I appear to be what you call reckless'), or flippant ('Oh, I'm a seduced milliner, anything you like'), while when Mayhew was descending the social ladder of prostitution, the humour could be downright frightening. When one prostitute was asked if she was passionate, she retorted, 'Passionate! I believe yer. I knocked my father down and well nigh killed him with a flat-iron before I wor twelve years old ... you see this public; well, I've smashed up this place before now.'

The language of reportage, so different from the purple prose of the handbooks and fun guides ('The twin hillocks of delight are redundantly stocked with lactiferous tubes, and swell prominently rich with love's choicest sweets') or the argot that sometimes permeates the handbooks, is the other side of the coin. One introducing house, Madame Audray's, of Church Street, Soho, is described throughout in terms of an abattoir. Although unpleasant, it is a *tour de force* of a kind:

This abbess has just put the kipehook on all other purveyors of the French flesh market. She does not keep her meat too long on the hooks, though she will have her price; but nothing is allowed to get stale here. You may have your meat dressed to your own liking, and there is no need of cutting twice from one joint; and if it suits your taste, you may kill your own lamb or mutton, for her flock is in prime condition, and always ready for sticking. When any of them are fried they are turned out to grass, and sent to the hammer, or disposed of by private contract, but never bought in again; consequently, the rot, bots, glanders, and other diseases incidental to cattle, are not generally known here, though there are instances of the awful enemy lodging itself here through some private jobbing in overtime.

Such a book as *The Man of Pleasure's Pocket Book*, from which these extracts have been taken, served a twofold purpose. They were whores' directories, and they were pornography; as in most pornography the writing is either: (a) overblown, or (b) Rabelaisian. The nonsense of the lactiferous tubes type is of historical interest. Stylistically, it followed the lines of Cleland's

Fanny Hill, drubbed out *ad lib* for an avid half-educated market. The Rabelaisian style, however, had a good deal of verve :

. . . The nuns of this convent can chaunt a tidy stave, grind the piano – and that is not the only slum they can grind. They dance, and are card players; they play a pretty game at all-fours, and when they cut they are safe to turn up Jack. The abbess, who is a slashing piece, is good at cribbage, though she will let you peg her; she is safe to bilk your crib, and hole you in spite of your play . . .

The class of person who made use of the information in the handbooks and pocketbooks kept its attention to certain specified localities. It was buying a West End commodity at West End prices; it might penetrate to Chelsea and Kensington, but rarely south of the river or east of St Paul's. The aristocratic whoremongers treated this class with contempt – they did not need little books to tell them where to go for their fun. Class, in true Victorian style, had triumphed again.

The basic unit of the profession was the streetwalker. The girls who were featured in the handbooks and the pocketbooks were, by and large, homesters who waited for the knock on the door. One of them is specifically mentioned as being fond of dancing but never allows any one to escort her home from the dances. In the West End the streetwalker was almost indistinguishable from the lady, as throughout the century London women were noted for their lack of a colour sense (green combined with red was highly thought of), and a gaudy ensemble meant little. The more expensive streetwalkers worked to a system. In the winter when it was cold they would congregate in Burlington Arcade, that still exclusive thoroughfare with its own uniformed attendant, and when their coy signals were responded to, would glide into prearranged shops to sort out details.

One prostitute's system was this : She would get up at four o'clock in the afternoon, walk the streets for one or two hours, and take men home or not take men home whatever the luck was that particular day. She would then go dancing, taking a man home, if possible. If no man was forthcoming she would go to the Haymarket, the centre of the streetwalkers, and circulate from café to café, 'Sally's to the Carlton, from Barn's to Sam's'. The Haymarket was known as 'Hell Corner'. It had gin palaces and oyster shops, and during the high period it was full of 'half-tipsy, half-amorous sirens'. Charles Dickens's magazine *Household Words* gave a jolly picture of the Haymarket, with its 'sporting gents and painted cheeks and brandy-sparkling eyes', though Dr Acton saw it as being 'haunted by rouged and whitewashed creatures, with painted lips and eyebrows and false hair'.

The prostitute proved a useful focus of attention for the inhibited who wished to rail at something. One of these was Francis William Newman, younger brother of the John Henry Newman who split the Church of England from top to bottom when he defected to the Roman Catholic Church. The tone of Francis William Newman is one of sustained truculence with a running bass of angry whine, so different from the almost supernatural angelic tone of his brother. He railed against the upper classes and hoped that the infidels from the lower classes would come and drub some sense into them, he railed at young men who took to prostitutes, and railed at the prostitutes. Late in life – when he was eighty-four – he brought out *Remedies for the Great Social Evil*. Was it, he asked plaintively, 'just in a man to expect in a wife an antenuptial chastity, if he do not come chaste to her, should he not feel degraded by what he would regard as self-degradation in her?' Of course, part of the blame lay in 'School Classics', which 'perniciously inflame passions in boys and young men', a rather surprising view from a man who had been professor of Latin at University College, London, for seventeen years. In the shadow of his great brother, one must make allowances for Francis William Newman. It was suggested that he was a prude. He was indignant – 'with 8,000 harlots in London alone, what utter nonsense is such talk!' Alas, the situation was even worse than he supposed; no one, except the police in one of their frequent periods of self-deception and self-defence, put the figure as low as 8,000.

The degree of moral indignation felt can often be gauged by the word used for prostitute. It is strange that a self-proclaimed

Christian such as F. W. Newman (his best known book is
Phases of Faith, 1853) should resort to harlot while the warlike
Duke of Wellington should have been contented with the
compassionate 'Unfortunate', though the python grip of middle-
class morality often had an odd effect on semantics as the century progressed (it would have been difficult for Newman to
get away with harlot had it not been consecrated by the Bible –
it was more usual for a circumlocution to be adopted rather than
discarded).

Any stick was good enough to beat the prostitutes with.
Why did women become prostitutes? Dr Tait supplied any
number of reasons – licentiousness of disposition, irritability of
temper, pride and love of dress, dishonesty and love of property,
indolence, seduction, ill-assorted marriages, low wages, want of
employment, intemperance, poverty, defective education, bad
example of parents, and obscene publications.

One of the favourite methods was deception followed by
seduction. Many 'good' girls were induced to leave home by
offers of jobs as governesses and ladies' companions. The governess was a position girls of good breeding could hold without
loss of face – indeed, one of the few jobs in this category. An
advertisement for a governess would be responded to over-
whelmingly. Being a governess was second best to being married,
and as the proportion of single women to the total population
increased, so did the replies to carefully worded advertisements.
In 1851 there were 2,765,000 single women over 15; in 1861,
2,956,000; in 1871, 3,228,700. This was an increase over 20 years
of 16·8 per cent, much higher than population growth over the
period. In 1851 there were 25,000 governesses – an insignificant
total when one considers the numbers of girls anxious and able
to do such work.

Many men liked their prostitutes to be genteel; the *nostalgie
pour la boue* was not universal. More important, when mistresses were kept, it was often necessary for them to entertain
friends, run a house efficiently, and, in fact, act as a quandam
wife. The French writer Taine noted with surprise the large
number of wealthy men who kept mistresses in the outer
suburbs of London and in what we now call dormitory towns,

going to them Friday night and returning to their businesses (and their town houses) on Monday morning. It was evident that no one was suited for this role better than an ex-governess or failed governess – a girl educated and genteel, a girl who could cope with the empty weekdays, a girl who would not be tempted to turn to drink, a girl who would be grateful to her provider even if the provisions had not included marriage.

The governess was therefore an easy mark for speculators, especially when they were enticed to places like Cologne, only to find that the so-safe jobs promised them were illusory. Of course, it was suggested to them, there was a way out of the dilemma ...

Occasionally the enticement of governesses was brought to the notice of the British public:

> I was standing on a railway platform at – with a friend waiting for a train, when two ladies came into the station. I was acquainted with one of them, the younger, well. She told me she was going to London, having been fortunate enough to get a liberal engagement as governess in the family of the lady under whose charge she was then, and who had even taken the trouble to come into the country to see her and her friends, to ascertain that she was likely in all respects to suit. The train coming in sight, the fares were paid, the elder lady paying both. 'Well, I will say you country gentlemen are pretty independent of public opinion. You are not ashamed of your little transactions being known!'
>
> 'What do you mean?'
>
> 'Well, then, I can tell you, her friend is Madame — one of the most noted procuresses in London, and she has got hold of a new victim, if she is a victim, and no mistake.'

Thus a letter to *The Times* in 1855.

This girl was rescued from the fate worse than death, but asked the writer, 'How many are lost?' How many, indeed? The market for 'fresh meat' was more booming than the market for governesses. With this in mind, governesses who had not succeeded in getting placed were encouraged to emigrate – Miss Rye founded the 'Female Middle Class Emigration Society' in 1862. The governess class, as can be seen in the novels of Dickens and the loves of the Brontë sisters, was an underprivileged one (as early as 1841 the Governesses' Benevolent Institution had been formed to 'afford assistance privately and delicately to ladies in temporary distress').

These girls, often the daughters of clergymen and the professional classes, were handicapped by the rigid standards of morals imposed on them by their education. One act of sexual intercourse spelled, to them, ruin (this was even true of married women of the respectable middle class – one lapse and they would often plead for divorce to wash out the sin). This attitude was reinforced by the habit of best-selling novelists of making one act of intercourse spell baby (present-day opinion avers that the incidence is more like one every twenty-five times to one every fifty times, and even this may be an underestimate).

However many governesses were seduced, under whatever hardships they were suffering, there was never lacking a body of opinion to say that they should have known better, being girls of good education and background. For every governess who was 'betrayed', there were dozens of female domestic servants, dressmakers and seamstresses. In 1851 there were 905,165 domestic servants in Britain, 270,000 dressmakers, and 72,940 seamstresses, all at the mercy of employers and the sharks of the big cities. For many of the rising middle classes who would not deign to make use of a common prostitute, their servants, the nurserymaids, and skivvies earning a few pounds a year were fair game. Even if the servants protested, even if the employers forced themselves on them, redress was difficult to obtain. Regarding rape, one judge said that there was 'no charge so easy to make, none so difficult to disprove'. Or, when it came to the lowly, prove.

The sharks of the big cities were always on the lookout for a new batch of innocents (it must be remembered that probably eight per cent of *all women* in London were prostitutes). As agents they used small shopkeepers, lodging house keepers, laundresses and charwomen; as a front the agents organized 'Servants' Bazars' at which procuresses and bawds could sort out new talents. Always lurking were the 'spooneys' – the ponces – and the 'fancy men'. Where a pretty servant girl failed to rise to the lure of money, then a smartly dressed fancy man might pretend to fall in love with her, and so began a chain of events that was fairly predictable, especially if the girl came from the country where a very strenuous form of courting called 'bundling' made premarital intercourse the rule.

Between the prostitutes and the police there existed a curious love-hate relationship. At the start of Victoria's reign, the police force was a relatively new instrument; they still wore funny hats and were known as 'Peelers' or 'Bobbies', after Sir Robert Peel who had initiated the force in 1829 (the Metropolitan Police Act). Three thousand constables were recruited, and their jurisdiction extended over an area having a radius of twelve miles from Charing Cross. The River Thames was governed by entirely different laws – only one example of the inefficiency of the 1829 act, which was succeeded by a more useful act in 1839. In the meantime, in 1833, a dramatic clash had occurred between the police and the mob, and established for the poor a *modus vivendi* that lasted for many years.

The two principal police figures were Colonel Rowan and Sir Henry Maine; they were known as the Escalus and Angelo of Scotland Yard, and pressure was put on them to clean up prostitution, a task that was beyond them (and would have been well nigh beyond anybody). The prostitutes gained sympathy from the public, quick to cry out against persecution. 'God forbid that I should stand forth as the champion and defender of a disgraceful mode of living,' trumpeted one editorial – hypocritically, as it happened (the editorial was in the scabrous weekly the *Town*, which doted on the doings of prostitutes) 'but low, wretched, degraded and miserable as the prostitute may be, there is a point at which the law may become oppressive to her'.

The law interferred as little as possible consistent with discretion, especially as it was difficult to pick out prostitutes except when they were soliciting. 'There are hundreds of girls in London,' wrote an anonymous J. B. in 1851, 'who can blush and look as modest as a maid, who are nothing but sly whores.' In the golden mile of whoredom, in the streets around the Haymarket, nothing changed. There were advertisements,

'Beds to Let', and there were subtle differences of wording significant only to those who were in the know – 'For private apartments, ladies' was more inviting than 'private apartments for ladies'. Brothels in the area went under massage rooms, baths, foreign language schools and rheumatism cures, and the more enterprising whores advertised their wares on the sandwich boards of men who promenaded up and down Regent Street and Bond Street.

In 1837, the year of the accession of Queen Victoria, the police arrested 3,103 prostitutes, and carefully analysed their findings. Of these women 1,773 could not read or write, 1,237 could read and write 'imperfectly', 89 could read and write well, and four had had a good education. These last two categories totalling 93 must have been singularly maladroit not to wriggle through the clumsy meshes of the inefficient Metropolitan Police of that period. The police force was hardly more efficient than the Society for the Suppression of Vice in London (though it got 10,493 obscene prints repressed in three years) or the various do-good organizations – like Miss Burdett-Coutts's – pecking at a huge cake. Throughout the whole of Victoria's reign, pressures were applied upon the Metropolitan Police to do something about the Great Social Evil ('the fouled hindquarters of English life' the Frenchman Taine had called it). Occasionally these pressures were heavier, and then there would be a Royal Commission to investigate the London police; they would come up with predictable conclusions – 'the main difficulty in enforcing the law (as to solicitation) is caused by the over-sensitivity and impatience of the public whenever there seems ground, however slight, for alleging that there has been a mistake in arresting a woman on a charge of solicitation'. To the vast majority of the British public, what went on between man and maid was something for their own consciences, whether it was the 'chaste courtship and passionless marriage' of Victorian legend, whether it was the rouged girl who came up to a man at the Casino in Great Windmill Street ('May I have the pleasure of paying my addresses to you?'), or whether it was the notorious park woman, right at the bottom of the pile, whose 'disgusting practices' were only 'gratifying to men of morbid and diseased imagination'. You paid your money and you took your choice. For some, there was no question where their inclinations lay:

> Ye jolly mots of London,
>   What strolls about at ease,
> How many a chummy's undone
>   By hearts and eyes like these;
> Your wriggling twists and caracoles,
>   And ribbons bright and gay,
> We melts in the streets,
>   And you bears our hearts away!

The Demi-Semi-Monde

The legislature of Great Britain has always found it difficult to deal with the question of prostitution, and many people looked across the English Channel during the nineteenth century to see how the French dealt with the situation. To a considerable number, it appeared that the French were handling the problem more sensibly than the British, by allowing certain brothels to exist (the *maisons de tolérance* for residents, and the *maisons de passe* for transients), by having prostitutes examined at either weekly or fortnightly intervals, and by the registration of prostitutes, voluntary by those not arrested, compulsory by the arrested. Hospital treatment was also arranged for diseased prostitutes. The disadvantage of this efficient if ungallant arrangement was that its operation was entirely in the hands of the police. Infringements of these arrangements could be punished by a year in jail – again, at the sole instigation of the police. In 1876 two women of Reims refused to be examined, the case came to court, the judge found in their favour, and he was promptly dismissed from his post.

The attitude of the British legislature was not so clear-cut. Although prostitution was looked upon with more severity than was the case in France, the grounds of prostitution were simply that it was no more than a public nuisance. An act of 1755

(25 Geo. II) was passed 'for encouraging prosecutions against persons keeping bawdy-houses'. Two ratepayers could go with a constable before a justice and obtain an order to proceed against the offenders. Another act in 1818 enabled parish officials to deal with any vipers in their bosoms, but the crowning glory was the Vagrancy Act, passed thirteen years before Victoria came to the throne, which enabled the police to proceed against 'common prostitutes for behaving in a riotous or indecent manner'. In 1839 this Vagrancy Act was given more teeth, though it applied to London only; this would prevent 'loitering for the purpose of prostitution or solicitation, to the annoyance of passengers or inhabitants'. The year 1847 brought an act making it an offence for publicans to allow 'common prostitutes to assemble and continue' in licensed premises, and although this act was confirmed with the Licensing Act of 1872, its practical use, like the previous acts, was virtually nil. Unless a prostitute was kicking up merry hell, she stood little more chance of being arrested than a respectable woman – even, on occasions, when the prostitute was known to have the backing of a gang of roughs, a pimp, a brothel keeper, or a 'gentleman friend', less.

Being a prostitute in the West End in the early and mid-years of Victoria's reign was a lucrative and secure business. There was not much chance of being chivvied by the police, and the only break in the routine promenade/-dance/-bed, promenade/-dance/-bed, would be the occasional rash intrusion of clergymen or do-gooders. Organizations that contained heavy guns were too often inclined to include prostitution under an umbrella of sin that included profanation of Sundays, blasphemous publications, obscene literature and fortune tellers. Average earnings among the higher classes of streetwalkers were between £20 and £30 a week, but the legendary reckless improvidence of the whoring class appears to have had some basis in fact, and as much as £10 to £12 of this went in the casinos and the gin palaces. A drawing room floor of a house in favoured Queen Street would cost between £3 and £4 a week.

The décor of the best establishments was not stinted. One set of rooms to which the diligent Henry Mayhew penetrated had Coburg chairs, sofas, glass chandeliers, and handsome green curtains, though he does not seem to have come across the more lavish set-ups, with the usual bric-a-brac of libertinism – the mirrors above the bed, the obscene prints and paintings (reversible), and the bawdy books on the table. Sometimes one has the impression that Mayhew is shrinking in the anteroom, fearful of being tempted; on the other hand, many prostitutes took him for a 'dodger' (i.e., parson), an easily understandable error, for in the primitive age of sociology, who would want to visit a whore to *talk* to if he were not a cleric? The whores were also pleased because Mayhew did not try to reform them, but considered him 'an inquisitive old party' (Mayhew was in his forties).

It took a considerable effort of will for outsiders to realize that prostitutes *liked* their trade, that they did not feel sordid or degraded, that the joy with which they manipulated their limbs was not simulated, and that their longings for sexual intercourse were often insatiable. Mentally, these were inconvenient irritations of the nervous system, and physically there had been on the market a number of articles – excluding men – for a considerable time which would act as a calamine lotion for these carnal itchings, articles such as *godemiches, consolateurs, bijoux indiscrets*, dildoes (or dildols). These were either imitation penises or spheres to be entrapped in the vulva. The ladies of Japan were very adept in the manipulation of two spheres.[15]

It was very tempting to wish an attitude on to the prostitutes, to see them as sinners wanting nothing better than repentance. The journalist William Stead put the basic attitude in a nutshell: 'Never do I walk the streets, but I see wretched ruins of humanity, women trampled and crushed into devils by society, and my heart has been racked with anguish for these victims of our juggernaut.' This fragile highly strung young man with Congregational tendencies had looked around Darlington where he was working, and saw all this. The prostitute as a subspecies of Homo sapiens was thus pigeonholed, and that was that, a view that was confirmed by the occasional dramatic self-disgust of a prostitute (or a journalist posing as one). Those of the Stead ilk would nod with satisfaction at these 'Verses for my tombstone if ever I should have one'.

Daily debased to stifle my disgust
Of forced enjoyment in affected lust.
Covered with guilt, infection, debt and want,
My home a brothel and the streets my haunt,
For seven long years of infamy I've pined,
And fondled, loathed, and preyed upon mankind,
Till, the full course of sin and vice gone through,
My shattered fabric failed at twenty-two.

There was a brisk traffic between London and Paris. During the Franco-Prussian War of 1870–71, many French *demi-mondaines* came to London. A couple of them, demure and charming, were reported to have been introduced to Dean Liddell (father of the 'Alice' of Lewis Carroll's *Alice in Wonderland*) at Oxford as respectable foreign ladies. A *demi-mondaine* of the previous generation, Laura Honey, had been one of the many to go to Paris to pick up experience and the higher wages of sin that prevailed in Paris. She was not impressed by the French gallants; she assured 'her less pretending countrymen that the tripe-coloured mousquetaires who infest this capital are not capable of making anything about her *heave* – except her *stomach*'. So much for *l'amour*.

The literary men of the time were not immune to temptation, though attitudes toward temptation took strange forms. Lewis Carroll, that strange unique creature for ever doomed to seek his love object in little girls, went to the theatre to see Dion Boucicault's play *Faust and Marguerite*. In one of the scenes, Marguerite is at prayer, then 'tosses about like a fascinated animal trying to escape from a snake. ... This scene, with her low despairing shrieks, was as dreadful as anything I have seen on the stage. ... I don't think this ultra-realising of things to us (at present) abstractions, can tend to good: it must lean far more to infidelity.' [16]

Similarly, the Reverend F. W. Robertson was as remote from the temptations of the ladies in the Haymarket. Women were 'beings that floated before me, robed in vestures more delicate than mine ... beings of another order. The thought of one of them becoming mine was not rapture but pain.' [17]

At the extreme from this was the private life of Samuel Butler. Samuel Butler is unfortunate in that he left us carefully documented evidence that he was rather a nasty piece of work, though his account of his day is pathetic, and echoed by thousands of bachelor writers before and since:

I get up about seven and immediately and in my nightshirt go into my sitting-room and light my fire. I put the kettle on and set some dry sticks under it so that it soon heats enough to give me warm water for my bath. At eight I make my tea and cook my breakfast — eggs and bacon, sausages, a chop, a bit of fish or whatever it may be, and by eight-thirty I have done my breakfast and cleaned it away...

His love life was organized with the same scrupulous attention to detail. In his early years, he was inclined to adopt the persona of a man about town ('I have a little needle-woman, a good little thing. I have given her a sewing-machine'), but later he picked up a Madame Dumas in Islington. Madame Dumas was not a regular streetwalker but for many years Butler went to her every Wednesday at 2.30 p.m., took his pleasure, paid her £1, and returned to his quarters at five o'clock. His servant recorded that he walked both ways. Madame Dumas was a large dark woman, and Butler was good enough to share her with his friend and biographer, Festing Jones, who, if anything, must have been more of a trial to Madame Dumas than Butler. Festing Jones, who paid his visit and his pound on a Tuesday, was 'always crying', always obsessed with his ailments, which included rheumatism, nervous exhaustion, eczema, impetigo, carbuncles and piles, while he shared with Butler diarrhoea and boils. Never, one thinks, did a prostitute earn £2 so laboriously.

Not many literary people recorded their lives so prosaically, and few are so unsympathetic as Samuel Butler, though one must forgive him much for his semi-autobiographical novel *The Way of All Flesh*. Possibly Gissing comes close in sheer unlikeability. ('Gissing at parties was an unforgettable spectacle of misery. He would sit in a corner of the room, crouched together like a wet bird, silent and strangely watchful' [18]). Gissing, like Butler, gave a girl he lived with a sewing machine, a talisman

that must have replaced horses and ostrich feathers as the right
thing to give to one's mistress.

The more astute writers went to Paris for their pleasures, and
if they had official biographers so watchful as John Forster
(as Dickens had) then they could kick over the traces without
anyone caring. Even the girls at the *Moulin Rouge* could address
the Prince of Wales "Ullo Wales!' with impunity (and drinks
all round). The painter-poet Dante Gabriel Rossetti also visited
Paris, avid and eager. At Valentino's he saw the cancan, later
to become an epitome of nineties-naughtiness; in 1849, Rossetti
was less impressed:

> For me,
> I confess, William, and avow to thee,
> (Soft in thine ear) that such sweet female whims
> As nasty backsides out and wriggled limbs
> Nor bitch-squeaks, nor the smell of heated quims
> Are not a passion of mine naturally.[19]

The entertainments of Paris were often emulated in London.
The Archery Rooms, situated in what was then called the New
Road (now Euston Road and Warren Street), were a cross between the strip-tease of the *tableaux vivants* and a brothel. As
for the archery, 'not that there is not a deal of archery going on,
too, but the targets being animated, and fixed upon locomotive
crutches, why they may naturally be allowed to put in a negative as to being shot at indiscriminately; and there can be little
doubt that steel-pointed shafts would be not altogether so congenial as those of softer construction and tipped with gold'. There
were 'servant girls' dressed '*à la Greque*', girls who wore 'fig
leaves in a state of expansion', and there were 'opera dancers
whose utmost art is to *double shuffle*'.

It did not quite suit the taste of the English *bon viveur*; the
motto of the early and mid Victorian whore seeker might well
have been 'Go to it'. The impression one gets from the pocketbooks and handbooks is of an endless stream of young bucks,
ever in heat, anxious to placate their desires in double-quick
time, without much aptitude for the finer subtleties of sex, and
subsequently only interested in '(1) On the best method of treat-

ing the slight accidents to which men about town are peculiarly liable (2) on the mode of preventing and curing intoxication (3) on the prevention of infection from *impure* sexual intercourse.' Does one detect that note of shame and disquiet later to expand into a giant organ swell?

As the century progressed, the centres of what was elegantly described as oscillatory prostitution shifted, and the language of the pick-up changed. At the Casino a favourite form of advance had been (from the woman), 'May I have the pleasure of paying my addresses to you?' Later a preferable form was 'Are you good-natured, dear?' The changes in the West End were accelerated by greatly increased property values, and houses, gin palaces and cafés were swept aside and replaced by stores and other commercial enterprises. The ascendancy of the Strand as a shopping centre was being challenged by Regent Street and Oxford Street.

Another casualty was the cigar divan.

Until lately, gentlemen visiting London hardly knew how to amuse themselves in the early part of the evening, and were under the necessity of sitting over their wine till the opening of the theatres. This is now obviated by the introduction of a number of Cigar Divans, or Saloons, elegantly fitted up and furnished with Magazines, Reviews, Newspapers and Periodicals of every class. In addition to these, there are chess, draughts, and backgammon boards; also, musical clocks which play a variety of popular tunes. The charge for entrance is *one shilling*, which includes an excellent cigar and a noble cup of coffee. Here you may sit and read, on a dull afternoon, for hours together, secure from noise and interruption. The principal Divans are in the Strand, Bedford Street, King Street, Pall-Mall and Regent Street. Some of these charge only sixpence for entrance.

The divan was not, as this early notice (*Kidd's London Directory and Amusement Guide*, 1831) might lead one to believe, an exclusively male preserve.

The notion of prostitution as a crime is, in the abstract, rather an odd one. It is possible that persistent solicitation could be a 'public nuisance', and that in its extreme form it could be something of a trial to the over-sensitive. In Norton Street,

Marylebone, prostitutes would appear naked at the windows, would lounge on the window sills, run into the street with one undergarment on, and, when the occasions were auspicious, drag men in. This could be defined as a public nuisance. In its usual form, however, the approaches of the Victorian prostitute were no more irritating than the inconveniences that we of the twentieth century take for granted – the Irish labourer cadging sixpence on Waterloo Bridge for a cup of tea, the methylated spirits drinker shunting beneath the railway arches, pneumatic drills and simple traffic noises, or the crunch of noble Italianate edifices demolished to make way for office blocks.

The respectable classes of the nineteenth century were cushioned against everything that threatened to intrude on their rose-coloured world. One member of a celebrated club had a hobby that consisted of looking out of the window of his club watching the rabble outside getting wet in the rain; Princess Beatrice was shocked when she found that shops in Windsor were openly selling stays. The flaunting of their trade by street-walkers was a rash intrusion into the respectables' crassly sensitive world. It was too strong a reminder of the other side of life. These were the lower orders daring to make their presence known without using the convenient no man's land of the servant class; a cat could, indeed, not only look at a king, but might even tempt him to do something he might afterwards regret. A Frenchman wrote to his friend Hippolyte Taine: 'Shall I tell you what struck me most in this country? The torpor of their nervous system.' If this torpor were allowed to be disturbed, what might not result?

The streetwalker was a social offender, an affront, a disturbing influence, upsetting the properties of decent life. To women, the streetwalker was an ever-present threat to the sanctity of married life (one could never tell with those poor wretches, husbands). The pursuit of the fallen was carried out with far more assiduity by women than men. Gladstone was in a minority, but occasionally they had the temerity to tackle the root causes.

The attitude of the tolerant man of the world to prostitution was live and let live; the women were, after all, only providing a service which one was at liberty to refuse. In certain circumstances they provided a splash of colour, were as essential to the overall effect as a tapestry or wallpaper. Such was the case at the Empire, Leicester Square.

No London square has undergone as many vicissitudes as Leicester Square from the days when it was the haunt of royalty and painters, through its period as a duelling ground (there was a duel to the death in 1699) to its chequered nineteenth-century state when it 'gradually presented that aspect of ruin which is said to have given rise to Ledru Rollin's work on the decadence of England'.[20] It was a place of panoramas, freaks, waxworks, taverns and acrobatic feats; it also possessed an unfortunate statue of George I that was a focus for practical jokers, who painted it, decorated it and abused it in many unedifying ways.

It also had a music hall, the El Dorado, which was burned down in 1865. The Prince of Wales, who was something of a pyromaniac, was always eager to go to fires, and he was on the scene in the guise of a fire officer, riding on the fire engine. In 1884 the Empire Theatre of Varieties was erected on the site, an ornate building in a mixture of Greek and Roman styles, with a long veranda at the front topped by flowering shrubs and supported by spindly shafts. At the back of the dress circle was a spacious promenade, and this rapidly became the haunt of whores plying their trade; this became one of the characteristics of the place, and few complained (after all, was not amusement the aim of a Theatre of Varieties?).

However, some did complain, and in 1894 Mrs Ormiston Chant opposed the renewal of the licence 'on the ground that the place at night is the habitual resort of prostitutes in pursuit of their traffic'. Fashionable life was aghast at this interference in their pleasures. A retired police inspector employed to patrol the promenade reported, predictably, that he had never come across any solicitation or drunkenness, evidence vitiated by Mrs Chant, who, with that curious ambivalence that do-gooders were subject to, had gone to the promenade herself on three occasions, once dressed quietly, twice dressed gaily ('but not fast') and had been accosted, much to her satisfaction.

It was evident that Mrs Chant had proved her point. The

question was what to do about it. The first thing was to make the subject a theme for a popular song:

> Prudes on the prowl! Boys, down with their cant!
> Let us march onwards with this for our chant –
> Let them be puritans! We will be free!

Then it was an appropriate occasion to launch another attack on the trade of prostitution; prostitutes were the 'transient darlings of bad men who minister unchecked to the demands of lust'. However, these were the permissive nineties, and Mrs Chant and her colleagues found that a powerful body of opinion was against them. The freemasonry of the theatrical profession, The Grand Order of Water Rats, was solidly against her, and to a theatrical newspaper Mrs Chant and her company were 'lachrymose nobodies and childless spinsters ... merely moody fanatics whose greasy minds see evil in everything'. The clergyman who was later to go bail for Oscar Wilde prayed for 'God [to] give us a prompt deliverance' from interferers, had a broker who had a place on the council concerned with the renewal of licences and who was incautious enough to support Mrs Chant was thrown into the street by his fellows of the Stock Exchange. Intolerance, then as now, worked both ways. W. G. Grace, the great bearded cricketer of legend, formed a 'Sporting League' to keep the 'wrong 'uns' out of the council, the wrong 'uns being those who voted against the Empire. The management of the Empire was in the hands of George Edwardes (proprietor of Edwardes Menu Company), who was torn between his duty to his patrons, most of whom wished the whores the best of luck, and his fear of closure; and in the tradition of British compromise had erected a screen of lath and plaster between the dress circle and the promenade. One evening a young man sardonically poked his walking stick through this partition, and many of his companions followed suit (these included the young Winston Churchill). In a bacchanalian rapture they tore down the screens and carried the wreckage in triumph through Piccadilly; virtue had been defeated yet again.

Facts and Figures

In Victorian England, prostitution through desperation was more common by far than prostitution through choice. In the industrial north of England there was often a stark choice – starvation or prostitution, and the meagre wages of the man were commonly supplemented by a few shillings earned by his wife on the street corner, perquisites the gaining of which held no moral stigma. As Dr Peter Gaskell, a Manchester surgeon, wrote in *The Manufacturing Population of England* (1833), 'The chastity of marriage is but little known or exercised; husband and wife sin equally, and an habitual indifference to sexual rights is generated, which adds one other stem to assist in the destruction of domestic habits.' In the midlands, in the coal-yielding iron-making purgatory known as the Black Country, men swapped wives as they wended their boozy way back from the public houses. In Wales, the Reverend J. W. Trevor, chaplain to the Bishop of Bangor, was disgusted by working class sex : 'Fornication was not regarded as vice, scarcely as a frailty, by the common people in Wales.'

Throughout the rural areas of Great Britain, a form of courtship known as bundling held sway. Lord Chelmsford – Solicitor General 1844, Attorney General 1845, Lord Chancellor 1858 and 1866 – was aghast at these curious customs ('It is a very extraordinary state of society'). Parents would not allow daytime visits by young men coming a-courting, but at night it was all right, and in barns and outhouses there would literally be rolling in the hay, with the full approval of parents who in the daytime exercised an almost Calvinist hold upon their offspring Bundling, in its oddest form, might be defined as courting in bed. Between the pair there would be a bolster or some other impediment. How efficient these barriers were can be judged by the comment of Dr John Mitchell Strachan, who had thirty-eight years of experience in Stirlingshire, Scotland, that nine tenths of girls at marriage had children by the bridegroom or were pregnant through courting in bed. Courting in bed, 'at late hours, leads to familiarities, and that leads to fornication'. It would have been a more extraordinary state of society had it been otherwise.[21]

These agricultural pursuits made Royal Commissions scratch their heads. The Royal Commission on the Laws of Marriage of 1868 decided that 'to mere carnal intercourse, if preceded by a *written* promise of future marriage, or by a promise, afterwards confessed on oath, the effect of marriage is practically given'. It is hardly to be wondered at that Lord Chelmsford and his legal colleagues found the boundaries of marriage difficult to locate. Bundling, in effect, was sanctioned premarital sex – sanctioned not only by parents, but by rural society (and half of society *was* rural); and the artificial barrier – (the bolster between the couple or even a specially prepared board) – was easily surmountable. The only people who were left out of this amiable and enviable pattern of behaviour were the servants at the farms; farmers' daughters might be permitted to indulge in bundling, but not the servants, who would be certain to be promiscuous, and who thus had to be protected from their own wanton impulses by having their bedroom windows barred.

It is against this permissive background that Victorian prostitution must be seen. The workman hiring out his wife to a mate for a pint of beer was no more a fancy man than the Eskimo for whom hospitality to a guest includes the guest's use of his wife. In Nottingham, a working man sold his wife in the market for a shilling, and this included the length of rope around her neck. Nothing very extraordinary was seen in this transaction. The sanctities of marriage for the vast mass of the labouring population were dubious entities.

One is not surprised that the statistics for prostitution during the midnineteenth century are so contradictory. Where did promiscuity end and prostitution begin, and in the slums of the East End and in the industrial towns did promiscuity end at all? The police statisticians made efforts to divide prostitutes into 'regulars' and 'irregulars' (as well as the subdivisions 'could not read or write', 'could read or write imperfectly', 'could read and write well', 'good education'). In the West End the irregulars were scorned – the nursemaids in the parks who attracted the soldiers were 'dollymops' – but in the East End the categories tended to merge, and so baffling were the figures to an age without computers that many authorities tended to cook the books, or make wild guesses, or botch what reliable figures they had. Twenty-five per cent of all prostitutes were said to 'amalgamate' each year with the 'respectable' population. But how could such assumptions be arrived at? Dr Acton, one of the less unreliable of the early Victorian specialists, stated that one in thirteeen or fourteen of unmarried women of full age was immoral, but this statement contradicts other data.

It was naïvely hoped that the census would help, but 'a very singular fact in connection with the census is that there is not a single individual returned as a prostitute'.[22] In an age fanatically attached to the divine pursuit of facts, the incredible fatuity of some of the statistics relating to prostitution led to despair, and many experts came to rely only on data collected in those hospitals that specialized in venereal disease. The Lock Hospital, Edinburgh, from the firm evidence of their admission registers, stated that nine tenths of prostitutes disappeared by the age of thirty.

During one of the forays into the mysterious world of statistics where the principal technical tool would appear to be the abacus, figures were produced in one report that were so distressingly self-contradictory that investigations were made into the accuracy of the report. This was an almost unique circumstance, as errors of arithmetic, if they were discovered, were gilded over or 'allowed for'. There is a network of compliance that enables clerical errors to be smilingly dismissed, and it is still considered bad form to be good at simple arithmetic. The poor unfortunate clerk was put to the question; 'Unfortunately the clerk who made [the report] out, a very inefficient one, omitted in some cases diseases not contracted in the district; in some cases he put it in, and in others he left it out.' (The report dealt with incidence of venereal disease at army and navy establishments 1868–9).

Sometimes, figures relating to prostitution and venereal disease are used with a near-surrealist logic, so much so that one is inclined to wonder whether the mathematically inclined don, the Reverend Charles Dodgson ('Lewis Carroll') had this in mind when he wrote his *Euclid and His Modern Rivals* (1879) or his *Curiosa Mathematica* (1888–93). Suppose, one writer speculated, there are 50,000 prostitutes in London, and one in a hundred has venereal disease. This means that there are 500 prostitutes in London with VD; let us suppose, further, that of these 500, one in five is in hospital undergoing treatment; this leaves 400 prostitutes on the rampage. The writer then went into mystical doodling, in which (a) affects (b) and (b) affects (c) and (c) affects (d), and so on until 'it will follow that there will be 4,000 men infected every night, and consequently 1,460,000 in the year'. Every night 400 women would be infected by these men, leading to 182,500 prostitutes having VD, a grand total of 1,625,500 having venereal disease! The rapture of the writer (in the *Medico-Chirurgical Review*) unfortunately affected his mathematics (1,460,000 + 182,500 = 1,642,500).

This anonymous medical man, no doubt proud of his inability to add two figures together, was only one of the many who went into hysteria at the very mention of venereal disease. The suffragette leader, Mrs Pankhurst, believed that 75 per cent of all men had venereal disease, but as many of the outer fringe of the emancipation movement believed also that when women got the vote they would cease to menstruate, one must not pay too much attention to such views.

In 1868 Sir John Simon entered into the lists as a speculator upon prostitution and venereal disease. His view was that there were 18,000 prostitutes in London, of whom one third were diseased; his figures were based on those of a Mr Curgenven. He estimated that there were 3,000 prostitutes in hospital (i.e. conveniently half the diseased), and this was costing the ratepayer £100,000 per annum. Of the sick poor under the poor law, 7 per cent had venereal disease, and one fifth of the sick children had inherited syphilis. In ten years 118,590 children had passed through the children's hospital in Great Ormond Street, London, and 1½ per cent of *these* had VD.

Sir John Simon's *Privy Council Report* of 1868 was only one of many reports to be issued about this time. The early years of

Victorian England are fairly well documented regarding prostitution data, but gradually a blanket of silence begins to fall over 'the Great Social Evil'. The passing of the Contagious Diseases Acts (1864–9) broke this silence in a dramatic way.

These acts were an attempt to deal with prostitution in so far as it affected the army and the navy. The venereal disease rate in the army was an estimated one fifth, in the navy it was one seventh, and in the merchant navy it was two sevenths. It was necessary to do something about this, and for the first time in Britain since the first Elizabeth – and the controlled brothels or 'stews' on the south bank of the Thames – a *logical* attempt was made to exert some kind of control on prostitution. The acts catered for only a minute portion of the population – much less than 1 per cent. In 1869 the total strength of the army and navy of Great Britain was 269,000; much of the army was perpetually involved overseas.

The furore aroused by the Contagious Diseases Acts [23] was incredibly ferocious, and philanthropic bodies that had been mostly concerned with reclaiming the fallen of London diverted their attentions to the repeal of the acts. In between his manifold duties Gladstone had a word to say about the acts, refreshingly against the current: 'Personally I would rather extend than restrict the operation of these Acts, but I admit that there is considerable difficulty in defending a system which can only be partially applied as these Acts have been.'

As in France, the enforcement of the acts left much power in the hands of the police, especially the somewhat 1984-ish Morals Police, which acquired a fascist-like reputation as badgerers of innocent women, subjecting them to humiliating medical examinations and informing on them to employers. There was a certain climate of hunting the whore, and this was taken up with glee by many self-righteous clergymen. The basic idea behind the acts was registration and examination; the basic idea of the repealers was that: (a) it infringed on the rights of free subjects; (b) it was humiliating; (c) it hardened the prostitutes, making their reclamation more difficult; and finally (d) it did not work.

Because the numbers were fairly small, it formed a microcosm of national prostitution, though the prostitutes who frequented the naval and military stations were the rough and tough professionals, and the incidence of venereal disease among them was considerably higher than elsewhere. The repealers produced a *Critical Summary of the Evidence before the Royal Commission upon the Contagious Diseases Acts 1866–1869, prepared* with rare skill by Douglas Kingsford of the Middle Temple.

It was soon discovered by Mr Kingsford and his band of workers that prostitutes had minds of their own; they had 'a horror of going into the union (i.e., the workhouse)', and they had an independence that was uncontrollable, whether they had syphilis or not. At the ports, when a ship came in, hospitalized prostitutes would leave whether they were cured or not. It was desirable, everyone agreed, for diseased prostitutes to have treatment; however, there were insufficient beds to go round. Mr Lane, of London lock hospital (a hospital devoted to the treatment of venereal disease), said that he had 'about thirty beds for females on the voluntary side' and that they had always been filled, and twice that many could be filled, so that he could only admit the 'most malignant and complicated cases'. In the London hospitals, between 23 and 25 per cent of patients discharged themselves without being fully cured.

It was also a fallacy to believe that women who had venereal disease were prostitutes or, indeed, in any way immoral – 30 per cent of the women in London who had VD were *not* prostitutes. In St Bartholomew's Hospital, London, in 1869, of 373 women who were admitted to the venereal ward, 61 discharged themselves. In Devonport, one of the ports frequented by navy men, a hospital had been built at a cost of £15,000 on a site given by the War Office, and so intent were the authorities on the purpose of this hospital that 'honest women' were refused aid.

The manageable proportions of the problem are revealed by the Army and Navy Estimates of 1870–71, in which £40,000 were set aside for 2,700 registered prostitutes in 18 military and naval stations. The police, somewhat cynical at the foolhardy intrusion of the military and naval authorities into their preserves, produced on occasions some weird statistics. The Portsmouth–Devonport complex came up with dramatic returns. At Portsmouth, a Captain Harris produced official figures that seemed to indicate a phenomenal reduction in the VD rate since the instigation of the acts – from 76·24 per cent in 1866 to 8·19 per cent. Here was proof positive that the acts, far from being the resounding flop the repealers claimed, had actually produced miraculous results. Or was it so?

Alas, no. The 1866 figures relate that of 462 prostitutes examined, 326 were found to have VD – agreed, a proportion of 76·24 per cent. But of these 462 prostitutes, *all were believed to be diseased*! That was the reason for their examination. In 1870, 11,633 prostitutes were examined, and 730 were found to have VD, and agreed 8·19 per cent. But these 11,633 prostitutes were *all* the prostitutes, a gigantic round-up, and the comparisons mean, in fact, absolutely nothing. Figures can be made to prove anything, and Captain Harris certainly succeeded in pulling the wool over the eyes of visiting Surgeon Parsons, who reported uncategorically that there were fewer cases in 1870 than in 1866. In Portsmouth–Devonport it is difficult not to believe that the statistics were unmercifully rigged; the 11,633 prostitutes were spread out over a year, in fortnightly examinations (the average intake runs out at 447 a time). Inspector Anniss, of Devonport, was sceptical of the whole project; since the acts, he declared, prostitutes were 'living in rather easy circumstances'. There might be some excuse for his somewhat offhand attitude, as Portsmouth–Devonport was one of the largest of the naval establishments, with 18,000 seamen.

The acts, effective or not by and large, and productive as they were of masses of unreliable data, did have beneficial side effects. The inspection of sailors and soldiers which had been discontinued despairingly in 1859 was recommended to 'give fair play to the Acts', and sanitary arrangements were given a salutary examination. Washing the penis after intercourse might not do much good against the more virulent micro-organisms being circulated around naval and military stations, but at least there might be more incentive to do this were the washroom facilities other than 'an old horse trough ... an iron barrack coal box' customarily used for the ablutions.

When the prostitutes had been taken from their promenading and from their beds they may well have benefited from the advice given to them. The surgeon at the huge camp at Aldershot had the 'custom of instructing women to keep themselves clean, to use injections and lotions, and to do all they can towards keeping themselves and the soldiers free from disease'. He handed out free syringes and lotions. The 'Queen's women', as they were called, had never had it so good.

Douglas Kingsford in his *Critical Summary* focused much of his attention on the Portsmouth–Devonport connurbation, and found a convenient chopping block in Inspector Anniss, who might well have been set up as a kind of stooge, a lay figure to prove that the police were a bad lot who would manipulate evidence to suit their book. In Castle Street, Devonport, Inspector Anniss declared, before the act nearly every house was a brothel. In 1865, he stated, there were 356 brothels in Devonport. That was before the acts. In 1870, there were 121. Unfortunately for the inspector, there were rival figures (40 brothels in 1865, 39 in 1870). Asked how he got his figures, Anniss was pressed to admit that certain of these houses were 'suspected by him', others were 'registered', while the rest, he confessed quite frankly, were 'guess work'.

Not only, it was suggested, did Inspector Anniss manipulate facts. He was also apparently incapable of carrying out the simple operation of having prostitutes registered. Mr Williams of the Rescue Society, 'whose experience and means of information have been exceptionally great', was brought into the fray, and he reported that of forty-eight prostitutes reclaimed by one lady in Portsmouth only five were registered prostitutes. One hesitates to doubt the word of Mr Williams of the Rescue Society, but like Inspector Anniss he belonged to a committed group. The acts were a menace to the ceaseless do-goodery of the lady in Portsmouth and others of her kind. Why shouldn't a little white lie help the cause?

Working-Class Prostitution

'I have seen the lowest quarters of Marseilles, Antwerp and Paris: they come nowhere near this. Squat houses, wretched streets of brick under red roofs crossing each other in all directions and leading dismally down to the river. Beggars, thieves and prostitutes, especially the latter, swarm in Shadwell Street ...'

So wrote the French visitor to England, Hippolyte Taine, in 1872. He went on to note the grating music from gin cellars, the view of unmade beds through uncurtained windows, women fighting, and 'their most horrible attribute ... the voice – thin, shrill, cracked, like that of a sick owl'. He was almost as shocked as when, on Derby Day at Ascot, he saw well-dressed gentlemen urinating against the wheels of carriages while ladies idly watched. Although Taine was not immune to a certain self-satisfaction, there is no question that when he visited dockland his objectivity was not at fault. It was a frightful place. Even today there are vestiges of this squalor and putrescence. Visitors to the Tower of London who take the riverside promenade, past the cannons, past the impressive ramparts of Tower Bridge, may happen to pass out of the Tower grounds into a narrow street, overshadowed by the huge cliffs of nineteenth-century warehouses, unchanged for nearly a century. This is St Katherine's Way, dating from the late 1820s, and it leads directly into a genuine period slum, Wapping High Street. The maze of mean streets that lead off will do nothing to reassure the visitor anxious to get back to civilization; there are streets and alleys that might well be roped off as specimens of Victorian slumdom.

If the Haymarket was the centre of West End vice, so did dockland vice circulate around a few choice streets – Frederick Street, Brunswick Street, Ratcliffe Highway, Shadwell High Street. It was here that the 'leggers' motts', the sailors' women, plied their trade – 'Poor Jack is thought fair game by most of the prowlers in Ratcliffe Highway' wrote a journalist in *Chambers's*

Journal sympathetically. The 'leggers' motts' catered for the dregs of five oceans, some of them making arrangements with the men, remaining with them for their time on land, taking care of their money. Others were more spry, wheedling from the seamen their money and leaving them broke and happily drunk. At any one time there were many tens of thousands of sailors on the loose in the dock area; at any one time there were several thousand ships in the docks, most of which were overburdened and out of date (West India Dock dates from 1802, London Dock from 1805). To the not-too-close observer it was a romantic region, with its forests of masts (in 1853 the tonnage of steamers was only 250,000).

However, even the most courageous and optimistic of reformers tended to give the dock area a wide berth, though Henry Mayhew ventured into it in the late fifties. In High Street, Shadwell, he found a public house called 'The White Swan', known colloquially as 'Paddy's Goose', and was amused by the fact that during the Crimean War the landlord had recruited sailors by having a small steamer pottering up and down the Thames, flags flying, streamers fluttering in the breeze, martial music playing (the landlord also ran a chain of thirty brothels). Mayhew had become used to low life, but, like Taine, the streets around the docks nonplussed even him. A house in Bluegate Fields he pronounced 'really low'. The woman who occupied it paid five shillings a week rent, charging prostitutes four shillings a week for their room. On the day of his visit, Mayhew found a Lascar smoking opium along with a woman, who was grimy, and unwashed, who had bloodshot eyes, matted hair, and features mangled by syphilis. 'Mustard-and-cress could be sown upon her hands,' commented Mayhew. There was also an Irish woman who cleaned out the lavatories for free rent, though one suspects that lavatories was a polite word for very free and easy arrangements.

He also came across China Emma (also known as Chaney Emm), a woman who had taken up with a sailor who had been inconsiderate enough to die in the West Indies. She had taken to drink, and her new man, Appoo, had thrown her into the gutter after tying her legs and arms together to cure her of this noxious habit. She had tried to commit suicide, jumping out of a first-floor window in Jamaica Place, but she bungled this, and a boatman had hooked her out of the river like some strange sea fish, giving her to the police. This cost China Emma a month in prison.

The whores of the area 'flaunting about bare-headed, in dirty-white muslin and greasy, cheap blue silk, with originally ugly faces horribly seamed with small-pox, and disfigured by vice' had curious names – Cocoa Bet, Salmony-faced Mary Anne. They did their parading in short nightgowns and nightjackets, and had their favourite public houses, the Half Moon and Seven Stars in Ratcliffe Highway, the Ship and Shears and the Duke of York in Shadwell High Street, and the Shakespeare's Head in Shadwell Walk. The endless revelry at night was described as 'the Highway has woke up'.

One of the most notorious of all sailors' women was Black Sarah, who lived in Bluegate Fields, which led off Ratcliffe Highway and which faced a gin shop and a pawnbrokers. It was conveniently near the East India Company's Chinese and Lascar barracks – Black Sarah, 'the far-famed *mollisher*', did not stipulate colour, race, or creed. She was a 'Dutch-built piratical schooner carrying on a free trade under the black flag' and 'many and many a stout and lusty lugger has borne down upon, and hoisted the British standard over, our sable privateer, Black Sall'.[24] She was made the subject of a little verse:

> The lady with diamonds and laces,
>> By day may heighten her charms,
> But Sall without any such graces,
>> At night lies as warm in your arms.

> The night when her sable o'ershades us,
>> Will veil all the pomp of the day,
> Then Sall is as good as my lady,
>> And cats are all equally grey.

It was in this area that Lushing Loo circulated, apparently ladylike, though haggard. As her name suggests, part of her downfall was drink, though in her case she went one better than the normal beverage of the class, gin. Her preference was 'a drain of pale' (i.e., pale brandy), and when the assiduous Mayhew cornered her, she sang him a comic song:

> The first I met a cornet was
> In a regiment of dragoons,
> I gave him what he didn't like,
> And stole his silver spoons.

Life in Victorian London was at its most carnivorous in the dock area. Wrote Taine:

Three times in ten minutes I saw crowds collect round doorways, attracted by fights, especially by fights between women. One of them, her face covered with blood, tears in her eyes, drunk, was trying to fly at a man while the mob watched and laughed. And as if the uproar were a signal, the population of neighbouring 'lanes' came pouring into the street, children in rags, paupers, street women, as if a human sewer were suddenly clearing itself.[25]

It says much for Victorian philanthropy that even in this morass someone was trying to do something – an attempt to give a series of lectures, with singing by a hundred schoolchildren, though it is doubtful whether many officials of the handsomely endowed (first year more than £20,000 in gifts) Metropolitan Visiting and Relief Association entered this ghetto, an area where the willingness of 'the higher classes of society to mingle with, and take an active part in the improvement of the London poor' might well be in doubt. The whores and toughs of the Ratcliffe Highway belonged to what Mary Carpenter called in 1851, the 'Perishing and Dangerous Classes', and if some way had been found to slice off this lump of land and float it out to sea few would have objected.

Amid all this, the dockers and their families lived. In August 1889 the dockers struck for a minimum wage of sixpence an hour. Led by the pioneer trade unionist John Burns, they paraded through the City of London, with an array of forty-one banners, some of them mere red rags, others topped with onions, fish heads, and pieces of rotting meat, to demonstrate what the dockers ate. The poverty of the dockers was a necessary concomitant to the complete degradation of the district. 'It is the sense of helplessness that tries everyone,' wrote the sociologist Charles Booth, 'they are so uncomplaining, so simple, and so dignified about their sorrows,' so much in 'continual contact with the realities of life'. Their lives 'lay hidden from view behind a curtain on which were painted terrible pictures; starving children, suffering women, overworked men; horrors of drunkenness and vice, monsters and demons of inhumanity . . .'[26]

Charles Booth was a sentimentalist, a rich Liverpool businessman with time to spare for the simple annals of the poor. His *Labour and Life of the People in London* (17 volumes, 1889–1903) is the quintessence of misplaced industry, drab and boring, lacking the sparkle that makes Mayhew's *London Labour and the London Poor* (1851–62) such an eminently readable work. Booth looked at the poor through middle-class pince-nez, even when he was lodging with them as part of his fieldwork ('What a drama, it is!' he wrote, marvelling as he passed round the common mug of beer, marvelling at this 'wholesome pleasant family life, very simple food, very regular habits, healthy bodies and healthy minds'). As he put it himself, 'To the rich the very poor are a sentimental interest.'

Poverty and prostitution went together in the nineteenth century with a ready click, and one is in a border country where promiscuity and prostitution combine with apathy to produce an effect that is ethically colourless. Promiscuous sex was a simple corollary of working-class childhood, where from five to thirteen slept in one bed. 'The sleeping of boys and girls, young men and young women, in beds almost touching one another, must have the effect of breaking down the great barriers between the sexes . . . such as necessarily to create early and illicit familiarity between the sexes.' So wrote A. Austin, an assistant Poor Law commissioner. These were simple facts, without overtones, though 'illicit' might seem an odd word to use in this connection. The clergy brought in the good-bad element: 'I do not choose to put on paper the disgusting scenes that I have known to occur from the promiscuous crowding of the sexes together.' This, from the Reverend S. O. Osborne, creates the tone with which one is so familiar; the main thing, for Osborne, was that he was disgusted, that his sensibilities had been upset so much so that he could not trust words to paper.

As for the lodging houses:

> Obscenity and blasphemy are the staple conversation of the inmates, every indecency is openly performed, the girls recite aloud their experiences of life; ten or a dozen sleep in one bed, many in a state of nudity. Indeed, the details of these places are horrible beyond description. Unmitigated vice and lustful orgies reign, unchecked by precept or example, and the point of rivalry is as to who shall excel in filth and abomination.

Thus wrote Mr Austin, assistant Poor Law commissioner, and again we are in a world of loaded language, the prurient and slightly excited middle class looking on. There is also a striking note of disapproval; one is reminded of the anecdote of the duchess in bed ('Do the lower classes know about this? ... it's much too good for them!'). Mr Austin's words echo those of Mrs Elizabeth Fry when she visited Newgate in February 1813: 'Nearly three hundred women, every gradation of crime, 120 in ward, no matting, nearly naked, all drunk ... her ears were offended by the most terrible imprecations.' To Mrs Fry, to Mr Austin, to Charles Booth, and to myriads more, the poor were too often satellites in too close proximity who offended one. The incomprehension of the poor when confronted with evidence of their wicked deeds was, to their 'betters', only proof of the utter degradation of the 'lower orders', much as they tried to hide these sentiments when it was time to put pen to paper.

The poor were a race apart, who were to be investigated like a lost species. In the early years of the reign, with Mayhew and Chadwick, there was a genuine effort to get at facts. Edwin Chadwick's *Report on the Sanitary Condition of the Labouring Population* (1842) is first-rate reportage: 'With broken panes in every window-frame, and filth and vermin in every nook, with the walls unwhitewashed for years, black with smoke of foul chimneys, without water ...' floors unwashed year after year, one to two feet of filth outside, stagnant puddles. 'Adult life,' observed Chadwick sagely, 'exposed to such miamata, gives way.'

He also noted that the poor were often better off than they appeared, that they had money but did not know how to make use of it properly. Chadwick was one of the earliest to see that the trouble often lay in improvidence rather than in poverty, and drew attention to a tailor who earned £3 a week, then a handsome wage, yet who never had had tables, chairs, or bedding. He slept on straw, his table was a square block of wood, and his only other possessions were a three-legged stool and an old tea caddy. Most of his money had gone on drink.

Thirty years later, in 1876, the same kind of cases were turning up, usually as a result of court proceedings. William Vaughan of Brandon Street, Walworth (the notorious Elephant and Castle district), was a tradesman – a boot clicker – whose furniture consisted of four chairs and a broken table (on which he slept). There was no mattress, no bed-clothing – only rags. There were also four children, ages three, six, eight and eleven, who were left alone all day while the father drank himself silly. 'The stench was frightful,' reported the *South London Press*. William Vaughan got six months' hard labour for neglect.

The lives of the poor were, indeed, nasty, short and brutish, and few shared the viewpoint of Booth ('I perhaps build too much on my slight experience, but I see nothing improbable in the general view that the simple natural lives of working-class people tend to their own and their children's happiness more than the artificial complicated existence of the rich.'). The manufacturers knew better, or thought that they did. Speaking of Booth's statistics, the proprietor of Simmons' Perambulator Manufactory, believed that they 'tend to foster discontent among the poor, and instead of directing them to exercise the discipline, industry, and thrift by which their condition might be bettered, rather suggest that while such multitudes are poor, and so few rich, the many might plunder the rich . . .'

The poor – whether they were called the labouring classes, the working classes, the indigent, or the lower orders – were beings to whom things were done, or for whom things were done. They were a class for ever being proffered advice from their betters – 'it should be as universal a rule that working men should support their parents, as that they should support their children. If this rule were allowed, we might see some revival of that genial spirit of charity and social duty among the poor, whose extinction we are apt to mourn.' So wrote Harriet Martineau, professional invalid and eccentric. As the century progressed, many well-meaning philanthropists gave the poor up as utterly incorrigible. The money pouring in from all sources was being diverted into the gin palaces. The Reverend William Stone found himself with £8,000 to distribute in Spitalfields, and was inundated with paupers from all over the East End, who took his money and spent it on drink or on baubles. The popularity of gin can be judged by the number of names it went under – 'blue ruin', 'max', 'duke', 'gatter', and 'jacky'. A measure of gin cost three halfpennies a time, and was taken in the extravagant luxury of the gin palace, gaudy with mirrors, corinthian pillars, and ormolu candelabra. 'The Whitechapel gin-drinkers brawl and screech horribly. Blows are freely exchanged, and sometimes pewter measures fly through the air like Shrapnel shells.'[27]

Violence and cruelty were essential ingredients of working-class life. Workmen repairing Bognor sea wall set a dog onto a four-year-old child – twelve or fourteen men urging the dog to 'Bite him! Bite him!' The dog did, fastening on to the child's knee. A performing bear in Battersea was tormented almost to death, and in Sunderland a Dr Abrath was fined one shilling and costs for advertising a public exhibition of experiments on animals. In Sheffield a bricklayer attacked his wife, destroying an eye, beat her cruelly, and drove her, half naked, into the street, covered with blood. At Southwark board school, children were punished by being put into a dark cupboard; one poor child, Emma Black, age six, died. The manner in which this was covered up by all concerned is not a pretty story; it only came to light when two boys told a local churchwarden.

Much of this violence and cruelty could be overlooked. What could not be passed over was the sexual immorality of the poor. A fall from virtue, wrote Booth, was 'a subject that it is polite to ignore', while Friedrich Engels, pioneer communist, wrote that 'Next to intemperance in the enjoyment of intoxicating liquors, one of the principal faults of English working-men is sexual licence'[28] (though Engels had taken to the English way of life and had two mistresses of his own).

It was often overlooked that to many young girls life in a brothel was infinitely better than life at home with drunken parents, no food, and nothing to wear but rags. The women who ran brothels at least clothed them and fed them. As Mother Willit of Gerrard Street put it, 'So help her kidneys, she *al'us* turned her gals out with a clean arse and a good tog; and as she turned 'em out, she didn't care who turned 'em up, 'cause 'em vos as clean as a smelt and as fresh as a daisy – she vouldn't have a speck'd 'un if she know'd it.' The fruits of vice were, in fact, what should have been the fruits of virtue – reasonably clean living conditions, food and good clothing. The fact that the girls had to open their legs to a succession of strange men was a matter of minor importance. The morality of prostitution was at no time so ambiguous as it was in the nineteenth-century brothel, where the abbess was an all-pervading mother figure both to the inmates and to the visitors.

At its most mundane level, the prostitutes were answering the ordinary needs of ordinary man. When the abbesses and the governesses of the brothels and the establishments enter into the picture, a new element enters, the sharing of an experience with a third uncommitted party. Perversions in the brothels were frequently carried out in groups, with the abbess playing a role part voyeur part organizer. Masochists found that the more people who viewed their 'misery', the more efficacious was the treatment. Sadists were more inclined to be loners; they were not a group greatly liked by brothel keepers, who often acted *in loco parentis* to their girls, and made use of the lowest kind of prostitute, the park girl. It was impossible for Victorian writers to speak more fully of what they called the 'disgusting practices' of the park women, which were 'alone gratifying to men of morbid and diseased imaginations'.

Unquestionably sexual practices are governed by the climate of opinion of the time, and married men of the Victorian age resorted to prostitutes when their wives refused to countenance pursuits that are part and parcel of twentieth-century everyday sexual activity. Victorian woman, wrote Dr Acton, 'submits to her husband's embraces, but principally to gratify him, and were it not for the desire of maternity, would far rather be relieved from his attentions'. This attitude of wife towards sex had been established since the beginning of Victoria's reign. Thus *woman as she is, and as she should be*, an anonymous publication of 1835: 'With grace to bear even warmth and peevishness, she must learn and adopt his tastes, study his disposition, and submit in short, to all his desires with that grateful compliance, which in a wife is the surest sign of a sound understanding.' Not surprisingly, men who were simply bored with their married life turned their attentions to women who might well display some gratification. Whether it was real or assumed was of no matter.

When the sado-masochistic instincts were isolated, then the lowest and most disposable of the prostitutes were placed in great danger, and ignorant and foolish creatures helped to act out fantasies for which they would receive a few coppers at best, and at worst a cut throat. Occasionally, this situation was reversed, and the more adventurous sadists and masochists were hoist with their own petards – literally. Rich masochists had their own 'torture chamber', with spiked collars, handcuffs, and whipping machines; particularly favoured were pulleys, by which the man was raised and lowered according to the whims of the prostitute who was usually one of the properties. One prostitute's whim was to go out shopping, forgetting that her employer was at that time suspended in space; she got back to find him half-strangled. In the 1790s a case occurred in London, in which a musician named Kotzwarra had himself strung up by a Covent Garden prostitute named Susanna Hill, who had earlier refused 'to split his genitals into two parts'. Requested to suspend Kotzwarra, she did this so efficiently that he died. She was put on trial for murder but was acquitted.

Child Prostitution

The most nauseating chapter in any account of Victorian life is that which deals with the exploitation of children, and the most nauseating section of that chapter is the one that deals with child prostitution. Strangely, even the most kindhearted of men thought this a subject for humour. Speaking of Leonard Smithers, the publisher of Aubrey Beardsley and miscellaneous erotica, Oscar Wilde said, 'He loves first editions, especially of women: little girls are his passion.' To Wilde, Smithers' pursuits if not laudable, were of no great public concern; Smithers was only one of the many who delighted in young virgins.

Smithers and his ilk were aided and abetted by the astonishing law that made the age of consent twelve, at a time when puberty was occurring at a later age in Britain than today. English law in respect of the relationship between the sexes was 'a maze of flighty fancies and misapplied logic'.[29] It had been even worse before Lord Hardwicke's marriage bill of 1753, when a boy of fourteen could marry a girl of twelve in a tavern before two friends. At the May Fair marriage could be arranged at a moment's notice. The age of twelve was accepted as an age when a girl was fit for sex. This legal fiction made it difficult for organizations such as the London Society for the Protection of Young Females to make headway, even though there were children of eleven in brothels.

This same society recorded that in three London hospitals in eight years there were 2,700 cases of venereal disease among girls between the ages of eleven and sixteen. In 1835 the Society stated: 'It has been proved that 400 individuals procure a livelihood by trepanning females from eleven to fifteen years of age for the purposes of prostitution,' and one brothel keeper confessed that there was a branch establishment 'over the water' where youngsters were broken in. In 1871 a Royal Commission was instructed to look into the question, and like most Royal Commissions it came through with the enlightened answer:

The traffic in children for infamous purposes is notoriously considerable in London and other large towns. We think that a child of twelve can hardly be deemed capable of giving consent, and should not have the power of yielding up her person. We therefore recommend the absolute protection of female children to the age of fourteen years, making the age of consent to commence at fourteen instead of twelve as under the existing law.

However, like most enlightened answers, the promulgation was vastly different from its accomplishment. The nature of the sexuality of man partly lies in the urge to deflower; the apex of a man's sexual life is supposed to be his bridal night and the ravishing of a virgin bride. In the way of marriage, such an encounter could not occur more than two or three times (supposing that on divorce or a wife's death the man acquires a virgin bride again). The answer, to the rich man with this primeval urge, was to acquire a succession of virgins; and in the only class such a man had access to – the working class – the thing was to catch them young. At fourteen or fifteen the odds were against a working girl being a virgin anyway.

Thus the trade in virgins, the cost of which ran out about £20 a time. It was an area where women had a vested interest, and into the arena came a number of excellent ladies, aghast at what they had discovered (it was reckoned that in Liverpool there were five hundred prostitutes under the age of thirteen). Like so many organizations, these women, admirable as their intentions were, tended to collect all the sins and put them under one umbrella. One of the leaders of these women, Josephine Butler, 'has a tendency to confuse the issues' (so said Gladstone), and others (such as Florence Nightingale, a bedridden spinster, and Harriet Martineau, ill, deaf, and eccentric) were dabbling in matters about which they knew little because they were on the side of the goodies versus the baddies. Again we have the enthusiastic collection of data for the sake of data, and it needed the scientific voice of T. H. Huxley to declare that such material meant little, if anything. In any event, the virgins were still being bought, and the men were still enjoying what was described as 'green fruit'.

The exploitation of children in one way or another was carried through all classes. The children of the rich were to behave as miniature ladies and gentlemen and were forced, often with considerable cruelty into moulds for this purpose; the children of the poor were beasts of burden. In 1842 a Royal Commission reported on the employment of poor children in mines and collieries, and 'a mass of misery and depravity was unveiled of which even the warmest friends of the labouring

classes had hitherto but a faint conception'. Many children began to toil in the mines when only four or five, acting as
'trappers' for twelve and fourteen hours on end. The job of a
trapper was to open and close passage doors before and after
each coal carriage so that no draught of air could cause fire or
noxious gases. During this spell of twelve hours or more the
child was quite alone. 'Many of the mines were infested with
rats, mice, beetles, and other vermin, and stories are told of
rats so bold, that they would eat the horses' food in the presence
of the miners, and have been known to run off with the lighted
candles in their mouth and explode the gas.' [30] Should the child
drop off to sleep or stray from his post, he, or she, was beaten
unmercifully. Not only that. 'These gloomy and loathsome
caverns are made the scenes of the most bestial debauchery. If
a man and a woman meet in them and are excited by passion
at the moment, they indulge in it.' What a spectacle for a child!

A computer would unquestionably come out with the answer
that the situation of a child in the coal mines was more tolerable
than the situation of a child of twelve faced with defloration. No
way has yet been found to feed into computers the taboos and
guilt feelings that the average man has towards the violation of
virgins, an act sanctified by the contract of marriage. In one of
his brief moments of logic, de Sade stated that in fornication
every man wants to play the tyrant; in very many marriages the
woman puts up a pretence at resistance, so that the husband
may indulge in quasi-rape. The twelve-year-old virgin is therefore a somewhat ambiguous figure; a primeval urge to deflower
is at odds with the constrictions and new patterns of behaviour
imposed by civilization. Few situations therefore arouse such
passions as the violated child. At its most acceptable, one has
the spectacle of the child wife, that hybrid beloved by the Victorian readers of Dickens, in which defloration is made acceptable by: (a) the marriage contract; and (b) compliance. In
physical circumstances there is little difference between the bridal
night of a Dickens child bride and the enforced defloration
(often under chloroform) of the twelve-year-old girl bribed from
parents for £20 or so.

At its extreme and most repulsive is the situation of the

young child raped and murdered, and nothing, not even the
worst atrocities of war or the most appalling torture, can create
the anger aroused by this situation. One of the most frightful
of such cases in Victorian times was the Blackburn murder of
1876, in which a twenty-five-year-old barber named William Fish
murdered Emily Holland, age seven to eight. His own account
is as follows: 'I asked her to bring me one half-ounce of tobacco from Con's shop. She went and brought it to me. I asked
her to go into my shop. She did. I asked her to go up stairs, and
she did. I went up with her. I tried to abuse her and she was
nearly dead. I then cut her throat with a razor.'

Unfortunately, William Fish was not unique. The disappearance of a child in the nineteenth century was not, as today, a
signal for a massive police search. Baby farming was an established industry, and for half a crown a week unwanted children
were nurtured by strangers; many of the girls ended up as
prostitutes. The William Fishes of the world often proclaimed
their proclivities to the public when their activities had not
concluded with murder. One of these in *My Secret Life*, goes
into great detail when he tells the tale of his violation of a ten-
year-old girl, with the full approval of her mother (who was
stout, 'full-sized', good-looking, dark, certainly forty, dressed
like a well-to-do tradeswoman).

In the capital, the London Society for the Protection of Young
Females had an impossible task. The twilight world of the procuresses of young girls could not be combated by high principles
and ideals, and for the more practical members of the society
the outlets for the trade were too various to cover adequately.
There were reckoned to be, in the 1840s and 1850s, 5,000 brothels
or houses of assignation, each avid for a fresh supply of youngsters and willing to pay, as agents, charwomen, shopkeepers,
and laundresses. The workhouses also made their contribution.
In June 1848 *The Times* noted that the female children in the
metropolitan workhouse were happy and healthy, that they
went off at fourteen as servants with all the prospects of a reasonable life, but that nine out of ten took to the streets.

Vice in London was then difficult to combat if only on account of the vastness of the city. In early Victorian days it was the only city in the world that topped the million mark; its nearest rival was Paris with 881,000 (1835). With its inadequate system of government, based on the archaic unit of the 'vestry', it was already becoming a disorganized sprawl. In the provinces, it was different. The towns were of reasonable size and could be seen in their entirety, though they grew faster than any one foresaw. In Birmingham, Joseph Chamberlain determined that the city should be 'parked, paved, assized, marketed, gas-and-watered, and improved'.

Birmingham is the mirror of the industrial revolution. The Soho Foundry was the first modern industrial plant in the world, and industrialists and scientists of the calibre of Watt, Boulton, and Priestley set their seal on the city. In 1801 the population was 73,000, and although this increased at a startling rate the city was not enfranchised until 1832. In 1851 the population was 232,841; in 1861, 296,076; in 1869, 360,846; and in 1891 it was 478,113. It speedily produced more than its fair share of slums, still preserved in all their pristine period glory, and it also produced its share of vice. However, unlike London where the police were inclined to wash their hands of vice except during purges, a war on prostitution was carried on with zeal, aided and abetted by the puritanical strain inherent in the city.

To judge by the figures, the war on vice was successful, but, as in London, one is suspicious of the Victorian cavalier attitude towards statistics. In 1862 in Birmingham there were said to be 184 brothels and houses of ill-fame, fifty-one prostitutes under sixteen, and 377 over sixteen, of whom 171 were summarily convicted. Once again, one searches the records of the hospitals for reliable data. In the year 1861–2 the General Hospital had thirty-one inpatients suffering from venereal disease, and 573 outpatients; the Queen's Hospital forty-two inpatients and 327 outpatients, while Dr Robinson, the surgeon to the workhouse (that concomitant to every large city) stated that admissions to the workhouse infirmary included 166 suffering from venereal disease.

As the century drew nearer to its close, prostitution became a major problem to the city fathers who had had Birmingham paved and watered, who had had a new main street cutting through the worst of the slums, and who had already had a square dedicated to their hero, Joseph Chamberlain. In particular, child prostitution was on the increase, despite the optimistic statement of the chief of police that there were only three girls who were immoral in the whole of the city – a proclamation that was a gift to journalists who declared with astonishment that they had come across the entire trio in one fell swoop.

One of the organizations which set out to put an end to the trade in young girls was the Birmingham and Midland Counties Vigilance Association for the Repression of Criminal Vice and Public Immorality, the first annual report of which came out in 1888. The association had, initially, 114 subscribers; the largest subscriptions were given by the Quaker kings of the chocolate empire, the Cadburys, George and Richard, who gave fifteen guineas each.

The Vigilance Association was characteristic of the associations and societies of the period, but unusual in that it is well documented by virtue of their lucid publications, and even more unusual in that it did not claim to do the impossible on a budget that was never more than the ludicrously inadequate (it folded up in 1893 – subscriptions that year came to £291 13s. 6d.). Although it did not *claim* to do the impossible, it tried to. Besides the subjugation of child prostitution, it also tried to suppress houses of ill fame, indecent performances in concert halls, the exposure of indecent pictures on the doors of theatres, music halls, in shops, and on walls, quack advertisements, and the circulation of 'impure' literature. The Vigilance Association had the aura of witch hunting, made no better by their request in each of their publications: 'If you should know or hear of any case of criminal vice or public immorality, in which you think this Association can render advice or help, you are requested to communicate with the Secretary. ... All such communications will be regarded as strictly confidential.'

This helped to deal with John Hammersley, guilty of indecent behaviour with little girls in Aston Park, for which he got two months' hard labour. 'It has evidently become the practice of a certain class of persons, whom a brutal lust has deprived of all sense of decency and manliness to entice little children into a public park, and to attempt by promises or threats to induce them to submit to outrage. There is no need to emphasize the heinousness of the offence.' The Reverend J. F. T. Hallowes also discovered another heinous offence. Going round Birmingham, 'one saw placards in which the revolver and the dagger were displayed'. This is the faintly risible side of the Vigilance Association; nor can one take the junior branch of the Vigilance Association very seriously, with its title of the 'Snowdrop Band'.

The year 1893 was the *annus mirabilis* of Birmingham vice, the year in which virtue 'seem'd but Shipwrack'd on so base a Coast' leading the Birmingham and Midland Counties Vigilance Association to throw up its hands in despair and die. It had never been the same since 1890 when Arthur John Naish, chairman of the executive, had 'passed into a world where there is no need for the services which he so unweariedly rendered in this'. It was 1893 that the chief of police averred that there were but three child prostitutes in Birmingham.

A court case focused the attention of the *Modern Review* in 1893 on Birmingham. The *Modern Review* was one of the slightly dotty magazines that flourished in the nineties, full of Celtic-fringe poems and half-crazed articles on the pros and cons of women's rights. However, the journalist who descended on Birmingham to write 'Sin of our Cities III' was one of the few who actually boarded a train at Euston to find out what sin in the provinces really amounted to.

The case in question dealt with Mary Ann Jennings, age thirteen, and Nellie Greatrix, age twelve, who had been arrested outside the Grand Theatre, Birmingham, for picking pockets. In their possession were three purses and a bottle of rum. Their cover for their sinister little game was that they were hawking matches, but upon their arrest it was found that this was not the extent of their sales. They said that they had received up to a sovereign apiece for prostituting themselves; on examination it was discovered that they were *virgo intacta*, and it was 'suggested that their immorality took a more unnatural form'.

The journalist perked up his ears, and loitered in one of the new streets of brighter Birmingham, where he overheard a conversation:

> 'Sarah, how much do you charge the fellows now?'
> 'Anythink they like, a penny, or I'd even take a ha'penny.'

He was soon accosted by a young girl, who 'speedily revealed her horrible profession', requiring him to take her home. Asked the writer:

> 'Who lives with you?'
> 'Uncle and his missus.'
> 'Will they let me come with you?'
> 'Oh, they wouldn't care, especially if you was to give 'em a drink.'

These young girls invariably used match selling as their ostensible pursuit. In Stephenson Square there were a dozen under the age of thirteen 'selling matches', and at New Street station a match seller 'asked whether she should come into the carriage in which I was sitting'. A curious aspect of vice in the Birmingham of the nineties was the 'whore train' that steamed out at eleven o'clock every Saturday night to the fashionable residential districts of Moseley and Camp Hill. 'When the train steams out of the station one hears a discordant medley of cheers, groans, screams, and songs from innumerable voices.'

Promiscuity through continuity was a factor noted in 1892 by an inspector of the Society for the Prevention of Cruelty to Children.

> I know that the conditions under which many children are raised in Birmingham must tend to corrupt them and deprive them of any sense of morality, or decency, or modesty. The one-room and two-room tenements are most common; they may be found in street after street in numerous localities. The condition of life for children in these tenements is shocking, and I hear of terrible cases of unnatural outrage and vice. The cases are very difficult to prove, yet I know they exist.
>
> There is no modesty, no reserve, no delicacy in our slums, and the passions of children are prematurely developed, while eye and ear are fed with disgusting sights and words which make morality, and not its opposite, a mystery.

The Stead Case

William Thomas Stead was a professional champion of causes, and his innate qualities as a catalyst made him a unique figure in nineteenth-century history. The son of a Congregational minister, he gravitated to journalism via letters to an editor on the subject of prostitution and the 'victims of our juggernaut', couched in the melodramatic tone of the new journalism. These letters appeared in the provincial newspaper the *Northern Echo*, and thus encouraged Stead to ask the editor if contributors were paid; they were not – the *Northern Echo* was too poor for that – but Stead had made his mark, and when the editor left in 1871 Stead became his successor at a salary of £150 a year (increased to £200 a year two years later). He speedily established a reputation as a character, riding through the Darlington grime on a pony, and as a journalist with a rare flair (he was quoted by *The Times*).

Towards the end of the 1870s, the Salvation army [31] came to Darlington in the persons of Captain Rose and Lieutenant Annie. The quasi-military set-up of the Salvation Army held few charms for Stead, and the theology struck no new notes, reflecting as it did the harsh neo-Calvinism made fashionable by Rev. Charles Spurgeon at his Tabernacle. The courage of Captain Rose and Lieutenant Annie, however, did draw from him reluctant admiration and he reproached William Booth ('Holy Willie'), the founder of the Army, for sending his soldiers into such alien territory. Booth retorted that Stead would not make general if he dared not risk human lives in battle. This was the level of repartee that Stead was to love, the grand gesture, the flamboyant words, and although he said the Army's methods were 'to many minds simply revolting', it was evident that the army touched off chords in his own nature, whether it was the flag, the motto ('Blood and Fire'), the processions, or the 'Hallelujah Lasses'. He was also impressed by the fact that local publicans were said to be offering the 'Lasses' £300 to desist from their fiery talk.

During this period, there was a revival of interest in the subject of child prostitution, and especially on the age of consent, the raising of which was perpetually wrecked on Lord Coleridge's dictum that the age *must* be twelve because this was the age, at common law, at which a woman could marry. Many progressive politicians were keen to raise the age of consent, in particular Russell Gurney (of Married Women's Property Act fame), and his bill passed the first reading, again to founder.

The centre of child prostitution was Brussels. Wrote Josephine Butler in May 1880:

In some houses in Belgium there are immured little children, English girls of some twelve to fifteen years, lovely creatures (for they do not care to take any who are not beautiful), innocent creatures who, stolen, kidnapped, betrayed, got from English country villages by artifice are sold to these human shambles. ... The secret is known to none except the wealthy *debauchés* who can pay large sums of money for the sacrifice of these innocents.[32]

Brussels provided all the data necessary for an exposé of the trade in young girls, and 'tortures endured at hands of clients' coupled with 'painful and revolting' hospital treatment. If the English police were suspect, how much more so were the Belgian police. Josephine Butler drew up an impressive indictment: 'There is reason to believe that the conduct of the chief of police encourages the keepers, not only to receive minors, but in some cases ... to provide children for the gratification of their fastidious clients.' One high-ranking police official sold wine to brothels under the trade name of his son, and when any inspections were due of the brothels the youngsters were moved out. The children had no street clothes, were given no pens or paper, and the doors opened only one way. Oddly enough, the Belgian law was a good deal more firm on seduction of under-age girls than British law, but this acted to the advantage of the brothel keepers, Couriers visited Somerset House, where all births are recorded, and made notes of suitable names and addresses of girls who were born twenty-one or twenty-two years before; these names were then wished on the girls who were being exported from Britain. In acquiring these names the girls were committing an offence, and this was held over their heads as a threat. The only person, it would seem, who was not cognizant of this trade was the British consul in Brussels, who declared, 'I myself believe it is impossible for a virtuous girl to be admitted into one of these houses. I do not believe it for a moment.'

This was a situation ready-made for Stead, with his unique psychological make-up and true Victorian gift of self-deception. Soon after the Salvation Army lassies had visited Darlington he had been offered the assistant editorship of the *Pall Mall Gazette* under John Morley. Morley as a journalist was stodgy, and it took him three years to decide that up against the ebullient Stead he was nowhere. So he retired from the editorship. Stead had gone to London with almost Salvationist rapture: 'If God needs an Editor of enthusiasm in London, I will serve His turn best.' There were also his readers to serve, and then, as now, there was no easier way than vice as main dish, which, in journalistic terms, meant that the *Pall Mall Gazette* must be 'lively, amusing, and newsy'.

This involved getting up to all kinds of stunts, some of which became established as standard newspaper procedure. Stead was a pioneer of the interview and the 'extra', and created a new dimension in popular journalism in 1884, the year he took over as full editor, by going down to Southampton and obtaining an interview with General 'Chinese' Gordon. Stead was England's equivalent to the American Hearst; he might well have been instrumental in starting a European war ('... Chamberlain is very jingo on the Egyptian question, and wants "to have a go in" at Bismark and France, by which I suppose he means a European war ...').

Stead was also a precursor of a new style of journalism in that he saw facts not so much as pieces in a jigsaw puzzle but as pieces of putty waiting to be manipulated, but most of all he must bear responsibility for that creature of the present, the pseudo-event. In both of these activities, he pulled the wool securely over the eyes of his ex-chief Morley, who wrote of him that he was 'abounding in journalistic resource, eager in convictions, infintely bold, candid, laborious in surefooted mastery of all the facts ...'[33] The poet and critic Matthew Arnold was more perspicacious about the new journalism, which threw out 'assertions at a venture because it wishes them to be true'.

Parallel with the lively journalism of the *Pall Mall Gazette* was the lively religion of the Salvation Army, which was beginning to find itself in hot water. The women's rights campaigner – the huge, man-faced Frances Power Cobbe – put a common point of view in an article in the *Contemporary Review*: 'There is no doubt that the mischief done is deplorable when Prayer and Praise are parodied in the streets, and Repentance turned into the standing jest of a gin palace.' Hostile clergymen noted that the meetings of the Salvation Army created over-excitement, and drew laborious inferences from the filling maternity wards of Hackney, a popular centre of Salvation Army activities. The same thing had occurred during the heyday of Spurgeon (who on the day of National Humiliation for the Indian Mutiny of 1857 addressed 24,000 people, many of whom achieved the same degree of euphoria as those subjected to the stirring words of the Lieutenant Annies of Victorian England).

In 1885 City Chamberlain Benjamin Scott went to see Stead at the offices of the *Pall Mall Gazette* to see if Stead would stir up public opinion on behalf of the girls who were being exported like so many heads of cattle, though it was not likely that Stead was ignorant of the matter. Stead, with a display of high indignation, went to see the Archbishop of Canterbury, the Bishop of London, and the Roman Catholic Cardinal Manning, and put forward his scheme. Stead had the idea in his head that there would be no reason for keeping the age of consent at twelve if it could be proved that there was a trade in young girls in London.

Benjamin Scott, the City Chamberlain, had been in conference with Bramwell Booth of the Salvation Army, and it was Booth who introduced Stead to the most important of his leads, Rebecca Jarrett. Age thirty-six, Rebecca Jarrett was something of an expert on child prostitution, as she had been a whore herself at the age of twelve. She was the eldest of thirteen children, her father had walked out on the family, and the mother drank. At Cremorne Gardens, Rebecca had been seduced, a glass of wine having been included in the entrance fee. Her sailor brother had turned her out of the house, she worked in a laundry, broke her leg, met a commercial traveller named Sullivan who set her up in Marylebone High Street, from which circumstance she was rescued by Captain 'Hawker' Jones.

Stead proposed to go through the motions of buying a young virgin, using Rebecca Jarrett as his agent. He also did fieldwork, during which a Member of Parliament is alleged to have offered him a hundred virgins at £25 apiece. The politician and editor of *Truth*, Henry Labouchere, gave Stead advice: 'I had a conversation with him when he was full of what he was going to do. I told him that his facts must be cast iron; and that he was not to believe all he was told when drinking champagne with questionable characters.'

The young virgin in question was Eliza Armstrong, and she was obtained by Jarrett from a Mrs Broughton. Eliza turned up in a dark long travelling dress and a Duchess of Devonshire hat adorned with a yellow feather, accompanied by her mother, who had a cut mouth, the 'father' apparently having objected. It transpired much later that he was not Eliza's father. Stead had the girl cleaned up, had doubts about her hair style (which was in what was known as a 'Piccadilly bang'), and had her taken to a Madame Mourez who examined her, and pronounced her *virgo intacta*. Stead took a cab to a house in Poland Street, where they were to have rooms, and ordered drinks so that the landlady could see how young Eliza was. Rebecca put Eliza to bed, chloroformed, and Stead entered the room, final proof that it was possible to buy a virgin for a fiver. Rebecca had forgotten her erstwhile trade, and had not succeeded in chloroforming Eliza adequately. Eliza woke up when Stead was in the room, and Stead retired in some confusion. The project was now complete; all that was needed was to keep Eliza out of the way (he sent her to Paris) and write up his experiences and the experiences of his stout band of helpers, including a Salvation Army girl who went to live in a brothel as if to the manner born and who, by preserving a fastidious distaste for customers and by paying the brothel keeper, retained her virtue.

Spice was not lacking in the London newspaper world of the

eighties. *Lloyd's Newspaper* and the *Pink 'Un* kept their readers titallated; exposures, however, in the *Pall Mall Gazette* were different; the *Gazette* had a respectable reputation dating from the Morley régime.

In his eagnerness to lap up a good story, Stead had ignored one aspect – the effect of all this on the thirteen-year-old Eliza Armstrong, who had been whisked away from her mother, seen her mother with a cut lip caused by this whisking away, trundled across London and examined by the short fat beady-eyed Madame Mourez in a most indelicate way, taken to a house and chloroformed, awakened to find the not very prepossessing person of Stead in the room, then examined again by a doctor to ascertain that Stead had not fallen prey to his desires, then sent to Paris. The world must have seemed an extraordinary place to the girl. Later in life, Stead appears to have had doubts: 'Even at this day,' he wrote, 'I stand amazed at the audacity with which I carried the thing through.' At the time he was quite confident that he had done the right thing. 'Beyond the momentary surprise of the midwife's examination, which was necessary to prove that a little harlot had not been palmed off upon us, she experienced not the slightest inconvenience.'

This carefully arranged pseudo-event also gave Stead the opportunity for self-dramatization, the projection of a persona that no one could fail to love. 'Oh, Mrs Butler,' he declared to Josephine Butler, 'let me weep, let me weep, or my heart will break.' To Mrs Butler, Stead was an agent of God ('I never believed that you could have got the age of protection raised this session by a 'fluke', as it were. God sees further than we do'). He was also a means of making life exciting ('. . . the memory is ever present of a dark night in which I entered his office, after a day of hand-to-hand wrestling with the powers of Hell. We stumbled up the narrow dark stairs; the lights were out, not a soul was there, it was midnight . . .').

On 4 July 1885, Stead issued a trailer of things to come:

We have determined with a full sense of responsibility attaching to such a decision to publish the Report of a Special and Secret Commission of Enquiry which we appointed to examine into the whole subject. . . . Nothing but the most imperious sense of public duty would justify its publication. ... We say quite frankly to-day that all those who are squeamish, and all those who are prudish, and all those who prefer to live in a fool's paradise of imaginary innocence and purity, selfishly oblivious of the horrible realities which torment those whose lives are passed in the London Inferno, will do well not to read the *Pall Mall Gazette* of Monday and the three following days.

So Stead jumped into the twentieth century. The 6 July issue dealt out all the clichés one is now familiar with: 'shuddering horror ... terrible as is the exposure ... maelstrom of vice'; or the chapter headings – 'The Violation of Virgins', 'Confessions of a Brothel-Keeper', 'Strapping Girls Down'. Stead was using the weapons of pornography to right a wrong; it was the death knell of responsible journalism, both in its approach and in its embellishment of the facts. The mother, in real life Mrs Armstrong, became a 'poor, dissolute', woman, 'indifferent to everything but drink', and Eliza had her name changed. How far do means justify the ends? In this case, there were strong doubts. Wrote Bernard Shaw:

We backed him up over the Maiden Tribute only to discover that the Eliza Armstrong case was a put-up job of his. After that, it was clear that he was a man who could not work with anybody; and nobody would work with him. When he was set up years after as the editor of a new London daily he had learnt nothing and forgotten nothing, being so hopelessly out of date journalistically that the paper collapsed almost at once.

During the articles in the *Pall Mall Gazette* (reprinted in pamphlet form as *The Maiden Tribute of Modern Babylon,* an allusion to the myth of the Minotaur and its quota of virgin sacrifices) Stead became infatuated with his own abilities and his effect on the world. His articles, he claimed, 'set London and the whole country in a blaze of indignation'. The second series carried on the tradition, with headings 'Delivered for Seduction', 'Where Maids are Picked Up', 'Procuration in the West-end', and 'A Close Time for Girls'. The Member of Parliament for Whitehaven asked the Home Secretary 'whether any means exist of subjecting the author and publisher of these obscene articles in a paper called the *Pall Mall Gazette* to a criminal

prosecution'. Such a notion would have been laughed to scorn by
Stead. For his part, he thought that the Home Secretary should
'tell the House that the *Pall Mall Gazette* had covered itself with
everlasting glory'. His delusions of grandeur were not pricked
by rival newspapers – the *St. James's Gazette* declared that the
articles were 'the vilest parcel of obscenity'. The demand for
the subsequent issues of the *Pall Mall Gazette* was greater than
the supply, and the *Globe* obliged by lending Stead paper. The
mobs jostled for the *Gazette*, which W. H. Smith and Sons had
inconsiderately decided that they would no longer stock.

Mrs Armstrong not surprisingly had read the articles, discovering to her amazement that 'Lily' could be no other than
her daughter Eliza, who was still in Paris. She herself did not
emerge with much credit from the articles, and she complained
to the magistrate at Marylebone who sent her on to Scotland
Yard. A reporter of the scurrilous *Lloyd's Newspaper* had picked
her up at Marylebone Police Court, and from then onward Mrs
Armstrong had a sympathetic ally, a ready ear for her grievances.
Lloyd's Newspaper followed the trail, accompanied by the *St.
James's Gazette*, discovering Madame Mourez, and Mr Armstrong, who was dispatched to Paris and got lost in the brothels.
In the meantime, Eliza had been surreptitiously sent back to
England – and was discovered with Stead in a garden in Wim-
bledon.

There can never have been a more willing martyr than Stead
when he found that proceedings were to be taken against him.
To Bramwell Booth Stead was a 'modern Galahad', to the suffragette extremist Mrs Fawcett he was 'the hero saint who in
every age of the world's history has been picked out for misrepresentation'. To the proprietors of the *Pall Mall Gazette*, he
was the editor who had lifted circulation to an all time high,
and to the authorities he was a nuisance.

The pseudo-event had gone slightly awry. Stead had omitted
to get Armstrong's permission to take away Eliza, and he had
led Mrs Armstrong to believe that Eliza was going into service.
To the legal minds the substantial question was whether or not
Eliza had been taken 'fraudulently' out of possession of the
parents, the axiom being that all fraud annuls all consent. It

was a question admitting of only one answer. Madame Mourez and Rebecca Jarrett got six months each, Stead three months, the news of which, related his daughter in her memoir *My Father*, 'struck like setting a match to gunpowder. The effect was instantaneous, explosive, seeming to liberate the pent-up horror that had gripped the whole country while the deadly drama was slowly being unfolded.' Over-dramatic, perhaps, especially as Stead had preferential treatment. Prayers were offered up, telegrams of protest sped to and fro, and the jubilant *St. James's Gazette* did a cynical post-mortem: 'Mr Stead was probably intoxicated when he took into his mind certain details worked into this story ...'

As a 'first-class misdemeanant' he was removed from Coldbath Fields to Holloway (now a woman's prison). Morley visited his former assistant editor, and found him 'in a strangely exalted mood'. Stead enjoyed his incarceration; after all (as he had told Morley) was he not 'the man of most importance now alive'? He had an armchair, a blazing fire, a comfortable bed, his own hearth-rug, a writing-desk and a 'cosy little tea table'. 'Never,' he wrote, 'had I a happier lot than the two months I spent in Happy Holloway.'

An enviable achievement. The Criminal Law Amendment Act of 1885 raised the age of consent to sixteen, made procuration a criminal offence, and the penalty for assault on a girl under thirteen either whipping or penal servitude. Would this have been done without the impetus of Stead's sensationalist articles? How mixed were his motives? To a modern writer, Roy Jenkins, Stead was a puritan fascinated by sex. His megalomania cannot be overlooked, nor can his extraordinary behaviour every 10 November. On this day he dressed in his prison garb, boarded his train at Wimbledon, got out at Waterloo, and walked across Waterloo Bridge in the persona of a convict, no doubt remembering the exalted mood of his manic days.

The *Pall Mall Gazette* took him back, provided there 'were no more virgins', but he left this after a while and founded a monthly, the *Review of Reviews*, started cheap reprints (*Penny Poets* and *Prose Classics*), and threw himself into another twilight world, the world of the spooks and the table rappers (his spiritualist paper *Borderland* lasted four years). He started with Annie Besant the *Link*, 'A journal for the Servants of Man', which serialized 'The Story of Trafalgar Square', hardly the kind of thing for Stead. Odd books were produced – *If Christ Came to Chicago* of 1893 and *The Americanization of the World* of 1902. He supported the Boer side during the Boer War, and Cecil Rhodes crossed him off his list of friends. His demise came in a suitably dramatic way; he went down in the *Titanic* in 1912. The 'man of most importance now alive' had gone under with the ship that could not sink.

The Stead coup and the subsequent trial have had their full share of publicity since those dramatic days in eighty-five, though they have yet to be made the subject of a musical, the final proof of an event having arrived. There is almost a full-scale libretto by Stead for such a project ('the daughters of the people ... served up as dainty morsels to minister to the passions of the rich ...'). In such a work, Stead would fall readily into the role of hero. However, the disturbing fact remains that this journalist who prodded an unwilling judiciary into passing a law that was wholly good was not, as he thought, merely a messianic instrument of the Lord. Driven into a frenzy as he was by the dire doings of noble lords, it did not escape the attentions of objective observers that Stead was hardly less aberrated than the pursuers of twelve-year-old virgins. Mrs Lynn Linton, the never-tiring chastiser of the New Woman, commented shrewdly that 'he exudes semen through the skin', and the opinions of two exceptionally cool-headed men of the period are worth mentioning.

Viscount Wolseley was a professional soldier of sterling qualities. Both on the field of battle and as an administrator he was quite of the first order; in 1870 he put down the Indian rising at the Red River in Canada without losing a man. In 1890, Stead visited him for breakfast; Stead was on one of his religious fugues at the time, and Wolseley listened to him with interest, as he told his wife:

His idea is there should be one universal religion, that of trying individually to be like Christ, and in all relations in life to act as you think Christ would have acted under similar circumstances. This he thinks would be a bond of religious union between Roman Catholics and all denominations of Protestants. [Nothing very harmful in these sentiments, but something else struck Lord Wolseley.] He is a sort of man who in days of active revolution might be a serious danger. I looked at him, thinking if it should ever be my lot to have to hang or shoot him.[34]

It was nearly a decade later when Reginald Brett, Viscount Esher, spoke of Stead. Viscount Esher was one of the great organization men of the last quarter of the nineteenth century, and from the Office of Works he had his finger on the pulse of politics and all that appertained thereto, applying subtle pressures when he thought they were needed. When there were processions that needed the managerial hand, when the machinery of government was becoming clogged through intertia or through incompetence, Reginald Brett, the intimate of Lord Rosebery and Sir William Harcourt, was never far away. A superior civil servant, he was the kind of man the nineteenth century was desperately short of.

He had been in touch with Stead for a number of years. He had been impressed by the 'Extra' Stead had brought out at the time of the Gordon disaster, and he had never overlooked Stead's flair. On 5 May 1899 he wrote to his son:

... To-day I lunched with Mr Stead whom I had not seen for four months. He is off to Russia to see the Tzar again – on Monday. He is wild and odd as ever, and thinks he has inherited the spirit of Charles II, who – through him – is making amends for his previous life on earth!

Pretty good loony! All his female friends he endows with the attributes of Charles's mistresses! If he wasn't so sane in other matters he would have to be shut up.[35]

Doubts about the sanity of a man throw doubts about his veracity. At the time of the *Pall Mall Gazette* furore, the *St. James's Gazette* declared: 'Our distinct opinion is that four-fifths of the narrative is mere imposture.' How much further would it have gone were it known that Stead was on the border and maybe sliding into insanity?

It is clear that there was a demand for young virgins, but

whether it was on the scale claimed by Stead is open to doubt. A refugee from the Nonconformist north of England is always open to the conviction that the flesh pots of London are fleshier than they actually are. Stead's new journalism was inner conviction wrapped around a small kernel of fact. He did not need to drink champagne with questionable characters to find out the facts; he only had to sit down with a pen and let his mind dwell on the subject. He was a happy accident. It was further fortunate that he had as allies men and women who were equally impressionable.

The Whitechapel Murders

A fashionable West End prostitute could earn more in a night than a working man could earn in a month. A drab in Drury Lane could earn in twenty minutes against a wall as much as a dock labourer could earn in five hours of back-breaking toil. The rates for the semi-professionals in Whitechapel and Bethnal Green just about tallied with the wages paid to unskilled labour. It was not all easy money. There was disease, humiliation and danger, though the danger varied in inverse ratio to the amounts of money received. The higher-priced whores had to cope with the eccentric demands of the aristocracy where there was some element of risk, while the perverts were inclined to favour the medium-range supplier. At the bottom of the pile the semi-professionals were the most vulnerable, without pimps or protectors, frequently living in common lodging houses with or without husbands, at the mercy of sadists, and the most potent of that group, the sexual murderers. These women were a class that was expendable, drifting itinerants who were difficult to protect, and during 1888 and 1889 they were the special prey of the Whitechapel murderer known as Jack the Ripper.

The crime of murder has never been particularly common in Britain, and during Victoria's reign the statistics are curiously consistent. Until 1876, the figures run at something over two hundred a year, from 1877 rather less than two hundred a year.

In 1888, when Jack the Ripper was at his peak, there were 190 murders. At this time, the police force of London was settling in after an era of uncertainty and dissatisfaction. In 1878 there had been a danger of the Metropolitan Police falling apart through inadequate pay (thirty shillings a week for a constable); but this had been partly rectified, 20,000 special whistles had been made and issued in 1884, and in 1886 much-needed re-arrangements of organization were carried out. At the end of 1888, for a population of 5,490,576 there was a police force of 14,261, consisting of thirty superintendents, 837 inspectors, 1,369 sergeants, and 12,025 constables. During the crucial year of 1888, twenty-seven policemen had died, mainly of exposure to the elements, and 131 had been taken off their beats with sore feet. They arrested 75,807 people, of whom 22,711 were subsequently discharged (a depressingly high ratio), but amongst this number was not Jack the Ripper, though one or two men came forward proclaiming that they were. Compared with the present police force, the Metropolitan Police of the eighties was like the Keystone Cops compared to the unfailing heroes of innumerable television series. They found clues where there were none, they assiduously tracked down leads that were not leads, and they signally failed to reassure the population of Whitechapel.

There were eight murders in 1888 by Jack the Ripper. They were sexually motivated, and the main purpose was to remove the womb. At one time, it was hazarded that there was an economic motivation for the murders when it was found that an American was offering £20 a womb for medical research, but this notion did not persist. The first murder occurred in April, but it did not receive wide publicity. On the second murder in August the press went to town. They were to suffer from a surfeit of murders and what with a constant stream of inquests and investigations, editors and reporters – and consequently readers – were to become confused, and the cases overlapped in a haphazard fashion so that it is difficult today to discern which murder is being discussed.

Confusion was assisted by the repetition of a pattern. The women were almost interchangeable, in their thirties or forties,

part-time prostitutes with a penchant for the bottle, living rough
or living in lodging houses. They also went by a variety of
names. Martha Turner went by the name of Emma, she was
aged about thirty-five, and lived at 4 Star Place, Star Street,
Commercial Road. Her husband had left her thirteen years before, and an initial allotment of twelve shillings a week had
been reduced to two and sixpence. To make ends meet, Mrs
Turner had gone on the streets. She was the second Whitechapel murder, and no connection was seen with the first of the
murders, that of Mrs Smith on 3 April. A friend of Mrs Turner's, 'Pearly Poll', declared that on August bank holiday the
pair of them had been to a public house with a couple of soldiers
from Wellington Barracks, and dutifully she went with the
police to the barracks and picked out two. Mrs .Turner died
from thirty-nine stab wounds.

On Friday morning, 31 August, a third body was discovered
by a carman of the firm of Pickford's. 'She looks to me to be
either dead or drunk,' he said when he went to summon help,
'but, for my part, I think she is dead.' The head had been almost
severed from the body; the gash was an inch wide. The lower
part of the abdomen had been ripped open. The Criminal Investigation Officer declared that 'the injuries are such that they
could only have been inflicted by a madman'. In her pockets
was a comb and soap; from her woollen flannel petticoat there
was an indication that she had been or was an inmate of a workhouse. The police surgeon, Dr Ralph Llewellyn, said, 'I have
never seen so horrible a case. She was ripped open just as you
see a dead calf at a butcher's shop. The murder was done by
someone very handy with the knife.' One of the local residents
had heard a call, 'Murder! Police!' not once, but five times, but
knowing the neighbourhood – Buck's Row, off Whitechapel
Road – she did not trouble to find out what it was all about, and
was pleased rather than otherwise when the shouts for help died
away.

The first policeman on the scene had been Police Constable
John Neil, number 97J. He stated that the body was lying on its
back, with clothes disarranged. The eyes were open, the bonnet
was off. She was wearing a reddish brown ulster with seven large

brass buttons, a brown dress that looked new, and a pair of stays. The first person to discover that the woman had been disembowelled was Inspector Spratley who went to the mortuary and casually turned up her clothes. For some reason, a theory was mooted that she was the victim of a 'High Rip' gang that specialized in blackmail.

A week later, Emily Annie Shiftney or Chapman was discovered in a passage leading to a common lodging house at 29 Hanbury Street, Spitalfields. She had been disembowelled and her entrails had been tied around her neck. Mrs Chapman was (apparently) about forty-five, five feet tall, with brown wavy hair. She had two teeth knocked out of her lower jaw, and rings had been wrenched off her third finger left hand. She was wearing lace-up boots, striped stockings, and two cotton petticoats. Like the previous victims she had no money on her – nothing but a handkerchief and two small combs – and like the others she was a low-cost prostitute. She lived at a common lodging house in Dorset Street with a sieve maker (known as Sievey), though, said the lodging house keeper, 'as a rule she occupied number 29 bed by herself'. The passage leading to the lodging house was always open, and was used by prostitutes regularly. Mrs Elizabeth Bell who lived at 31 Hanbury Street said: 'The house is open all night next door, and this poor creature was taken into the yard, and butchered, no doubt, by the same man who committed the others.' This time there seemed to be clues, and rumours circulated that at the scene of the crime there was a leather apron and a knive. This seemed to be confirmed when it was known that in the area there lived a man known as Leather Apron (the nickname is characteristic of the primitive or closely integrated society, whether it is Whitechapel in the dark days of the eighties or the Marlborough House set of the Prince of Wales). Leather Apron was lucky not to get lynched, as he was a born victim – about thirty, five foot three, dark, sallow, black hair and moustache, Jewish features, thickset, wearing old dirty clothing. His real name was John Piser, and he was arrested, but released when he convinced the police that he had nothing to do with the murder. Panic was spreading through the district, and through the police; arrests were carried out by large bands of constables – as many as fourteen men took part in one apprehension.

Mrs Chapman had gone out of the house at 1.45 a.m., saying, 'I'll soon be back again; I'll soon get the money for my doss.' One of the first on the scene was John Davis, who lived on the top floor. 'What was lying beside her I cannot describe – it was part of her body.' He called across to men who were making packing cases, 'Here's a sight; a woman must have been murdered.' James Kent reported, 'Her clothes were thrown back, but her face was visible. Her apron seemed to be thrown back over her clothes. I could see from the feet up to the knees. She had a handkerchief of some kind round her throat, which seemed sucked into her throat ... it seemed as if her inside had been pulled from her, and thrown at her. It was lying over her left shoulder.'

The public was fascinated. The Whitechapel murders had all the ingredients of high drama – they were lurid, sufficiently near to chill the spine but far enough away to be comforting; there was macabre detail that lent itself to headlines; and there was an ambivalence about it all, sexual and moral, the kind of provoking kinkiness that had made Stead's crusade into the white slave traffic such a best seller. The Whitechapel murders also gave newspaper editors the chance to use their unique double morality; they could cash in on the extra sales and yet wax choleric at sensationalism. *Reynold's Newspaper* had grown fat on yellow journalism, but it took time off, in the person of 'Northumbrian', to be scathing at its equivalent in another medium: 'Take an ordinary bill-posting hoarding, for example. It is decorated with bills printed with the greatest realism, representing murder and crime in every form. Here is a woman with blood gushing all over her dress in a bright crimson stream, the assassin standing above her, knife in hand, the gore dripping from the blade in large spots.' One of *Reynold's Newspaper*'s tame poets wrote it up: 'For murder is stalking red handed 'mid the homes of the weary poor.' The news boys ran up and down the streets calling out 'Latest Hawful Horror. A woman cut in pieces – full details – speshul,' and urchins played at cut-throats in the streets.

The murders gave scope for the racialists, and bands of hooligans went through Whitechapel with slogans – 'Down with the Jews'; 'It was a Jew who did it'; 'No Englishman did it.' A youth was chased through the streets, and the cry went up, 'The murderer is caught!'; and a blind man was grabbed when he struck a woman. The locals formed vigilantes, and woe betide anyone who looked suspicious. Someone, it was said, had written with chalk 'I have now done three, and intend to do nine more, and give myself up, and at the same time give my reasons for doing the murders,' and four people reported that they had seen this, though there is little evidence that there was at any time such a chalked message. Three medical students dressed up as women as decoys, concealing on their persons revolvers and daggers, and little men who had suffered all their lives under the indignity of being unnoticed blossomed – such as Mr Lusk the builder, who headed the Mile End Road Vigilance Committee.

The prostitutes who had died were treated sentimentally. At the inquest of one of them, the coroner asked the father 'Was she fast?' The father replied, 'No; I never heard of anything of that sort. She used to go with some young women and men that she knew, but I never heard of anything improper ... I don't think she had any enemies; she was too good for that.' The prostitutes themselves were more phlegmatic: 'Well, suppose I do get killed, it will be a good thing for me, for the winter is coming on and the life is awful. I can't leave it; nobody would employ me.' She had been on the game for twenty years – so much for the early Victorians' theories that three years on the streets killed them off.

Another thing that came to light was the barbaric state of Whitechapel amenities. In Whitechapel there was no mortuary, and bodies were taken to a shed adjoining the workhouse. In Battersea, too, bodies were left in a shed, where they decomposed to the disgust of the local inhabitants. There was also a curious feature of police procedure in that the examination of the body of 'Polly' Nicholls was carried out in an extremely haphazard way. The body was stripped in the 'mortuary' by two inmates of the workhouse without permission or authority. One of these men, a man named Hatfield, was asked, 'What did you take off first?' 'An ulster, which I put side on the ground. We then took the jacket off, and put it in the same place. The outside dress was loose, and we did not cut it. The bands of the petticoats were cut, and I then tore them down with my hand. I tore the chemise down the front. There were no stays.' It was stated at the inquest that the mortuary keeper was prone to fits. No wonder. When one considers the chaotic state of London before the reforms of 1894, it becomes remarkable that the police managed to function at all; had they managed to catch the Whitechapel murderer amidst the overlapping authorities and loyalties, the machinations of the vestries and the corruption of the notorious Metropolitan Board of Works, then it would have been a wonder indeed. It is interesting that in this year 1888 a parliamentary committee was enquiring into allegations that the existing authorities in London were spending ratepayers' monies to fight reform (said to be £19,550 between 1882 and 1885). The brickbats thrown at the Metropolitan Police for not catching Jack the Ripper were undeserved. The police were operating as efficiently as they were allowed to under the diabolical conditions of the London octopus.

Surprise, as Jean Cocteau has remarked, only works once. The murders continued, but the indignation evaporated. An arm floating down the Thames was greeted with languid imperturbability. Two more murders followed in late September, and in November Mary Jane Kelly was cut up in Dorset Street, Spitalfields, the street where Mrs Chapman had lodged. Toward the end of December, Rose Milettor Davis was killed in Poplar. Nothing else happened, and the East Enders began to breathe more easily. Then in July, Alice M'Kenzie was found murdered in Castle Alley off Whitechapel High Street. She was lying on her back, with her skirt and petticoat up, and a gash in her abdomen; it was not a deep wound, and it seemed as if the murderer had been interrupted. Like the previous locales, Castle Alley was dim, menacing, a place avoided by the respectable, and it contained the barrows of costermongers and tradesmen's carts. It was 180 yards long, but only a yard wide. The odds were against a discovery, especially as the man who normally minded the barrows until one o'clock in the morning had gone home ill at 11.30 p.m. The body was discovered at 12.50 a.m. by Police Constable Andrews.

The quiescent fears were aroused, and on the scene came Mr Monro, the commissioner of police, and he organized a proficient search of near-by lodging houses, though there remained no clues. The woman was like the others, about forty, five feet five, dark brown hair, and it was considered significant that like her predecessors she had a tooth missing; like the others, she was a semi-professional, living with a drunken loafer, John M'Cormack, for six or seven years, who had seen her last in the afternoon in bed. 'How came you in bed at four o'clock?' he was asked. He said that he was drunk. He gave her one shilling and eightpence, the eightpence being for the night's rent, but she did not pay the rent. Between ten and eleven o'clock in the evening, M'Cormack rose from his stupor sufficiently to ask, 'What am I to do? Am I to go and walk the streets as well?' Apparently not. His paramour went off, and consequently was murdered. 'I recognize her by her thumb,' said M'Cormack, 'which had been crushed at the top by a machine.'

Alice M'Kenzie was found, said the police, with her clothes up to her chin; her 'legs and body were exposed'. She was wearing odd stockings, a shawl, but no hat, which was also considered significant, as was the fact that she smoked a pipe in bed. She had been seen in Gun Street, Buck Lane and Dorset Street, no doubt touting for custom. Despite the personal intervention of the commissioner of police, the murderer was no nearer to being caught, though the vigilance committees that had fallen into lethargy during the six months since the last killing sprang into action. On Friday a man was seen struggling with a woman at Aldgate East underground station, and the vigilantes caught him, while a lively mob yelled, 'Lynch him!' The woman crawled away, and the man turned out to be a sailor from South Shields who declared that he had been robbed by the woman he was assaulting. A man named Brodie did not need any pursuit; he gave himself up. 'This is the ninth murder that I have committed in Whitechapel,' he told the police, 'but none of them have caused any trouble to my mind except the last one. What with that and a worm in my head that wriggles about I cannot stand it any longer.' Somewhat disappointed, the police categorized him as a 'wandering lunatic', and, more to the point, he had only been in England a fortnight having served a long spell of penal servitude abroad. At Leystown, in the Isle of Sheppey in the Thames estuary, Mrs Sarah Mortley had a shock. Falling asleep in a field she 'awoke with a sudden sensation of pain and found a strange man dressed in black in the act of cutting her throat with a knife'. However, it was a false alarm. It was not Jack the Ripper, but a relatively harmless interloper named George Cooper who was later arrested.

The Whitechapel murders created irrational panic, irrespective of the well-documented fact that all the victims belonged to a clearly-defined substratum of East End life. The most optimistic answer to the crimes was to disperse the entire population of Whitechapel, though the Reverend S. Barnett came up with a four-part solution:

(a) efficient police supervision for small thoroughfares
(b) adequate light and cleaning
(c) the removal of public slaughter houses 'the sights of which tend to brutalise a thickly crowded population, and to debase the children'
(d) tenements to be controlled by responsible landlords without sub-leases.

The general public were not given clinical details of the mutilations, though the popular press left little to the imagination. In the *British Medical Journal* of 29 September 1888, the injuries inflicted in the victim Chapman were enumerated. The following were removed by the murderer:

The central portion of the abdominal wall including the navel
Two-thirds of the bladder
One-third of the vagina and the connection with the womb
The womb.

The *British Medical Journal* also took seriously the notion that there was to be issued a gynecological book which included in its purchase price a womb.

In an October issue, the *BMJ* came out with a diatribe of the kind usually indulged in by the ecclesiasticals: 'We have had the heavy fringes of a vast population packed into dark places, festering in ignorance, in dirt, in moral degradation, accustomed to violence and crime, born and bred within touch of habitual immorality and coarse obscenity.'

The theory that the murders had medical backing was pursued in the pages of *The Scotsman* by Dr Batty Tuke in terms that make the writer's Christian name marginally apposite: 'Moreover, there is an incentive to wickedness productive of crime analogous to those now under consideration, which only those very intimately acquainted with the dark records of medical jurisprudence know of.'

The Whitechapel murders have never been completely forgotten, and Jack the Ripper has joined Sweeny Todd in the irreducible mythology of East End low life.

7

Perversion

Crimes Against the Person

'RAPE' was not a word much used in Victorian England, and none of the euphemisms so dear to the heart of the nineteenth-century journalist, whether he was writing for the august *Times* or the shoddy *Illustrated Police News* (the official-sounding title is entirely spurious), fits this most extreme of sexual crimes – with the exception of sexual murder. 'Outrage' was the favour-ite, but the roll of indignation-arousing nouns and adjectives was too often exhausted by minor misdemeanours, as witness, the Valentine Baker case of 1876, where a kiss and an arm round a waist was described by a member of parliament as 'one of the most scandalous and atrocious crimes ever committed'.

Rape has always enjoyed a somewhat ambiguous position in England. De Sade's dictum that every man wants to play the tyrant when he fornicates, the acceptance that defloration is one of the perquisites – for the man – of the bridal night, neither of these sits comfortably on the image of sexual intercourse as a pursuit of a kind or married virginity that reached its apotheosis in Victorian England, and its final manic epode in Coventry Patmore's poetical glorification of married love. English law over the centuries betrays this uncertainty over rape. The Romans introduced their own fierce civil law, in which rape was punished by death and the confiscation of goods, the Saxons perpetuated this code, but the Normans were more merciful – the rapist's testicles were cut off and his eyes were gouged out. A statute of Westminster of 1275 inexplicably dropped rape to the status of a trespass (two years' imprisonment plus a fine at the king's discretion) but, not surprisingly, this created such a vogue for rape that it was only in existence for ten years, whereupon rape was made a felony. In 1841 rape was made punishable by transportation (transportation was used as a punishment until 1846), and in 1861 the Offences against the Person Act made rape punishable by penal servitude, from a period of almost laughable inadequacy to life. Clearly a judgement on rape depended on circumstances. The law of England regarded it – and still does – as immaterial whether the woman raped is a young virgin in her prime or an old whore from the East End rookeries, and it was worse if rape was accompanied by threats of death, or if consent was won by fraud, misrepresentation, or impersonation of a woman's husband (in the darkness, as one philosopher maintained, all cats are grey).

It is a crime that has plummeted bright young lawyers into gloom and despondency. The German expert Dr Magnus Hirschfeld in the 1930s pronounced the verdict of many when he said that,

twenty-five years of practice in forensic medicine has convinced me that no allegation deserves to be treated with greater suspicion than that frequently made by girls, including pregnant girls, that they have been violated or raped ... Genuine experts on the subject are all agreed that it is extraordinarily difficult, if not impossible, to deflorate a woman or make her pregnant by the employment of sheer physical force, except where the woman's arms and legs are held by others or, as frequently happened during the last war [i.e., the First World War], she is tied down to a piece of furniture or the like.

All the facts regarding rape in Britain in the nineteenth century are suspect. Cases of genuine rape were unquestionably suppressed because of the shame; this was especially true during the last three decades of the century, when universal education meant that the more spicy cases were endlessly reported in periodicals devoted just for this purpose. Dubious cases of rape were also kept away from the prying eyes of outsiders. The statement 'Daddy I have been raped and there is a baby on the way' must have struck horror in middle-class hearts, and in such a case the odds are that no one outside the family ever heard of it. Similarly, the rape that failed was only haphazardly recorded; when there was no chance of catching the culprit, it was considered better to accept the indignity and avoid notoriety.

Henry Mayhew declared brightly that 'the number of rapes in England seems to be governed by excess of men over women', though it is difficult to see how he arrived at this conslusion. During the period he covered (1841–1850) the number of reported rapes was as follows:

1841   78
1842   118
1843   127
1844   127
1845   86
1846   139 (most in Middlesex and Yorkshire)
1847   97
1848   124 (Monmouth the worst county)
1849   121 (Nottinghamshire the best county)
1850   137

During this period, Mayhew maintains, the cases for 'carnally abusing' girls between the ages of ten and twelve were a mere fifty-six. This statement one simply cannot believe. References in the scurrilous periodicals to men with a taste for 'unripe fruit', and the existence of many establishments specializing in young girls, would seem to indicate there was more than one case of carnal abuse of a young girl every two months, as Mayhew maintains. 'Who is the greatest patron of the den of infantine prostitution, kept by Madame Marie, the French milliner, in Conduit Street?' asked the *Town* rhetorically (the answer is the Duke of Beaufort; and equally famous as a provider of female children (and young virgins were the *raison d'être* for these places) was 'Mother' Jacobs of Pickering-place. One woman of Bury-street, St James, was brash enough to advertise: 'Madame Dentiché, presenting compliments to Mr —, is anxious to inform him that she has just received a fresh importation of pretty little girls from Paris, and shall be extremely happy if Mr — will favour her with a visit, to see them.' In an effort to establish that old men were most partial to children, Thomson in his *Lectures on Medical Jurisprudence* found that of 1,000 seductions examined, 350 were by old men, and of these 318 were of children under twelve. If Mayhew's figures for the abuse of children are suspect, so are his figures for rape.

In the doggy world of working-class sex, rape shaded imperceptibly into other crimes against the person, and was rarely brought to the attention of the police except when murder was combined with rape. Crimes on the verge of murder were treated by magistrates with a bland good humour. A case occurred in 1876 when James Lane, a fishmonger, stabbed his 'paramour', Eliza Hitchin ('He shoved a knife into my back three times, but it did not hurt me much'). The magistrate's clerk commented sagely, 'Ah, you want to beg him off.' Lane had followed up this attack on his woman by stabbing her daughter three times in the back, and once in the arm. He was sent to prison for twelve months. In such circles as these, rape was a crime of hardly more than theoretical importance if it did not lead to death; on certain occasions, if it did lead to death, it could be glossed over as indecent assault. A curious case where this happened occurred in 1871 in Bathgate, near Edinburgh, where Mr Macpherson and his wife were over from Ireland for the harvest. They took holdings in a brothel, and while Mrs Macpherson 'was lying beside her husband who was dead drunk, several men abused her in a manner too shocking for publication, from the effects of which she died'. This seems to us unequivocal rape. However, the mystery deepens; her husband, who had been lying 'dead drunk' beside her and therefore presumably was in no position to say yea or nay to the other inmates of the brothel was fined seven shilling and sixpence, or seven days, for 'breach of the peace', while the three men who 'abused her in a manner too shocking for publication' were collared for 'indecent assault'.

This interesting and revealing case was reported in a fairly short-lived scabrous journal called *Day and Night* (1871–2), which carried on the tradition of the pornographic magazines by having a line engraving of a Titian or a Raphael nude on the cover. Where the pornographic journals had no hesitation about calling a spade a spade, *Day and Night* was deftly suggestive; like its contemporary *Reynold's*, it was content to imply the worst, and at the same time it conducted vendettas against rival newspapers and periodicals, and, in particular, *Sporting Life*, which drew its net over what even its most fervent devotees would hesitate to call sport. The odd facing-both-ways attitude of the Victorian press is demonstrated by the ethos of *Day and Night*; although its existence depended on the amount of scandal and violence it could compress into its columns, it could look askance at a recent edition of the seventeenth-century playwright John Webster in which 'all the words' were printed *in full* with as much indignation as the hoariest critic in the *Saturday Review*.

That rape is not an easy thing to accomplish *solus* was found out by James Rundle, a pit man, who intercepted in autumn 1876 a Miss Mary Smurthwaite, aged eighteen, who was returning home from church across the fields. Rundle pulled a red handkerchief over the lower part of his face, took his coat off, and threw it over Miss Smurthwaite's head. He put a rope with a slipknot over her right wrist, and threw her on her face; she asked if he was going to kill her. He carried her into a field of stubble, but she struggled, and he tied her clothes about her – they were voluminous and this cannot have been an easy operation – and dragged her through the stubble by her ankles. The girl continued to scream, and kicked at him, and Rundle was unable to accomplish what he set out to do. He simply went away. The girl, no doubt distressed, saw him adjusting his clothes in a nearby turnip field. When he was brought to court, it also counted against Rundle that he had stolen her umbrella as well as trying to commit rape, and offences against property, of course, were treated far more severely than offences against the person. .

What must not be overlooked are the mechanics of rape in Victorian England. The upper-class and middle-class ladies were, with their masses of enveloping and bulky clothing, one might surmise, almost rape-proof. In the fifties, the well-dressed lady wore from four to six petticoats of cambric. The crinoline on its wire or cane frame, forty-eight yards of material in one gown, bustles and half-bustles, corsets which were almost chastity belts, and combinations ('a new style of combining chemise and drawers') made of chamois leather, all these combined over the period to defeat the most valiant efforts to abuse a lady. Rape and attempted rape of a *lady* was quite rare. Although the lower orders were clad in the cast-offs of their betters, the almost paranoiac padding up and petticoating that made a lady's maid a necessity rather than a luxury for the well-heeled was not for them. On the debit side was the fact that drawers did not come into general use until Queen Vicoria was well and truly settled on the throne, and that when they did come in, they were 'split drawers', two legs. As the King of Sardinia remarked to the French Empress when a lady-in-waiting tripped over her crinoline, 'I am delighted to see, Madame, that your ladies do not wear drawers, and that the gates of paradise are always open.' 'He'll frighten the Queen [i.e., Victoria] out of her senses if he goes on so with her,' commented an English observer of this little tableau.

Rape was a product of the time, the place, and drink. One August evening at seven o'clock, Frederick Bonser, a private in the Coldstream Guards, 'effected his purposes' on Lucy Kercher, the wife of a labourer, in the neighbourhood of Aldershot. The time and the place had led Bonser to the belief that Mrs Kercher was easy game. 'A witness named Lee admitted that he passed the spot at the time, and that the prosecutrix called to him for help, but he passed on, making a coarse remark, which, with a subsequent explanation to the magistrate, showed that the witness had an exceedingly low opinion of the morality of the district.' Frederick Bonser was, in fact, unfortunate, in that he had picked on one of the rare lone women in the vicinity of Aldershot who was virtuous. The low opinion that the witness Lee had of the district – notwithstanding the cutting remarks of the magistrate, who, like most magistrates of the period, lived in the sliced-off world of the upper and middle-classes – was unquestionably justified.

About the same time, Ellen Bailey, a widow, was found

lying near Guildford Railway Station with her skull seriously fractured, the victim of rape or attempted rape. She had been harvesting – the harvesters were employed on a casual basis, their collective morality was low, and women travelling alone were fair game. On arrival at Guildford station she had asked the porter the time of the next train to Weybridge; there was no train until 6.40 a.m. the next day. George Walker, an engine cleaner, came up and said to her, 'I'll take you on my engine to Weybridge,' a fantasy that Mrs Bailey surprisingly believed (or so the case would indicate). He took her over the railway bridge, and on to a railway locomotive, where he 'attempted to take liberties with her'. Not succeeding, he turned the engine hose on her, called her names, and threw a ginger beer bottle at her, hitting her on the temple. When she was discovered, her life was despaired of. Walker was apprehended, and confronted with his victim; somewhat astonishingly, he was allowed to cross-examine her and accused her of being drunk; this accusation she denied. It was one of the characteristics of Victorian crime reporting that cases were picked up and dropped as the editor pleased, and that as soon as the juice was squeezed out they were discarded. Hence today's reader does not know of the outcome. Perhaps Mrs Bailey died, perhaps she had been drunk, perhaps she knew that the notion of riding to Weybridge on a locomotive was just a lark, perhaps it was a simple seduction that had gone awry – no doubt the engine cleaner had had previous experience of women harvesters who were travelling alone.

No such ambiguity exists about the Jane Shore case. Jane Shore, aged thirty-five, lived in Shoreditch, and was the wife of an engineer in China. On her way to see a friend she visited the Lord Napier public house in Clapton, and rapidly downed a succession of ale, beer and gin. Five men volunteered to see her to her friend's home. On the way, a foreman of an oil works intercepted the party. 'What are you going to do with that woman?' he asked. 'Oh, she likes it,' one of the men replied. They threw Mrs Shore down a twenty-five-foot hollow, and, watched by a considerable crowd, the five men raped her and beat her, without anyone interfering, until she was nearly dead.

The prosecution criticized the onlookers for not interfering, but the bewigged and supercilious lawyers did not live in the jungle. 'It is not in country,' wrote the sociologist Charles Booth, 'but in town that "terra incognita" needs to be written on our social maps.'

In most cases in the nineteenth century, rape was not the coefficient of sadism. It was a product of circumstances, the circumstances being poverty (in the mid 1880s in London this condition ran at thirty-five per cent of the population) and ignorance and their concomitants – dirt, amorality and brutality. In Southwark in 1891 between Blackfriars Bridge and London Bridge the poverty level was sixty-eight per cent. Rape was an extension of the general sexual ethos of the poorest, and the poorest were those who did not work or who spent the bulk of their money on drink. The prospect of never working produced a level of immorality that has few echoes in the twentieth century, an immorality that reflected a complete oblivion to right and wrong, to any kind of social adjustment, to any kind of logical behaviour pattern. The pressures that had kept the lowest classes down were no longer applied; from the middle of the century onward there existed a substratum of the unemployed and the unemployable that was not amenable to the help of the philanthropists and was always in danger of eruption, either on the grand scale, such as the Hyde Park riots in the late sixties, or the Trafalgar Square riots of 1886 (which even alarmed left-wing extremists with a vested interest in upsetting the established order – H. M. Hyndman called it 'monstrous'), or on a smaller scale, manifesting itself in pointless brutality, extreme promiscuity, and their extensions, fortified by cheap and plentiful drink, incest and rape.

Each age has its subterranean layer, including our own. In the back streets of Whitechapel and Walworth, in Cable Street and the ghettos of Notting Hill and North Kensington, London displays in the twentieth century a life that differs from nineteenth-century slumdom only in the pigmentation of the inhabitants. The French journalist, Francis Wey, one of the most perspicacious of foreigners who came prying into London's cesspools in the fifties, noted with disgust the filthy condition of the working classes, their clothes caked with layers of shining grime, and their women lying about 'higgledy piggledy in the mud, hollow-eyed and purple cheeked, their ragged clothing plastered with muck'. What was rape in this milieu? Hardly more, indeed, than trespass.

Rape was clearly a crime against the person, but its punishment depended entirely on what class the person raped belonged to. The rape perpetrated by a working-class man on a working-class woman was treated by magistrates as a rather humorous interlude – if the case ever arrived in court at all. 'Sexual assault' is a euphemism for the rape that fails, and it was more a province of the higher reaches of society, if only because its intent was foiled by stronger inhibitions. Sexual assault depended on the time and place. It is clear from innumerable cases appearing in such periodicals as the *Illustrated Police News* that most assaults were unpremeditated and were carried out in conditions where repressions were lifted.

The coming of the railways provided such an environment. The solitary girl or woman in a railway carriage became a prey for the Victorian sybarite, a circumstance that was not overlooked by the pornographers – as, for example, *Raped on the Railway* of 1894, about the girl who was raped and flagellated on the 'Scotch express'. Three factors combined to make the railway carriage an ideal site for sexual adventure: (a) no means of immediate access for rescuers of the assaulted girl – the corridor train is a fairly recent innovation; (b) the extraordinary fact of a man being alone with a young woman whom he did not know; and (c) the darkness of a tunnel (lit railway carriages were rare). This triple combination was sufficient, more than sufficient, to set middle-aged and middle-class pulses racing.

It is clear that many so-called assaults were never brought to court, that many so-called assaults were bogus, and that many neurotic women imagined that they had been interfered with in the unlighted sojourn of the tunnels of the British railway system. A new type of woman arose, one with a demure and innocent face who was aware that not only was rape the hardest thing to prove in a court of law, but one of the hardest to disprove. For magistrates and juries, indecent assault on the railway was replete with problems.

Characteristic was the case of Samuel Harry, a respectable innkeeper, who was accused of indecently assaulting Mary Kennedy in an unlighted railway carriage on the Furness Railway as it was passing through a mile-long tunnel. He was fined £9 14s., or two months in jail. Thomas Higginbottom did much the same thing to Rachel Kerwin. Defending counsel claimed that the charge was trumped up, and that Rachel Kerwin kept a house of ill-fame; this was proved to be true – she had a stable of eight or nine girls. Nevertheless, Higginbottom was fined £4 or four months (a curiously unbalanced equation). Mr Greenwood, trying the case, told Higginbottom that had the woman been respectable he would have given him six months. He also delivered a homily; he himself 'always made it a rule to leave any railway carriage where he was left alone with a woman and he should advise all gentlemen to do the same'.

One man who most heartily would have wished that he had carried out this injunction was Colonel Valentine Baker.

Valentine Baker was a professional soldier, interested not only in the perquisites of officer life, but in the study of military history and tactics. He emerged from a minor war in Africa and a major war in Europe – the Crimean War – with credit; he was not much over thirty when he acquired his lieutenant colonelship. He visited Persia, noted the power of Russia in the Middle East, and wrote a book about it; with a rich wife and a handy selection of powerful friends, his appointment as assistant quartermaster general at Aldershot opened up the widest of vistas. Nothing, it would seem, was needed to fill his cup.

On 17 June 1876, he boarded a train at Liphook for London. The first-class carriage he entered contained a single occupant, Miss Dickinson, aged twenty-two. Not having read the advice of an obscure provincial law-giver, Colonel Baker did not retrace his steps. He sat down opposite the girl, and asked if she would like the window shut. They chatted in a civilized manner, and in Colonel Baker's eyes the acquaintanceship was blooming nicely. From mere trivialities, the conversation, on his part, took a more personal turn, and past Woking he was sufficiently encouraged to put his arm round her waist and kiss her. Miss Dickinson pulled the communication bell, or tried to, but with typical railway perversity it was broken. Outside each carriage was a footboard, and Miss Dickinson clambered on to this, while Baker held her there, stopping her from falling off the train. During this time, Miss Dickinson was screaming for help. 'If you get in,' Baker told her (Miss Dickinson's evidence), 'I will get out by the other door. Then everything will be all right.' Not for Miss Dickinson. When the train was eventually brought to a halt – a man working on the railway line had observed her hanging from the carriage and had raised the alarm – Baker asked, 'Please don't say anything about what has happened, or you will get me into trouble. Just tell the guard you were frightened.' This was not good enough for the girl. When the guard asked her why she was hanging in a perilous position from a carriage footboard, she said, 'This man has insulted me, and will not leave me alone.'

A clergyman accompanied Miss Dickinson during the rest of the run to London, and two gentlemen sat guard over Baker, who was beginning to realize the enormity of his offence – he had actually *kissed* a young unmarried lady without permission. Miss Dickinson did not press any charges until she had talked it over with three brothers, a doctor, a lawyer and a subaltern in an inferior regiment (Colonel Baker had hailed from the Tenth Hussars, a lordly prestige-laden regiment). On his arrest, Colonel Baker declared, 'If by any act of mine I have caused Miss Dickinson annoyance, I beg to express my most unqualified regret. Still, I solemnly declare that what she has told you has been under the influence of exaggerated fear and alarm.' Throughout the trial, he steadfastly refused to let his counsel cross-examine Miss Dickinson, and she was handled with kid gloves by everyone concerned. She had herself a field day. She had been held by the waist and kissed. What was the nature of this kiss, and how high was it in the annals of crime? Should a kiss in a railway compartment, and not even a tunnel, be more heinous than a kiss at a party or a kiss in bed? How should it compare against another crime against the railway? (In the following month a labourer got seven years' penal servitude for throwing a stone at the property of the Great Western Railway – insults to the railway companies and damage to their image were indeed subject to grotesque punishment.)

The judge at the trial of Baker ponderously fulminated on kissing:

If a man kisses a woman against her will, and with criminal passion or intent, such an act is an indecent assault. As you know, there are some kisses which are entirely proper. Thus, the kiss of a daughter by her father is a holy one, and the kiss of a playful assembly of young people may be perfectly harmless. But a kiss that gratifies or excites passion is undoubtedly indecent. Therefore, if you think that such was the reason of the conduct with which the accused is charged, you should find a bill for indecent assault. You must then also find a bill for common assault, since the mere laying of a man's hand upon a woman without her consent amounts to this.

The judge was Mr Justice Brett, and it never seemed to occur to him that here was a case that was farcical in the extreme, even though Colonel Baker could scarcely be described as 'a playful assembly of young people'. The Baker case was the triumph of Victorian triviality, the cumbrous machinery of law directed on behalf of a rather smug period damsel against a distinguished fifty-year-old man who had had a rush of blood to the head and who was destined to be ruined by the most minor of peccadilloes. Mr Justice Brett played the case up to its utmost; so commented sardonically the author of *London in the Sixties*:

when Mr Justice Brett began his charge to the jury with, 'A man we looked to as protector of our women and children' there was not a soldier present who did not internally vow that henceforth – be it a first-class or third-class compartment, be it in Piccadilly Circus or the British Museum, – a woman should be his constant care, and, if necessary, any tadpole that lawfully pertained to her.

The Miss Dickinsons of the period come and go, like so many phantoms:

a winsome young lady of distinctly prepossessing appearance. Her costume was of dark silk, trimmed with beads and bugles, a feathered black hat, and lavender gloves. She gave her evidence in a silvery musical voice, and without the slightest hesitation. It was clear that she had nerved herself for the very trying ordeal confronting her, and her modest and ladylike demeanour won the sympathy of all.

What, one wonders, was she getting out of it? Colonel Baker was an honourable soldier – his refusal to put Miss Dickinson in an embarrassing position is some proof of this. It is possible that she afterward regretted her precipitate action, though after the trial she slid into utter obscurity; one does not know whether this traumatic experience did anything to her. Henry Hawkins, counsel for the defence, could do hardly more than make a pathetic appeal to the jury, constrained as he was by his client's refusal to hammer at Miss Dickinson, and comment on the ribald enthusiasm of the mob who liked nothing better than the spectacle of one of their betters biting the dust of humiliation. Hawkins seems to have revelled in this humiliation; Baker had 'a deeply contrite heart . . . professes the most profound regret . . . deep and lasting remorse . . . terrible anxiety'. The judge went one better:

Prisoner at the bar, when this appalling story was first published, a thrill of horror rang through the country at learning that a young and innocent girl, travelling by a public conveyance, had been compelled to risk her life in order to protect herself from gross outrage. . . . It may perhaps be suggested that this libertine outrage has defiled this virtuous victim. It has not done so. Miss Dickinson leaves this court as pure and as innocent as ever; and, not only without a stain on her character, but with an added lustre – a fresh measure of glory – to her equipment of youth and beauty . . .

The jury, no doubt wishing, individually, that they could get Miss Dickinson alone in a railway carriage, fell for this rodomontade, and found Baker guilty. The judge awarded him a year's imprisonment, plus a fine of £500, plus the costs of the prosecution. To some, this was not enough. 'The description which the lady gave of the transaction was calculated to excite a feeling of the highest indignation, and that indignation would be increased by the sentence, which was really no punishment at all, for one of the most scandalous and atrocious crimes ever committed.' So spoke the honourable Member of Parliament for Stoke, Edward Kenealy, a lawyer who had been disbarred be-

cause of dubious practices during the notorious Tichborne
claimant case and who was disliked so much that when he was
elected to the House of Commons he could find no member to
introduce him (he had also done a year in prison through ill-
treating his illegitimate son). Charles Reade, novelist and one-
time trader in violins, who had been flogged silly as a schoolboy,
and thereafter was always a supporter of the underdog, put his
finger on the mixed moralities of the period: 'Every day men of
the lower orders commit two thousand such assaults on women
of the lower orders, and it is thought so little of that they are
rarely brought to justice. When they are, it is to a magistrate,
and not to a jury, that the women apply. It is dealt with on the
spot by a small fine or a very short imprisonment.'

For a man who had been through the terrors of the Crimean
War, a year's imprisonment was no great privation, especially
as he was 'a first-class misdemeanant', which meant that he had
a room and not a cell, could eat food from an outside restaurant
and not bother with the prison gruel, and could receive visitors
every day, though not pay visits. The Duke of Cambridge who
had, early in Baker's career, paid reluctant tribute to the sheer
professionalism of the man, tried to ease Baker's suffering by
advising the Queen to accept Baker's resignation. The Queen,
however, kind as she was over the fall of sparrows – such as the
lowly on her staff, the errant chambermaid, the fornicating
coachman – was severe on those who should know better.
In the *London Gazette* of 2 August 1875 final doom was pronounced: 'Lieut.-Colonel and Brevet-Colonel Valentine Baker,
half-pay, late Tenth Hussars, has been removed from the
Army, her Majesty having no further occasion for his services.'

Baker, announced the *South London Press* in lordly fashion
in between frowning at the spectacle of a performing bear in
Battersea and cock fighting in the north of England, 'purged
his misdoing by a painful incarceration'. Eventually, he was re-
habilitated. His old regiment welcomed him back, the clubs
sacred to the armed forces of the Crown readmitted him into
their precincts, though the Queen held on to her crumbling
ground; she had never quite forgotten that it was a group of
army officers that had first got the Prince of Wales into trouble

(and that, fifteen years ago, had precipitated her husband's death, or so she had believed).

After his wife's death, Baker hired himself out as a mercenary and became a lieutenant-general in the service of the Sultan of Turkey, and when he died in 1887 he was inspector-general of the Egyptian constabulary. Colonel Baker had been spiked on the spears of Victorian hypocrisy as surely as if his head had been placed on Temple Bar. When every officer in India had his kept native woman, when Aldershot itself was not exempt from the incursions of the high-priced lady of pleasure, Colonel Baker had, by propositioning a demure twenty-two-year-old girl in a first-class carriage, made himself a martyr. He should have travelled third-class – where the women were not so fussy about a bit of slap and tickle.

No one today would proclaim that Valentine Baker's sin was particularly heinous. Is, as the judge put it, 'a kiss that gratifies or excites passion ... undoubtedly indecent'? In this view he was not in a minority. Would that he and his like could have made the logical extensions, would that he could have proposed that a beating that gratifies or excites passion was undoubtedly indecent. Corporal punishment in the nineteenth century was not only a means of keeping order among the naturally rebellious, but a pleasure with strong sexual overtones. As the victims were usually children, it was an occupation that suited the self-righteous who had the backing of that most disgusting maxim, 'Spare the rod and spoil the child'. Workhouse masters and men in charge of orphanages waxed joyfully in this situation. In January 1885 Labouchere's journal *Truth* uncovered an unpleasant scandal at the ironically named House of Rest for Suffering Children near Bristol. A young child had been beaten, and, surprisingly, the case had come to court. The magistrate related:

The complainant was brought to my house by a policeman, and I had her stripped. I found very heavy bruises on both arms, and also a very heavy bruise on her lip. Her two hands were badly bruised and bleeding, and she also had the mark of a blow on the forehead. There were marks on the shoulder blades. The marks were black and blue, and all kinds of colour.

The complacency of the defendant beggars description: 'The wickedness found in young children is almost incredible. I found two children two years of age using the most profane language, and clamouring for the gin bottle.' This view that children of two were arbiters of their own destiny was not, alas, uncommon.

Some parents found themselves unable to dish out the whippings and the beatings that they thought society demanded and expected, and considered that this argued some weakness in themselves. They therefore sought for a surrogate; they did not have far to look, for in the advertisement columns of the newspapers there were women like Mrs Walter, of 53 Oakfield Road, Clifton, Bristol, who provided a respectable chastising service for unruly daughters at £100 a year, or a little more for girls over twenty.

The ambiguously worded advertisement was spotted by a newspaper editor, who replied in the person of a lady who wanted her daughter disciplined. He also sent a reporter to see Mrs Walter. Mrs Walter was tall and strong, wearing a dress reminiscent of one of the nursing orders, and displayed a medallion representing the Good Shepherd. Becomingly reticent in the presence of reporters, to those in need of her professional services she was revealing to a degree that possibly she did not realize.

The props of her discipline were 'a strong narrow table, straps (waistband with sliding straps, anklets, and wristlets), cushions, and good long pliable birch rod'. She told the girl 'to prepare by removing her dress, knickers, and corset, and putting on the dressing gown (hind part before)'. There is a familiar ring about Mrs Walter in action; both pornography and the reminiscences of public school masters and boys are echoed:

Taking the birch, I measure my distance, and, standing at the side, proceed to strike slowly but firmly. By moving gently forward each stroke is differently placed, and six strokes may be enough if well given with full force. If the fault has been such as to need severe correction, then I begin on the other side and work back again. For screams, increased strokes must be given. If a girl tries very hard to bear it bravely, then, perhaps, I give ten instead of twelve.

This place was an ostensibly respectable establishment that advertised openly, that was not ashamed of its prospectus, that existed and was tolerated in a high-class residential district. Today the motivations of Mrs Walter, real name Smith, are easy to ascertain. It is difficult to discern any difference in tone between this proud exposé of a service to harassed mothers and an extract from one of the hack works on flagellation:

What a difference between high and low life in this particular! To see a vulgar woman, when provoked by her children, seize them as a tiger would a lamb, rudely expose their posteriors, and correct them with an open hand, or a rod more like a broom than a neat collection of twigs elegantly tied together; while a well-bred lady coolly and deliberately brings her child or pupil to task; and when in error, so as to deserve punishment, commands the incorrigible Miss to bring her the rod, go on her knees, and beg, with uplifted hands, an excellent whipping. . .

The extensive literature of flagellation can be seen not to be just fantasy but a reflection of life that really existed in Victorian suburbia.

Flagellation

Primarily intended as a punishment, flagellation became, for generations of schoolboys, a form of sexual pleasure; it was also looked upon as one of the weapons in the relatively sparse medical cabinet. In 1839 Dr J. G. Milligan wrote in his *Curiosities of Medical Experience*, 'As a remedy it was supposed to reanimate the torpid circulation of the capillary or cutaneous vessels, to increase muscular energy, promote absorption, and favour the necessary secretions of our nature ... flagellation draws the circulation from the centre of our system to the periphery.' To Dr Milligan flagellation was somewhere at the level of urtication – stinging with nettles – which was also designed to reanimate 'the torpid circulation of the capillary or cutaneous vessels'. In reality, Milligan was only one of many for whom flagellation was a somewhat dubious remedy. He does not mention it as an instrument of education.

If one accepts the premise that ninety-nine per cent of the important politicians in the nineteenth century went to a public school, then one must accept the fact that almost ninety-nine per cent of politicians were acquainted with the pains and the pleasures of the block. To get through the public schools – especially Eton – without a whipping, was a considerable achievement. In any case, the fact of being flogged brought a certain cachet; *vide* the Eton Block Club, membership of which was confined to those who had undergone 'ordeal by birch' on not less than three occasions. (In 1836 three Old Etonians, including the Marquis of Waterford, went to Eton and stole the dreaded block so that it could serve as the official throne of the president of the club.)

The discovery that pain and pleasure are qualities that can, on occasions, be interchangeable was one that was made many centuries ago but was hardly thought a suitable matter to cogitate upon. At its simplest level, a thrashing is an uncomfortable business – if it is left off at a certain point. If a thrashing is persisted in, and if the whole affair is carried out as a ritual, then strange elements creep in. Few writers have written about the actual sensations of flagellation; one of the most acute is the psychologist E. Wulffen writing in 1913:

... Although the heavy blows may not at first induce erotic pleasure, the initial pain soon gives way to a sensation of warmth which envelops the whole of the seat like a soft, warm blanket, producing a pleasurable sensation and this may easily connect up with the sexual area. Boys after a sound thrashing are often surprised by the subsequent pleasant sensation of warmth in the seat and for this reason they sometimes endeavour to obtain a repetition of the chastisement which may ultimately affect them sexually.

The ritual flagellations of the public schools were part of the ethos that included fagging, filth and frugality. The bullying of small boys by big boys often verged on torture. One writer, Rowland Williams, was literally scalped as a denizen in the notorious Long Chamber and was disfigured for life through being tossed in a blanket. For many, years at Eton remained etched in the memory throughout life, often laying down a subsequent pattern of existence. For James Fitzjames Stephen, later a great legal luminary, 'the process taught me for life the lesson that to be weak is to be wretched, that the state of nature is a state of war'.[1] His brother, Leslie, instigator of the *Dictionary of National Biography*, professional agnostic, and father of Virginia Woolf said that bullying would not cease until men stopped 'dwelling more fondly upon their schooldays in proportion to the remoteness of their memory'.[2]

The most notorious figure in the annals of Etonian floggery is unquestionably Dr John Keate, and although his reign ended before Victoria assumed the throne, his effect remained on many nineteenth-century worthies. In 1841, a very special Eton dinner was held in Willis' Rooms to commemorate four centuries of the school. Present was Gladstone, who had himself been, rather startlingly, flogged at Eton. He was sitting nearly opposite the aged Dr Keate, who had abandoned 'the fancy dress, partly resembling the costume of Napoleon and partly that of a widow woman' and 'was now garbed as a commonplace Early Victorian parson'.[3] Gladstone wrote that 'in those days at public dinners, cheering was marked by gradations'. Queen Victoria was going through an unpopular phase, and applause for her was unenthusiastic. Wrote Gladstone:

I suppose it to be beyond doubt that of the assembled company the vastly predominating majority had been under his sway at Eton ... it is equally beyond doubt that to the persons of the whole of them, with the rarest exceptions, it had been the case of Dr Keate to administer the salutary correction of the birch. But upon this occasion, when his name had been announced, the scene was indescribable. ... The roar of cheering had a beginning, but never knew satiety or end. Like the huge waves of Biarritz, the floods of cheering continually recommenced; the whole process was such that we seemed all to have lost our self-possession and to be hardly able to keep our seats.[4]

Gladstone as a supporter of systematic flagellation is a figure that comes to one as a slight surprise (was his obsession for chopping down trees some kind of compensation formula?).

Dr Keate, standing a little over five feet in height, brought to the art of flagellation a manic devotion. His record is said to have been ninety at one swoop, and even if there were no secret smokers or drinkers or dullards at their Latin grammars Keate would be sure to find an excuse for a flogging. He administered the birch to a number of candidates for confirmation, and when one of them protested, Keate declared 'You are only adding to your offence by profanity and lying.' The scene had something of the air of a gladiatorial bout of ancient Rome. As the Reverend W. H. Tucker stated, 'The execution hour was an amusement; and there was usually a large attendance of Fourths and Removes, with a scanty sprinkling of Lower Fifths, to see their friends under the amelioration system, and to note how they bore it. Occasionally an Upper Fifth came under the triangle, and the attendance in that case was considerably enlarged.'

'A cry arose behind me: "Hullo! there's going to be a swishing!" and a general rush was made towards the upper end of the schoolroom ... several dozens of fellows clambered upon forms and desks to see Neville corrected, and I got a front place, my heart thumping, and seeming to make great leaps within me, as if it were a bird trying to fly away through my throat.' So wrote James Brinsley-Richards (*Seven Years at Eton*, 1883). The master here was a Mr Carter, and the victim was a curly-headed boy with a squint ('which enhanced the comical expression of his countenance').

There were two 'holders down', and during Brinsley-Richards' time (1857–64) the rod, which he imagined as a handful of twigs, was nearly five feet long, three feet of handle and two of 'bush'. The sound of the six lashes inflicted on the unfortunate Neville was 'like the splashings of so many buckets of water'. To his credit, the scene made Brinsley-Richards feel almost faint, but the stoicism of the public schoolboy soon came to his rescue and he could watch subsequent executions 'not only with indifference, but with amusement'. This aspect of flagellation – the pleasure given to the spectators – is one that has rarely been written about, and it is rather surprising that in consequence of it, the educated portion of the nineteenth century were not wholly *voyeurs*. It is evident that the physiological sensations of young Brinsley-Richards watching the whipping of Neville were akin to those of his elders viewing the *poses plastiques* of the West End of London or of empire-builders viewing donkey-and-woman exhibitions in Cairo or the performances laid on in India.

The opportunities for being swished in nineteenth-century Eton were many and various. One of the most curious was the performance known as 'shirking'. Schoolboys were allowed to boat on the river, they were allowed to walk on the terrace of Windsor Castle, but *all* approaches to the river or the terrace were out of bounds. Even more idiotic, the approaches to the shops were out of bounds. Every schoolboy was therefore, in the eyes of Eton jurisdiction, a felon, when he went to cash a money-order or when he went to purchase a new pair of stockings. However, there was a way out of this *impasse*; if a boy saw a master approaching he would pop into a nearby shop, and the master would pretend that he had not noticed him. This was known as shirking. If the boy was too slow or too half-witted and the master came on to him in a manner that made recognition imperative, then the boy would be whipped for 'not shirking'.

The mania for corporal punishment was not governed by common sense or age. 'I had the honour this morning of soundly flogging a major in His Majesty's service,' declared the eighteenth-century headmaster Goodall complacently. There were occasions when the unwritten laws revolving around the block were contravened. In 1856 a boy named Morgan Thomas was caught smoking, a heinous sin for which a flogging was the just deserts. During this period, Dr Goodford was headmaster, and, preparing to ply the rod, he was aghast to find that the culprit refused to submit, pleading prior instructions from his father. Dr Goodford promptly expelled the boy, confidently expecting the father to back him on account of the boy's manifest cowardice. Mr Thomas, however, demanded that his son should return to Eton. A violent correspondence broke out in the columns of *The Times*; an editorial article in *The Times* made the point that Mr Thomas had 'no right to send his boys to Eton with a secret proviso that they will not submit to the system of discipline there enforced, and then to complain when, under such circumstances, they are summarily dismissed'. It would have only been fair of *The Times* to supply Mr Thomas with a list of the top schools where flogging was not the system of discipline enforced. Even Dr Arnold's new Christian school for the rising middle classes, Rugby, used the whip as the ultimate deterrent.

There were few nineteenth-century writers of autobiographies who had been to Eton and who did not confess with sometimes nauseating coyness that they had been whipped by this or that personage. Or, indeed, any other school. In 1845 the historian J. R. Green went to Magdalen Grammar School, which was in the precincts of the Oxford college. 'I was set to learn Latin grammar from a grammar in Latin! and a flogging every week did little to help me. I was simply stupefied, – for my father had never struck me, and at first the cane hurt me like a blow, – but the "stupid stage" soon came, and I used to fling away my grammar into old churchyards, and go up for my "spinning" as doggedly as the rest.'[5] During the Thomas controversy, one elderly flagellant wrote to the *Morning Post*:

Now, I can vouch that, from the earliest ages to the days of the immortal Keate, and thence to those of the present headmaster, they have, one and all, appealed to the *very seat of honour*. 'Experientia docet.' And, mark me, flogging, used with sound judgment, is the only *fundamental* principle upon which our large schools can be properly conducted. I am all the better for it, and am, therefore – ONE WHO HAS BEEN WELL SWISHED.

The Latin tag inserted into the body of the text is the hall-mark of this type. Latin and Greek were virtually the only two subjects taught at Eton; even mathematics was lowly, and the master who took it was considered of a mediocre cast of mind. *Punch* adopted the progressive standpoint and in doing so probably lost many thousands of readers. 'When we find a manly sentimentalist advocating the rod, we generally discover that he has been at a public school; and we see pretty clearly that his eulogy of flogging proceeds from an opinion that it has made an

exceedingly fine and clever fellow of himself; an opinion sometimes very erroneous.'

It was perhaps fortunate that flogging was only one element
in the maelstrom of cruelty in which the public schoolboy incessantly whirled, and could not therefore be isolated except by those few who found it a transgressing experience.
At Winchester, the newest arrival – known as the 'junior in
chambers' – had to light the fire, call all the boys in the room,
and put out the prefects' washing gear. The fire was laid on
'dog irons' and was difficult to light, as no tongs were allowed in
the ritual. When the boy arrived he was given a pair of 'tin
gloves' – one of the elder boys took a red-hot brand, and made a
mark down all the fingers and around the wrists. If, in the
future, he made a mess of his fire-lighting, the 'tin gloves' would
be reapplied. The elder boys also organized 'bolstering matches'
between the youngsters; the object of the bolstering match was
to take the skin off one's opponent's nose with the rough end of
the bolster. At Harrow in 1853, a monitor named Platt gave a
younger boy Stewart thirty-one cuts with a cane, disfigur-
ing him and injuring him so much that he had to be removed
from the school. It was doubtful whether there was much to
choose between the amenities of the nineteenth-century public
schools, whether it was Harrow with its 'bare and dirty rough-
cast corridors, ill drained latrines, the stuffy studies with wired
windows, the cheerless refectory'[6] or Eton where, said the historian Sir Edward Creasy, 'the lads underwent privations that
might have broken down a cabin-boy, and would be thought
inhuman if inflicted on a galley slave'.

Each school had its special rods. The Winchester rods consisted of four apple twigs tied fast into grooves at the top of a
wooden handle, and it was believed that they were boiled with
mutton to get grease into them and then tucked up the college
chimney to toughen. 'By Jove!' wrote the naturalist Frank
Buckland, marvelling, 'they were tough as whalebone!'[7]

There were few masters immune from the flogging fever. Of
Ridding of Winchester, related his successor, Dr Wordsworth,
'it was not unusual of him after morning school to castigate not
less than fifty boys at a time'. Dr Wooll of Rugby 'polished

off' thirty-eight delinquents in fifteen minutes, and at Harrow Dr Longley flogged fifty boys one morning for going to a steeplechase. When Keate died in 1852 the *Annual Register* described him as 'the eminent former of the minds of the most intellectual and aristocratic youth of Britain'. The floggers were truly a sacred order; 'Let us meet,' said one to another – Dr Gabell to Dr Parr – 'and quaff a bumper to the good cause of flogging.' The minor schools emulated this tradition; the hack novelist R. E. Francillon relates of his own school that 'it was a common thing to see a boy seized by the collar of his jacket and, for some infinitesimal offence, publicly and savagely flogged all over the schoolroom, to the scattering of spectators and the upsetting of forms, till the splintered cane could do its work no more'.[8]

Flogging in the nineteenth-century public schools was sadism sanctioned by society, sometimes a sado-masochistic pact between the teacher and the taught. One enterprising lad had the face of his executant painted on his buttocks before the event; another boy, to avoid pain, used a prophylactic ointment that turned his buttocks black. Flagellation in the public schools was a conspiracy, a ritual that marked off the upper classes with a savage precision, a tribal procedure that was almost as good as circumcision in denoting the transition from one stage to another. In other respects, school days were easygoing; if one could avoid the trip wires that led to punishment (such as 'not shirking') then, indeed, especially if one had the ability to learn Greek and Latin parrot fashion, schooling was not onerous in terms of boy-hours spent learning.

The ceremony was sometimes carried out with a cosy informality. At lesser times, the lower master was called upon to officiate. On one occasion the lower master was a man named Durnford, and he was once heard to enquire of a boy on the block, 'Have you seen your uncle lately?' a question that has an almost surrealist ring, as have the pet jokes of these strange men. 'On one occasion,' wrote the Reverend A. G. l'Estrange (*Eton Days*) 'when a fellow was being punished for playing cards, as the Doctor (Hawtrey) was "letting it in" he said, "Play whist, will you?" (swish). "Odd tricks indeed!" (swish). "Oh yes – all right – you shuffle, and I'll cut." (swish).' Such are the words of a man who was, according to his contemporaries, full of harmless fun.

Few people have held the power or were treated with such awe as the headmasters of the great public schools of the nineteenth century. After forty years, Sir Charles Bruce, Governor of Mauritius, trembled when he recalled Dr Vaughan's castigations, 'Cast forth that evil person from among you.' The extent to which they were responsible for the prevalence of 'the English vice' during the nineteenth century is difficult to estimate. Very few of those men who passed through the public schools were keen to broadcast the fact that they had acquired a taste for the whip. Unquestionably some headmasters were only doing their duty and received little satisfaction of a sexual nature from the 'discipline' they were enforcing; it may be that corporal punishment was a valid treatment of drinking, smoking and whoring. It is very doubtful, however, whether even the most unwordly headmaster failed to realize the power he had to form an addiction, an addiction sanctioned by English literature ('I was so us'd to 't at Westminster School I cou'd never leave it off since' – Thomas Shadwell, 1676). One cannot say whether Goodford, Hawtrey, and their like were acquainted with the considerable body of literature on the subject (Hawtrey spent £30,000 on his library, so it is possible). Perhaps it is a pity that French as a language did not share the kudos of Greek and Latin, for otherwise the sober judgement of Rousseau might well have given the masters a queasy conscience ('Who would have believed that this childhood punishment would have determined my tastes, my desires, my passions for the rest of my life?').

As he was under the tyranny of a cruel taste; that of an ardent desire to being unmercifully scourged himself but of others so. . . . what increases the oddity of this strange fancy, was the gentleman's being young; whereas if generally attacks, it seems, such as are, through age, obliged to have recourse to this experiment, for quickening the circulation of their sluggish spirits. . .

Thus John Cleland in his *Fanny Hill* of 1750. The 'tyranny of a cruel taste' gradually included more and more young men among its subjects. In 1838, the publisher Cannon declared in a preface to one of his list that flagellation 'is, however, a letch which has existed from time immemorial, and is so extensively indulged in London at this day, that no less than twenty splendid establishments are supported entirely by its practice'.

The most professional of the 'governesses' who ran the brothels for flagellants was Mrs Theresa Berkley of 28 Charlotte Street, who made £10,000 in the eight years from 1828, when she invented a flogging machine called 'the Berkley Horse', until she died in 1836. Bloch in his *History of English Sexual Morals* (1938 translation) wrote that 'she was in the habit of finding out and satisfying every idea, every caprice, every wish of her clients, provided she was sure of commensurate remuneration'. Her stock in trade included a massive variety of 'instruments of chastisement' – whips with a dozen thongs, cats o' nine tails studded with sharp points, flexible switches, straps decorated with tin tacks, and a variety of flora including the ubiquitous stinging nettle for urtication. An etching found among her effects at her death shows an illustration of the 'Berkley Horse' (sometimes known as the *chevalet*) in action.

The popularity of flagellation – known on the continent as 'the English vice' – created a large corpus of literature on the subject, ranging from the insipid to the ultrasadistic, an example of the latter being 'Colonel Spanker's' *Experimental Lecture* 'on the exciting and voluptuous pleasures to be derived from crushing and humiliating the spirit of a beautiful and modest young lady', and of this, the great Victorian authority on erotology, H. S. Ashbee (alias 'Pisanus Fraxi'), was so distrustful that he handed over all criticism to an unnamed expert (or another alias). 'It seems to be the wild dream, or rather nightmare, of some vicious, used-up, old rake, who, positively worn out, and his hide tanned and whipped to insensibility by diurnal flogging, has gone mad on the subject of beastly flagellation.' This kind of abhorrence is a rare, and refreshing, break in the *savoir faire* of the experts, who are usually able to deal with this pornography as if it were neglected master work.

The literature created for the flagellants, and the flagellant *voyeurs*, is essentially esoteric. The performances are repeated endlessly, and are of a sameness and monotony that beggars description. The 'victim' is either willing or unwilling; if the latter, and if female, 'she is pinned by powerful arms, dragged back, and forced face downwards on the chair. In the act of kneeling, Mama whisks up her skirts behind, packs them tight-drawn beneath the captor's hands, lifts and tucks in the pendant front, and moulds the doomed posteriors to a crescent form.' Thus one of the inevitable sequences in *Romance of Chastisements* (1866), a series of short stories interspersed with episodes in verse, by St George H. Stock, which is about the most articulate and 'literary' production in this curious genre. Of the practitioners, wrote Stock:

Some are too tender-hearted, others too chaste or too timid, but – their scruples overcome and vengeance safe – they know no measure in the cruel sport, that, under the name of duty, gives rein to passion and gratifies two lusts at every lunge ... the rapport, as the magnetisers have it, was so strong that I could divine her thoughts. ... ere he can trace the cause, the snow turns crimson, neath the rapid rod; the air is shrill with stripes, cut follows cut, and groan succeeds to groan.

One might cavil at the metaphor 'shrill with stripes' but there is no question that St George H. Stock was a committed writer. The block he described in one of these yarns 'proved to be a heavy stool, riveted, I believe, to the floor, with an upright front, in shape somewhat like an executioner's block, whereon the culprit knelt low and erect to receive the discipline.'

The prose writing qua writing is, of course, rubbish, but the verse interludes have a certain verve, though technically St George H. Stock did not have the ear of his fellow enthusiast, Swinburne, and even the extravagant use of the literary device of elision cannot make some of the lines scan:

> Vain all her writhings and contortions odd,
> The licking lady with sardonic grin
> Withholds, but only for a space, the rod,
> Watching the happy moment to whip *in*
> As whip she will, or soon or late, of course,
> Seeing the deadly purpose in her eye,

> Her victim turns the reluctant thigh,
> When down it comes with desolating force,
> And worn to fragments, is again renewed,
> Tho' half a glance the punisher had told
> Before the kicking devil was subdued,
> That Rush for such correction was too old.

The tales and the verses have so little consequence that it is vain to guess who Rush was. The following is a good deal more saucy, and one is reminded of the period of extreme licence that extended during the early years of Victoria's reign (*Romance of Chastisements* dates from the middle of the Swinburne period):

> Ann lifts her left leg on a lounging chair
> And over it she turns, as you may guess,
> The part she wants exalted in the air,
> Split, equipoised, and destitute of dress,
> The end that should be upper, so no more,
> Is pendant now, black curls strew the floor,
> And tho' 'our love is but a lassie yet'
> We faintly trace a stencilling of jet.

The other 'classic' of the period is *The Merry Order of St Bridget* (1868). Whereas *Romance of Chastisements* deals with a variety of environments, usually centred in schoolrooms, *The Merry Order of St Bridget* by 'Margaret Anson' is a leisurely narrative of a closed order of female flagellants pursuing their desires in what sounds like an extended film set. It is utterly dotty, and has its own surrealist touches: 'With that she opened the window, broke off some slender sprigs from a myrtle which grew outside, completely spoiling the bush by doing it. ... Every lady held a rod in her hand, made of lithe and strong twigs, tied up with ribbons which corresponded with the colours of her dress. ... I always garter above the knee, and that is one secret of keeping the leg a good shape; your knee loses its roundness if the garter is below it.'

The widespread demand for books for the flagellant market led hack writers to turn their attention to 'histories' of the rod. One of these writers was James G. Bertram alias 'Reverend W. M. Cooper', who started off his literary career as a novelist

(*The Story of a Stolen Heir*, three volumes, 1838), went on to *The Language of Flowers* (1864), on to piscine matters, *Harvest of the Sea* ('*a contribution to the natural and economic history of the British food fishes,*' 1865), then on to *A History of the Rod* (1870), a most tedious stringing together of anecdotes and facts. 'Cooper', after this brief foray into pseudopornography, went back to the sea, and *The Unappreciated Fisher Folk* came out in 1883.

The prevalence of the cult of the whip led to extended essays in verse, whimsically entitled 'rodiads', 'whippiads, and 'birchiads', as well as to a two-act comic opera, the *dramatis personæ* of which features the Duches of Picklerod, Lady Castigate, the Countess of Greenbirch, and Miss Stoutback. The scene setting of this opera is a most curious illustration of modern fetishism – in the centre of the stage was a bunch of birches in the form of a tree, and this was apostrophized thus:

> All hail, lovely Rod! twigs of yonder Birch Tree,
> Which surely, dear Busby, was planted by thee,
> Enraptured I kiss it, and bow to the shrine:
> What comes from thy hand must be ever divine!

Busby was the headmaster of Westminster in the seventeenth century, a grandfather figure for the flagellants. This was followed by a chorus:

> All shall yield to the lovely Birch Tree,
>   Bend to thee
>   Immortal tree.
>   None like thee,
>   The world agree,
> E'er gave such sweet felicity.

Inane is the politest adjective one can use on this verse. Of more vivacity was a pantomime that came out in 1879, *Harlequin Prince Cherrytop*, which had the quatrain:

> Here, take the wand; whene'er you find him flagging
> And disinclined for after-dinner shagging,
> Give him three dozen, dear, with all your might,
> And he'll be fresh as on his wedding night.

It might be supposed from pantomimes, comic operas, rodiads, and romances centred on girls' schools that flagella-

tion was a fun game that might be a viable alternative to ortho-
dox sex. However, there were extremes – as in 'Colonel
Spanker' and his *Lecture* (1878) with its unbridled sadism,
which, although fiction, had its mirror images in real life. During the Eyre case in Jamaica, a certain Dr Sandwich created his
niche in history by flogging natives with whips made of piano
wire, first trying them on women, whose backs 'were easier cut
than those of men'. Earlier, James Miles, master of the Hoo
Union workhouse, got his kicks by flogging twelve- and thirteen-
year-old girls under his aegis. Connoisseurs, such as Swinburne,
collected interesting cases, watching the daily press like hawks.

In the *Guardian* there appeared in 1876 the following advertisement: 'A widow, a great invalid, wishes to place two of
her daughters, aged twelve and thirteen, under the charge of a
lady, who would, when necessary, administer the birch-rod, as
they are extremely troublesome. Terms liberal.' The *Englishwoman's Domestic Magazine* ran a long series on flogging,
with masses of letters coming in from the most unlikely sources
(many of them were hoaxes, not spotted by the somewhat half-
witted editor). That great nineteenth-century instrument of reaction, the *Saturday Review*, declared petulantly, 'Is it possible
that before long the only creatures in Europe, besides cattle,'
that will be flogged will be 'English criminals and English
girls?' Ominously, the review asked, 'is the whole of this amazing correspondence fictitious? Is it nothing more than an elaborate and vulgar hoax?'

Alas, no. English women of the respectable classes were taking a most unhealthy interest in flagellation just at a time
when flogging was gradually being dropped in the armed forces
(it began to be reduced from 1863, when of 18,659 men court-
martialled, 518 were flogged, a reduction stimulated by the
regulation passed in 1859 when only soldiers and sailors convicted of serious offences were flogged). At schools some masters
had serious doubts about the efficacy of the whip, while C. H.
Pinches, proprietor of Clarendon House School, stated, 'I object
to the accompaniments of the Rod – that is, taking the trousers
down, and so on . . .'

It is perhaps significant that the head of an establishment

devoted to flagellation was often called a 'governess', while the head of a brothel was an 'abbess', and it is curious that the flagellation jargon includes terms such as 'discipline' and 'castigation'. Discipline and castigation for *what?* one may ask. When a reason was needed to satisfy the psyche of a 'victim' small pseudo-crimes were thought up. The motives of the flagellants were even more mixed than those of other perversions; it may be argued that often flagellation had nothing at all to do with sex, that – as in the numerous church orders that have used flagellation as one of the disciplines – whipping was indulged in to assuage a feeling of guilt and that the whippings carried out still in the more esoteric areas of religion have nothing in common with a perversion of the sexual instinct beyond the mechanism.

The desire to be whipped might also on occasions be a regression. In an age when to spare the rod was maybe to spoil the child, the feelings of a child towards the parent who was doing the castigation might well have had a certain ambience. A love–hate relationship might well be harked back to in later life if normal sex had proved uninteresting; the desire to be whipped might mean a reversion to the role of child in a parent–child relationship (and it must be noted that the 'governess' as a term was sometimes replaced by 'mamma' – the 'governess' as a mother substitute is surely a valid concept). The urge to whip, rather than be whipped, has more ramifications still; it could be construed as: (a) simple revenge against (1) certain people, (2) society in general; (b) a genuine perversion of the sexual instinct leading to (1) intercourse, (2) an orgasm without intercourse; (c) the need to wield power and to be seen to wield power; (d) the need to keep discipline in school, home, prison, or armed services; or (e) an outlet for the animal in man. No other activity of man (or woman) as a sexual being raises so many questions as flagellation. Has the flagellation sanctified by religion any relationship *at all* with flagellation as practised in the brothel or in private?

There is a curious area where religious fustigation and sexual flagellation meet. During the intense suspicion of the activities of the Roman Catholic Church in Great Britain in the nineteenth century, great play was made of the various rites and ceremonies of the church, and in particular it was believed that nuns were engaged in an endless succession of dubious pursuits. Even more under suspicion were the establishments of the ritualistic sectors of the Church of England, especially the nunneries. In his *Manual for Confessors* of 1878, Dr E. B. Pusey recommended as a penance, 'for mortifications, the Discipline for about a quarter of an hour a day'. The discipline was a whip, though sometimes believed by the aghast to be an instrument of 'spiked steel'. The 'confessions' of the nuns formerly immured in the Church of England nunneries of the nineteenth century are couched in the language one is familiar with from the literary productions of 'Margaret Anson' and Stock. 'Sister Mary Agnes OSB' had been a nun under the control of the Reverend J. L. Lyne, alias Father Ignatius, and her *Nunnery Life in the Church of England* (*circa* 1880) was a rich source of material to those who saw the flirtation of the High Church with Rome as disastrous:

All left the sacristy but myself, the Mother Superior, and one Nun, who was ordered to be present at the casting out of the devil. I was commanded first to strip. I saw '*the Discipline*', with its seven lashes of knotted whipcord in her hand, and I knew that one lash given (or taken by oneself) was in reality seven. I should mention that at certain times *it was the rule to Discipline oneself*. .... Then I began to undress; but when I came to my vest, shame again overcame me. 'Take that thing off,' said the Mother Superior. I replied, 'I cannot, reverend Mother; it's too tight.' The Nun who was present was told to help me to get it off. A deep feeling of shame came over me at being half-nude. The Mother then ordered the Nun to say the '*Miserere*', and while it was recited *she lashed me several times with all her strength*. I was determined not to utter a sound, but at last I could not restrain a smothered groan, whereat she gave me one last and cruel lash, and then ceased.

How does this differ from *The Merry Order of St Bridget* or the *Romance of Chastisements* save in the *mise en scène*? How could the chosen instrument of 'the English vice' be at the same time an instrument for the casting out of vices, English and otherwise? Indeed, it is a question that might be posed to 'One who enjoys far more than any farce/The writing of a flagellated arse.' Few activities illustrate so clearly the danger of defining the areas of pleasure and pain or the extraordinary psychological make-up of Homo sapiens.

The mechanisms of the pleasure wrought by being whipped were set down by the Victorian erotologist John Davenport in his *Aphrodisiacs and Anti-Aphrodisiacs* dated 1869: 'As an erotic stimulant, more particularly, it may be observed that, considering the many intimate and sympathetic relations existing between the nervous branches of the extremity of the spinal marrow, it is impossible to doubt that flagellation exercised upon the buttocks and the adjacent parts, has a powerful effect upon the organs of generation.' The connoisseurs could by the experts in Mrs Berkley's harem – Miss Ring, Hannah Jones, Sally Taylor, One-eyed Peg, Bauld-cunted Poll or Ebony Bet – be 'birched, whipped, fustigated, scourged, needle-picked, half-hung, holly-brushed, furse-brushed, butcher-brushed, stinging-nettled, curry-combed, phlebotomized', and, amazing as all this is to an outsider, it could be, literally, a deadly business. The 'Epitaph on a Young Lady who was Birched to Death' is whimsical, though it needs an odd sort of humour to be ribald on such a subject:

> They laid her flat on a gorse down pillow,
> And scourged her arse with twigs of willow,
> Her bottom so white grew pink, then red,
> Then bloody, then raw, and her spirit fled.

This style of writing was not only indulged in by hacks, but by fine poets. Swinburne left Eton with a firm belief in the efficacy of the whipping block and tendencies that were to rule out for the rest of his life any participation in normal sexual relations. In 1863, he wrote, 'Once, before giving me a swishing that I had the marks of for more than a month, the tutor let me saturate my face with eau-de-cologne. ... He meant to stimulate and excite the senses by that preliminary pleasure so as to inflict the acuter pain afterwards on their awaked and intensified susceptibility ...'[9] Swinburne was also birched in a fir wood near Eton, when wet from bathing.

These tendencies were confirmed when Swinburne discovered the writings of de Sade. He was introduced to them through his friend Richard Monckton Milnes, whose collection of erotica was so famous that his country seat at Fryston Hall was known as 'Aphrodisiopolis', and although Swinburne could laugh at the 'most abominable bawdry books that ever were written … sodomy mixed with murder and hideous cruelty …'[10] he was continually harking back to them in his correspondence.

Swinburne made use of an 'establishment' at 7 Circus Road, St. John's Wood, where, for a consideration, two outwardly respectable ladies, rouged and golden-haired, 'consented to chastise' gentlemen 'guests'. Lady floggers 'must have a quick and intuitive method of observing the various aberrations of the human mind, and be ready and quick to humour and relieve them … when an elegant high bred woman wields (the birch) with dignity of mien and grace of attitude, then both the practice and suffering becomes a real pleasure …' (*Romance of Chastisements* by St George H. Stock).

These 'governesses' were powerful figures in this sub-world. After the death of Mrs Berkley, a number of them vied for the first place as queen of the flagellants. Among the most famous was Mrs James, of 7 Carlisle Street, Soho, who retired to live in great luxury in Notting Hill, and others included Mrs Emma Lee, of 50 Margaret Street, Regent Street; Mrs Phillips of 11 Upper Belgrave Place; Mrs Shepherd of 25 Gilbert Street; and Mrs Sarah Potter alias Stewart.

It was very much of a closed earnest circle, with little of the gay abandon of the swells and the men about town; the victims were elderly men who needed some gingering up, genuine sadists and masochists, and those who had been diverted by unfortunate experiences at school. The humour – what there is of it – is either sick and macabre or donnish. One quiet bit of humour is perhaps worth recording. When the poet Coleridge heard of his old schoolmaster's death he remarked that it was lucky that the cherubim who took him to Heaven were nothing but faces and wings, or he would infallibly have flogged them by the way.

Two Facets of Perversion

Perversion is a word that has no final meaning. What might be a perversion one century can be normal in the following. It helps to consider it as a subjective term, denude it of its ethical overtones, and ask of a specific perversion: What physical harm does it do? Then ask a subsequent question: What psychological harm does it do *beyond satisfying the wishes of the protagonists*?

The perversions of the Victorian age have now become part and parcel of the *via sexualis*. That the following pursuit would ever be encouraged by respectable sex manuals of the 1960s would have shattered the Victorian worthy. The extract is from *The Boudoir* (1860):

Charlie was on his knees in a moment, paying his devotions to that divinely, delicate-looking, pinky slit. His tongue divided its juicy lips, searching out her pretty clitoris, which at once stiffened under the lascivious osculation. It was more like a rabbit's prick than anything, and his fingers could just uncover its rosy head as he gently frigged it, sucking at the same time.

The most harmless of Victorian sexual perversions was fetishism. This was not confined to the literate class – Richard von Kraft-Ebing in *Psychopathia Sexualis* (1886) told of the workman who collected women's shoes, the shoemaker who accumulated night caps, garters and women's underwear, and the labourer who had in his possession a hundred ladies' handkerchiefs. Fetishism is not an anomaly only found in societies where fashion decrees the highly ornate, though this helps.

The psychologist A. Binet (1857–1911) explained fetishism in terms of what a man (or, more rarely, a woman) saw during an early sexual experience. Krafft-Ebing drew attention to the separate type of fetishism stimulated by materials rather than articles of clothing, materials that were particularly popular during the nineteenth century (furs, leather, velvet, and silk).

L. von Sacher-Masoch (1835–95) in his *Venus in Furs* endeavoured to explain why the stroking of fur stimulated him erotically. Certain items can become fetishes by virtue of the smell; to those with curious olfactory tastes, the chamois leather combinations of the late seventies must have been irresistible, and it must be noted that some fetishists are only interested in worn or soiled underwear. As early as 1821, in *Kalogynomia, or the laws of female beauty*, Dr T. Bell had written 'the musky odour ... of the armpits and generative parts (and they are perfectly musky in cleanly persons of warm temperament) is a powerful stimulus to sexual love'.

Fetishist objects may be so because they are (a) associated with an early sexual experience; (b) replacements for the genitalia; or (c) made of a lubricous material. The neurologist J. M. Charcot (1825–93) recorded the case of the man who came from a hereditarily insane family, who had his first erection at the age of five when a male relation of thirty in whose room he was sleeping put on his night cap. He was also excited when, later, an aged retainer tied the ribbons of her night cap. At twenty-one he married, but could not carry out intercourse until he imagined his wife to be an old woman in a night cap; this device accompanied him through many years of married life, though he did not tell his wife as he considered the fantasy was degrading.

That a certain degree of fetishism is 'normal' is evident from the general masculine preoccupation with lingerie. There are few grounds to doubt that a *soupçon* of underwear of one kind or another is a norm. As the anonymous author of *Lady Pokingham* put it: 'The ladies were now also divested of everything, till the complete party were in a state of buff, excepting the pretty boots and stockings, which I always think look far sweeter than naked legs and feet,' or the author of *Miss Coote's Confessions* (1879): '... she had such a beautiful brunette complexion, her almost black hair hanging all down her back to her loins, her pretty white rounded globes, with dark brown nipples looking impudently above her chemisette, which only reached a little way down her thighs.'

The disrobing of woman prior to intercourse was brought to

The Worm in the Bud

a fine pitch by the more expensive £5-a-time prostitutes of the 1850s. Jane Fowler had 'a peculiar method of disrobing, and possesses excellent tact in managing a charming repulse to the eager advance of a vigorous gallant for the purpose of enhancing the enjoyment'. The art of undressing in a salacious manner is the key to the expert stripper, and that the items concerned should be isolated from the ultimate object of the exercise, i.e., intercourse, is not surprising; even less astonishing is that the undergarments should be isolated, as it were, in transit. Again, from *Miss Coote's Confessions*, 'I assisted to tie her up, and unfastening her drawers, Jane drew them well down, whilst Mr Mansell pinned up her chemise, fully exposing the broad expanse of her glorious buttocks, the brilliant whiteness of her skin showing to perfection by the dazzling glare of the well lighted room.'

Complete undressing for copulation appears to have been the ultimate in naughtiness during the nineteenth century. After the most extravagant sexual tricks, the final ace played by the pornographic writer was the removal of (in early Victorian England) the lady's shift, or (in late Victorian England) the lady's chemise. In extramarital sex, the fact that the whore or kept woman wore selected undergarments during intercourse was a tradition taken over from France, where many of the English whores had undergone their apprenticeship. For example, from *The Three Chums*:

A quiver of delight thrilled through her frame as he gained complete insertion, her lovely legs encased in delicate knickerbocker drawers fringed with lace, and set off by rose-coloured silk stockings and high-heeled Parisian boots, were thrown amorously over his manly buttocks, whilst his hands clasped round her lovely rump as it rose in agitated heaves in response to his vigorous thrusts.

The removal of the undergarments was one of the key operations of the sadistic and flagellation sagas of the period: 'The landlady now quickly unbuttoned the band of Bessie's drawers, pulling them down to her knees, and tucking the tail of the thin cambric chemise out of the way under her corset, both before and behind, so as to give a full view of a truly magnificent white rump, and all the stock-in-trade of a handsome and pretty young whore as one could wish to see' (*Adventures and Amours of a Barmaid*, 1860).

Or in third-generation (the eighties onward) pornography (*The Secret Life of Linda Brent*, 1882):

They seize her. One by one her garments are taken off, in spite of her struggles, disclosing first her beautiful polished shoulders, her round firm swelling virgin breasts, with a valley between them where cupid himself might nestle his head in rapture. Her beautiful moulded arms, ripe, well-formed waist, which, as she moved and writhed in their hands, showed suppleness of a most voluptuous character; and, at last, she stands before them panting, naked but for her drawers, which she tenaciously clung round her, her beautiful eyes flashing with anger.

Garment fetishism has been called by specialists in this field tragicomic. The participants are not truly anti-social, except when they happened to be kleptomaniacs. Some of the forms of fetishism merge into transvestism; the love affair with a chemise can lead into the man wearing it, especially when he has some inner confusion as to his sexual role.

The chief fetish of the age became the shoes. During the period of the crinoline, the hem of the dress, responsive to goodness knows what obscure whim of fashion, rose three inches. No doubt officials connected with the Great Exhibition of 1851 were grateful that this had not happened during the term of that exhibition (the cleaning machine of so many housemaid power had not been necessary as lady visitors kept the floor spotless, their long skirts acting as dusters). Three inches may not seem a lot, but to ogling Victorian men a new dimension of foot and ankle was opened up to them. Children who genuinely believed that woman went down to the ground in one piece like the trunk of a tree were disillusioned. Samuel Butler's anecdote was not so farcical as it might seem:

A little boy and a little girl were looking at a picture of Adam and Eve.

'Which is Adam and which is Eve?' said one.

'I do not know,' said the other, 'but I could tell if they had their clothes on.'

At the beginning of Victoria's reign, shoes had a rectangular front. Twenty years later there was little basic difference, except that shoes broadened out. There was no difference between the left foot and the right foot. They were flat-heeled and, for formal day wear, were made in black satin, for evening dress, white satin, and for casual wear, leather or cloth. In the fifties heels appeared of about an inch high, and in 1862 one sees the introduction of coloured shoes; that decade introduced fancy accessories to shoes – bows, rosettes, or steel buckles. The decline of the elastic-sided boots coincided with higher heels, the so-called 'Louis' heels of up to two inches in height. Walking shoes were now laced over the instep. The eighties saw boots going higher up the ladies' legs until in the nineties the boots had accumulated as many as sixteen buttons. This boot might have been specifically designed for the erotically over-excitable.

'There are certain things which are hidden in order to be shown,' commented the sixteenth-century essayist Montaigne, and the shoe and the boot assuredly belonged in the last century to this category. The display of foot and ankle had an odd mock-modesty about it ('Modesty,' wrote Havelock Ellis in *Studies in the Psychology of Sex* (1901–10), 'may be provisionally defined as an almost instinctive fear prompting to concealment and usually centring around the sexual process'). The foot became a new and attractive erogenous area, and particularly useful in that it could be written about and sung about. The number of times foot, ankle and boot occurred in music hall songs is incredible. The boot and shoe had a double appeal – as an indication of this novel sexual territory and as sexual symbols in their own right. 'Pocket books, ring, arm band, furs, stockings, gloves, are articles having in common the feature that something is stuck into them,' wrote William Stekel in *Peculiarities of Behaviour* (1925), and in the context in which he was writing he did not have to specify the symbolic something, nor did he have to ram his lesson home with the most obvious article of all, the shoe/boot.

The implications were not lost on the purveyors of smut:

> A snob fitting on a pair of boots for a young lady –
> On his knees and at it, put it in, and pat it;

'Is it in?' says he;
'Oh, yes,' said she,
'As nice as nice can be, and I like it.'

At a more innocent level were the music hall songs:

I say, lads, have you seen my Molly?
Have you seen her chignon made of artificial hair?
I say, lads, have you seen my Molly?
She is a little beauty, and the pet of Leicester Square.

She wears a mantle, dress and shawl,
That cost a crown complete,
And sports the new Flexura Boot,
They sell in Oxford Street.

The symbolism was constantly being evoked by traditional *tableaux* – the swells who drank champagne from chorus girls' slippers, the shoe as a symbol of both the vagina and of submission or dictatorship.

Few people came to any harm through fetishism, though one reserves judgement on the man who demanded of his wife that she bandage his penis with a small strap, rub it with eau de cologne, and stamp on it with the heels of Russian boots. Perversions such as flagellation, on the contrary, left their mark in every sense of the word, and masochism and sadism in their more extreme forms could end in violent death. The twentieth century has been more free in its investigation of such circumstances, and in January 1935 Mr Justice Atkin read an interesting paper to the Medico-Legal Society on 'Murder from the Point of View of the Psychiatrist' in which he said: 'In masochism the man or woman derives sex gratification from physical discomfort or pain and moral humiliation. Sir Bernard Spilsbury has called attention recently to accidental deaths in men due to this cause, and considers it possible that some cases of suspected murder may be due to masochistic practices.'

Perversions occur when sexual impulses are diverted into other than heterosexual channels, and some are subject to criminal proceedings, when they are called unnatural offences. Until the Offences against the Person Act of 1861 the law was in some confusion, but even in 1861 there were anomalies; one law for the man, one for the woman worked in this case to the advantage of the woman. Tribadism (i.e., Lesbianism) was not considered a crime, whereas sodomy assuredly was – section 61 reads: 'Whosoever shall be convicted of the abominable crime of buggery, committed either with mankind or with any animal, shall be liable, at the discretion of the court, to be kept in penal servitude for life or for any term not less than ten years.'

Buggery with such animals as the cow, mare and she-ass were not unknown and not particularly uncommon, as cases turned up fairly regularly at the assizes, though they were not reported. It might be mentioned that a British regiment stationed in India was known as the 'sheep shaggers'. In most of the cases that came to the notice of the law, the men or youths were caught *flagrante delicto*.

In one case tried at the assizes, where a man was charged with having had unnatural intercourse with a cow, the prosecution was able to show that some short coloured hairs found on the prisoner's person resembled those of the animal. In another case (*R. v. Brinkley* Lincoln Assizes, April 1887) Sir Thomas Stevenson found the peculiar coloured hairs of a mare upon the prisoner's clothing, and spermatozoa on his trouser-flap.

Experts in medical jurisprudence did their best to understand the motivations of men who committed bestiality. It was admitted that sexual passions were stronger in some than in others, and that the condition among older men known as the 'enlarged prostate' might encourage bestiality. It was generally considered, however, that men who had connection with animals were more fit for a lunatic asylum than a prison.

If masturbation and indecent exposure are at one end of the perversion spectrum, incestuous rape and sodomy are at the other. At the Liverpool Summer Assizes of 1887 Thomas Woods, a blind man age forty-three, was accused of committing sodomy on his son, age nine. He was found guilty and sentenced to ten years' penal servitude. On 20 April 1895 Michael Crowley, age twenty-four, raped his four-year-old daughter Catherine, after having nine or ten pints of beer that afternoon.

The mother had gone out for a short time, and on her return noticed that the child's eyes were blackened. She asked Crowley what he had been doing. Crowley said that it was not her eyes, but that she was 'bleeding below'. The account continues: 'The mother then saw that the child was naked, and that her privates were torn and bleeding. She charged the prisoner with having done it, and threatening to inform the police, wrapped the child up in her apron and took her to the Northern Hospital.'

Crowley went to the 'nearest bridewell' and told the officer of his wife's accusation. He was detained, and the house searched. A bucket of bloody water was found. The child's condition was ascertained, and it was found that she was badly lacerated internally. Crowley was taken to the detective office and interrogated; he asked to be examined by Police Surgeon Lowndes, who found about Crowley's genitals no signs of violence, no stains, no blood, no semen, and no dirt – in fact, they were cleaner than the rest of his body. He was charged with having carnal knowledge of his daughter, and replied, 'I know nothing whatever about it.' The apron in which the girl had been wrapped was examined, and blood and spermatozoa were found.

At the police court, Crowley elected to make a statement. He stated that he was washing the child in the bucket when she fell astride it, the injuries being caused in this way. The daughter was interviewed, but she was mentally backward and seemed to confirm what her father had told the court; she told her mother that 'daddy had done bad in the bucket'. The provisions of the Criminal Law Amendment Act 1885 made it possible for Mrs Crowley to give evidence against her husband, and this she did. Crowley was found guilty at the Liverpool Assizes of May 1895 and sentenced to ten years' penal servitude.

If this case is considered extraordinary, what is one to make of the rape in 1840 of a female infant of eleven months by a soldier, 'in which the violence to the genitals proved fatal'? Man can be, indeed, a strange and terrible animal.

The Cult of the Little Girl

When a man sustains a disappointment in love he is inclined to take as his love object: (a) a carbon copy of his lost love but more amenable; (b) someone reminiscent of his mother, a person with whom disappointment is difficult to associate; (c) someone whose qualities and dimensions preclude the timbre of disappointment once experienced – a child. The last two categories represent regression, the tendency to adhere to a premature state, what psychoanalysis calls the 'law of psychic gravitation'. The nineteenth century was especially replete with gentlemen who had for girl children an overwhelming penchant, and when these men were respectable such attachments were treated as if they were ordained by God. When these men were of the literary persuasion, the rationalization became even more involved, and the refusal to face the fact that passionate involvements with immature girls argued some personality defect resulted in some curious and tortuous thinking.

This was helped by the dichotomy in the way little girls were looked at. As has been pointed out, the extent to which children were looked upon as direct sexual objects in the nineteenth century was frightening. There were child brothels in all parts of London, and particularly in the East End (Maxwell in Betty Street, Commercial Road, and Catherine Keeley in Dock Street, Commercial Road), and, wrote a correspondent of *Figaro*, 'every evening towards midnight more than five hundred girls in ages between twelve and fifteen years parade between Piccadilly Circus and Waterloo Place, that is on a stretch of ground no more than three hundred yards long'. The exploitation of young girls is the most repellent aspect of Victorian sex. In Iwan Bloch's *Sexual Life in England* (1938 edition) a woman in the West End is reported as saying that 'In my house you can gloat over the cries of the girls with the certainty that no one will hear them besides yourself,' and this odious statement was confirmed by other sources. The odd notion that the rape of a virgin

cured venereal disease can only have carried weight with pro-
fligates who were far gone with that prime reward of promiscuity, general paralysis of the insane, but girl virgins were
highly prized in these circles, and there were ingenious restric-
tions of virginity. Astringent plants, broken glass, leeches, and
sponges soaked in blood were used to simulate loss of virginity.

At the other extreme, little girls were looked on with a reverence that would have been applicable to angels, and, indeed,
many of the more committed waded about in soggy sentimentality thoroughly convinced that there was some strong connection. This confusion exasperated outsiders who looked upon
children as children, as it exasperated Harry Furniss when he
had been commissioned by Lewis Carroll to provide illustrations for *Sylvie and Bruno* (1889–93). Lewis Carroll wrote to
him:

> I think I had better explain part of the plot, as to these two – Sylvie
> and Bruno. They are not fairies right through the book – but *children*.
> All these conditions make their *dress* rather a puzzle. They mustn't
> have *wings*; that is clear. And it must be *quite* the common dress of
> London life. It should be as fanciful as possible, so as *just* to be pre-
> sentable in Society.[11]

Furniss, best known for a long series of cartoons for *Punch*, was
a graphic artist not outstanding for his subtlety. He looked on
himself as a caricaturist, and like many other illustrators he
began to regret being involved with the hypercritical Lewis
Carroll, who tried to dispatch him all over the country to see a
succession of sweet little girls whom he had observed or photographed or from whom he had received their likenesses. Carroll
penned his own pictures of Sylvie, but he did not have the technical equipment to do justice to his ideal. He continued to bom-
bard Furniss with suggestions:

> I *wish* I dared dispense with all costume; naked children are so
> perfectly pure and lovely, but Mrs Grundy would be furious – it
> would never do. Then the question is, how little dress will content
> her? Bare legs and feet we *must* have, at any rate. I so entirely detest
> that monstrous fashion *high heels* (and in fact have planned an attack
> on it in this very book), that I cannot possibly allow my sweet little
> heroine to be victimised by it.

As to your Sylvie. I am charmed with your idea of dressing her in *white*; it exactly fits my own idea of her; I want her to be a sort of embodiment of Purity.

Furniss apparently came up with a beauty, and the impassioned Carroll wrote to him: 'How old is your model for Sylvie? And may I have her name and address?' Furniss was amused, for he was basing his designs on an idealized version of his own daughter – professionals did not dash off to Scotland, as Carroll wanted him to do, to reverently copy a pretty girl who had turned up there. That there was a market in cherubs is clear from Carroll. 'My friend, Miss E. G. Thomson, an artist great in "fairies", would be glad to know of her, I'm sure.' Miss Thomson was a pupil of the Pre-Raphaelite fellow-traveller Shields; she was once hauled over the coals by Christina Rossetti for 'indecent' fairies, though Miss Rossetti had her own notions of what constituted indecency. In many ways she was the embodiment of aggrieved spinsterhood. Later in the century there was to be a market for cherubic little boys sparked off by Millais' 'Bubbles',[12] the painting used by Pear's Soap in one of the first of the adman coups. No doubt Furniss was glad to get back to the cosy pages of *Punch*, sharing honours with another graphic artist, John Tenniel, whose drawings for the *Alice* books have had more impact on subsequent generations than all the acres of political cartoons he executed for *Punch*.

Little girls in pen, pencil and water-colour were more amenable than little girls in the flesh. The latter had one great disadvantage; they grew up. Admittedly they did not grow up like little boys:

Can you persist in telling me that this fair-haired innocent – this little sportive, prattling, lovable child, with dimpled, dumpling hands that almost fold themselves spontaneously into the attitude of supplication and prayer; with cherry lip – 'some bee has stung it newly' – lisping thanksgiving and love; with arms that long to embrace; with eyes beaming confidence, joy, pity, tenderness – am I to be told that this infant is father to yon hulking, sodden, sallow-faced, blue-gilled, crop-haired, leaden-eyed, livid-lipped, bow-shouldered, shrunken-legged, swollen-handed convict, in a hideous gray uniform branded with the broad arrow, with ribbed worsted hose and fetters at his ankles. . .[13]

Thus G. A. Sala (writing in 1883), described by Vernon Lee as a 'red, bloated, bottle-nosed creature who poured out anecdotes in a stentorian voice', but who was nevertheless one of the greatest journalists of the age (the sustained performance above has a Jamesian virtuosity). Little girls grew up and grew out of their mentors whose efforts to join in with their fun was no longer seen as flattering but ridiculous. Ruskin, for instance, had connected himself with a girls' school at Winnington. He wrote to his father: 'We had such a game of hide-and-seek yesterday in the attics and empty rooms ... today we have been playing at prisoners' base till I'm stiff with running!' No doubt the girls found this participation acceptable, but it is possible that they were slightly bored when Ruskin was persuading them to 'act out' the poems of James Russell Lowell ('I got a nice blue-eyed girl to be Minerva ... I had studied curtseying all the afternoon before in order to get myself nicely up as Venus').

The motivations for a fixation on young girls were various. The failure of an adult relationship or the inability to enter into an adult relationship were frequently combined with simple nostalgia for the past, with awareness of the gulf of time, with envy at the range of years that lay before the youngsters. This was briefly mentioned in the verse preface to Carroll's *Through the Looking-Glass* (1872):

> We are but older children, dear,
> Who fret to find our bedtime near.

By committing themselves to the young, many unquestionably sought to retain their own youthful vision, and threw away the qualities of maturity – experience and judgement. Purity and Innocence were regarded as the supreme Goods, and intellectual virtues were gladly relinquished. It was rare when intellectuality and sentimentality thrived in harness, as they did in the *Alice* books where the fact that Carroll was a mathematician and a logician is everywhere evident.

Ruskin's preoccupation with young girls is amply documented, not least by himself. His first traumatic experience occurred when he was sixteen or seventeen, when the daughters of his father's partner in the family Cherry firm descended upon him. He himself was

virtually convent bred more closely than the maids themselves, without a single sisterly or cousinly affection for refuge or lightning rod, and having no athletic skill or pleasure to check my dreaming, I was thrown, bound hand and foot, in my unaccomplished simplicity into the fiery furnace, or fiery cross, of these four girls – who, of course, reduced me to a mere heap of ashes in four days.[14]

The complacency, the 'of course' was conditioned by half a century of being perennially reduced to ashes by one or other of his girl friends. The favourite of the four was Adèle, and she was fifteen. This was a key age for Ruskin, who was affected more by sexual blossoming than was Carroll, who rejected his girls when they were, as he put it, entering the awkward transitional stage.

The image makers have dealt with any breath of scandal that might have lingered around Ruskin. Had he been less of a sage, had parents not been gratified by the excessive interest taken by Ruskin in their daughters, had his presents to them been less respectable (he gave them drawings and Bibles), then more suspicion might have fallen on him. Magistrates were very keen on men who took an unnatural interest in children, provided that they were not well connected, were not famous, or were not clergymen. Phillip Lyne, of West Dulwich, was none of these, and the only thing in his favour was that he had had a 'superior education'. He had no occupation, was forty-nine, and loitered in the Crystal Palace and its purlieus with an opera glass, with which he was said to entice little girls. They described it as a 'thing with two eyes to look through'. He had something of a reputation in 1876 among the petty officials of the Crystal Palace, and was known as 'The Pest of the Palace'. What did Phillip Lyne do? It seems, very little. He touched the leg of one little girl with a stick, put his arm around the waist of the youngest of them, gave them roses, and a penny to buy foodstuffs, and once caught hold of a leg. 'He seemed a very pleasant gentleman, and I did not think he meant any harm,' one of the girls said. There were rumours that he had behaved with impropriety at the swings in the Crystal Palace pleasure garden and had 'interfered' in apparently a mild way with a young woman who was married and had made no complaint. This seemed to be the extent of his misdoings, but to the chairman of the court he was a monster of infamy;

You have been an utter hypocrite leading a most disgraceful existence quite apart from your respectable dealings with friends and your wife and family. ... I cannot feel the smallest doubt that a very great criminal, a great polluter of innocent children and young women, now stands at the bar ... For my own part, I do not think the sentence sufficiently heavy for behaving as you have behaved, but the law limits me.

For what seems very small beer in the context of Victorian nastiness, Lyne received two years of hard labour.

There was not only one law for the rich and one for the poor. There was one for the aristocrat and one for the middle class, one for the clergyman and one for the layman. *Truth* in 1885 disinterred a court case entombed in obscure provincial newspapers:

The Kesteven Magistrates have odd ideas of justice. A curate was charged before them with indecently assaulting a child. He admitted his guilt, and was fined £20. The reverend gentleman's counsel pleaded for mercy on the ground that a sentence of imprisonment would give pain to the offender's wife and child, and would lead to his being deprived of his curacy. I am curious to know whether the Established Church is still to benefit by the ministrations of this pastor?

One of the most shocking instances of influence in high places occurred four years later, when the brother-in-law of Lord Salisbury, Lord Galloway, was involved in a case in Dumfries. Lord Salisbury was at the time Prime Minister, and the case was disposed of in a hurried four minutes. What seems to have happened is that Lord Galloway was accused of having his hand up the dress of ten-year-old Jane Gibson. The impression given by Galloway was that they were 'gathering brambles'. A Mrs Moffat was not so impressed: 'For shame, you old blackguard! What have you been doing?' The Galloway side collected a group of witnesses, and an architect said that there were sixty windows overlooking the site, all within 150 yards, though he admitted that the nearest was sixty yards, a considerable range at which to detect all but the most blatant sexual behaviour. Lord Galloway's brother was recruited to affirm that Galloway was fond of children, and the official who was mainly concerned with the case, aware that his political career hung by a thread, declared that it was not the Act that was the crime, but the Intention and Motive. This was the substitute sheriff of the area; no doubt he made sheriff eventually. 'This little girl suffered no injury at the hands of the accused,' he pointed out soothingly, 'and she was of such a tender age that it was not likely that she would understand the lewd motive of the way in which she was treated, assuming, of course, that it was done from a lewd motive.' What other motives could induce a man of fifty-four to put his hand up the skirt of a girl of ten?

The rapidity with which the court dealt with the case, the speedy not guilty verdict – these encouraged closer scrutiny. The journal *Scottish Leader* was the initiator of indignation and it was leaned on by those in high places. The Galloway case had some of the ingredients of a *cause célèbre*, and its fame was echoed in the *New York Herald*, which reported that

The club gossips, and some few of the Society papers have lately interested themselves very strongly in a reported scandal concerning a well-known Scottish peer and near relative of two of our greatest politicians. The whole thing has now been shown to have arisen through a misunderstanding, and a very serious charge was founded upon a very trivial incident. The large number of society people interested in this case will be glad to know that nothing more will be heard of it.

This extract was quoted in the *North London Press* of 5 October 1889. Its editor thought that quoting was less hazardous than reporting. Two months later he found himself involved in a libel case concerning the Cleveland Street scandal (he accused Lord Euston of making use of a homosexual introducing house) and was sent to prison for a lengthy spell. Newspapers were powerful, but they had to watch their step. The divinity that hedged kings (and queens) did not extend to humble editors, and they played the Galloway case cautiously.

That there was something nasty in the woodpile was clear, that there was a miscarriage of justice was a possibility, a possibility that remained just that if one sees this case in isolation. But in January 1890 a tiny paragraph appeared in the newspapers. Lord Galloway appeared at Glasgow Central Police court, charged with having molested Margaret Brown, aged sixteen. He had been seen at four in the afternoon behaving in an odd fashion, and a man, having no idea of the eminence of the molester, had warned him off, telling a policeman when Lord Galloway was obdurate. Two policemen arrested Galloway. The case was declared 'not proven', that ingenious compromise that indicates that there is insufficient proof for a conviction.

There were other court cases at the same time that seem to affirm the ability of men of mark to escape scot free from charges that might land lesser creatures in prison for extended sentences. Mr Brodie, a justice of the peace, did not manage to creep away by virtue of his status, and got eight months for indecent assault, but it was thought scandalous that he should have been released after a mere three months, a period spent in the infirmary. The authorities found it difficult to be consistent. Many magistrates, confronted by lurid offences — especially against property — considered indecent assault hardly more than a peccadillo, and the sentences they passed were governed by the way they personally felt towards the immolation of children. In rural Walsgrave, near Coventry, a labourer named Olerenshaw was convicted of indecent assault of young children and was given six months' imprisonment; when he repeated the offence he was given eighteen months. 'Cannot the police lay hands on these scourges of society,' wrote a local reporter, 'and make an example of some of them before the public, so that they may be spurned by society, and kept out of every office of public trust?' This was not a problem likely to be set before the labourer Olerenshaw, but it was a question that troubled many, not only reporters anxious for copy. Magistrates were also upset by the tendency of the public to find indecent assault funny. James Crumbie was charged with offences to boys. Laughter from the public gallery caused the stipendiary magistrate to rebuke: 'The allegations were most disgusting, and how anyone could laugh he could not conceive', and when the case was put forward at the Warwickshire Assizes, Lord Chief Justice Coleridge was moved to the same sort of admonition. 'This case is disgusting enough,' he said sternly to the same sort of hilarious spectators, 'but, my God, that you should laugh makes one ashamed of one's kind.' The humour of the situation must have escaped Crumbie; he got two years.

The euphemisms of 'indecent assault', 'interference with young children', 'the violation of innocence', 'the despoliation of purity' – for many these were incidents of no importance in the lives of the poor. Well-meaning mothers who sent their daughters out on the streets thought starvation a more terrible prospect than the loss of virginity or the enacting of the services perverted elderly men demanded. Men of the world thought the attention paid to lost innocence excessive and were cynical about what Wyndham Lewis in another context called the 'strange tone of almost drivelling righteousness'. Magistrates not only were extravagantly influenced in their findings; by their own feelings regarding indecent assault they also had to be aware that many young girls and their mothers knew that there was a market in mock rape and mock interference. Dr Lawson Tait, a medical man with great experience in this field, examined over a period seventy young girls who claimed to have been assaulted sexually, and he advised a prosecution in only six of these instances. He was sceptical of their collective innocence: 'There is not a piece of sexual argot that ever had before reached my ears but was used by these children in the descriptions given by them of what had been done to them, and they introduced, in addition, quite a new vocabulary on the subject. The minute and detailed description of the sexual act given by chits of ten and eleven would do credit to the pages of Mirabeau.' [15]

The committed adorers of little girls refused steadfastly to see any other side of the coin than the one that they had selected. If Ruskin had been permitted into the dormitories of the girl pupils at his favourite school at Winnington, he would no doubt have been shocked by what he heard, though it is possible that he might have included any indiscretions in his pre-packed vision of maidenly purity without realizing the implications – there was none so blind as Ruskin when he would not see.

The commercials cashed in on the appeal of young children, and especially girls. If the public wanted pictures of young girls in mob caps, said Millais contemptuously, he would give them them, and he made between £30,000 and £40,000 a year doing just that. 'My First Sermon' sparked off the Archbishop of Canterbury:

Art has, and ever will have, a high and noble mission to fulfil. That man, I think, is little to be envied who can pass through these rooms and go forth without being in some sense a better and happier man; if at least it be so (as I do believe it to be) that we feel ourselves the better and the happier when our hearts are enlarged as we sympathize with the joys and sorrows of our fellow-men, faithfully delineated on the canvas; when our spirits are touched by the playfulness, the innocence, the purity, and may I not add the piety of childhood.

Incompetent artists could also make a tolerable living by catering to the sentimental taste, artists such as Kate Greenaway, a 'gentle, bespectacled, middle-aged lady, garbed in black' who spent her life painting sickly sweet water-colours of girls in a kind of Jane Austen setting. She was taken up by Ruskin, who allowed his sentimental inclinations to overcome his critical faculties to such an extent that Miss Greenaway was the subject for lectures to all-knowing Oxford dons and undergraduates. It was not only Ruskin who swallowed technical incompetence for the content. *Kate Greenaway's Birthday Book* of 1879, with verses by a Mrs Sale Barker, sold 128,000 copies in English,

13,500 in French, and 8,500 in German. Frederick Locker-Lampson, himself not impartial to childish whimsy, wrote to her, without a hint of tongue in cheek, 'It has occurred to me that you are about the only English artist who has ever been the fashion in France.' It was not everyone who was drawn into this conspiracy. The magazine *Fun* was started as opposition to *Punch*, though it rapidly went into decline, fond as it equally was of the basic unit of Victorian jokery, the pun. It related:

> A picture by Miss Greenaway (we scarcely like a bit of it)
> Is rightly titled 'Misses' for she hasn't made a hit of it.

Kate Greenaway turned out water-colours of little girls as they turned out copper-plate alphabets, but even the most deliriously intoxicated of her admirers seemed to sense that as works of art there was something lacking. A collection of 292 of her drawings mounted and bound in a morocco-covered box were sold by a bookseller for no more than £300; this would never have done for Turner.

When Ruskin was going through his spell of infatuation for Miss Greenaway's products, he was in a mental eclipse. He had a drawing of a girl with a doll put on glass. 'It will be a nursery window when you are next here,' he wrote to Kate Greenaway (in 1882), 'but it might be, as rightly, part of a cathedral window.' Occasionally his critical capability rears its head when confronted by more spectacular incompetence. 'But I wish some of the children had bare feet – and that the shoes of the others weren't *quite* so like mussel-shells.' However, for most of the time, like the Archbishop of Canterbury, he considered content was all. Here is the most influential art critic of the time writing in 1884 of one of Miss Greenaway's pieces:

> Of course the Queen of them all is the little one in front – but she's just a month or six weeks too young for me. Then there's the staff bearer on the right (– the left, as they come) turning round!!!! but she's just three days and a minute or two too *old* for me. Then there's the divine one with the dark hair, and the beatific one with the brown – but I think *they've both* got lovers already . . .[16]

Sickening as are these sentiments, puerile as is the language in which they are set out, Ruskin did not commit the final idiocy. He did not marry one of them. Others had. George Frederick Watts ('a great fellow or I am much mistaken' – Ruskin) in his late forties had married a chit of a girl thirty years younger than himself (Ellen Terry), a marriage that never got off the ground sufficiently to be called disastrous. Watts was the son of an unsuccessful piano maker in Marylebone, and found his *métier* as a painter of allegory, coming down to earth sufficiently to become a member of the Anti-Tight-Lacing Society. Nor did he like women's boots, which made the foot a 'crumpled clump of deformity'. But for chance, his giant symbolic 'Physical Energy' might to this day be on the Thames Embankment cheek by jowl with 'Boadicea'. Instead, it ended up in Rhodesia, as a token of Watts's admiration for Cecil Rhodes.

The motives of the child worshippers are ineluctably mixed. There was nostalgia for lost innocence; there was adult guilt at the mess they were making of the century, and children were seen as a hope for the future. The money-grubbers saw the young as phantoms of their former selves. Progress had proved to be a bitter thing, bought at a prohibitive price. The East End of London was an open festering sore, the whores of the Haymarket vaunted their wares with ever more assurance. The golden age of the New Britain had proved to be a hollow sham, and to many it seemed that the industrial revolution and its aftermath had resulted in nothing but dirt, degradation and disease. At times, it seemed that chaos was overwhelming the country. 'The unemployed are getting somewhat unpleasant,' said *Town Topics* nervously in 1894.

There were waves of revulsion at the way the country was going. Chauvinism, opportunism, incompetence at every level from the political down, mismanaged wars of conquest – these impelled a yearning for the lost delights of the early years. Tennyson was most popular when he was being escapist and yodelling the praises of King Arthur's England. There were grounds for panic. The desire to revert to a never-never land without chimneys and factory grime was understandable. At one time, it appeared that industrial Britain was a melancholy failure. In the seventies, when the cult of innocence, purity and all the other qualities symbolized by the image of the little girl was at its prime, Britain was in danger of being overwhelmed by the blight of civilization. In 1872, exports totalled £256,000,000; unemployment ran at 1 per cent. In 1879, exports were down to £192,000,000, and unemployment was 12 per cent. Was there a connection between these depressing figures and the refusal to look at life as it was, the preoccupation with sentiment and charm? It is interesting to note that in 1879, the most popular picture was Millais's 'Cherry Ripe', the essence of undiffused sentimentality, that in 1880 colour reproductions that appeared in the *Graphic* sold 600,000 copies. For every man stuck in a certain state of sexual development, for whom a young girl was a valid substitute for a mature partner, there were dozens who went misty-eyed at the young girl as a symbol for what-might-have-been. They made veneration for immaturity respectable.

The people who retained the objective eye were the girls themselves. Crisp and detached, they looked about them. Louisa Haldane, born 1863, watched as her governess was scolded for not eating trifle that she had taken on to her plate at lunch and heard with some curiosity the reason – the governess had taken a temperance pledge for the sake of her brother who 'needed all the help she could give him'. When she was very young, Louisa Haldane was troubled by a young boy who 'used to get under the table at nursery tea and pinch my legs. I did not complain because I wanted to deal with the nuisance myself, and hoped to kick him hard enough to make him stop; but when he got his hand up my drawers I had to complain, and was scolded for not doing so earlier.' [17] Girls were made of sterner stuff than their parents realized. Parents were frequently hermetically sealed from their brood by nurses, governesses, and a battery of servants, their parental duties thus confined to supplying food and living and sleeping quarters and to keeping the youngsters pure by providing them with unexceptionable reading matter, such as Mrs Trimmer's *History of the Robins* and *Conrad the Squirrel*. Being more ingenious than their elders supposed, the girls often got hold of more inflammatory literature – Louisa Haldane thought that she was very dashing to have acquired *Lilian's Golden Hours*, a sentimental tale for schoolgirls. When certain books were receiving undue attention, they were banned; this happened to Louisa with *The Infant's Magazine* after she had betrayed too much interest in the fate of the young hero. A now forgotten popular book of the seventies was the *Bibliothèque Rose*, a succession of paperbacks by Madame de Ségur, but glee on the part of the young was tempered by the discretion of the adults who inked out or pasted over doubtful portions.

The excessive interest taken in them by some men was puzzling rather than alarming. Arthur Arnold, the brother of the poet Edwin Arnold whose *The Light of Asia* was once a best-seller, and who was in himself an eminently respectable figure (later M.P. for Salford and an early chairman of the London County Council), was suitably crushed when he wanted to take Louisa Haldane for a picnic – it 'wouldn't do at all' Louisa's mother declared, though she would not tell the man herself. Governesses could be either mice or tyrants. 'When I think of our violent teachers ... I am surprised that we knew as much as we did and my parents' helplessness bewilders me.' [18] So wrote Margot Asquith née Tennant (born 1864). Lucy Lyttelton (1841–1925) had a governess named Miss Nicholson, who was 'over-severe and apt to whip me for obstinacy when I was only dense, letting me see her partiality for the other two, and punishing too often'. When the family was at Brighton, Miss Nicholson's favourite punishment for Miss Lyttelton was making her walk on the Parade with her hands tied behind her back, and threatening her with the prospect of meeting a policeman. A more refined torture was putting the girl in a large deep old-fashioned bath in a corner of the schoolroom, in the dark. 'I was continually put between the doors and often whipped,' wrote Lucy Lyttelton. The mother also had a curious form of punishment when it occurred to her to take an interest in her children; she crushed their hands in 'a thing for pressing letters together; a bronze hand it was, which pinched us slightly, leaving the dents of the fingers on the back of one's hand ...' [19] The pretty bright-eyed maidens who captivated the hearts of elderly gentlemen often went through a hell on earth behind nursery and schoolroom shutters.

This cruel indoctrination was often done for the best. A disobedient churlish child reflected badly on the governess, who would therefore stand a good chance of being dismissed in an age when the supply of governesses was greater than the demand. If the girl's sins were more than usually vicious or unmentionable then the punishment was consequently the greater. If the girl was more than usually angelic on the other hand, it might be better for her not to have to face the temptations of the wicked world outside. An early grave preserved the image. In *A Toy Tragedy* (1894) by Mrs Henry de la Pasture, the heroine 'died a little, sinless child; the gay blue eyes closed beneath the cloudless sky of innocence – who could wish them to open on the "pomps and vanities of this wicked world"?'

A man's rejection of the adult world can take many forms, whether it was the Duke of Devonshire who built beneath his estate at Welbeck Abbey a maze of underground passages so that he would not have to meet people, or the lower-class hermits who hid up like moles in cave and tenement, or those who went quietly and uncomplainingly mad, or those who found themselves hooked on a vision of childhood and spent their lives describing it, writing about it, or painting it. The cult of the little girl could be carried out in a sly knowing way. Max Beerbohm had a rather camp attachment to an adolescent music-hall star, Cissie Loftus, and was very shocked when Miss Loftus one day emerged rouged and with a curled fringe.

The clergy were particularly captivated by childish innocence. In 1875 the clergyman Francis Kilvert was at a fair, and 'a girl came up to me with a beseeching look in her eyes and an irresistible request for a swing. She was a perfect little beauty with a plump rosy face, dark hair, and lovely soft dark eyes melting with tenderness and a sweet little mouth as pretty as a rosebud.' Her clothes became tangled up in the seat of the swing, and to the amusement of the spectators it was seen that she was wearing no drawers. 'We hustled her out of the swing and her clothes into their proper place as soon as possible,' described Kilvert, 'and perhaps she did not know what a spectacle she had presented.' It had made Kilvert's day, however – 'her flesh was plump and smooth and in excellent whipping condition' [20] – surely no comment is necessary.

Samuel Rutherford Crockett was a Scottish Free Church minister, but resigned when he was thirty-five to be an author. He harnessed his talent to a very effective star; the cult of the little girl cannot have had a much more persuasive expositor, as shown by this passage from *Sweetheart Travellers* (1895);

My Sweetheart is sweet. Also she is my heart of hearts. To look into her eyes is to break a hole in the clouds and see into heaven, and the sunshine lies asleep upon her hair. As men and women, care-weighted with the world, look upon her, you can see the smiles break over their faces. Yet am I not jealous when my Sweetheart smiles back at them. For my Sweetheart is but four years, old and does not know that there is a shadow on all God's world. To spend a day with her in the open air is to get a glimpse into a sinless paradise. For there is no Eden anywhere like a little child's soul.

A long way, indeed, from an advertisement of 1889: 'Unruly Girls Received, by a Lady of Experience. Advice by letter five shillings, with "Hints on Management". Hints eight pence. Birch Rods supplied,' or the approval of such advertisements by *Reynold's Newspaper*: 'For the unruly girl is far worse than the unruly boy, just in proportion as she is more ingenious.' Yet there is a common factor. The sentimentality and gush, the cruelty and the harshness, reflect an inability to see things as they are, a preference for the lazy pre-packaged notions, a reluctance to come to terms with not only children as they were and not as embodiments of one's own virtues and vices, but with life as it was in an age that had killed off God and had not fulfilled its promise.

The whippings and chastisements inflicted by such as the 'Lady of Experience' and the governesses of the idle rich could only occur in an age when parents had contracted out of their obligations. Upper-class ladies had their society commitments, their vapours, and psychosomatic illnesses and considered it ill-befitting their dignities to discipline their children. With the wealth of servants, the upper classes reasoned, why keep a dog and bark oneself? The middle-class mothers were harassed and badgered by what they imagined to be their social duties. They modelled their attitude toward their children on what they imagined the upper classes did; too close an involvement with their progeny was ill-bred and beneath their dignity. Children were to be seen and not heard, though if obedience could be instilled into them they might prove useful status symbols.

It was not until the nineties, as in many other things, that the iron hand in the velvet glove finally succumbed to rust. Papa and mama gave way to mummy and daddy, unnatural sentimentality to natural sentiment. It was a change of emphasis that was long overdue.

8

Pornography

Pornography

IN the mid 1860s, the publisher William Dugdale advertised one of his list, *Nunnery Tales or Cruising under False Colours* (priced two guineas) in the following terms: 'every stretch of voluptuous imagination is here fully depicted, rogering, ramming, one unbounded scene of lust, lechery and licentiousness'. In brief, *Nunnery Tales* had the qualities of every pornographic book of the period, including the high price. Such books were published in limited editions under false imprints; some of the imprints were whimsical, such as the Society of Vice, Paris and London, and some were misleading (*Cythera's Hymnal*, a repository of lewd and blasphemous parody, was advertised as a product of the University of Oxford). *Raped on the Railway*, where a lady was raped and then flagellated 'on the Scotch express' was published in an edition of three hundred copies, and a curious volume published in 1898, *White Stains – the Literary Remains of George Archibald Bishop, a Neuropath of the Second Empire*,[1] a book of poems, was restricted to a hundred copies.

Similarly, the pornographic magazines were expensive and restricted. The *Boudoir*, of 1860, cost fifteen shillings per volume of thirty-two pages. The *Cremorne*, with obscene and incredibly incompetent illustrations, dated 1851 but really of 1882, cost a guinea, was privately published in, the title page states, Cheyne Walk, and was issued in an edition of three hundred copies. For the extremes of pornography there is nothing quite the equal of these magazines, the *Cremorne*, the *Boudoir*, and the *Pearl* (1879–80); and earlier obscene magazines of the 1840s, such as the *Exquisite*, have an almost cleanly mien alongside these salacious products, in which every conceivable perversion, position and anomaly are presented with a brusque candour, whether it is sodomy, incest, buggery, or the fashionable 'French' vice clinically called *cunnilicto* and its corresponding variation, *fellatio*.

These magazines were divided into several sections, but the standard feature was a serial, with titles such as *The Adventures and Amours of a Barmaid* and *Miss Coote's Confessions*. There were also jokes, usually in the form of anecdotes, obscene verses, often in the form of a parody of a well-known poem or hymn, and limericks, which were then known as nursery rhymes. There were sometimes references, especially in the anecdotes and poems, to local events; the easier divorce allowed by the Divorce Act of 1857 led to an almost endless stream of jokes about adultery, which was believed to necessarily increase because of the new laws, and the Contagious Diseases Acts of 1864 onward – and especially the repealers – caused much hilarity.

The Pearl was subtitled 'A journal of Facetiae and Voluptuous Reading', and although some of the writing is witty enough, much of the prose has the committed air not of hack writers but of eager participants in the fun and games they describe. *Miss Coote's Confessions* includes much flagellation material ('She goes on counting and thrashing the poor girl over her back, ribs, loins and thighs, wealing her everywhere, as well as the posteriors. All the spectators are greatly moved, and seem to enjoy the sight of Selica's blood dripping down till her stockings are saturated and it forms little pools beneath her on the floor.') This is no exceptional extract, and page after page reveals the same *ethos*. After this flogging, the girl has tar laid on her buttocks ('This will heal your bruises, and prevent the flies getting at your sore bottom this warm weather').

My French Friend, published in the *Boudoir*, has not got quite these sadistic overtones, and the writing is of a higher calibre, though again, everything goes for the benefit of the three hundred readers, as one can judge from this description: 'pretty little morsel, ripe and melting as a plum, acquiescent and charming, ready to make the beast with two backs, to play the game of sixty-nine, to exercise the delicate manipulation of her soft fingers, or do the lolly-pop trick with her ripe lips at a moment's notice'. There is a section where 'I had to go to Coventry. There, unlike Mr Tennyson, I did not hang with grooms and porters on the bridge, but I made up to my little dark-eyed chambermaid, and hung on to her with all the tenacity I was capable of.' This extract tells one or two things; that the writer could use current high art props with a certain assurance, and he was writing for an audience that would appreciate such references, to whom Mr Tennyson, if not exactly a familiar – though Tennyson liked smutty stories – was one of their kind. This same writer was adept at the Victorian device of the pun. 'He would knock down a gendarme, bilk a cocher or a garçon, and rumple the linen of a laundress with equal equanimity. He raised so many bellies in the gay capital that the registrar of births had to increase their staff owing to the way he had exercised his.'

Following this tale, was the serial, and once again one sees the prevalence of the pun:

Before many minutes had passed the coy lady was spread upon the heath couch, and Capias was duly 'entering an appearance' in a court in which he had not practised before; but which, as there was no 'bar' to his 'pleadings', he contrived to make a very sensible impression. His few 'motions' were rewarded with a verdict of approval; his 'attachment' was pronounced a valid one, and soft caresses, murmured thanks, and close endearments rewarded him for his successful issue into the 'court of love',

a cumbersome description of the sex act in legalistic terms. It might be a clever trick, but, who, one thinks, could possibly care? Who would want to pay fifteen shillings for thirty-two pages of this kind of twaddle?

There is perhaps a clue in a later volume of this magazine, when the same serial, *Adventures and Amours of a Barmaid*, is pursuing its same nutty amorous way:

Taking a walk early one summer's morning she entered Kensington Gardens, and sat down by herself on a chair in a rather secluded spot, closing her eyes as various pleasant reveries floated before her vision. 'What a lovely leg! Alas! Get thee hence, Satan!' she heard ejaculated in low trembling tones, and suddenly opening her eyes, fixed them on an elderly gentleman, whom she at once recognized as a particularly pious Earl.

This is low-level stuff by any table of values. The girl takes the earl home, and while she prepares herself ,'it was amusing to her to watch the variations of his face as picking up a decidedly naughty book he eagerly scanned its contents.' So this was the audience the *Boudoir* and the other naughty books were aimed at!

When the writer of the tales was not being particularly motivated, the style has a wishy-washy women's magazine air:

Jane and the housekeeper had already stripped off the blue silk, and were proceeding to remove the under skirts of white linen, trimmed with broad lace; the bouquet had fallen to the floor, and presently the submissive victim stood with only chemise and drawers. What a glance I had of her splendid white neck and bosom, what deliciously full and rounded legs, with pink silk stockings and handsome garters.

Why, one can get more from advertising hand-outs. Sometimes, the style can sink to a level of ineptitude that must have made even the most hag-ridden purchaser wonder what, exactly, he was getting for his sixpence a page. Thus *Sub-Umbra, or Sport Amongst the She-Noodles* (1879): 'After luncheon, Frank smoked his cigarette in my room, the events of the morning had left both of us in a most unsettled and excited state. "I say, old fellow," he exclaimed, "by Jove! it's quite impossible for me to wait till to-morrow for the chance of enjoying that delicious Rosa ..."' One would have thought that Rosa was some wine recently imported from Cyprus, but no, Rosa is a woman, and, like all women in these stories, up to any trick. Another character in *Sub-Umbra* (one wonders, at times, who Umbra is) is Sophie. ' "How lovely the honeysuckle smells!" sighed Sophie, as I drew them both down by my side in the corner, and began a most delicious kissing and groping in the dim obscurity. ...' This is the inevitable standard of this class of literature, a standard that perks up slightly for the prosaic four-lettered one-syllabled descriptions of *fellatio*, ordinary common-or-garden fornicating (quite a *rara avis*), with the occasional lash of a casual whip.

Some of the sex jokes have a certain period flavour, though, like most sex jokes, the material tends to be stretched out. In one case, a daughter is asking her father for permission to marry a young man by whom she is three months pregnant. Retorts the father:

'Egad! Do you think I'll ever have that penniless puppy?'

'Oh, oh, Papa!' cries the girl, 'but the puppy's had me, and there's a baby coming.'

'Well, I'm buggered.'

'Father, Father! Don't say that, we're such an unfortunate family.'

One of the events commemorated in bawdy verse was the siting of New-Temple-Bar; old Temple Bar, built by Sir Christopher Wren to mark the traditional boundary of the City of London, stretched across the road and made the traffic problems of the nineteenth century insurmountable. The whole impressive edifice, on which the heads of traitors were once wont to be put, was taken down in 1878 and moved in what was then a fairly novel way to Theobald's Park, Herefordshire in 1888. The man entrusted with the New-Temple-Bar was one Truscott; as the verse tells one, he had problems:

It has without doubt been Truscott's ambition
To get the New-Temple-Bar in position.
He thought of it by day, dreamt of it by night
And one morning woke in a terrible fright
'I dreamt, my dear love, that this came to pass,
That the public had shoved Temple-Bar up my arse;
That they greeted me loudly with hisses and calls,
And the dragon grew lively and bit off my balls.'

In the stories and serials, the mechanical repetition of descriptions of the necessarily limited rota of sexual activities make for boring reading. When women are brainless toys ever capable of being brought to heat by the brandishing of a penis, and when men are a set of genitals attached to a chunk of beef, then it can hardly be otherwise. The dialogue has the asinine ring that today one tends to find only in television serials and put in mainly so that women could pronounce the *verboten* words, then more numerous than they are today, or to speed the action from one bed to another.

Writers on the subject, such as H. S. Ashbee, often speculated as to why French erotic writing should be so superior to English, when the English language has a much greater vocabulary and is so much richer by virtue of the various strains that have been introduced into it via Latin, Greek, and French. It would seem that the English language of sex is a basic language, depriving itself of influences that in other spheres have made English the most flexible tongue in the world. The English language of sex is curt and Anglo-Saxon – hardly words to fit into an elegiac content – and the Latin equivalents are still just that, Latin equivalents – 'copulate' (*co* together *apere* to join), 'penis' (a tail), 'vagina' (a sheath), while other Latin terms, such as 'vulva', still have the air of only just coming out of the italic stage.

English erotic prose was stretched on the procrustean bed of the literary and the prosaic, and few masters have ever arisen to grapple with this problem, though in this century D. H. Lawrence did his fumbling best. Most of the writers of erotica remain anonymous, and the few names that do come down to us hardly have the ring of genius; they come down to us often because they were eccentric, perverted, or half-mad – such as Edward Sellon, whose *Ups and Downs of Life* of 1867 is the nearest thing to a classic Victorian erotology has. There is not a great deal known about Sellon; he dabbled in Hindu literature and archaeology, taught fencing, drove a mail coach between London and Cambridge, and at the age of forty-eight he blew out his brains.

The name of Henry Smith of 37 Holywell Street, Strand, is

prominent in early Victorian smut. His list was almost entirely obscene. In the forties this included:

Tales of Twilight: or the Amorous Adventures of a company of Ladies before Marriage (10/6, 8 fine coloured plates)

The Royal Wedding Jester or all the Fun and Facetiae of the Wedding Night with all the good things said, sung, or done on that joyous occasion (reduced price 2/6)

Onanism Unveiled, or the Private Pleasures and Practices of the youth of both Sexes exposed, The Connubial Guide, or Married People's Best Friend (price 6d)

The Spreeish Spouter or Flash Cove's Slap-Up Reciter

The Voluptuarian Cabinet or Man of Pleasure's Miscellany (5 plates, 3/6)

The Wedding Night or the Battle of Venus

The Jolly Companion, Woman Disrobed (a most capital tale)

Adventures of a Bedstead

Venus in the Cloisters, or the Jesuit and the Nun

Julia or I Have Saved My Rose.

All these were timid excursions into pornography, harmless schoolboy smut. The bestiality, the buggery and the extremes of pornography came later.

Collecting erotica in Victorian England had its own perils, and the books contained in the British Museum's Private Cases are accompanied by plaintive little letters from executors who found this or that book in the library of 'a gentleman in the country' and thought that the British Museum was the safest place for it, away from the prurient eyes of those whom Carlyle contemptuously designated 'the goats'. Collecting erotica was principally a mid- and late-Victorian pursuit; for this market there was a ready supply of material – *The Romance of Lust* (1873),[2] in which the hero relates his couplings with his sister (who also happens to be his daughter), *The Story of a Dildoe* (1880), *Kate Handcock or A Young Girl's Introduction to Fast Life* (1882), *Laura Middleton, Her Brother and Her Lover* (1890), or *Venus in India or Love Adventures in Hindustan* (1889). Empire builders had brought back information from the East, and these were rehashed in fictional form – *A Night in a*

Moorish Harem depicted a stallion-and-woman congress, and dates from the nineties.

The curious with friends at the British Museum – such as the lawyer and *bon viveur* Sir William Hardman – had access to many of these books, his interest was concealed under the pseudonym of anthropology or 'the cult of Priapus' (Hardman's own particular kink).

Occasionally the collectors [3] were themselves writers of pornography, and speculations that the learned and supercilious Ashbee indulged are not lacking. Another expert, James Campbell Reddie, was certainly the author of *The Amatory Experiences of a Surgeon* (1881), and one is at a loss to reconcile Reddie's assertion that he viewed erotic literature from a philosophical point of view, as illuminating human nature and its ramifications, with the hysterical squeakings of his own work. Reddie was particularly interested in semen; the narrator would 'drench her little stomach and thighs with almost a supernatural flood of sperm ... heavy pattering sounds announced the return of the fluid which fell in large drops upon the carpet, and ran in rills down her beautiful thighs'. *Nostalgie pour la boue* mixed with fantasy and a disguised sadism is the blissful quintessence of the Reddie vision, and Ashbee might well have awarded his colleague the accolade he granted another: 'The copulations which occur at every page are of the most tedious sameness; the details are frequently crapulous and disgusting, seldom voluptuous ... gross, material, dull and monotonous' (of *Letters from a Friend in Paris*, 1874). At times one thinks that Ashbee went into erotology as a penance; his heavy air of disapproval of almost everything he comes across makes one wonder why he did not invest his time in something more congenial, such as the study of earthworms. Indeed, one cannot envy anyone the task of plodding through one of the landmarks of Victorian pornography, the 4,200 pages of the anonymous *My Secret Life* of 1888, or the lesser masters of the genre (Ashbe left a total of 15,299 books to the British Museum).

This territory was an ideal hunting ground for the amateur scholar, such as Ashbee. The last quarter of the nineteenth century was the golden age of the amateur scholar and the amateur archaeologist, and monthly magazines such as the *Antiquary* containing articles such as 'Guernsey Folk Lore' and 'Curious Corporation Customs' enjoyed considerable success. A large proportion of these crypto-experts were clergymen, especially those placed by circumstances and influential relatives in sinecures; others were successful businessmen whose duties did not lie too heavy, and others were businessmen who had made a packet and retired from the rat race at an early age, like Ashbee. A common characteristic of the amateur scholar is that learning does not lie lightly on him, but more conforms to heavy armour; there is a good deal of ostentatious quoting – especially of foreign languages – and there is a heavy donnishness as protective colouring. The three books by Ashbee are named *Index Librorum Prohibitorum* (1877), *Centuria Librorum Absconditorum* (1879), *Catena Librorum Tacendorum* (1885). The first of the three is a whimsical take-off of the prohibited book list of the Roman Catholic Church (Ashbee was rabidly anti cleric), and one wonders whether these three titles are more or less pretentious than Joseph Octave Delepierre's earlier *Pornodidascaliana*. One is inclined to award the laurels to Ashbee on account of the subtitle of *Index Librorum Prohibitorum – being Notes Bio-Biblio-Icono-graphical and Critical, on Curious and Uncommon Books* – and to be irreverently reminded of Polonius in *Hamlet* ('The best actors in the world, either for tragedy, comedy, history, pastoral, pastoral-comical, historical-pastoral, tragical-historical, tragical-comical-historical-pastoral, scene individable, or poem unlimited').

Indeed, Polonius might have been a suitable pseudonym for Ashbee had he not chosen 'Pisanus Fraxi' as it could be construed as having lewd overtones. Oscar Wilde once commented that a dirty mind is a perpetual feast, and no doubt Ashbee got a considerable kick out of the scatological invention Pis-anus.[4] Ashbee must have thought it very droll to call a book *Index Librorum Prohibitorum* (though the game of knocking the Catholics was then rather old hat) and very scholarly to have pages with but one line of text, the rest of the paper covered by aimless and often irrestrainable notes, a sort of bibliographical diarrhoea in a variety of languages.

The interest of the respectable in pornography was often disguised. As the genuine scholar, A. H. Bullen wrote from the Residence, the British Museum, on 12 October 1885: 'Of late the demand for bawdy books has become startlingly large. If the study of "Anthropology" goes on at this rate, heaven only knows what we shall reach in the next generation.' The appeal of pornography was not difficult to understand; the Victorian age was a muddled age, an emancipated age, and – as Victorians acutely recognized – an age of transition. Although businessmen were honest because they still believed in God and thought they would fry if cheated, religion no longer had an iron grip on the sophisticated; there was no longer a regiment of angels looking over their shoulders to see what they were reading. Among the intellectuals there existed, in the words of Pater, an 'inexhaustible discontent, languor, and homesickness'. Pornography was a way out; it was a new interest, the forbidden forthcoming, and a guide to the new freedom released by the slackening hold of organized religion.

'The prospect of a book which can produce horripilation is refreshing,' said Sir Richard Burton breezily, but it was generally not the man of action who was addicted to the gooseflesh so raised, but the modest, the retiring and the discreet. Many must have been the burnings of the books that accompanied the deaths of quiet country gentlemen, and no one can say with certainty the extent of the distribution of pornography, as the publishers were playing a game of their own that involved covering their tracks whenever conceivable. Dugdale, the nastiest of all the publishers, used a variety of aliases – including Henry Smith. Born in Stockton, he was involved in the Cato Street Conspiracy (the idea was a mass assassination of politicians at a cabinet dinner; the main protagonists of which were arrested in 1820 and executed as traitors). Many of Dugdale's advertising methods anticipate those of the twentieth century; the blurb for *Betsy Thoughtless* – 'a most spicey and piquant Narrative of a Young Girl obliged to excoriate her sweetheart's bum before he could ravish her Maidenhead'.

Since the publicity given to it by Steven Marcus in *The Other Victorians* (1964), perhaps the most famous Victorian porno-

graphic book is *My Secret Life*, published in Amsterdam in the
nineties. It purports to be a diary of a man's complete sexual life.
The language is prosaic and factual, but a man with but one
idea in his head rapidly becomes a bore, and eleven volumes,
more than 4,000 pages, is surely carrying egotism a little too far,
and the diarist's claim that he had 'had women of twenty-seven
Empires, Kingdoms or Countries' has a grip on one's imagination that is hardly more than marginal. Whatever the merits of
My Secret Life, they certainly do not vie in interest with the un-
exampled fervour with which erotologists treat this work, in
which error is compounded with error, and in which assumption and presumption bring scholarship to a grinding halt.

My Secret Life is part of the submerged iceberg of Victorian
low life, and the author takes his place alongside his milder
brethren, John Addington Symonds, who was castigated by the
Contemporary Review for 'the total denial of any moral restraint on any human impulses' or Swinburne, 'tuning his lyre
in a stye ... nameless, shameless abominations', cramming his
Poems and Ballads 'with pieces which many a professional ven-
dor of filthy prints might blush to sell'. It was fortunate that
John Morley, who wrote this of Swinburne, was not called upon
to review *My Secret Life*.

We enter diffracted areas when we enter the realm of pornographic verse; whereas pornographic prose is pretty sad stuff, the
verse can be either uninspired stodge or poetry of the highest
calibre. The Ruskins and the Carlyles did not write pornography; the Tennysons and the Rossettis did. The Victorians
used verse as a genuine medium of expression, and they used it
with unparalleled virtuosity; often they were too clever for their
own good, and the exponents have received less than their due
deserts. This is particularly true of the writers of smutty verse
and *vers de société*.

Pornographic verse can be more extreme than pornographic
prose, and at its furthest ends presents an apocalyptic blasphemy
that has few parallels elsewhere – the 'spooney Jews' mastur-
bating upon Christ on the cross is one of these extreme concepts,
and this is by no means the ultimate image created by the

curious set who used verse to free themselves from their repressions. Although the pornographic books frequently use large
slabs of verse either as a prelude to a tale or as a piece of free-
wheeling pornography in its own right, the writers of verse
pornography can be seen to have a different attitude towards
their task as compared with their colleagues in prose. Prose pornography is a product for a market, as well as being a release for
the writers; verse pornography is not only a release, but a life-
enhancing exercise in a viable art form. The constrictions of the
line and the stanza tend to damp down the turgid frenzy that
characterizes so much of the prose; the writer of dirty verse has
to consider his message so that it can be formalised for the
medium; this formalisation also tends to take away the 'real'
elements of the raw material, so that extreme concepts can be
presented in a more or less acceptable form, though occasionally
these do overstep the mark (as in the religious example quoted
above). Verse pornography is superior to prose pornography for
several reasons; in the first place, its composition needs a *certain*
literacy, if only to rhyme 'sleep' with 'deep'; in the second place,
verse can use the humour of sexual behaviour in a way that
prose cannot. The pornographic novel or the tale is not very
funny, except unintentionally; the doggy air is almost impossible
to eliminate. When funniness is there, it tends to drift off into
the grindingly facetious.

The quintessence of pornographic verse is contained in the
Oxford-orientated *Cythera's Hymnal* of 1870. The British
Museum's copy of this – a pre-war photostat facsimile [5] – was
presented by the scholarly Alfred Rose (pseudonym: Rolf S.
Reade).[6] The bulk of the verses are parodies of poems in the
standard repertoire, nursery rhymes and popular ballads, and
hymns. The Victorian age was a great period for anthologies,
and the most famous of them all, Palgrave's *Golden Treasury*,
had appeared nine years before the publication of *Cythera's
Hymnal*. It was also a wonderful time for the parody, of which
the Victorians were masters – just as they had succeeded in
parodying, without quite realizing it, Gothic and Renaissance
styles in Architecture, so they had triumphed in parodying Tennyson and earlier writers. The greatest master of the parody was

Lewis Carroll, and *Cythera's Hymnal* was published when Carroll was at his peak, midway between the two *Alice* books, and shortly after his *Phantasmagoria*. The anonymous composers of these verses might have learned a thing or two from Carroll, the leading exponent of this genre and one of the key figures in the Oxford of the time. Some of the parodies are so good that one is tempted to assign them to Lewis Carroll, though there is no evidence that he did have a hand in any of them, as all kinds of smut were alien to the mathematical don.

The specialized pornography of this period was ribaldly anti-religious, especially in Oxford, a town that had been the centre of the move of the established church towards Rome. The confessional had been taken over by many High Church clerics, and this was a cause of either concern (as it was to Ashbee who devoted a large chunk of *Centuria Librorum Absconditorum* to *The Confessional Unmasked*) or amusement, as it was to a versifier in *Cythera's Hymnal*:

> The Reverend Pimlico Poole was a saint
> Who averted from sinners their doom,
> By confessing the ladies until they felt faint,
> All alone in a little dark room.
>
> Now this little dark room was a sight to behold,
> So becurtained a brothel did seem,
> With a well padded sofa, and I also am told,
> On a shelf stood a pot of cold cream.
>
> Chorus:
> But they never confessed, and it never was known
> What was done in that little dark room all alone.
>
> And all these confessions, so shocking to hear,
> Never shocked Mr Poole in the least,
> But arranging his person, he sat in his chair,
> While his Tommy kept rising like yeast.

A virtuoso piece, a parody of the hymn that is still the staple diet of the English country church:

See him rise, with pride ascending,
  Oft in favoured sinners lain,
Thousand thousand crabs attending
  Swell the triumph of his train;
    Hallelujah! Hallelujah!
Rises prick to fall again.

Virgin eyes with fear behold him
  Rise in dreadful majesty;
Claps that set at nought and sold him,
  Pox that burned him grievously,
    Never fears he, never fears he,
In the bliss of venery.

and on to more. It is interesting that so many of these poems
find a macabre humour in syphilis and gonorrhoea, diseases
that in the fun books are glossed over, quite understandably.
Pox was the Russian roulette of the Oxford gay set:

It was evening, I lay dozing,
Spirit wandering, frame reposing,
  But one thought would never leave me
    Till poetic form it bore;
Though to you it may appear, Sir,
For a poet rather queer, Sir,
'Twas about the gonorrhoea, Sir,
  That I'd caught a week before,
And I write these warning stanzas,
  As I trickled down before,
    Trickle, trickle, evermore!

I remembered how I wandered,
Nor on consequences pondered,
  Where Haymarket lamps shone brightly
    Over many a nighthouse door;
Came a hoarse though jovial maiden,
Who with brandy seemed o'erladen,
To address an old and staid 'un
  Said 'Old chap, we've met before,'
Touched the garments that arrayed one
  Where they buttoned up before,
    Fingered them, and something more!

This was a parody of what passed as high art – Edgar Allan Poe's 'The Raven' of 1845, and excellent it is, too. The Oxford element in *Cythera's Hymnal* betrays itself in the following, not because of the localized terms used ('the High', 'Big Tom', 'bull-dogs'), but because the author assumed that such terms needed no introduction or explanation. The more expensive and exclusive pornography was directed at an in group who did not have to have the i's dotted or the t's crossed, an in group that *knew* that the High was High Street, Oxford, just as the Corn was Cornmarket Street and the Broad was Broad Street. Big Tom was the great bell of Christ Church – never called Christ Church College, but more usually The House – which was rung by hand at 9.5 p.m. 101 times to indicate it was time to close the college gates. One hundred and one, naturally enough, was the number of students Christ Church at one time possessed. This close-knit terminology was a reflection of this celibacy-orientated community, just as the flash language of the swells of London betrayed their predominant inclinations. The Oxford bulldog was not an animal, but a proctor's attendant.

> Three Students went slumming out into the High,
>   Out into the High, as Big Tom went down,
> Determined to slum till their taps ran dry,
>   And the bull-dogs stood watching them right thro' the town,
> For men must slum, and women will try
> To gain a small pittance by walking the High,
>   While Peter stiff is standing.[7]

A couple of stanzas from a parody of the nursery rhyme *There was a little man who had a little gun* might well present the amiable cleverness of these anonymous Oxford poets:

> It's a strawberry, said Eve, or a carrot, I believe
>   Or a cucumber, or something of that breed, breed, breed,
> But now I come to scan it, I think it's pomegranate,
>   Because it is so very full of seed, seed, seed.
>
> So he gave him Eve to lay with, but he said, You musn't play with
>   This pretty little fruit that you see here, here, here;
> But all the rest you may indulge in night and day,
>   Until you both do get the diarrhoea, rhoea, rhoea.

Unfortunately, the second verse does not scan, but, then, even Homer nods.

The verse contained in the magazines varies widely in quality, and is often of a startlingly innocuous ingenuousness considering the events it is portraying and the way these events are celebrated in prose. This is especially true of the earlier magazines, when dirt was beginning to rear its head from the somnolence of the Prince Albert period.

> Ye Gods! the raptures of that night!
> What fierce convulsions of delight!
> How in each other's arms involv'd,
> We lay confounded, and dissolv'd!
> Bodies mingling, sexes blending,
> Which should most be lost contending;
> Darting fierce, and flaming kisses,
> Plunging into boundless blisses;
> Our bodies and our souls on fire,
> Tost by a tempest of desire;
> 'Till with the utmost fury dow'n,
> Down, at once, we sunk to heav'n.

In the magazines, the verse forms are not ambitious. Thus the simplest of trochaic measures:

> For a time her rich protector,
>   Lavished on her lots of wealth,
> But his ways so funny wrecked her
>   Hopes, and played hell with her health.

Occasionally disaster struck these humble poetasters. Invention was there, but technique failed:

> I don't like to see women wear dirty smocks
> Nor a boy of fifteen laid up with the pox;
> And I don't like to see – it's a fact by my life –
> A married man grinding another man's wife.

> Nor I don't like to see, though it's really a lark,
> A clergyman poking a girl in the park;
> Nor a young lady, wishing to be thought discreet,
> Looking at printshops in Holywell-street.

I don't like to see, coming out of Cremorne,
A girl with her muslin much crumpled and torn,
Arm in arm with a fellow who's had the mishap,
To forget, when he shagged her, to button his flap.

I don't like to see – it's a fact that I utter
That nasty word—written upon a shutter;
And I don't like to see a man, drunk as an earl,
Getting into a lamp post think it's a girl.

At its best, the journeyman verse has a rollicking swing that
it would be churlish to overlook:

And then his house he showed his spouse
And lined her again on a box in the garret,
He showed her the cellar, and with his umbrella
He shoved her backside through a dozen of claret.
He then took the bitch in, and showed her the kitchen,
And his plunges made every spoon, dish, and plate clink;
He lined her in dining-room, bed-room, or snoring-room,
Pantry, larder and parlour, and privy and sink.

Laughter is the surest way of obtaining release from the in-
congruity of sex, and the savagery of the male in pursuit of the
female quite in palaeolithic style is rendered acceptable by the
mocking awareness of the absurdity of it all. The laughter en-
gendered by humorous pornographic verse (and the bulk of pornographic verse is humorous) partly stems from this realization
– the animal in man confronted by the sophistication of centuries and isolated in a frame. If pornography can be said to be
beneficial, then verse must be the most favoured facet.

When the need arose for sexual excitation in private the clum-
siest medium became acceptable; photography was still a bant-
ling, and was only available in two forms – the print and the
lantern slide. No economic way had been found to reproduce
photographic prints in magazine or book; when they were used
– as they were extensively on sheet-music covers – the print was
stuck on with glue. Therefore, for most of the period, the pornographic book had to be content without illustrations or with
engravings or coloured lithographs.

The Boudoir of 1860 contained in each issue one page-size

engraving, any one of which would have been quite acceptable in any Royal Academy exhibition of the time. The engraving was of a nude or partly nude woman, devoid of any characteristics, done with skill but without salaciousness, hack work of slightly above average quality. The woman would be posed in a decent classical arrangement; occasionally a second woman would be introduced with the possible suggestion, betrayed by a certain coyness in the facial expression, that they were more than friends; very rarely a man would enter the *mise en scène* but he played no part in the proceedings unless the subject was from mythology (a favourite dodge of the respectable artists to portray nudes). This engraving was a boasted selling point in the advertising campaign of *The Boudoir*, and the eagerness of the public to have dirty or pseudo-dirty pictures in their dubious literature is rather pathetic (Dr Armstrong's *The Economy of Love* of the early forties was advertised as possessing 'a fine engraving of the Titian Venus'). For whom, one wonders, did these engravings *do* anything?

The Cremorne of 1882, sold at a guinea a copy, contained lewd coloured lithographs of a flagellation scene with a man standing by, penis ready, a woman lying on a bed with her legs apart, and a sixty-nine position. These lithographs are incompetent in the extreme, so badly drawn as to be clearly the work of men without any art training, and the colour is gaudy and out of synchronization. This bad workmanship is difficult to believe when one considers the extensive history of the pornographic print in Britain; in 1845 one dealer was arrested, having in his possession 12,346 obscene prints, 393 books, 351 copper plates, 188 lithograph stones, and 33½ hundredweights of set type. That the producers of the *Cremorne* could not do better than they did savours of sharp practice.

The essence of pornography is secrecy. Its aim is to make – in Sir Alan Herbert's phrase – the reader as randy as possible as often as possible, and its mechanisms do not alter much over the years:

Her lovely thighs and heavy mount of love, shaded by the softest golden-haired down, whilst one finger was fairly hidden within the fair lips of the pinkiest possible slit below the dewy moisture from which glistened in the light... the battering ram of love had to be vigorously applied before a breach was made sufficient to effect a lodgement. What sighs, what murmurs of love and endearment were mixed with her moans of pain.

This extract from *The Three Chums* (from the *Boudoir* 1860) has its parallel in the present-day pornography, both in the vocabulary and in the curious grammatical formations. Similarly, conventionally unrespectable procedure – conventionally not actually (*vide* Kinsey) – are presented with almost Tennysonian sweetness: 'Side by side on the sofa, with heads reversed, they sucked each other's parts like two bees, till the last drop of honey of love had been extracted' (also from *The Three Chums*).

However, there is frequently a squeaking note that was peculiar to the age: 'You naughty man, you shall tell me what I want to know this time. How do babies come? What is the parsley bed the nurses and doctors say they come out of? Is it not a curly lot of hair at the bottom of the woman's belly? I know that's what Lucy's got, and I've seen you kiss it, Sir?' (*Sub-Umbra, or Sport Amongst the She-Noodles* – the *Pearl* (1879–80). The *cognoscenti* of pornography were more likely to be shy and timid than otherwise. Wish-fulfilment played their part:

Haven't you tasted the choice juice of Jew and Gentile? haven't you revelled between the thighs of the lovely Circassian; penetrated the busy forest of a moustachoe'd Spanish woman; parted the fair curls of a German frow; touched the cold clammy interior of a New Orleans negress; penetrated the musk-smelling secret corner of a mandarin's wife; and drove home the vitals of a Scotch fish wife?

Sadly, the reader must have shaken his head as he went on from lubricity to what can only be described as women's magazine journalese:

Who, without agonies of desire, could see breasts round and hard as an apple; a skin whiter than the driven snow, suffused with a glowing warmth, that brightened the colour and heightened the temptation, softer than the down of swans and sweeter than all the balmy spices of Arabia. [1813]

Their sparkling eyes, slightly flushed faces, and above all the dazzling beauties of their teeth, as they indulged in gay laughter at our badinage, set all of us in a flame. [1880]

He could see at times up to my knee ... He was evidently getting excited. [1904]

The Pornography Trade

PORNOGRAPHY is a trade like any other, needing a manufacturer, a distributor, and a consumer. In any society there have always been hacks ready to string words together for a specialty market, and the Victorian hacks were fortunate in that their anonymity was respected; they had no one like Alexander Pope to probe them from their burrows and castigate them.

By and large, the writers of pornographic fiction were not very talented. Occasionally, however, a 'real' writer emerges from the fog to write pornography for bread and butter, and one of these was Arthur Machen, who enjoyed a reputation in the nineties and the Edwardian era as a writer of horror stories by using the simple device of piling up adjectives like 'unnameable' and 'unutterable' and then not qualifying them. Machen started his literary career translating the *Heptameron* of Margaret of Navarre (1492–1549), which was a fashionable mixture of religious fervour and refined voluptuousness, and no writer who has been dead for four hundred years could be less than respectable. The *Heptameron* had been modelled on Boccaccio's *Decameron*, which rings few bells in our sophisticated days. Machen did this translation for a man named Redway, who ran an indecent lending library.

Like many young men who fell under the spell of the curious and the naughty, Machen frequented the Reading Room of the British Museum, and was one of the set which was freethinking and vaguely subtopian. He married in 1887 a certain Amelia Hogg, who, wrote the humourist Jerome K. Jerome (*Three Men in a Boat*), 'frequented restaurants and aerated bread-shops and had many men friends; all of which was considered very shocking in those days'. Machen became friendly with A. E. Waite, author of *The Real History of the Rosicrucians* (it was one of those circles), and eked out a sparse existence as a cataloguer for a Coventry Street bookseller at £80 a year. To earn extra money, he turned his attention to translating Casanova's *Memoirs*, and then *Le Moyen de Parvenir* by Béroalde de Verville, a coarse imitator of Rabelais. During this operation, what must have been a very lowering incident took place – after eighty pages of Machen's translations, the printers, shocked to their honest English marrows, laid down the tools of their trade and refused to carry on.

Throughout the century, French pornography, either in the original or in translation, enjoyed a consistent vogue, and occasional sallies by the Society for the Suppression of Vice, especially against accepted classics like Rabelais, only served to whet their appetites. When malicious critics got their teeth into the Society, then there was little these well-meaning people could do except mumble. In 1875, the Society ran a crusade against 'The book entitled Rabelais', and in one of the century's masterpieces of sustained invective, Swinburne, hurt himself at the hands of the suppressors, launched himself at the Society for the Suppression of Vice, which had had the misfortune to declare that 'the book entitled Rabelais ... is scarcely understood even by accomplished French scholars by reason of its antiquated phraseology.' What, asked Swinburne, was the Society going to do about 'the book entitled the Bible' and 'the book entitled Shakespeare'? Somewhat shamefacedly, the Society admitted that they had no plans for suppressing the Bible or Shakespeare. What, retorted Swinburne indignantly, 'It will allow Shakespeare to be hawked in public, – to be exposed on the Vestal altar of a railway stall!' So the controversy raged in the learned pages of the *Athenaeum*. It is agreeable to see Swinburne getting his own back on his critics; he also had a point. Where does censorship stop? What does one do, what does even the most soul-searching society do, over the saucier pages of *Romeo and Juliet*? It was a question that no one was able to answer with any degree of persuasion. The analogy was carried to painting. 'Picture,' declared Lord Lyndhurst, 'a woman stark naked, lying down, and a satyr standing by her with an expression on his face which shows most distinctly what his feelings are, and what is his object'. Lord Lyndhurst, in his valiant effort to stem the flood of prudery, was merely describing Correggio's *Jupiter and Antiope*.

It was easy for the sophisticated to make fun of the honest attempt to stop the distribution of obscene literature, especially when the decision as to whether a given work was obscene was left to the discretion of local magistrates, many of whom were ever anxious to exercise their newly acquired muscles. In pre-industrial days the fragmentation of English society had meant that outside the hub of London, the country was largely in the hands of the country élite so far as local government was concerned, an élite that was Oxford or Cambridge educated, literate, yet knew one end of a horse from the other and was not averse at times to setting mantraps for poachers. The justice of peace was a well-bred man with common sense who could chuckle at bawdy with the best of them.

Industrial times threw up a different kind of justiciary – the middle-class man who had done well in business and was something of a zealot, and who knew what he liked and could pick out smut at a hundred paces. The Obscene Publications Act of 1857 held that magistrates throughout the country had the power to order the destruction of 'any obscene publication held for sale or distribution on information laid before a court of summary jurisdiction'.

The man who was responsible for this act was Lord Campbell, a learned and industrious gentleman who made up for lack of sparkle with glum determination. He had early fancied himself as a writer, and after a short incubatory period as a candidate for the church and then as a tutor, he joined the *Morning Chronicle* for a spell before throwing himself fully into the business of law. His conscientious perseverance made him modestly formidable, but the briefs did not flow in, and he did not obtain 'silk' until he was nearly fifty. He was a man who flowered late; he entered parliament in 1830, spoke lengthily on every conceivable subject, a zeal that was forgiven him as he put in sterling work on projects that less enthusiastic members shirked

— the Fines and Recoveries Abolition Act of 1833, the Inheritance Act and the Dower Act of the same year, the Wills Act of 1837. His main admirable object, however, was to get rid of the cumbersome technicalities that bogged down the law in primeval mire.

He became Attorney General in 1834, and speedily took action against the bookseller Hetherington for blasphemous libel, an action he blithely justified on the ground that 'the vast bulk of the population believe that morality depends entirely on revelation; and if a doubt could be raised among them that the ten commandments were given by God from Mount Sinai, men would think they were at liberty to steal, and women would consider themselves absolved from the restraints of chastity'. This extraordinary statement is one of the clearest demonstrations of the view that morality has no real existence, but is dependent on the fear of divine chastisement. Here, plainly, was the man every magistrate would love, but much water was to go under the bridge before he was to give every half-baked magistrate the chance to play David against the Goliath of obscenity and impurity, and in the meantime he was to make his mark as a historian (or, rather, a smudge – Lord Campbell's *The Lives of the Lord Chancellors and Keepers of the Great Seal of England from the earliest times till the reign of King George IV*, seven vols, 1849, might well be the ultimate in unreadability). Undeterred, Campbell went on to the *Lives of the Chief Justices of England, from the Norman Conquest till the death of Lord Mansfield*. Of these works, Sir Charles Wetherell repeated a witticism of an earlier age – 'his noble and biographical friend had added a new terror to death'. Had he stopped there, Lord Campbell would have gone down in history as a useful, if tiresome, political hack who knew his way around the law, even though he later failed, at Queen Victoria's pathetic behest, to get divorce proceedings banned from the popular press. This considerable body of literary work, the quantity of which, if not the quality, many full-time writers would have envied, did not wholly take up Lord Campbell's time, and he took up arms against the sea of troubles represented by the opposition (one is partially mollified by the stand he took against Peel's Income

Tax Bill of 1842). As the Chief Justice of the Queen's Bench he was inclined to histrionics (as a tyro reporter on the *Morning Chronicle* he had 'done' drama), and he was accused – as a Chief Justice should not be – of unduly influencing juries, as well as concealing purple passages for gallery applause. Here was the man who made himself arbiter of the fate of literature. He was not the kind of person to be thwarted by the difficulty of defining obscenity.

One definition was 'something offensive to modesty or decency, or expressing or suggesting unchaste or lustful ideas or being impure, indecent or lewd'. Modesty, decency, unchastity, lust, impurity, indecency, lewdness – one would be at a loss to conjure up concepts that were more subject to the vagaries of taste and the inscrutable workings of time. In 1868 Chief Justice Cockburn made his bid : 'the tendency of the matter charged as obscenity is to deprave and corrupt those whose minds are open to corruption and into whose hands a publication of this sort may fall', and until recently this definition has remained the guiding light when a prosecution for obscenity has been mooted.

The power to expunge from the register any work that offended the delicate sensibilities of magistrates resulted in some odd verdicts. In 1888 the publisher Vizetelly was fined £100 and bound over for twelve months for publishing the English translation of Emile Zola's *La Terre*, a book in which the crowning erotic incident is the bringing of cow to bull. A member of parliament 'believed nothing more diabolical has ever been written by the pen of man', and it did not end there, for Vizetelly with a courage and persistence that does him credit brought out the book again, and was sent to prison for three months, harsh testimony to the efficacy of French literature, though Zola would have cut little ice with the *cognoscenti* – even less in a translation, for part of the appeal of French erotic literature was in the notion that it could not be translated, that the language was inviolable, and that it could be handled by English translators only at their peril.

The appeal of French erotic literature was very wide, and the enthusiasts included such figures as General Studholme Hodgson, an elderly libertine. 'Have you read Mademoiselle de

Maupin [8] which the Parisian ladies rave about?' he asked. 'It was recommended to me by quite a young woman – It is beautiful French, but a perfectly bawdy book. I cannot conceive how the censorship has allowed it to appear'. In most cases the censorship had no option, as there was an undercover connection between publisher and distributor, distributor and collector that left few chinks for officialdom to poke around in.

A key distributor was Frederick Hankey, who lived in Paris, 'a second de Sade without the intellect' (or so Ashbee commented). Ashbee met him in company with a forgotten figure, Octave Uzanne, and the century's most talented pornographic artist, Félicien Rops, whose engravings are still to be found, strangely enough, on the open shelves of London's public libraries. There were very few in the pornographic market who did not know Hankey; Sir Richard Burton had promised him the skin of a Negress (preferably torn off a live one), and wrote to Richard Monckton Milnes from Dahomey with news of the project: 'I have been here three days and am grievously disappointed. Not a man killed, nor a fellow tortured. The canoe floating in blood is a myth of myths. Poor Hankey must still wait for his peau de femme.' Hankey was one off the bottom of the pack for Burton.

Hankey was born in the late 1820s, the son of a Malta general and a Corfu Greek mother, and was forever in the shadow of his eminently successful elder brother, Thomson, who was making a name for himself in the Bank of England before Frederick was fledged. When an inadequate nature finds itself beset by such a situation, it flees; so Frederick made his home in Paris, frequenting dubious book sales while in his late teens, early realizing that here was a way of disporting his talents. Although Hankey did not have the aristocratic connections to make whoopee like his hero, de Sade, there is evidence that the inclinations were not lacking, that his request to Burton for a Negress's skin was by no means an idle one. When two murderers were publicly hanged, Hankey and a friend took a couple of girls along so that they could have intercourse during the event.

In 1862 Hankey made the acquaintance of the de Goncourts

in Paris; the de Goncourts were a two-brother team who recorded events and their reactions to these events with precision and objectivity. Jules had a penchant for the low life, the bizarre, and the creepy, and after he died, the journal took on a certain tone, though Edmond recorded his brother's decline and death with a suavity that was hardly fraternal. Unfortunately this unique document (would that Victorian England had had its de Goncourts), the de Goncourt journal, runs to 900,000 words, and far too often English editions are fey and too intent on accentuating period Frenchiness. Hankey, noted the de Goncourts, was about thirty when they met him, rather bald, with temples swollen like an orange. His eyes were blue, clear, piercing; his skin was delicate, and the veins shewed through. His mien was that of an ecstatic young priest, and he moved stiffly and mechanically, though elegantly; he was well bred, very polite, and he had a sweet, gentle manner.

In appearance, he was probably very much like his English opposite number, Monckton Milnes who, wrote Disraeli, 'was unfortunately short, with a face like a Herculaneum masque, or a countenance cut out of an orange',[9] with his mouth (said George Smythe) 'one long slit'. However, Hankey had no aspirations to political power, as Monckton Milnes had, nor his tendency to sing comic songs at the drop of a hat (Milnes actually wrote a pop song in 1836, 'I wandered by the brookside, I wandered by the mill'). Hankey had, considered Ashbee, 'given himself up body and soul to the erotic mania'. It was not a scholarly mania, and no holds were barred; when Hankey's book binder proved refractory, Hankey provided him with access to young girls, and in doing so ruined the man's marriage. Ashbee provides another glimpse of Hankey, dressed in a 'short velvet coat, shirt without necktie, thin trowsers, thinner socks, and slippers',[10] in an apartment where there was no fire, and where it was cold. 'What of Hankey?' wrote Burton, 'what of poor old Hankey?' Hankey died in 1882.

Hankey used several couriers to get the obscene books through to England, some of the methods anticipating those of the fictional spies of our own day. One of them was via his cousin Arthur's valet – cousin Arthur had friends in high places.

Not infrequently the books were carried in the British embassy bag (Hankey had a friend in the Foreign Office), but the best of the couriers, Hankey maintained, was Mr Harris, manager of Covent Garden. 'He is not only devoted to me but a very good hand at passing quarto volumes as he has done several times for me in the *bend* of his *back*.' Hankey was fascinated by all aspects of erotica, and nineteenth-century Paris was adept at producing them – e.g., porcelain ink wells in the form of a pair of female breasts with detachable nipples, and even the noble house of Sèvres had been induced to dabble in erotic statuary at one time.

It is difficult at this late date to determine how important Hankey was, and it is hard to believe that all the cloak-and-dagger stuff was really necessary, though it is certain that Monckton Milnes liked to shroud things with an air of mystery. Hankey is indicative of a certain climate of opinion, and a type such as he could hardly flourish at a time when pornography is very much in the open, as it is in our time, when in back-street bookshops the eager can thumb through openly imported books – such as *Petting* from Denmark – in which there are photographs of couples copulating, or skim through boxes of photographs, which are divided into sections (homosexual, Lesbian, heterosexual,[11] and so on). Paris has ceased to be the centre of the pornographic trade, and the Hankey-type with couriers has long been obsolete. Furthermore, French is no longer a favoured language for pornography; today it is difficult to believe that French was used as an everyday language by the English far into the nineteenth century as a means of communication, not merely to show off, not merely to tell one's wants to the natives, not merely to acquire education. The letter writers of the last century dropped into and out of French with almost insolent ease. For those with an interest in erotic literature it was a 'secret' language that was yet easy to understand, a means of separating 'us' from 'them', with many of the connoisseurs scorning those to whom – because of a lack of knowledge of French – the ultimate in pornography was represented by the flagellation dramas and the dreary copulation epics of Dugdale and his colleagues.

The publishers of pornography of the nineteenth century share a general miasma of carelessness, haste and incompetence. Many of the writers were unable to understand the function of the apostrophe:

> Such breeding hussy's are a pest
> A neighbour's wife is far the best.

These errors were passed over by the publisher's reader. Cloak-and-dagger techniques were not only used in the transportation of obscene literature but in the production as well – a knock on the compositor's door and the stick of type would scatter across the floor, fallen from a shaky guilty hand. At various times, when, as Bernard Shaw said, the British public was indulging in one of its bouts of morality, the firm hand of the law, aided and abetted by the more staid press, came down upon publishers with more than usual venom. Whatever they printed today, few publishers would be sent to prison as Vizetelly was, while the pursuit of those publishers who dared to inform the poor of techniques in birth control that their betters had known for decades bordered on the insane (raids on publishers and booksellers where innocuous books such as *The Freethinker's Text Book* and *Jesus, Shelley, and Malthus* were seized strike one as quite ludicrous).

The stern attitude of the police towards anything that savoured of the lubricous frightened off the more timid respectable publishers. After the howls of execration that greeted Swinburne's *Poems and Ballads* Payne of Moxton's dropped him like a hot brick, and ever afterwards was an especial object of Swinburne's scorn ('that pellet of decomposed dung technically known as Payne ... that bottomless and drainless cesspool of lies and counterlies, the mouth of Mr J. B. Payne').[12] When Hotten took over the property, it was not an occasion of unqualified joy for Swinburne; although Hotten did publish respectable work he also published dirt, and consequently was burdened with carelessness and incompetence, qualities that cling to pornography like incubus and succubus. Whereas most of Hotten's writers were not overly particular about the setting up of their work, Swinburne was different, and his plaintive appeals to Hotten wring the heart:

I saw at Reading station a copy for sale with the hideous misprint 'bowers' for 'hours' – *pray* let no others get abroad, as nothing could more annoy me... you can hardly have looked at the proofs you send, or you would have seen that they are identical with those sent in the autumn, corrected, and returned. Not one misprint has been corrected, not one omission supplied, by the printers. At this rate we may go on for ever. . .[13]

Hotten did not have many poets on his books; publishing Swinburne was full of hazards, as witness an advertisement in *The Times* of 20 June 1867: 'LOST, 10 to 20 BLUE FOOLSCAP LEAVES of PAPER roughly written upon in verse (partly dialogue). Missed between April 15–May 10. May have been left in a cab. Of no use to anybody but the owner. Small REWARD will be given upon restoration by Mr Hotten, 47 Piccadilly, W.'

John Camden Hotten was born in Clerkenwell, London – a district notorious for horse stealing – in 1832 and acquired an early interest in books, being allowed to frequent the shop of John Petheram, a minor Anglo-Saxon grammarian and bookseller of Chancery Lane, where he once had the distinction of being struck by the historian Macaulay. In 1848 he and his brother went to the United States. John was enabled by this trip and subsequent sojourn to become an expert on American literature. On his return to London he opened up a shop at 151b Piccadilly, speedily revealing his interests by publishing a *Dictionary of Modern Slang Cant and Vulgar Words* (1859), and his versatility by publishing Lowell, Artemus Ward, Holmes, Leland, and Bret Harte (whose heathen Chinee was once believed to be the last word in nineteenth-century American verse). Not content with this, Hotten wrote biographies of Thackeray and Dickens, a *History of Signboards* (in collaboration), and involved himself in the vexed question of literary copyright, a subject of hardly more than academic interest as Hotten was hardly a respecter of other people's literary rights, and one of his authors, John Davenport, was a shameless appropriator of other writers' productions (his *Aphrodisiacs and Anti-Aphrodisiacs* and *Curiositates Eroticae Physiologiae* are prime examples of the dullness of pseudo-scholarly pornography). Ashbee had a soft spot for Hotten and Davenport, whose *Aphrodisiacs and Anti-*

Aphrodisiacs he considered 'an able and erudite work'. Hotten died at the age of forty-one from 'brain fever',[14] having delivered himself of a *Golden Treasury of Thought*, and the final fruits of his American expedition, the editing of the 'Original List' of those who went from Great Britain to 'the American Plantations' between 1600 and 1700, laudable projects now forgotten.

Hotten was as crafty as his more singleminded colleagues. One of his advertisements, for *Aphrodisiacs*, runs: 'Beautifully printed on toned paper, and only ONE HUNDRED COPIES, for private distribution. ... £2 10 shillings.' Ashbee relates that 250 were in fact issued steaming hot from the press, half of which were exported immediately to New York. However, Hotten as a writer was modest and respectable – not like his colleague, Dugdale alias H. Smith, who was responsible for some of the nastier passages in the *Boudoir*, the three-volumed magazine published by this *alter ego*, H. Smith. Dugdale was a thoroughly disagreeable person, blackmailer and pornographer, adman and publisher, and the slime of his trail has been all but obliterated by the years. He died in the House of Correction just off the Gray's Inn Road in 1868, wondering, no doubt, what frolics could be got up to with a prison as the locale.

Ashbee's three books were published before the heyday of the pioneer of aesthetic pornography, Smithers was unfortunate enough to flourish at a time when the authorities had got the bit between their teeth and were hammering publishers and booksellers alike, using informers and plainclothesmen to get convictions. Leonard Charles Smithers was born in Sheffield in 1861 and went into law. In 1891 he and a friend, H. S. Nichols, migrated to London to start up a publishing business with money left to Smithers by his father, who had recently died. In London, Smithers kept on a solicitor's practice at 174 Wardour Street and dabbled in art. Nichols had been concerned in Burton's *Arabian Nights* (1885–8), and was the professional partner. They began business in Soho Square, later moving to 3 Charing Cross Road, where, as the Walpole Press, the place was raided by the police, who confiscated two tons of set type. Nichols, allowed bail, fled to Paris, where he issued obscene pamphlets, an activity that was not appreciated, for he was forced out of the country and went to New York.

Smithers rapidly established himself, and soon had acquired, according to his son, a house in Bedford Square, a flat in Paris and a flat in Brussels, and for something like a year a large house at Walton-on-the-Naze. He gathered around him a group of talented writers and artists, many of whom were engaged in pornography – Ernest Dowson, who wrote poetry and who translated obscene French works; Reginald Bacchus, who wrote goody-goody stories for an English religious journal and pornography for the French market; and the man who made Smithers's name: Aubrey Beardsley. Beardsley had established himself as an illustrator of great talent in the *Yellow Book*, which is often supposed to conjure up the decadence of the nineties but is really quite harmless. The *Yellow Book* (1894) was published by John Lane, a publisher of high repute; the first number contained *A Defence of Cosmetics* by Max Beerbohm, which was considered rather daring, for reasons which are difficult now to see.

The *Yellow Book* was, if anything, a gathering of Victorian respectability, the contributors including Sir Frederic Leighton, president of the Royal Academy, the ultrafashionable portrait painter John Singer Sargent, and the venerable Henry James – not to mention such stalwarts of the Establishment as Professor Saintsbury and Dr Richard Garnett. Beardsley was the fly in the ointment. Although Leighton was a great admirer of Beardsley's techniques, the moral lapses of the Beardsley message were only too evident, and William Watson – knighted in 1917 for the immaculacy of his poetic genius if for little else – sent the editor, Henry Harland, and the publisher, John Lane, an ultimatum. If Beardsley was to continue befouling the *Yellow Book* with his naughty drawings, he, William Watson would have nothing more to do with it. Surprisingly, Watson won, and Lane and Harland – a novelist who had been weaned from early sensational fiction under the name of 'Sidney Luska' and was now writing sentimental rubbish such as *Mademoiselle Miss* – chose safety (just as Payne of Moxon had done a generation earlier).

The Role of Hotten was now played by Smithers, described – probably not accurately – as 'the most learned erotomaniac in Europe'[15] and, by the antiquarian bookseller Quaritch as 'the cleverest publisher in London'. The introduction of Beardsley and Smithers was effected by Arthur Symons, a professional *fin de siècle* operator, who littered the nineties with the corpses of his decadent verse – *Silhouettes* (1892), *London Nights* (1895), *Amoris victima* (1897) (he, too, had been struck down by the Latin blight). Symons, basically a Celtic fringer, had been instrumental in getting the French poet Verlaine to come to lecture in Oxford and London – Verlaine, of whose sonnets Ashbee had pronounced the learned judgement, 'pretty, but display no great talent'.

Whereas the *Yellow Book* was an amalgam of very diverse talents, the new project the *Savoy*, was a projection of the Beardsley ethos; Beardsley set to work on illustrations to Pope's *Rape of the Lock* and an erotic romance *Under the Hill*, in which a new note sounds in English pornographic fiction. Gone are the four-letter words and the robustious copulations and floggings; the swish of the whip is replaced by the delicate skimmings of 'fans of big living moths', the heavy contorted features of Miss Coote and Miss Floggem are replaced by 'masks of coloured glass', and the receding hair of elderly gentlemen waiting to be chastised by 'governesses' is challenged by the new concept in naughtiness, 'wigs of black and scarlet wools'. The mark of tuberculosis on him, Beardsley turned out material, delicate, naughty, obscene, with a virtuosity that even the supercilious Whistler admired ('Aubrey, I have made a mistake. You are a great artist'). With his black satchel, that gave him the look of 'a man from the Prudential', Beardsley was one of the stalwarts of the nineties, prevented, in the true decadent style, from carrying out any of the stylistic perversions he drew by virtue of his illness.

Smithers, assimilating the obscene drawings along with the respectable material for the *Savoy*, was no hole-in-the-corner operator like Dugdale. He stares out of the photographs of the period with a modern quizzical elegance; clean-shaven in an age that ran to beards like fungoid growths, natty in a check cap and striped bow tie, pale-faced and fair-haired, Smithers had 'singularly clear cut aristocratic features'. He sported a monocle, was well-bred and at ease with his curious stable of artists and writers. However, he had his problems: As his contemporary Arthur Symons put it, 'Have you ever thought of the frightful thing it is to shift one's centre? That is, what it is to love a woman.' [16] Smithers' centre shifted several times. It was unfortunate that he married a woman who turned into a raving alcoholic, and it was unfortunate that he acquired a taste for young girls, much to the amusement of Wilde, whom Smithers also published; Smithers also had himself photographed while copulating with the wife of a friend in Shepherds Bush,[17] a friend who was also in the dirty-book business and who had a printing press in the basement of his house. Smithers went bankrupt in 1900, his wife went into a drunken retirement, and he moved to squalid Cubitt Street, Islington; he died in 1907, a pauper, a curio from another age. Smithers had flourished for a mere decade, but he impressed his personality upon it, though after his death there was more interest in what had happened to the obscene Beardsley drawings he had possessed. In 1898, when he was dying, Beardsley had written to Smithers from the south of France:

Jesus is our Lord and Judge
I implore you to destroy all copies of Lysistrata and bad drawings ...
By all that is holy all obscene drawings

Did Smithers comply, or was he a good business man? Did he salt them away, or were they stolen, as was made out at the time? Why, when he died, was there no furniture in the house except the bed he was placed on, two empty hampers, and fifty bottles of chlorodyne?

Sexual Humour

The Victorians had highly developed senses of humour when they were not engaged in standing on their dignity. The English

sense of humour itself is a labyrinth through which even the
minotaur might stalk at his peril. When dealt with pedantic-
ally, it can be rubbed out of existence; philologists who deal
with it so usually betray a marked lack of understanding of
the various ramifications of the language, and occasionally the
language itself. When the editor of the *Encyclopaedia Britannica*, eleventh edition (1910–11) decided to get someone to write
on 'Humour' he picked on David Hannay, a former vice-consul
at Barcelona and author of a *Short History of the Royal Navy*.
So was humour served in the classic reference books. Hannay
contented himself with a brisk summary of humour as per Dr
Johnson's dictionary, with a diatribe against practical jokes.

In *Lectures on the English Comic Writers*, Hazlitt drew a
distinction between humour and wit. 'Humour is the describing
the ludicrous as it is in itself; wit is the exposing it, by compar-
ing or contrasting it with something else.' In the late sixties,
Rossetti had his foot bitten by Olaf, a dog belonging to his
friend William Bell Scott (who went through life believing
that he had committed the great sin against the Holy Ghost
without quite knowing what the sin was). 'He suddenly sprang
up from the hearth and produced an indented pattern in the
style of Morris and Company round the toe of my boot – the
different ornaments comprising it being varied in the fanciful
style of that firm so as to avoid monotony – some mere depres-
sions of the surface and others complete perforations.' [18] So
wrote Rossetti in a casual letter. This is wit of quality.

People objected to Professor Dingo, when we were staying in the
North of Devon, after our marriage, that he disfigured some of the
public buildings by chipping off fragments of those edifices with his
little geological hammer. But the the Professor replied that he knew
of no building save the Temple of Science. 'Finely expressed' said
Mr Badger. The Professor made the same remark in his last illness
when (his mind wandering) he insisted on keeping his little geological hammer under the pillow, and chipping at the countenances
of his attendants.

This, from Dickens, is quality humour. Hazlitt's rough and
ready distinction between humour and wit may be assailed, but
it brought a certain amount of order into a difficult subject.

Victorian sexual humour, likewise, is humorous or witty. It is predominantly written humour. When visual it is frequently coarse and burdensome, taking on the mantle of one of the few English masters of the visually ribald, Thomas Rowlandson, who died in 1827, or it is insufficient, needing amplification by caption (such as the cartoons in *Punch*). Visual humour accentuates the ludicrous aspects of sex; the dirty seaside postcard is the enervated modern equivalent of the Victorian dirty-funny print – both illustrate stock themes: the gent whose age runs counter to his desire, who is confronted by vast breasts and buttocks and who lacks the wherewithal to satisfy their owners; the perspiring ruddy-face woman whose bottom is in itself risible (in present-day seaside postcards clad in tight red bathing costume, in Victorian prints, bare). The dirty engraving is not usually very competent, and some doubt must exist as to the original intentions, whether it is meant to excite or amuse. When it is not captioned, it presents a static situation which almost always indicates, 'This is man and woman engaged in sexual intercourse. Isn't it funny?' Sometimes there are all kinds of weird positions and perversions. 'Isn't this even funnier?' is implied.

Verbal sexual humour uses all the conveniences that the English language has acquired, all the literary devices, all the incredible wealth of analogies and metaphors that an immense vocabulary – conservatively estimated at 500,000 items – has given ground to. The spoonerism, the malapropism, euphemism, hyperbole, meiosis, and, above all, the pun, all were recruited in the cause of sexual humour, sometimes with stunning effect. The Reverend W. A. Spooner of New College, Oxford, had a lot to answer for, though the transposition of initial letters did not really need donnish authority – verbal humour is delighted in by all classes.

The early Victorian period is noteworthy for its ability to produce sexual humour without using sex words. This example is from the early forties:

'When the flesh rebels against the spirit,' said a monk to his prior, 'What do you?'

'I take my breviary and read it through,' he replied.

'And I,' said a sanctified frater, "jump into cold water.'

'For my part,' observed a young fellow, who was listening to them, 'I settle the matter at once, without all that ceremony – I knock the brains out of the evil one.'

or: 'Madam, I should like to pay a visit to your gro(o)ve of sweet retirement.' The first example demonstrates a sophisticated sort of *double-entendre* set in a somewhat prolix and arch context. It is characteristic one-shot humour, with the punch at the end.

Other humour of the forties is also adept at analogies. Often it rumbles along like a juggernaut, particularly when it is humour directed at certain people, or when it is centred about a specific situation. The wedding night of Queen Victoria was treated in many ways – as an essay in horse-riding,[19] as an exploratory foray, as a military operation. February 1840, brought forth 'An Historical Chapter':

Maidenhead is a small town, twenty-six miles west of London, not far from Stoney-bottom, and in daily communication with Staines and Slough. On the morning of the eventful eleventh of February, the breach having been deemed practicable, Field Marshal Prince Albert mounted, and, with his truncheon in hand, succeeded in maintaining a position in Maidenhead-thicket. For a considerable period the resistance was exceedingly obstinate; the enemy, by a series of successful movements, contrived to gall the besiegers from the covered way; while the Prince continued to batter in breach with most untiring efforts. At length the beseiged began to slacken fire, and the Prince advanced from the thicket and got possession of the covered way. At this critical moment the Prince's imagination failed him, and his forces appeared to be spent with fatigue and exertion. The Maidenhead troops advanced, and, extending their flanks, for a time threatened destruction to the Prince; he, however, speedily rallied, and at half-past three in the morning, he made a triumphant entry into the town. There was no considerable bloodshed, as may be seen from the following official return: – killed, none; wounded, two privates; missing, one rank and file.

When analogies are pursued, there is no holding back, as is evident from 'Animals at Ascot' in which selected rakes, impotent old lords, and their women are let loose into this stylized paddock:

Lord Alfred Paget drove a *mail* and Fitzroy Somerset a *female*...
Louisa Turner swore the Marquis should not *drive* her any more,
until he chose to drive to church with her – Blessington was *driven*
by d'Orsay, apparently very much to her satisfaction, for *her* face
beamed with a smile, and his with an expression of *unutterable* im-
port – Mrs Norton *tooled* her own *vehicle*, and declared, upon her
husband's honour and her own, she had not had a single *drive* since
her last *turn up* with Lord Melbourne.

The flowery diction of the period combined with the content
often produced a ponderous irony:

Thomas Bradley, the physiological phenomenon, is said to sleep for
forty, fifty, and a hundred hours, without waking. When Prince
Albert was told of this extraordinary circumstance, he expressed
great surprise, and declared that there was a vast difference between
the dormant faculties of poor Bradley and his little beloved Vic, who,
he said, never slept more than an hour at a time, and who would not
return again to sleep without he instantly rose, and gave Her
Majesty what she is so dearly fond of viz. the Albert Cordial, which,
upon all occasions, immediately composes and stimulates Her Majesty
to sleep.

The sledge-hammer style is one of the great staples of English humour, and was particularly suited to that variety of
sexual humour that was cumulative, building up to a climax.
Its devotees included, in the past, Swift and de Quincey (1785–
1859) whose *On Murder, Considered as One of the Fine Arts* –
one section includes an account of a murder in terms of a box-
ing match – anticipated many of the newer elements in sexual
humour – a sadistic or sick tone, the mixture of poetic speech
and the vulgar idiom, the extended account of an event in
terms of another. The heavy irony that figured so much in
satirical sexual humour, where scandal-mongering newspapers
were attacking the lewd aristocracy, and which was rendered
null simply because of the incompetence of the journalists and
their inability to utilize all the weapons at their disposal, this
irony was anticipated in very great measure by de Quincey.
Dealing with murderees of the past de Quincey encounters the
philosopher, Hobbes:

Hobbes – but why, or on what principle I never could understand – was not murdered. This was a capital oversight of the professional men in the seventeenth century; because in every light he was a fine subject for murder, except, indeed, he was lean and skinny: for I can prove that he had money, and (what is funny) he had no right to make the least resistance; since, according to himself, irresistible power creates the very highest species of right, so that it is rebellion of the blackest dye to refuse to be murdered when a competent force appears to murder you.

This kind of logic became a prime element of sexual humour. In unintentional humour even more so. The ideal of pornographic writers was perpetual sexual intercourse; this logically led to the high jinks of *The Romance of Lust* of the seventies: 'Our second double couplings were, myself in my aunt's cunt, which incest stimulated uncle to a stand, and he took to his wife's arse while her nephew incestuously fucked her cunt. The Count took to the delicious and most exciting tight cunt of the Dale, while her son shoved his prick into his mother's arse, to her unspeakable satisfaction.'

This is seriously intended, but the author's intense preoccupation with what is objectively an extreme situation only succeeds in producing merriment. By excluding from their repertoire everything that was left, the writers of hard-core pornography built up a series of *tableaux* that had no reference to any real situation that the reader might come across. A reader was therefore confronted by abstractions disguised as people engaged in a long-winded parody of what people do get up to. Similarly, the people who act as demand and response in sex jokes never existed on land or sea; they are conveniences of two kinds: He and She.

The favourite device of sexual humour is undoubtedly the pun. The long-drawn-out analogies, such as 'An Historical Chapter' above, are extended puns. The present cloud under which the pun rests is partly a reaction against the prestige which this form of wit enjoyed for many centuries. Charles Lamb wished his last breath to be exhaled in a pun; though he pointed out the perils. 'A pun and its recognitory laugh must be co-instantaneous. The one is the brisk lightning, and the other the fierce thunder.

A moment's interval, and the link is snapped.' 'Where the common people like puns, and make them,' declared G. C. Lichtenberg, 'the nation is on a high level of culture,' and Boswell maintained that 'a good pun may be admitted among the small excellencies of lively conversation'. The nineteenth century did all it could to reduce the pun to limpness. Hack journalists found puns easy to churn out, and where there was half a column to fill, nothing was more convenient than half a dozen well-chosen ones. They could be adopted to current events and names in the news. The scandal weeklies made an easy killing by going through the marriages recently promulgated, and making ribald play with the names of the protagonists:

Mr Thomas Fortescue to Lady Louisa Grace Butler:
> In Cupid's service Lady Grace
> Fills nightly her appointed station,
> And takes in bed – delightful place –
> An under-*butler's* situation.

Theodosia Mariner to John Symonds:
> May Providence send to the fortunate pair,
> With the brightest of weather, the fairest of gales,
> While in quest of the anxiously sought *sun* and *air*,
> On the billows of Hymen the *mariner* sails.

J. V. Gibbs to Mary Anne Elizabeth Catchpole:
> Thrice-lucky, Mary Anne, we say
> If Gibbs hath power and will,
> At night of every married day
> To make you 'Catch-pole' still.

Edward Dower to Miss Mead of Bath:
> Now for a ride the charming fair,
> Will never stand in need
> For nightly with a *rattling pair*
> He'll drive *across* the *mead*.

Nathaniel Forte to Arabella Chorasse Millard:
> Nat and his wife may day and night
> In love's soft dalliance sport;
> She'll find that *getting over her*
> Is quite her husband's *forte*.

Reverend J. Ellaby of Milston Rectory, Wilts, to Emma Field:
> To air and exercise, if prone,
> He need not seek a weald,
> But gently jerk himself at home
> By getting in the *field*.

H. F. Broadwood to Juliana Maria Birch:
> Strip, was the awful word at school,
> Behind the strokes we bore;
> Broadwood adopts but half the rule,
> And takes the *Birch* before.

W. H. Moare of Strand to Miss Parsons of Stalbridge, Dorset:
> Oh, Moare, religious man, 'tis clear,
> On piety how firm you fastens;
> For these cold wintry nights so drear,
> You kneel between a *pair* of *Parsons*.

Metcalf Larkin at the British Embassy, Paris, to Emily Comb:
> Metcalf will part those curly locks,
> Which *Comb* was never parting;
> And if rudeness Emy shocks
> He'll swear he's only *Larkin*(g).

Henry Forrester to Louisa Holmes:
> How merrily I live, *a Forrester*,
> To Louisa's coppice often hie,
> And *perdu* in the thicket lie,
> In a sweet little valley, two hills between –
> O mine is a right merry life, I ween.

This is the common people making puns with a vengeance. More elegantly, Rossetti to Swinburne that 'the provincial form of All Souls could only have been discovered by a Bulgarian Columbus' [20] (bugger comes from *Bulgarus*, a Bulgarian, via French *bougre*; in 1870, when Rosetti was writing, the Bulgarians were in bad odour, due to a spate of atrocities, both real and imagined). The respectable pun was deified by *Punch*, and a brisk browse through any volume of the eighties will dispel any surprise that Skeat in his authoritative *Etymological Dictionary* of 1898 should be so supercilious about the word 'pun', a pun on pound, in the sense 'to pound words, to beat

them into new senses, to hammer at forced similes'. One suspects that Skeat was being less than objective. Very few puns
stand the test of time; when they are hooked on to contemporary
events or people, they need to be exceptionally good to be
worth a chuckle. 'Will that naughty Cole end in smoke?' asked
the *Tomahawk* rhetorically in 1870 (Cole was involved in a
notorious divorce case). An 1840 journalist thought he had a
bright naughty idea: 'Where do you hang out to-morrow
night?' 'Furnavels-in' (Furnivel's Inn). A writer in John Cor-
lett's short-lived *Bird o' Freedom* decided that if he invented a
girl named Mattie he could work up a modestly saucy pun:

> His Mattie is a pretty girl – as fair as fair can be;
> And every time he comes to call he has a Mat-on-knee.

An even more cumbersome effort is from the same periodical:

> Willie kissed Susan under the rose –
> The rose was in bloom and the corn in the ear –
> And the tiny rouge spot on the tip of his nose
> Remained with Willie as Sue veneer

A better example from the same issue (29 January 1890):
'The average ballet-girl is something of a philosopher. She believes in gauze and effect.'

Worthier of admiration are specimens where the effect is
made by using a word in its prosaic and then in its abstract
form: 'She certainly had a pretty foot, but after all it did not
make so much impression on him as the old man's.' Or 'I was so
bright as a boy that my mother used to look at me through
smoked glass.' This superior class of pun leads on to the intellectual level of transposition. 'What is the difference between
a photograph and influenza? One makes facsimiles, the other
sick families.' In 1874, the venerated American preacher Henry
Ward Beecher was involved in an unsavoury affair with the
wife of Theodore Tilton. 'What is the difference between Mrs
Tilton and a Singer sewing machine? The machine tucks and
fells, Mrs Tilton fucks and tells.' This is a straightforward
spoonerism; a similar mechanism is revealed in the transposition
of words ('A Question of Lunacy', 1879).

A lady the other day, wishing to get an imbecile son into an asylum consulted a doctor about a certificate, and he naturally enquired as to the actions of the alleged lunatic.

Lady: I must tell you that lately at Christmas, he would get up at night and eat all the mince-pies in the pantry.

Doctor: That is only gluttony.

Lady: There's something awfully shocking to tell: The other day he threw the servant down on the stairs and fucked her.

Doctor: Mere depravity, that's all. Now allow me to explain the difference to you, madam! If you had told me that your son had eaten the servant and fucked the mince-pies, there could have been no doubt about the necessity of confining him in an asylum.

The innate tendency of the anecdote is to be stretched out to inordinate lengths, so as to render the final punch more conclusive. When this blow is feather light, one's curiosity is aroused by the anecdote being printed at all:

Lord E. T—e, when a youth, asked his mother the following question: 'Mamma, dear,' said he, 'what is the meaning of the word bugger?'

'Bugger, my child, why do you ask?'

'Because I heard my tutor call the coachman a damned bugger.'

'Well, my child,' replied the Marchioness, 'a bugger is a person who does his fellow an injury behind his back.'

The elements that made this feeble anecdote worth the printing consist of the spurious air of authority – Lord E. T—e rather than A Noble Lord, plus the mild sadism of saddling A Noble Lady with the responsibility of: (a) saying forbidden words; and (b) being put in an embarrassing position. These are characteristic of the bulk of Victorian pornography, which is resolutely anti-clerical, anti-genteel, and anti-privilege. The anti-church tone is allied with a general anti-humanism; anything savouring of education or improvement is drastically dealt with. The mock lecture announcement was a favoured format for anti-clerical humour:

The Reverend Newmann Hall will lecture on 'The Conduct of Lot and his Daughters' December 20th. Illustrated with Dissolving Views of the Paternal Pego entering the Daughters' Cuns. Also January

3rd: 'Salomon in all His Glory' with 700 wives and 300 concubines; being an attempt to eludicate the mystery of how he gave satisfaction to them all.

The odd spelling may spring from the vagaries of the continental printers. The desire to push the clergy into humiliating positions reflects the power that the church still held, even though churchgoing was no longer the prime Sunday activity of the mass of the people. The pornographers had a vested interest in holding the clergy up to ridicule, as the clergy formed the bulwark of the Society for the Suppression of Vice. In 1870 the Reverend Lloyd James of this society reported that up to date the haul consisted of:

129,681 prints
16,220 illustrated books
5 tons of letter press
large quantities of infidel and blasphemous publications
16,005 sheets of song
5,503 cards, snuff boxes, etc.
844 engraved copper plates
428 lithograph stones
95 wood blocks
11 printing presses
28 cwt [hundredweight] of type 'including stereotype of several entire works of the grossest immorality'.

The clergyman as a butt featured throughout nineteenth-century humour. It was taken for granted that in any act of sex he would be ridiculous. To the sexologists, H. S. Ashbee in particular, the clergy had even more to answer for; not only did they confiscate and have burned the volumes that the prurient Ashbee was desirous of collecting, but 'every system of theology has, sooner or later, become alloyed with immoral doctrines, impure rites, or obscene practices and customs', Ashbee then indulges in a manic diatribe directed especially against the Catholics '... the blunders, crimes and follies of the infallible popes; the vices and hypocrisy of many of the clergy, both regular and secular; the duplicity, lax teaching, infamous doctrines, and dishonest commercial dealings of the jesuits ... the terrible system of auricular confession, and the abuse which has been made of it; the coarse, scurrilous, abusive and licentious discourses ...' Ashbee must have been exceedingly bitter that when a valuable exposé of the confessional was published – *The Confessional Unmasked: Showing the Depravity of the Romish Priesthood, the Iniquity of the Confessional and the Question put to Females in Confession* – it was pounced on by the trail-blazing Wolverhampton magistrate Hicklin in 1868, who ordered its destruction; no doubt he would have liked to have ordered the destruction of the purveyor of this book, one Henry Scott, described as a zealot, but Scott only lost 250 copies. In his lengthy review of the confessional situation, Ashbee is so appalled that he leaves the naughty words in Latin (his readers he naturally assumes are polyglots).

The best way to make fun of a clergyman was to put him in a wedding night situation:

> Instead of jumping in the sheets,
> Where on my back extended
> In expectation of these sweets
> Nature for us intended,
> He dropped upon his bended knees.
> I cursed the marriage vow, Sir,
> Is this your method, Sir, to please?
> None of your praying now, Sir.

The second best way was to get the clergyman into a tizzy during confessionals – 'the Reverend Pimlico Poole' who confessed 'the ladies until they felt faint, All alone in a little dark room'. That there was a viable target here was admitted by Dr Pusey, an advocate of the confessional in the Church of England. He wrote in his *Manual for Confessors*:

It is a sad sight to see Confessors giving their whole morning to young women devotees, while they dismiss men or married women, who have, perhaps, left their household affairs with difficulty to find themselves rejected with, 'I am busy, go to someone else!' so that, perhaps, such people will go on for months or years without the Sacraments. This is not hearing Confessions for God's sake, but for one's own.[21]

As for the 'Reverend Pimlico Poole', '... at length Mr Poole's constitution gave way. And his clock-weights hung down to his knees.'

The sixties anecdotes ran to prolixity, and elaborate scene setting is essential. Sometimes it worked admirably:

A gentleman was in the habit, whenever attending a public dinner, of always when called upon for a toast of giving 'The Church'. His wife, who was rather deaf, got tired of this continual repetition, and told him that the next time he gave it she would expose him. The husband taking the hint upon the next occasion gave 'The Ladies'. The wife mistaking this for the old toast astonished the company by rising and saying – 'I told my husband that if he again gave this toast I would expose him – I assure you he has not been in one for a very long time, and the last time he was, he came out before it was half over!'

This was an analogy making in a consistent format, and rare in that it did not exist *in vacuo*; the build-up received its just deserts. Far too often, the conclusion did not justify the groundwork:

'Mary,' said Mrs Robinson to her servant, 'I believe you are in the family way!'

'Yes, marm; and so are you!'

'But, girl, you don't understand!; I'm married, and have a father for my child.'

'Yes, marm; and so have I.'

'You don't understand; my husband is the father of my child.'

'And so he is of mine, marm.'

'For shame, you hussey; why, my husband wouldn't touch you with a pair of tongs.'

'No, marm, but he did with his little poker!'

Exit Mrs Robinson for an explanation with the gay old deceiver.

Making most of available material was an art well known by music hall artists, such as The Great Macdermott, famed for his 'By Jingo' crusade during Anglo-Russian troubles in 1878 (like the Prince of Wales, he would have liked a war). In evening dress, blue silk tie, white waistcoat, red silk handkerchief, gold chain, he was the essence of dandydom for his audience. One of his songs was 'Jeremiah Jones', the jaunty rhythm of which he stressed with his elbows and hands. It was a song of cumulative effect. The first verse and chorus went:

> My name is Jeremiah Jones, and when I was a child,
> I used to play a little game which drove my mother wild.
> I'd take the bellows on my knee, to blow the fire I'd try,
> And when the fire began to blaze, I lustily would cry:
>
>> Jeremiah, blow the fire, puff, puff, puff;
>> First you do it gently, then you come it rather rough.
>> Jeremiah, blow the fire, puff, puff, puff!

Innocuous enough, though the surrealist inconsecutiveness of this action predicts the final verses:

> In time I loved a pretty girl, and strange though it may be,
> The lady in her younger days was just the same as me.
> And when I asked her to be mine, she bowed her lovely head,
> And as I pressed my lips to hers, in artful tones she said:
>
>> Jeremiah, blow the fire, puff, puff, puff;
>> First you do it gently, then you come it rather rough.
>> Jeremiah, blow the fire, puff, puff, puff!

This extensive, and what seems to us laborious framework is consistent with laughter theory, and the pleasure–pain principle. As William James stated, 'If a movement feels agreeable, we repeat and repeat it as long as the pleasure lasts ... there are many pleasures which, when once we have begun to taste them, make it all but obligatory to keep up the activity to which they are due ...' [22] The humour of sex is an acquired taste, but when it is acquired auditors frequently cannot have too much of it. In the closed situation of the music hall, filled with the mingled odours of tipsy men and women bent on being titilated, the nearer the artist could go to the bone with innuendo without really laying sex on the line the more the audience was pleased. The rapport between the talented entertainer and the audience can be sensed in the usually expurgated pages of reminiscences. It was a rapport assisted by the custom of having waiters ply the audience with liquor between the numbers, by a studied informality, by the device of a chairman who confirmed with high-flown oratory the rapport between performer and auditor, by a flexible programme that meant that surprise was always possible. When a talented artist of the calibre of 'The Great Vance', MacDermott, or Leybourne was going great guns, there must have been an empathy with the audience that one occasionally encounters today in a jazz cellar. This was reinforced by the semi-private language; the 'all was Cockney, with its own special lingo. One of Vance's songs ran:

> I'm a Chickaleary bloke, with my vun-two-three –
> Vitechapel was the village I was born in;
>   To catch me on the hop
>   Or on my tibby drop
> You must vake up very early in the mornin'!

By this, Vance (who flourished in the 1870s) and his colleagues assured the audience that they were all one happy family, that there was an understanding between them, that they were all one under the skin, though they were not of course – the mugs and mashers who were thrilled to sit at the chairman's table were fleeced. Leybourne, who came to the fore in 1867, earned at least fifty times as much money as most of his admirers – he asked £25 a night for singing 'Champagne Charlie' and got it, and the warmth the artists propagated dissipated with astonishing rapidity, unlike the goodheartedness of the 'tender' school of music hall entertainers such as Albert Chevalier, who came to the music hall in 1891, in whom the acrid sauce of the earlier men was diluted in the milk of human kindness.

The long-drawn-out songs were frequently an excuse for the spoken smut between verses, and the longer-drawn-out they were, the better. Sexual humour is a humour of release. It parallels the sex act; the longer the climax is postponed the more enhancing is the experience. Sexual humour is also the humour of an in-group. When an interloper intrudes, the atmosphere for the telling of risqué anecdotes can be dispelled like a flash. Jowett, one-time Master of Balliol – known at school as Miss Jowett – was a professional caster-down of raconteurs. 'I think there is more dirt than wit in that story', he cut down one incautious wit. On another occasion, when his friend Sir Robert

Morier was indulging in highly spiced reminiscences of St Petersburg, 'Jowett said with a twinkle in his eye, and in the most dulcet tones, "Morier, shall we adjourn this conversation to the drawing-room?" ' [23]

It is interesting to look at general laughter theory in so far as it applies to sexual humour. One of the most reasonable and convincing expositions of laughter theory was put forward to *Nature* in 1903 by a psychologist whose ineluctable common sense has succeeded in giving later generations an undeserved impression of a drudge, William McDougall. McDougall dismissed as inadequate Herbert Spencer's theory that laughter is an overflow of surplus nervous energy, pointing out that laughter involves complex highly coordinated systems of movement. He also looked askance at Henri Bergson's notion as laughter being a servant of social discipline 'because we naturally laugh at whatever in behaviour is stiff, clumsy, or machine-like'. The first questions McDougall asked are, 'What biological service does laughter perform? What advantage does it bring? What is its survival value?' The key question, however, was 'What does laughter do for us?'

Laughter does us good; we enjoy laughing, it prevents gloomy thinking, melancholy brooding by: (a) raising blood pressure, stimulating the respiration; (b) breaking up every train of thinking and every sustained activity, bodily or mental. 'The nervous channels of laughter drain off energy from all others.' Laughter is relaxation from all effort, and 'this being so, it is obvious why we seek the objects and situations that make us laugh; we seek the ludicrous, the grotesque, the absurd, the ridiculous, not because they are in themselves pleasing, but because they make us laugh'. McDougall draws a distinction between the smile and the laugh – 'the smile is the natural expression of the satisfaction that attends the success of any striving'. [24]

We laugh at the ludicrous. Why? Because: (a) the ludicrous involves some maladjustment, something inappropriate – if we did not laugh it would be displeasing; (b) if the ludicrous situation happened to *us* it would distress us – if we did not laugh we should suffer disappointment, embarrassment, distress, or humiliation. 'A human being, deprived of the capacity for laughter, but otherwise normally constituted and leading a normal social life, would suffer very frequently from sympathetic pain and depression.' Laughter, by breaking up a train of mental activity, preventing the dwelling on a distressing situation, by physiologically stimulating respiration and circulation, is 'one of the most delicate and beautiful of all Nature's adjustments'.

McDougall regards humour as arising from man's ability to laugh at himself, 'the capacity to stand aside and contemplate one's self and one's minor mishaps ... humour is essentially laughter at ourselves, at one's own individual self, or one's self as included in humanity at large or some group or class.' Nietzsche put it succinctly: 'Perhaps I know best why it is man alone who laughs; he alone suffers so deeply that he had to invent laughter. The most unhappy and melancholy animal is, as is reasonable, the cheerfulest.'[25] to conclude his survey, McDougall states crisply: 'Laughter is the antidote to sympathy ... if we are pleased when we laugh, we are pleased because we laugh.'

Sexual humour gives rise to laughter, sexual wit to the smile. Sexual humour is concerned with images – the Reverend Poole whose testicles have become metamorphosed into clockweights, or the 1860 anecdote: 'It chanced during the rapturous embraces of a wedding night the bride unfortunately broke wind upon which, says the ignorant husband, "Rot me, if this ain't too bad, for a bran new utensil to crack the first time of using."'

Sexual wit is more inclined to make one smile at the cleverness of the progenitor, at the adroitness with which he manipulates the elements of language. It is more inclined to be written than oral, and is frequently exclusively visual, such as the acrostic:

> C ome love, and dwell with me
> U nder the greenwood tree,
> N one can more happy be,
> T han I shall be, if bless'd with thee!

As McDougall states, laughter is the antidote to sympathy; it is also the antidote to commitment. The ring-around-a-rosy copulative sequence quoted from *The Romance of Lust* is meant to excite. Laughing at it – or smiling at it, depending on taste (they surely, despite what McDougall says, can be quantitative) – immediately denudes it of any excitable qualities. A sex situation treated humorously is like a frame from a movie stilled and examined with amusement coupled with curiosity; such a single frame can be analysed and redistributed by the various formal devices of language. In such cases, commitment is twice removed, and even extreme situations can be treated in such a manner that one's susceptibilities are not offended. Heavily formalized media are therefore particularly suited to exploring situations that, in themselves, are perverted, disgusting, or disquieting. The medium most adapted for the humour of the extreme situation was the limerick, formerly called the 'nursery rhyme':

> There was a young man of Peru
> Who had nothing whatever to do;
> So he whipped out his carrot
> And buggered his parrot,
> And sent the result to the Zoo.
> There was a young lady of Diss
> Who went on the river to piss;
> The man in the punt
> Shoved the pole up her cunt,
> And gave her most exquisite bliss.

Ludicrous, of course, but it must be recalled that this kind of thing happens in the seriously intended and avowedly stimulating sadistic literature of the period. By compressing the content into a stylized five-line stanza, all emotive tone has been squeezed out of it.

The personages in the anecdotes – the noble lords and ladies, the cooks and footmen, engaged in persiflage or the most outrageous of acrobatic exploits – are ciphers. The analogies are remote, and because remote, funny. When the situation is insufficiently depersonalized, then sex humour can be objectionable, such as this riddle:

Question: When is a newly married lady like the *Victory* at Trafalgar?
Answer: When her cock-pit is full of bloody semen.

Although this pun is ingenious enough, the context in which it is set disobeys the rules. It has a twofold reference to the real world and real events, and the twin images conjured up are too vivid to enjoy conjunction. Laughter, if laughter there were in this instance, would be hardly 'breaking up a train of mental activity, preventing the dwelling on a distressing situation'. The humour of this riddle is in the tradition of sick humour – Swift, whose answer to the Irish problems of famine and overpopulation was for the Irish to eat their children, is a good example. McDougall mentioned this type of humour in passing, but being pre-Freudian in spirit if not strictly speaking chronology, he is at a loss to account for it:

There is a strange type of laughter which has puzzled and shocked many who have experienced or witnessed it; namely, the laughter sometimes provoked by the recital of a catalogue of human disasters. This occurs when disasters are recited which are great and horrible, but which afflict persons so remote from us in time and place, so unfamiliar, that their great mishaps affect us only in the same mild degree as the minor mishaps of those nearer to us.

McDougall seems to have been fortunate in that a great area of the human psyche was hidden from him. If he had been one of Carlyle's 'goats' or one of the eminent who had friends in the British Museum and who therefore had access to the forbidden literature not available to the general reader, he would have found that the humour he found puzzling and shocking was everyday chit-chat to a band of dedicated writers and their publishers, writers who had lost their sense of the ludicrous; what passed in the mundane world as humour and what did not with these the writers had lost touch. Not having a sense of the ludicrous the committed pornographic author handled humour at his peril; in his Utopian world of human daisy chains he would have been indignant at the very thought that sexual behaviour could be funny.

The Language of Victorian Sex

The channels of communication between the nineteenth and the twentieth century are entirely visual, the written and the pictorial, and to a certain extent we today are conditioned by this. We are fortunate in that there were masters of language who can convey the sound of Victorian man and woman, but they are a second best, and no substitute for recording disc, sound tracks, or recording tape. The 'ums' and the 'ers', the intonation, the hesitancies, all are absent, and we are confronted by an approximation that is significant but can never be definitive. The media that could have opened up another channel were distrusted and used for parlour games. The talking machine of Thomas Edison was repellent even to those who might passably be called scholars or historians. On 18 January 1899 Stopford Brooke heard the gramophone, 'a vile concoction of the scientific people'. He objected to its being used to reproduce music-hall songs, but he also objected to it as an instrument of information:

To put by and reproduce the voice of the dead, can the meanest imagination conceive anything more insolent, more insulting to the dead than that? The folk that are beyond are silent, let them keep silence. It is not their living voice we hear; it is the voice of a thin ghost, squeaking like a rat behind the arras. To hear it is to violate the sacred silence of the dead.[26]

There speaks the voice of the *status quo*.

The language of *Pickwick Papers* might well be taken to be the language of the people of the time, but Dickens himself realized that this was language expurgated ('throughout this book, no incident or expression occurs which could call a blush into the most delicate cheek or wound the feelings of the most sensitive person')[27]. Mary Mitford, apostle of genteel rural femininity, declared that *Pickwick Papers* was fun 'but without anything unpleasant: a lady might read it all *aloud*'.[28]

One must constantly be sceptical of dialogue and 'realism' as put out by nineteenth-century writers. Their corporate aim was not to bring a blush to the innocent cheek, save in the case of the pornographic writers, where the reverse was true, but who were equally suspect. Because the pornographic writers were men of minor talents, and often were working under some powerful compulsions, their demonstrations of the language of sex do not replace the hiatuses conscientiously left by Dickens and the respectable – in so far as their writings went – writers.

The everyday language of the Victorians was a good deal racier than is often supposed by a generation that considers itself the last word in vividness and open-mindedness. The 'thees' and 'thous' that pop up like little spikes in the pseudo-religiose, the circumlocutions of affectation, the inflated rhetoric of the politicians, these do not reflect the language of humdrum life. That Victorian spoken language is viewed as something akin to poetic diction represents the triumph of inadequate historical teaching, and the victory of that kind of laziness that prefers the stereotype to the reality.

Raciness was a quality many of the celebrities tried to eradicate from the annals for the benefit of posterity. For example, Lady Dorothy Nevill was one of the great survivals of an earlier way of life; her reminiscences are interesting without being particularly captivating. Yet when her conversation was recalled by one of the most lively reporters of the late Victorian scene, E. F. Benson, then it fairly crackles.

She preserved in her conversation many of the devices of the fifties – still considered good form in huntin'-fishin' circles (one of them is, anyway) – the absence of the final 'g', and the omission of the initial aspirate. Speaking of the new race of girls she said: 'Look at the girls nowadays, playin' golf in their thumpin' boots with never a veil or a pair of gloves till their skin's like a bit of mahogany veneer. I should think the young men would as soon think of kissin' a kipper. And to make it worse they are beginnin' to dab themselves with lip-salve and muck. I never saw such a mess.'

Or of her culinary preferences: 'Guinea-pig, there's a tasty dish for you, but it was always a job to make your cook do it.

They want bakin' same as the gipsies serve the hedgehogs. I tried eatin' donkey, too, but I had to stop that, for it made me stink.' [29] This was how the aristocracy spoke when they were not playing at being aristocrats for the wider public and for posterity.

Similarly, Tennyson when he was not the Great Poet. Mary Gladstone, who was the slightly priggish daughter of the Grand Old Man, wrote in her diary of 1879 that Tennyson 'makes us a little hot sometimes, says near the wind things, but all in an odd, childlike way'.[30] Once he was giving an audience to one of his fervent female admirers. Silence fell; the girl was enwrapped by the Presence, and could not say anything. Tennyson broke the silence with the remark, 'Your stays creak.' Shocked, the girl fled, only to find the great poet stalking her. Diving behind trees, doubling back along obscure paths, she hurried into the kitchen garden for refuge, only to find she had entered a desolate no man's land of asparagus and cabbage from which there was no exit. Fortunately, there was a potting shed, and she tried to hide in there, but it was locked, and Tennyson closed on her, saying: 'I beg your pardon, it was my braces.'

On another occasion, a composer had gone down to see Tennyson about a setting he was doing of a Tennyson verse. Tennyson liked reading his own verse (he even did it to the dreaded gramophone, and the results are in the archives of the British Broadcasting Corporation), and the composer was a sitting duck. At a pause in the reading the composer said, 'That's an awfully jolly stanza.' 'Don't say "awfully,"' admonished Tennyson. 'What shall I say, then?' asked the composer. 'Say "bloody",' replied Tennyson. So is the reality more compelling than the polite fictions.

Ruskin could also falter, though what he said on 27 September 1869 can only be conjectured upon. 'I talk naughtily and frighten poor Joan, who cries.' Joan was Joan Severn, his cousin and housekeeper. He could be shocked by anything but the most innocuous. 'Violet calls herself a "disreputable baggage". Modern Education!' (*Diary*, 2 August 1873.) The effort not to shock delicate sensibilities could also be ludicrous. In a letter to Julia Wedgewood, 3 September 1864, Robert Browning spoke

studiously of 'the perfection of what Virgil calls "exsertae mam-
mae",' and it is evident that an aptitude for being shocked could
be switched on and off, as could the aptitude for shocking. It
depended on the time, the place, and the person. With the Queen,
for instance, Tennyson could hardly be other than reverent.
When he paced the Mausoleum with her, his sole preoccupation
was that his shoes squeaked. That most raffish of Victorian perverts, Simeon Solomon, had, said his friend Henry Holiday, a
'conscientious objection to using stronger language than "Drat
it!"' and Swinburne's outbursts of respectability were well
known. Gosse ('Dear, cunning, cat like, crafty, old Gosse,' said
R. L. Stevenson) amusingly recounted one such incident of
February 1875:

It was magnificent to see him, when Purnell, who was a reckless
speaker, 'went too far', bringing back the conversation into the paths
of decorum. He was so severe, so unwontedly and phenomenally
severe, that Purnell sulked, and taking out a churchwarden left us at
table and smoked in the chimney corner. Our shock was the bill –
portentous! Swinburne, in 'organizing', had made no arrangements
as to price, and when we trooped out into the frosty midnight, there
were five long faces of impecunious men of letters.

There was no general agreement on what would shock, and
what would not shock. Damn was still frequently written d—n,
and bloody was an adjective that was simply not written down.
William Hardman was an urbane man of the world, anxious to
get among the dirty books of the British Museum, but he had
doubts about telling in mixed company what he described as a
'good but slightly blasphemous story', a duty that was taken over
by his friend Shirley Brooks (one of *Punch*'s brood). The format
in which Hardiman reproduces the story is also worthy of note:

This is the story: 'The Enemy of Human Souls' was playing at dice
with 'the Second Person in the Trinity', for what stake I know not.
Of course, the devil, who can do all that doth beseem a man, threw
sixes with perfect facility. But the other party instantly threw *sevens*.
'Come, now,' said ye Devil, 'play fair: let's have none of your damned
miracles!'

The ladies, we are told, 'were slightly shocked, but laughed nevertheless most heartily'. And good for them. At a slightly lower social level – this gathering was of middle-class semi-Bohemians – they would have been thrown into a tizzy of embarrassment.

Because there was no general agreement on what would shock, what was taboo, what was printable, ambiguity often ruled the roost. In the famous Dilke case, Dilke, it was claimed, called at Bailey's Hotel, Gloucester Road. There, said the injured lady, 'he made love to me and kissed me but nothing more'. This, of course, could mean anything.

In high literature, the flash language of the forties and fifties never makes an appearance. Much of this is worth recording on account of its vividness:

Academician	whore in a brothel
Altitude, to be in his	drunk
Ankle, sprained her	pregnant
Apple dumplings	breasts
Backgammon	sodomy
Ballum ranorum	dance of naked whores
Biddy	young whore
Bing we to rumville	go to London
Bobtail	whore
Bunter	whore
Bung-up	woman lying on her back
Cat	drunken prostitute
Charvering crib	accommodation house
Cock-chafer	whore
Corinth	brothel
Corinthian	whoremonger
Frow	whore
Flymy	up to anything
Glue	veneral disease
Hussington	'old fellow who can only feel and grope'
Jock gaggers	men who live on wives or whores
Leather	vulva
Lumber	room for fornicating in
Muzpot	chamber pot
Pavé thumper	whore
Pegging crib	brothel
Queer blowen	ugly whore

Queer ogles	squinting eyes
Rolling it	out on a spree
Spifflicated	swindled
Swells' ken	accommodation house
Trooper	prostitute

In addition, there were innumerable synonyms for money: 'soskins', 'posh', 'dimmock', 'tin', 'moppusses', 'denaly', 'blunt'.

However, the trend of the language of sex was mainly in the other direction. 'Tits', 'teats', 'titties', and 'dugs' were out; in were 'milk-shop', 'feeding bottle', 'baby's public house', 'globes', 'hemispheres'. Medical terms began to appear in the ordinary vocabulary – 'genitalia', 'private parts', along with a procession of dimunitives and coynesses. 'Sit-me-down' and 'botty' for hind-quarters; for the penis any number of male names (favourite – 'John Thomas'), and for the vulva any number of female names (favourite possibly 'Fanny', though 'Mary Jane' and 'Lady Jane' were also popular during the earlier years of Victoria's reign). This nomenclature can lead to some confusion; 'Fanny' in America has different connotations altogether. As London was spreading out, there was a good deal of ingenuity used in applying new districts to the female parts. The new London district of Mount Pleasant was a gift to these specialist philologists.

Urination has always had quasi-sexual overtones, and has always resulted in cumbersome disguises. 'Plant a sweet pea' is nineteenth century, as is 'shake hands with an old friend', and the Victorian propensity for erecting huge numbers of cast iron green urinals and sombre daunting lavatories evoked the pretty phrase, 'spend a penny' (still a favourite). 'Micturate' never quite made it, but 'wee wee' as a diminutive assuredly did. Why people should get worked up at the mention of 'lavatory' is something that will never cease to amuse. 'Convenience', 'little house', 'smallest room', 'Sir John', 'john', 'WC', 'cloaca', 'chapel (of ease)', all have had their supporters, and the synonyms for sexual intercourse are legion. Having a 'four-legged frolic', 'nibble', 'crumpet', 'getting hulled (or holed) between wind and water', 'doing a spread', 'doing the naughty', 'giving the old man his supper' are a few.

A universe separates the mildly sexually shocking from the

deeply shocking. The music hall song 'Little Things' by J. Wood titillated the groundlings in the eighties:

> The little ladies of the day
> Their little figures dash on,
> They have such funny little ways
> And they like a little fashion.
> And as they cross the little streets
> They look like little pegs,
> And when they raise their little skirts
> They show their little legs.
>
> There was a little maid,
> Looked like a little dove,
> This little maid felt very queer,
> She felt a little love.
> There was a very little man,
> Said he felt a little smart,
> He told this pretty maid
> That she'd stole his heart.
>
> And now this very little maid,
> So says my little song;
> She believed this little man,
> And she'd done a little wrong.
> And, oh, this pretty little maid,
> She grew a little wavy,
> And so after a little time
> She found a little baby.
>
> And now this very little man,
> After the little wrong he'd done,
> From this naughty little maid
> This little man did run.
> Oh! he would not a little pay,
> To buy little baby frocks,
> They sent him then a little way,
> To crack the little rocks.

The nursery rhyme nuances of this song are apparent. This was a device used in rather less innocent verses. To the tune of 'Mountain Daisy':

> When the birds are sweetly singing,
>   As in summer oft they do,
> Would you, dearest, be offended
>   If I lay on top of you?
>   [chorus] No, Sir, No, Sir, No.

or this extract from a saga:

> Eve was so very curious, she fingered Adam furious,
> Till he dibbed in with might and main his root, root, root;
> Said Eve, I do not know, but I think the thing will grow,
> Because I most distinctly felt it shoot, shoot, shoot.
>
> They hardly had the time to wipe away the slime,
> When God down on 'em like a hammer bore, bore, bore;
> And caught the guilty pair with flushed face and tumbled hair,
> And an enormous fig-leaf poultice clapped before-ore-ore.
>
> Out of Eden, roared out God, with an awful rod
> Kept cracking up old Adam's poor behind-hind-hind
> Till his prick began to harden, and against the gates of the garden,
> He stirred up Eve with another joyous grind, grind, grind.

Writers had great trouble with what might be termed the language of bed. The professional pornographers had the greatest, as they were working in some kind of Arcadia in which nothing is real, least of all the dialogue. *A Town-Bull or the Elysian Fields* adopts the affection of being printed in New Orleans, but was really published on the continent. Is this the language of 1893?

> See me, a sensual slave to all the lust you can pour into me. . . . Talk bawdy, vulgarly, wildly, lecherously, teach me all you know of lustful pleasure. Even the most outré. Order me around as you would a common strumpet. . . . I am your slave, your whore, your harlot, ready to be whored out in the public streets, if you want to. I only live to be whored. I will die for it!

More convincing is the narrator of *My Secret Life*. He has just returned from one of his archetypal adventures with street women; this time it was a threesome with a whore and a sailor. He returns home to his wife, worried about having possibly contracted syphilis. But after washing his penis, recollections of his recent amours arouse him, and although his wife is a burden and he is waiting for her to die so that he can inherit her money, he decides to have her.

'I shan't let you – what do you wake me for, and come to me in such a hurry after you have not been near me for a couple of months – I shan't – I dare say you know where to go.'

But I jumped into bed, and forcing her on to her back, drove my prick up her. It must have been stiff, and I violent, for she cried out that I hurt her. 'Don't do it so hard, – what are you about!' But I felt that I could murder her with my prick, and drove, and drove, and spent up her cursing. While I fucked her I hated her, – she was my spunk-emptier. 'Get off, you've done it, – and your language is most revolting.' Off I went into my bedroom for the night.

As *My Secret Life* (1888) was privately printed in very small numbers – not more than twenty-five copies – there was little chance of it becoming an in-book, and similarly the pornographic magazines of a slightly earlier period did not reach a public that would have bought them had they been able to. Books of an erotic nature that were published openly had a guarded air. Smithers, who made considerable sums of money from erotica posing as high literature, transposed material to avoid offending what he called the *amour propre* of English readers, John Addington Symonds in translating the *Memoirs* of Count Carlo Gozzi was bidden to be cautious ('Think how bored I must have been, boiling him down and trimming him up'),[31] and one of the few people who made a sensational killing out of this type of literature was Sir Richard Burton, who between 1885 and 1888 published his translation of the *Arabian Nights* (ten volumes, six supplements), though later his energetic wife published an expurgated edition in which concubines figure as assistant wives.

Burton was a curious man, voracious in the search for knowledge, not averse to a little knockabout sadism (as Her Majesty's consul in Fernando Po he flogged the natives – thirty-six lashes), and not unwilling to cash in on African chieftains' partialities for kinky sexual behaviour (Burton dished out photographs of naked white women for their edification). *Arabian Nights* made

£11,000, and his footnotes have a decidedly un-Victorian bias – one relates his belief in sexual education for young men in 'how to satisfy the physical woman'. Isobel Burton sent out 34,000 circulars without having read the book; when she did read it, she decided that something must be done about it. She also was a person out of the usual run; upon her husband's death she had erected a tomb in the shape of a tent. It cost £688, and she spent 22 January 1894 in it, before deciding that seances with a Miss Goodrich Freer would prove more efficacious.

Nevertheless, despite the success of Burton's translation, one swallow does not make a summer. The conspiracy to keep sex where it belonged – in silence and between sheets – was difficult to break. There was hardly room at all for prosaic sex; where sex was mentioned it was in nutty, esoteric, exotic, ego-vaunting, pseudo-scientific, ultra-romantic contexts. The extract quoted from *My Secret Life* is the expression of an extremely rare genus. A further specimen is found in 'The Morning Poke' (*circa* 1870), the first part of which is the *reductio ad absurdum* of the fancy erotics of the pornocracy:

> Though with lust urging wine-cups at night we grow warm,
> Yet morn, says the sage, is the time to perform;
> 'Tis then you should join in venereal bliss,
> And greet your chaste spouse with a cuddle and kiss.
> 'Tis true a thick paste has grown up on your tongue,
> And your teeth with a yellowish slime are o'erhung;
> 'Tis true that your lips may be dry, cracked and peeling,
> As you lie on your back, uncertain to know
> If't had best be sent upwards, or let out below,
> By a strain for a vomit 't would quicker escape, or
> A spluttering stool that wants oceans of paper;
> 'Tis true that your nose with thick mucus is choked up,
> And your nails are begrimed with the filth you have rolled up…

This was the side of life that no one wanted to know about.

9
The Psychology of Victorian Sex

Anxiety

WHAT is anxiety? 'All the symptoms are exaggerations or distortions of the normal physiological accompaniments of fear. The whole neurosis is a perversion of the fear instinct.' Thus the psychoanalyst Ernest Jones.[1] It is the view of psychoanalysis that desire, if repressed, tends to lead to its opposite, fear. Repression was part of the pattern of Victorian sexual life, and anxiety flourished, abetted by the doctors; there was anxiety over masturbation, anxiety over too much sex, anxiety over no sex at all.

Regarding anxiety over masturbation, it is the opinion of the twentieth century that masturbation is so widespread, both by male and female, as to be normal rather than abnormal. H. Rohleder (1921) put the figure at 90 per cent under twenty years, M. Marcuse (1923) 98 per cent, Meirowsky 88.7 per cent (precision indeed!), M. Hirschfeld (1944) 96 per cent; and more recent researches by Kinsey confirm these findings. Dr Acton established the medical opinion. He believed that the class most subject to temptation was the talented, scholarship-winning, intelligent, brought up on dubious Latin authors:

He reads in them of the pleasures, nothing of the penalties, of sexual indulgence. He is not intuitively aware that, if the sexual desires are excited, it will require greater power of will to master them than falls to the lot of most lads; that if indulged in, the man will and must pay the penalty for the errors of the boy; that for one that escapes, ten will suffer; that an awful risk attends abnormal substitutes for sexual intercourse; and that self-indulgence, long pursued, tends ultimately, if carried far enough, to early death or self-destruction (1857).

These boys at school or university were confused. To avoid temptation they frequently mutilated themselves. In the anonymous *Man and Woman in a State of Marriage* from the early forties:

In speaking of Puberty, we shall view men who have coolly sacrificed to a pretended tranquility the organs which gave them disturbance.... Fanaticism, love of tranquility and dread of disease were, among men, considered as sufficient incitements to seize on the organs of their virility with hardy hands, and to destroy those very organs by a cruel and painful operation from which even death might result.

Young men muddled up sexual anxiety with religious doubt. Charles Kingsley was typical of this generation. In 1839 he met his future wife, Fanny Grenfell, who described the encounter: 'He was then full of religious doubt, and his face, with its unsatisfied hungering look, bore witness to the state of his mind.' [2] Kingsley declared that he was 'saved — saved from the wild pride and darkling tempests of scepticism, and from the sensuality and dissipation into which my own rashness and vanity had hurried me before I knew you'. What this sensuality and dissipation was, one can only conjecture, but in 1855 a Cambridge contemporary of Kingsley told the politician John Bright about Kingsley's passion for making 'drawings such as no pure man would have made or could have allowed himself to show or look at'.

Not only young men. Even more deplorable was masturbation among girls. As late as 1901, Bernard Macfadden in *The Power and Beauty of Superb Womanhood* could speak forebodingly of the exponents, 'You see its victims everywhere. Their white faces, thin voices, lustreless eyes, and emaciated or obese bodies tell the tale more plainly than words ever could.' These poor girls, he went on, were dying by the thousands ostensibly from consumption, but really from self-abuse, or onanism, as it was often called. Masturbation would also arrest growth, distort the pelvis, and prevent the development of the breasts.

Obviously Macfadden had learned a thing or two from Acton's *Functions and Disorders of the Reproductive Organs* of half a century earlier: 'The frame is stunted and weak, the muscles undeveloped, the eye is sunken and heavy, the complexion is sallow, pasty or covered with spots of acne, the hands are damp and cold, and the skin moist.' Acton and his contemporaries were working from false premises. Many writers on sexual physiology were convinced that man was equipped with a certain amount of semen 'to spend'. Other writers considered the testicles to be a kind of accessory to the stomach ('the seminal liquor, being prepared before the man has given any ailments to his stomach is in the reservoirs which are destined for it'). If too much semen was 'spent', it was believed, nothing but tragedy could result. Acton recognized that anxiety brought about by masturbation could be tied up with religion ('... in the acute attack resulting from this cause ... religion forms a noted subject of conversation or delusion').

It may be that to the Victorians, masturbation was the ultimate in the unspeakable. As outspoken a work as *Don Leon* could be almost deferential on this subject: 'While some in corners make themselves a heaven.' Self-excitation by accident was frequently dealt with in a hysterical manner:

A lady putting on her riding trousers becomes, consciously or unconsciously, akin to a hoydem assuming man's clothes, or nearer still, to a ballet girl drawing on her tights. She is subject to contact of the most perilous kind. The warm close substance that passes close to her flesh, that clasps her loins, and embraces her bum, and insinuates itself between her thighs, has, all senseless leather, cloth, or silk, as the case may be, something of the nature of a man's hand in it.

So does pornography (*The Mysteries of Verbena House or Miss Bellasis Birched for Thieving*, 1882) nod across to the world of Dr Acton. The paucity of authentic confessional material in Victorian England, save in pornography, is not surprising. One can draw inferences, but this is a dangerous procedure; one might mention, without comment, the curious extracts from a note-book Florence Nightingale kept in 1850 when she was abroad. Early in life she had enjoyed an over-romantic friendship with Marianne Nicholson, encouraging Marianne's brother to make polite advances to her so that the relationship could continue. This caused her guilt of one kind; but what of this?

March 15th:
> God has delivered me from the great offence and the constant murderer of all my thoughts.

March 21st:
> Undisturbed by my great enemy.

June 7th:
> ... But this long moral death, this failure of all attempts to cure. I think I have never been so bad as this last week ...

June 10th:
> The Lord spoke to me; He said 'Give me five minutes every hour to the thought of Me. Couldst thou but love Me as Lizzie loves her husband, how happy wouldst thou be.' But Lizzie does not give five minutes every hour to the thought of her husband, she thinks of him every minute, spontaneously.

June 17th:
> After a sleepless night physically and morally ill and broken down, a slave – glad to leave Athens. I have no wish on earth but to sleep ...

June 18th:
> ... I had no wish, no enemy, I longed but for *sleep*. ... My enemy is too strong for me, everything has been tried. ... All, all is in vain.

June 21st:
> Two delightful days in Corfu. My enemy let me go, and I was free. I lived again both in body and mind. Oh to-day how lovely, how poetic it was – and I was *free*.

June 24th:

> Here too (Trieste) I was free.

June 29th:

> Four long days of absolute slavery.

June 30th:

> I cannot write a letter, can do nothing.

July 1st:

> I lay in bed and called on God to save me.

In its treatment of anxiety and hysteria, neurasthenia and repression, the nineteenth century took a firm step backward,
though there were men who were explaining anxiety states in
terms that have only recently begun to make sense. Thus J. L.
W. Thudichum in *A Treatise on the Chemical Constitution of
the Brain* (1884): 'Morbid phenomena of mind, incomprehensible to the physiologist and inscrutable to the pathologist, may be
intimately dependent upon minute changes in the organic chemical constitution of brain matter affecting not only the quantity
and quality but distribution of the nerve and psychical force . . .'
This was a lone voice. Too often, medical men were content to
utter platitudes: 'Anxious forebodings wrinkle many brows'
(*Medical Times*, 10 January 1885). The age of reason had been
more acute. Dr J. Cheyne in *The English Malady* (1733) had
spoken of the 'apprehension and remorse . . . a perpetual anxiety
and inquietude . . . a melancholy fright and panic'. Dr R. Whytt
in *Observations on the Nature, Causes and Cure of Those Disorders Which Have Commonly Been Called Nervous, Hypo-
chondriac, and Hysteric* (1764) noted the 'fearfulness . . . uneasiness not to be described', and those who were 'hypped and
vapoured with imaginary or trifling evils'. Dr David Macbride
in 1772 observed that 'anxiety excites the motion of some im-
pending evil' and could be precipitated by 'fear, grief, revenge,
disappointment'. These eighteenth-century men observed but
could do little about it. Victorian doctors could do far more, but
they preferred to pooh-pooh anxiety and its train of troubles,
though they had access to the successes of the pharmaceutical
revolution, which had seen morphine, strychnine, chloroform,
narcotine being produced in commercial quantities. Unfortun-

ately few of the new additions to the pharmacopoeia were perfectly safe, and naturally doctors were reluctant to prescribe something that could sink a patient in two minutes flat. They were also concerned with addiction, especially to laudanum (tincture of opium), and were thankful when a new 'non-addictive' drug was introduced towards the close of the century. This drug was heroin.

Today, it is recognized that no hard line separates one neurosis from another. The Victorians liked to categorize; they liked the new concept of neurasthenia as being respectable, and a logical extension of the Regency 'vapours'. Neurasthenia was an upper-class complaint and was therefore worth money to the medical profession. On hysteria, doctors were inclined to be hawkish. During a fit, it was a good idea if cold water was thrown at the hysteric 'or poured in a stream upon the head for a few minutes at a time'. Mustard plasters near the base of the spine might prove efficacious. It was not recommended that 'as sometimes is done, severe and violent remedies should be proposed within hearing of the patient with the view of frightening her out of the fit' (*Dictionary of Domestic Medicine* by Spencer Thomson, 1856). Thomson believed that hysteria was solely a woman's disease. Continental medical people thought hysteria merely an extension of the essential nature of women; one, Dr E. Kraepelin (1856–1926), considered 70 per cent of all adult women to be hysterical. To Dr C. S. Féré, the hysterical subject was 'the frog of psychology'. Pierre Janet (born 1859), a greatly underrated psychologist, thrown into the shade by his contemporary, Sigmund Freud, considered hysteria 'a form of mental depression characterised by the retraction of the field of personal consciousness and a tendency to the dissociation and emancipation of the systems of ideas and functions that constitute personality'.

Hysteria was in the side lines of every spinster pushing thirty. There were many cures: electricity, strychnine, belladonna, camphor, arsenic, zinc, ergot, Indian hemp, claret, burgundy, cod liver oil, koumiss (a fermented milk). Electricity was available in two versions: the galvanic belt and 'faradization'. Answers were therefore not difficult to find in the closing years of the old century. Choleric medical men were still of the opinion that there was nothing like a cold bath, and, presented with this diabolical roll call of killer drugs, they may well have been right.

Repression

Each epoch has its forbidden subjects. We may chuckle at the Victorians' attitude towards sex, but we must remember that they would be no less amused by our hesitant and mealy-mouthed posture regarding death, an event they could treat in a melodramatic big-production way or casually, as the occasion demanded – just as we, in fact, come to terms with sex. Francis Wey, one of those useful foreigners who visited England in the traumatic fifties (useful in that he saw and recorded diligently and accurately) was shocked by the English way of death. 'In no Christian country is irreverence towards death so shocking.' He was passing by Westminster Abbey one Sunday where there was a bustling crowd of Londoners sampling the sunshine. He wrote:

As I drew near the side door of the Abbey, I noticed a workman digging a trench, as they do in France to find an escape of gas, and I stood rooted to the spot with astonishment at such manual labour being performed on the Lord's Sabbath! While the man worked people sauntered or hurried past, treading in the fresh earth as he threw it out of the pit. A few people were loitering round watching him, but the crowd scarcely glanced his way. As I came nearer an onlooker moved aside, and I was amazed to see a coffin balanced on the edge of the hole. A black cloth had been carelessly thrown half across it, and there it lay like a packing-case waiting to be shipped. . . . The loiterers were the relations, jostled by the crowd who all but tripped over the corpse. At my feet lay a fragment of the shin bone of some previous occupier of the grave, which had just been thrown out among a spadeful of rubble.[3]

It is an incident worth recording at length. Placed alongside the tearful deathbed scenes of innumerable Victorian worthies, heroines, and children, it illustrates the willingness with which the nineteenth century confronted death. The furtive death scenes of the twentieth century, funeral services treated as though they were obscene rites, the cortèges of Rolls-Royces and Daimlers through supermarket-lined streets that everyone ostensibly ignores (the raised hat of the casual spectator is now decidedly *outré*) has made the major factor of life slightly shameful. The nineteenth century would have seen our attitude as ludicrous; it ill becomes us to mock them for their cautious handling of sex. Earlier ages, candid regarding both sex and death, have had their forbidden subjects, too (religion and the supernatural). The Victorians did not burn their prostitutes at stakes.

Many Victorians would have liked copulation to have been a criminal offence. If this were impossible, it was better not to talk about it. This was difficult, because there were always numbers of people who continued to make a great song and dance about it whether or not it was a nice subject. There were the pagan free lovers in their hideaways who wanted sex to be free and untrammelled, there were the poets who endeavoured to express the inexpressible, there were the journalists, especially those of the radical persuasion, who were never so happy as when penning the scandals and debaucheries of the idle rich, and there were the marriage and divorce reformers who made it almost impossible for the subject of sex to be pushed away into the back of the mind. It was possible not to talk about sex; it was more difficult not to think about it. One had to pretend one was not thinking about it.

The result was repression. Wishes of a sexual nature that were not acceptable to the conscious mind were pushed underground; it is in the nature of such wishes that they collect together and form a complex, and it is also in their nature to try and express themselves. Freud and his followers – psychoanalysis is a form of psychology framed for the Victorian mentality – postulated the existence of a censor, the embodiment of high thinking and respectability, which would prevent the nucleus of sexual wishes from appearing at a conscious level. To avoid the censor, these wishes presented themselves to the outside world in a more acceptable form, in disguised or distorted shapes – in dreams, in word slips, or projected onto neutral features. When a word slip had sexual connotations, the efforts made to shut the stable door after the horse had bolted were frequently hysterical. The highly respectable *Daily Telegraph* was the victim of an innocuous misprint: 'Women's tights must not be pushed too far, nor stretched too wide,' which should have read 'women's rights'. This scandalous assertion caused the proprietor of the *Telegraph*, Joseph Moses Levy, to create the position of chief reviser, so that such nasty things should not happen again. Even worse befell *The Times* on 23 January 1882, when in an account of parliamentary proceedings there occurred the direful pronouncement: 'The speaker then said he felt inclined for a bit of fucking.' This was inserted by a rebellious printer, who found the mechanism of a deliberate *faux pas* satisfying.

Thwarted sexuality displayed itself in a number of surrealist ways. One of the clichés of the period was the way sexual disgruntlement was expressed by hiding the legs of pianos and tables with coverings. Furniture legs were equated with human legs, and were given a peculiar sexual charisma, made psychic equivalents. This led to a sauciness about this spurious sexuality, as in the music hall riddle

> Dressed in white, wears drawers,
> Smart legs, but ugly claws –
> *Answer:* A tea table.

Furniture received ratings on its capacity for sexual arousal from 'Mr and Mrs John Brown' by Winford Hallington Pollington Gullamore, 1871):

> The piano in fact
> Tho' its notes were half crack'd
> Look'd like some primmy old maid,
> 'Twas quite veil'd from sight
> In a dress quite a fright,
> And appear'd to be all in the shade.

One effect of this strenuous deception was that real legs acquired a fascination that can only be described as lurid, and even pornographic magazines, with the whole gamut of sensations to play with, could get worked up by the merest mention of legs. Thus *The Pearl* (1879–80):

It has frequently been remarked by travellers, that in no nation of the world are the ladies nicer and more curious about their legs than in England; and to do them justice, there is perhaps no nation in the world where the ladies have greater reason to show them like pretty girls in dirty weather, when the fear of passing for draggletails causes the pretty creatures to hold their petticoats up behind and to display their lovely calves and ancles.

Sexual repression caused many people to put on a front of being extravagantly shocked. Violet Paget, alias Vernon Lee, was reluctant to admit to herself that she had Lesbian characteristics. Sexual envy is manifest in her description of a typical aesthetic group of the eighties: 'There were some most crazy looking creatures: one with crinkled gauze all tied close about her and visibly no underclothing (and a gold laurel wreath); another with ivy leaves tied by each others' stalks on short red hair.' Also prim clergy went to the exhibitions each year at Burlington House with, it seems, the purpose of being outraged by nudes.

Surreptitious ways of exciting the animal in man popped up in the most amazing guises. In January 1872, at Stalybridge Borough Court, Samuel Parkinson was brought to task for 'exposing for sale a number of indecently stamped pieces of confectionery in the Victoria Market on the sixth inst.'. Inspector Bottoms [*sic*!] bought some cough lozenges and observed a 'number of cakes of boiled sugar, on which were stamped the figures of men and women in the most disgusting positions'. A warrant was obtained, Parkinson's house was searched, and the offending moulds were found. A clear case for the full vigour of the law – Parkinson received a month's imprisonment with hard labour.

Numbers of obscene watches were made for the English market, in which the mechanism activated a tiny man and woman in the process of copulation. One proud possessor had his watch stolen, and when it was recovered, notwithstanding the sacred laws of property, the police refused to let him have it back, and it was confiscated. Rather less harmful was 'The Bachelor's Scarf Pin – containing secret Photographs of Pretty Women', which could be bought for 'Twenty Stamps' of C. Nash of Bristol. There was also a considerable trade in saucy literature, inoffensive yet vaguely naughty. These were usually advertised at less than their published price, and characteristic of this genre was *All About Kisses*, a hundred illustrations, nearly 250 pages, published at six shillings, offered at three – 'What is a Kiss. Convenient subjects for Kissing. How to Kiss. Kisses in courtship. When to Kiss and when not. Throwing Kisses. Kisses per post. Forbidden Fruit. Lips. Kisses at Marriage and Two Hundred other kinds of Kisses'.

These little dodges served to satisfy urges that had become suppressed or refined; they were less honest than the aphrodisiacs and the inciters to masturbatory fantasies – the nude engravings, the obscene photographs, the pornography, the *tableaux vivants*. They were also cheaper and more easily obtained. The purchasing of hard-core pornography in Victorian England was a project of some complexity. The repressed therefore had to be satisfied with conciliating material of the second order, with the saucy and not the naughty. There was a good deal of shame involved in falling prey to temptation; Ruskin, for example, could reproach himself for reading Mrs Braddon's *Lady Audley's Secret* (1862).[4] The shame at being secretly excited could be projected elsewhere, and being stimulated could be rationalized into being disgusted. The statement by a minor man of letters, George Brimley, that French novels were 'the properly styled literature of prostitution'[5] tells us more about Brimley than about French novels; the strong feeling tone of Charlotte Brontë in her advice to a Miss Lewis on reading Shakespeare and Byron strikes one as not being commensurate with the facts: '... you will know how to choose the good, and to avoid the evil; the finest passages are always the purest, the bad are invariably revolting; you will never wish to read them over twice.'[6]

Repression works in curious ways. Combining with guilt and anxiety it can drive a person to the edge of insanity and beyond. The painter William Bell Scott was dogged throughout his life by the conviction that he had committed the supreme sin against the Holy Ghost without quite knowing what this sin was; Rossetti on holiday thought that a bird he saw fluttering about was the spirit of his dead wife; the homosexual John Addington Symonds could attack the 'dram-drinker, slave to secret vice, the victim of habitual excesses, the adulterous couple, the obscene dreamer, the nympholeph of unnatural erethism'. He could, in the couplet of Samuel Butler:

> Compound for sins they are inclined to
> By damning those they have no mind to.

The trouble George Meredith had with his first wife, who was, Holman Hunt, the Pre-Raphaelite painter declared, 'a dashing type of horse-woman who attracted much notice from the "bloods" of the day', found its apotheosis in psychosomatic digestive troubles, and its cure in strenuous writing. This abre-action, the working off of repressions, was more difficult for women, often condemned to an endless round of social visits and needlework. Men, at least, could do something about it; too frequently, women who suffered from sexual repression were pinned like butterflies in transparent cases. When they did try to squirm free, it could be an embarrassing and hazardous business, especially as in most cases they had not the slightest notion of their motivations.

A favourite break-out was through hysteria. A very astute medical man, Robert Brudenell Carter, noted this in 1853. His *On the Pathology and Treatment of Hysteria* was far ahead of contemporary psychology. Carter became an eye specialist, de-spite his early interest in psychiatry.

It is evident that a young woman whose chief enjoyment rests either upon a complacent contemplation of her own perfections, mingled with an angry sense of the neglect shown to them by her associates, or else upon an imagined gratification of her sexual desires, is not in the best possible frame of mind for withstanding the pressure of a new temptation; such as is held out by the discovery that she can, at will, produce an apparently serious illness, and thus make herself an object of great attention to all around her, and possibly, among others, to the individual who has been uppermost in her thoughts.

Carter made the point that this kind of imitation hysteria was very widespread. However, watchful observers could differenti-ate between the two:

Attacks of this kind may be distinguished from primary hysteria by the frequency with which they occur in the absence of any exciting cause; by their never being produced under circumstances which would expose the patient to serious discomfort or real danger, but at a time and place discreetly chosen for the purpose; and by observing many little arrangements contrived in order to add to their effect. Thus the hair will often be so fastened as to fall at the slightest touch, in most 'admired disorder'; and many analogous devices will be had recourse to, their number and variety depending upon the ingenuity of the performer, and the extent of her resources.

This is all very well, and due credit to Carter for perspicacity. But it rarely crossed his mind that girls with this desire to cause an effect should be commiserated with, that pseudo-hysteria was not merely a whim of flighty upper-class maidens who were bored by not being paid attention to, that beneath the play acting something was prompting the girls to behave in this manner. He was aggrieved rather than startled by the cunning methods pseudo-hystericals adopted to make themselves convincing – leeches inside the mouth to induce bleeding, tight bandages to swell joints, chafing oneself to produce interesting scratches. He was most shocked – the year, after all, was 1853 – by the readiness with which pseudo-hystericals produced symptoms that made it necessary for the doctor to examine the sexual organs. He was decidedly against the use of the speculum. 'No one who has realized the amount of moral evil wrought in girls ... whose prurient desires have been increased by Indian hemp and partially gratified by medical manipulations, can deny that remedy is worse than disease.' The mention of Indian hemp as an aid to spinsterly erotics is most interesting. Carter had 'seen young unmarried women, of the middle-class society, reduced by the constant use of the speculum, to the mental and moral condition of prostitutes; seeking to give themselves the same indulgence by the practice of solitary vice; and asking every medical practitioner ... to institute an examination of the sexual organs'.

Pretending to have a hysterical attack was a way through the inhibitions of the upper and middle classes. For a time, it was not necessary to conform to a standard of behaviour. No doubt such 'attacks', despite the disapproval of the medical profession, released the internal tensions; they let off steam, they were the respectable and demure maiden's Saturnalia and could be dignified by the appellation 'the vapours'. The structure of society made other exhibitions rare. English society, Henry James wrote to his mother in the seventies, was 'a collection of mediocrities, mounted upon the pedestal of their wealth, their family, their respectability, their consecrated habits etc.'. The sons and daughters were hemmed in, and explosions of inner impulses and desires were not only not welcomed, but were not understood. Repression was one of the consecrated habits of which James spoke. 'The upper classes are too refined,' he also wrote. Their girls had too few outlets for their budding sexuality; visiting Warwickshire, James, perhaps the most detached 'foreign' observer the Victorian scene ever had, commented that 'the women dance ill, but they are soft and clinging'.[7] It was not every day that a handsome American came to do them homage.

Extremely characterisitic of the age was the suppressed hysteric. In his curiously entitled *Fat and Blood* (1877), an early handbook to the fashionable neurasthenia, S. Weir Mitchell depicts the typical suppressed hysteric:

The woman grows pale and thin, eats little, or if she eats does not profit by it. Everything wearies her, – to sew, to write, to read, to walk, – and by and by the sofa or the bed is her only comfort. Every effort is paid for dearly, and she describes herself as aching and sore, as sleeping ill, and as needing constant stimulus and endless tonics. Then comes the mischievous role of bromides, opium, chloral and brandy.

Many women were able to surmount the desire to retreat to sofa and bed to escape from both themselves and the world, and sublimated their sexual energies in 'good works' (Florence Nightingale managed to do both of these in the course of her long life). One of the most outstanding of these women was Octavia Hill, who appears to have completely avoided any sexual commitments by helping the poor, building them homes, hero-worshipping a succession of Victorian worthies, and ruling a series of do-gooding young ladies with amiable despotism. She had a vision of purity, and the excesses of the poor she regarded as due to her own deficiencies. Regarding the girls who dragged out their lives in the squalid courts, she thought 'they wanted to be told that "wild, unmanageable feeling" was their curse, from which they ought to free themselves. I said that the best of them aspired towards an ideal of wisdom, temperance, and quiet self-control, which they were often told they could not reach.' [8] She was able to read into the situation aspirations that she herself had but that the poor under her aegis decidedly did not have. Because she was doing a good job (by the 1880s there were 378 families in Octavia Hill schemes), no one would disillusion her. It is characteristic of the repressed and the thwarted that their own complexes act as smoked or rose-tinted glasses distorting life as it is.

It was not a sympathetic era for the repressed. Parents were urged by doctors to be always on the watch for the 'sexual temperament'. How did one discern the sexual temperament? 'The restless bashful eye and changing complexion, in presence of a person of the opposite sex, and a nervous restlessness of body, ever on the move, turning and twisting on sofa or chair, are the best indications of sexual temperament' (*Uterine and Ovarian Inflammation*, Edward Tilt, 1862). Or there was Olive Schreiner, who in a letter declared to Havelock Ellis, 'The pain in my stomach that I used to get when I had to eat before people, was really asthma in the stomach, caused by the terrible excitement of my heart from nervousness and misery.' Or there was the acquaintance of Violet Paget (Vernon Lee), Anna Hélène, 'forever lying about on sofas, or just rushing away shrieking *tendresses*'. Or Julia Kavanagh, a 'little almost dwarfish figure ... not deformed – that is, not hunch-backed, but long-armed and with a large head, and (at first sight) a strange face'. Miss Kavanagh was a novelist who supported her feeble-minded mother and was destined for celibacy. The Victorians were cruel to the physically unattractive. When a lack of beauty was combined with perverse tendencies, then, indeed, a woman had good cause to bemoan her lot. Thus Edith Simcox, in thrall to Marian Evans (George Eliot): 'I cried a little behind my spectacles over a notebook' – she was doing research at the British Museum on

Egyptian history – 'and my heart ached sorely, but that was not for long – to love her and do what work one can – that is my "formule de la vie".' Something of the same sort afflicted Miss Eliza Mary Ann Savage, who for some reason conceived a passion for Samuel Butler. Miss Savage was plain, an ex-governess, and lame. She met Butler at Heatherley's School of Art, came across him in Berners Street eating cherries; he offered her a handful, and she went on her way 'rejoicing'. Cryptically she declared 'I was like Peter Bell and the primrose with the yellow brim.' Her passion for the equally physically unattractive author ('I knew myself to be plebeian in appearance') was not required. Butler himself had homosexual tendencies, which he intermittently suppressed and rationalized; he and his Boswell, Festing Jones, shared a Platonic love for Hans Falsch ('out dear little fellow'). They each had a lock of his hair. Jones gave his to Falsch's fiancée, upon which Butler gallantly suggested that they share his. Falsch did not live up to expectations and in 1903 was murdered by his discarded mistress. It is perhaps significant that Festing Jones and Butler, besides sharing the doubtful affections of Falsch and the same whore, composed between them an opera called *Narcissus*. Certainly Miss Savage got little change out of Butler. When Festing Jones looked her over as one of Butler's properties, he thought her 'a shock and a disappointment'. She reminded him of ladies who had been at school with his mother. After her death, Butler hung kettle holders she had made for him over his mantelpiece, no doubt to propitiate her.

Men who suffered from the equivalent to the woman's sexual temperament were conditioned to keep a stiff upper lip against all comers. Edward Burne-Jones, painter of langour, and whose official biography (by his wife) is perhaps the dullest of the period bias 'I hold it a point of honour with every gentleman to conceal himself, and make a fair show before people, to ease life for everyone.' One could get a certain satisfaction from suppressing natural grief, as in 'Lines' by James Thomson (1878):

> I had a love; it was so long ago,
> So many long sad years:
> She died; and then a waste of arid woe,
> Never refreshed by tears.

James Thomson sought his consolation in drink – he was hardly ever sober.

Others endeavoured to find release in religion. In December 1857 Octavia Hill went to a working men's church service sponsored by Spottiswoode the printer. She described the preacher:

See him, then, a pattern Puseyite, pale worn face (wasted with fasting), evidently with fears and sorrows about the intense wickedness of the world and its ways, probably a believer in the superior righteousness of celibacy. Great large dark eyes, large forehead, very small chin, smooth, short black hair parted in the middle, and so smoothed and pressed that evidently no hair could have a will of its own. Strange type was it of the complete subjection of the man's spirit, all human nature, good and bad alike, subdued and kept in order, and still his great dark eyes saying how wicked he thought himself.[10]

It would be imprudent to inquire into the motivations of many of the ritualistic (i.e., Puseyite, those who were adopting the forms and ceremonies of the Roman Catholic Church) clergymen. One of them, the Reverend Alfred Poole, overstepped himself by asking outrageous questions of his lady penitents. He is immortalized in many a pornographic saga. Bishop Tait withdrew Poole's licence as curate. One is also suspicious of the motives of the Reverend Bryan King, who instituted about the same time a holy war against sin and sinners, and whose attitude towards the 'seething mass of evil and sin by which [he] was encompassed'[11] verged on the paranoid. It was easier to cast out the devils in others than in oneself.

Some degree of repression is a condition of the human species, though unfashionable today in a country swinging its way if not to perdition at least to a mindless vacuity. Scratch a Victorian personage be it ever so lightly, and we are sure to find something nasty under the façade. Those in positions of power not only tried to appear better than they were, but managed to convince themselves they were, with occasional contrite interludes when they managed to view the scene objectively. There is a smugness, a cocky self-righteousness, a gluey sanctimoniousness about the 'great men' of the age, especially in the field of morals, that contrasts nauseatingly with their more prosaic actions, where expediency and the law of *status quo* are king. One set of ethics was for the rich, one for the poor. Beatrice Webb could refer to the 'aborigines' of the East End but pointedly neglect the West End, with its accommodation houses for rich women with a taste for extramarital sex and its thousands of high-priced whores. Occasionally it was necessary to make a scape-goat of someone *pour encourager les autres*. *The Times* lifted the lid to have a go at Parnell, who was incautious enough to play around at a public level with Mrs O'Shea: 'Domestic treachery, systematic and long continued deception, the whole squalid apparatus of letters written with the intent of misleading, houses taken under false names, disguises and aliases, secret visits and sudden flights, make up a story of dull and ignoble infidelity ...'

The contradiction in the Victorian way of life were fre-quently not even sensed by the natives; when they were, they were pasted over. What would be the result eventually, asked Henry James, of the 'fermenting idiosyncrasies'? It was fortunate, and, indeed, odd, that repression did not become a national condi-tioned reflex. Something happened in the eighties and nineties to halt the triumph of brainless conformity to ludicrous stan-dards of behaviour and morals. The lemmings stopped in their mad rush to the sea; and it was time, too.

Victorian Dream Theory

Modern man does not care to confess that he does not know. Each generation that comes along is modern, and the men of the 1850s and 1860s conformed to pattern. Because they were afflicted by inner uncertainties, their dogma has an irritating smugness, an arrogance that ill befits only their partial use of data available. Dream theory was a subject about which many of the eminent held forth.

Present-day lay views are those held by Freud more than half a century ago, voiced by him in *The Interpretation of Dreams* in no uncertain terms: 'The more one is occupied with the solution of dreams, the more willing one must become to acknowledge that the majority of the dreams of adults treat of sexual material and give expression to erotic wishes.' The dream, he states elsewhere, is 'the royal road to the unconscious'. Contemporary academic psychology is inclined to treat Freud with scant ceremony – he is an eccentric Jewish meddler, his theories as amusing but odd, and the unconscious as an unverified hypothesis. The sexual element in the dream, nevertheless, cannot be wished away by the fact that the principal modern writer on the subject is unfashionable. Kinsey's researches indicate that more than 80 per cent of men have had sex dreams of sufficient potency to reach an involuntary orgasm; the figure for women is slightly less – 65 per cent of the Kinsey sample admitted to overtly sexual dreams, 20 per cent of these to the point of orgasm.

For Victorian writers on the dream, there was no place at all for sex, except the insane. There was not much place, in fact, for the dream itself, which was considered evidence of ill health or the harbinger of madness. This attitude was especially an English one; on the continent, the view was refreshingly objective.

One of the best ways to gauge the way the mediocre and the middle-of-the-road men were thinking is to con the various periodicals devoted to the professions. Although psychology was only marginally a separate subject, it had its own journal, the *Psychological Journal*, edited by Dr Forbes Benignus Winslow (1810–74). His second Christian name does not reflect his attitude; his tone is usually morose and sombre, he has little regard for anything straying from his modest norm, and this tone is mirrored by the contributors to his magazine. Over 1856 and 1857 Forbes Winslow used in his journal a series of articles on dreams, anonymously contributed, though there are echoes of these papers in his own unutterably depressing *Obscure Diseases of the Brain and Mind* (1863).

It was necessary to examine dreams in their context, as part of the pattern of human life, as a cog in the machinery of the body. The mechanism of man was worked by a nervous fluid, the 'vis nervosa'; this nervous fluid was contained in a metaphorical well and could be exhausted if the bucket went in too deeply and too frequently – in the sedentary by too much mental occupation, leading to digestion troubles and the derangement of organic functions, in the sanguine by excessive exercise, leading to fatigue. These states would lead to unsound sleep, and in such sleep dreams would occur. For the truly healthy, there was no such thing as a dream.

Delving into the rag bag of illustrations, the writer in the *Psychological Journal* drew on an obscure case of 1821 to show that dreaming was a nasty thing and unnatural. Dr Perquin, a French doctor participating in the affairs of Montpelier Hospital, had under his charge a woman of twenty-six who had lost part of the scalp and skull and the brain covering through the inroads of syphilis, and whose brain was therefore exposed to view. During dreamless sleep, the brain was undisturbed, but when dreams occurred 'her brain moved and protruded within the cranium, forming a cerebral hernia'. The only part of the brain that should be activated during the sleeping hours, pointed out the writer sternly, was the base, which continued to supply nervous energy to the heart and lungs.

Early editions of the *Encyclopaedia Britannica*, faced by the necessity of including dreams in its curriculum but honestly doubting, half-solved the problem of the dream by rhetorical questioning: 'What parts of the human being are active, and what dormant when he dreams? Why does not he always dream when asleep? Or why dreams he at all? Do any circumstances in our constitution, situation, and peculiar character determine the nature of our dreams?'

Dr John Abercrombie (1780–1844), acknowledged the first consulting physician in Scotland, divided the impulses of dreams into four parts:

1. Wrong association of new events
2. Trains of thought from bodily associations
3. Revival of associations
4. Casual fulfilment of a dream [whatever that might mean]

This was confirmed by other writers. There were primary

impressions (sight, smell, taste, touch, hearing), physical sensations (cold, heat, currents of air), ill health, and the use of narcotics and stimulants, alcohol in particular, which induced 'animal and prurient associations'. In any case, in a state of grace there would be no dreams. Unfortunately, there was one class of dream that had to be included in the canon and one special class of dreamer. There were too many saintly dreamers in the Bible for the whole dreamer species to be dismissed out of hand. There were the hallowed dreams of prophecy to be somehow dealt with. This was not too difficult, as cited by Abercrombie, *Pathological and Practical Researches on Diseases of the Brain and Spinal Cord* (1828):

for Omnipotence may excite material organs in a definite manner, so as to convey true prophecies. The phantoms themselves may be referrible to motions of the organs of the brain, like ocular spectra in the retina, or the imaginary sounds and noises that some nervous people hear. But the coincidences between the dream and the event which it seemed to predict, constitute the astonishing part, and render them miraculous.

So did psychologists have to make polite obeisance to the power of Victorian religion.

The dreams that writers liked to deal with (and for every page of theory there are sure to be up to half a dozen pages of examples) were simple dreams, sparked off or borne to a conclusion by evidence of the senses. One dream study in the *Psychological Journal* of 1856 is possibly more interesting as an illustration of the hazardous life of the itinerant doctor of the period than as a fascinating dream. A Birmingham doctor was visiting Coventry and was housed by a cheesemonger. It was an old building in a narrow street with low rooms, through which percolated the smell of 'strong old American cheese'. The doctor dreamed that he had been imprisoned for an unknown political offence in a large cheese, and there were rats biting through the cheese, eventually biting through to him. He awoke to find that there were, indeed, rats biting through to the room. Strong evidence that the dream was sponsored by the senses of smell and hearing.

Another example is quoted of a dreamer who was asking for a Mr Jones at a large house up a flight of steps. A 'little pert dwarf-like figure' appeared suddenly at the dreamer's side, asking 'What Jones? What Jones?' The dreamer awoke. Outside there was a man shouting, 'Hot rolls! Hot rolls!' These kinds of dreams were acceptable. It was rather odd that a respectable person like a doctor should imagine that he was imprisoned in a cheese, but his environment was hardly conducive to sound dreamless sleep. What about the more dubious types of dream?

These were suffered by those with a 'nervo-bilious' temperament, and were caused by lying on the back, which 'by heating the *cerebellum,* will ... be a cause of prurient associations, from the afflux of blood to that organ'. Nightmares were 'nocturnal phantasmata, which disturb the soft embraces of Morpheus with their playful and visionary forms', and are 'suggested often by pain, by sounds, and various bodily sensations, in the same manner as are trains of waking thoughts'. The theory that a rush of blood to the brain caused nightmares was echoed by the Frenchman, B. A. Morel in 1860, who went one further than his English contemporaries in implanting dread: 'Frightful dreams indicate a determination of blood to the head making delirium. If a person sees in dreams frightful figures making grimaces, the person is menaced with an intestinal malady, or an affection of the liver.'

The notion that dreaming was the province of the ill or the maladjusted was one that could not hold up to any kind of examination. So how was it that a sane well-adjusted man could conjure up such odd and frequently lower-class and vulgar dreams? The simplest answer was that the brain, observed to be in two sections of comparable size and configuration, ran in tandem; one half was a spare, only coming into operation when the other half was not functioning, i.e., when it was sleeping. This curious theory held sway with a surprisingly large number of medical men in Britain. On the continent, the attitude towards dreams was more pragmatic. As early as 1839 Leuret and Gratiolet (*Anatomie Comparée du système Nerveux*) were considering the dream in a manner that was decades in advance of their time: 'In certain respects, dreams ought to be attentively studied: natural instinct can, in certain cases, while inciting the imagination to certain ideas, induce useful dreams, containing salutary warnings.' If, to a closed circuit of medical men, the dream was a symptom of malaise, to others, especially those involved in literature, the occult, and its various manifestations, it was proof positive of the existence of the soul, of a psyche that was freed during the sleeping hours for all kinds of activities – visiting foreign parts or friends. As we can see from the massive documentation of F. W. H. Myers and his friend Edmund Gurney, it was quite all right for a man to visit, as a 'phantasm of the living', the bedroom of an unmarried girl. This theory of a free-wheeling spirit is quite prosaically stated in Myers's *Human Personality* (1904): 'I do not think (in view of the telaesthetic evidence now collected)' – Myers was inordinately fond of coining words – 'we can any longer dismiss as a mere *bizarrerie* of dream-imagery the constant recurrence of the idea of visiting in sleep some distant scene, – with the acquisition thereby of new facts not otherwise accessible'.

Dreams became a hobbyhorse, and the professionals produced theories like rabbits from a hat. 'He who dreams turns his back upon the world of waking consciousness,' declared L. Strümpell (*Die Natur und Entstehung der Träume*, 1877); but he was contradicted sixteen years later by a colleague, W. Weygandt, 'Apparently in the great majority of dreams . . . they lead us directly back into everyday life, instead of releasing us from it' (*Entstehung der Träume*, 1893). Certain dreams were handed down, were exchanged like medical case histories; some of them were apocryphal with built-in impossibilities (the man who dreamed that he was being guillotined, and when the blade came down, he died – how could he have told the dream when he was dead?). This example probably derives from a dream by an indefatigable experimenter, A. Maury, who had this dream and was then hit on the neck by part of his collapsing bed. Maury recounted his experiences in *Le Sommeil et les Rêves* of 1878; he was tickled with feathers on lips and nose – he dreamed that he was undergoing awful torture, and that a mask of pitch was torn off his face; he had *eau de cologne* applied to his nose – he dreamed that he was having 'mad adventures' in Cairo; he had his neck pinched – he dreamed that he had a blistering plaster.

The literature of the dream was paraded by Freud in the first chapter of his *Interpretation of Dreams* (1914) without much comment. It had little relevance to his own train of thought, the preoccupation with symbolism in dreams, and the twofold layer (the manifest content – what the dream states, the latent content – what the dream means). Earlier writers had recorded dreams without realizing that any kind of substitution had been made. One example by Forbes Winslow (1863) is the dream of a neurotic woman: 'I sleep upon scorpions, my bed is full of horrible reptiles, adders are in my pillow, and clinging round my neck.' An even more explicit symbolic dream is recounted by R. von Krafft-Ebing in 1888. The patient was suffering from a curious painful configuration of the skin beneath her breast, in the form of a W and a B, brought on by a dream: 'Last night an old man came to me; he looked like a priest and came in company with a Sister of Charity, on whose collet there was a large golden B. I was afraid of her. The old man was amiable and friendly. He dipped a pen in the sister's pocket, and with it wrote a W and a B on my skin under the left breast. Once he dipped his pen badly and made a blot in the middle of the figure . . .' If one is inclined to doubt the general truth of dream symbolism, one only has to glance at accounts of dreams that Freud could not possibly have got hold of – in particular, Ruskin's dreams that he jotted down in his journal, a journal that has only recently been published.

In most of the writings about dreams, there is one great group that is neglected – the overtly erotic dream. In the present century, as well, there is a paucity of such dreams, if only for the fact that the dreamers are reluctant to talk about them. Erotic dreams often clashed with the dreamer's daytime persona. Florence Nightingale was ashamed of her dreaming; there is no question that they had a strong erotic content. The inhibitions on relating to the doctor such dreams are released when the dreamer is highly neurotic or insane. This led many to believe that erotic dreaming was a concomitant to insanity. In the West Riding Asylum Report of 1876, J. M. Fothergill was inclined to be superior about such dreamers: 'These dreams are much more frequent than is ordinarily thought, and are the cause of a great deal of nervous depression among women. Women of a highly nervous diathesis suffer much more from these dreams than robust women. Not only are these involuntary orgasms more frequent among such women, but they cause more disturbance of the general health in them than in other women.' Fothergill was here saying that orgasms through erotic dreams are not only ethically dubious, but one of the steps to madness. This is odd, when one considers the high proportion of women who have had orgasms consequent upon erotic dreaming, but it was an attitude that held sway until the fact-finding American sociologists of the twentieth century. It was an attitude that was even more forbidding in so far as women who have erotic dreams are in the age groups or in the environmental situations that tend to cause neurosis, i.e., toward the menopause, in middle life when their sexual energies are not satisfied by marital intercourse, in old age when sex *qua* sex has passed them by, or in closed communities (prisons, etc.). The guilt suffered by having erotic dreams has also meant that dream theory is incomplete; the bookish accounts of dreams have usually come from people suffering from some degree of neurosis, leading to repression, leading to a degree of imposed symbolism that is not necessary for healthy erotic dreamers. Why should dreamers bother with symbols when they are out to enjoy their dreams? Unquestionably, the scant attention paid to the erotic dream has led many of the leading psychologists to theories rendered inapposite by the very absence of this vital element. For example, Alfred Adler saw the dream as proof of aggression; possibly this is because more dreams of this nature were related to him. The erotic dreams were not told him.

Not all erotic dreams are happy dreams. In one survey, erotic dreams at puberty were split into four classes: anxiety 37 per cent, desire 17 per cent, fear 14 per cent, pleasure 32 per cent. Not surprisingly, up to ninety per cent of erotic dreams are described as vivid. Curmudgeonly as is the response of the experts to such dreams leading to orgasm, the Roman Catholic Church has taken a rational view of these phenomena. There is no fault or sin provided the dreams are not deliberately induced by thought and deed, not consciously welcomed or enjoyed. If such dreams and such results come from the 'chaste conversation' beforehand with someone of the opposite sex, there is still no fault, nor is there if dream and orgasm is consequent upon 'a rather suitable position on the bed'. The hammering that the Catholic Church has received on account of allegedly obscurantist dogma might well be mitigated by consideration for their enlightened position on the topic of erotic dreams.

Women are less prone to the erotic dream than men. Havelock Ellis maintained that generally they are more copious dreamers, quoting Sante de Sanctis in support (*I Sogni*). Thirty-three per cent of women always dream as against 13 per cent of men. They are more inclined to dream in colour – 75 per cent against 54 per cent; and in sound, 58 per cent against 30 per cent. Dreams of fulfilled wishes reinforce this trend: 43 per cent women, 23 per cent men; and, in the footsteps of Cassandra, their dreams are more frequently prophetic – 24 per cent against 7 per cent. The secret night life of women is therefore considerably more interesting than that of the men, and it is unfortunate that a source of innocent pleasure should have been dealt with with such thoughtless callousness by the experts, who, notwithstanding their qualifications, did not succeed in creating a viable theory of dreams, and only managed to inculcate guilt, repression and fear.

The Dream World of Ruskin

Ruskin today is not a writer much read, and the fact that his collected works run into thirty nine volumes is one more reason why we tend to pass by on the other side. Such fecundity is suspect in the twentieth century, and beyond acknowledging that Ruskin was a master of English prose style, we would rather leave these volumes with the obscurantist titles where they seem to belong (*viz.* in the second-hand book shops). Even the assertion that Ruskin was a master of style is open to doubt; in 1932

R. H. Wilenski roundly stated that 'Ruskin could not write for toffy' but added that 'he had a devil of a lot to say'.

Writing, for Ruskin, was a substitute for loving. His early romances were effectively squashed by his parents, especially his overbearing possessive mother, and the rest of his life was a nostalgic harking back. His marriage with Effie Gray was never consummated.

Until Wilenski rediscovered Ruskin in the 1930s, he was of little interest to scholars and historians, but since then he has been well served by many admirable writers. His books still remain unread, but his life is a source of endless fascination; madness in great ones, especially when combined with a mysterious sex life, is ever a topic of interest, and the etiology of madness has never been so documented. With the decline of letter writing, a modish reluctance to keep diaries, and the presence of the evil genius of the twentieth century – the telephone – it is doubtful whether any future great man will leave so many clues to his imbalance.

Not that the image makers did not try to present an unsullied picture of Ruskin to posterity. One of his official biographers, E. T. Cook, destroyed material that was unpalatable; Ruskin's last conquest, Miss Olander, destroyed at Cook's request one of her own letters in which she was rather tart about Ruskin's housekeeping cousin Mrs Severn. The image makers faltered when they had to strike a balance. The author of the 'popular' biography of Ruskin, W. G. Collingwood – the first edition was written in 1892 when Ruskin was still, nominally, alive, and was later revised to include the later phase –preferred Ruskin to be mad rather than bad. 'Without a life of singular temperance, without unusual moral principle and self-command, he would long ago have fallen like other men of genius of his passionate type,' wrote Collingwood, a curious and indeed fatuous judgement upon one of the most tragic of Victorian sages. Journalists took their cue from Collingwood. 'The occasional reports of his failing mind were mainly wide of the truth,' wrote an anonymous obituarist in the short-lived illustrated magazine the *King*.

Wilenski put his finger on the Ruskin nub. 'He was a man of

action, who was condemned by an unlucky accident to act for the most part by means of words and sentences.' Large chunks of the words and sentences are now meaningless. Many of Ruskin's books are drivel. His championship of a pretty-pretty children's book illustrator when he was Slade Professor of Fine Arts made many of his colleagues rub their eyes, made others uncomfortably aware that this lauding of the merits of Miss Kate Greenaway was not the action of a man altogether *in compos mentis*. His airy-fairy bourgeois socialism led to acres of arid pamphleteering in the guise of hard-cover books.

In 1931 there occurred the notorious Brantwood sale. At his Lake District home, Ruskin relics, dead and buried for thirty years, were exhumed. Books were wrapped up in invaluable Ruskinian letters and notes; annotated volumes by the master were sold in job lots while eager beaver dealers lurched among the bric-a-brac looking for Turner drawings. It is a comfort to know that they bought indifferent copies of Turner drawings by Ruskin's cousin's shadowy husband. Fortunately among the people there was J. H. Whitehouse. He bought the Ruskin diaries, and in due course Joan Evans and he selected and edited them for the Oxford University Press.

The material is rich. Ruskin was introspective and viewed his bodily functions with the same interest and trepidation as Dr Johnson. He also recorded his dreams. For one period his diary is entirely taken up with accounts of such dreams.

These dreams are studied with the symbolism that Freud was later to make fashionable. Many of them have a weird Gothic macabre quality, such as the dream of 7 April 1867: 'A singular night, last night, dreaming of a haunted castle, and of a bright apartment in it, looking out on a lovely view, with two skeletons standing, one at the window, one at the side of the room — very ghastly. The whole, I suppose, the result of eating too much porridge.' It was characteristic not only of Ruskin but of the way of life he represented that there was an effort to apportion praise and blame to dreams and dreaming (*Diary*, 9 August 1867):

A most singular dream last night. I was laying out a garden somewhere and a little child, half like a monkey, brought me a bunch of keys to sell. I looked at them and saw they were ivory and silver, and of exquisite old pattern, but I could not make out on what terms they were to be sold. Then I was in a theatre, and a girl of some far-away nation – half like Japanese, but prettier – was dancing, and she had never been used to show her face or neck, and was ashamed; and behind there was a small gallery full of children of the same foreign type, singing, and the one who brought me the keys was one of them, and my father was there with me. And then it came back – the dream – to the keys, and I was talking about them with some one who said they were the keys of a great old Arabian fortress; and suddenly we were at the gate of it, and we could not agree about the keys; and at last the person who held them said: 'Would it not be better no one should have them?' and I said, 'Yes'; and he took a stone, and crushed them to pieces, and I thought no one could now ever get into the fortress for its treasures, and it would all moulder into ruin; and I was sorry, and woke.

Except that my watch-key had got awkwardly entangled with my other keys, when I wound up my watch, I have no clue to this ridiculous dream, at all.

At this time, Ruskin was in love with Rose La Touche, the most important of his child-women. In her teens she acquired religious melancholy and died early. Her quintessence for Ruskin was at the age of ten when she was

neither tall nor short for her age; a little stiff in her way of standing. The eyes rather deep blue at that time, and fuller and softer than afterwards. Lips perfectly lovely in profile – a little too wide, and hard in edge, seen in front; the rest of the features what a fair well-bred Irish girl's usually are; the hair, perhaps more graceful in short curls round the forehead, and softer than one sees often in the close-bound tresses above the neck.

The feeling tone here is evidently of the order that the average man associates with a mature woman. Rose figured in the dreams of 1867. It was a hot, sultry August. Ruskin was 'terribly nervous and ill about letters and all things'. He dreamed of Rose being in a boat, looking pained when she saw him on the shore, and rowing away from him. 'No noble dreams yet,' he commented. 'Base and paltry. Must see to reason of this, and conquer it.' His diary entries were frequently prefaced with a quotation from the Bible, opened at random and selected from. It is difficult to tell whether they represented an appeasement or a comfort. Against this particular day, 14 August 1867, there was a number – 984. In 984 days, Rose La Touche would be twenty-one; then, Ruskin hoped, he would marry her. This hope was dashed by the machinations of his ex-wife, who wrote to Rose's parents telling them of the wedding night debacle.

Towards the end of August Ruskin returned to London from the Lake District (*Diary*, 30 August 1867):

Dream of being at court of Louis XV, in consequence of reading *Ormond*. Getting into King's private room; courtiers lying to save me, I wanting to tell truth, but not able to speak. King at last telling me he had just seen a lovely Irish girl, whose name was Rose, who had been terribly and brightly startled, hearing my name. I go wild upon this, and wake just as King is looking kind.

1868 opened sombrely. Rose had been in a nursing home, and Ruskin managed to see her. He asked her to marry him, and she refused. The symbolism of Ruskin's dreams becomes more explicit:

Dream of being with some embassy to Russia, and getting into a scrape about their church service. Then of four serpents in a tub, supplied as an article of luxury in one's bedroom by Russian chambermaid, with warning that they must be fed with fish pulled off the bones and put into their mouths, for if they ate the bones they would choke themselves. (Remembered, with remorse, having killed a serpent by that carelessness some time before).

It is not clear whether this bracketed comment is part of the dream, or whether Ruskin was in the habit of feeding serpents with fish. The sexual symbolism of the serpent is self-evident. During this period, Ruskin was seeing sex in everything. 'Saw Gustave Doré's drawing of the lark and her young ones, in *Fables* of La Fontaine. In speaking of the plant larkspur, give the metaphysical character of this disgusting drawing; his dwelling on the spur, and the bald heads.' The dream Ruskin records of 26 February has curious overtones:

Between four and six this morning, dreamed of being in large room at a party, busy eating; called to listen to a piece on piano, played by the family. The piano was twice as wide as usual, and at the side of it there was a square hole cut, just enough for a little girl-baby to sit in, who played on about seven keys, set across the other keys, all for herself. Then the grandmama played the great keys and the mama played on a deep soup-plate, with a knife handle, all very prettily; and I was standing leaning against a sort of kitchen dresser, with my knife and fork stuck out awkwardly at the musicians till I thought I had better put them down; so I did, on the dresser; and then the cook, behind me, began finding fault with my coat collar and asking leave to put it right and brush it, and as he was brushing he cried out at something, and I looked to see what he meant, and the lappet of my waistcoat was all stained with blood, and I thought I had been going about all the evening like that, and so I woke.

The sexual symbolism here is densely packed. Playing the piano is a frequent symbol for sexual intercourse, the 'deep soup-plate' of the mother, played on 'with a knife handle' has one obvious interpretation, the 'knife and fork stuck out awkwardly' another. The knife is almost as often used as a pistol as an analogy of the penis.

On 9 March Ruskin defended the content of the recorded dream by announcing that he had taken too much wine:

Dreamed of walk with Joan and Connie, in which I took all the short cuts over the fields, and sent them round by the road, and then came back with them jumping up and down banks of earth, which I saw at last were washed away below by a stream. Then of showing Joanna a beautiful snake, which I told her was an innocent one; it had a slender neck and a green ring round it, and I made her feel its scales. Then she made me feel it, and it became a fat thing, like a leech, and adhered to my hand, so that I could hardly pull it off – and so I awoke.

If one accepts to any degree at all Freudian theories regarding the dream, there can scarcely be a dream more explicitly sexual. It also raises an intriguing point: With this key dream in mind, is there an implied sexual relationship between Ruskin and his cousin Joan? At this time, she was Joan Agnew, having not yet married Arthur Severn; she was a poor relation who served as a kind of companion to Ruskin's mother, after whose death she was to Ruskin to a large extent *in loco parentis*. It was Ruskin who brought her to London after his father had died, for a week, and she stayed seven years, until her marriage, but even then she was not allowed to move outside the Ruskin orbit. She and her insipid husband were destined to be nature's satellite. Was this latter dream wish-fulfilment – did the continual presence of this young high-spirited girl act as a corrosive on Ruskin?

On 23 March Ruskin recorded a dream in which he and his father were walking in fields, coming 'to a narrow glacier, shut in between walls: very beautiful in soft ridges of snow. My father wondering at its narrowness and feebleness, for it wound far away between rows of trees'. On 24 March he wrote:

Dreamed first of having to take care of two children in a wood walk. It was marshy, and I kept them on a hill gathering flowers, with pools of water round; I with an uneasy feeling of its being unwholesome for them. Then I was driving in a carriage with an old English gentleman who was the landlord of the shops in the street down which we drove, and he jumped up suddenly and shook his fist at a Scotch confectioner, because he had his shop open on Sunday. I said we weren't sure he was really selling anything; I had better go back and see. So I went, but couldn't find anything I liked to buy. At last I found two little sponge cakes and they were halfpenny each, and small at the price, to which I objecting, the Scotch confectioner said it was difficult to 'lay sponge cakes down' because the 'almonds and milk' were so dear. And then I was suddenly in a room, with my mother, writing a letter to somebody, I don't know whom, describing some girls bathing in a pool surrounded by bulrushes and I was very long about it and my mother was terribly angry at my wasting time; and I wouldn't stop, but wrote a great deal, of which I remember only a single sentence: that 'one of the girls when she saw her brother, jumped up and gave him such a kiss that she made the bulrushes shake, all round the pool.'

The public picture of Ruskin was far from the private one. Shuddering on the edge of nervous breakdown as is revealed in his diaries, he nevertheless went in May to Ireland to deliver at the Royal College of Science a lecture, 'The Mystery of Life and its Arts'. To Dubliners he was the oracle from across the seas, the epitome of the nineteenth-century complete man. On his return, Ruskin went to France, where he assuaged his restlessness by much sketching, and projected his own disturbed psyche into the things he saw. In St Riquier, the carving on the church 'is elaborately stupid and vulgar, the last phase of flamboyant, monstrously, and to sickness, rich without design'. The confusion of morals and aesthetics was not peculiar to Ruskin, though Ruskin read into the external world more than most. He dreamed of a 'great naval engagement, and black steamer running away' and 'the most strangely happy dream: [Rose]', took photographs, and sketched with a manic persistence. He began speculating on the use of black in paintings, and how this led to evil (*Diary*, 30 September 1868): 'Dreams always now of going to court, note this: the other night I was at French emperor's, and was sitting talking beside the empress. I had got one foot crossed over the other so as to crush her dress a little, and some Frenchman came in and was ready to faint with horror and amazement – and I couldn't uncross my foot, do what I would ...'

In Abbeville he had what seemed to be a chill, during which 'wall papers all turning into faces'. This, he considered, a sign of weakness. On his return to England, he noted that: 'Singularly, I have had no disgusting or serpent dreams lately.' An extended visit to Italy and a rediscovery of the wonders of Italian art occupied his attentions, and there is a hiatus in his dream reportage. In September 1869 he recorded a curious dream, the second part of which might well be deserving of attention:

Ate cheese and mushrooms last night – very sleepless. At last, dreamed of going to Westminster school to see a tutor whose name was Mr Selby. Shown upstairs into narrow little wooden schoolroom – no Mr Selby, only an old lady and some young boys and a dog. Gave my card to be taken to Mr Selby. Boys looked at it and came and talked pleasantly, and the little dog fondled me; but gnawed me tiresomely, as puppies do; and the boys were telling me all they were reading, and expecting me to know all about it, and I didn't, and was terrified lest they should find out, and no Mr Selby ever coming – till I woke with the worry.

Next, I was going down a long spiral stair in a tower, broken and difficult, till a cobweb came across my face, and I thought 'I can't have come *up* this way, or I should have broken that'; and so I tried to get up again and did, with difficulty, and got out on a balcony, where there was no way down at all. But it opened into a pleasant room at last, and I awoke.

The psychoanalytical school has frequently been accused of making far-fetched interpretations. Assuredly, they would have referred the second section of this dream to the traumatic bridal night. In October, Ruskin's dreams were 'vexatious and ugly'. On the sixteenth:

Bad sleep – stomach wholly wrong at night. Woke at 3; dozed into the usual absurd but – for once – not unpleasant dreams, which I forget, all but the end. I was playing the piano in Ann's room [Ann was Ruskin's old nurse], or rather in a large room belonging to Ann, in a different house from this. Ann was asleep on a little bed in the corner, but presently jumped up, rather in déshabillé, and rubbed her eyes, and saw me, and said, 'Bless me, is that a fly!' When she found it wasn't, she opened the window to see what sort of morning it was, and there was one of the loveliest mountain scenes I ever saw, up a little green dingle with a snowy mountain beyond, under the most intense light conceivable; but when I had looked a little while, I could not make up my mind whether it was sunlight or moonlight before dawn, and so I awoke. . .

Social embarrassment features largely in the Ruskin dream. He dreamed that he had lost his return ticket and had to turn out his pockets while everyone waited for him. On 24 October he related:

Sleep broken. Dreamed I was going up a lovely mountain ravine and met a party of Germans, four very ugly women and their papa and mamma – indefinite – and they were arranging themselves to pic-nic, as I thought, with their backs to the beautiful view. But when I looked, I saw they were settling themselves to see Punch, and wanted me out of the way lest I should get any of it gratis; and I was going on up the ravine contemptuously, when, Punch appearing on the stage, I looked back for a minute and was startled by his immediately knocking down his wife without dancing with her first, which new reading of the play made me stop to see how it went on; and then I saw it was an Italian Punch, modernized, and that there was no idea of humour in it, but all the interest was in a mad struggle of the wife for the stick, and in her being afterwards beaten slowly, crying out, and with a stuffed body, which seemed to bruise under the blows, so as to make the whole as horrible and nasty as possible. So I awoke, and wondered much at the foolishness, coherence, uselessness, ludicrous and *mean* unpleasantness of it all.

On 1 November:

Got restless – taste in mouth – and had the most horrible serpent dream I ever had yet in my life. The deadliest came out into the room under a door. It rose up like a Cobra – with horrible round eyes and had woman's, or at least Medusa's, breasts. It was coming after me, out of one room, like our back drawing room at Herne Hill, into another; but I got some pieces of marble off a table and threw at it, and that cowed it and it went back; but another small one fastened on my neck like a leech, and nothing would pull it off. I believe the most part of it was from taking a biscuit and glass of sherry for lunch, and partly mental evil taking that form.

In December, he 'dreamed of huge spider running over table and dropping on the floor with a "thud" like a toad, and then scrambling away into corners where I couldn't get at it.' The following night he dreamed of 'Christy minstrels, made of leather, playing very merrily and grimacing with leathern faces, superbly cut, and twisted by wires at the noses and wrinkles – one partly in imitation of death's head'.

During 1869 Ruskin's habit of introspection had often been total, and for lengthy periods he had viewed the world through the diffracting lens of his obsessions. He had published one of his more eccentric books, *Queen of the Air*. During his visit to Italy, he had acquired an infatuation for Carpaccio's St Ursula, and, Collingwood states, Ruskin was afterwards accustomed to ask himself when faced with distress and discouragement, 'What would St Ursula say?' Collingwood, much to one's surprise, did not see anything at all odd in this.

On 7 January Rose passed Ruskin in the street without speaking to him, an incident that gnawed at him. It was hardly an auspicious time to begin his lectures as Slade Professor of Fine Arts at £358 a year. His audience was so large that the customary venue had to be altered to the Sheldonian Theatre at Oxford. In his stiff blue frock coat, high collar, long thin gold chain to his watch, he was, ostensibly, 'a plain old-English gentleman, neither fashionable bourgeois nor artistic mountebank'. His lecture methods were freakish; when he talked about birds, he acted them. In March he and Rose were brought together, and in April he found himself writing a children's story of unprecedented coyness: 'Twice upon a time this happened which I am going to tell you; and it happened twice upon a time to two little girls, so that was four times altogether. And then it happened once more upon a time to both the little girls at once: and I don't know how many times that was.' Towards the end of 1870 he dreamed that he was flirting with a girl, and a witch threatened him from a recess high up 'like a ghost'. He threw stones at the witch.

In 1871 he had a mental and physical breakdown. Joan Agnew married; his old nurse Ann Strachan died; he bought, site unseen, Brantwood on Coniston Water in the Lake District; and his mother died. She was ninety. Ann Strachan had been a Calvinist of the deepest dye. 'If ever a woman in this world was possessed by the Devil, Ann was that woman,' Mrs Ruskin had said. Ann's influence on Ruskin may have been crucial. She would have approved of his strictures on Michelangelo when, in 1872, he went to Rome: 'The Judith, David and Brazen serpent especially to be noted, and the artifices for showing of legs.' And his attitude towards a fairly harmless comedy *Frou-Frou* ('dreadful'). In 1872 Ruskin and Rose La Touche, despite the efforts of Rose's mother to break up the relationship, came together, but Rose was teetering on the brink of madness.

The disappearance from the scene of the old time arbiters of his fate – his mother and his old nurse – did not achieve any psychic break-through for Ruskin. He retreated to Brantwood. In December he recorded a sombre dream:

Dreamed that I had charge of a little girl, who was eating at the same table with the spirit of Wisdom and of Death, and they were both cold, and I was terrified lest she should touch them. They were both beautiful, only, if Death smiled, he showed his teeth; and the little girl noticed that they never smiled and asked them why; then Death smiled, and showed his teeth more than he ought to, but the little girl did not notice – and I awoke, for fear she should.

Serpents figure again in his dreams. Others are 'very terrible, and touching on deepest feelings of which I would not write in such connection, about my parents'. There was 'an old woman with ducks' bills instead of feet. (Singularly diabolic form of disturbed brain, as I hold it).' Of course, he was right.

The Oxford dons were amused by his sudden espousing of the cause of Botticelli (prompted by engravings that were not even by Botticelli); to Carlyle he was the 'Ethereal Ruskin;' and to philanthropists he was a source of comfort, light, and money. He went to Eton to do his celebrated lecture on birds, and no doubt amused the boys, ever eager for eccentrics to come and relieve the monotony. However, the beginning of 1874 saw him in 'failing strength, care, and hope'. He wrote a peoem, beginning 'Love, it is a wrathful peace/A free acquittance, without release.' Clearly the long-hoped-for union with Rose La Touche was now out of the question; he sought diversion in childish entertainment – the pantomime. He saw Kate Vaughan (a refugee from burlesque where she had popularized and made something of a sexual fetish of black gloves) in *Cinderella* and Violet Cameron in *Jack in the Box*. He looked at himself with a painful jocularity : 'Now hopelessly a man of the world – of that woeful outside one, I mean. It is now Sunday; half-past eleven in the morning. Everybody else is gone to church – and I am left alone with the cat, in the world of sin.'

The world in which Ruskin was to gyrate was increasingly egocentric. He retreated into the inner world of madness, where dark clouds were assumed to be visual warnings of the wrath to come, and where the serpents not only appeared in dreams, but took control. 'The true secret of happiness,' he wrote to Mrs Acland in 1855, 'would be to bolt one's gates, lie on the grass all day, take care not to eat too much dinner.' He tried to bolt the gate when it was too late. Occasionally, the madness lifted, and he returned to Oxford to lecture. They were absurd, fatuous lectures. 'He had found two young Italian artists,' wrote a reporter, 'in whom the true spirit of old Italian art had yet lived. No hand like theirs had been put to paper since Lippi and Leonardo.' These were two now totally unknown hacks – Boni and Alessandri. The *Spectator* referred to Ruskin's 'gifts of insight and power of reaching the best feelings and highest hopes of our too indifferent generation', but more astute observers realized that this Ruskin was a shell of his former self. When Oxford proposed to sponsor a move to endow vivisection, Ruskin resigned from his professorship, and his friends breathed more easily.

The madness stemming from his early disappointments in love was mingled with senility. He lived to a great age. Despite the illness and the misery that he recorded so diligently in his diaries, it was an influenza epidemic that finally overcame him. His last sane or sanish years were occupied with his autobiography. He looked back at his first love with an objectivity that had been lacking in his Oxford lectures and his forays into the world of economics. 'My mother, who looked upon the idea of my marrying a Roman Catholic as too monstrous to be possible in the decrees of Heaven, and too preposterous to be guarded against on earth, was rather annoyed at the whole business, as she would have been if one of her chimneys had begun smoking.' By hook and by crook, Mrs Ruskin had tried to keep her clever son damped down. That she succeeded was not to her credit.

10

Against the Norm

Homosexuality

THE term 'homosexual'[1] was first introduced by a Hungarian physician named Benkert in 1869. He defined it as 'a sexual fixation which renders them both physically and mentally incapable of achieving normal sexual erection and inspires them with horror of the opposite sex, while they are irresistibly under the spell of their own sex.' Towards the end of the nineteenth century there was great interest in the phenomenon; between 1898 and 1908 more than 1,000 works on homosexuality were published, though statistics remained unreliable. The present-day estimate of the percentage of the male homosexual population has been put by Kinsey at 6 per cent. There is no reason to suppose that this figure has greatly altered over the last century. Havelock Ellis put the figure at between 2 per cent and 5 per cent. More astounding are Kinsey's figures for those males who have at some time or another participated in homosexual behaviour: '37 per cent of the total male population has *at least some overt homosexual experience* to the point of orgasm between adolescence and old age. This accounts for nearly two males out of every five that one may meet' (*Sexual Behaviour in the Human Male*, 1948). Most of these men eventually eschew such behaviour, but it does emphasize the fact – if Kinsey's figures are correct – that more than a third of the male population is bisexual. The climate of opinion has altered drastically – in no sphere of sexual activity so much; whereas the position of the prostitute is less accepted, the homosexual is treated as a person and not as a criminal. The state of the law in the nineteenth century meant that repression was almost universal (except in the public schools, where homosexuality thrived unabated, and was often sponsored by masters and tutors who were themselves homosexual), and this resulted in severe nervous ills, and, when the occasion offered itself, excessive violence. As Krafft-Ebing stated in *Homosexuality and the Law*: 'The homosexual urge may sometimes enforce satisfaction with such violence that control becomes impossible. It has even been said that the excitements and dangers entailed by the prohibition of homosexual acts may easily intensify nervous and sexual irritability.' In these conditions, the male prostitute flourished; many of them were heterosexual and belong to a group known as pseudo-homosexuals who offer their services for money and remain uninterested in the proceedings.

Many attempts were made in England towards the end of the last century to make homosexuality respectable, and numbers of books were written by homosexuals who thought that by a change of terminology miracles would be achieved – among the contenders have been 'homogenic love', 'contrasexuality', 'homoerotism', 'similisexualism', 'uranism', 'sexual inversion', 'intersexuality' and 'the third sex'. Uranism was a concept thought up by Carl Heinrich Ulrich in the sixties, and the exponents of it were called 'urnings' and 'dionings'; the philosophical form of this was 'Uranismus', the female soul in the male body, and for a time the term 'urning' had a fairly wide currency among the initiates. 'What a number of Urnings are being portrayed in novels now!' wrote J. A. Symonds to Edmund Gosse.

There are four basic types of homosexuality, manual, oral, femoral and anal. Manual homosexuality is mutual masturbation; this is possibly the most widespread form of active homosexual behaviour. Oral homosexuality is almost as common – this is *fellatio*, the stimulation of the penis with tongue and palate. In its feminine form, this is a form of excitation widely

practised by Lesbians, often combined with the use of an artificial penis (in the 1840s *godemiches* of india rubber that fitted
on the chin of the female partner were sold for £2 10s).
Femoral homosexuality is performed by the passive male partner
lying like a woman while the active participant ejaculates into
the fissure between the scrotum and the thighs. Occasionally a
pseudovagina may be worn. The fourth type, anal, although it
represents to the lay mind the typical image of homosexual
behaviour, is not believed to be very common. This is pedication,
the introduction of the penis into the anus, and in many countries this form of homosexuality was the only illegal one. Magnus Hirshchfeld estimated in this century that only 8 per cent of
active homosexuals use this form of intercourse.

Until 1828, pedication was punishable by death, but the witness had to have *seen* penetration. As pedication was such a
heavily prohibited crime, much blackmail was attempted, and
the courts were faced with a grotesque predicament, and there
was an understandable reluctance to use the supreme penalty.
During this period, young men who were homosexually inclined
and were aware of the penalty for sodomy frequently committed
self-mutilation.

Public personages were particularly vulnerable, and in 1833 a
Member of Parliament, W. Bankes, figured in a sensational
case. He was discovered and accused of 'standing behind the
screen of a place for making water against Westminster Abbey
walls, in company with a soldier named Flower, and of having
been surprised with his breeches and braces unbuttoned at ten
at night, his companion's dress being in similar disorder.'

Homosexuality was ignored by the well-bred and scourged by
others. In a handbook for men about town, *The Yokel's Preceptor*, published in the fifties, the writer goes into high indignation over the presence of homosexuals in a civilized city:
'Why has the pillory been abolished? Would it not be found
very salutary for such beasts as these? for can they be too much
held up to public degradation and public punishment? Will the
reader credit it, but such is nevertheless the fact, that these
monsters actually walk the streets the same as the whores, looking for a chance.' Fleet Street, Holborn, and the Strand were

favourite sites for the homosexual prostitute, and there were signs in the public houses near Charing Cross, 'Beware of Sods'. 'When they see what they imagine to be a chance, they place their fingers in a peculiar manner underneath the tails of their coats, and wag them about – their method of giving their office.' They were known during early and mid Victorian times as 'margeries' and 'pooffs', and the act itself was referred to as 'backgammon'. Had society realized the extent of homosexual behaviour, it might earlier have come to a *modus vivendi* and resisted the successful efforts of the prurient and the police to make examples of the sexually maladjusted, though conveniently homosexual behaviour of the powerful and the high in office was not observed. Canning, it is said, made overtures to any pretty youths in the House of Commons, and Disraeli's behaviour, if not homosexual, was unquestionably camp. When in Spain, he played the role up to the hilt: 'I also have my fan,' he wrote home, 'which makes my cane extremely jealous.'[2] Others had doubts about Browning, later the exponent of masculine and rugged verse, who as a young man was given to wearing his hair in ringlets.

For the man aware of his tendencies, there were three possible attitudes: to vaunt them, to keep them quiet, or to attack those with similar tendencies. This could create curious situations. Of the first group, a classic example is Simeon Solomon, friend of Swinburne, a painter and poet, whose brother was a respectable Royal Academician (Abraham Solomon, ARA). He was born in 1841, and mixed for a time in the highest artistic circles. He had friends including Albert Moore, ultra-fashionable painter Marcus Stone, the aesthetician Pater, and Burne-Jones. Solomon's father was a rich importer of hats, and became the first Jewish freeman of the City of London. His paintings, said Swinburne, showed 'the latent relations of pain and pleasure, the subtle conspiracies of good with evil, of attraction and abhorrence', and he encouraged Solomon in this naughty vein. Solomon was unashamedly homosexual and perverse:

I should doubtless be vigorously judged by two widely different classes of my fellow men, namely, those whose passionless temperaments are incapable of being excited by anything in heaven above, or if you will allow me the expression, in the hell beneath the earth; the other class is composed of those persons, and their name is legion, who find a delight in visiting casinos, and other dull, disreputable resports of the like nature, and an amusement, nay, a satisfaction in copulating with vulgar and often diseased persons of the opposite sex. ... I will at once candidly unbosom to my readers, my affections are divided between the boy and the birch.

While his brother Abraham was turning out genre paintings with titles such as 'First Class', 'Second Class' and 'Waiting for the Verdict', Simeon was living it up, interspersed with trips to undiscovered Wales – 'I suppose they turn this off at night,' he said of a cascade, Rhaiadr-y-Wenol, adding laconically, 'you might be a hundred miles in the country'. In the circles in which Solomon and Swinburne moved there was no need for the reticence that formed a fog over Victorian England, but Solomon's behaviour was too *outré* even for Swinburne, who wrote to his friend George Powell, a Welsh squire and de Sade enthusiast, 'I suppose there is no doubt the poor unhappy little fellow has really been out of his mind and *done* things amenable to law such as done by a sane man would make it impossible for anyone to keep up his acquaintance and not be cut by the rest of the world as an accomplice?' Later, Swinburne was even more on the side of the angels: Solomon was 'a thing unmentionable alike by men and women, as equally abhorrent to either – nay, to the very beasts – raising money by the sale of my letters to him in past years, which must doubtless contain much foolish burlesque and now regrettable nonsense never meant for any stranger's eye ...' Even Swinburne drew the line somewhere. Solomon sank lower and lower and died in squalor in a workhouse in 1905.

For those homosexuals who kept their traits hidden, the image-makers have frequently managed to keep the subject untarnished, and occasional spots of rust have the power to surprise. The propensities of Edmund Gosse, literary figure *in excelsis*, were effectively hidden, and it was unfortunate that a fellow homosexual managed to pick out the flaw, J. A. Symonds. The vision of Gosse looking through pictures of male nudes during the funeral service of Robert Browning in Westminster Abbey is decidedly surrealist.

For many of the upper classes, homosexuality approached them in stocking feet via the passionate friendship that was the done thing in the public schools. Homosexual experiences were the rule rather than the exception, and it was rare for a boy to get through without some traumatic event occurring, though Arthur Stanley, the friend of Benjamin Jowett and a copious writer on religious matters, managed it, despite his nickname of 'Nancy'. (His sister probably knew more about homosexuality than he did, as she was married to one, Dr Charles Vaughan, headmaster of Harrow, and pleaded to a doctor who had threatened to expose him.) The passionate friendship was frequently idealized in retrospect; the first Earl of Selborne, an ex-Lord Chancellor, wrote of his relationship with Frederick Faber, hymn writer, founder of the Brompton Oratory, and an important convert of Newman's to Roman Catholicism: 'Our affection for each other became not only strong, but passionate. There is a place for passion, even in friendship; it was so among the Greeks; and the love of Jonathan for David was "wonderful, passing the love of woman".'[3] Sanctified as it was by the Bible and the Classics (at Rugby in the sixties, seventeen hours out of a total of twenty-two learning hours were devoted to Greek and Latin), love between youth and youth was acceptable. Occasionally this could produce a masterpiece, as it did in Tennyson's 'In Memoriam' (1850) for Arthur Hallam; the *cri de coeur* of anguished adolescence:

> My Arthur, whom I shall not see
> Till all my widow'd race be run;
> Dear as the mother to the son,
> More than my brothers are to me.

Posterity has not found the sentiments expressed in Tennyson's poem of 131 sections improper, but the affection of Tennyson for Hallam can only have differed in degree from more dubious associations. At Harrow, it was customary for pretty boys to be given feminine names, and they were accepted as the 'bitches' of the older boys. Jowett advised 'a cuff on the ear' to those boys who propositioned the younger, but this was not always possible in the power politics of school life at a time when brutality reigned and was sanctioned. At Augustus Hare's first day school, he related, 'Eve's apple was quite eaten up – the leaves of the Tree of Knowledge were stripped bare.' Hare turned into a gossipy spinsterish type tied to his mother's apron strings; it is possible that early sexual experiences savouring of indecent assault produced this. Monitorial systems, fagging and the advent of muscular Christianity gave ill-advised power to the already strong. School life was a farrago of beating, buggery and boredom, and it needed either an extraordinary personality or an equally extraordinary lack of perception to look back at it with complacency, as, for example, Sir William Gregory did in his *Autobiography* of 1894: 'Harrow was a fine manly place. It was a little world in itself, and boys were the arbiters of their happiness or unhappiness in it ... but woe betide the sneak and the snob.' True, the public school was a little world, with its own ethos and its own pattern of sexual adjustment. It was a world that sent out censored dispatches, presided over by ambisexual men such as Oscar Browning of Eton, or the ambiguous G. H. Shorting of Rugby with his 'Arcadian' tastes, or the blissfully ignorant Dr Percival of Clifton College, 'very ready to discuss and anxious to be informed.'

It was rare for a headmaster to be caught out, though Dr Vaughan assuredly was. He became headmaster of Harrow in 1844, when he was in his late twenties, and this post he retained for fifteen years. It was his aim to produce an 'English Christian gentleman'. Harrow was a consolation prize; he had missed getting Rugby by one vote. He speedily recognized that his charges were not behaving like Christian gentlemen, but were in the habit of passing compromising notes from one to the other, and gave the boys a stern talking-to, also forbidding the use of feminine names for the 'bitches', backing these measures up with floggings and lines.

In 1858, Vaughan selected as his love object a boy, Alfred Proctor, who did not have his own capacities for reticence, and Proctor wrote John Addington Symonds that he was having an affair with the headmaster. Young Symonds told his father, and

Dr Symonds wrote to Vaughan. Vaughan resigned the head-mastership under this pressure and was warned not to take the bishopric of Rochester five years later when Palmerston offered it to him. This caused much interest, and at a dinner party a lady told Bishop Wilberforce of Oxford the reason for the rejection of Palmerston's offer. In 1869 Vaughan became Master of the Temple, and in old age, Dean of Llandaff – his tormentor, Dr Symonds, was no longer alive to apply his veto. After Vaughan's departure, Harrow was offered to Dr Henry Butler, also a young man in his twenties, 'fond of popularity and eager [as was the case with Vaughan] to keep up the external prosperity of the School at the cost of concealing any of its internal corruptions'.[4] So wrote Symonds, beset with his own temptations. The case of Dr Vaughan is a salutary one. Public school life was not just *Tom Brown's Schooldays* or *Eric, or Little by Little*.

School is possibly what one makes of it, possibly not. Gladstone, according to his adoring biographer John Morley, 'did not stand aside from the harmless gaieties of boyish life, but he rigidly refused any part in boyish indecorums' – the harmless gaieties consisted of chess and cards in the evening, with an occasional turn on the river. 'When I was at Eton,' Gladstone recorded, 'we knew very little, indeed, but we knew it accurately.' Many parents were aware of the temptations of the public school. Sir James Stephen took a house at Windsor so that his two sons could go to Eton as day boys, and so avoid the obscure sins that afflicted the boarders. But even parents who had possibly undergone a fate worse than death at the hands of the older boys continued to send their own sons to those pyres of happy innocence, the public schools. A handful of public schools were more than status symbols; attendance at one or other of them was essential for a boy who was to make any kind of mark in the establishment world. The more philosophical fathers considered that it was a good thing to send a son to public school, as it would assuredly make the rest of his days reasonably happy – no horror could overtake the cruelties, humiliations and curious sexual practices that the boy came up against at Harrow, Eton, Winchester, Shrewsbury, Rugby or wherever. There were few alternatives to the public school; the grammar schools were in decline, though towards the end of the century many of them had their kudos restored when the demand for a superior popular education became too over-whelming for the authorities to ignore. At one endowed gram-mar school, Whitgift's Hospital, Croydon, there were simply no pupils, and there had not been for thirty years.

At what point did the normal adolescent friendship slide over into passionate friendship, at what point did the passionate friendship shade into overtly homosexual behaviour? The mas-ters did not know, and most did not care. The Reverend Wil-liam Dobson of Cheltenham College insulated himself from both masters and boys, his only known recreation long biweekly tramps over the country with an iron bar as a walking stick. The morals of his 585 pupils did not concern him. For him, the purpose of his College, which he had brought up from nothing, was a powerhouse not exactly of learning but of examina-tion techniques. Butler of Harrow was elegant in cambric and complacent. Edward Hawtrey of Eton was a licensed eccentric, an act of God. Thomas Arnold of Rugby, endeavouring to make this the first great public school for the middle classes, also fell into line. The headmasters were munificently paid, and tradi-tion was all.

'At school friendship is a passion. It entrances the being; it tears the soul.' Thus wrote Disraeli in his novel *Coningsby*. Oscar Browning felt such a friendship when he wrote in his diary upon his seventeenth birthday:

Today I received the greatest pleasure that for many days I have received, indeed a noble birthday gift, an hour of Prothero's society. For the last three weeks have I prayed to God that his heart might have changes and he might love, and my prayer hath been answered. For today I met him and walked with him. I told him that it was my birthday, and his lips wished me many happy returns of the day. Surely God will receive that prayer, surely I am blessed in that wish. Why I should love Prothero as I do I cannot tell, but I do love him and I believe that that love ennobles me and purifies me. It gives me an object for my work and my affections, truly a noble one.[5]

A year later, Browning was more circumspect: 'My object is not love, but love without his wings, friendship. A half or two ago I saw a boy named Dunmore. I was struck by his eyes. I have been more so by his manner and everything about him. My wishes, my hopes and fears begin and terminate in him. I have found that he is a lord, but I loved him before. I never shall have a chance of knowing him, perhaps not one of speaking to him.'[6] Later, Browning became a master at Eton and was involved in a feud with the headmaster of the day, who, prompted by the tutor, interfered with Browning's friendship with the young George Nathaniel Curzon, to whom, said the tutor, Browning's 'irrepressible attentions' were causing mirth and merriment among the boys. 'Spooning' between master and boy was a subject for cruel jest. But it was also accepted as part of the order of things.

Sentimental hindsight often succeeded in robbing boyish amours of their distasteful side, though sometimes the years did not deflect the trauma. 'I remember well my first day or two at Eton,' wrote Edward Vesey Bligh, 'and the catechism of oaths and bad words and doings, which I had to learn quickly in the Pandemonium of my Tutor's House. He was half, and his Wife fully mad; and the boys were a wicked lot generally and not looked after at all.'[7] That the myth of the public school as a Christian gentlemanly world in miniature was not exploded says much for the fortitude and forbearance of the English upper classes of the nineteenth century.

Pitchforked into *mores* far removed from home life, the young boys had to make a great effort at reorientation. If homosexuality is implanted in early adolescence, no ground was more fruitful than the public school. The editor William Stead recognized this when he wrote in his *Review of Reviews* after the Oscar Wilde case: 'Should everyone found guilty of Oscar Wilde's crime be imprisoned, there would be a very surprising emigration from Eton, Harrow, Rugby and Winchester to the jails of Pentonville and Holloway. Until then, boys are free to pick up tendencies and habits in public schools for which they may be sentenced to hard labour later on.' From one closed community, the public school boys moved to another one, the university, and seeds that were sewn at school unequivocally blossomed. While Oscar Browning was being over-friendly with

George Curzon at Eton, Oscar Wilde was at Oxford. Wilde was unquestionably attracted to women at Oxford, and his attitude towards a companion, Charles John Todd, was thoroughly conformist and heterosexual: '. . . saw Todd and young Wood the choir boy in a private box together. . . . Myself I believe Todd is extremely moral and only mentally spoons the boy, but I think he is foolish to go about with one, if he is bringing this boy about with him.'[8] Todd became a chaplain in the Royal Navy in 1881 and died at a great age in 1939.

If masters and tutors at public school were remote, scorned, or amorous, the dons at the universities were inclined to play up their little foibles and their eccentricities. G. A. Simcox was accustomed to give tutorials in his nightshirt and burst into maniacal laughter in church (in 1905 he went on a walking tour of Ireland and never returned). The formidable Mark Pattison, rector of Lincoln College, Oxford, from 1861, was a remote ascetic to timid undergraduates, for whom the summons to a walk with the rector was no more agreeable than a death knell. One anecdote refers to the undergraduate who on one of the dreaded walks could only venture into conversation by volunteering that 'the irony of Sophocles is greater than the irony of Euripides'. 'The rector seemed lost in thought over the statement,' recalled the Reverend Andrew Clark in his *Lincoln College*, 'and made no answer till the two turned at Iffley to come back. Then he said. "Quote." Quotations not being forthcoming, the return and the parting took place in silence.' Were such as Simcox, Pattison or Newman close observers of sexual life at the universities? Hardly. Were they the kind of people worried undergraduates who discovered that they had irrevocable homosexual tendencies would go to? Hardly. Were there any influences at the universities (particularly Oxford – 2,972 undergraduates in 1888 and Cambridge – 3,059 undergraduates in 1888) for, if not the good, at least the normal? Perhaps Jowett, who as Master of Balliol exerted great influence on the whole of university life. In a letter to Professor Lewis Campbell, Jowett's official biographer, Josephine Butler pointed out this little-known facet of Jowett's life. At one time there was an outbreak of abnormal immorality among a few of the young men in Oxford. To such he was (I know) the wisest, most prudent and gentlest of counsellors. He was extremely severe and tender at the same time. We had the unhappiness of having to try and guide for a time one of these youths (now dead) and thus I got to know how implicitly such misguided or guilty creatures might confide in him, and seek and follow his advice ... I always admired Mr Jowett's wonderful reticence and refinement coupled with sternness and *swift, decided action* when needful, in cases where moral corruption called for drastic measures.

Life at Oxford, Jowett stated elsewhere, was like 'living in a hot-house'. At one time in Oxford, to be slightly camp was the best way to gain friends and influence people; when the 'hearties' and the 'aesthetes' were developing into two mutually exclusive power blocks, the uncommitted found the aesthetes more interesting. What Hilaire Belloc called 'Remote and ineffectual Don' watched these new manifestations with alternate disinterest and malignity, while 'Repulsive Don — Don past all bearing' joined in, frequently starting movements of their own. One of these was Walter Pater, aesthete-in-chief, hunch-backed (at school it was known as the 'Pater Poke'), heavy-jowled, decidedly odd, who looked forward to 'a strange complex of conditions where, as in some medicated air, exotic flowers of sentiment expand, among people of a remote and unaccustomed beauty, somnambulistic, frail, androgynous, the light almost shining through them'. Jowett was suspicious of the way of life Pater represented, and strove hard to stop Pater from getting a position of real power, though we are today inclined to see them both as sexual outsiders, who did not participate in any heterosexual or homosexual games, but watched, sometimes slightly goggling, from the side lines. The 'exotic flowers of sentiment' expanded, for many undergraduates, in a way that Pater did not anticipate.

Yet the university population was a small one, and in no way represented the ways of the common people. The behaviour of certain undergraduates did lead to certain assumptions — that when normal sexual outlets are stemmed, sexual activity tends to revolve around the people who are most handy. Not that

Oxford was inaccessible – there was a perfectly good train service to London – but the atmosphere of the hot-house tended to the obfuscation of normal sexual instincts. There was also a certain amount of confusion in the undergraduate mind as to what constituted normal sexual activity, nurtured as they had been on Plato, for whom free homosexual love was one of the good things one could take for granted. The dons also had fixations on the Greeks, and many of them had immense difficulty in keeping the style and the message in logic-tight compartments. 'What Plato says of the loves of men must be transferred to the loves of women, before we can attach any serious meaning to his words,' wrote Jowett in some perplexity. 'Had he lived in our times he would have made the transposition himself.' [9] For young men who indulged in homosexuality, they had their own holy writ, Plato's dialogue *Phaedrus*, which glorifies love between a man and a boy or a younger man; however, they must abstain from the crudest mutual pleasures – they may embrace and kiss, but must stop there (and so Plato gave a multi-purpose adjective, platonic, to the English language). The approval of Plato led to the elimination of guilt.

The world of Oxford and Cambridge was a young world. At one time in the nineteenth century, many colleges deprived their dons of their fellowships when they married. In 1856 at All Souls the average of the forty fellows was thirty-four. It was a celibate all-male society in which it would be surprising had not the tinder raised the occasional spark.

In London, homosexual society was like 'feasting with panthers'. There were the homosexual brothels – one was next to Albany Street barracks, kept by a Mrs Truman – and there were the homosexual clubs, such as the 'Hundred Guineas', where the guests were given girls' names. There was a small select market for homosexual pornography, such as *The Sins of the Cities of the Plain: or the Recollections of a Mary-Anne*, which cost four guineas (less than a hundred pages), in which the participants live it up on champagne and oysters. It was a branch of literature known as 'Socratic'. There was a magazine called *The Chameleon* in which the seduction of a choir boy is described in detail – choir boys and soldiers are staple elements in the diet – and literary homosexual men sought clues in other writers to find out if they were that way inclined, too. The tone of F. W. Myers was felt by Symonds to be 'radically wrong in matters of passion'; the homosexual Roden Noel, son of the Earl of Gainsborough, was felt to betray himself in *A Little Child's Monument*; and Gosse's *With Viols and Flute* indicated 'a strong and tender sympathy with the beauty of men as well as women'. Walt Whitman, when approached delicately as to the state of his sex life, bragged of six illegitimate children.

It was a twilight world occasionally illuminated when an outsider stumbled into it and made indignant noises, leading to court cases, described in great detail in a way that would be difficult today by newspapers who specialized in that sort of thing, such as *Reynold's Newspaper*. In the last half of the reign, there were three cases of prime importance – the Boulton and Park transvestitism case of 1870, the Cleveland Street scandal of 1889, and the Oscar Wilde case, which represents for many the apogee of the late Victorian way of life.

At Oxford, Wilde had been influenced by Walter Pater. As an aesthete he had been dumped by a group of hearties on a hill outside Oxford ('Yes,' he told them, 'the view is very charming'), and although he dressed in an extravagant manner – velvet coat with silver buttons, knee breeches, white stockings, buckled shoes, hair parted in the middle in High Church style – Oxford scandal passed him by. In London, Wilde stole the thunder of the group that had formed around Whistler; in 1881 he went to America on a lecture tour; in 1884 he married the cool conventional Constance Lloyd, daughter of an Irish lawyer. In 1886 he is believed to have had his first homosexual adventure with Robert Ross. This date is interesting, for in 1885 the Criminal Law Amendment Act had been passed to protect minors from procuration. An amendment to this stated: 'Any male person who in public or private commits or is party to the commission, or attempts to procure the commission by any male person, of any act of gross indecency with another male person, shall be guilty of a misdemeanour.' The penalty was two years' imprisonment, with or without hard labour. This amendment, said J. A. Symonds, was a 'disgrace to legislation by its vagueness of diction and the obvious incitement to false accusation'. It was now exceedingly rash to pick up guardsmen outside Albany Barracks, view pretty choir boys, frequent the Knightsbridge skating rink, or eye men bathers at the Serpentine in Hyde Park or in the Victoria Swimming Baths – all places favoured by homosexuals on the rampage. Artists with Arcadian tastes had to watch their p's and q's when they hired male models for late Victorian high art.

Wilde, as if encouraging the wrath of authority, camped it up, an Oedipus inviting divine retribution. From his Oxford friends, Frank Miles, Reginald ('Kitten') Harding; his newer London friends, Norman Forbes-Robertson (brother of the famous actor), and Harry Marillier; he went on to a working-class lad with artistic pretensions, John Gray; the artist couple Ricketts and Shannon; a queer office boy Edward Shelley; and, of course, Lord Alfred Douglas ('Bosie'). As Wilde wrote, 'tired of being on the heights, I deliberately went to the depths in the search for new sensations'. He graduated to a succession of stable boys, pseudo-homosexuals, and villains, some of whom had backers not averse to a spot of blackmail. There was Frederick Atkins, an ex-billiard marker, with his blackmailing protector James Burton ('Uncle Burton'); a small-time crook, Alfred Wood; Sidney Mavor ('Jenny'), who later became a clergyman; and the Parker brothers, a valet and a groom respectively.

The insensate appetite of Wilde had been predicted by the journalist H. W. Nevinson who had met him at Oxford, and had noted his 'mouth like a shark's in formlessness and appetite'.[10] Despite the proclivities of these young men with their tendency to steal compromising letters and form into commercial blackmailing syndicates, it was Lord Alfred Douglas who proved the weakest link. When 'Bosie's' father, the eighth Marquis of Queensberry, left his curious note at the Albemarle Club, 'To Oscar Wilde posing as a sodomite', when Wilde instituted libel proceedings, the richer homosexuals of the Wilde circle left England by the steamerload. The panthers had turned into pussy cats.

The Boulton and Park Case

Ernest Boulton was the son of a respectable Peckham gent, and was employed by his uncle, who was a stockbroker. He was a good-looking young man with a voice that was described as soprano, and his role in life had early been established by his mother, who from the age of six dressed him as a girl. Frederick William Park was articled to a solicitor. Louis Charles Hurt was a post office clerk, John Salford Fisk was a merchant. In May 1871 they were charged 'with conspiring and inciting persons to commit an unnatural offence'. There were four others, named Somerville, Cumming and Thomas, and Lord Arthur Clinton, the third son of the fifth Duke of Newcastle; but as the trial had been postponed for more than a year, three of them had not come forward, and Arthur Clinton had committed suicide in June 1870.

It was a big case, with the Attorney General and the Solicitor General appearing for the prosecution. The Attorney General opened the case: 'It is at all times an unpleasant duty to have to conduct a prosecution, but when it is conducted against four gentlemen, and such they are, and well educated, two of whom have certainly borne a high character, it is with the utmost pain and sorrow that I feel constrained to accuse them as I have to do; but I have no alternative.' Despite these commendable sentiments, the Attorney General launched into the case with gusto. Boulton and Park were accustomed to dress up as women in private theatricals; this, the Attorney General pointed out handsomely, was not in itself an offence, but this habit of dressing up as women was carried over into their every day lives. They had been seen in the Alhambra, in Leicester Square, in the Surrey Theatre south of the river, and in Burlington Arcade, where the higher-priced prostitutes plied their trade. Boulton had also lived with Lord Arthur Clifton for a month or two in 1868.

Boulton and Park lived up to their appearance with consummate skill, though they gave the game away to servants by turning up sometimes as men, sometimes as women, creating confusion. A Mr Cox had flirted with Boulton in a public house in the City, believing him to be a woman, and thinking himself no end of a swell by having succeeded in enticing Boulton to his office ('You City birds have good fun in your offices, and have champagne,' Boulton had speculated). 'I kissed him, she, or it, believing at the time it was a woman,' Cox had deposed, understandably uncertain about his pronouns. His deposition was read at trial because he too had died between the offence and the trial. Boulton had also played the piano, and at the railway station he had given Cox his photograph. Some indication was later given to Cox that all was not as it should be, and he encountered Boulton and Lord Arthur in the celebrated Evans's in Covent Garden. 'You damned set of infernal scoundrels, you ought to be kicked out of this place!' he is reported as saying in true melodramatic style, no doubt appreciated by the regular patrons of Evans's, but Cox had admitted that at no time had Boulton said that he was a woman, though Boulton had made no resistance when Cox kissed him.

The prosecution then delved into a medley of amorous letters between Boulton and Lord Arthur ('I am consoling myself in your absence by getting screwed'); Boulton had the advantage over jealous heterosexual wives in that, when he was annoyed, he could relapse into his male persona. As a lover he signed himself 'Stella', as an injured party he could sign himself, 'Yours, Ernest Boulton'. There were also letters between Park (who signed himself 'Fanny') and Lord Arthur. In the pseudo-marital tiff between Boulton and Lord Arthur, Park tried to pour oil on to the troubled waters ('As to all the things she said to you the other night, she may have been tight and did not know all she was saying'). Lord Arthur proposed coming over to see Park. Park replied saying that he would be pleased to see the couple at any time, asked if his umbrella handle was repaired 'as the weather has turned so showery that I can't get out without a dread of my back hair coming out of curl'.

Boulton was also Stella to Somerville ('Willy'), one of the three who had not surrendered, who wrote to him: 'You imagine I do not love you. I wish to God it was so; but tell me how I can prove it, and I will willingly do so.' A curious letter is from 'Harry' to Boulton, containing the postscript: 'Of course I have as usual left a few little things behind, such as the glycerine &c. – that don't matter – but cannot find (oh, horror!) those filthy photos nor Louis' [Hurt's] likeness. I do hope they are not lying about your room.' Fiske in Edinburgh was also writing to Boulton: 'I have eleven photographs of you (and expecting more to-morrow) which I look at over and over again. I have four little notes which I have sealed up in a packet. I have a heart full of love and longing, and my photographs, my four little notes, and my memory are all that I have of you. ... Believe me, darling, a word of remembrance from you can never come amiss.' Fiske (or Fisk – both surnames were used indiscriminately during the proceedings) ended his letter '*A un ange qu'on nomme Ernie Boulton, Londres*'. Hurt wrote to Fiske about high jinks in London, and Fiske wrote further to Boulton: 'He tells me you are living in drag. What a wonderful child it is! I have three minds to come to London and see your magnificence with my own eyes. Would you welcome me? Probably it is better I should stay at home and dream of you. But the thought of you – Lais and Antinous in one – is ravishing.'

Hugh Mundell met Boulton and Park at the Surrey Theatre. He was convinced that they were women dressed as men and gave them advice on how to make the imposture more accurate – they should swing their arms more. He met them again at the Surrey Theatre, and gave them a rose each; they were now dressed as women, but Boulton gave him a note saying that they were men dressed as women, which Mundell thought was a capital joke. Boulton was still 'Stella' alias 'Mrs Graham', but Park was called 'Jane' by Boulton. Mundell and another man, whose name he did not know, took the 'girls' for a meal at the Globe, near the Haymarket. The sands were running out for Boulton and Park. On 28 April 1870, William Chamberlain of the detective police force followed the pair in a cab to the Strand Theatre, where Park went to the ladies' room to have some lace pinned up. During the performance they had brandy and sherry. Afterwards as they were about to enter the cab, Chamberlain arrested them. Boulton was wearing a scarlet dress and white muslin shawl, Park a white dress. Both wore false hair, and Boulton had on a bracelet and necklet. His dress, commented Chamberlain, was very low cut. Boulton also wore a couple of rings, white gloves, and ladies' white boots, while Park was wearing earrings. Chamberlain had seen the pair on a number of previous occasions, at Holborn casino and elsewhere; once they were 'larking about' in Brunswick Square, and Chamberlain, believing Boulton to be a woman, told him his white dress was dirty.

There was ample evidence that Boulton and Park did not trouble to cover up their propensities for dressing up as women. The woman with whom they lodged had been aware of the masquerade for a long time, but she had never noticed any impropriety. The spectators in the court pricked up their ears when a large chest was brought into court; it was opened to reveal sixteen silk dresses, twenty chignons, and a variety of boots and gloves. A female attendant at the Lyceum Theatre told that she had seen Boulton and Park there – Park in a green dress, Boulton in mauve satin – and she took them for fast women.

Fiske and Hurt were drawn into the net, and in June, Frederick Holland, an Edinburgh police officer, searched Fiske's apartment, finding letters and photographs. Fiske was alarmed: 'I have written some foolish notes to Boulton,' he admitted, 'but I meant no harm by them.'

Upon their arrest by Chamberlain, Boulton and Park were taken to Bow Street. They were examined by the magistrate, and James Paul, surgeon to the Metropolitan Police E Division, was called in. Dr Paul ordered Boulton to take his clothes off behind a screen, and Boulton did so. He was wearing drawers and silk stockings. Dr Paul examined Boulton's anus for evidence of pedication, noting 'extreme dilation of the posterior' and relaxed muscles – 'The relaxation was such as I had never seen before.' He also examined Park in the same way. 'The result with reference to him was extreme dilation of the orifice.' Dr Paul admitted that he had no experience in the field of unnatural vice, but 'there were the same symptoms in these men as

I should expect to find in men that had committed unnatural crimes'. The judge was somewhat perturbed by this tourist and cavalier attitude of the police doctor ('I imagined I had to examine them for everything, seeing them in women's clothes') and asked him, 'Did you not think you ought to have an order from the magistrate?' Dr Paul replied, 'No, my lord; I never wait for a magistrate's order in any case.' This did not do the prosecution's case any good. The London juryman had a wholesome dislike of police impudence.

In June, J. R. Gibson, surgeon to Newgate Gaol, examined the two men for evidence of pedication, and was subject to a long cross-examination. There was no indication that either of the two men had had pedication, and the phenomena that had so struck Dr Paul, who admitted that he had been reviewing the subject on the very day of the trial, could result from natural events. In May, Boulton and Park had had their own expert, Le Gros Clark, examiner at the Royal College of Surgeons, and he gave them a clean bill. Hurt and Fiske were also examined.

Other evidence came from Charles Reeves, superintendent of the Alhambra, who told the court that he had thrown Boulton and Park out when they came dressed as women, with their faces powdered and painted, and when they came as men their conduct was no less objectionable – 'they were giggling and chirping to each other, and chucking each other under the chin'. Comic relief was supplied by George Smith, a beadle in the Burlington Arcade, who was more concerned with explaining his habit of taking money from whores so that they could promenade through the Arcade. A one-time policeman, he had also been an omnibus conductor and a ticket collector for the Metropolitan Railway. Cross-examined, he proved another cross for the prosecution to bear: 'He decidedly told the police that he would do all he could to assist them in getting up evidence in the interest of justice.' What was he doing now? Nothing. 'He resigned [from the Arcade], but it was almost forcible [laughter].' A note of truculence came into his evidence as Mr Seymour for the defence goaded him. 'He could not say how much he received a week. His wages were twenty-one shillings per week. He always took what money was offered to him. He should like to see the man who would refuse it. The directors' order was that such women were not to be admitted; and if refused, the tradesmen would complain that he had turned out their best customers. He lived up to what he got.'

When he summed up, Lord Chief Justice Cockburn was faced with a dilemma. Layman's homosexuality – penetration – had decidedly not been proved; Hurt and Fiske, he maintained, despite their fulsome letters, should not be in the dock at all; the police had behaved in a crass manner. Not only had their surgeon behaved in a most improper way, but the London police had actually overstepped their jurisdiction by going to Edinburgh on their own authority, without the warrant or authority of any Scottish judge or magistrate, and taking possession of papers. Scotland had, and has, its own laws; the Metropolitan Police had looked on it as an appendage of England, and goodness knows what principle this would establish. As for Dr Paul, police surgeon of E Division, 'if it had been the case of two strong, instead of two effeminate men [he] might have met with summary punishment for such unwarrantable conduct'.

What was left? Merely that a couple of men had dressed in drag.

It is impossible to speak in terms of sufficient reprobation of indecent conduct of this description. No one can doubt it is an outrage not only of public morality but also of decency, and one that deserves in some way or other not only reprehension, but actual and severe punishment, and that without the suggestion of any ulterior sinister purpose. It is an outrage against public decency that ought to offend any right-minded person of either sex, and ought not to be tolerated; and in my opinion, when it is done even as a frolic, it ought to be the subject of severe and summary punishment. It is one of those incidents to which the provisions of a most useful Act for the prevention of public indecency might be extended. If the law cannot reach it as it is, it ought to be made the subject of such legislation, and a punishment of two or three months' imprisonment, with the treadmill attached to it, with, in case of repetition of the offence, a little wholesome corporal discipline, would, I think, be effective, not only in such cases, but in all cases of outrage against public decency.

There is no question where Cockburn stood. The prosecution, when they heard this squeaking indignation, must have felt that this was the last straw. The jury had heard of police behaviour on the borders of perjury (relating to the beadle of Burlington Arcade), of the insolence of the police in venturing into a neighbouring country to pluck forth evidence, of their culminating impudence in examing the bottoms of two young men who happened to be dressed as women. After fifty-three minutes, the jury returned a verdict of not guilty. It was an expression of live and let live, of the late nineteenth-century rejection of an outdated penal code, of the treadmill and the whip that Cockburn had promised for future offenders against public decency.

The jury might have turned in a not guilty verdict, but the world outside knew differently, and a limerick soon appeared:

> There was an old person of Sark
> Who buggered a pig in the dark;
> The swine in surprise
> Murmured: 'God blast your eyes,
> Do you take me for Boulton or Park!'

The behaviour of Boulton and Park was not understood by the legal lights of 1871. The evidence of Boulton's mother that she encouraged her son to dress as a girl from the age of six, and later prompted him to wait on table as a maidservant, might well have been deserving of a closer scrutiny. The complacent way in which Boulton and Park permutated between man and woman must surely have convinced them that eventually society would turn upon them, that it would not be the superintendent of the Alhambra who would eject them but a detective of the Metropolitan Police who would gather up all the innumerable and all too explicit loose ends and tug them into a police station. Lord Chief Justice Cockburn does not make it clear what he thought, whether it was an unwholesome frolic, or whether it was a fullfledged homosexual circle lacking only observation of the ultimate rites. The surprising thing, to us, is that Boulton and Park's extrovert behaviour should have gone unchecked for so long as it did; they let things rip in no uncertain manner. The machinery of the law eventually ground them small; ejected as pips, they fell into a complete oblivion.

The Cleveland Street Scandal

In the summer of 1889 sums of money were missed from the General Post Office, London, and a telegraph boy who seemed to have more money to spend than he earned was suspected, and questioned. Under interrogation, he said that the money had been given to him by Charles Hammond of 18 Cleveland Street, and that he was not the only one to receive such payments for services rendered. Many other telegraph boys were involved, not to mention members of the Household Cavalry. In brief, 19 Cleveland Street, like the establishment at 13 Little College Street to which Oscar Wilde had been introduced, was a homosexual introduction house and brothel.

The house was raided, and a minister, Veck, age forty, was put on trial, together with Newlove, an eighteen-year-old clerk. Veck got four months' imprisonment, Newlove nine months. Hammond had, to use the reporter's vivid term, 'levanted'. It was thanks to a reporter that the case was ever noted, a reporter on the newly born *North London Press*, a modest weekly devoting most of its space to local government affairs, the comic opera machinations of London's units of administration, the vestries, and their minions, the guardians. The rest of the *North London Press* was concerned with harmless anecdotes, an incompetent cartoon, and appeals on behalf of the various submerged classes. The dockers had emerged victorious from their strike, and the *North London Press* was urging like consideration for the postmen ('second-class' postmen earned from fourteen to sixteen shillings a week rising to twenty-two or twenty-three shillings) and for insurance agents.

Homosexuality was the sin no one could overlook. No one realized that the incidence was probably one in twenty. But the case in question was hustled in and out of the court with almost indecent haste, and the *North London Press* began to probe; why had Veck and Newlove got off so lightly, when twelve months before a Hackney minister had been sent to prison for life for such offences? How was it that Hammond had managed to get away, Hammond who owned the place and was the main figure? It was soon evident that Hammond had had a tip-off, and that people in high places were keen that he should not be apprehended.

It was on 4 July that the telegraph boy was questioned. On 9 July Constable Sladden was set to watch the house and observed 'a great many gentlemen' coming and going. On 10 July he noted that furniture was being removed – Hammond was on the move. It was not likely that the men involved would say anything about their proclivities, but the telegraph boys were different. So Arthur Newton, a solicitor, and an interpreter at Marlborough Street police court named De Gallo, operating through Newton's clerk, took five of them away from their homes and installed them in lodgings, from which they would be sent to start a new life in Australia, along with a new outfit, £20 down each, and a pound a week for three years. One of the boys, Alleys, was told: 'The reason we want to get you away is so you should not give evidence against you know whom.'

However, the boys were not kept sufficiently *in camera*. One of them, a lad named Swinscow, wrote to his mother, and she told the police. De Gallo advised the boys to go home – if the five could not be exported to Australia in one batch, there was no point in sending three or four of them. The key witness was Algernon Alleys, who had received compromising letters from a 'Mr Brown', and who was grabbed by the police and kept in a 'state of distress' in a small coffee house in Houndsditch.

Charles Hammond was safe on the continent, or reasonably so, though two Scotland Yard men were following him, as he wrote to his sister-in-law: 'One of the two men that followed in from France has gone away, and a Belgium man has come in his place. If we only go across the road from the Hotel they follow us. If I ask any questions they go and ask the people what I said to them. It makes me feel so ill I can scarcely eat my meals. I wish to god I knew what they are going to do.' After Europe, Hammond proposed going to America; he wrote to his wife to organize the details of such a move: 'You must buy another large basket like the large one you have got to pack the Bed Linnen and Velvet Curtains in And the two yellow silk Pillows. You can pack the best Dresden Vases that are on my Mantle Glass And the few best plates there these two large round ones and the Blue Dresden Dish that hangs on the walls.' As an afterthought he asked about his piano, wondering how much it would cost. He had £800 to play about with.

The editor of the *North London Press*, Ernest Parke, had a scoop on his hands. The case had built-in audience appeal. Being a keen advocate of the rights of the common man, Parke could also stress that here was a startling and shocking illustration of the adage that there was one law for the rich and one for the poor. Why had a Hackney minister been sent to prison for life, while Veck and Newlove had received ridiculously mild sentences, and the principals were being protected by who-knows-whom?

Who were the principals? When the case first came to light, Parke was content to hint, but the people he had in mind were the Earl of Euston and eldest son of the Duke of Grafton, and Lord H. Arthur G. Somerset, the younger son of the Duke of Beaufort, and assistant equerry to the Prince of Wales. Lord Arthur Somerset was a safe bet for any editor; he was the 'Mr Brown' who had written disgraceful letters to young Alleys, though Alleys had destroyed many of these letters in response to an anonymous letter. On 12 September only eight days after the questioning of the telegraph boy, a warrant was issued against Lord Arthur, who speedily revealed his guilt by fleeing to Boulogne, whence he made his way to Constantinople where he offered his services to the Sultan (in what capacity has not been revealed). Lord Arthur was a sitting pigeon, and the *North London Press* printed a poem about him:

> My Lord Gomorrah sat in his chair
>   Sipping his costly wine;
> He was safe in France, that's called the fair,
>   In a city some call 'Boo-line.'

He poked the blaze, and he warmed his toes,
And, as the sparks from the logs arose,
He laid one finger beside his nose –
  And my Lord Gomorrah smiled.

He thought of the wretched, vulgar tools
  Of his faederastian joys, [*sic*]
How they lay in prison, poor scapegoat fools!
  Raw, cash-corrupted boys.
While he and his 'pals' the 'office' got
From a 'friend at Court', and were off like a shot,
Out of reach of Law, Justice, and 'that — rot,'
  And my Lord Gomorrah smiled.

Had Ernest Parke restricted his brief to Lord Arthur, he unquestionably would have remained content, though the staider newspapers were being superior: 'The less that has to be said in these columns of the terrible scandal in London the better we shall be pleased' said the *Birmingham Daily Post*. It was a *cause célèbre* that was echoing widely. Louis Jennings, Conservative M.P. for Stockport was poking around, and behind the scenes it was believed that the Prince of Wales was concerned with this 'hideous and foetid gangrene', if only on account of the fact that his assistant equerry had been exposed as a practising homosexual. The lower orders also watched the miasma develop with scarcely controlled glee. At a meeting of the London Fields Radical Club, J. Knifton of the Borough of Shoreditch Club drew attention to the gulf that divided working-class *mores* from those of the aristocracy. 'Working men,' he proclaimed in ringing tones, 'are free from the taint.' But, he added, 'for gold laid down our boys might be tempted to their fall'.

It was doubtful how long Lord Euston remained in the dark about the rumours that were circulating about him. On 26 October a Mr Dudford told him about them. Lord Euston consulted with Lord Dungarvan as to his course of action, and sued the editor of the *North London Press* for libel. No doubt Parke was surprised by this, as the Marquis of Queensberry was no doubt astonished when Oscar Wilde adopted the same attitude towards him, but he was quite confident, as there was no question that Lord Euston had visited 19 Cleveland Street. Lord Euston was also acquainted with Lord Arthur Somerset.

Toward the end of May, Lord Euston had been in the Piccadilly area, and had been offered a card which stated that *poses plastiques* were being held at Cleveland Street. So far as he knew, he had been the only one to be offered a card, though it was late at night – between ten-thirty and eleven o'clock – and he was not certain whether he had been especially honoured. He retained the card, and several days later he went to the address, knocked on the door, which was opened. He was asked for a sovereign, which he paid, and then the man who opened the door made an 'indecent proposal'. Lord Euston called the man an 'infernal scoundrel ... threatened to knock him down if he did not at once allow him to leave the house'. The man did not demur, and Lord Euston, puffing righteously, went out into the night. This recital was believed by the respectable; the *New York Herald* was interested in the Cleveland Street Scandal, but it accepted the Euston line: 'There is not the least reason to doubt that some of the gentlemen – to give them their conventional names – who have been traced to the abominable house went there innocently. They were taken there by friends, merely to see what was going on, and it is possible that some of them thought it was a gambling house.'

Before he appeared for trial, the editor of the *North London Press* noted sardonically that the newspapers and periodicals that usually went in for revelations, such as William Stead's *Pall Mall Gazette* and *Lloyd's Newspaper* remained silent. *Reynold's Newspaper* had timidly quoted the early forays of the *North London Press* but had done nothing for itself. No doubt these worthies thought that Parke was dancing on thin ice; they did not know of the ace that Parke was hiding up his sleeve, nor did they know that the police were working hard on the job of exposing Lord Euston and collaborating with Parke's hidden sources.

A fund was raised for Parke, the Fair Trial Fund, organized by the young H. W. Massingham, who was later to be one of the great journalists of the age. Heading the lists of donors was T. P. O'Connor, journalist, Irish Nationalist, and M.P. for

Liverpool since 1885, a popular revolutionary with a penchant for founding and running newspapers. One of the more curious of the contributors was 'Ye see yon birkie ca'd a lord' who sent ten shillings, sixpence, while 'Mr and Mrs Badcock' sent five shillings each. (A birkie is a strutting swaggering fellow – in the Scottish idiom; Lord Euston was a convenient scapegoat for the lesser folk.)

It was soon seen that this was to be a night of the long knives for Parke and that the establishment meant to crush him. In accord with civilized procedure, he gave himself up at Bow Street police station, prepared to put up bail of £1,500. There was no magistrate available, and he was put in the cells until Monday, behaviour on the part of Bow Street that was inexcusable (Bow Street was the station that had stepped out of line during the Boulton and Park case nearly twenty years earlier). This action was widely deplored by the press.

The case was postponed until January 1890. It was time for Parke to produce his ace, and for the police to reveal their findings. Just as they had been over-enthusiastic in the Boulton and Park case, so were they in their endeavours to staple Lord Euston to the mat. Witnesses of the goings-on in Cleveland Street were taken over London in cabs so that they could pick out and recognize Lord Euston at various sites. Captain Webb at Westminster Inquiry Office had showed photographs of Lord Euston to witnesses so that identification could be facilitated. Unfortunately he had omitted to supply photographs of full length with a foot scale delineated thereon. The general consensus was that Lord Euston was a man of medium height, stout, face clean-shaven, dark moustache, thin on top (there was a variant – fair hair). Even Mrs Morgan, who kept a tobacco and sweet shop at 22 Cleveland Street, opposite number 19, agreed with this. Lord Euston on his appearance in the witness stand must have confounded many of them, for he was six feet four inches tall.

That there was a wide divergence between the way lawyers looked at the outside world and the way men of the world did was plain from the cross-examination. It was made to seem that there was something diabolical in a mature man (Lord Euston was forty-one) going to see *poses plastiques* (strip tease), and the lawyers made great play with the admitted fact that Lord Euston had been acquainted with this phenomenon. Somewhat exasperatedly Lord Euston had maintained that *poses plastiques* could be quite artistic. This out-of-touchness of magistrates and judges was made clear by the inquiry in 1889 of magistrate Hannay at Marlborough Street police court, who asked 'What is the meaning of "Mary Anne"?' A police officer had replied in delicate language suited to an outsider, 'Men that get a living by bad practices.'

Ernest Parke's ace was produced with appropriate drama. This was John Saul, age twenty-six or twenty-eight, with a 'stagey manner and a peculiar effeminate voice'. Saul said that in May 1887 he had taken Lord Euston to 19 Cleveland Street; Lord Euston he knew as 'The Duke'. The prosecution prodded Saul with some curiosity not unmixed with disgust – this was the genus queer without doubt. They remarked upon the ring on his finger – presumably it had come from some rich protector? No, said Saul, he was at present living with Mr Violet, 'a respectable man' in Brixton, and the ring was paste. Well, then, how about the silver-headed cane which he was flaunting. This was surely of great value, donated by some grateful pervert? No, said Saul, he had bought this for one shilling and sixpence in the Brixton Road. He was questioned about his background. He admitted his erstwhile vocation, but he had also been an actor at the Drury Lane Theatre, playing in *Royal Oak*. Saul did not do well under cross-examination, and had to confess that the police had let him alone on condition that he would play ball with them. The witnesses and the police had not taken account of Lord Euston's stature; the police and Parke had not realized the basic unreliability and bad image of their key witness. Now thoroughly alarmed, Parke intervened. He had other material, other sources that would prove he had been stating the truth, that Lord Euston had been in the habit of frequenting 19 Cleveland Street, but, when encouraged by Lord Justice Hawkins to tell all, Parke said that he could not betray his sources.

Lord Justice Hawkins summed up. Lord Euston was accused of 'heinous crimes revolting to one's common notions of all that was decent in human nature'. It was for the jury to decide whether the accusations were just, whether Parke was justified in his allegations. The jury was out for half an hour, and found Parke guilty of libel. Hawkins sentenced him to a year's imprisonment. This was unduly harsh said the *North London Press* in a subdued tone, bereft of its editor, and this was echoed by those papers who had supported Parke in his role as vigilante. The *North London Press* died without a murmur.

Other newspapers and periodicals were not so sympathetic. The *Saturday Review* said that Parke had ministered 'to a foul taste with fouler lies; he deserves as much mercy as a pole-cat'. The *People* said that 'Lord Euston has earned the gratitude of society for enabling the law to stamp upon a miscreant who, if he had his deserts, should be whipped at the cart's tail from one end of London to the other.' The most difficult judgement for Parke to bear came from Champion in the *Labour Elector*. Parke had made a business of supporting the underdog; he had given the dockers wide publicity in their troubles, he had made heroes of Burns and other figures involved in the dockers' strike, he had started a union for underprivileged postmen, and he had been probing into the callous mechanisms of the insurance companies vis-à-vis their agents. The *Labour Elector* knifed him in the back with manic glee:

If Lord Euston had gone to the *Star* office and there and then physically twisted the little wretch's neck, nobody would have blamed him. We are not, as a rule, in favour of Lynch Law, but there are undoubtedly cases in which it is permissible, and this was one. Penal servitude for life or for a lengthened period of years might have met the justice of the case; but twelve months' imprisonment, without hard labour, is little better than mockery.

The Cleveland Street Scandal still has the power to intrigue. Was Parke merely another editor interested in pushing up the circulation of his little weekly by salacious tidbits, or was it a genuine case of David versus Goliath? Did he really have other undisclosed sources? Did the police have additional information which they did not bring forth at the trial, and did they expect Saul to be the brand of fire to excise Lord Euston? If

Saul was right, if Lord Euston was known as 'The Duke' and had been at 19 Cleveland Street as early as 1887 – Lord Euston steadfastly maintained that he had only been there on that one occasion in 1889 and then for a matter of five minutes – then Parke was right and his year's imprisonment was a gross miscarriage of justice. If Saul was lying – and there is every reason to suppose that he was, living as he was at the mercy of the law – why was he not immediately indicted for perjury?

Whatever the pros and cons were, the trial was a salutary warning to other editors – when dealing with high-placed personages, watch out.

Lesbianism

Lesbianism is not, nor has been, a crime in Britain, but this is not because of a permissive or forward-looking policy on the parts of mysterious legislators of the past. This state of affairs was largely accidental; when the Criminal Law Amendment Act of 1885 was amended to make homosexual acts in private a crime it referred only to men – no one could think of a way to explain to Queen Victoria what homosexual acts between women were.

Female homosexuality is less common than male homosexuality (the ratio is probably between two to one and three to one) but there is a large area where it shades into socially acceptable behaviour. Dr A. Forel wrote that 'kisses, embraces, and caresses in bed seem far less peculiar among girls than among boys, and the normal woman submits to such tenderness with far less nausea'. Whereas 'among men, intellectual or spiritual friendship is completely divorced from physical intimacy of any kind ... in women it often rouses a desire for kissing, embracing, and caresses, and produces a sensation of sensual pleasure, though this may not be localized'. To outsiders, female homosexuality has appeared more aesthetic than male homosexuality, and the lawmakers have frequently felt the phenomenon beneath their notice, though there is a reference in the Bible (*Romans* 1, xxvi) to this 'vile affection'.

Allusions to male homosexuality in Victorian England resulted almost entirely from court cases, and men without homosexual tendencies became acquainted, much to their surprise, with this other side of the heterosexual coin solely through reading newspaper reports of the various unsavoury cases that were sure-fire circulation raisers for the Sundays. Many of them remained in the dark about the precise activities, though for clinical details of the Boulton and Park case left little room for conjecture. If the man in the street was oblivious to homosexuality in men, how much more was he so in respect of homosexuality in women. George Meredith, of whom no one could say he was imperceptive, could write of a Lesbian attachment in *Liana of the Crossways* without realizing what exactly he was doing.

Those who did speculate were probing in a stygian gloom. The pornographic writers projected their own feelings into the recreation of Lesbianism, and few of them, if any, had any experience of female homosexuality as it was and not as it appeared through the distorted visor of male sexuality. To men, it was clear that in the absence of a real penis, an imitation product was vitally necessary for the transaction of any pleasurable experiences, and it was necessary to incorporate in every Lesbian saga an artificial penis, the dildo. Although there were dildoes – there were even dildoes made to fit to the chin of the 'male' partner (the 'butch') – they were rare, and not in the trousseau of every female homosexual. If they were used, it was more likely to be in a masturbatory situation, as recorded by Swinburne in one of his dirtier fantasies:

> This is a dildo the Queen used
> Once in a pinch in an office,
> Quite unaware it had *been* used
> First, by a housemaid erratic.
> Soon, though obese and lymphatic,
> Symptoms she felt all that month as it went on
> What sort of parties had used it and spent on.[11]

When there is no law against something, looking upon it as wrong becomes difficult. Whereas male homosexuals found an added zest in their pursuits when the Criminal Law Amendment Act was brought to fruition, women tended to drift in a mystified ignorance, a slightly naughty hinterland without any of the proscriptions that one would expect. 'Is it my fault,' wrote one Lesbian, Edith Simcox, 'that every wholesome, natural, reasonable passion I have felt from the young ambitions of the tomboy to the fierce worship of Her lover – is it my fault that all without exception have been choked off by a churlish fate and I hurled back upon the one inexhaustible gospel of Renunciation?' [12] Although male homosexuality was spoken of (by Lord Alfred Douglas) as the love that did not dare speak its name, female homosexuality was the love that could not speak its name simply because the state was undefined. Many women found themselves, often to their surprise, the subject of a physical and erotic adoration. They shrugged off their lady admirers with embarrassment, or gave in with puzzlement, often becoming alarmed when their own sleeping sensitivities were awakened.

The one class who cultivated this area were the prostitutes. Satiated by men, they indulged in violent erotic transports with other girls with relish:

> Men hire our persons for the night,
> Keep us awake, and kiss and teaze,
> But ah! how different the delight
> I have in cuddling dear Elise.

Although the dildo was not prominent in Lesbian activities, mouth–genital contacts were. Oral manipulation of the breasts were frequent, as well as manual excitation of the clitoris, and the *labia majora* and *labia minora*. Because women are aware of their own psychological make-up, orgasms between homosexual women are more easily wrought than in heterosexual intercourse; unactivated by preconceived notions, Lesbians can exploit the genuine erotogenic zones, rather than the 'accepted' ones (it is widely believed by men, for instance, that the vagina is such a zone, when in fact the vagina is almost totally insensitive, as is proved by the ability of surgeons to operate in this area without any anaesthetic, local or otherwise). Of the modern

Lesbians surveyed by Kinsey, 70 per cent are glad that they are so. In present-day society, there is no stigma attached to being such, nor any disadvantage. Certain organizations might well have been formed for the express purpose of satisfying the butch type – the transport services where masculine women can indulge in a quasi-male uniform, or the women's army.

Certain dominant women were willy-nilly placed in the centre of the picture. An attachment to other women could be sublimated. The uncritical and sickeningly sentimental adoration given to Queen Victoria by large numbers of her Ladies-in-Waiting was frequently a projection of the inner psyche. Particularly prone to the assiduous attentions of younger women were those ladies who had a masculine appearance. One of these women was Marian Evans, known throughout her life as the novelist George Eliot. 'Have you seen a horse, sir? Then you have seen George Eliot' was an anecdote recorded by Sidney Colvin. Sensitive girls who remained outside her potent spell found her distasteful. Alice James, the doomed sister of Henry James, who, even before her fatal illness, was regarded as a professional invalid variously awarded by doctors with 'rheumatic gout', 'spinal neurosis' and 'nervous hyperanesthesia', spoke of her 'dank moaning features ... she makes upon me the impression, morally and physically, of mildew, or some morbid growth – a fungus of a pendulous shape, or as of something damp to the touch'.

George Eliot the woman has long been neglected in favour of George Eliot the novelist. Her *Adam Bede* and *The Mill on the Floss* are watersheds of English literature, the crosses innumerable schoolchildren have to bear, as they are ideal set subjects for examination, being lugubrious without being particularly nasty. She was born in 1819, her father was a land agent, and she early betrayed intellectual tendencies. One of her first contacts with the great outside world was a phrenologist named Bray, and after her father's death in 1849 she threw off the trammels of provincial life and went with Mr and Mrs Bray to Geneva. In London she met John Chapman, a man with an un-Victorian *ménage à trois* – his mistress Elizabeth Tilley lived with him and his wife in corporeal bliss. Marian Evans and

Chapman baited the philosopher Herbert Spencer, and it was in the cards that Spencer would marry her.

Marian Evans soon met G. H. Lewes, philosopher, actor *manqué*, and a dramatic critic of the Teutonic persuasion. He was a refugee from an early episode in communal sex – his wife had two children by the journalist Thornton Hunt during this blissful period. Marian Evans exerted a profound spell over Lewes, and he left his wife; and for the rest of his life he and Marian Evans regarded themselves as man and wife, a phenomenon that for no very specific reason writers on the period treat with reverent awe. It was soon clear that Marian Evans was a honeypot around whom the bees – of both sexes – thronged. She particularly attracted women. Among these were Elma Stuart, whose husband had died young, and Edith Simcox. More restrained adorers included Mrs Mark Pattison (later Lady Dilke), Georgina Burne-Jones and Frances Wedgwood. The magnetism of George Eliot for her own sex extended over the seas. In 1869 Mrs Charles Sanders Pierce, the wife of the founder of the philosophy Pragmatism, wrote from America:

Dearest –

You will not be bored by another love letter – a little one? It is three whole years since I wrote to you before, and you sent me such a grave, kind, precious little answer. O how wise thou art! Where didst thou learn it all?

Edith Simcox was born in 1844. One of her brothers was the eccentric G. A. Simcox of university legend who disappeared one year in Ireland on a walking holiday. He and the other two brothers were effeminate. Edith was 'passionate and spoonily fond of my mother and easily attached myself to older girls or women, if, as at school, intimacy was achieved in spite of my shyness. My affection was of a demonstrative "fondling" sort, not at all deeply sentimental.'

She was small and bespectacled. She was, she wrote in exasperation, that kind of woman who might find a husband if she took more care with her appearance. When she met Marian Evans she was completely captivated and vied for her affections with her rivals. Edith Simcox was in her late twenties, assuredly on the shelf; Marian Evans was fifty-three. Edith spent days writing letters of appalling sentimentality to her goddess, making vows in her diary ('and I will lie on the rug and kiss her feet – whether she likes it or not') and counting off the days when she could visit ('I dream of all sorts of new ways of wooing her – if I could feel that she was learning to know and love me more'). There was one disadvantage – the ubiquitous G. H. Lewes, but he could be accommodated. It was clear that he wanted to join in, no doubt having happy memories of the *ménage à trois* he had forsaken in earlier decades. Miss Simcox was rather dubious of the propriety of this:

There was something very innocently boyish about Mr Lewes and it did not seem to me unnatural that he should expect to be kissed or petted a little when he was ill, but when he was well, in the palace of Truth, I think I should have betrayed an impression that he was rather too hairy for the purpose. But since he thought it appropriate to our relationship as brother worshippers at one dear shrine, I had nothing against it . . .

In the rapport between Edith Simcox and Marian Evans, Lewes has the air of a slightly excited observer. In November 1878 Miss Simcox wrote in her diary:

When I said I wanted to kiss her feet he said he would let me do it as much as I liked – or – correcting himself – as much as she liked. He could enter into the desire though she couldn't. I did in spite of her protests lie down before the fire and for one short moment give the passionate kisses that filled my eyes with tears – and for the rest of the evening her feet avoided the footstools where I had found them then. Still, though I would rather have the kisses ungrudged, I would rather have the memory of them thus than not at all.

Among her friends, Marian Evans had had a penchant for the sexually odd, ambiguous, or neuter – Edmund Gurney, the spiritualist who committed suicide, F. W. Myers, Oscar Browning. She accepted the adoration of her young friend with a certain complacency. In November, 1878, Lewes died. Edith Simcox haunted the purlieus of the Lewes–Evans establishment, hoping for the summons in unequivocal language from her lover. Unknown to her, rivals had beaten her to it, had already broken into the widowhood with their commiserations.

In March 1880 Miss Simcox achieved the summit of her goal – a reaction on the part of Miss Evans:

I kissed her again and again and murmured broken words of love. She bade me not exaggerate. I said I didn't – nor could, and then scolded her for not being satisfied with letting me love her as I did – as in present reality – and proposing instead that I should save my love for some imaginary he. She said – expressly what she has often before implied to my distress – that the love of men and women for each other must always be more and better than any other and bade me not wish to be wiser than 'God who made me' – in pious phrase. I hung over her caressingly and she bade me not think too much of her – she knew all her own frailty and if I went on, she would have to confess some of it to me.

Marian Evans said that she had never cared very much for women, and that the friendship and intimacy of men was more important to her. She told Edith Simcox that girls and women had always looked upon her as 'uncanny'. Edith was not deterred, and continued to kiss the older woman – it must be remembered that Marian Evans was sixty. 'I asked her to kiss me,' recorded Miss Simcox in her diary, 'let a trembling lover tell of the intense consciousness of the first deliberate touch of the dear one's lips. I returned the kiss to the lips that gave it and started to go – she waved me a farewell.'

It was a pathetic end to the affair. Two months later, Marian Evans became a genuine married woman at last, marrying a much younger man, John Cross. It was a short marriage; six months later Marian Cross died. 'The perfect Union I always longed for', wrote Miss Simcox, had not been reached. It was time to join hands with the rivals. A Mrs Congreve 'had loved my Darling lover-wise too'. In their private requiems, John Cross (whom they knew as 'Johnny') was very much of an outsider. Edith Simcox did a passionate pilgrimage to the scenes of Marian Cross's early life. It was possible that she would do the official biography. But this task was taken up by Cross.

Death had taken away her love, but this could possibly be

alleviated. In December 1882 Edith Simcox went to Highgate Cemetery, where Marian Cross was buried, to see about a plot, 'so that one may lie at Her feet'. She found that such a plot would cost fifteen guineas. But even this scheme did not come to fruition; her thunder was stolen by one of her rivals, Elma Stuart, on whose tombstone was engraved, 'One who for eight and a half blessed years George Eliot called by the sweet name of Daughter'.

Was this the appeal of George Eliot alias Marian Evans alias Marian Lewes alias Marian Cross, as a mother-figure for Victorian spinsters and young widows? Was it her fate to be associated with the sexually incomplete? What part in all this did G. H. Lewes play, and was it not odd that he should have left the impregnation of his real wife to a minor journalist, Thornton Hunt? Although Edna Simcox regarded herself as the central figure, her experiences were unquestionably paralleled by Mrs Congreve and Mrs Stuart, though probably the intensity with which Miss Simcox loved Marian Evans had been partly drained off through marriage. It may be that Miss Simcox was a pseudo-Lesbian – that her erotic energies were directed at Marian Evans because, on account of her plainness and the pressures of nineteenth-century conformity, no man was available. It is evident that Miss Simcox was not unacquainted with her own state: there was 'no practical doubt that the melancholia which darkened many years of my life was due to what I may call the emotional inanition of spinsterhood'. Her love for Marian Evans was a bright spot in almost unrelieved gloom – 'Everything else,' she wrote, 'pales in comparison with real worship.'

Her life was not solely one of obsequious maudlin sentimentality. With another girl, Mary Hamilton, Edith Simcox ran a successful cooperative shirt factory for eight years. As an occasional journalist she was tireless in research. Though Miss Simcox would be a minor figure in any tableau, there must be some doubt, however, whether Marian Evans was justified in making such emotional hay of her, and whether the sly prurience of Miss Evans's consort, Lewes, was entirely in accordance with his stern philosophical tenets. From their commonplace villa in

St John's Wood, the pair of them represented a still centre in a flux, and a parallel might be drawn between one elderly lady holding court amid her maidenly acolytes, and another, in stuffy seclusion among the relics of dear Albert at Windsor. Queen Victoria had the same abilities to attract the adoration of women. 'I was with Her at twelve-thirty,' wrote Lady Augusta Bruce, 'and She wished me to write for Her in Her journal, the beloved hand being powerless.' The Queen was 'our beloved one, our Benefactress, our second Mother', and when she wrote to Lady Augusta asking her to accept a post in the household, Lady Augusta 'could not restrain the passionate burst of weeping – Such words, such thoughts! I felt that it was Her spirit – Her heart – and then when my own trembled at the thought of Her love that is sheltering me, but of my own unworthiness and weakness and felt that it all came in answer to other prayers.'[13] The relationship between the Queen and Lady Augusta was of the utmost respectability, but the quality and timbre of gush is not so different from that with which Edith Simcox greeted Marian Evans. Sorting out the relationships between Victorian women is very much a question of treading between the puddles of tears.

The concept of 'the masculine protest' was evolved by Alfred Adler, a pupil of Freud who later defected to frame his 'individual psychology'. It might have been custom-made for one type of Victorian woman. The little girl grew up with the idea that she was expected to be weak, that it was a man's world, that her value was in being different, as different as possible from the idea of the manly man. Many were drilled into the notion that they could not cope until the idea became the reality, and they could only prevent themselves from falling into chaos by clutching at the forms – such a class – which rapidly assumed an ossified character far removed from their original purpose (class was a useful prop in stabilizing a culture). This kind of woman became a common subspecies, intent on standing on ceremony because ceremony was the only thing that stopped her from dropping into a dangerous marsh. Alice James in her diary recorded the case of a genteel woman of this ilk who was gradually reduced to living on ten shillings a week, 'a blurred vague ant … on this little heap of social ruin, however, the *Gentlewoman* was impregnably entrenched'.

Less timid girls realized that life was a giant confidence trick fostered by men, and consciously played roles demonstrating naïveté, helplessness and foolishness, at the same time using what Adler called 'feminine weapons' (cunning, insincerity, treachery) to gain their own ends. These were the women who ran their homes, ran their husbands, and unobtrusively ran the century. They were contemptuous of the women who made themselves miserable by trying to play the role of man – not so much the votes-for-women enthusiasts, but the members of their own sex who were trying hard to be otherwise. Consequently there is a large corpus of Victorian women folk who were being masculine for doctrinaire reasons, and these are extremely difficult to separate from the genuine deviants, who were masculine because this was the way their psyche worked. Of this second group, Mrs Harriet Grote, wife of the historian of Greece, is an instance. She was a woman unquestionably shading into man, 'like a Grenadier in Petticoats', said John Addington Symonds. 'She stands at least six feet in her shoes, wears no crinolines, mounts a huge plume of ostrich feathers above an auburn wig, and rolls fierce ogreish eyes while she devolves her periods in a deep bass voice.' Although formed in the Regency, she lived well into Victoria's reign. Of the Grotes, Sydney Smith, witty irreverent dean of St Paul's, said, 'I like them. I like him, he is so ladylike, and I like her, she's such a perfect gentleman.' [14] He observed Mrs Grote at a country house, stick in hand, man's hat on head, a coachman's box coat of drab hue hunched on her martial form, and topped by an exotic turban. 'Now I know the meaning of the word grotesque,' he commented. Mrs Grote was the classic butch type, and her love object was a dancer-prostitute, Fanny Elssler, ex-mistress of the King of Naples's brother, and currently mistress of diplomat and man of fashion Marquis de la Valette. 'Between us,' wrote Mrs Grote delicately, 'there exists a lively and tender tie based on a romantic attachment on our side, and a grateful affection borne us by her.' Fanny Elssler had one child, the identity of whose father was in doubt.

Fanny was not exactly an ideal choice, though she had her own code of ethics – she would not run two men at the same time. Although a man named Wikoff was after her, she 'scrupulously respected' her attachment to de la Valette. Mrs Grote chased her to Paris, but it did not suffice; in 1840 Fanny went to America, though she had qualms about taking her child. 'Well, Fanny,' wrote Mrs Grote, 'send the brat to me; I don't ask you whose child it is, and I don't care, so long as it isn't that fool d'Orsay's.' (D'Orsay was the gigolo lover of the celebrated Lady Blessington.)

Grote was the essence of scholasticism, with lank dishevelled hair, an abstracted air, and a 'spout mouth'. He had, said Carlyle, 'greatly the look of a prosperous Dissenting minister'. While he delved into the more obscure Greek myths (his *History of Greece* 1846–56 is a monument to diligence and assiduity) his dramatic wife Harriet looked around her, took up Jenny Lind, 'the Swedish nightingale', but she proved disappointing, and Mrs Grote refers to her as 'a hussy'.

The unwomanly mien of Mrs Grote did not commend itself to Herbert Spencer. With his curious penchant for seeing qualities in men that few others did (Grote had 'extreme suavity') he was, however, in agreement with others regarding Mrs Grote: 'She was a masculine woman, alike in size, aspect, character, and behaviour; and I greatly dislike masculine women.' [15] Gladstone was more appreciative, as she had told him that the only two subjects worth discussing were religion and politics, a true Gladstonian view. While preparing for press his elaborate *Plato and the other Companions of Socrates*, Grote became infatuated with a Miss Durant. It was, said Mrs Grote amiably, a 'visitation of disease'. Grote was then seventy. After his death, Mrs Grote set to work on his biography, and, when she herself died, her personality had struck Lady Eastlake, wife of one of the dullest of Royal Academicians, sufficiently for her to do one of her.

Harriet Grote was a masculine soul in a womanly (or passably womanly) body. She had little in common with Edith Simcox, more with Olive Schreiner, who fluctuated uneasily between the two sexes. Edward Carpenter found Olive Schreiner something of a peach, with her 'charming girl face, of *viant* Italian type ... and wonderful beauty and vivacity, a lightning-quick mind, fine eyes, a resolute mobile mouth', though his appreciation of her 'determined little square-set body' might not have been shared by the majority of Victorian woman admirers. A different picture is presented by her one-time lover, Havelock Ellis, who noted her curly hair at the forehead, lace at her throat, her strongly corseted body. Olive also appealed to the gentle Professor Donkin to whom she had gone for treatment of hypertension, and whose therapy included proposing to her; and to the hypochondriacal professor of statistics, Karl Pearson, who was convinced that he was dying of tuberculosis (these were the eighteen-eighties – Pearson died in 1936 at the age of seventy-nine).

Olive Schreiner would have liked to have been a man. This she sublimated by means of her heroine Rebekah in her novel *From Man to Man*:

> She tucked one hand under her cheek and after a while closed her eyes. Her thoughts ran around in a dreamy way now. How nice it would be to be a man. She fancied she was one until she felt her body grow strong and hard, and shaped like a man's. She felt the great freedom opened to her; no place shut off from her, the long chain broken, all work possible for her, no law to say this and this is for woman.

That this was not just a fictional longing is clear from letters she wrote to Havelock Ellis. 'I want to wear boys' clothes, and *will* as soon as I can get other women to join me' (9 August 1884), and in 1888 she plaintively requested whomever her executors happened to be not to have her buried in a place where there were women. 'I've not been a woman, really, although I've seemed like one.' That she was something of a handful for the repressed Ellis is indicated by his summary: 'She possessed a powerfully and physically passionate temperament which craved an answering impulse and might even under other circumstances – for of this I could have no personal experience – be capable of carrying her beyond the creed of right and wrong which she herself fiercely held and preached.' Although Olive Schreiner married and bore a child, this did not make her any the more attached to her own sex; as late as 1912 she railed to Ellis about women. 'Who farm little babies and starve them to death? Women in most cases and not men. Who keep brothels and betray young children and girls into a life which means disease and generally early death, without motherhood or wifehood or love? Women!! ... I don't for one moment believe in the moral superiority of women.' As usual, Olive Schreiner was overcharging the account. Women did run brothels, did corrupt young children, but they were only supplying a service demanded by men. Ellis did not tell Miss Schreiner about one of his cases – a Wolverhampton woman who raped a young girl held down by two other women. If he had, Olive Schreiner's cup would have been filled.

She did not come to terms with her impulses. Still less did Violet Paget, who, like Marian Evans, wrote under a male pseudonym, Vernon Lee. Her little books on aesthetics were once staple features of every second-hand bookshop. Violet Paget was a prim-looking little woman with round-lensed spectacles and the air of an outsider looking in. Passionately devoted as she was to a series of women friends, physical intimacy frightened her, and like Ruskin and Lewis Carroll she was thrown into a panic by works of art that activated her innermost instincts. In Cranach's 'The Choice of Paris' Mercury was 'all wrinkled and grimacing with brutal lust'. Her curious and perverse novel *Miss Brown* (three volumes, 1884) has an interesting episode when the heroine is confronted by drawings of people 'stark naked'. Like her originator, Miss Brown does not quite know where to put herself, but is clearly interested despite the tut-tutting conventional noises she makes. Similarly, when she is offered Gautier's *Mademoiselle de Maupin*, Miss Brown retorts: 'I have often heard that it is a book which a man does not offer a woman except as an insult.' The episode was put in just to point the unexceptional sentiments of the heroine.

George Moore, eager to instil a Zolaesque quality into English fiction, was interested in *Miss Brown* and wanted to publish excerpts. He had seen that this novel was Miss Paget exposing herself in public; she did not see this. Henry James did, and told her so: 'You have impregnated all those people too much with the sexual, the basely erotic preoccupation.' This was not putting it too strongly, as the following shows: ' "There is passion of all sorts," said Chough, pulling his long black whiskers: "the passion of the pure animal, the passion of the mere human creature, and the passion of divine essences." ' Chough, who is a kind of decadent villain figure (if such a strange work of fiction can be said to boast a villain), is keen on introducing Miss Brown to a series of naughtiness, during which, 'the ladies went to sleep, or pretended to do so, over the descriptions of the kisses of cruel, blossom-mouthed women, who sucked out their lovers' hearts, bit their lips, and strewed their apartments with coral-like drops of blood'.

Henry James was not alone in seeing something not very nice in all this. In her rejection of one suitor, Miss Brown's 'soul recoiled from contact with his as her body might have recoiled from the forced embrace of a corpse', as it did from the queer multisexual Madame Elaguine, in 'a crimson plush coat and a big man's cravat of Flanders lace, but all bursting out, by every conceivable slashing and gap, into a mass of lace, which hung about her like a cloud of thistle down, beneath which her thin and nervous little body seemed to twist and writhe with every word'. Madame Elaguine made advances to the prissy Miss Brown:

'Dear Annie,' she murmured, pulling an arm round Miss Brown's neck, in her childish way, and which yet affected Anne as might the caress of a lamia's clammy scales [and later] Madame Elaguine suddenly jumped up from her chair and flung her arms round Miss Brown's neck and kissed her, with such violence that Anne felt her lips almost like leeches and her teeth pressing into her cheek. . . . Anne felt a horror, a kind of fear of death.

There is a description of a woman attempting the rape of a youth that has the feverish glassiness one finds in pornography of the period: 'A beautiful naked youth was clutched by a huge haggard woman, her torn dress licking his body into flames, her lips greedily advancing to his delicate face, which shrank back, like a flower withering in the heat of a furnace.'

In real life, Violet Paget was not Anne Brown. In the novel Miss Brown gets affianced in the last pages, though Violet Paget makes it clear that she has been trapped; as the couple drive off into the night, the hero is displaying pleasure at his cleverness in catching Miss Brown. Violet Paget was wiser; man's love, she considered, was 'acquisitive, possessive, and BESTIAL!' Her affections lay with a series of women, for example, Annie Meyer, with whom she had a passionate friendship lasting two years and whose photograph she kept above her bed through subsequent amours. 'Things went quickly with a woman of her ardent impatient, imperious temper,' described Miss Paget with inscrutable ambiguity; 'things usually go quickly with a woman so imaginatively impressionable, as passionate, wayward and vain as myself – perhaps I should add as naked?'

Another of Violet Paget's passionate friendships was with Mary Robinson, who let her down – as passionate friends are apt to do – by becoming engaged in 1887 to James Darmsteter, upon which Violet Paget had a nervous collapse. The qualities Miss Paget sought were contained in Kit Anstruther-Thomson, 'a semi-painter, semi-sculptor, handsome creature ... a picturesque personality, paints very well, dressed *crâne* and rather fast, drives tandem and plays polo ... who talks slang like a schoolboy and cares in reality for nothing but pictures, and trees and grass ...'

The urges that Violet Page felt had not been codified. She utilized them by fitting them into the acceptable format of a novel, the residue splitting off into sentimental non-physical relationships on the one hand and spiteful acrimony on the other. For women who were accommodating themselves to the world as it was, Violet Paget was venomous. For instance, Miss Thackeray, novelist, eldest daughter of the author of *Vanity Fair*, was described by Miss Paget as 'the thin, sentimental leering, fleshy, idealistic old person who would marry her godson, and who seems quite brimming over at the idea of having babies at an age when she ought to be ashamed of it'. True, Miss Thackeray had married a young man (her cousin), but she was only forty. Envy and jealousy were part of the price Miss Paget paid for trying to run her Lesbian urges in harness with Victorian respectability.

Mrs Havelock Ellis was more fortunate. By associating herself with the free love movement, by marrying a man with ambiguous sexual interests, she was enabled to pursue her own leanings. 'The beauty and intimacy of our relationships,' related Ellis in *My Life*, 'was built on our separations, separations without which the relationship might perhaps have dissolved.' In return for the sexual freedom that her husband gave to her, Edith Ellis was awarded a place as Miss H. in case 42 of Ellis's gargantuan encyclopedia of sexual curiosities and misfortunes. It is interesting to note that Ellis tampered with the facts, did not mention his mother-in-law's death, the existence of a stepmother-in-law, a father-in-law's cruelty to the young Edith, thus throwing doubt on the accuracy and reliability of the other innumerable 'case histories'.[16]

At one time, the couple lived in an office building of an abandoned mine at Lelant in Cornwall. Mrs Ellis bought miners' cottages, dressed them up, put furniture in them, and let them to summer visitors. It was in Cornwall that she had one of her affairs, with Lily, an amateur artist who lived with an elder sister in St Ives. Lily read poetry and was generally 'artistic'. Being Paris-trained, she was something of a local celebrity. She would hurry to the Ellis home 'with her little nightdress at a late hour when she had almost been given up'. Doubtless it was a convenient ménage, but notwithstanding an exceptionally understanding husband, the stresses of a dual life told on Mrs Ellis, and on one occasion she tried to commit suicide.

The etiology of Lesbianism may or may not be the same as male homosexuality, though there is a facet of it that has no analogue in its fraternal deviation: 'organ inferiority' and the need to compensate for the lack of possession of a penis. Where the girl is a tomboy, this deprivation may seem to be more than usually cruel. As E. Wexberg said in his *Individual Psychology* (1933), 'the extreme type of masculine protest occurs most frequently where a little girl is crowded from the normal line of development by a trick of nature — by external masculine characteristics, such as ugliness, facial hair, masculine body, a deep voice and the like'.

The shading of girlish affection into erotic high jinks also has no parallel in male homosexuality. There is nothing other than affection implied when Mary Gladstone wrote in her diary: 'Adelaide in bed; sat by her a long time principally occupied in admiring her as she lay with her hair all wild about the pillow.' [17] The romantic friendships that swarm through Victorian popular novels are just that.

If Meredith could depict a Lesbian relationship without realizing it, young ladies could so likewise fall into a grand passion without being aware of the implications. 'I never loved but one person with passion in my life and that was her,' Florence Nightingale wrote of her cousin Marianne Nicholson, admitting elsewhere, 'The truth is I was afraid of her.' The close romantic relationships of well-bred young ladies were rendered more potent by the enforced idleness in which most of them lived, what another of Florence Nightingale's passions, Mary Clarke, an English salon queen of Paris, called 'faddling twaddling and the endless tweedling of nosegays in jugs'.

For boys, Eton, Winchester, Rugby and Harrow proved a breeding ground for homosexual tendencies. It was not usual for girls to be sent away from home for their education, and it was considered dashing and daring for parents to send their daughters to boarding schools, even more to coeducational schools such as Bedales (in 1900 there were sixty-eight boy pupils, seven girl pupils, instructed by six men and three women). The 'crushes' of girl for girl had no sinful implications, except to the more perceptive observers. The prising open of the universities to women students was treated with suspicion; in 1873 the first students moved in to Girton (prematurely – there were few doors and even less windows); by this time, twenty-two out of thirty-four university professors at Cambridge were admitting women to their lectures. This unique woman-orientated education was thought to be unnatural – the girls would find themselves incapable of 'performing their functions as women', and in the schools, 'vices with which they ought to have been absolutely unfamiliar were openly discussed and in a language that savoured of the gutter'. Among the opponents of female education *en masse* was the venerable and powerful authority on Victorian madness, Dr Henry Maudsley. For such as Dr Maudsley the hall of residence was the last straw. Nevertheless,

Somerville and Lady Margaret Hall came into being, and although the inhabitants could not go to lectures without chaperons, and were cautioned to 'dress carefully and have gentle manners' the moral dangers came not from lascivious undergraduate males but from the novel incarceration of young ladies together in unprecedented proximity. The high incidence of homosexuality in women's prisons had already been noted by sociologists, but those who did observe this phenomenon were satisfied that it was due to the depravity of the prisoners.

At University College, London, the first of the lady propagandists of birth control for suburban folk, Marie Stopes, was subject to the pressures of this new environment. An unnamed woman to whom Miss Stopes had admitted she was having an affair replied, 'You have outgrown me, little one, and our life streams make different windings. ... I still consider you my property, the feeling is akin to that of an old hen towards the duckling she hatched. As regards the subject of your last letter — a sickening dread came over me as I read. The thing ought not to have happened, Marie ... it is like a stain on your garment of purity.' Such reproaches were frequently made by women who were not aware of the transitional states of the passionate friendships. The flighty flirtatiousness of young girls confronted by the heavy drama of older women's affections, especially older women who had been rejected by men and who had found a second best in girls and younger women, could create unintentional havoc. The schoolgirl crush did not always have flippant overtones.

Edward Carpenter and the Intermediate Sex

'You should make a point of trying every experience once, excepting incest and folk-dancing,'[18] a Scotsman is supposed to have once said, an anecdote the composer Arnold Bax noted down approvingly. Had the Scotsman been writing in 1895 he might well have added a third occupation — sodomy. The furore aroused by the Wilde case was no academic exercise in public

indignation. It triggered off a response in the most unlikely
people, including the powerful enemy of cant and hypocrisy,
Henry Labouchere, whose journal *Truth* probably exposed more
schemes and scandals per hundred pages than any other organ.
Labouchere had a vested interest in the trial as it was he who
had helped frame the law. As he wrote in *Truth* :

Wilde and Taylor were tried on a clause in the Criminal Law
Amendment Act which I had inserted in order to render it possible
for the law to take cognisance of proceedings like theirs. I took the
clause *mutatis mutandis* from the French Code. As I had drafted it
the maximum sentence was seven years. The then Home Secretary
and Attorney-General, both most experienced men, suggested to me
that in such cases convictions are always difficult and that it would
be better were the maximum to be two years. Hence the insufficiency
of the severest sentence that the law allows.

He went on to say: 'In view of the mischief that such a man
does, the sentence he has received compares but lightly with
those almost every day awarded for infinitely less pernicious
crimes.'

Labouchere was no proselytizing crusader. To his contemporaries he had been almost lewdly frank about himself, his
whoremongering, his ventures into the brothels, his gambling,
his duelling, his living with an actress before he married her.
He was one of the few men who succeeded in evoking the same
conditioned response in both the Prince of Wales and his mother
('That viper Labouchere,' said the Prince; 'that horrible lying
Labouchere,' said Queen Victoria).

The frame of mind that could treat the situation objectively
or with levity was rare. The noble lord who, it is said, commented that he did not mind what Wilde did as long as he did
not do it in the streets and frighten the horses, was exceptional.
Frank Harris, as one might expect, was not shocked; he was
more amused, no doubt trying out the phrases he would eventually set down in his life of Wilde. In the more Bohemian
circles, homosexuality became a great talking point. When
prodded, Harris retorted: 'Unnatural vice! I know nothing of
the joys of unnatural vice. You must ask my friend Oscar about
them.' However, since Harris had always considered that he had

a special corner in Shakespeare, and it was a general article of faith that Shakespeare had had homosexual experiences, he therefore added, 'But had Shakespeare asked me, I should have had to submit!' Max Beerbohm did one of his most eloquent cartoons on this theme.

The attention given to the Wilde case perturbed those who believed that homosexuality had cosmic implications. The woman in a man's body was a philosophical concept that appealed to those who were trying out new terms for this condition, and remained of interest long after the echoes of the Wilde case had died away. In about 1910 *The Intersexes: A History of Similisexualism as a Problem in Social Life* included a questionnaire so that the reader could find out whether he belonged to the elect, whether he was a Uranian, or, if the reader was female, whether she was a Uraniad. One of the questions was, 'Can you readily separate the great toe from its fellows by its *own* force?'

Many of the Uranians or Urnings (favourite term among the literati) were disgusted by the physical manifestations of their tendencies, if they even knew about them. The choice tidbits in the homosexual pornography of the time were not for them. One character in *Teleny, or the Reverse of the Medal* (1893) has his hand on his friend's penis, a hand 'as soft as a child's, as expert as a whore's, as strong as a fencer's'. This was not for the delicately minded Urnings, who were proud of the womanly qualities they had discovered in themselves because it was reckoned among the experts that a taint of femininity was essential to make a genius, 'for genius carries us into a region where the strongly-differentiated signs of masculinity or femininity, having their end in procreation, are of little significance'.[19] The literary and philosophical Urnings had been indoctrinated into a belief in woman's inherent superiority. 'It is through woman and her pangs that man is to receive the life of the soul, as well as of the body. Man's life is their gift, who are sunk to hell without a chance.'[20] James Hilton wrote this in 1875. Urnings were pleased that they had a share of this divine charisma. Again, Hinton made his point: 'Genius is inability to keep out Nature, and is the woman in man.'[21]

Those who thought that they had a flavour of this commodity, genius, were only too pleased to cultivate their little garden of womanliness. This could lead to grotesqueries. Anarchist, market gardener, poet and sandal maker Edward Carpenter had set up house at Millthorpe, near Sheffield, in 1883. His housemate at one time was George Merrill. Carpenter 'knew of course that George had an instinctive genius for housework, and that in all probability he would keep house better than most women would'.[22] Photographs reveal that George had a long rather soppy face, the weakness accentuated rather than hidden by a spreading walrus moustache. George was a failed Jack-of-all-trades; he had worked in a newspaper office, a hotel, and an ironworks. As a housekeeper to the fairly well-off Carpenter he was content to fill the rooms with flowers, do the baking and washing. It was a camp relationship that has its many parallels in today's life, two rather prissy bachelors living a mutually absorbed self-intoxicating wide-blue-yonder existence. Wrote Carpenter in his autobiography:

On one occasion he was standing at the door of our cottage, looking down the garden brilliant in the sun, when a missionary sort of man arrived with a tract and wanted to put it in his hand. 'Keep your tract,' said George. 'I don't want it.' 'But don't you wish to know the way to heaven?' said the man. 'No, I don't,' was the reply, 'can't you see that *we're in heaven here* – we don't *want* any better than this, so go away!'

It was clear that this relationship had nothing of the squalid character of Boulton and Park, Wilde and Lord Alfred Douglas, and it was clear most of all to Carpenter. People came to Millthorpe, which Carpenter described as a cottage though it was really a substantial rural residence, where 'architects, railway clerks, engine-drivers, signalmen, naval and military officers, Cambridge and Oxford dons, students, advanced women, suffragettes, professors and provision-merchants ... parsons and positives, printers and authors, scythesmiths and surgeons, bank managers and quarrymen. ... Young colliers from the neighbouring mines put on the boxing-gloves with sprigs of aristocracy; learned professors sat down to table with farm lads.' [23] Nothing wrong with this surely, or was this what the actively queer called a symposium on a grand rustic scale?

To Carpenter, this was Whitman's love of comrades made manifest. Love that 'has the same exalting, purifying, redeeming effects' [24] as heterosexual love, 'although it is less focussed, more suffused: it hallows friendship, sanctifies brotherly service, haloes lowly manhood with a divine nimbus ...' Frequently the expression of this hallowed state (hardly haloed) is a looking upward, and there is an interesting specimen in Carpenter's own poetry, in one of the Whitmanesque pieces that make up his *Towards Democracy* (part 1 1883, parts 2 and 3 1892, part 4 1902). The hero of this particular poem is a hard-pressed tailor, 'stitching, stitching twelve hours a day', who

> To a casual little club which once a week he was in the habit
>   of attending, there came one night a new member,
> Of athletic strength and beauty, yet gentle in his manners,
> And with a face like a star – so steadfast, clear and true that he,
>   the sufferer, felt renewed by merely looking on it.

The tailor is flabbergasted when this stranger notices him and makes a friend of him. 'Great waves of health and strength come to him', and under the power of this friendship, the tailor throws up his job and gets work in the open air, and his 'little heart gathers and knits itself together, and sings, sings, sings'. All this drivel, of course, is harmless enough, but the sentimentality of this and other grand friendships recorded diligently by Carpenter in this odd work, is sufficiently sickly for one to take especial notice of the motivations. This trend was also manifest in Carpenter's *Iolaüs, an Anthology of Friendship* (1902).

Carpenter might be termed on the fringe of homosexuality. He did not tempt the fates as Symonds did, did not claim that the male form was richer in 'lovely qualities' than the female. Still, even the tepid sentiments of *Towards Democracy* aroused the ire of the *Saturday Review* in March, 1886. 'The blank monotony ... is only relieved here and there by a few passages which it would be undesirable to quote, and which it is not wholesome to read.'

Early in 1894 Carpenter decided that he would make some

contributions to sexology, and, aware of the reluctance of reputable publishers in this field, he had them printed and issued by the Manchester Labour Press, a small left-wing outfit. *Sex-love, Woman* and *Marriage* sold 3,000 or 4,000 copies each; *Towards Democracy* had sold seven hundred – in seven years. The publishers of *Towards Democracy* were willing to take a chance with *Love's Coming of Age*. In January 1895 Carpenter had published by the Manchester Labour Press *Homogenic Love* dealing with homosexuality, and marked on the title page 'printed for private circulation only'. The news of this reached Fisher Unwin, who was setting up *Love's Coming of Age*, and he cancelled the contract with Carpenter. Not only that – he also refused any longer to have anything to do with *Towards Democracy*.

Despite the title of his pamphlet on homosexuality, Carpenter was to prefer the term, 'the intermediate sex'. The perfect prototype of this genus he had already set down in 'O Child of Uranus' in *Towards Democracy*:

O child of Uranus, wanderer down all times,
Darkling, from farthest ages of the Earth the same
Strange tender figure, full of grace and pity,
Yet outcast and misunderstood of men –
Thy Woman-soul within a Man's form dwelling,
So gentle, gracious, dignified, complete,
With man's strength to perform, and pride to suffer without sign,
And feminine sensitiveness to the last fibre of being;
Strange twice-born, having entrance to both worlds –
Loved, loved by either sex,
And free of all their lore!

Obviously it was a Good Thing to be one of these. 'They became students of life and nature, inventors and teachers of arts and crafts' – yes, we know them – 'or wizards and sorcerers; they became diviners and seers, or revealers of the gods and religion; they became medicine-men and healers, prophets and prophetesses.' (*Intermediate Types among Primitive Folk*, 1914). Pretty well anything that advanced civilization was the province of the intermediate sex, or so Carpenter would appear to claim. He maintained that the intermediate sex had had a raw deal and were perennially misunderstood, and the future should make more provision for them, such as 'the restoration and full recognition of the heroic friendships of Greek and primitive times', which 'bred ideals of heroism, courage, resource, and endurance among the men, and exalted these virtues into the highest place of public honour'.[25] One of Carpenter's biographers, Edward Lewis, was most insistent on what he described as 'Dorian Friendship' – 'when two persons love each other with a passionate affection transcending the plane on which sex, as usually understood, operates, there is with them That which is the only solvent of human ills, the only triumphant leader of human progress'.

Membership in the intermediate sex was an excellent excuse for contracting out of society and any sexual embroilment. It was a group that could be joined with tongue in cheek – the ambiguities are endless. What were the motivations of William Sharp, who called himself Fiona Macleod? R. E. Francillon was plainly baffled. 'I cannot share in the solemnly nonsensical theory that Sharp's body was actually and without metaphor the abode of two separate, independent, and violently contrasted, if not mutually antagonistic, souls'[26] – i.e., the Uranian as schizoid. When a young lady wrote to 'Fiona' asking for 'her' photograph, Sharp sent her a photograph of a pretty girl. Merely practical jokery?

'Are you laughed at, are you scorned? Do they gaze at you and giggle to each other as you pass by? Do they despise you because you are misshapen, because you are awkward, because you are peculiar, because you fail in everything you do – and you know it is true?'[27] It is not a contemporary ad, but Carpenter addressing his reader. Unquestionably were he living today he would have made a great name for himself in the English advertising industry – he had that kind of a prose style. There is also little doubt that Carpenter himself *was* peculiar, and that this extract might well be an apostrophe to him.

His appearance was reported by one of his biographers – 'erect, lithe, athletic in appearance, sandalled, with free stride and high step; he wore a soft hat tilted a little to one side in the half-rakish fashion of Walt Whitman'.[28] Related another, Ernest

Crosby: 'There is a sweet reasonableness in his wildest assertion, and a twinkle of merriment in his eye when his thought
is at its deepest.'[29] The twentieth century has seen these too
often on television to be impressed by them. Olive Schreiner,
who first met Carpenter about 1883, was more prosaic: 'A
slight man of middle height, plain rather than handsome, nothing remarkable in face or figure, and dressing as the ordinary
working men dress.' She makes the point that he possessed
considerable magnetism, and this was affirmed by a hard-boiled
journalist, H. W. Nevinson, who first saw Carpenter at an
intellectualist rally in 1896:

He is certainly a very beautiful and attractive person; tall and slim,
and fairly straight; loose hair, and beard just grizzled; strong, dark
eye-brows, dark eyes, hooked nose, and thin cheeks of palish brown;
the whole face very like Carlyle at forty-five – a Carlyle fined down
and 'cultured'; he has one little trick of licking his thumb; was
dressed in loose greys, with a blue shirt, and tie in a large bow;
voice soft but strong enough without effort; spoke from a few notes
and went slowly ahead in almost perfect grammar.[30]

Sex was only a sideline for Carpenter. His grand scheme was
'the bringing of the Races of the world together, the gradual
evolution of a Non-governmental form of Society'. One of his
notions, 'the extension of the monogamic Marriage into some
kind of group-alliance', was enthusiastically acted upon by an
Anarchist group who rented eighteen acres near Newcastle, led
by a man named Kapper who thought he was starting a great
social revolution. Each man got up in the morning, and decided
for himself what work he was going to do that day, if any.
When Nevinson visited this establishment he saw leeks, cab-
bages, rhubarb, celery, strawberries, roses, pansies – the horticul-
tural variety – and mushrooms, about a hundred chickens, a
score of ducks, three cows, half a dozen goats, two horses, some
rabbits, a dog, one woman, and three children. 'All was very
dirty and unkempt, ill-weeded and unorganised,' recorded
Nevinson. The last two adjectives might well be the final words
on the Anarchist movement in Great Britain. In Russia, according to Prince Kropotkin, the high priest of the movement, men
and women were 'broadly and delicately humane in their

mutual relations'; in America, under the name of syndicalism it was inflammatory and dangerous; in Britain it was ill-weeded and unorganized. In fact, like Carpenter himself.

At this late stage, it is difficult to say how important he was to his contemporaries. He does not figure in any of the 'standard' memoirs of the time. His pamphlets on sex have achieved a sort of notoriety by being mentioned in Alfred Rose's *Registrum librorum eroticorum* (two volumes, 1936). Like Hinton, Carpenter was keen on open-ended sex relationships, but, like Hinton, he does not appear to have done much about it. He skated very prettily over the thin ice of the Wilde scandal, going out of his way to stress that he had never met Wilde. Carpenter knew William Morris and Annie Besant ('she gave the general mind a wholesome shock on the Malthusian question'), the Havelock Ellises, and an odd group who called themselves the New Fellowship and who had their own journal (*Seed-time*). He had a particularly special relationship with Mrs Ellis, who, before she married, set up her own essay in communal living, 'a co-operative boarding-house' near Mecklenburgh Square. Other sympathetic fringe members included J. L. Joynes, son of Swinburne's birch-happy tutor. J. L. Joynes went campaigning in Ireland in the early eighties and got himself arrested, an event that spelled finish to his teaching career at Eton. Another odd bird was Henry Salt, and he and Carpenter composed 'A Church Service for the use of the Respectable Classes'. Carpenter also included among his allies the Hermetic Society; the Hermetic Society was a *ménage à trois* consisting of Edward Maitland, Anna Kingsford, and her husband. Mrs Kingsford was a late Victorian beauty. When he met her – he was fifty, she was in her twenties – Maitland described her as 'tall, slender and graceful in form; fair and exquisite in complexion; bright and sunny in expression. The hair long and golden, but the brows and lashes dark, and the eyes deep-set and hazel, and by turns dreamy and penetrating. The mouth rich, full, and exquisitely formed.' From the outsider, Carpenter, there was the snide comment of her 'generous and undisguised use of cosmetics'. The Hermetic Society wrote, among the three of them, *The Perfect Way, Clothed with the Sun*, the *Virgin of the World*, some of it under trance conditions. Mrs Kingsford, confessed Carpenter reluctantly, had access to 'astral intelligence or earth memory'.

Except to students of rural socialism, Carpenter can never again be of abiding interest. That he was of some importance stresses the uncommon degree to which late Victorian and Edwardian England was preoccupied with sex and particularly homosexuality. To a certain extent, Carpenter, with his concept of the intermediate sex, lent respectability to homosexuality; the feminine soul in the male body did not exclude heroism and a host of medieval attributes, and the sentimental altruism of the Carpenter set led to waves of fine feeling, later to eddy around the ambiguous personages of Rupert Brooke (1887–1915) and T. E. Lawrence (1888–1935).

Carpenter felt that he himself had this access to 'astral intelligence or earth memory'. He considered that he was free to pontificate on a whole world of sexual subjects about which he knew very little (unless the image makers have done a *very* special job on him). Compared with Havelock Ellis, who had medical training, a passion for facts, and a *schema* that was measured in decades rather than years, Carpenter, as a writer on homosexuality, was a babbler. Kinsey, in his *Sexual Behaviour in the Human Female* (1950), taxed Carpenter (as well as Ellis) for statistically unsupported presumptions. That Carpenter features three times in the index of Kinsey's book, the very antithesis of his own studies in sex, is a fact that is somewhat surprising. It would have startled *him*, however, that he did not get a chapter to himself.

Bachelors

'What was Canon Liddon like as a boy of seventeen?' asked Frederic Harrison rhetorically in the *Pall Mall Gazette* in 1890. 'Well, so far as I can remember, he was at seventeen just what he was at twenty-seven, or thirty-seven, or forty-seven – sweet, grave, thoughtful, complete ...'[31] In reference books, Canon

Liddon gets a disproportionate amount of space as the liberal supporter of High Church doctrines, but he is perhaps of more interest as a prime example of that characteristic Victorian figure, the sexual outsider, the nonparticipant who viewed the game from the side lines. Harrison wrote in what was in fact Liddon's obituary:

As a schoolboy, I always thought he looked just what he did as a priest. There was the same expression of sweet, somewhat fatherly, somewhat melancholy interest ... I do not think that he ever joined in any game or even looked on at any game; I am sure that he never took part in the rough-and-tumble horseplay common amongst boys; and I am certain he never returned a blow or a practical joke at his expense.

Liddon was clearly not of the usual run. 'I distinctly remember the howl of indignation which rose when a boy, mistaking him for another, once roughly struck him from behind in a rude jest. When he turned with a look of sorrowful expostulation, without a sharp word, we felt somewhat ashamed of our companion, who, I think, was carried off and judicially pommelled.' Liddon must have been singularly fortunate in his choice of school (King's College School, London), and it may have been that its motto, *'Sancte et sapienter'*, had exerted a mesmeric affect on its quota of small boys, not usually given to consideration for the weak and scholarly.

Liddon was one of nature's celibates, a type of Homo sapiens not now in fashion. The nineteenth century accommodated the species with a good deal more comfort. The notion that a Church of England priest should cut himself off from all kinds of sexual connection was not considered astonishing or disgusting. Scholarship was indissolubly connected with celibacy. In 1863 Arthur Stanley married Lady Augusta Bruce, as a mother substitute (she had died the previous year), an event – his friend Benjamin Jowett called it an experiment that 'among his friends at Oxford' was greeted with 'almost unmixed dismay'. Impressed by the success of this experiment, Stanley advised Jowett to take the plunge. 'I could not marry without giving up Balliol,' [32] wrote Jowett, and in any case he was made of stronger stuff than Dean Stanley, after whose wife's death in 1873 other women had to provide the household duties Lady Augusta had managed so well in the tradition of her dead mother-in-law ('His frugal breakfast was prepared as Lady Augusta had prepared it, and his *Times* taken from him and read aloud, lest, absorbed in its contents, he should altogether omit the meal'). Jowett could not marry without giving up Balliol because under an 1857 ordinance, only one fellow was permitted marriage; the rest of them, so far as the ordinance was concerned, had to burn or leave. The universities were strictly speaking ecclesiastical units, powerhouses of faith.

Jowett was a professional celibate who was never too sure that he had made the right decision. This uncertainty he often concealed under whimsy on the subject of marriage. When Margot Asquith was probing him *vis-à-vis* his relationship with Florence Nightingale (Had he loved? What did he feel about love?), he took refuge in a little verse:

> 'Tis said that marriages are made above –
> It may be so, some few, perhaps, for love.
> But from the smell of sulphur I should say
> They must be making *matches* here all day.[33]

A decade earlier, when he was sixty-six, Jowett found himself regressing. 'Some passing vanity or semi-sensuality is constantly interrupting me in prayer, or in other serious thought', and, a little later, 'thoughts of evil, day-dreams, love fancies, easily find an abode in the mind',[34] a strange confession by perhaps the greatest of university celebrities of the period. Jowett assuaged any problems caused by his celibacy by gossip, by a slightly prurient interest in The Great Social Evil of prostitution, in straightening out young men who were straying from the straight and narrow. Other outsiders fell prey to harmless eccentricities. The Reverend C. L. Dodgson ('Lewis Carroll') transferred his repressions on to little girls, whom he photographed in fancy dress or in no dress at all. Pernickety, precise, he was a hoarder and a collector of things. In his Oxford rooms there were watches, clocks, a microscope, a pocket sundial, a chess set, an artist's model of hand and foot, two pairs of dumb bells, a musical album, six travelling pots, an 'ammoniaphone' for voice cultivation, a 'nyctograph' invented by himself for making notes in the dark, and two boxes of homeopathic medicines. His background was not so dissimilar to Liddon's, though he unfortunately was at Rugby, a school that took less kindly than King's College to a sub-specie boy that was known as a 'muff'.

Even in Victorian England, families were inclined to poke around when their menfolk remained assiduously celibate. It was the opinion of Dodgson's family, 'that Uncle Charles had had a disappointment in love'. Dodgson, amiable, good-looking, thoroughly presentable, was regarded as a contender in the marriage stakes, and his attention to the Liddell girls – one of whom was the original of *Alice in Wonderland* – was looked upon as a smoke screen so that he could get near to their governess, Miss Prickett (who somewhat improbably became the proprietress of the Mitre Hotel, Oxford), though, whatever Miss Prickett might have thought, she was then past the age of Dodgson's interest, which was puberty. This was strictly the limit. When puberty occurred among his many little girl friends his interest evaporated; even 'Alice' was subject to this immutable law. 'Alice seems changed a good deal,' he wrote on 11 May 1865, 'and hardly for the better – probably going through the usual awkward stage of transition.' That his biographers considered that there was something that needed covering up is evident from his nephew S. D. Collingwood's gloss: 'But those who loved him would not wish to lift the veil from these dead sanctities, nor would any purpose be served by so doing. The proper use of sympathy is not to weep over sorrows that are over ...' One wonders why Dodgson troubled to copy out some maudlin verse from an old issue of *All the Year Round*:

> And fast and free these pulses played
> When last I met that gentle maid,
> When last her hand in mine was laid

The rejection of a mature sexual relationship is manifest in countless episodes in the life of Dodgson and in innumerable documents. Like Ruskin, he read more into the external world and its artifacts than his more humdrum contemporaries. As one knows, the Victorian theatre had its nether regions, and it is perhaps fortunate that Dodgson did not come across this damned area. When he did go to the theatre, it was to the respectable middle-class variety to see such dramas as *The Little Treasure* by Augustus Glossop Harris. 'A great objection to such plays is the insult they offer to human nature by simulating its noblest passions – those which redeem it from mere sensual brute life. It is a profanation of things we should rather revere.'[35] This is from a young man in his early twenties. Is it mere priggishness, or is Dodgson being confronted by matter he has consciously expunged from his own private world picture?

The last of Dodgson's child friends, Mrs Shawyer, declared that 'the Victorian mind saw possible evil in the association of a child of twelve with an old man of sixty-three'. Perhaps. Yet Dodgson was only one of many bachelors who sought solace in the companionship of young girls without the evil intent of the licentious virgin takers. These bachelors created sunny memories in the minds of children often awed by unapproachable father and servant-insulated mother (Mrs Shawyer, for example, was permitted by Dodgson to strike the great bell in Tom Tower, and this provided a unique experience for her). Another ecclesiastic who was extremely fond of young girls was Francis Kilvert. In his diary of 3 May 1870 he recounts a visit to the village school of Newchurch.

Janet was doing simple division and said she had done five sums, whereupon I kissed her and she was nothing loth. Moreover I offered to give her a kiss for every sum, at which she laughed. As I stood by the window making notes of things in general in my pocket book Janet kept interrupting her work to glance round at me shyly but saucily with her mischievous beautiful grey eyes. Shall I confess that I travelled ten miles today over the hills for a kiss, to kiss that child's sweet face. Ten miles for a kiss.

On 9 July Kilvert was describing the charmingly named Bird's Nest Lane, and how 'sometimes my darling child Gipsy comes down to school this way ... often and often must those tiny feet have trodden this stony narrow green-arched lane, and those sweet blue eyes have looked down this vista to the blue mountains and those little hands have gathered flowers along these banks'. The twentieth century sees an unnatural preoccupation with young girls in such journals, while being smugly aware that the clergy has never been averse to sentimentality. Sometimes Kilvert crossed the border line from sentimentality into a more suspect area. In personalizing the sun as 'he' (*Diary*, 11 July 187—), Kilvert perhaps was incautious:

... he has stolen into her bedroom and crept along the wall from chair to chair till he has reached the bed, and has kissed the fair hand and arm that lies upon the coverlet and the white bosom that heaves half uncovered after the restlessness of the sultry night, and has kissed her mouth whose scarlet lips, just parting in a smile and pouting like rosebuds to be kissed, show the pearly gleam of the white teeth, and has kissed the sweet face and the blue veined silky lashed eyelids and the white brow and the soft bright tangled hair, till she has unclosed the sweetest eyes that ever opened to the dawn, and risen and un-fastened the casement and stood awhile breathing the fresh fragrant mountain air as it blows cool upon her flushed cheek and her half veiled bosom, and lifts and ruffles her bright hair which still keeps the kiss of the sun.

This joins hands with conventional pornographic purple prose of the same epoch: 'Her rounded, softly moulded chin, gradu-ally merging into the white column of her neck, the last gradually swelling until it ended in two round swelling breasts, parted between and crowned each with a delicious pink bud, their very colour (a dusky brown) but added to my delight.'

Kilvert would not have deigned to have written or even have noticed such work (from the *Boudoir* of 1860), but he introduces the same mechanism, a literary voyeurism, protecting himself by projecting his own feelings on to an anthropomorphic sun. Yet there is no evidence that Kilvert was other than a gentle helpful country parson, or that he saw anything at all repre-hensible in these confessions. He visited the sick and gave them consolation, and his account of his visit to the celebrated and notorious Father Ignatius is a model of accurate reportage. Kil-vert has an interesting relationship with the gossipy Augustus Hare – Hare had been a pupil of Kilvert's father. Hare, tied to his mother's apron strings as if they were leather reins, is one of the archetypal male spinsters.

Like Dodgson, Kilvert was excited by erotic and crypto-erotic high art. Although a country parson he did not disdain the delights of the metropolis. He described with relish one picture he saw (unnamed) at a London gallery:

The beautiful girl stripped naked of her blue robe and stabbed in the side under the left breast is sailing through the air and reclines half standing, half lying back, supported tenderly in the arms of her lover who has been stabbed in the same place. The naked girl is writhing and drawing up one of her legs in an agony – but her arms are thrown back and clasped passionately round her lover's neck.[36]

Sex and pain were intimately related in Victorian pornography (in any pornography), and whatever picture this was and by whomever it was painted no doubt it activated far less deserving cases than Kilvert. However, Kilvert was soon back in his parish, ogling the housemaids and intoxicated by the beauty of little girls. But even rural idylls have their seamy side: '. . . I had a horrible dream that I was married to Mrs Danzey and living as curate at Gwythian . . .'

It is unfortunate that Kilvert's diary has never been published in full, though in 1938 William Plomer's three-volume selection from the diaries was published. Kilvert wrote in twenty-two notebooks, and, if transcribed into printed form, these would fill nine volumes. Like many bachelors who seem to be coursing through life without any prospect of marrying, Kilvert faltered at the last hurdle, which would seem to come about the age of forty. In August 1879 he married Elizabeth Rowland, a woman of thirty-three, whom he had met on a visit to Paris. It was short-lived bliss; they spent their honeymoon in Scotland, but shortly afterwards, on 23 September, Kilvert died suddenly of peritonitis.

Another man who was reluctant to enter into the battle of the sexes was Kenneth Grahame, who resolutely entrenched himself in childhood. 'I too have always kept a scrap-book,' he wrote, 'of places where I'm going to live "when I'm grown up".' Nothing extraordinary about this fantasy except that Grahame was thirty-eight when he wrote it. Grahame led a curious double life. His sexual conflicts he sublimated in that classic children's book *Wind in the Willows* which, like the *Alice* books of

Lewis Carroll, exists on any number of levels, though, of course, it is of nowhere near the calibre of Carroll's masterpieces. Grahame used his books not only to extirpate sexual problems but to wreak vengeance on the adult world, with which he could never identify. The adult world included burdensome relatives, and in 1891, when he was in his early thirties, Grahame wrote *Justifiable Homicide*, slightly sick jokery, advocating the putting down of relatives, who 'have crammed their victim [i.e., Grahame] full of precepts, rules of conduct, moral maxims, and most miscellaneous counsel; all which he intuitively suspected at the time, and has ascertained by subsequent experience, to be utterly worthless'. It is characteristic of writers who use their craft as a means of working out intimate problems of life that they can be alternately slushy and crisply brutal without realizing it, and if they do realize it they can relapse into the persona of a child 'who didn't really mean it'. So *Justified Homicide* takes its place alongside the same writer's gushing *Dream Days*, and the concealed savagery of *Alice's Adventures in Wonderland* rides alongside the sickening sentimentality of Carroll's *Sylvie and Bruno*.

While he was desperately trying to root himself in a non-adult world, using animals as substitutes for men and women – as he put it himself, 'using the animal to get away ... from weary sex-problems', Grahame was at the same time a person of note in the City – secretary of the Bank of England. Unlike Kilvert or the other clerical celibates, Grahame was not all of a piece. His fear of sex had not been faced, and this indeterminateness led him eventually and reluctantly at the age of about forty to the altar. He was led there by Elspeth Thomson, a bluestocking opiniated woman, described in a graphic phrase as a 'superficial and twilight woman', and she was aided by Grahame's being ill, during which period she got her father to send him a consignment of ancient port and the offer of a carriage.

It was hardly a tempestuous courtship. Miss Thomson had to share him with his passion for 'messing about in boats' in the West Country. In his new role as a fiancé, Grahame was at something of a loss, and he resolved the situation by regressing and adopting in his letters to Miss Thomson baby talk :

Darlin Minkie ope youre makin steddy progress & beginnin ter think of oppin outer your nest & avin a short fly round.... Don't bovver to let loose enny muvverly large people on me I dont want to be muvvered just now if I do theres a chambermade wot'll take it on. ... I could play at frowin' you over – over the cliff I mean, but I woodn't do it reely – and you cood play at bandonin me artlessly for nuther – but you wouldn't do that neither.

This was a convenient method of dealing with a novel problem. It told Miss Thomson to keep off the grass until he had come to terms with the idea of marriage, and it could release inner conflict – the notion of throwing his fiancée over the cliff – through a formula that could not cause offence; the baby talk nullifies the content.

The concept of an ordinary bourgeois marriage was not to Grahame's liking: 'Darlin,' he wrote, 'ow'd you like ter go on living at Ons: Sq.; [i.e., Onslow Square] & cum away wif me fer week-ends? Then [a part here is illegible] and you needn't rite no notes & it wood be so nice & immoril & yet nobody coodnt find no forlt not even arnts.' Grahame seems to have been particularly dogged by relatives, especially aunts. 'Arnt' in this instance clearly represented adult disapproval. Despite all the auguries, Elspeth pressed on, the marriage was promulgated and consummated, though the couple speedily agreed that sex was not for them. In this brief period of what might pass for passion, Mrs Grahame conceived and bore a boy, Alastair, who was blind in one eye and had a squint in the other. In their courtship, Grahame had simulated desire; in their marriage, his wife led. Marriage was for Grahame a traumatic experience; his literary output dried up. It was seven years before the springs started flowing again, though when they did, Grahame came up with his best book, *The Wind in the Willows*, in which animals personify people, a book sparked off by stories he told his young son.

The Grahame marriage might be a salutary warning to bachelor authors tempted by wanton impulses. Predictably, Elspeth Grahame saw her son not as he was but as she wanted him to be, and when the First World War broke out in 1914 she thought it was quite in the cards that Alastair would have to go and fight, completely ignoring the reason that would make this impossible – his eyes. Alastair and his mother ganged up against Grahame; very significantly, the boy's nickname for his father was 'Inferiority'. In his later years – Kenneth Grahame did not die until 1932 – he stared out from photographs with a curiously vulnerable boyish innocence from behind a dashing military moustache. He long outlived his son. Alastair committed suicide, run over by a train. Elspeth became a village eccentric, stomping around in *sabots* brought back from France, rarely up before eleven, spending much time on a sofa, sipping endless gallons of hot water while the local mice made merry in the larder.

Born bachelors are inclined to gather around them others of the same ilk, and Kenneth Grahame was no exception. Among his scholar friends was Robinson Ellis, tall, shabby, with obsessions concerning his feet. His boots were slashed open at the toes to give them room, and landladies at the seaside resorts that he favoured – they included Whitby, Saltburn and Bognor, traditionally havens for the lower middle classes and not scholars – were bidden to look at his feet. They said that there was not much to see. 'That is what makes me uneasy,' was Ellis's response. Perhaps this was a harmless exhibitionism. Of more moment in Victorian letters was another of Grahame's acquaintances, F. J. Furnivall, immortalized by Swinburne as 'Brothelsdyke', founder of innumerable literary societies, members of which he occasionally excommunicated with a printed 'I am glad to be rid of you', a man seen today as something of a tiresome pedant but who was in fact an eccentric extrovert who took slum children to Kew Gardens, tramped round London in a red shirt, was for a time closely connected with F. D. Maurice and his mixed bag of Christian Socialists, and who thought that the answer to prostitution was to get the girls sculling on the Thames. If feet was Ellis's obsession, Furnivall's was sculling; his first question to new acquaintances was 'Can you scull?' Grahame could and was therefore favoured.

The solitary life tends to bring in its train nervous disorders. Herbert Spencer suffered from unformulated neuroses throughout most of his life. On one occasion in 1856 he was put in a haunted room – 'rather a sharp test for one labouring under a nervous disorder, whose nights were always broken by long waking intervals'. Spencer was very fond of fishing, and one day he got his line, as fishermen do, in a tangle. Losing patience, he swore, as fisherman do. But Spencer reflected, after a man in the boat with him, a cleric of the Calvinist persuasion, reproved him. 'I suppose it was the oddity of this incident which drew my attention to the fact that, being thirty-six years of age, I had never before been betrayed into intemperate speech of such kind.' Spencer pondered on this and wrote to a friend: 'I want a keeper, to be always taking care that I do not overstep the limits on one side or the other; for a consequence of my present condition is that I lack judgement and presence of mind, and commit some imprudence or other before I am aware of it.' 'Under a lowered condition of the nervous system,' decided Spencer, 'failure is first manifest in the highest intellectual coordinations and in the highest emotional coordinations.' Though introspective, Spencer was never other than rational and lucid; he tried to solve his problem by extra activities and by what he describes as restless wandering. He did not try marriage, though this was recommended to him by the philosopher Comte whom he met in Paris ('the sympathetic companionship of a wife would have a curative influence'). It was also characteristic of Victorian bachelors that they discussed their neurasthenic aches and pains with anyone who would listen. T. H. Huxley also advised his friend Spencer to marry to cure his nervous debility, facetiously terming it 'gynoeopathy', though he admitted 'that the remedy had the serious inconvenience that it could not be left off if it proved unsuitable'.

Few autobiographies and journals of bachelors are free from a preoccupation with what the twentieth century affectionately dubs 'nerves'. 'After dinner today,' wrote Kilvert (14 March 1872) 'I was seized with a strange fit of nervous restlessness such as I never felt before. I should think it must have been something like the peculiar restlessness that comes shortly before death. I could not sit still or rest for a minute in any posture. The limbs all kept jumping and twitching and I should have liked to set to a run only I felt so weak and wretched.' An extreme example of the power of 'nerves' over the bachelor is furnished by Frederick Shields, a painter of modest talents, and a close friend of Rossetti. Shields was introspective and self-critical to a high degree. His diary is full of pleas: 'O Lord, crush and break my hasty, unmortified temper, Amen, for Thy Glory's Sake, that my light may shine before men undimmed' – rather extravagant for a young man in his mid-twenties. He reproached himself for 'too much levity and griggishness', and turned out harmless and sentimental pseudo-religious pictures. His self-conscious asceticism provided an admirable foil to the Rabelaisian indecencies of Rossetti, but it was an asceticism only at a price. 'When nervousness and debility supervene take wine,' suggested Ford Madox Brown. Shields was troubled by sleeplessness. 'Stillman who is here has given me the name of a splendid sleeping potion,' Madox Brown informed him, 'Hydrate of Chloral 1 dram in 1 oz. of water, and take one to four teaspoonfuls as needed.' Shields took this up, and became an addict for several years. Ford Madox Brown's son Oliver also came up with advice for their neurotic friend, 'A dose of *Chloral* Monday, *Sour Milk* Tuesday, *Laudanum* Wednesdays, on Thursday a little Spirits (Irish whisky is best for sleep-producing purposes), while on Friday you might modestly content yourself with fifteen to twenty drops of Chlorodyne."

Shields became involved in the close meticulous work that is the prerogative of Victorian minor artists and was associated with the photographer M'Lachlan in a massive Windsor Castle group depicting *all* Victoria's descendants – this was, said Shields, 'hateful slavery', and he was at it for two years. When he was forty, for no very clear reason Shields married a sixteen-year-old girl who was acting as a model. This, Madox Brown told him, 'will do much to alleviate the nervous troubles and anxieties you have suffered from'. Like Huxley, Madox Brown believed in 'gynoeopathy', though it is rather odd that the picture he gave Shields as a wedding present should have had the lugubrious title, 'The Way of Sorrow', though this may have been a tradition among the Rossetti circle. Shields gave William Michael Rossetti, the stodgiest of the set, his own mournful 'The Sacrifice of Manoah' (and most of Shields' pictures are mournful

– he objected to any levity in art; in 1870 he had collected signatures to stop a prize being awarded to what he considered an 'improper picture').

Whatever the poor girl was expecting from her nuptials, it was surely not immediately being left alone in the rambling house Shields had bought, with the housekeeper, while Shields went off with his photographer colleague M'Lachlan to Blackpool, a visit that did him 'wonderfully good'. Even worse was to come. While Shields was struggling with the epic picture of the tribe of Hanover and Saxe-Coburg ('Fighting with Lorne and Hesse. Got Prince of Wales pinned up') his wife was sent off to school, the boarding school run by Miss Bell – a friend of Ruskin, short, stout, bespectacled – and Miss Bradford – tall, thin, delicate, hair in Grecian plaits. Shields believed in having an educated wife; he would not have wanted to emulate George Gissing 'condemned for ever to associate with inferiors – and so crassly unintelligent. Never a word exchanged on anything but the paltry everyday life of the household. Never a word to me, from anyone, of understanding sympathy – or of encouragement.' Shields did not want, as Gissing had, a wife who said 'amusing' when she meant 'interesting', or who had never heard of *The Pilgrim's Progress*.

Mrs Shields would have appeared to have been a ringer for Dora of Dickens's *David Copperfield*, but there are rumbles of discontent. 'The Lord preserve us both from the worst evil, a sinful disobedient will,' Shields wrote to her ominously, '... may He who is the only refuge of Sinners – the God of all Consolation – cleanse and deliver you from all sin and comfort you with His Holy Spirit' – difficult counsel for the immured child wife especially as Shields was writing from Florence, a city famous for its high life and its fun-loving English colony. 'Above all,' Shields went on, '*obey* and submit yourself to the school rules as if you were my child.' This was because 'your mind has been so neglected that for a long while you will have to be busy uprooting the weeds of ignorance'. Was Shields looking for a daughter by proxy? Certainly he did not treat his wife like a spouse, and his behaviour did not get any the less odd. He adopted Mrs Shields's sister Jessie as a daughter, and eventually –

one assumes in despair – the two girls joined the Salvation Army.

Shields was one of those doomed to trials and tribulations. Before his marriage he had bought Ordsall Old Hall, Manchester, but as soon as he had settled in neighbouring land was bought by an oilcloth company and inundated with 'great cartloads of stinking oyster shells'. Existing property was brought crashing to the ground. 'If the Parthenon itself stood here,' wrote Shields bitterly, 'and these speculators could clear five pounds by its demolition, it would go.' In 1876, two years after this 'marriage', Shields sought for a place in London, and fancied 7 Lodge Place. Swinburne's lawyer friend, and Rossetti's aide in the matter of clearing a forged cheque, Theodore Watts, carried out the purchase with his customary efficiency, only to find Shields not so appreciative as he had anticipated. Shields had discovered a house he liked even more, at West Drayton. An expedition to see his house had also been fraught with problems – Shields was thrown into a panic by having lost his railway tickets. The place he had bought was no Arcadia – 'every day,' he recorded mordantly, 'I find out some new trouble about floors, drainage, roofage, or something.'

It is difficult not to feel sorry for Frederick Shields, always worried about the state of his soul, pondering on sins that he may or may not have had, reduced even further by his dependence on chloral, involved in a marriage that was probably never a marriage, and, to cap it, the portion of his life that he considered to be above reproach – his art – was even under suspicion because one of his pupils happened to design some child fairies. These child fairies were seen by the Rossetti sister, Christina who, after two broken romances and after exophthalmic bronchocele had destroyed her looks and complexion, took a very dim view of anything approaching the salacious. These included child fairies. 'I do admire the grace and beauty of the designs, but I do not think that to call a figure a "fairy" settles the right and wrong of such figures,' she wrote to Shields, implying that Shields was to blame for the suspect pupil. She might well have felt confirmed in her judgement when Miss Beale, headmistress of Cheltenham Ladies' College, instructed

Shields to cover a Cupid he had designed for stained glass windows with, of all things, roses.

As for Christina, as she said in 'Repining':

> She sat alway through the long day
> Spinning the weary thread away;
> And ever said in undertone,
> 'Come, that I be no more alone.'

Aloneness was not a circumstance alien to Shields. It is evident from the canny cautiousness of his official biographer, Ernestine Mills, that Mrs Shields was something of a problem; even more from a letter Shields wrote in 1898 to unnamed young friend about to be married: 'At the first sentence of your letter a great gulp of anguish choked me, so that I put it away unread for two days, self-tormenting with dread for you. For marriage holds within itself such terrible possibilities of unmitigated misery that I shook with fear for you.' It is not recorded what particular picture Shields sent with this woeful letter.

The connection between William Bell Scott and Frederick Shields is Rossetti; both were close friends of his. Dante Gabriel Rossetti had a personality that transgressed his limitations as a painter and made his rather indifferent corpus of poetry seem better than it was. If a nineteenth-century personage was born a century ahead of his time it was surely Rossetti. He was an octopus who grabbed at people with an amiable brutality; he used Ruskin with brazen insouciance (it helped that Ruskin was in thrall to his wife), and he prodded Swinburne in his alcoholic days with a curious interest as to what made Swinburne tick. People who crawled out from beneath Rossetti's tentacles were never quite the same afterwards.

Although William Bell Scott was married, he might just as well have not have been. His wife had had an attack of typhoid, and this had affected her mind. While she remained in London, her husband lived in a genuinely period castle called Penkill with battlements, drawbridge, portcullis and mullioned windows. Scott suffered from the disadvantage that early in life he had, he believed, committed the supreme sin against the Holy Ghost without knowing what this sin was. He had amplified this by stealing a book from Puttick and Simpson. This, Rossetti told him maliciously, was 'an act that has doubtless been photographed by the Recording Angel'. Scott lived at Penkill Castle in a platonic and spiritual relationship with Miss Alice Boyd. It was a communion of souls that Shields might well have envied. The nineteenth century is a treasure house of such quaint and endearing ways of life.

One's knowledge of the bachelor of the nineteenth century is lopsided, in so far as it is orientated to the literary and the articulate. Almost every village had its bachelor, just as nearly every village had its idiot, with his fixed place in the community. When scarlet fever, cholera, typhoid fever and 'the white plague' (tuberculosis) took such a toll of young ladies in their prime, there was a considerable body of fiancés who mourned for the rest of their lives. Such figures had the sympathy of the village. There were others who felt no urge to marry, who were crippled, ugly, diseased, or for whom there were no available women, others who were homosexual, others who sought connection with animals (an ill-documented area even in sexology). 'Full many a flower is born to blush unseen,' and the village bachelor was no exception.

The aristocracy also had its quota of sexual outsiders, such as Lord Crewe, the brother-in-law of Monckton Milnes. Crewe had received a traumatic shock when he saw his tutor commit suicide. He was pathologically shy, and 'would stick his face in a holly bush sooner than meet a party of his neighbours'. He regularly turned up to three sermons on a Sunday, was fascinated by strange flowers, and, that perquisite of most bachelors, he was fond of arguing with himself. His dislike of children was only excelled in ferocity by his passion for the family manse, Crewe Hall, though he could watch it burning down with something like detachment, saying to his sister, 'Well, Annabel, you have always said Crewe was a cold house but you can't call it cold now.'

Lord Crewe was too self-sufficient to be pressurized into marriage, but natural celibates with more forceful relatives were driven into anguished marriages. It was their duty to propagate, and propagate they would. The scandalous liaisons of the nineteenth-century aristocracy arose not only from women marrying men to whom they were ill-suited, but from women marrying men who did not want to get married at all. When the great families moved in on some timid elder son who only wanted to be left alone with his books or his crucifix any opposition he was likely to put up to the notion of marriage with some lady sprig of nobility was destined to be short-lived.

Natural inclinations towards marriage were often thwarted by some constitutional weakness. Christina Rossetti's constitutional weakness was that she could not countenance marriage with anyone whose religious views did not tally with her own, the poet James Thomson's (who wrote under the initials 'B. V.') that he was hardly ever sober. It is difficult to distinguish between natural spinsters who use carefully staged pseudo-events to justify their solitary state, and unmarried women who have not had offers or whose offers have been blighted.

There was, as there always is, a considerable body of men who looked at marriage as objectively as they could, rejecting it consciously in favour of (a) celibacy; (b) casual alliances; (c) an extended relationship outside marriage. To the nineteenth century, marriage was a terminal stage. In England in 1870, the divorce rate was eight per million, in 1880 fifteen per million. In 1880, only 116 divorced persons remarried. The inherently timid looked about them. The 'nice girls', as Henry James called them – the quotes are his – coming in from lawn tennis 'flushed a little and a little dishevelled, they might have passed for the attendant nymphs of Diana flocking in from the chase', these were seen to be transformed almost overnight into tyrants and viragos. Many Victorian men remained outsiders from choice, and should their sexual urges prove inconvenient there were plenty of women in the Haymarket and all points north, south, east and west.

A Trio of Oddities

The first of the professional aesthetes was Walter Pater. It was his aim to get 'as many pulsations as possible into the given time ... to burn always with this hard, gemlike flame', and he was prepared to throw out what others considered essentials. 'Great passions,' he admitted, 'may give us this quickened sense of life, ecstasy and sorrow of love, the various forms of enthusiastic activity, disinterested or otherwise, which come naturally to many of us.' But he was not in favour of them.

Pater himself did not burn with this hard, gemlike flame; he flickered. Personality defects and foibles did not permit him to lead a 'normal' life, and he might be termed the sexual outsider *par excellence*. There are indications in his adolescence that he had urges, but his ugliness and an almost pathological shyness kept him restrained to the verge of inarticulateness.

At King's School, Canterbury, he betrayed an aversion to small-boy pursuits – 'I do not seem to want a black eye,' he said. He had macabre and portentous dreams, 'wild weird dreams of grave or shroud', and took a soulful interest in the many religious processions and events that Canterbury was prone to. He made friends with two rather creepy boys, McQueen and Dombrain, and was unpopular at school, so much so that he was savagely attacked by his fellow pupils, an attack that left him with a permanent aversion to the hearty life and something of a limp. When he left, the headmaster offered him a backhanded compliment: 'I cannot say that you have been an active monitor in suppressing turbulence, in punishing the refractory, but you have always set in your own person an example of good discipline, obedience and order, and ever set your schoolfellows an example of Christian forbearance, a meek and quiet spirit.'

It might be supposed that Oxford, in the mellow twilight of the Newman era, with its sensibility and religious fervour, was the ideal place for Pater, but he lost his faith, gave away all his religious books, and decided to try a new image by growing a huge moustache. He is supposed to have said that he would give ten years of his life to be handsome. In 1862 he took a not very good degree, and in 1864 was elected Fellow of Brasenose; as tutor to what he described as 'young tigers at play', Pater exerted an incredible influence on his charges, and was an indefatigable prodder of the considerable number of homosexuals and suspect men who came within his orbit, including Simeon Solomon and

Wilde. Many of these young men were to horrify him by resolutely refusing to distinguish between art and life, burning not in the regulation gemlike manner but like Bunsen burners.

In 1869, Pater moved from his modish rooms in the college – with their pale apple-green walls, stained and varnished floors, and Oriental rugs – to live with his sisters in Bradmore Road. His sisters were devoted and artistic, wearing aesthetic dresses of the Girl of the Period era, and their views tended to parallel those of their brother. When a visitor to tea went into raptures over a sunset of unusual beauty, one of the Miss Paters put up her spectacles and said gently, 'Yes – yes – perhaps, but rather crude, don't you think?' They were the originals of what was described as the 'Passionate Brompton' school (abbreviated by the in-group as the PBs.

Watching from his Balliol fastness, the greatest university figure of the age, Benjamin Jowett, was anxious. Had Pater been just a not very competent tutor cramming his disciples with the ecstasy of the artistic life instead of the felicities of Homer he would have been merely another second-rater who had found a sinecure within dreaming Oxford. But he was not. Beside his sense of inferiority, his awareness that intellectually he was not of the first order, he had a lingering preoccupation with death and the perverse, and his writings were to foster eventually the decadents of the nineties. The central figure of Fra Angelico's *Coronation of the Virgin* was 'corpse-like in her refinement', and of a piece of Pre-Raphaelite poetry, 'the colouring is intricate and delirious as of "scarlet lilies". The influence of summer is like a poison in the blood.' It was of no matter that his was a paper naughtiness, that any kind of perverse behaviour in the external world was anathema to him. He had the power to corrupt youth and his maxims and aphorisms were quoted by the marvelling young. George Moore called him a 'vicarage Verlaine'. Oscar Wilde modelled his style on Pater's, but Pater was not altogether grateful, referring to 'the strange vulgarity which Mr Wilde mistakes for cleverness'.

Pater lived in a vacuum-sealed world. A crabbed Narcissus, he did not notice things as others did. He could write a long piece on the poetry of Michelangelo without observing that its matter was homosexual. Women were a closed book to him, a circumstance to which he responded with anger. 'Women,' he declared, 'can perceive neither truth when they encounter it, nor beauty where it really exists.' His value is as a catalyst; this ugly little man wracked with feelings of inferiority was in the right place at the right time. He was the high priest of camp who would not get his surplice dirty. When Solomon got arrested in 1873 for buggery, while the Eton schoolmaster Oscar Browning was being delicately accused of 'Socratic' behaviour their mutual friend, Walter Pater, floated blissfully through life, not knowing very much what went on and unaware of the seeds he had inadvertently sown.

At the opposite end of the spectrum was Lord Leighton, one of the most assured exponents of Victorian high art, whose public life was one of assured impeccability, and whose private life seems to have been as shiny and unsullied as the nudes he so delighted in painting. In 1890 the nation gave £1,000 for Leighton's sexy and luscious 'The Bath of Psyche'; no one thought it odd that this handsome and dynamic artist had not married, that his name had never been associated with any woman, and that he should have spent his life painting what in any other context but the late nineteenth century would be blatantly erotic pictures.

It would appear that Lord Leighton was too good to be true. He never failed a friend in need – and his friends ranged from the Prince of Wales down to the homosexual cartoonist 'Ape' of *Vanity Fair* – and he was not known ever to have done an ungentlemanly deed. Born in Scarborough in 1830, Frederick Leighton was the son of a well-to-do doctor who, on account of deafness, gratefully threw down the burden of work in order to devote his life to parlour metaphysics. His mother was a fashionable invalid who took refuge in a multitude of psychosomatic disorders when she was bored, and from whom Leighton was glad to escape. Until he was thirty he lived mainly abroad, mostly in Rome, a welcome member of the expatriate English-speaking society there. His mother bombarded him with exhortations. 'My precious child,' she wrote in 1852, 'if one sinful mortal's prayer for another could avail, how carefully would you be preserved from moral evil (the greatest of all evil).' Not surprisingly, Leighton selected a mother substitute in place of his real mother, Mrs Adelaide Sartoris, sister of the actress Fanny Kemble, grotesquely fat with a large aquiline nose. Leighton also acquired in the person of Henry Greville, one-time court gossip, a substitute father. Greville offered him advice about the nudes Leighton was so energetically painting. Pan and Venus were heaven-sent subjects. Said Greville:

If such personages were to be painted, it was not possible to clothe them in crinoline or in green gauze drawers. . . . it makes me so sick, all that cant about impropriety, but there is so much of it as to make the sale of 'nude figures' very improbable, and therefore I hope you will turn your thoughts entirely to well-covered limbs, and paint no more *Venuses* for some time to come.

Leighton pooh-poohed the advice, though when he sent some paintings over to America for Mrs Sartoris's sister, Fanny Kemble, to dispose of, they were so risqué that they were locked up in a cupboard. Leighton's biographer, Mrs Russell Barrington (*Life and Letters*, 1906), was at pains to emphasise the pure thought of Leighton. 'In his undraped figures there is the same total absence of the work of the degenerate as there is in everything he did and was; no remote hint of any *double-entendre* veiled by aesthetic refinement.'

Are we to take Mrs Barrington's words at their face value? Certainly the creation of erotic art is frequently left to those whose sexual impulses are sublimated or repressed or bizarre. One need only think of Etty or Rops. Leighton also had a penchant for drawing handsome boys; one of his favourite boy models was John Hanson Walker. Walker had some talent in drawing, and on the strength of this he tried to get Leighton to sponsor him as a curator. Leighton refused ('. . . the Curator is expected to be able when required to *advise and direct the pupils*, and I cannot in candour conceal from you that your age and experience do not appear to me yet to qualify you for that part of the duties'). Did Walker have some hold over Leighton that made him think that this request would be acceded to? There is support for this in the tradition that during the Oscar Wilde trial in 1895, Leighton left the country to avoid being involved. True, he did leave the country, but he was a sick man, and died the following year. Yet on May 1895 he wrote a letter to his sister Lina that bears a number of stylish interpretations: 'I am grieved that you should have been worried – as well you might – by that idiotic report that I should not return to society or my profession (I wonder who invented it!), but you were fortunately soon relieved.'

When Leighton's biographer rises to the defence of her subject, her fever knows no bounds. The four Misses Pullen were orphans used by Leighton as models. Wrote Mrs Barrington:

It is almost unnecessary, as it is distasteful, to mention that this beautiful paternal attitude Leighton displayed towards these orphans was made the subject of ugly gossip – for are there not always the *misérables* of the world who seek the ugly rather than the beautiful? misinterpreting the beautiful so that it should come within the range of their scandalous arrows, more especially when the darts attack a man in the high position Leighton held.

It would seem that there were some who had not fallen under the Leighton spell. But not many. 'He declares he has never seen a girl he could marry,' Leighton's mother wrote when he was in his early thirties. She added, 'Of course this shows he is unreasonably fastidious.' Was it really 'of course', Mrs Leighton?

The bond between Pater and Leighton is that they were bachelors whose private lives were, ostensibly, irreproachable. This is not true of John Ruskin, who was, like G. F. Watts and Frederick Shields, a basic bachelor who was unfortunate enough to get himself married. No marriage has been subjected to so much searching light over the last decade or so, and from publishers' lists it might appear that Ruskin has taken over from the Bible as the prime topic to pontificate upon.

As a young man, Ruskin had been interested in a number of young ladies, but any romance had been squashed by Ruskin's possessive mother. Reluctantly she gave a qualified blessing to Ruskin's courtship of Effie Gray, but was less sanguine when it was known that Miss Gray's father was on the edge of bankruptcy. The couple were married on 10 April 1848; she was nearly twenty, Ruskin was twenty-nine. 'Immediately after our marriage,' wrote Ruskin, 'we agreed that we would not consummate it, at all events for some little time; in order that my wife's state of health might not interfere with a proposed journey on the Continent. Soon afterwards we agreed that the marriage should not be consummated until my wife was five and twenty.'

Odd perhaps? On the first night, declared Ruskin, 'My own passion was also much subdued by anxiety; and I had no difficulty in refraining from consummation.' On the second night they talked about it. Why did Ruskin abstain? 'It may be thought strange that I *could* abstain from a woman who to most people was so attractive. But though her face was beautiful, her person was not formed to excite passion. On the contrary, there were certain circumstances in her person which completely checked it.' Yet Effie was in no way deformed and was everything a normal healthy woman should be. What were the circumstances? Effie was almost certainly the first and last naked woman Ruskin ever saw, and it is likely that he was taken aback by her pubic hair, an eventuality his acquaintance with art had not prepared him for. On the bridal night, he was also aware of his own lack of experience in this area. 'I did not think either, that there could be anything in my own person particularly attractive to *her*: but believed that she loved me, as I loved her, with little mingling of desire.'

From 1848 to 1853 Effie Ruskin had a double problem – to repress her sexuality and to put on a pose to the world that everything was all right. In Scotland in 1853 the Ruskins had John Millais as company; Millais told Ruskin that he was patently neglecting his wife, but Ruskin disdained the idea, and threw the pair of them together. Millais fell in love with Mrs Ruskin, she with him, and the machinations began, blissfully ignored by Ruskin as members of the grand world pecked with rabid interest, lining themselves up into two diametrically opposing groups. Effie Ruskin had the most support when the stunned world realized that her flighty and vivacious persona was a cover for enforced virginity, while the most fervent of her myrmidons were those who wanted to score off Ruskin.

When Effie confided the truth to her parents, their main worry was that Ruskin would get some whisper of a scheme to get the marriage quashed, and make an effort to consummate it – it must be remembered that there is no such crime as a rape upon a wife. Effie's method to prevent Ruskin having any such idea was to be as hostile and belligerent as possible – from Christmas Day 1853, alleged Ruskin, her attitude had been one of 'resolute anger – venting itself in unexplained insults; and rejecting every attempt of mine to caress her as if I had been a wild beast'.

The nullity suit was carried through. Ruskin behaved with dignity, and was willing to let the annulment rule that the marriage was void through non-consummation due to his impotence, but at the time he stressed his own virility, though he appears to have confused two issues: (a) the ability to achieve an orgasm; (b) the ability to engage in coition. That he could achieve orgasm he was probably prepared to prove, and there is a key phrase in a later letter to Lady Mount-Temple (formerly Mrs Cowper Temple):

Have I not often told you that I was another Rousseau? – except in this – that the end of my life will be the best – has been – already – not best only – but redeemed from the evil that was its death. But long before I knew her, [i.e., Rose La Touche, a sick, bewildered adolescent whom Ruskin wished to marry] I was, what she and you always have believed me to be: & I am – and shall be – worthy of you.

Rousseau in his *Confessions* had admitted to the habit of masturbation.

On 30 May 1854 Effie had been examined by Drs Charles Locock and Robert Lee, who stated: 'We found that the usual signs of virginity are perfect and that she is naturally and perfectly formed and there are no impediments on her part to a proper consummation of the marriage.' This kind of detail is characteristic of the Ruskin case. No Victorian marriage has been subjected to such close scrutiny; it is the Rosetta stone to the intellectual marriage that failed.

For the last half of his long life Ruskin continued to fall in love with a series of young girls, and in 1878, born of repression, madness overtook him. This madness, a manic-depressive psychosis, was intermittent, and his last affair with a young girl dates from 1888; darkness then descended for the rest of his days. Ruskin was an authentic casualty of the Victorian way of love. He sought release from the pangs not only of despised love but of unacknowledged lusts and frustrated urges by compulsive writing. Others found release in the creation of something outside themselves. Victorian repression was represented not only by young girls lovingly embroidering gentlemen's braces or making skirts for pianofortes, not only by the nudes of Victorian high art coyly parading in a never-never land of fanciful mythology and the hundreds of thousands of obscene photographs and prints still locked up in private collections, but also by the seemingly indestructible architectural fantasies like St Pancras Station. In its agonized steeples and tortuous passageways it is a living metaphor of Victorian sex.

Conclusion

That the Victorian age was not all of a piece is evident. In many circles, the Regency ethos lasted until the 1860s, and the simple divisions, early, mid and late Victorian, are often mere conveniences. We are gradually realizing that it is no longer good enough to browse through the catalogue of the Great Exhibition of 1851 and proclaim that it represents what the climate of taste and opinion was, as writers have been inclined to do in the past. Similarly, the image of the age as one of ever greater economic expansion can play one false; the nineteenth century had disastrous slumps, and had governments and oppositions had balance-of-payments difficulties, as at present, cabinets would have fallen like ninepins. Increased competition from the United States and the continent had sliced into profit margins, had made warfare for the sake of trade a happy folk memory. Although the volume of exports had doubled between 1855 and 1875, the subsequent quarter of a century was an uphill fight against the new economic facts of life.

In terms of technological history, the age may in future be seen as a transitory one between the eras of the mechanical and the electronic, in terms of anthropology as the age in which the roles of man and woman began to be confused. In the long run, the machinations of the suffragettes in the early years of this century, prefaced by the phenomena of the new woman and the girl of the period, may be observed as an evolutionary process, showing that the attempt to obtain equality for the sexes was instinctive rather than rational. Historians of the period are increasingly aware that at no time was the age free-running; advances in industry, welfare and simple living were clogged, intuitively and deliberately, and at no time has the peculiar propensity of the English to imagine that in no matter what area they know best been brought so much into play.

The Victorians had their think-tanks, but they were bedevilled by the necessity of appeasing the establishment, and great minds were rendered ineffectual by the obdurate conservatism of the highly placed. There is no reason why the internal combustion engine was not invented in the 1850s, or why, in 1882, the electrical industry was merely lighting a few buildings like the British Museum and the Savoy Theatre. Nineteenth-century man was not attuned to what he could do. In 1869 Ruskin wrote in a letter to Lady Mount-Temple, 'Half the power of the world is lost, because people are not trained to accuracy of obedience enough to be able to act with certainty.' The will and the power to operate efficiently were vitiated by intense mental conflicts resulting from an archiac programming of people's minds. The church and parents inculcated the need to believe in a supra-national father figure, and this created all kinds of problems to those who only wanted to see clearly and get things done, even those who consciously rejected the idea of a god as a doubtful hypothesis. Preoccupation with sexual problems ran off libido that could more usefully have been adapted to the improvement of life, and there were few who were not equipped with emotional balls and chains. England was full of Pavlov dogs who would react in appallingly stereotyped ways to whatever was done or said.

The entrustment of the voice of the age was given largely to the middle classes; it was difficult for the working classes to expound their point of view or their ethos, and propagandists for the lower orders were more usually expatriate middle-class people, like George Gissing, who were spiritually slumming. The basic attitude towards sexual matters of the middle classes was compounded of fear and alarm and shame, and this was affirmed by the middle-class experts in the field – the doctors, who scornfully rejected the honest-to-goodness approach, especially in hysteria and related areas, of their eighteenth-century predecessors. Those who wanted to let in a little fresh air on to this forbidden topic – Carlile, Place, Drysdale, Bradlaugh – were considered guilty of something worse than obscenity, something analogous to high treason. Doctors who dabbled in sexual enlightenment had let down their own class, had done something worse than anything propounded by Hippocrates.

Fear, alarm, and shame meant that when anything approached sex in the course of conversation, the shutters of the mind came down with a great slam. Fermenting complexes were unscrupulously used by the writers of pornography and the journalist who made sexual misdemeanours the staple diet of the popular Sunday newspaper. How did these mental shutters work? Recent research by Drs D. E. Broadbent and Margaret Gregory at the Applied Psychology Research Unit of Cambridge has thrown a fascinating light on this subject. After a series of experiments, it was found that 'neutral' words were heard more clearly than obscene ones; in subsequent experiments, Cambridge housewives were subjected to a series of common one-syllabled words, *good* ('lawn', 'mirth', 'neat', 'peach') *bad* ('fog', 'fright', 'grief', 'guilt') and *neutral* ('hut', 'mode', 'moist', 'plough', 'puff', 'purse'). These words had been shuffled into a random order, tape recorded, and mixed with random noise. Neutral words were heard more distinctly than good words, good words more clearly than bad words. The scientists wrote up their discoveries in Nature, and expressed great satisfaction with the results. 'Frankly,' they wrote, 'we were not expecting these results, and they have been described at an informal level as showing that Freud was right after all.' Theorizing from this, the scientists put forward an interesting theory of perception; the brain matches what it hears at each instant against stored target words, and the reception of a certain sequence of sounds makes the target word stand out more clearly so that it is fastened on by the conscious mind, and the incoming word is accepted and recognized. Emotionally loaded words may be stored as moving targets, fluctuating in prominence more wildly than neutral words; consequently they are less likely to be appropriated correctly in this recognition process.

If this can happen today, when the heavens do not tumble when a four-letter word is heard by millions, how more often did it happen in the Victorian age?

It is evident that this function of the censor mechanism is not mere squeamishness or prudery. 'It is really quite likely,' wrote Dr Broadbent to me in August 1967, 'on general grounds that people have to have some way of economising effort in dealing with the world, and develop frameworks and biases of this kind afresh in each era.' It is clear that people were activated to an extraordinary extent in the nineteenth century by the judicious handling of emotionally loaded words and sentences, whether it was John Morley reading with baffled rage Swinburne's *Poems and Ballads*, flagellation maniacs reading the same poet's *The Whippingham Papers*, or, more pertinent, the music hall audiences reacting to the innuendo of Marie Lloyd. In the tones of the experts, the innocuous could acquire emotional loading (such as Marie Lloyd's rendering of *Come Into the Garden, Maud*).

The spoken word has more power to disturb than the written word in that it is more immediate; the photograph has far greater potency than the painting – if Bosch's paintings were transcribed into photographic terms they would be unbearable – because photography is more 'real'. Professional communicators of the nineteenth century had to always watch their step.

Although the present century has its own share of aberrations, we are still very much inclined to award praise and blame to what were conditioned reflexes of Victorian man and woman. The decline of the family as a unit has been put forward as a reason for all kinds of sociological ailments, and here we are tending to load the dice against ourselves, letting sentimentality cloud an important factor. In Victorian England, the family was a power unit, an instrument of *Realpolitik*; that family is a *good* word, in the Broadbent–Gregory sense, is undeniable – we are as much victims of the 'you and me and baby makes three' syndrome as the Victorian paterfamilias was.

The guilt and the shame that Victorians felt when confronted with sexual matters are related to a major premise – the devout belief and trust in a norm of sexual behaviour; sex more than twice a week was an unequivocal sign of the beast, and it was as heretical to dispute this as it would have been for a medieval monk to wonder about arguing with his abbot about the existence of the Trinity. That a large percentage did indulge themselves at above the norm, that they did experiment with sexual positions, that they did not heed conventional proscriptions (e.g., no intercourse during the latter stages of pregnancy), put them, in their own minds, in invicious straits, confirming their shame in the memory of having, in puberty, committed the unmentionable – 'self-abuse', this very phrase having given masturbation ominous overtones. 'Man is as beast when shame stands off from him,' proclaims a character in Swinburne's *Phaedra*, echoing an overriding motif of the age. When one considers all the factors that encompassed Victorian man and woman, it is not surprising that their attitude towards sex was what it was; nor is it surprising that this attitude was constantly thwarted by their own instincts. The world of love became a closed compartment in the mind, sinister and unventilated; for many, internal pressures blew out the walls, while others managed to construct safety valves, whether it was Patmore making the curious equation that copulation was an earthly version of divine love, or middle-class man doing his damnedest to build up a big family because a family was a Good Thing and almost holy – copulation, in fact, in the service of society.

It is difficult to say how much the complex of evasions and rationalizations, doublethink and defensive hypocrisy basic to the Victorian way of sex permeated other fields, whether the tortuous modes of political behaviour, tempering the wind to the shorn foreigner, own much to the devious pattern of thought enforced by domestic issues. If the morality of the private man is shifty – if his sexual behaviour is at odds with the prescriptions of conventional decent society – how far does this influence the morality of public man? To judge by certain examples, considerably. When sexual behaviour was *seen* to be at odds with conventional morality, as it was with Dilke and the three-in-a-bed case (and the three-in-a-bed situation is not at all uncommon, *vide* contemporary sexologists), then the fury of outraged middle classdom was unlimited. It was a way of atoning for their own sexual peccadilloes; it did not even matter that Dilke was probably innocent.

Victorian England, rich in artists and writers, was also repléte with those other concomitants of a modern western civilization – idleness and incompetence. The sexual pattern of an age depends to some extent on the time the practitioners have on their hands to do it or think about it. The three broadest spectrums of Victorian idleness were: (a) the enforced idleness of the unemployed and half-employed working classes; (b) the socially necessary idleness of middle-class wives and daughters; and (c) the languid idleness of an effete aristocracy. Unemployment was a brutalizing influence on the working classes; when the philanthropic organizations handed out money – characteristically it was easier for the middle classes to dish out money rather than clothing and food (it was too much trouble to do the more socially advantageous) – it predictably went into drink. Drink begat violence and promiscuity, and starving daughters went automatically on to the street, where they provided fun for the middle-class young men – who understood that they were more acceptable to their awesome fathers than respectable girls who would want marriage – and the poorer members of the aristocracy. Middle-class wives and daughters were the victims of conspicuous display; their absurd dresses, yards and yards of material, their bustles, their crinolines, their white gloves, their dotty hats and bonnets – all combined to demonstrate that this was not a class which would soil its hands with that nasty four-letter word, 'work'. What were they to do to pass the empty hours? 'Their needlework was beautiful and they turned out piles of it, generally for charitable purposes,' wrote Lord Ernest Hamilton (*The Halcyon Era*, 1933). If needlework and watercolours became wearisome, there was always harmless flirtation with those members of the equivalent class who were provided by providence for this very purpose, minor clergymen. *Noli me tangere* love making led many into dire straits, into emotional distress, hysteria and fashionable neurathenia, into self-titillation.

If a middle-class woman really went off the rails, it meant social death; a daughter was the prey of the aristocracy, and the seduced nice girl became the staple diet of novel readers who themselves were dimly aching for the same kind of excitement. The fatuous three decker novels of the time provided a kind of pornography for these unfortunate girls.

The upper classes were born into idleness, and could better cope with it, along with their preempted mental somnolence, a weakness which made them dependent on what Lord Ernest Hamilton called 'the unintelligent orders' – butlers, housekeepers, estate agents (in the old sense), solicitors, doctors, and tradesmen. The fawning tradesmen could frequently achieve their great ambition – upgrading into the middle class – by merciless over-charging of the upper classes, who considered it not only ill-bred to check bills but an inordinate claim on their mental processes.

This unwillingness of the 'intelligent orders' to apply themselves to the job in hand led to a scarcity of organization men in almost every area of life. For every efficient and assiduous Lord Wolseley in the army there were a dozen Lord Cardigans; for every diligent, though morally speckled, Gladstone there were a dozen half-baked Members of Parliament who hardly knew where the Houses of Parliament were; for every Lord Esher in the Civil Service there were a score of aristocratic dunces who rather fancied the gay life in St Petersburg. In the professions, it was less trouble to work by rote and cling to the traditions than take advantage of new discoveries and the new technology. Doctors found it convenient to let their patients meddle with newly found panaceas like prussic acid, and when the new 'non-addictive' drug, heroin, was evolved towards the close of the nineteenth century, few bothered to find out whether it really was non-addictive. Similarly, in sexual matters, doctors clung to the old stereotypes, that too much sex, masturbation, would drive one mad, blind, or both and that birth control would lead to bestiality or cancer; unfounded speculations were taken up eagerly by a most un-idle species, the medical journalist, who had their own not particular disinterested motivations in mind when promulgating these doubtful hypotheses.

Overall, the Victorians opted for comfort, cosiness and the womb-like life of the family villa. In an age when respectable publications spelled damn d—n and 'stays' was almost a dirty word, they peered out from behind their lace curtains at a world that was becoming more alien. This way of life had its advantages, but prurience and timidity brought with it a lopsided way of looking at life, and the twentieth century is still left with its fruits.

Notes on Sources

LITTLE advantage would accrue from a complete biography. It would surely be of more use to indicate where the material relating to Victorian sexuality lies.

The most sensational material is contained in the Private Cases of the British Museum, a euphemism that hides one of the largest collections of erotica in the world. In August 1966, I wrote to R. A. Wilson, who was then the Principal Keeper of Printed Books, asking for access to books in the Private Cases. On 5 August, 1966, I received the following letter:

Dear Sir,

I note that you have been commissioned to write a book on Victorian sexuality, and shall have no hesitation in allowing you to read the books kept in the so-called Private Cases in this Library. I cannot, however, allow you to have immediate access to the cases themselves.

Not all the books are entered yet in the General Catalogue. You should therefore not assume, if you do not find an entry in the General Catalogue of the book you want, that it is not available.

Yours faithfully
(signed) R. A. Wilson
Principal Keeper

This letter proved to be a kind of visa, but a rereading will reveal a sobering state of affairs, for *under no circumstances* can a member of the public see the catalogue to the Private Cases. At this stage I was fortunate in being given a lead, and was referred to four works:

History of English Erotic Literature by C. R. Dawes (1943)

Index Librorum Prohibitorum by 'Pisanus Fraxi' (1877) (P C 18 b 9)

Centuria Librorum Absconditorum by 'Pisanus Fraxi' (1879) (P C 18 b 9*)

Catena Librorum Tacendorum by 'Pisanus Fraxi' (1885) (P C 18 b 9**)

These four books are bibliographies. The books they refer to may or may not be in the Private Cases of the British Museum. Of more practical use was *Registrum librorum eroticorum* by Alfred Rose (1936), which contains the catalogue numbers. A copy of this useful book, two volumes, more than 5,000 entries, can actually be taken home and read by members of the London Library (yearly subscription fourteen guineas). At this point I was perused by British Museum officials and those connected with the *terra incognita* to see if I was a fit and proper person to have access to these naughty books. I was asked if my book was to be 'sociological'. As I had no idea what exactly this meant I replied that I did not know. This lack of precision, surprisingly, did not lead to permission being withdrawn.

The officials at the Reading Room of the British Museum did their job affably and politely, but did not go out of their way to be helpful, an attitude apparently shared by long-term writers on sexology, who seem to resent intruders in their preserve. One is struck by the different atmosphere that prevailed at the Newspaper Library of the British Museum at Colindale, north London, where I was not only allowed to know what was in their 'private cases', but even allowed to see the books – mainly old bound copies of the *Police Gazette* and newspapers and weeklies of dubious propriety – in their setting.

Beside the British Museum Reading Room and the British Museum Newspaper Library there are other exceptionally useful providers of primary material – the Manuscript Room of the British Museum, the Wellcome Historical Medical Museum in Euston Road, the London Library, and innumerable reference libraries throughout the country; particularly the Birmingham Reference Library, the Wandsworth Reference Library near the Elephant and Castle (a bit subfusc but very interesting), the Islington Reference Library in Holloway Road, and the Westminster Reference Library near Charing Cross. In an age when one is accustomed to peering at period newspapers through the irritating medium of the microfilm scanner, the huge bound copies of that invaluable guide to south London low life, the *South London Press*, to be found at the Wandsworth library, are a delight.

All these libraries are free with the exception of the London library. The librarian of the London library takes the enlightened view that anyone who can afford their subscription is not likely to run amok with scissors even when he or she has the book at home, though he admitted that occasionally especially juicy photographs were found missing from books. The Manuscript Room of the British Museum is different from the Reading Room in that one can usually get a seat (the Reading Room is filled up with the world's students by noon). Many researchers fight shy of it, justifiably put off by the *Guide* to the Manuscript Room. It was here that the Swinburne scholar, Cecil Y. Lang, was struck with amused awe by the reluctance of the officials to let him browse among the more sensational Swinburne letters.

The best of all places to research in is the Wellcome Historical Medical Museum, where the staff are helpful in a way that is regrettably rare.

Although we may not be living in an age of great creative writing, it is often overlooked that this is an age of great scholarship. Biographies of nineteenth-century men and women are immeasurably better now than they were between the wars, when objectivity got lost in self-opinionated smugness; and there is no comparison at all in the collation and editing of letters and diaries, where the kudos must often go to American scholarship. Among many dedicated projects, the following are particularly noteworthy – *The Swinburne Letters* (Yale University Press, 1962), and the *Letters of Dante Gabriel Rossetti* (Oxford University Press, 1965). Among the biographies of especially key figures must be commended *John Addington Symonds* by Phyllis Grosskurth (Longman, 1964), James Pope-Hennessy's two books on Richard Monckton Milnes *The Years of Promise* (1949) and *The Fight of Youth* (1951), and Dr Joan Evans' superb biography of John Ruskin. Her edition of the Ruskin *Diaries* can scarcely be overvalued; it opens a new window on possibly the most interesting of all nineteenth-century figures.

Regarding Victorian sexuality *per se* one is less enthusiastic. Many of the books, especially those written for the paperback market, are content to track over the same old ground, errors multiply, speculations harden into half-baked dogma. Certain books are treated as if they had the authority of holy writ; others have a fearsome built-in reputation, if only for the massive slabs of untranslated material that spread over the pages like mine fields – one thinks of Mario Praz's *The Romantic Agony* (1933). There are some books on specialized subjects that are so good that it seems almost impertinent to proceed further along these lines. Although it was published thirty years ago, Norman E. Himes's *Medical History of Contraception* (Williams and Wilkins, 1936) remains the definitive work on the historical aspects of birth control.

Despite the large number of excellent biographies issuing from the presses, there are subjects of the most impelling interest who have been dealt with, if at all, almost inaudibly – Lord Leighton, Furnivall, Simeon Solomon (one hopes that the biography that Lionel Lambourne is writing will throw light on this curious phenomenon.) The time is more than ripe for a definitive biography of Walter Pater. However, for many thousands of Victorian personages one must be thankful for the various lives and letters, pious, irritating, and misleading, as they often are. Fortunately they are more revealing than was realized at the time; omissions often serve as beacons guiding one to some interesting cross-checking.

The true mirror of the age was the journalist. If we read *Day and Night* we read the submerged literature of the thousands, not the submerged literature of a couple of hundred freaks – as when we read nineteenth-century hard-core pornography. For many millions the Sundays of today are given over to the reading of court cases of sexual misbehaviour. Exact parallels are provided with *Reynolds' News* (circulation 300,000), a powerful instrument of systematic prurience throughout the last quarter of the century. The hard-cover books, the memoirs, the lives and letters, the apologia for this or that, these represent the triumph of the image maker; the newspapers illustrated their defeat.

Notes and References

Chapter 1

1 Letters of Prince Albert to Prince Ernest, quoted in *Albert the Good* by Hector Bolitho, 1932.
2 *Letters of Queen Victoria 1837–1861*, 1908, three vols.
3 ibid.
4 ibid.
5 ibid.
6 Monteith is an interesting little-known period figure; his happy personality can be judged from this extract from a letter he wrote in September 1838: 'I am very happy today. I have resisted a very irresistible adultery – thank God – I only fear I shall reward myself now by yielding.'
7 Quoted in *The Years of Promise* by James Pope-Hennessy, 1949.
8 Extracts mainly from the *Town*, edited by 'Baron' Renton Nicholson, who often wrote his editorials from prison, to which he was frequently committed. He later organized an entertainment called 'Judge and Jury' at the Garrick's Head Hotel in Bow Street. This was a mock trial, with Nicholson attired as judge, the audience acting as jury, and salacious trials were acted out, especially those involving 'crim. con.' (adultery) and sexual offences. His writers included John Dalrymple, wrongfully arrested for 'uttering forgeries on Chelsea Hospital', Henry Pellatt, John Canning, and Edward Blanchard. These unknown journalists produced a formidable body of witty and scurrilous material for the *Town* and other journals.

9 Spavins = a disease of horses.
   Crowdie = a mixture of meal and water.

10 Mag = a halfpenny; therefore magless = penniless. Wight = 'a creature or a person – used chiefly in sport or irony' (*Chambers's Twentieth Century Dictionary*).

11 Letter from Lady Holland to Henry Fox (later Fourth Lord Holland) 18 February 1840.

12 *Letters of Queen Victoria 1837–1861*, 1908, three vols.

13 *Life of Dickens* by John Forster, 1871–4.

14 *Memoirs* by Charles Greville, 1875–87.

15 The disenchanted popular press turned morosely to the Queen's relations ('Here's a toast to the Duchess of Kent and the rest of the royal flues').

16 The Queen's attitude toward Palmerston was ever after conditioned by this incident.

17 *Life of the Prince Consort* by Theodore Martin, 1874–80, five vols.

18 *Mary Ponsonby* by Magdalen Ponsonby, 1927.

19 *The Early Days of Prince Albert* by Lord Grey, 1867.

20 *The Manufacturing Population of England* by Peter Gaskell, 1833.

21 Letter from Lady Holland to Henry Fox (later Fourth Lord Holland), 29 March 1844.

22 *Mary Ponsonby* by Magdalen Ponsonby, 1927.

23 Letter from Queen Victoria to the Princess Royal, 10 August 1859.

24 Letter from Queen Victoria to the Queen of Prussia, 6 October 1856.

25 Letter from Prince Albert to Prince Frederick William, 4 January 1860.

26 *Life of the Prince Consort* by Theodore Martin, 1874–80, five vols.

27 Letter from Queen Victoria to the Princess Royal, 27 December 1861.

28 *My Dear Duchess*, Social and Political Letters to the Duchess of Manchester 1858–69, edited by A. L. Kennedy, 1956.

29 Letter from Jane Welsh Carlyle to Grace Welsh, 17 March 1863.

30 Throughout most of the reign £1 = 5 dollars.

31 *Impressions and Memories* by Lord Ribblesdale, 1927.

32 Queen Victoria believed in the hereafter; her relationship with the rough Highland servant John Brown can only be fully understood if one realizes that he represented a psychic link with the dead Prince Albert.

33 Letter from Queen Victoria to the Prince of Wales, 17 January

1868. Royal Archives Z 448/186, quoted in *King Edward the Seventh* by Sir Philip Magnus, 1964.

34 Royal Archives Z 449/80, quoted ibid.

35 *Diary* by Lady Frederick Cavendish, 1927, two vols.

36 Lillie Langtry's own statement.

37 *The Private Life of Mr Gladstone* by Richard Deacon, 1965. Lord Rosebery (Prime Minister in 1894) was another admirer of Lillie Langtry.

38 *Mr and Mrs Bancroft* by themselves, 1889.

39 *Tomahawk*, 7 May 1870.

40 ibid., 2 May 1868.

41 ibid., 21 May 1870.

42 *Memories* by Lord Redesdale, 1915.

43 Edwardian practical jokes are related with great approval by 'Anon' alias Julian Osgood Field (1849?–1925) who convulsed – he thought – London society in the 1920s with *Uncensored Recollections*, *More Uncensored Recollections*, and *Things I Shouldn't Tell*.

44 *Fraser's Magazine*, 1867. Francis Newman, the 'immeasurably inferior brother', was described by the great Oxford celebrity Benjamin Jowett as 'a good man who is always in the wrong'.

45 *Life of Joseph Chamberlain* by Louis Creswicke, 1904, four vols.

46 Anecdote by Julian Osgood Field.

47 *As We Were* by E. F. Benson, 1930.

Chapter 2

1 *Autobiographic Memoirs* by Frederic Harrison, 1911, two vols.

2 *My Recollections* by the Countess of Cardigan, 1909.

3 *Under Five Reigns* by Lady Dorothy Nevill, 1910.

4 Oh, Captain Shaw!
   Type of true love kept under!
    Could thy Brigade
    With cold cascade
Quench my great love, I wonder!

5 *Life of Sir William Harcourt* by D. G. Gardiner, 1923, two vols.

6 *Impressions and Memories* by Lord Ribblesdale, 1927.

7 *Life of John Cobden* by John Morley, 1906.

8 A comment made to the journalist W. T. Stead, quoted in *Life of W. T. Stead* by F. Whyte, 1925, two vols.

9   *London in the Sixties* by D. Shaw, 1908.

10 ibid.

11 *The Gentlewoman in Society* by Lady Greville, 1892.

12 ibid.

13 *My Wanderings and Memories* by Lady Norah Bentinck, 1924.

14 *The Nineteenth Century*, March, 1894.

15 *Chambers's Journal*, anonymous.

16 ibid.

17 Letter of 7 March, 1854, quoted in *The Order of Release* by Sir William James, 1947.

18 *The New Art of Love*, anonymous, *circa* 1841.

19 Published in the Cambridge University magazine *Granta*, June 1891.

20 None of these songs was published with dates. This one is a strong echo of W. S. Gilbert's songs in the operetta *Patience* (1881). Nelly Farren was a great mistress of burlesque, at her best playing boys' roles. She retired from the stage in 1892 and died in 1904.

21 *Reminiscences* by Lady Dorothy Nevill, 1906.

22 A seasonal request in time for Christmas – published 23 December 1871.

23 A song certainly not earlier than 1876 when Westminster Aquarium was completed, after the success of the Crystal Palace Aquarium opened in 1872. Fish soon took second place to amusements and exhibitions. The quotes around zoo mean nothing, as the Zoological Gardens of Regent's Park had been a popular draw for many decades, and in the 1850s had been attracting more than 300,000 visitors a year.

24 Maria Taglioni (1804–84) was a celebrated *danseuse*, début 1827. Sims Reeves (1818–1900), the first English tenor with a continental reputation; he left the stage in 1860 to concentrate on concerts and oratorio.

25 Spooney, spoony = silly, weakly affectionate, foolishly fond.

26 This was the traditional camp attitude towards the lower orders; the grandfather of camp, in its English sense, was probably Disraeli, who depersonalized his own standpoint by inventing the concept of 'the two nations'.

27 Pierce Egan (1771–1849) is better known as the first systematic chronicler of pugilism.

28 Another example is 'The Funny He = She Ladies'.

We have had female sailors not a few,
And Mary Walker the female barman too,
But I never heard such a sport, did you,
As these swells toy'd out as ladies.

They are well known round Regent Square
And Paddington I do declare,
Round Bruton Street, and Berkeley Square,
Round Tulse Hill, and the lord knows where.

The reference is to the Boulton and Park case (see Chapter 10, part 2, on them).

29 Pickford's were, and are, one of the major moving firms. William Marwood was the public hangman; he died 1883, which makes the song no later than that year. Although he was known as the public hangman, public executions ended in 1868. Marwood took over in 1871 from John Calcraft, executioner since 1828.

30 'donah' is Cockney slang – root obviously *donna*.

31 In its reference this song is extremely sophisticated. *Patience* (1881), the operetta by W. S. Gilbert and Arthur Sullivan in which Oscar Wilde figures under the name of Bunthorne. 'Colonely' a reference to *The Colonel* by F. C. Burnard, produced in 1881, in which Wilde features as Lambert Streyke.

Chapter 3

1 *From Grave to Gay* by H. Cholmondeley-Pennell, 1884.
2 From the pornographic magazine the *Exquisite*, 1842–44, three vols.
3 *Rosenberg's Little Journal*, 2 October 1886.
4 Therefore a magistrate. Bow Street=Bow Street police court.
5 Steven Marcus in *The Other Victorians* (1964) describes *La Rose d'Amour* as an American pornographic novelette.
6 *An Autobiography* by Herbert Spencer, 1904, two vols.
7 *Man and Woman* by Havelock Ellis, 1894.
8 *Nineteenth Century*, March 1894.
9 ibid., May 1892.
10 *Diary* by Alice James, edited Leon Edel, 1965.
11 *Household Words*, 10 April 1852.

12 These accounts are contained in the notes to the mid-Victorian publication of *Don Leon*, supposedly by Lord Byron.

13 *Life and Letters of Frederick W. Robertson*, edited by Stopford Brooke, 1891, two vols.

14 *Life of Archbishop Tait* by Randall Davidson, 1891, two vols.

15 ibid.

16 *Rod, Root, and Flower* by Coventry Patmore, 1895.

17 By isolating themselves Prince and his followers escaped the hilarity of the populace. The Walworth Jumpers were more vulnerable. The locals of the area (the notorious Elephant and Castle district) joined in the fun. At one of the meetings there was a fracas, leading to appearances in court. The magistrate was curious: 'Do you have dancing in the services?' he asked. 'No. There are "manifestations" which might appear to others as dancing, but it was not so on this occasion,' replied a Jumper. 'Do these manifestations take the form of knocking on the tops of hats?' asked the magistrate. 'No, not on the part of our friends,' was the reply.

18 *Henry James: The Conquest of London* by Leon Edel, 1962.

19 *Eton Sixty Years Ago* by A. C. Ainger, 1917.

20 From *Ionica, Poems*, 1857.

21 *Eton Sixty Years Ago* by A. C. Ainger, 1917.

22 Symonds's diary is an interesting document. It has never been published and is held by the London Library, which gives access to it.

23 Quoted in *Charles Dickens* by Una Pope-Hennessy, 1945. The deficiencies of the 'official' biography are well illustrated by the fact that Maria does not even appear in John Forster's biography of Dickens (1871–74).

24 *As We Were* by E. F. Benson, 1930.

25 Some of the odder Victorian properties play havoc with the understanding. A bandoline is 'a gummy substance used for stiffening the hair and keeping it in shape'.

26 Originally in 1539 there were Six Articles, decreeing the acknowledgement of transubstantiation, communion, vows of chastity, private masses, celibacy of the clergy, and auricular confession. Offenders were punished as heretics. In 1551 forty-two were published, modified to thirty-nine in 1563. As Oxford University in the nineteenth century was, strictly speaking, an ecclesiastical organization, the teaching staff were obliged to sign the Thirty-Nine Articles. In November 1871 this obligation ceased.

27 By Lord Tennyson.

28 *The Letters of D. G. Rossetti*, edited by Oswald Doughty and J. R. Wahl, 1965.

29 *Saturday Review*, 9 September 1871.

30 ibid., 9 December 1865.

31 *Nineteenth Century*, March 1894.

32 *Queen*, 7 August 1875.

33 *Cythera's Hymnal*, an anthology of pornographic verse, published in Oxford, 1870.

34 In *The Pre-Raphaelite Tragedy*, 1942.

35 In a letter to Theodore Martin, then engaged in writing his life of Prince Albert.

36 Edward Knatchbull-Hugessen's opposition was so malevolent that he even used children's stories as a vehicle. In *The Pig-Faced Queen* unbelievers in women's rights are shaved, stripped, and washed in hogwash before an audience. That he was not completely in *compos mentis* might be deduced from his *Stories for my Children* (1869), where a farmer is hung by his chin from a hook, a priest is hung next to him with his throat cut from ear to ear, and as for the instruction of an ogre, 'Bleed the girl to death, that her flesh may be as white as possible', one is hard put to it to find its like in the most nauseating pornography of the time.

37 *The Art of Beauty* by Mrs H. R. Haweis, 1878.

38 *Autobiography* by Margot Asquith, 1920.

39 For classic activation, see Kilvert's *Diary*, 21 May 1873: 'I went to Dore's Picture Gallery in New Bond Street. There was a new picture there, an Andromeda, a handsome graceful girl life size, well painted, the flesh tints very natural. The slender girlish form is bowed and shrinking from the monster, the white feet are washed by the lap of the green waves, the manacled hands and wrists are straining at the chain and the rich brown hair is blown wildly forward from the bowed back and beautiful shoulders across the horror-stricken face.'

40 Lecture given on 26 May 1883, published in *The Art of England*, 1898.

41 *Autobiography* by John Gibson, no date.

42 *My Autobiography and Reminiscences* by W. P. Frith, 1887, two vols.

43 *The Art of England* by John Ruskin, 1898.

44 *Leaves from Journal* by Henry Greville, 1884.

45 It has been speculated that the author was the well-known journalist G. A. Sala.

46 An interesting clue to the dimensions of a *real* Victorian woman is contained in paper patterns; thus 1858, cutting out a bodice:

waist	24 inches
bust	34 inches
across shoulders	16 inches
across back	14 inches
length of back	15½ inches

In the 1890s, the ideal vital statistics:

waist	22 inches
bust	36 inches
hips	40 inches

47 *Notes from the Life of an Ordinary Mortal* by A. G. C. Liddell, 1911.

48 Quoted in *Man and Woman* by Havelock Ellis, 1894.

49 To most men, the presence of the corset gave an agreeable sense of continuity. Thus *Bird o' Freedom*, 5 February 1890:

> That fashions come and go like dreams
> 'Tis said, as swift to pass away;
> But when the corset came, it seems,
> It came to stay.

Chapter 4

1 Lord Byron's *Journal*, 30 November 1813.
2 *Journal of Clarissa Trant*, edited by C. G. Luard, 1925.
3 Letter, Fanny Nightingale to Mary Clarke, quoted in *Florence Nightingale* by Cecil Woodham-Smith, 1950.
4 *Diary* by Lady Frederick Cavendish, 1927, two vols.
5 *Lady Geraldine's Courtship*, 1844.
6 *Life and Letters of Rev. John Bacchus Dykes* by J. T. Fowler, 1897.
7 Letter from Jane Welsh Carlyle to Miss Barnes, 24 August 1859.
8 *An Autobiography* by Herbert Spencer, 1904, two vols.
9 *Charles Booth* by T. S. and M. B. Simey, 1960.
10 Advertisement in *The Times*, January 1840.
11 *Life and Work of the Seventh Earl of Shaftesbury* by Edward Hodder, 1887.
12 ibid.

13 *Life of Edward Bouverie Pusey* by H. P. Liddon, 1893–7, four vols.

14 *Life and Letters of Mandell Creighton D.D.*, by Louise Creighton, 1905, two vols.

15 *Memoirs of Coventry Patmore* by Basil Champneys, 1901, two vols.

16 *Life and Letters of Frederick W. Robertson*, edited by Stopford Brooke, 1887, two vols.

17 *Fragments of Inner Life* by F. H. Myers, 1904.

18 *Times Literary Supplement*, 12 May 1932.

19 From *The Angel in the House*, 1845–66.

20 *Reminiscences* by Lady Dorothy Nevill, 1906.

21 *Household Words*, 29 October 1853.

22 *Letters of Lady Augusta Stanley*, 1927.

23 *Reminiscences* by Lady Dorothy Nevill, 1906.

24 *A Mid-Victorian Pepys* by S. M. Ellis, 1923.

25 *Letters of Lady Augusta Stanley*, 1927.

26 The authority is Jane Welsh Carlyle writing to Miss Grace Welsh on 17 May 1863; she 'heard it'. Mrs Carlyle was invariably accurate when it came to gossip. She was one of the first to have some inkling of the facts behind the Ruskin marriage fiasco.

27 Anecdotes recorded in *Chambers's Journal*, 21 September 1889.

28 *Fifty Years of My Life* by Sir John Astley, 1895.

29 *Life and Letters of Mandell Creighton, D.D.*, by Louise Creighton, 1905, two vols.

30 'The Birth Mark' by E. W. Pierce, published in the humorous weekly *Here and There*, 1872.

31 This particular version comes from *The Life of Richard, Lord Westbury* by T. A. Nash, 1888, two vols.

32 *Life and Letters of Mandell Creighton, D.D.*, by Louise Creighton, 1905, two vols.

33 *Letters of Queen Victoria 1837–1861*, 1908, three vols.

34 Crim-con was the usual term for criminal conversation.

35 *Three Modern Seers* by Mrs Havelock Ellis, 1910.

36 *Praeterita* by John Ruskin, 1899.

37 *Three Modern Seers* by Mrs Havelock Ellis, 1910.

38 ibid.

39 *Religio Poetae* by Coventry Patmore, 1893.

40 *Towards Democracy* by Edward Carpenter, 1883.

41 *An Autobiography* by Herbert Spencer, 1904, two vols.

42 *Collected Letters of Bernard Shaw 1874–1907*, edited by Dan H. Laurence, 1965.

43 ibid.

44 ibid.

45 Letter, Bernard Shaw to Amy C. Morant 13 December 1895. Amy Morant was a characteristic 'new woman'; she studied economics and politics at Bedford College and Newnham College, was organizer for the Women's Liberal Federation, and was associated with both the Social-Democratic Federation and the Independent Labour Party. In the *Labour Leader* of December 1895 she challenged Shaw to a public debate, which he declined.

46 Ernest Belfort Bax was an interesting figure, if less important than he believed. A muddled writer on metaphysics and sociology, he and William Morris put together what was described as a distressingly bad book, *Socialism. Its Growth and Outcome*, of which a reviewer said, 'Each of these authors must have consented to send this work to press solely for fear of offending the other.'

47 Letter, Bernard Shaw to Ellen Terry, 28 May 1897.

48 In 'The Princess'.

49 *Religio Poetae* by Coventry Patmore, 1893.

50 *Journals of Arnold Bennett 1896–1910*, 1932.

Chapter 5

No notes.

Chapter 6

1 Mrs Cornwallis West was a professional beauty, a 'shop-window celebrity'. Professional beauties were put into plays merely to lounge about looking pretty, their photographs were sold, and they advertised commodities. Among Mrs West's contemporaries were Evelyn Rayne, Lillie Langtry, and Maud Branscombe, who advertised toothpaste with the slogan 'Nun nicer'.

2 Wilfred Scawen Blunt (1840–1922) – attaché and secretary to British embassies – married granddaughter of Byron 1869,

travelled through Spain, Egypt, Algeria and Syria 1887–8, imprisoned in Ireland because of subversive activities.

3 The issues of the *Englishwoman's Domestic Magazine* that might have created excitement (volumes 5–9, 1868–70) were moved to the famous Private Cases of the British Museum.

4 Known as the 'Pocket Venus'.

5 *History of Prostitution* by William W. Sanger, 1910.

6 An official figure, unquestionably greatly underestimated.

7 Black prostitutes were highly favoured by the *cognoscenti*. Of 'Mary Mitchell the Black Mot' – 'mot' and 'mott' are used indiscriminately – the *Yokel's Preceptor* (circa 1850) reported: 'This fair paviour used to hang out in the vicinity of Unity Court, Westminster, and used to pad the Haymarket. She did a vast deal of business; but being too fond of tape she often figured before the beak. She was a good-hearted mot and used to support her aged parents by her button-hole stitching. She has hooked it in a wooden box.'

8 'He is very nearly six feet high; part of his hand is eaten away by a certain disease; very attenuated legs; dark hair and eyes, rather a long nose, and very offensive breath. His *tout ensemble* has obtained him the cognomen of the Vampire, even amongst his own associates.' *Town*, 9 September 1837.

9 An attempt was made near Florence in 1850 to rear ostriches commercially.

10 *Journal* of Queen Victoria, 8 April 1837.

11 *Journal* of Queen Victoria, 5 May 1837. One wishes that the habit of a monarch publishing a diary had not lapsed, though Queen Victoria's journal was edited drastically by one of her daughters for publication.

12 *A Mid-Victorian Pepys* by S. M. Ellis, 1923.

13 The nobility had 'minders' when they visited the East End of London. The high-born adventurers were known as 'Corinthians'. The 'minders' merged with the 'bullies', two of the most famous being Negroes – 'Kangaroo' and 'Plantagenet Green'.

14 Lord Ossulston is a typical figure of the period. Born 10 January 1810, educated at Harrow (1823–6) and Christ Church, Oxford, took Bachelor of Arts degree 1831, married in 1850. He inherited the Tankerville title, the estate in 1883 comprising 28,930 acres in Northumberland, and 2,493 acres in Shropshire, producing £33,650 a year. He died in 1899; his will was proved at more than £85,000. His widow died as recently as 1922, age 92.

15 So Havelock Ellis tells us in *Studies in the Psychology of Sex*, 1901–10.
16 *Journal* of Lewis Carroll, 16 September 1857.
17 *Life and Letters of Frederick W. Robertson*, edited by Stopford Brooke, 1891, two vols.
18 *Thoughts and Memories* by Austin Harrison, 1926.
19 Letters from D. G. Rossetti to W. M. Rosetti, 8 October 1849.
20 *Walks in London* by Augustus Hare, 1878.
21 Bundling produced its own sartorial requirement – the bundling stocking, a one-piece garment that came up to the waist of the girl.
22 *London Labour and the London Poor* by Henry Mayhew, 1851–62.
23 The Contagious Diseases Acts covered: Aldershot, Canterbury, Chatham, Colchester, Down, Gravesend, Maidstone, Plymouth and Devonport, Portsmouth, Sheerness, Shorncliffe, Southampton, Windsor, Woolwich, The Curragh, Cork, Queenstown.
24 *Town*, 8 July 1837.
25 *Notes on England* by Hippolyte Taine, 1860–70, translated by Edward Hyams, 1957.
26 *Labour and Life of the People in London* by Charles Booth, 1889–1903, seventeen vols.
27 *Household Words*, 1 November 1851.
28 *Conditions of the Working Class in 1844* by Friedrich Engels, 1892.
29 *History of English Law* by F. Pollock and F. W. Maitland, 1898.
30 *Life and Work of the Seventh Earl of Shaftesbury* by Edward Hodder, 1887.
31 Formed for 'the evangelization of the very lowest classes'.
32 A letter in the *Shield*, the organ of repeal of the Contagious Diseases Acts.
33 *Recollections* by John Morley, 1917, two vols.
34 *Letters* of Lord and Lady Wolseley, 1922.
35 *Journals and Letters of Viscount Esher*, edited by Maurice V. Brett, 1934, two vols.

Chapter 7

1 *Life of Sir James Fitzjames Stephen* by Sir Leslie Stephen, 1895.
2 *Cornhill Magazine*, March 1873.
3 *Eothen* by Alexander Kinglake, 1844.
4 *Life of Gladstone* by John Morley, 1908, two vols.
5 *Letters* of J. R. Green, 1901.
6 *Memories* by Lord Redesdale, 1915.
7 *Life of Frank Buckland* by George C. Bompas, 1885.
8 *Mid-Victorian Memories* by R. E. Francillon, 1913.
9 Letter, A. C. Swinburne to R. Monkton Milnes, 10 February 1863.
10 *A Mid-Victorian Pepys* by S. M. Ellis, 1923.
11 *Recollections of a Caricaturist* by Harry Furniss, 1901.
12 It is said that if Mrs Millais, the former Mrs Ruskin, had remained married to Ruskin, Ruskin would have written 'Bubbles'.
13 *Dutch Pictures* by G. A. Sala, 1883.
14 *Praterita* by John Ruskin, 1899.
15 Quoted by Havelock Ellis in *Studies in the Psychology of Sex*, 1901–10.
16 *Life of Kate Greenaway* by M. H. Spielmann and G. S. Layard, 1905.
17 *Friends and Kindred* by L. K. Haldane, 1961.
18 *Autobiography* by Margot Asquith, 1920.
19 *Diary* of Lady Frederick Cavendish, 1927, two vols.
20 *Kilvert's Diary 1870–1879*, edited by William Plomer, 1944.

Chapter 8

1 Attributed by some to Aleister Crowley.
2 Said to be by William S. Potter 'and others'
3 Who were the collectors? Present day erotologists are reluctant to say. In the nineteenth century Lord Rosebery and Coventry Patmore were said to collect pornography.
4 The actual reason for 'Pisanus Fraxi' is more literary; it is an anagram of two Latin words, *fraxinus*=ash, and *apis*=bee.
5 The original is in the Bodleian Library, Oxford.

6 Alfred Rose was one of the few figures operating in this seedy area of Victoriana at whom one tips one's hat. As the author of *Registrum librorum eroticorum* (1936) he has done browsers in the Private Cases of the British Museum a service by supplying them with the catalogue numbers of a large number of private case books. The official catalogue of the Private Cases is not available to any member of the public. In Rose's book there are 5,061 entries. Many of these books are now on open sale, such as Frank Harris' *My Life and Loves* and the *Kama Sutra*. Nevertheless, the *registrum* still fills a need.

7 A parody of Charles Kingsley's then popular poem 'The Three Fishermen'.

8 By Théophile Gautier, 1835.

9 *Life of Disraeli* by W. F. Monypenny and G. E. Buckle, 1910–20.

10 *Catena Librorum Tacendorum* by 'Pisanus Fraxi', 1885.

11 Sold particularly in Soho.

12 *The Swinburne Letters*, edited by Cecil Y. Lang, 1962.

13 ibid.

14 Other authorities say 'a surfeit of pork chops'.

15 So his son relates in *The Early Life and Vicissitudes of Jack Smithers*, 1939.

16 *The Romantic Movement in English Poetry* by Arthur Symons, 1909.

17 The author has an interesting annotated copy of *The Early Life and Vicissitudes of Jack Smithers* in which the name of the road is given as Goldhawk Road (Smithers had substituted another one). Precise details of locale are not common in the late Victorian period.

18 *The Letters of D. G. Rossetti*, edited by Oswald Doughty and J. R. Wahl, 1965.

19 This analogy persists, e.g., *Pendulla Venus or the Girl Astride – Novel Studies in the Art of Equitation*, 1906.

20 *The Letters of D. G. Rossetti*, edited by Oswald Doughty and J. R. Wahl, 1965; Doughty and Wahl, op. cit.

21 It could be hazardous, too. The Rev. Arthur Tooth was a Church of England ritualist who was sent to prison for 'contumacy'. Ruskin called him 'Simpleton Tooth'.

22 *Text Book of Psychology* by William James, 1892.

23 *Reminiscences of Jowett* by A. L. S., No date.

24 *Outine of Psychology* by William McDougall, 1923.

25 *Will to Power* by F. Nietzsche, 1895–1901.

26 *Life and Letters of Stopford Brooke* by L. P. Jacks, 1917, two vols.

27 Introduction to *Pickwick Papers* by Charles Dickens, 1838.
28 *Life of Mary Russell Mitford*, 1870, five vols.
29 *As We Were* by E. F. Benson, 1930.
30 *Diary* by Mary Gladstone, 1930.
31 *Memories of a Clubman* by G. B. Burgen, 1922.

Chapter 9

1   Quoted in *Aids to Psychiatry* by W. S. Dawson, 1924.
2   *The Treasury of Modern Biography* by Robert Cochrane, 1878.
3   *Les Anglais chez Eux* by Francis Wey, *circa* 1856, translated by Valerie Piri, 1935.
4   *Lady Audley's Secret* of 1862, three volumes, was a novel of a golden-haired murderess. Enormously popular, it went through eight editions in three months.
5   *Essays* by George Brimley, 1882.
6   Letter, Charlotte Brontë to Miss Lewis, 16 March 1839.
7   *English Hours* by Henry James, 1905.
8   Letter to Mary Harris 22 December 1857, quoted in *Octavia Hill* by Emily S. Maurice, 1928.
9   *Memories and Notes* by Sidney Colvin, 1921.
10 *Octavia Hill* by Emily S. Maurice, 1928.
11 *Life of Archbishop Tait* by Randall Davidson, 1891, two vols.

Chapter 10

1   The *Oxford English Dictionary* cites Havelock Ellis 1897; Ellis thought it a 'barbarously hybrid word'.
2   Quoted in *Dizzy* by Hesketh Pearson, 1931.
3   *Jowett* by Geoffrey Faber, 1957.
4   Letter from J. A. Symonds to Graham Dakyns, 12 August 1866.
5   *Victorian Eton and Cambridge* by H. E. Wortham, 1927.
6   ibid.
7   *This Was a Man* by Esmé Wingfield-Stratford, 1949.
8   Letter, Oscar Wilde to William Ward, 6 August 1876.
9   Introduction to the 'Phaedrus' by Benjamin Jowett, 1871.
10 *Changes and Chances* by H. W. Nevinson, 1923.
11 Letter, A. C. Swinburne to D. G. Rossetti, 1 March 1870.

12 From Miss Simcox's diary 28 June 1889.

13 *Letters of Lady Augusta Stanley*, 1927.

14 Herbert Spencer ascribed this anecdote to Samuel Rogers.

15 *An Autobiography* by Herbert Spencer, 1904, two vols.

16 It cannot be emphasized too strongly that *all* Victorian case histories are suspect. There are a number of reasons. The basic one is that a specific went through a number of filters; by the time an 'event' had been transmitted from patient to doctor, doctor to notebook, notebook to casebook, and casebook to publisher, it was inevitably trimmed, emasculated, developed or interpreted. As so many case histories were continental in origin, the translator added yet another filter.

17 *Diaries and Letters* of Mary Gladstone, 1930.

18 *Farewell My Youth* by Arnold Bax, 1943.

19 *Man and Woman* by Havelock Ellis, 1894.

20 *Life and Letters of James Hinton*, 1878.

21 *James Hinton* by Mrs Havelock Ellis, 1918.

22 *My Days and Dreams* by Edward Carpenter, 1916.

23 ibid.

24 *Edward Carpenter* by Edward Lewis, 1915.

25 *My Days and Dreams* by Edward Carpenter, 1916.

26 *Mid-Victorian Memories* by R. E. Francillon, 1913.

27 *Towards Democracy* by Edward Carpenter, 1883–1902.

28 *Edward Carpenter* by Edward Lewis, 1915; *Lewis*, op cit.

29 *Edward Carpenter* by Tom Swan, 1910.

30 *Changes and Chances* by H. W. Nevinson, 1923.

31 *Life of Henry Parry Liddon* by J. O. Johnston, 1904.

32 *Life of Dean Stanley* by R. E. Prothero and Dean Bradley, 1894, two vols.

33 *Autobiography* by Margot Asquith, 1920.

34 'Private confessional notes' quoted by Geoffrey Faber in *Jowett*, 1957.

35 Diary of Lewis Carroll, 17 January 1856.

36 Diary of Francis Kilvert, 4 January 1872.

Bibliography of Periodicals and Journals

All the Year Round (*formerly* Household Words)
Bird o' Freedom
Boudoir
British Medical Journal
Chambers's Journal
Cremorne
Daily Telegraph
Day and Night
The Day's Work
Echo
Englishwoman's Domestic Magazine
Exquisite
Family Doctor
Graphic
Here and There
Illustrated London News
Illustrated Police News
Ladies' Pocket Magazine
Lancet
Lloyd's Newspaper

Man About Town
Modern Review
Nineteenth Century
North London Press
Pall Mall Gazette
Pearl
Police Gazette
Psychological Journal
Punch
Queen
Review of Reviews
Reynold's
Rosenberg's Little Journal
St James's Gazette
Saturday Review
Savoy
South London Press
Sporting Times (*known as the* Pink 'Un)
The Times
Tittle-Tattle
Tomahawk

Town

Town Topics

Truth

Vanity Fair

Westminster Review

Woman

World

Yellow Book

Index